Crim

KU-016-810

18

SWINDON COLLEGE

LEARNING RESOURCE CENTRE

The Elliott & Quinn Series
for the best start in law

This renowned author team draw on their extensive experience to bring an unbeatable selection of texts that provide total clarity on the core areas of law.

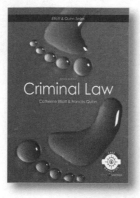

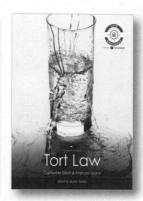

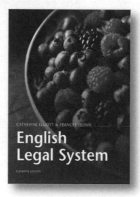

The Elliott & Quinn Series is supported by **mylawchamber** websites, which include regular updates to the law and a range of resources from interactive questions and exam advice to weblinks, for students to use throughout their course.

For further information or to order these books, please visit:
www.pearsoned.co.uk/law

8th edition

Criminal Law

Catherine Elliott and
Frances Quinn

SWINDON COLLEGE

LEARNING RESOURCE CENTRE

Longman
is an imprint of

Harlow, England • London • New York • Boston • San Francisco • Toronto
Sydney • Tokyo • Singapore • Hong Kong • Seoul • Taipei • New Delhi
Cape Town • Madrid • Mexico City • Amsterdam • Munich • Paris • Milan

Pearson Education Limited
Edinburgh Gate
Harlow
Essex CM20 2JE
England

and Associated Companies throughout the world

Visit us on the World Wide Web at:
www.pearsoned.co.uk

First published 1996
Second edition 1998
Third edition 2000
Fourth edition 2002
Fifth edition 2004
Sixth edition 2006
Seventh edition 2008
Eighth edition 2010

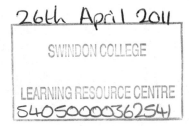

26th April 2011

SWINDON COLLEGE

LEARNING RESOURCE CENTRE
540500000362541

© Pearson Education Limited 1996, 2010

The rights of Catherine Elliott and Frances Quinn to be identified as authors
of this work have been asserted by them in accordance with the Copyright,
Designs and Patents Act 1988.

All rights reserved. No part of this publication may be reproduced, stored in
a retrieval system, or transmitted in any form or by any means, electronic,
mechanical, photocopying, recording or otherwise, without either the prior
written permission of the publisher or a licence permitting restricted copying
in the United Kingdom issued by the Copyright Licensing Agency Ltd,
Saffron House, 6–10 Kirby Street, London EC1N 8TS.

All trademarks used herein are the property of their respective owners. The
use of any trademark in this text does not vest in the author or publisher any
trademark ownership rights in such trademarks, nor does the use of such
trademarks imply any affiliation with or endorsement of this book by such owners.

Crown Copyright material is reproduced with the permission of the Controller
of HMSO and the Queen's Printer for Scotland.

Law Commission Reports are reproduced under the terms of the Click-Use Licence.

ISBN: 978-1-4082-3053-4

British Library Cataloguing-in-Publication Data
A catalogue record for this book is available from the British Library.

Library of Congress Cataloging-in-Publication Data

A catalog record for this book is available from the Library of Congress.

10 9 8 7 6 5 4 3 2 1
14 13 12 11 10

Typeset in 9.5/13pt Stone Sans by 35
Printed and bound by Ashford Colour Press

The publisher's policy is to use paper manufactured from sustainable forests.

Brief contents

Contents

Visit mylawchamber at **www.mylawchamber.co.uk/elliottcriminal**
to access a wealth of resources to support your studies and teaching
in **criminal law**. These include:

Companion website support

- Access to the accompanying Pearson eText – an electronic version of *Criminal Law* which you can personalise with your own notes. Extensive links are provided to the Pearson eText from all of the resources listed below, and it is fully searchable
- Multiple-choice questions, flashcards and practice exam questions to test yourself on each topic throughout the course
- Updates to major changes in the law to make sure you are ahead of the game by knowing the latest developments
- Live weblinks to help you read more widely around the subject, and really impress your lecturers

Case Navigator*

This unique online support helps you to improve your case reading and analysis skills.

- **Direct deep links** to the core cases in criminal law
- **Short introductions** provide guidance on what you should look out for while reading the case
- **Questions** help you to test your understanding of the case, and provide feedback on what you should have grasped
- **Summaries** contextualise the case and point you to further reading so that you are fully prepared for seminars and discussions

Use your access card to activate the unrivalled support for your studies. Online purchase is also available at **www.mylawchamber.co.uk/register**

* Case Navigator access is included with your mylawchamber registration. The LexisNexis element of Case Navigator is only available to those who currently subscribe to LexisNexis Butterworths online.

Guided tour

Chapter openings outline the key concepts to be discussed, and help organise your study.

Key case boxes summarise the leading cases in criminal law, and identify the related principles of law that arise from them.

To help explain more complex legal processes in more detail, **diagrams** and **flow charts** are used throughout.

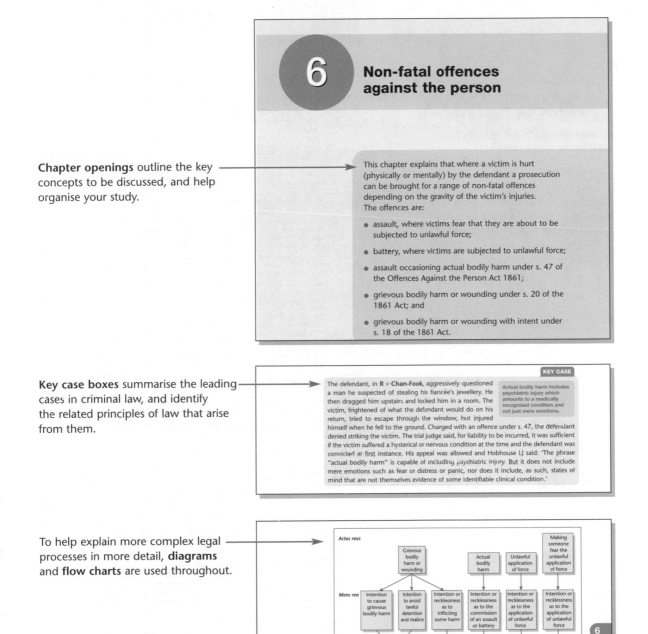

6 Non-fatal offences against the person

This chapter explains that where a victim is hurt (physically or mentally) by the defendant a prosecution can be brought for a range of non-fatal offences depending on the gravity of the victim's injuries. The offences are:

- assault, where victims fear that they are about to be subjected to unlawful force;
- battery, where victims are subjected to unlawful force;
- assault occasioning actual bodily harm under s. 47 of the Offences Against the Person Act 1861;
- grievous bodily harm or wounding under s. 20 of the 1861 Act; and
- grievous bodily harm or wounding with intent under s. 18 of the 1861 Act.

KEY CASE

The defendant, in **R v Chan-Fook**, aggressively questioned a man he suspected of stealing his fiancée's jewellery. He then dragged him upstairs and locked him in a room. The victim, frightened of what the defendant would do on his return, tried to escape through the window, but injured himself when he fell to the ground. Charged with an offence under s. 47, the defendant denied striking the victim. The trial judge said, for liability to be incurred, it was sufficient if the victim suffered a hysterical or nervous condition at the time and the defendant was convicted at first instance. His appeal was allowed and Hobhouse LJ said: 'The phrase "actual bodily harm" is capable of including psychiatric injury. But it does not include mere emotions such as fear or distress or panic, nor does it include, as such, states of mind that are not themselves evidence of some identifiable clinical condition.'

> Actual bodily harm includes psychiatric injury which amounts to a medically recognised condition and not just mere emotions.

Figure 6.3 Distinguishing the non-fatal offences

Topical issue boxes present examples of the law working in newsworthy or contentious situations, helping to demonstrate its relevance.

TOPICAL ISSUE

Incitement in the community

In 2006, there were two high-profile incitement cases before the courts. These two cases had very different outcomes and raised questions about the way the law is applied in practice. The first involved a prosecution of Nick Griffin, the leader of the British National Party. Mr Griffin was charged with four counts of inciting racial hatred under the Public Order Act 1986, following a TV documentary in which he was shown making derogatory comments about Muslims. He was acquitted on two counts but the jury failed to reach a verdict on the other two.

The second case involved a prosecution of Abu Hamza, an Islamic cleric. He was convicted of 15 charges of inciting racial hatred and murder after secret recordings had been made of his sermons in a London mosque.

Icons alerting you to more detailed examination of key cases via **Case Navigator** on the accompanying mylawchamber website.

prevented the defendant from having the *mens rea* of the offence. This will be the case where the *mens rea* of the offence is subjective, but where it is objective then a mistake is only likely to prevent the existence of the *mens rea* if it was reasonable. Following the case of **R v G and another** (2003), *mens rea* will normally be subjective.

In the case of **DPP v Morgan** (discussed at p. 174), the House of Lords looked at the issue of mistake in relation to the offence of rape. The House stated that if the accused honestly believed the complainant was consenting, they did not have the *mens rea* for rape, even though they were mistaken in that belief and their mistake could not even be said to be a reasonable one. The law in the context of rape has now been changed by

You can test your understanding of the subject by using the **exam style question and answer guidance** at the end of each chapter.

? Answering questions

1 F and G agreed to beat up X who had recently displaced G in G's former girlfriend's affections. F and G waited for X as he came home from work. They jumped on X. X punched F rendering him unconscious. X fought with G who fell and hit his head on a wall. X walked away leaving F and G on the pavement.

Advise the parties of their criminal liability. What difference, if any, would it make to your advice if (a) F, who had a thin skull, had died from X's blow; or, alternatively, (b) G had died of exposure? *(London External LLB)*

When F and G agreed to beat up X they entered into a criminal conspiracy to assault X, probably with actual or grievous bodily harm. When F and G jumped on X in furtherance of their agreement they committed offences under the Offences Against the Person Act 1861.

X punched F. This could have amounted to a non-fatal offence, the type of offence depending on the gravity of the harm actually caused. He will have a self defense or a public defence (see p. 346) as long as he only used a reasonable amount of force.

If F had died because he had a thin skull, the rule in **Blaue** would apply so that X would have to take his victim as he found him. The thin skull would not break the chain of causation and X could be liable for murder or manslaughter depending on his *mens rea* and the success of any public or private defence.

If G had died of exposure, you would need to consider whether X had a duty to act and seek help for his victims. You could look at the case of **R v Miller** at p. 13. On the issue of causation you could consider the test of foreseeability and the case of **Pagett** (see p. 56).

2 Maggie and Bert are both staying in a hospital. Maggie is expecting her first child and is of low intelligence. She is trying to read a book and Bert starts to taunt her about her inability to read and the fact that her unborn child is illegitimate. In a violent rage

Each chapter ends with a **summary** which helps you to recap and focus on the key themes from the chapter you've just read – a very useful tool for revision.

Ⅲ Summary

The inchoate offences – attempt, conspiracy and encouraging or assisting – are concerned with the preparatory stages of other criminal offences. The common law offence of incitement has been abolished by the Serious Crime Act 2007. A person may be convicted of an inchoate offence even if the main offence was never actually committed.

Attempt

Actus reus
Section 1(1) of the Criminal Attempts Act 1981 provides that: 'If with intent to commit an offence to which this section applies, a person does an act which is more than merely preparatory to the commission of the offence, he is guilty of attempting to commit the offence.' The question of whether an act is 'more than merely preparatory' is a matter of fact and, in a trial on indictment, will be for the jury to decide. Under s. 1(2) of the Act, people can be guilty of this offence even if the main offence they were attempting to commit was impossible.

Mens rea
Defendants can only be liable for an attempt if they act with the intention of committing the complete offence – recklessness as to the consequences of the act is not enough. Where the definition of the main offence includes circumstances, and recklessness as to these circumstances is sufficient for that aspect of the *mens rea*, then it will also be sufficient for an attempt to commit that offence (though intention will still be required for the rest of the *mens rea*).

Conspiracy

End of chapter **further reading sections** provide references to relevant hard copy and electronic resources which will be useful if you wish to study that area in more depth.

Reading list

Becker, B.C. (1974) 'Criminal attempts and the law of crimes', 3 *Philosophy and Public Affairs* 262.

Brady, J. (1980) 'Punishing attempts' 63 *The Monist* 246.

Glazebrook, P. (1969) 'Should we have a law of attempted crime?' 85 *Law Quarterly Review* 28.

Law Commission (2007) *Conspiracy and Attempts*, Consultation Paper No. 183, London: Law Commission.

Law Commission (2006) *Inchoate Liability for Assisting and Encouraging Crime*, Law Com. No. 300, London: Law Commission.

Ormerod, D. and Fortson, R. (2009) *Serious Crime Act 2007: the Part 2 offences* [2009] Crim LR 389.

Rogers, J. (2008) 'The codification of attempts and the case for "preparation"' [2008] *Criminal Law Review* 937.

Williams, G. (1983) 'The problems of reckless attempts' [1983] *Criminal Law Review* 365.

Reading on the internet

The Law Commission Report *Inchoate Liability for Assisting and Encouraging Crime* (2006) is available on the Law Commission's website at:
http://www.lawcom.gov.uk/lc_reports.htm

The **appendix** at the end of the book provides valuable advice on answering both problem and essay questions, which will help prepare you for success in your exams.

Appendix:
Answering examination questions

At the end of each chapter in this book, you will find detailed guidelines for answering exam questions on the topics covered. Many of the questions are taken from actual A level past papers, but they are equally relevant for candidates of all law examinations, as these questions are typical of the type of questions that examiners ask in the field.

In this section, we aim to give some general guidelines for answering questions on criminal law.

Citation of authorities

One of the most important requirements for answering questions on the law is that you must be able to back the points you make with authority, usually either a case or a statute. It is not good enough to state that the law is such and such, without stating the case or statute which lays down that law.

Visit mylawchamber at **www.mylawchamber.co.uk/elliottcriminal** to access your interactive Pearson eText version of *Criminal Law* which you can personalise to your study, and is linked to a wealth of supporting resources, including:

- Regular updates to the law
- Multiple choice questions to help test your knowledge
- Practice essay questions with answer guidance
- Flashcards to help with your revision
- Case Navigator to help improve your case reading and analysis skills.

Preface

This book is designed to provide a clear explanation of criminal law. As well as setting out the law itself, we look at the principles behind it and discuss some of the issues and debates arising from it. The criminal law is frequently the subject of heated public debate, and we hope that the material here will allow you to enter into this debate and develop your own views as to how the law should progress.

One of our priorities in writing this book has been to explain the material clearly, so that it is easy to understand, without lowering the quality of the content. Too often, law is avoided as a difficult subject, when the real difficulty is the vocabulary and style of legal textbooks. For that reason, we have aimed to use 'plain English' as far as possible, and explain the more complex legal terminology where it arises. In addition, chapters are structured so that material is in a systematic order for the purposes of both learning and revision, and clear subheadings make specific points easy to locate.

Although we hope that many readers will use this book to satisfy a general interest in the law, we recognise that the majority will be those who have to sit an examination on the subject. Therefore, each chapter features typical examination questions, with detailed guidance on answering them, using the material in the book. This is obviously useful at revision time, but we recommend that when first reading the book, you take the opportunity offered by the questions sections to think through the material that you have just read and look at it from different angles. This will help you to both understand and remember it. You will also find a section at the end of the book which gives useful general advice on answering examination questions on criminal law.

This book is part of a series produced by the authors. The other books in the series are *The English Legal System, English Legal System: Essential Cases and Materials, AS Law for OCR, AS Law for AQA, Contract Law* and *Tort Law*.

We have endeavoured to state the law as at 1 January 2010.

Catherine Elliott and Frances Quinn
London 2010

Publisher acknowledgements

We are grateful to the following for permission to reproduce copyright material:

Figures
Figure I.1: From Crime in England and Wales 2005/06, p. 49; Figure I.2: From Crime in England and Wales, 2008/09 Home Office Statistical Bulletin, p. 25; Figure I.3: From Crime in England and Wales, 2008/09 Home Office Statistical Bulletin, p. 24; Figure 3.1: From Crime in England and Wales 2007/08 Supplementary Volume 2: Homicide, Firearm Offences and Intimate Violence, p. 10; Figures 4.1 and 5.8: From Crime in England and Wales 2007/08, Supplementary Volume 2: Homicide, Firearm Offences and Intimate Violence, p. 12; Figure 5.2: From Crime in England and Wales 2007/08 Supplementary Volume 2: Homicide, Firearms Offences and Intimate Violence, p. 11; Figure 6.1: From Crime in England and Wales 2008/09 Home Office Statistical Bulletin, p. 45; Figure 6.4: From Crime in England and Wales 2008/09 Home Office Statistical Bulletin, p. 48; Figure 8.4: From Crime in England and Wales 2008/09 Home Office Statistical Bulletin, p. 27 and p. 31; Figure 8.5: From Crime in England and Wales 2006/07, p. 75; Figures 8.6, 8.9a, 8.9b, 8.9c and 8.9d: From Crime in England and Wales 2007/08, supplementary tables; Figure 8.7: From Crime in England and Wales 2008/09 Home Office Statistical Bulletin, p. 77; Figure 8.10: From Crime in England and Wales 2008/09 Home Office Statistical Bulletin, p. 79; Figure 9.1: From Crime in England and Wales 2007/08 Home Office Statistical Bulletin, p. 90; Figure 13.2: From Crime in England and Wales 2008/09 Home Office Statistical Bulletin, p. 71. Crown Copyright material is reproduced with permission under the terms of the Click-Use Licence.

Tables
Table 6.1 from Crime in England and Wales 2007/08: Supplementary Tables 5.2; Table 6.2 from Crime in England and Wales 2007/08 Supplementary Tables; Table I.1 from Crime in England and Wales 2008/09, Home Office Statistical Bulletin p. 41. Crown Copyright material is reproduced with permission under the terms of the Click-Use Licence.

Text
Pages 32, 132, 277, 301, 302, 389: Exam board questions from Oxford, Cambridge and RSA Examinations.

Photos
The publisher would like to thank the following for their kind permission to reproduce their photographs:

Publisher acknowledgements

Page 80: Rex Features; 89: © Bettmann / Corbis; 92 (left): Reuters / HO Old (left); 92 (right): Rex Features; 95: Rebecca Naden / Press Association Images; 316: Ron Edmonds / AP / Press Association Images.

Every effort has been made to trace the copyright holders and we apologise in advance for any unintentional omissions. We would be pleased to insert the appropriate acknowledgement in any subsequent edition of this publication.

Table of cases

Visit the *Criminal Law*, 8th edition **mylawchamber** site at
www.mylawchamber.co.uk/elliottcriminal to access unique online
support to improve your case reading and analysis skills.

Case Navigator provides:
- **Direct deep links** to the core cases in Criminal Law.
- **Short introductions** provide guidance on what you should look out
  for while reading the case.
- **Questions** help you to test your understanding of the case, and provide feedback on
  what you should have grasped.
- **Summaries** contextualise the case and point you to further reading so that you are
  fully prepared for seminars and discussions.

Please note that access to Case Navigator is free with the purchase of this book, but you must register
with us for access. Full registration instructions are available on the website. The LexisNexis element of
Case Navigator is only available to those who currently subscribe to LexisNexis Butterworths online.

Case Navigator cases are highlighted in bold.

Table of statutes

Table of treaties

Introduction

This introduction discusses:

- what amounts to a crime;

- the difference between reported crime, recorded crime and actual crime; and

- how to interpret statistics about crime.

Introduction

Criminal liability is imposed on conduct felt to be against the general interests of society. Obviously if millions of people have to live together, their lives will be more pleasant and peaceful if some measures are taken to prevent people from killing or physically attacking others, walking into their houses and taking things away, or smashing up someone else's car. Most of us would agree that these types of behaviour are anti-social, and we want them to be controlled. But there is not always agreement on what kinds of conduct should be considered criminal. Swearing in front of children is considered anti-social by many, along with eating smelly fast food on public transport, or wearing too much perfume or aftershave. Yet none of these constitutes a crime, and very few people would wish them to be. On the other hand, there are types of behaviour which may affect nobody but the people involved – smoking cannabis and failing to wear a seat belt are examples – which are nevertheless criminal acts.

The types of conduct which are considered criminal vary from society to society. In our own system, for example, homosexuality was once a crime, while, until 1991, it was not a crime for a man to rape his wife. As general attitudes change over time, so do attitudes to the kinds of behaviour we label as criminal. And at any stage in a society, there will be some kinds of behaviour about which there is dispute – at the moment, for example, smoking cannabis is a crime and some people argue that it should not be, while abortion (within certain rules) is not a crime, and some believe it should be. It is important therefore to realise that there is no absolute definition of criminal behaviour – 'criminal' is no more than a label attached to different types of behaviour at different times in different societies.

How much crime is there?

Official statistics on crime are published annually in the UK, and provide two main kinds of information: the number of crimes committed, as a whole and by type of crime; and certain characteristics, such as age and sex, of convicted offenders. The figures tend to be reported in the media under headlines such as 'Violent crime up 10 per cent', or 'Burglaries reduced by 25 per cent'. However, since the 1960s, increasing doubt has been shed on this interpretation of official statistics. We now know that when official figures say that, for example, burglaries are down by 25 per cent, it does not necessarily mean that there have been 25 per cent fewer burglaries than the year before. This is because these statistics do not measure the crime that has taken place, but the crimes that have been officially recorded, and they may be two very different things. The reason for this is that before a crime can be recorded, a series of processes must occur: a person (the victim, the police, or someone else) must be aware that it has happened; if the police have not discovered it, someone must report it; and the police must accept that the law has been broken. Each stage has implications as to whether the incident appears in the official statistics or not.

Awareness of crime

While in the case of crimes such as burglary or theft it will be clear to the victim that a crime has been committed, many offences do not have an obvious victim. For example, tax evasion victimises the whole community, because if dishonest people avoid paying their fair share, the rest of us have to pay more, but we are not likely to be aware of it happening. Unless the police, or other enforcement agencies, discover such crimes, nobody but the criminals will know that they have taken place.

Whether the police discover a crime depends heavily on where police officers are actually placed. Areas where police believe that crime is likely to occur are allocated higher policing levels, so crime is more likely to be discovered there, and presumably less likely to be discovered in areas not seen as likely to produce crime. Styles of policing may also play a part in this, as the sociologists Lea and Young point out in their book *What is to be Done About Law and Order?* In suburban and country areas, policing is more likely to be what Lea and Young describe as 'consensual', with officers seeing themselves as supporting the community in upholding the law. In cities, they see themselves as controlling the community, and preventing it from breaking the law. Lea and Young suggest that people are more likely to be stopped and searched in the second type of area, and thus more likely to be discovered if they do commit crime.

Reporting crime

Numerous studies have shown that the majority of crimes which take place are not reported to the police. Victimisation surveys ask respondents whether they have been the victim of crime over the previous year, whether they have reported it, and whether it was recorded by the police. The best known is the Home Office British Crime Survey, which takes place every couple of years. It regularly reveals a huge number of crimes which have not been reported to the police. The 2000 survey uncovered almost 15 million crimes, three times the official figure of 5.3 million. In addition, rates of reporting varied widely between different types of offence. Clearly this throws doubt on the official picture of which types of crime are committed most frequently; not only are the numbers wrong, but also the proportions.

What influences the decision to report? According to the British Crime Survey, the main reasons for not reporting are that the victim saw the offence as trivial, and/or believed that the police would not be able to do anything about it. People also tend to report crimes where there is an obvious advantage to them in doing so – 98 per cent of car thefts are reported, presumably because that is necessary in order to make an insurance claim. Other factors which the survey has highlighted are that some crimes are regarded as personal matters, to be sorted out between the individuals; victims may want to protect the offender, particularly in crimes such as child abuse or domestic violence; and victims may be too embarrassed to report to police, especially where the offence is of a sexual nature.

Kinsey, Lea and Young in *Losing the Fight Against Crime* provide additional reasons why crime may go unreported, and therefore unrecorded in official statistics. They argue that inner-city communities have little faith in the police, and this expresses itself in two ways: residents believe the police are biased against them, and they also fear reprisals from

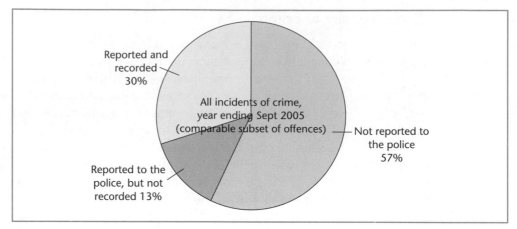

Figure I.1 Proportion of all crime reported to the police and recorded by them, year ending September 2005

Source: 'Crime in England and Wales 2005/06', p. 49.

criminals, against which the police will not be able to protect them. Another victimisation study, the Merseyside Crime Survey (Kinsey (1984)), has shown that the higher the crime in an area, the lower the willingness to report.

However, even victimisation studies probably underestimate the true amount of crime committed. They can only record certain types of crime – those with an obvious victim. They therefore do not include drugs offences, prostitution, tax, corporate or white-collar crime. Sexual offences are also likely to be underreported; although victims may be more likely to report these in the confidentiality of such surveys than they are to go to the police, many will still be too embarrassed to admit to them, especially as there may seem to be no practical point in doing so.

Victimisation surveys also rely on victims' memories, and their ability to define an act as a crime. Minor criminal acts may be forgotten, not regarded as serious enough to record, or not seen as crime.

Recording crime

Even where a crime is reported to (or discovered by) the police, it will not necessarily end up being recorded by them. Sociologists have suggested that whether the police perceive an individual's behaviour as a crime may depend on how they label the offender. An American study by Chambliss looked at two teenage groups, one working-class (known as the 'roughnecks') and one middle-class (the 'saints'). Despite the fact that the 'saints' committed more, and more serious, delinquent acts, they did not conform to the police image of young criminals, and were able to present their activities as harmless pranks. Whilst they were questioned, they were never charged, and therefore their activities were not recorded as crimes.

The proportions of different types of crime recorded in official statistics may be distorted by the fact that some acts potentially fall within the definitions of more than one crime – different types of assault, for example. Which crime is recorded may depend on

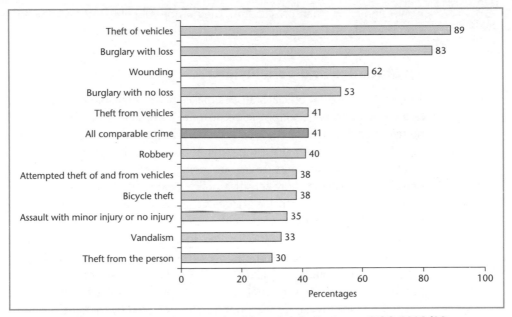

Figure I.2 Reporting rates for comparable subset of crimes, BCS 2008/09

Source: Crime in England and Wales, 2008/09, Home Office Statistical Bulletin, p. 25.

police discretion. In addition, different forces may have different attitudes to types of crime, reflecting the priorities of their senior officers. If the result is that forces concentrate resources on some crimes at the expense of others, this may make it appear that certain crimes are rising by comparison with others, when in fact they may simply be more likely to be detected.

White-collar and corporate crime

White-collar crime is the name given to criminal activities performed by those in fairly high-status occupations during the course of their work – fraud is the obvious example. Corporate crime is that committed by companies. Fraud also tends to be the area most associated with corporate crime, but sociologists such as Steven Box have argued that deaths and injuries caused by companies to employees or customers also often amount to crimes.

Neither white-collar nor corporate crimes are adequately reflected in official statistics, for two main reasons. First, there is low awareness of the fact that they have been committed. Many such offences victimise the community as a whole, or large groups of consumers. Where a company breaks safety legislation and an employee dies or is injured as a result, the situation is often viewed as accidental, so although the company may be sued for compensation, criminal charges are rarely brought. In cases of bribery and corruption, both parties may benefit, and both are liable to prosecution, so neither is likely to report the offence.

Secondly, these crimes are frequently investigated not by the police, but by regulatory authorities such as the Health and Safety Executive, who, as a matter of policy, rely on persuasion rather than prosecution; the number of companies who need 'persuading' to stop breaking the law is not recorded in the criminal statistics.

● Statistics and conclusions

These weaknesses of official statistics make them unreliable not only as a picture of current crime rates, but also for the purposes of comparison – which is a problem, given the huge media attention paid to such comparisons, and its influence on policy. For example, rape figures have risen since the early 1980s, but the figures themselves cannot show whether this means more rapes are being committed or more are being reported, perhaps as a result of more sensitive police treatment of victims. In addition, methods of gathering and/or categorising statistics may vary over time. Consequently, it is difficult to draw reliable conclusions from either apparent increases or decreases in the crime rate. A rise, for example, in the official crime statistics is usually seen as bad news. Yet it may not reflect more crimes committed, but more crimes reported, which may in turn be a result of higher public confidence in the police, and/or less tolerance by victims and others of crimes such as marital rape, child abuse or domestic violence.

Similar problems can be seen in the picture painted by the official statistics of offenders. They suggest that most crime is committed by young, working-class males, and that black people are more heavily represented than might be expected from the proportion of the population that they make up. Many important theories of criminology have been based on these findings, with experts accepting that working-class men are the main

Table I.1 Reasons for not reporting crime to the police, 2008/09

Percentages								
	Vandalism	Burglary	Thefts from vehicles and attempts	Other household theft	Other personal theft	All violence	Comparable crime	All BCS crime
Trivial/no loss/police would not/could not do anything	87	72	87	82	73	52	76	76
Private/dealt with ourselves	8	18	7	10	8	34	15	14
Inconvenient to report	4	4	7	5	7	5	5	5
Reported to other authorities	1	3	2	1	13	6	3	4
Common occurrence	2	4	1	1	2	5	3	2
Fear of reprisal	2	2	1	1	1	6	3	2
Dislike or fear of the police/ previous bad experience with the police or courts	1	0	1	1	0	3	1	1
Other	3	6	3	6	6	6	4	5

Source: *Crime in England and Wales 2008/09*, Home Office Statistical Bulletin p. 41.

offenders, and then setting out to explain what it was about these men that made them likely to commit crime.

However, in recent years, other criminologists, known as 'labelling theorists', have questioned these assumptions, asking whether it is in fact the case that some sections of society appear more frequently in the crime figures because they are more likely to be convicted, and not because they commit more crime. As we have seen, the offenders who appear in official statistics are likely to be a small proportion of actual offenders, given the amount of crime which is not reported or recorded. As Chambliss's research shows, some groups are more likely to appear in official statistics because of who they are, not what they have done. If young, working-class men are most likely to be stopped by police, or to have their activities defined as criminal, it is not surprising that this is reflected in the official statistics. Lea and Young have suggested that the police may also be more likely to stop and question black people, with the same result.

It has been argued that police behaviour to these two groups reflects the fact that they actually do commit more crime, but, even if this is the case, it ignores the fact that, in concentrating on some groups, the behaviour of others is not recorded, and so the balance presented in statistics is distorted. In other words, the targeted groups may commit more crime – but not as much more as statistics suggest.

The same applies to the absence of white-collar and corporate crime in official statistics. Box's study of these areas suggests that if the true picture of criminal activity were revealed, the assumption that crime is a working-class activity would soon be overturned.

A further problem with official statistics is that they aim to present a picture of crime as a whole, which may ignore the reality of crime statistics for some groups or geographical areas. For example, the Islington Crime Survey (1986) found that residents of that borough had much higher than average chances of being a victim of certain serious

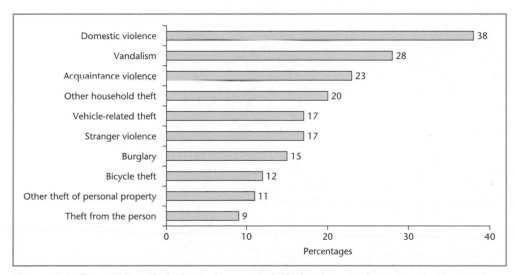

Figure I.3 Proportion of victims who were victimised more than once in the past year by offence, 2008/09, BCS 2008/09

Source: *Crime in England and Wales 2008/09*, p. 24.

crimes. Women were 40 per cent more likely to suffer non-sexual assault and rates of sexual assault were 14 times the national average. This was even though women were five times more likely than men to avoid going out alone after dark, and six times more likely to avoid going out alone. Burglary in the borough was five times the national average. Clearly this suggests that the national average rates underestimate the effects of crime in such areas and, by implication, overestimate its effects in other districts.

Similarly, the British Crime Survey reveals that many apparently separate instances of crime may involve the same victims over and over again; this is known as repeat victimisation. Regarding burglary, for example, the 2000 British Crime Survey found that 13 per cent of households suffering burglaries had done so twice in the year, and 7 per cent had been burgled three or more times. High-crime areas may not contain more victims, but a similar number to other places, who are victimised more often. Again, this is not reflected in the official statistics, but since these figures are used to help make decisions on policy and allocation of resources, such variations are important.

It seems clear that official statistics are not – and should not be regarded as – reliable, at least not in the role they are designed to perform. They may be very revealing about the assumptions used in defining crime, by police and others, but, as a picture of how much crime is committed and by whom, they are seriously flawed.

1 Elements of a crime

This chapter explains:

- that the defendant must usually have both committed an *actus reus* (a guilty act) and have a *mens rea* (a guilty mind) to be liable for a criminal offence;

- that criminal offences are not normally committed by an omission;

- the three main forms of *mens rea* are intention, recklessness and negligence;

- the doctrine of transferred malice; and

- the requirement that the *actus reus* and *mens rea* of a crime should usually both exist at the same point in time.

Introduction

A person cannot usually be found guilty of a criminal offence unless two elements are present: an *actus reus*, Latin for guilty act; and *mens rea*, Latin for guilty mind. Both these terms actually refer to more than just moral guilt, and each has a very specific meaning, which varies according to the crime, but the important thing to remember is that to be guilty of an offence, an accused must not only have behaved in a particular way, but must also usually have had a particular mental attitude to that behaviour. The exception to this rule is a small group of offences known as crimes of strict liability, which are discussed in the next chapter.

The definition of a particular crime, either in statute or under common law, will contain the required *actus reus* and *mens rea* for the offence. The prosecution has to prove both of these elements so that the magistrates or jury are satisfied beyond reasonable doubt of their existence. If this is not done, the person will be acquitted, as in English law all persons are presumed innocent until proven guilty – **Woolmington** *v* **DPP** (1935).

Figure 1.1 Elements of an offence

Actus reus

An *actus reus* can consist of more than just an act, it comprises all the elements of the offence other than the state of mind of the defendant. Depending on the offence, this may include the circumstances in which it was committed, and/or the consequences of what was done. For example, the crime of rape requires unlawful sexual intercourse by a man with a person without their consent. The lack of consent is a surrounding circumstance which exists independently of the accused's act.

Similarly, the same act may be part of the *actus reus* of different crimes, depending on its consequences. Stabbing someone, for example, may form the *actus reus* of murder if the victim dies, or of causing grievous bodily harm (GBH) if the victim survives; the accused's behaviour is the same in both cases, but the consequences of it dictate whether the *actus reus* of murder or GBH has been committed.

Conduct must be voluntary

If the accused is to be found guilty of a crime, his or her behaviour in committing the *actus reus* must have been voluntary. Behaviour will usually only be considered involuntary where the accused was not in control of his or her own body (when the defence of insanity or automatism may be available) or where there is extremely strong pressure from someone else, such as a threat that the accused will be killed if he or she does not commit a particular offence (when the defence of duress may be available).

Some accidents may be viewed by the court as amounting to involuntary conduct that does not give rise to criminal liability. However, in **R v Brady** (2006) the Court of Appeal considered the case where a young man had drunk heavily and taken drugs and then sat on a low railing on a balcony that overlooked a dance floor. He lost his balance and fell, breaking the neck of a dancer below who was subsequently wheelchair bound. While the fall was a tragic accident the Court of Appeal pointed to his earlier voluntary conduct of becoming heavily intoxicated and sitting precariously on the railing and considered that this voluntary conduct was sufficient to be treated as having caused the injuries.

In a much criticised decision of **R v Larsonneur** (1933), a Frenchwoman was arrested as an illegal immigrant by the authorities in Ireland and brought back to the UK in custody, where she was charged with being an alien illegally in the UK and convicted. This is not what most of us would describe as acting voluntarily, but it apparently fitted the courts' definition at the time. It is probably stricter than a decision would be today, but it is important to realise that the courts do define 'involuntary' quite narrowly at times.

Types of *actus reus*

Crimes can be divided into three types, depending on the nature of their *actus reus*.

Action crimes

The *actus reus* here is simply an act, the consequences of that act being immaterial. For example, perjury is committed whenever someone makes a statement which they do not believe to be true while on oath. Whether or not that statement makes a difference to the trial is not important to whether the offence of perjury has been committed.

State of affairs crimes

Here the *actus reus* consists of circumstances, and sometimes consequences, but no acts – they are 'being' rather than 'doing' offences. The offence committed in **R v Larsonneur** is an example of this, where the *actus reus* consisted of being a foreigner who had not been given permission to come to Britain and was found in the country.

Result crimes

The *actus reus* of these is distinguished by the fact that the accused's behaviour must produce a particular result – the most obvious being murder, where the accused's act must cause the death of a human being.

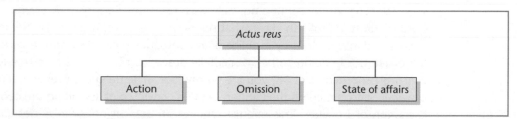

Figure 1.2 *Actus reus*

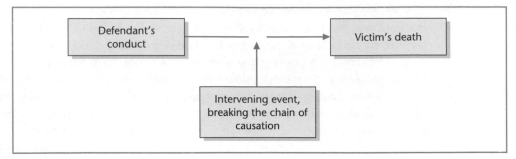

Figure 1.3 Breaking the chain of causation

Causation

Result crimes raise the issue of causation: the result must be proved to have been caused by the defendant's act. If the result is caused by an intervening act or event, which was completely unconnected with the defendant's act and which could not have been foreseen, the defendant will not be liable. Where the result is caused by a combination of the defendant's act and the intervening act, and the defendant's act remains a substantial cause, then he or she will still be liable. Much of the case law on the issue of causation has arisen in the context of murder, and therefore this issue will be discussed in detail in Chapter 3 on murder at p. 52. However, it should be remembered that the issue of causation is relevant to all result crimes.

Omissions

Criminal liability is rarely imposed for true omissions at common law, though there are situations where a non-lawyer would consider that there has been an omission but in law it will be treated as an act and liability will be imposed. There are also situations where the accused has a duty to act, and in these cases there may be liability for a true omission.

Act or omission?

It must first be decided whether in law you are dealing with an act or an omission. There are three situations where this question arises: continuing acts, supervening faults and euthanasia.

Continuing acts

The concept of a continuing act was used in **Fagan v Metropolitan Police Commissioner** (1969) to allow what seemed to be an omission to be treated as an act. The defendant was told by a police officer to park his car close to the kerb; he obeyed the order, but in doing so he accidentally drove his car on to the constable's foot. The constable shouted, 'Get off, you are on my foot.' The defendant replied, 'Fuck you, you can wait', and turned off the ignition. He was convicted of assaulting the constable in the execution of his duty. This offence requires an act; an omission is not sufficient. The defendant appealed on the grounds that at the time he committed the act of driving on to the officer's foot, he lacked *mens rea*, and though he had *mens rea* when he refused to remove the car, this was an omission, and the *actus reus* required an act. The appeal was dismissed, on the basis that driving on to the officer's foot and staying there was one single continuous act, rather than an act followed by an omission. So long as the defendant had the *mens rea* at some point during that continuing act, he was liable.

The same principle was held to apply in **Kaitamaki** (1985). The accused was charged with rape, and his defence was that at the time when he penetrated the woman, he had thought she was consenting. However, he did not withdraw when he realised that she was not consenting. The court held that the *actus reus* of rape was a continuing act, and so when Kaitamaki realised that his victim did not consent (and therefore formed the necessary *mens rea*) the *actus reus* was still in progress.

Supervening fault

A person who is aware that he or she has acted in a way that has endangered another's life or property, and does nothing to prevent the relevant harm occurring, may be criminally liable, with the original act being treated as the *actus reus* of the crime. In practice this principle can impose liability on defendants who do not have *mens rea* when they commit the original act, but do have it at the point when they fail to act to prevent the harm they have caused.

KEY CASE

This was the case in **R** *v* **Miller** (1982). The defendant was squatting in a building. He lay on a mattress, lit a cigarette and fell asleep. Some time later, he woke up to find the mattress on fire. Making no attempt to put the fire out, he simply moved into the next room and went back to sleep. The house suffered serious damage in the subsequent fire. Miller was convicted of arson. As the fire was his fault, the court was prepared to treat the *actus reus* of the offence as being his original act of dropping the cigarette.

> People who create a dangerous situation are under a duty to act to put a stop to that danger when they become aware of it.

A rare example of the principle in **Miller** being applied by the courts is the case of **Director of Public Prosecutions** *v* **Santra-Bermudez** (2003). A police officer had decided to undertake a search of the defendant, as she suspected that he was a ticket tout. Initially she had asked him to empty his pockets and in doing so he revealed that he was in possession of some syringes without needles attached to them. The police officer asked the defendant if he was in possession of any needles or sharp objects. He replied that he was not. The police officer proceeded to put her hand into the defendant's pocket to continue the search when her finger was pricked by a hypodermic needle. When challenged that he had said he was not in possession of any other sharp items, the defendant shrugged his shoulders and smirked at the police officer. The defendant was subsequently found guilty of an assault occasioning actual bodily harm (discussed on p. 145). This offence is defined as requiring the commission of an act, as opposed to an omission, but the appeal court applied the principles laid down in **Miller**. By informing the police officer that he was not in possession of any sharp items or needles, the defendant had created a dangerous situation; he was then under a duty to prevent the harm occurring. He had failed to carry out his duty by telling the police officer the truth.

A recent example of **Miller** being applied is **R** *v* **Evans** (2009). In that case the appellant was the elder half-sister of the victim. She had supplied the victim with heroin and after the victim had injected herself with the drug, the victim had shown signs of overdosing. The appellant had recognised those signs but had been frightened to call for medical assistance in case she or the victim got into trouble. She therefore put the victim to bed, wiped water on her face to cool her and hoped that she would sleep it off. In the morning the victim was dead. Following the case of **R** *v* **Kennedy (No. 2)** a prosecution for constructive manslaughter could not succeed because the requirement of causation would not be satisfied. Instead the appellant was successfully prosecuted for gross negligence manslaughter and her appeal dismissed. A duty to act was found relying on the case of **Miller**.

TOPICAL ISSUE

Euthanasia

Euthanasia is the name given to the practice of helping severely ill people to die, either at their request, or by taking the decision that life support should be withdrawn when the person is no longer capable of making that decision. In some countries euthanasia is legal but, in this country, intentionally causing someone's death can constitute murder, even if carried out for the most compassionate reasons. However, in the light of the case of **Airedale National Health Service Trust** *v* **Bland** (1993), liability will only be imposed in such cases for a positive act, and the courts will sometimes say there was a mere omission when strictly speaking there would appear to have been an act, in order to avoid imposing criminal liability. The case concerned Anthony Bland, who had been seriously injured in the Hillsborough football stadium disaster when only 17. As a result he suffered irreversible brain damage, leaving him in a persistent vegetative state, with no hope of recovery or improvement, though he was not actually brain-dead. His family and the health trust responsible for his medical treatment wanted to turn off his life-support machine but, in order to ensure that this did not make them liable for murder, they went to the High Court to seek a declaration that if they did this they would not be committing any criminal offence or civil wrong.

The declaration was granted by the High Court, and upheld by the House of Lords. Since the House was acting in its civil capacity, strictly speaking the case is not binding on the criminal courts, but it is highly persuasive. Part of the decision stated that turning off the life-support system should be viewed as an omission, rather than an act. Lord Goff said:

> I agree that the doctor's conduct in discontinuing life support can properly be categorised as an omission. It is true that it may be difficult to describe what the doctor actually does as an omission, for example where he takes some positive step to bring the life support to an end. But discontinuation of life support is, for present purposes, no different from not initiating life support in the first place. In each case, the doctor is simply allowing his patient to die in the sense that he is desisting from taking a step which might, in certain circumstances, prevent his patient from dying as a result of his pre-existing condition: and as a matter of general principle an omission such as this will not be unlawful unless it constitutes a breach of duty to the patient.

In this case, it was pointed out that there was no breach of duty, because it was no longer in Anthony Bland's interests to continue treatment as there was no hope of recovery.

The decision of **Bland** was found to conform with the European Convention on Human Rights by the High Court in **NHS Trust A** *v* **M** and **NHS Trust B** *v* **H** (2000). In particular, there was no violation of the right to life protected by Art. 2 of the Convention. The High Court stated that the scope of Art. 2 was restricted to positive acts, and did not apply to mere omissions.

Offences capable of being committed by omission

Where the conduct in question is genuinely an omission, and not one of the categories just discussed, the next question is whether the particular offence can, in law, be committed by omission. This depends on the definition of the offence. Some of the offences have been defined always to require an act; some can be committed by either an act or an omission. For example, murder and manslaughter can be committed by omission, but assault cannot (**Fagan** *v* **Metropolitan Police Commissioner**, above).

An example of the offence of murder being committed by an omission is **R** *v* **Gibbins and Proctor** (1918). In that case, a man and a woman were living together with the man's daughter. They failed to give the child food and she died. The judge directed that they were guilty of murder if they withheld food with intent to cause her grievous bodily harm, as a result of which she died. Their conviction was upheld by the Court of Appeal.

A duty to act

Where the offence is capable in law of being committed by an omission, it can only be committed by a person who was under a duty to act (in other words, a duty not to commit that omission). This is because English law places no general duty on people to help each other or save each other from harm. Thus, if a man sees a boy drowning in a lake, it is arguable that under English criminal law the man is under no duty to save him, and can walk past without incurring criminal liability for the child's subsequent death.

A duty to act will only be imposed where there is some kind of relationship between the two people, and the closer the relationship the more likely it is that a duty to act will exist. So far the courts have recognised a range of relationships as giving rise to a duty to act, and other relationships may in the future be recognised as so doing.

Special relationship

Special relationships tend to be implied between members of the same family. An obvious example of a special relationship giving rise to a duty to act is that of parents to their children. In **R** *v* **Lowe** (1973), a father failed to call a doctor when his nine-week-old baby became ill. He had a duty to act, though on the facts he lacked the *mens rea* of an offence partly because he was of low intelligence.

Voluntary acceptance of responsibility for another

People may choose to take on responsibility for another. They will then have a duty to act to protect that person if the person falls into difficulty. In **Gibbins and Proctor**, a woman lived with a man who had a daughter from an earlier relationship. He paid the woman money to buy food for the family. Sadly they did not feed the child, and the child died of starvation. The woman was found to have voluntarily accepted responsibility for the child and was liable, along with the child's father, for murder.

KEY CASE

In **R** v **Stone and Dobinson** (1977), Stone's sister, Fanny, lived with him and his girlfriend, Dobinson. Fanny was mentally ill, and became very anxious about putting on weight. She stopped eating properly and became bed bound. Realising that she was ill, the defendants had made

People may have a duty to act to protect another when they voluntarily assume responsibility for them.

half-hearted and unsuccessful attempts to get medical help and after several weeks she died. The couple's efforts were found to have been inadequate. The Court of Appeal said that they had accepted responsibility for Fanny as her carers, and that once she became bed bound the appellants were, in the circumstances, obliged either to summon help or else to care for her themselves. As they had done neither, they were both found to be liable for manslaughter.

Contract

A contract may give rise to a duty to act. This duty can extend not just for the benefit of the parties to the contract, but also to those who are not party to the contract, but are likely to be injured by failure to perform it. In **R** v **Pittwood** (1902), a gatekeeper of a railway crossing opened the gate to let a car through, and then forgot to shut it when he went off to lunch. As a result, a haycart crossed the line while a train was approaching, and was hit, causing the driver's death. The gatekeeper was convicted of manslaughter.

Statute

Some pieces of legislation impose duties to act on individuals. For example, s. 1 of the Children and Young Persons Act 1933 imposes a duty to provide for a child in one's care. Failure to do so constitutes an offence.

Defendant created a dangerous situation

Where a defendant has created a dangerous situation, they are under a duty to act to remedy this. This duty is illustrated by the case of **R** v **Miller**, which is discussed at p. 13.

Criticism

It will depend on the facts of each case whether the court is prepared to conclude that the relationship is sufficiently close to justify criminal liability for a failure to act to protect a victim. This approach has been heavily criticised by some academics, who argue that the moral basis of the law is undermined by a situation which allows people to ignore a drowning child whom they could have easily saved, and incur no criminal liability so long as they are strangers. In some countries, legislation has created special offences which impose liability on those who fail to take steps which could be taken without any personal risk to themselves in order to save another from death or serious personal injury. The offence created is not necessarily a homicide offence, but it is an acknowledgement by the criminal law that the individual should have taken action in these circumstances. Photographers involved in the death of Princess Diana were prosecuted for such an offence in France.

Table 1.1 Duty to act

Existence of a duty to act	Case authority
Special relationship	**R v Lowe**
Voluntary acceptance of responsibility for another	**R v Stone and Dobinson**
Contract	**R v Pittwood**
Statute	
Defendant created a dangerous situation	**R v Miller**

Termination of the duty

The duty to act will terminate when the special relationship ends, so a parent, for example, probably stops having a duty to act once the child is grown up.

Mens rea

Mens rea is the Latin for 'guilty mind' and traditionally refers to the state of mind of the person committing the crime. The required *mens rea* varies depending on the offence, but there are two main states of mind which separately or together can constitute the necessary *mens rea* of a criminal offence: intention and recklessness.

When discussing *mens rea*, we often refer to the difference between subjective and objective tests. Put simply, a subjective test involves looking at what the actual defendant was thinking (or, in practice, what the magistrates or jury believe the defendant was thinking), whereas an objective test considers what a reasonable person would have thought in the defendant's position. The courts today are showing a strong preference for subjective tests for *mens rea*.

Intention

Intention is a subjective concept: a court is concerned purely with what the particular defendant was intending at the time of the offence, and not what a reasonable person would have intended in the same circumstances.

To help comprehension of the legal meaning of intention, the concept can be divided into two: direct intention and indirect intention. Where the consequence of an intention is actually desired, it is called direct intent – where, for example, Ann shoots at Ben because Ann wants to kill Ben. However, a jury is also entitled to find intention where a defendant did not desire a result, but it is a virtually certain consequence of the act, and the accused realises this and goes ahead anyway. This is called indirect intention (or sometimes oblique intention). An example might be where Ann throws a rock at Ben through a closed window, hoping to hit Ben on the head with it. Ann may not actively want the window to smash, but knows that it will happen. Therefore, when Ann throws the rock Ann intends to break the window as well as to hit Ben. It should be noted that Lord Steyn suggested *obiter*, in the House of Lords judgment of **R** *v* **Woollin** (1998), that 'intention' did not necessarily have precisely the same meaning in every context in the criminal law. He suggested that for some offences nothing less than purpose (direct intention) would be sufficient. He gave a possible example as the case of **Steane** (1947) which concerned the offence of assisting the enemy with intent to do so. Steane had given a broadcast for the Nazis in order to save his family from being sent to concentration camps. The accused did not desire to help the Nazis and was found to be not guilty of the offence.

The developments in the law on intention have come about as a result of murder cases, and so we discuss intention more fully in Chapter 3.

● Recklessness

In everyday language, recklessness means taking an unjustified risk. Its legal definition has radically changed in recent years. It is now clear that it is a subjective form of *mens rea*, so the focus is on what the defendant was thinking. In 1981, in the case of **MPC** *v* **Caldwell**, Lord Diplock created an objective form of recklessness, but this was abolished in 2003 by the case of **R** *v* **G and another**.

A subjective test

Following the House of Lords judgment of **R** *v* **G and another**, recklessness will always be interpreted as requiring a subjective test. In that case, the House favoured the definition of recklessness provided by the Law Commission's Draft Criminal Code Bill in 1989:

> A person acts recklessly . . . with respect to –
> (i)   a circumstance when he is aware of a risk that it exists or will exist;
> (ii) a result when he is aware of a risk that it will occur;
> and it is, in the circumstances known to him, unreasonable to take the risk.

Defendants must always be aware of the risk in order to satisfy this test of recklessness. In addition, their conduct must have been unreasonable. It would appear that any level of awareness of a risk will be sufficient, provided the court finds the risk taking unreasonable.

Until the case of **R** *v* **G and another**, the leading case on subjective recklessness was **R** *v* **Cunningham** (1957). In **R** *v* **Cunningham**, the defendant broke a gas meter to steal the money in it, and the gas seeped out into the house next door. Cunningham's prospective mother-in-law was sleeping there, and became so ill that her life was endangered. Cunningham was charged under s. 23 of the Offences Against the Person Act 1861 with 'maliciously administering a noxious thing so as to endanger life'.

The Court of Appeal said that 'maliciously' meant intentionally or recklessly. They defined recklessness as where: 'the accused has foreseen that the particular kind of harm might be done and yet has gone on to take the risk of it'. This is called a subjective test: the accused must actually have had the required foresight. Cunningham would therefore have been reckless if he realised there was a risk of the gas escaping and endangering someone, and went ahead anyway. His conviction was in fact quashed because of a misdirection at the trial.

In order to define recklessness, the House of Lords in **R** v **G and another** preferred to use the words of the Law Commission's Draft Criminal Code Bill (the Draft Code), rather than its own earlier words in **Cunningham**. It is likely, therefore, in future that the Draft Code's definition will become the single definition of recklessness, and the phrasing in **Cunningham** will no longer be used.

There are three main differences between the definition of subjective recklessness in the Draft Code, and the definition in **Cunningham**. First, the **Cunningham** test only refers to taking risks as to a result and makes no mention of taking risks as to a circumstance. The Law Commission, in preparing its Draft Code, felt that this was a gap in the law. It therefore expressly applies the test of recklessness to the taking of risks in relation to a circumstance. Secondly, the Draft Code adds an additional restriction to a finding of recklessness: the defendant's risk taking must have been 'unreasonable'. To determine whether the risk taking was unreasonable the courts will balance such factors as the seriousness of the risk and the social value of the defendant's conduct. William Wilson (2003) observes that: 'Jumping a traffic light is likely to be deemed reckless if actuated by a desire to get home quickly for tea but not if the desire was to get a seriously ill person to hospital.' Thirdly, the **Cunningham** test for recklessness only requires foresight of the type of harm that actually occurred. It is arguable that the Law Commission's Draft Code requires awareness of the risk that the actual damage caused might occur (see Davies (2004) listed in the bibliography).

In **Booth** v **CPS** (2006) the High Court applied **R** v **G and another** and interpreted it as including where a person, being aware of a risk, chooses to close their mind to that risk. In that case the defendant had run onto a road without looking and caused damage to a car as a result. The High Court held that as the defendant was aware of the risks of running into the road and, being aware of those risks, put them out of his mind, he was reckless as to the causing of damage to property and was liable.

In the tragic case of **R** v **Brady** (2006) where a young intoxicated man in a nightclub fell from a balcony onto a dancer, breaking her neck, the man appealed against his conviction for causing a non fatal offence against the person on the basis that the jury had been misdirected on the issue of *mens rea*. He argued that the jury should have been told that recklessness for the purposes of **R** v **G and another** required foresight of an 'obvious and significant risk' of injury to another by his actions. This argument was rejected by the Court of Appeal which stated that foresight of some risk of harm was sufficient.

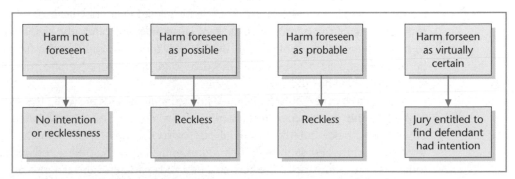

Figure 1.4 Foresight and *mens rea*

Caldwell recklessness abolished

In 1981, the case of **Metropolitan Police Commission** v **Caldwell** created a new and much wider test for recklessness. Caldwell was an ex-employee of a hotel and nursed a grudge against its owner. He started a fire at the hotel, which caused some damage, and was charged with arson. This offence is defined in the Criminal Damage Act 1971 as requiring either recklessness or intention.

On the facts, there was no intention and, on the issue of recklessness, Lord Diplock stated that the definition of recklessness in **Cunningham** was too narrow for the Criminal Damage Act 1971. For that Act, he said, recklessness should not only include the **Cunningham** meaning, but also go further. He said that a person was reckless as to whether any property would be destroyed or damaged if:

1 he does an act which in fact creates an obvious risk that property would be destroyed or damaged; and
2 when he does the act he either has not given any thought to the possibility of there being any such risk or has recognised that there was some risk involved and has nonetheless gone on to do it.

Thus, there were actually two potential ways that **Caldwell** recklessness could be proved. The first way was very similar to the **Cunningham** test: 'he does an act which in fact creates . . . a risk . . . and . . . has recognised that there was some risk'. The second way was the important extension to the meaning of recklessness: 'he does an act which in fact creates . . . an obvious risk . . . and . . . he has not given any thought to the possibility of there being any such risk'.

The first limb of this definition is essentially a subjective test, because it requires the defendant actually to see the risk – we will call this limb the 'advertent' limb as the defendant adverts to the risk; he or she sees the risk.

The second limb is more difficult to categorise. It has often been described as an objective test, because the defendant does not actually have to see the risk, so long as the risk was so obvious that a reasonable person would have seen it. For this reason, **Caldwell** recklessness as a whole is often described as an objective standard because, although its first limb is subjective, it is much easier for the prosecution to prove the second limb – it is more difficult to prove what was actually going through defendants' minds at any particular time than it is to prove what reasonable people would consider should have been going through their minds. However, the label 'objective' was criticised by the House of Lords in **R** v **Reid** (1990), on the basis that, even for the second limb, the actual state of mind of the particular defendant is still relevant, since the defendant is required to have given no thought to the risk. We will therefore call this the 'inadvertent' limb because essentially it means that the defendant failed to advert to the risk; he or she failed to think about the risk.

In **R** v **Lawrence** (1982), decided immediately after **Caldwell**, the House of Lords looked at the meaning of recklessness in the context of the old offence of reckless driving, and held that the **Caldwell** test of recklessness applied to this offence. They reformulated the test slightly in their judgment, so that the phrase 'obvious risk' became 'obvious and serious risk'. The test also had to be adapted to take into account the fact that the type of risk would inevitably be different for this different offence. Therefore, instead of talking about a risk that 'property would be destroyed or damaged', they spoke of a risk of 'injury to the person or of substantial damage to property'.

The **Caldwell** test was further adapted and analysed by the House of Lords in **R** v **Reid** (1990). Reid had been driving his car along a busy road near Hyde Park in London. He tried to overtake a car on the inside lane, but the inside lane narrowed to accommodate a taxi-drivers' hut. Reid's car hit the hut, and spun off into the oncoming traffic. His passenger was killed and he was charged with the old offence of causing death by reckless driving. The jury were directed in accordance with the **Caldwell/Lawrence** test, and he was convicted. An appeal against this conviction eventually reached the House of Lords; it was rejected, but the House tried to clarify certain issues relating to the **Caldwell** test. They made it clear that, while Lord Diplock had given a model direction in **Caldwell** (as amended by **Lawrence**), it was no longer necessary to use his exact words, for it could be adapted to fit the particular offence. Courts were free to move away from his words altogether if it would assist the jury to understand the meaning of the test.

Following Lord Goff's comments in **Reid**, it appears that when Lord Diplock spoke of the risk being 'obvious', the risk only needed to be obvious in relation to the inadvertent limb, and it need not be proved in relation to the advertent limb. The logic for this conclusion is that if the defendant actually personally saw the risk then it does not really matter whether a reasonable person would have seen it: the defendant is at fault for seeing the risk and going ahead anyway. On the other hand, both limbs of the test required that the risk must be serious.

Taking into account these points of clarification, Lord Diplock's model direction could be redrafted as follows:

> A person will be reckless if (1) he or she does an act which in fact creates a serious risk that property would be destroyed or damaged and (2) either (a) when he or she does the act he or she has not given any thought to the possibility of there being any such risk, and the risk was in fact obvious; or (b) has recognised that there was some risk of that kind involved and has nonetheless gone on to do it.

Where did *Caldwell* apply?

Following the decision of **Caldwell**, two tests for recklessness existed. **Cunningham** applied to most offences requiring recklessness and **Caldwell** applied to a small minority of offences. Initially it was thought that **Caldwell** would have a wide application. In **Seymour**, Watkins LJ stated that '[t]he *Lawrence* direction on recklessness is comprehensive and of general application to all offences . . .' unless otherwise specified by Parliament. In fact, **Caldwell** was only applied to a narrow range of offences. Thus, **Caldwell** was the *mens rea* for criminal damage, which was the offence in **Caldwell** itself. In **R** v **Seymour** (1983) it was used for a common law offence of reckless manslaughter, but later in **R** v **Adomako** (1994) the House of Lords held that this offence did not exist (see p. 119).

The *Caldwell* lacuna

The idea behind the test developed in **Caldwell** was to broaden the concept of recklessness, so that people who it was felt were morally at fault could not escape liability because it was impossible to prove their actual state of mind. Unfortunately, the test left a loophole, or 'lacuna', through which equally blameworthy conduct could escape liability. **Caldwell** recklessness imposed liability on those who either realised there was a risk and took it anyway, or who failed to see a risk that, by the standards of ordinary people, they ought to have seen. But what about the defendant who did consider whether there was a risk, but wrongly concluded that there was not? An example might be where a person is driving a car and wants to overtake a lorry. In approaching a bend, the car driver considers whether there is a risk involved in overtaking on this stretch of the road, and wrongly decides that there is not. In fact there is a risk and an accident is caused. In theory, the car driver in this situation would appear to fall outside Lord Diplock's two limbs of recklessness, yet most people would agree that the driver was at least as much at fault as a person who fell within the inadvertent recklessness limb by failing even to consider a risk.

The issue was eventually tackled by the House of Lords in **R** v **Reid**. The House recognised that the lacuna did in fact exist, but said that it was narrower than some academics had originally suggested. It was held that people would only fall within the lacuna if they thought about whether there was a risk and, due to a *bona fide* mistake (meaning a genuine, honest mistake), decided there was none; in such cases they would not be considered reckless. If they thought about whether there was a risk, and decided on the basis of a grossly negligent mistake that there was none, then they would still be reckless for the purposes of **Caldwell**. The logical conclusion seems to be, though the House of Lords did not specifically state this, that this last scenario actually created a third limb of **Caldwell** recklessness.

Problems with *Caldwell* recklessness

Two tests

Having two different tests for the same word caused confusion and was unnecessary. There was concern that the higher **Cunningham** standard applied to rape and the lower **Caldwell** standard applied to criminal damage. This meant that property was better protected than people.

Objective standard for mens rea

The adoption of **Caldwell** recklessness meant that a potentially objective standard was being applied to determine *mens rea*, while many academics and practitioners felt that a *mens rea* requirement should always be subjective. Lord Diplock argued that there were three good reasons for extending the test for recklessness in this way. First, a defendant may be reckless in the ordinary sense of the word, meaning careless, regardless or heedless of the possible consequences, even though the risk of harm had not crossed his or

Table 1.2 *Caldwell* recklessness

Think about the risk	See the risk	Mens rea
Yes	Yes	Subjective limb of **Caldwell** recklessness
No	No	Objective limb of **Caldwell** recklessness
Yes	No	Lacuna, not **Caldwell** recklessness

her mind. Secondly, a tribunal of fact cannot be expected to rule confidently on whether the accused's state of mind has crossed 'the narrow dividing line' between being aware of risk and not troubling to consider it. Thirdly, the latter state of mind was no less blameworthy than the former.

Overlap with negligence

The **Caldwell** test blurred the distinction between recklessness and negligence (discussed on p. **25**). Before **Caldwell**, there was an obvious difference: recklessness meant knowingly taking a risk; negligence traditionally meant unknowingly taking a risk of which you should have been aware. **Caldwell** clearly came very close to negligence.

The lacuna

A person who falls within the lacuna appears to be as morally at fault as a person who falls within the advertent limb of **Caldwell** recklessness. The case of **R** v **Merrick** has been criticised as unrealistic. In practice, replacing electrical equipment often creates a temporary danger which cannot be avoided, yet technically each time in criminal law the electrician is reckless.

Problems for juries

The **Caldwell**/**Lawrence** formula is notorious for being difficult for juries to understand.

Defendant incapable of seeing the risk

The harshness of the **Caldwell** test for recklessness was highlighted by the case of **Elliott** *v* **C**. That case drew attention to the fact that a defendant could be found to be reckless under **Caldwell** when they had not seen a risk and were incapable of seeing the risk because, for example, they were young and of low intelligence. The defendant was a 14-year-old girl, who was in a remedial class at school. Playing with matches and white spirit, she set fire to a neighbour's shed, which was destroyed. The magistrates found that she gave no thought to the risk of damage, but, even if she had, she would not have been capable of appreciating it. Consequently, she was acquitted of recklessly destroying the shed. The Divisional Court allowed an appeal by the prosecution, on the grounds that the **Caldwell** test was purely objective, and the fact that the girl was not capable of appreciating the risk was irrelevant to the issue of recklessness. When the court in **Caldwell** had talked about an obvious risk, it had meant obvious to a hypothetical reasonable person, and not obvious to the particular defendant if he or she had thought about it.

An attempt was made to moderate the harshness of the inadvertent test of recklessness in **R** *v* **R** (1991), a case in which marital rape was first recognised as a crime. Counsel for the accused unsuccessfully argued that in deciding what was obvious to the reasonable person, that reasonable person should be assumed to have the permanent, relevant characteristics of the accused. This method is used by the courts to moderate the objective test for the partial defence of provocation (see p. 84). The Court of Appeal held that there was no reason for bringing such an approach into the **Caldwell** test.

However, in **R** *v* **Reid** the harsh approach to this issue taken in these two cases was softened slightly. The House of Lords recognised that sometimes the issue of capacity

1

Elements of a crime

could be relevant, but the examples given were limited to situations where there was a sudden loss of capacity, such as a heart attack while driving. More recently in **R** *v* **Coles** (1994), a case involving arson committed by a youth of an allegedly low mental capacity, the Court of Appeal followed **Elliott** strictly. It stated that the only relevant capacity was that of the average person. This was the central issue in the leading case of **R** *v* **G and another** (2003).

In **R** *v* **G and another** (2003) two boys aged 11 and 12 had gone camping without their parents' permission. In the middle of the night they had entered the back yard of a

> The test for recklessness is subjective.

shop where they had found some bundles of newspaper. They had started to read the newspapers and had then set light to some of the papers. They put the burning newspapers underneath a large plastic wheelie bin and left the premises. A large fire resulted that caused £1 million-worth of damage. The boys had thought that the newspaper fire would extinguish itself on the concrete floor of the yard. Neither of them realised that there was any risk of the fire spreading as it did. The trial judge and the Court of Appeal both felt bound by the precedents and reluctantly convicted the boys of arson under the Criminal Damage Act 1971. The House of Lords, however, allowed the appeal and dramatically overruled **Caldwell**. The House considered the option of simply refining the **Caldwell** test in order to achieve justice in the case, by, for example, taking into account the actual characteristics of the defendant when determining whether there was an obvious risk. However, Lord Hutton concluded that Lord Diplock's speech in **Caldwell**:

> . . . has proved notoriously difficult to interpret and those difficulties would not have ended with any refinements which your Lordships might have made to the decision. Indeed those refinements themselves would almost inevitably have prompted further questions and appeals. In these circumstances the preferable course is to overrule **Caldwell**.

The House did not mince its words in criticising the **Caldwell** decision. It stated:

> The surest test of a new legal rule is not whether it satisfies a team of logicians but how it performs in the real world. With the benefit of hindsight the verdict must be that the rule laid down by the majority in **Caldwell** failed this test. It was severely criticised by academic lawyers of distinction. It did not command respect among practitioners and judges. Jurors found it difficult to understand; it also sometimes offended their sense of justice. Experience suggests that in **Caldwell** the law took a wrong turn.

Having abolished **Caldwell** recklessness, the court then quoted with approval the subjective definition of recklessness provided by the Draft Criminal Code Bill, discussed above.

A future for Caldwell recklessness?

In this chapter we have taken the view that **Caldwell** recklessness has been abolished and will no longer be applied in criminal law. However, an alternative interpretation of the impact of **R** *v* **G and another** (2003) has been put forward by the respected criminal law academics Simester and Sullivan (2007). They point out that Lord Bingham at the start of his judgment stated: 'I mean to make it as plain as I can that I am not addressing the meaning of "reckless" in any other statutory or common law context.' Relying on this statement Simester and Sullivan argue that **Caldwell** recklessness could theoretically still be applied to some statutory offences. They suggest that the most likely offences where this may occur are those where the recklessness refers to the *manner* in which an *actus reus* is performed (e.g. reckless driving).

This argument is not persuasive. The judges in the House of Lords pointed to fundamental problems with the old **Caldwell** test and, in the light of those criticisms, it seems unlikely that they would then decide that it was suitable to be applied in the future. The Court of Appeal has stated in **Attorney General's Reference No 3 of 2003** (2004) that **R** *v* **G and another** recklessness did not only apply to criminal damage and that it applied to conduct crimes (including misconduct in public office) as well as result crimes such as criminal damage. In practice, even before **R** *v* **G and another, Caldwell** was barely being applied by the criminal courts, the main offence to which it did apply was criminal damage. So even if Simester and Sullivan are right in their interpretation of **R** *v* **G and another** there could only be a very small range of offences to which **Caldwell** could be applied.

Negligence

Negligence is a concept that is most often found in civil law, but it does have some relevance to criminal law as well. The existence of negligence is traditionally determined according to an objective test, which asks whether the defendant's conduct has fallen below the standards of the reasonable person. Historically, the standard of the reasonable person for the purposes of criminal negligence took no account of the defendant's actual characteristics: in **McCrone** *v* **Riding** (1938), which concerned a charge of careless driving, it was held that the accused's driving could be considered careless if he had failed to come up to the standard of a reasonably experienced driver, even though he was himself a learner driver.

True crimes of negligence are rare in criminal law, though there are some statutory offences of negligence, particularly those concerned with motoring. More commonly, an offence of strict liability (where no *mens rea* is required) may allow the accused to use the defence of having acted with all due diligence: in other words, of not being negligent.

There is one important common law crime where negligence is an element of the offence: gross negligence manslaughter. Because this is a very serious offence, the courts are not just looking for negligence but for gross negligence. The leading case on the meaning of gross negligence is the House of Lords judgment of **R** *v* **Adomako** (1994). In that case the House stated that the question of whether gross negligence existed was a jury issue to be determined taking into account all the circumstances. The jury had to consider whether the defendant had been so negligent that their conduct went beyond a mere matter of compensation for the civil courts and justified criminal liability.

There is some academic debate as to whether negligence can be properly described as a form of *mens rea*. In **Attorney-General's Reference (No. 2 of 1999)** the Court of

Appeal stated it was not a form of *mens rea* as it could be proved without the jury having to look at the state of mind of the defendant. This case arose from the unsuccessful prosecution of Great Western Trains following the Southall train crash in 1997. While the Court of Appeal accepted that gross negligence was not a form of *mens rea*, a person's state of mind could still be relevant to proving gross negligence. It could be relevant because **Adomako** requires the jury, when deciding whether gross negligence exists, to consider all the circumstances of the case. But the jury were not required always to look at the mental state of the defendant; they might find that their physical conduct alone fell so far below the standards of the reasonable person that it justified criminal liability. For example, following the Hatfield railway disaster, a jury might find that the simple fact of not repairing the railway line constituted gross negligence, without needing to look at the mental state of any particular company employee.

We will consider the concept of gross negligence in much more detail when we look at the offence of gross negligence manslaughter at p. 111.

Transferred malice

If Ann shoots at Ben, intending to kill him, but happens to miss, and shoots and kills Chris instead, Ann will be liable for the murder of Chris. This is because of the principle known as transferred malice. Under this principle, if Ann has the *mens rea* of a particular crime and does the *actus reus* of the crime, Ann is guilty of the crime even though the *actus reus* may differ in some way from that intended. The *mens rea* is simply transferred to the new *actus reus*. Either intention or recklessness can be so transferred.

As a result the defendant will be liable for the same crime even if the victim is not the intended victim. In **Latimer** (1886), the defendant aimed a blow at someone with his belt. The belt recoiled off that person and hit the victim, who was severely injured. The court held that Latimer was liable for maliciously wounding the unexpected victim. His intention to wound the person he aimed at was transferred to the person actually injured.

Where the accused would have had a defence if the crime committed had been completed against the intended victim, that defence is also transferred. So if Ann shot at Ben in self-defence and hit and killed Chris instead, Ann would be able to rely on the defence if charged with Chris's murder.

In **Attorney-General's Reference (No. 3 of 1994)** the defendant stabbed his girlfriend who was to his knowledge between 22 and 24 weeks pregnant with their child. The girlfriend underwent an operation on a cut in the wall of her uterus but it was not realised at the time that the stabbing had damaged the foetus's abdomen. She subsequently gave birth prematurely to a baby girl who later died from the complications of a premature birth. Before the child's death the defendant was charged with the offence of wounding his girlfriend with intent to cause her grievous bodily harm to which he pleaded guilty. After the child died, he was in addition charged with murdering the child. At the close of the prosecution case the judge upheld a defence submission that the facts could not give rise to a conviction for murder or manslaughter and accordingly directed the jury to acquit. The Attorney-General referred the case to the Court of Appeal for a ruling to clarify the law in the field. The Court of Appeal considered the foetus to be an integral part of the mother until its birth. Thus any intention to injure the mother prior to its birth was treated as an intention to injure the foetus. If on birth the baby subsequently died, an intention to injure the baby could be found by applying the doctrine of transferred malice. This approach was rejected by the House of Lords. It held that the foetus was not an integral part of the mother, but a unique organism. The principle of transferred malice could not therefore be applied, and the direction was criticised as being of 'no sound intellectual basis'.

Coincidence of *actus reus* and *mens rea*

The *mens rea* of an offence must be present at the time the *actus reus* is committed. So if, for example, Ann intends to kill Ben on Friday night, but for some reason fails to do so, then quite accidentally runs Ben over on Saturday morning, Ann will not be liable for Ben's murder. However, there are two ways in which the courts have introduced flexibility into this area: continuing acts, which are described on p. 12, and the interpretation of a continuous series of acts as a single transaction. An example of the latter occurred in **Thabo Meli** *v* **R** (1954). The defendants had attempted to kill their victim by beating him over the head, then threw what they assumed was a dead body over a cliff. The victim did die, but from the fall and exposure, and not from the beating. Thus there was an argument that at the time of the *actus reus* the defendants no longer had the *mens rea*. The Privy Council held that throwing him over the cliff was part of one series of acts following through a preconceived plan of action, which therefore could not be seen as separate acts at all, but as a single transaction. The defendants had the required *mens rea* when that transaction began, and therefore *mens rea* and *actus reus* had coincided.

Another example of the single transaction doctrine is the case of **R** *v* **Le Brun** (1992). The defendant had punched his wife on the jaw, knocking her unconscious. He then tried to carry her from the garden into the house. As he attempted to carry her, he dropped her, fracturing her skull and it was this injury which caused her death. The defendant had the *mens rea* for manslaughter but he did not commit the *actus reus* until the later time when he dropped his wife. The Court of Appeal applied the single transaction doctrine and Le Brun's conviction for manslaughter was upheld. It noted, however, that the doctrine of a single transaction would not have applied if the defendant had been trying to help his wife when he subsequently dropped her.

Mens rea and motive

It is essential to realise that *mens rea* has nothing to do with motive. To illustrate this, take the example of a man who suffocates his wife with a pillow, intending to kill her because she is afflicted with a terminal disease which causes her terrible and constant pain. Many people would say that this man's motive is not a bad one – in fact many people would reject the label 'murder' for what he has done. But there is no doubt that he has the necessary *mens rea* for murder, because he intends to kill his wife, even if he does not want to do so. He may not have a guilty mind in the everyday sense, but he does have *mens rea*.

Motive may be relevant when the decision is made on whether or not to prosecute, or later for sentencing, but it makes no difference with regard to legal liability.

Proof of *mens rea*

Under s. 8 of the Criminal Justice Act 1967, where the definition of an offence requires the prosecution to prove that the accused intended or foresaw something, the question of whether that is proved is one for the court or jury to decide on the basis of all the evidence. The fact that a consequence is proved to be the natural and probable result of the accused's actions does not mean that it is proved that he or she intended or foresaw such a result; the jury or the court must decide.

Problems with the law on *mens rea*

Unclear terminology

The terminology used has become very unclear and uncertain. The same word may be defined differently in different offences. For example, 'malice' means one thing in relation to murder, another in the Offences Against the Person Act 1861 and yet another in relation to libel. Some clarity may have been provided by the decision of **R** v **G and another**, which seeks to give a single definition of recklessness.

Mens rea and morality

Problems arise because in practice the courts stretch the law in order to convict those whose conduct they see as blameworthy, while acquitting those whose behaviour they feel does not deserve the strongest censure. For example, the offence of murder requires a finding of intention to kill or to cause serious injury. The courts want to convict terrorists of murder when they kill, yet do they have the requisite *mens rea*? If you plant a bomb but give a warning, do you intend to kill or to cause serious injury? Assuming a fair warning, could death or serious injury be seen as a virtually certain consequence of your acts? What if a terrorist bomber gives a warning that would normally allow sufficient time to evacuate the relevant premises, but, owing to the negligence of the police, the evacuation fails to take place quickly enough and people are killed? The courts are likely to be reluctant to allow this to reduce the terrorist's liability, yet it is hard to see how this terrorist could be said to intend deaths or serious injury to occur – in fact the giving of a warning might suggest the opposite. The courts are equally reluctant to impose liability for murder where it is difficult to find real moral guilt, even though technically this should be irrelevant. The problem is linked to the fact that murder carries a mandatory life sentence, which prevents the judge from taking degrees of moral guilt into account in sentencing (see p. 66).

The academic Alan Norrie has written an exciting article on this subject called 'After Woollin'. He argues that the attempt of the law to separate the question of *mens rea* from broader issues of motive and morality is artificial and not possible in practice. He points to the fact that the jury are merely 'entitled to find' indirect intention and that for some offences (illustrated by **Steane**) only direct intention will suffice. In his view, through this flexibility the courts want to allow themselves the freedom to acquit in morally appropriate cases. Such moral judgments on the basis of the defendant's motive are traditionally excluded from decisions on *mens rea*.

George Fletcher (1978) has noted how historically there has been a development of the law from terms with a moral content such as 'malice' to the identification of 'specific mental states of intending and knowing'. Fletcher observes that:

> Descriptive theorists seek to minimise the normative content of the criminal law in order to render it, in their view, precise and free from the passions of subjective moral judgement. . . . [Such a concern] may impel courts and theorists towards value free rules and concepts; the reality of judgement, blame and punishment generates the contrary pressure and ensures that the quest for a value free science of law cannot succeed.

Making a judgement on someone that he is a 'murderer' and that he should have a life sentence are both moral judgements. Judges are constantly making judgments on right and wrong and what should happen to wrongdoers. But they have to render these judgments in specialist legal terms using concepts such as 'intention' and 'foresight'. These terms are different from everyday terms of moral judgement, but they are used to address moral issues. Norrie argues:

> . . . as a result of this, lawyers end up investing 'nominally descriptive terms with moral force'. Thus terms like 'intent', 'state of mind' and 'mental state' which appear to be descriptive are used to refer to issues that require normative judgement.

In Norrie's view the desire to exclude 'subjective moral judgement' really results from the desire in the past to safeguard a criminal code based on the protection of a particular social order. He considers that:

> . . . if one examines the historical development of the criminal law, one finds that a legal code designed to establish an order based on private property and individual right was legitimated by reference to the dangers of subjective anarchy. This argument was the ideological window-dressing justifying the profound institutional changes taking place.

Thus, he considers that the apparently impartial language used to describe *mens rea* is actually very partial and unfair to many. The law is based upon the supposed characteristics of the average person, stressing the free will of the individual. It ignores the 'substantive moral differences that exist between individuals as they are located across different social classes and according to other relevant divisions such as culture and gender'.

One way to avoid this tension between the legal rules and the moral reality is to develop the defences that are available. Defences such as duress (discussed at p. 358) explicitly allow moral issues to enter into the legal debate through questions of proportionality. Defendants in situations such as **Steane** should be able to avoid liability through the use of a defence such as duress rather than an inconsistent application of the law on *mens rea*.

1

Elements of a crime

Subjective principles in criminal law

In the case of **R** v **G and another** the House of Lords clearly stated that *mens rea* should consist of a subjective test. Lord Bingham observed:

> . . . it is a salutary principle that conviction of serious crime should depend on proof not simply that the defendant caused (by act or omission) an injurious result to another but that his state of mind when so acting was culpable . . . It is clearly blameworthy to take an obvious and significant risk of causing injury to another. But it is not clearly blameworthy to do something involving a risk of injury to another if (for reasons other than self-induced intoxication: **R** v **Majewski** [1977] AC 443) one genuinely does not perceive the risk. Such a person may fairly be accused of stupidity or lack of imagination, but neither of those failings should expose him to conviction of serious crime or the risk of punishment.

Has the House of Lords gone too far down the subjective route? Abandoning an objective form of recklessness assumes that a person who fails to think about a risk is less at fault than one who sees the risk and goes ahead and takes it. This assumption is open to debate. The great legal philosopher Hart observed that the role of *mens rea* was to ensure that defendants had a fair opportunity to exercise their physical and mental capacities to avoid infringing the law. Hart concluded:

> it does not appear unduly harsh, or a sign of archaic or unenlightened conceptions of responsibility to include gross, unthinking carelessness among the things for which we blame and punish.

It is certainly appropriate for the law to take into account the limited intellectual skills of a child or a mentally disabled person when determining their criminal liability. But is it unfair to apply an objective standard to ordinary citizens? Was Lord Diplock right in **Caldwell** to be worried that if a purely subjective test is applied, some people who are morally at fault would be able to avoid liability? Should the House of Lords have simply amended the **Caldwell** model direction so that the specific characteristics of the defendant (such as youth) could have been taken into account when deciding whether the risk was obvious?

The House of Lords in **R** v **G and another** were of the view that the criminal law was moving in the direction of applying subjective principles generally. Over the years, objective tests in criminal law have been supplemented with elements of subjectivity (this will be seen in the context of duress (at p. 361) and provocation (at p. 84) later in this book. In the context of age-based sexual offences (such as having sexual intercourse with a girl under the age of 16) the House of Lords held that liability would not be imposed if the defendant genuinely believed that the victim was over the relevant age: **B** v **DPP** (1998) and **R** v **K** (2001). However, Parliament has moved in the opposite direction, effectively overruling these cases in the Sexual Offences Act 2003. This Act also imposes a test of reasonableness for liability for some of the most serious sexual offences, including rape (discussed on p. 170). In addition, strict liability offences (discussed in Chapter 2) run contrary to the principle of subjectivity. It is arguable that *mens rea* should always be subjective, but defences (discussed in Chapter 13) can be objective: that a person should be able to avoid liability if their conduct objectively provides a justification or an excuse for their conduct.

In **R** *v* **Misra and Srivastava** (2004) and **R** *v* **Mark** (2004) the defence lawyers argued that following **R** *v* **G and another**, the offence of gross negligence manslaughter which applies an objective test to determine liability, should be replaced by subjective reckless manslaughter. This argument was rejected by the Court of Appeal.

? Answering questions

1 'Recklessness remains a difficult concept to explain to juries though it is only another way of saying that the defendant foresaw the results of what he was doing as possible and this gives rise to the offence.'

Discuss *(London External LLB)*

This is a straightforward essay question on recklessness. The essay could be divided into three parts:

- difficulties for the jury
- objective and subjective tests
- injustice.

You could use these as subheadings in your essay to make the structure of your essay clear to the reader.

Difficulties for the jury

The concept was extremely complex when two definitions of recklessness existed, and may have become easier for the jury following the decision of **R** *v* **G and another**. You could point out the complexities of Lord Diplock's model direction in **Caldwell**, which had been repeatedly changed by the courts. One of the reasons the courts moved away from **Caldwell** reckless manslaughter and replaced it with gross negligence manslaughter was because of the difficulties for the jury in understanding the test. The new test contained in **R** *v* **G and another** does itself contain some complexities which could cause problems for the jury.

Objective and subjective tests

You could discuss the fact that the law has been simplified following the case of **R** *v* **G and another**, which provides a single, subjective definition of recklessness. **Caldwell** had extended the law to cover where the defendant did not foresee the result, but a reasonable person would have foreseen the result. **Caldwell** has now been overruled.

Injustice

The concluding section of your essay could argue that the real difficulties with the concept of recklessness in the past was that **Caldwell** recklessness could cause injustice. You could point in particular to the problem that the law ignored the capacity of the actual defendant, as illustrated by the case of **Elliott**. The House of Lords hopes that the law contained in **R** *v* **G and another** will not cause such injustice.

1

Elements of a crime

2 Critically analyse the situations where a person can be liable in criminal law for an omission to act.

This is not a difficult question – the circumstances in which criminal liability will be imposed for true omissions are clearly explained above. You should also include the situations in which liability is imposed for conduct which would in everyday language be described as an omission, but which in law is an act, and vice versa. Remember that you are asked to analyse the law critically, so it is not good enough simply to provide a description; you should also evaluate the law by pointing out its strengths and weaknesses. For example, you could look at the issue of the drowning child and whether the law is adequate in this situation and you could also consider the approach taken by the courts to Tony Bland's case.

3 The term 'recklessness' plays a crucial role in determining criminal liability yet its meaning still appears uncertain. Critically assess the meaning of the term 'reckless' in criminal law. *(OCR)*

Most of the material discussed under the heading 'Recklessness' is relevant here. You might start by explaining why recklessness 'plays a crucial role in determining criminal liability'. To do so you could point out that most offences require proof of *mens rea*. In proving *mens rea* a distinction often has to be drawn between recklessness and intention because the more serious offences often require intention only, conviction for which would impose a higher sentence. For lesser offences recklessness is usually sufficient and a lighter sentence would be imposed.

The rest of your essay could be structured in much the same order as the relevant section of this book. In looking at the meaning of the term 'recklessness' you would have to discuss the meaning of recklessness in the light of **R v G and another**. As you are asked to 'critically assess', a mere description of the law will not be sufficient – you will need, in addition, to look at issues raised under the headings 'Problems with Caldwell recklessness' and whether recklessness should be restricted to a subjective test.

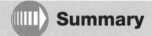 **Summary**

Actus reus

An *actus reus* can consist of more than just an act, it comprises all the elements of the offence other than the state of mind of the defendant.

Conduct must be voluntary

If the accused is to be found guilty of a crime, his or her behaviour in committing the *actus reus* must have been voluntary.

Types of *actus reus*

Crimes can be divided into three types, depending on the nature of their *actus reus*:

- action crimes
- state of affairs crimes
- result crimes.

Omissions

Criminal liability is rarely imposed for true omissions at common law. However, in some situations the accused has a duty to act, and in these cases there may be liability for a true omission. A duty to act will only be imposed where there is some kind of relationship between the two people, and the closer the relationship the more likely it is that a duty to act will exist. So far the courts have recognised a range of situations as giving rise to a duty to act. These are where:

- there is a special relationship
- there is voluntary acceptance of responsibility for another
- there is a contractual relationship
- statute imposes a duty
- the defendant created a dangerous situation.

Mens rea

Mens rea is the Latin for 'guilty mind' and traditionally refers to the state of mind of the person committing the crime.

Intention

Intention is a subjective concept. To help comprehension of the legal meaning of intention, the concept can be divided into two: direct intention and indirect intention. Where the consequence of an intention is actually desired, it is called direct intention. However, a jury is also entitled to find intention where a defendant did not desire a result, but it is a virtually certain consequence of the act, and the accused realises this and goes ahead anyway. This is called indirect intention.

Recklessness

In everyday language, recklessness means taking an unjustified risk. Its legal definition has radically changed in recent years. It is now clear, following the case of **R** v **G and another**, overruling **MPC** v **Caldwell**, that recklessness is a subjective form of *mens rea*.

Negligence

The existence of negligence is traditionally determined according to an objective test, which asks whether the defendant's conduct has fallen below the standards of the reasonable person. There is one important common law crime where negligence is an element of the offence: gross negligence manslaughter. The leading case on the meaning of gross negligence is the House of Lords judgment of **R** v **Adomako** (1994).

Transferred malice

Under the principle of transferred malice, if Ann has the *mens rea* of a particular crime and does the *actus reus* of the crime, Ann is guilty of the crime even though the *actus reus* may differ in some way from that intended. The *mens rea* is simply transferred to the new *actus reus*.

Coincidence of *actus reus* and *mens rea*

The *mens rea* of an offence must be present at the time the *actus reus* is committed.

Mens rea and motive

It is essential to realise that *mens rea* has nothing to do with motive.

Reading list

Crosby, C. (2008) 'Recklessness – the continuing search for a definition' [2008] *Journal of Criminal Law* 72, 313.

Hall, J. (1963) 'Negligent behaviour should be excluded from penal liability' 63 *Columbia Law Review* 632.

Haralambous, N. (2004) 'Retreating from Caldwell: Restoring subjectivism' [2004] *New Law Journal* 1712.

Padfield, N. (1995) 'Clean water and muddy causation: is causation a question of law or fact, or just a way of allocating blame?' [1995] *Criminal Law Review* 683.

Williams, G. (1991) 'Criminal omissions – the conventional view' 107 *Law Quarterly Review* 86.

Reading on the internet

The House of Lords' judgment of **R** *v* **Woollin** (1998) on intention is available on Parliament's website at:

> http://www.publications.parliament.uk/pa/ld199798/ldjudgmt/jd980722/wool.htm

The House of Lords' judgment of **R** *v* **G and another** (2003) on recklessness is available on Parliament's website at:

> http://www.publications.parliament.uk/pa/ld200203/ldjudgmt/jd031016/g-1.htm

---

Visit **www.mylawchamber.co.uk/elliottcriminal** to access multiple-choice questions, flashcards and practice exam questions to test yourself on this chapter.

Use **Case Navigator** to read in full some of the key cases referenced in this chapter:

- R *v* Adomako [1995] AC 171
- R *v* Cunningham [1957] 2 All ER 412
- Fagan *v* MPC [1968] 3 All ER 442
- R *v* G [2003] UKHL 50; [2004] 1 AC 1034
- Kennedy (No 2) [2005] EWCA Crim 685
- DPP *v* Majewski [1977] AC 443
- R *v* Woollin – [1998] 4 All ER 103

2 Strict liability

This chapter explains:

- that strict liability offences do not require *mens rea*;

- how the courts decide which crimes are ones of strict liability; and

- why the existence of strict liability offences is controversial.

Introduction

Some offences do not require *mens rea* or do not require *mens rea* to attach to an element of the *actus reus*. These are generally known as strict liability offences which is the term used in this chapter, though some lawyers refer to those offences requiring no *mens rea* at all as imposing absolute liability and those requiring no *mens rea* as to an element of the *actus reus* as imposing strict liability. Most of these offences have been created by statute.

Which crimes are crimes of strict liability?

Unfortunately, statutes are not always so obliging as to state 'this is a strict liability offence'. Occasionally the wording of an Act does make this clear, but otherwise the courts are left to decide for themselves. The principles on which this decision is made were considered in **Gammon (Hong Kong) Ltd** *v* **Attorney-General** (1985). The defendants were involved in building works in Hong Kong. Part of a building they were constructing fell down, and it was found that the collapse had occurred because the builders had failed to follow the original plans exactly. The Hong Kong building regulations prohibited deviating in any substantial way from such plans, and the defendants were charged with breaching the regulations, an offence punishable with a fine of up to $250,000 or three years' imprisonment. On appeal they argued that they were not liable because they had not known that the changes they made were substantial ones. However, the Privy Council held that the relevant regulations created offences of strict liability, and the convictions were upheld.

Explaining the principles on which they had based the decision, Lord Scarman confirmed that there is always a presumption of law that *mens rea* is required before a person can be held guilty of a criminal offence. The existence of this presumption was reaffirmed in very strong terms by the House of Lords in **B (a minor)** *v* **DPP (2000)**.

KEY CASE

In **B (a minor)** *v* **DPP** (2000) a 15-year-old boy had sat next to a 13-year-old girl and asked her to give him a 'shiner'. The trial judge observed that '[t]his, in the language of today's gilded youth, apparently means, not a black eye, but an act of oral sex'. The boy was charged with inciting a

> When interpreting a statute there is always a presumption of law that *mens rea* is required for an offence.

child under the age of 14 to commit an act of gross indecency. Both the trial judge and the Court of Appeal ruled that this was a strict liability offence and that there was therefore no defence available that the boy believed the girl to be over 14. The House of Lords confirmed that there was a presumption that *mens rea* was required, and ruled that the relevant offence was not actually one of strict liability. The House stated that in order to rebut the presumption that an offence required *mens rea*, there needed to be a 'compellingly clear implication' that Parliament intended the offence to be one of strict liability:

> . . . [T]he test is not whether it is a reasonable implication that the statute rules out *mens rea* as a constituent part of the crime – the test is whether it is a *necessary* implication.
>
> As the offence had a very broad *actus reus*, carried a serious social stigma and a heavy sentence it decided Parliament did not have this intention. Soon afterwards the House of Lords confirmed its reluctance to find strict liability offences in **R** *v* **K** (2001).

These cases have thrown doubt on the old case of **Prince** (1874) which had also been concerned with an offence against the person that could only be committed on a girl under a certain age. That offence had been treated as one of strict liability and the reasonable but mistaken belief of the defendant as to her age was therefore found to be irrelevant. The House of Lords described that case as 'unsound' and a 'relic from an age dead and gone'. In **R** *v* **K** the House of Lords described **Prince** as a 'spent force'.

KEY CASE

While there is a clear presumption that *mens rea* is required, if the courts find that Parliament had a clear intention to create a strict liability offence then strict liability will be imposed and the presumption will be rebutted. Thus in **R** *v* **G** (2008) the House of Lords held that an offence known as 'statutory rape' created by Parliament in s. 5 of the Sexual Offences Act 2003 was a strict liability offence. The offence is committed when a man has sexual intercourse with a child under the age of 13. The defendant in the case had only been 15 at the time of the alleged incident and the victim admitted that she had lied to him on an earlier occasion about her age. Despite this, the House of Lords still found the defendant liable because his mistake about her age was irrelevant since this was a strict liability offence.

> The presumption that *mens rea* is required will be rebutted if Parliament intended to create a strict liability offence.

There are certain factors which can, on their own or combined, displace the presumption that *mens rea* is required. These can be grouped into four categories which will be considered in turn.

● Regulatory offence

A regulatory offence is one in which no real moral issue is involved, and usually (though not always) one for which the maximum penalty is small – the mass of rules surrounding the sale of food are examples. In **Gammon** it was stated that the presumption that *mens rea* is required was less strong for regulatory offences than for truly criminal offences.

KEY CASE

This distinction between true crimes and regulatory offences was drawn in the case of **Sweet** v **Parsley** (1970). Ms Sweet, a teacher, took a sublease of a farmhouse outside Oxford. She rented the house to tenants, and rarely spent

> The presumption in favour of *mens rea* is less strong for regulatory offences.

any time there. Unknown to her, the tenants were smoking cannabis on the premises. When they were caught, she was found guilty of being concerned in the management of premises which were being used for the purpose of smoking cannabis, contrary to the Dangerous Drugs Act 1965 (now replaced by the Misuse of Drugs Act 1971).

Ms Sweet appealed, on the ground that she knew nothing about what the tenants were doing, and could not reasonably have been expected to have known. Lord Reid acknowledged that strict liability was appropriate for regulatory offences, or 'quasicrimes' – offences which are not criminal 'in any real sense', and are merely acts prohibited in the public interest. But, he said, the kind of crime to which a real social stigma is attached should usually require proof of *mens rea*; in the case of such offences it was not in the public interest that an innocent person should be prevented from proving their innocence in order to make it easier for guilty people to be convicted.

Since their Lordships regarded the offence under consideration as being a 'true crime' – the stigma had, for example, caused Ms Sweet to lose her job – they held that it was not a strict liability offence, and since Ms Sweet did not have the necessary *mens rea*, her conviction was overturned.

Unfortunately the courts have never laid down a list of those offences which they will consider to be regulatory offences rather than 'true crimes'. Those generally considered to be regulatory offences are the kind created by the rules on hygiene and measurement standards within the food and drink industry, and regulations designed to stop industry polluting the environment, but there are clearly some types of offences which will be more difficult to categorise.

● Issue of social concern

According to **Gammon**, where a statute is concerned with an issue of social concern (such as public safety), and the creation of strict liability will promote the purpose of the statute by encouraging potential offenders to take extra precautions against committing the prohibited act, the presumption in favour of *mens rea* can be rebutted. This category is obviously subject to the distinctions drawn by Lord Reid in **Sweet** v **Parsley** – the laws against murder and rape are to protect the public, but this type of true crime would not attract strict liability.

The types of offences that do fall into this category cover behaviour which could involve danger to the public, but which would not usually carry the same kind of stigma as a crime such as murder or even theft. The breach of the building regulations committed in **Gammon** is an example, as are offences relating to serious pollution of the environment. In **R** v **Blake** (1996) the defendant was accused of making broadcasts on a pirate radio station and was convicted of using wireless telegraphy equipment without a licence, contrary to s. 1(1) of the Wireless Telegraphy Act 1949. His conviction was upheld by the Court of Appeal which stated that this offence was one of strict liability. This conclusion was reached as the offence had been created in the interest of public safety, given the interference with the operation of the emergency services that could result from unauthorised broadcasting.

In **Harrow London Borough Council** v **Shah** (1999) the offence of selling National Lottery tickets to a person under the age of 16 was found to be an offence of strict liability. The Divisional Court justified this by stating that the legislation dealt with an issue of social concern.

These crimes overlap with regulatory offences in subject area but, unlike regulatory offences, may carry severe maximum penalties. Despite such higher penalties, strict liability is seen to be a necessary provision given the need to promote very high standards of care in areas of possible danger.

The wording of the Act

Gammon states that the presumption that *mens rea* is required for a criminal offence can be rebutted if the words of a statute suggest that strict liability is intended. The House of Lords said in **Sweet** v **Parsley**: 'the fact that other sections of the Act expressly required *mens rea*, for example, because they contain the word "knowingly", is not in itself sufficient to justify a decision that a section which is silent as to *mens rea* creates a [strict liability] offence'. At present it is not always clear whether a particular form of words will be interpreted as creating an offence of strict liability. However, some words have been interpreted fairly consistently, including the following.

'Cause'

In **Alphacell** v **Woodward** (1972) the defendants were a company accused of causing polluted matter to enter a river. They were using equipment designed to prevent any overflow into the river, but when the mechanism became clogged by leaves the pollution was able to escape. There was no evidence that the defendants had been negligent, or even knew that the pollution was leaking out. The House of Lords stated that where statutes create an offence of causing something to happen, the courts should adopt a common-sense approach – if reasonable people would say that the defendant has caused something to happen, regardless of whether he or she knew he or she was doing so, then no *mens rea* is required. Their Lordships held that in the normal meaning of the word, the company had 'caused' the pollution to enter the water, and their conviction was upheld.

'Possession'

There are many offences which are defined as 'being in possession of a prohibited item', the obvious example being drugs. They are frequently treated as strict liability offences. For example, s. 5 of the Firearms Act 1968 provides:

> A person commits an offence if, without the authority of the Defence Council . . . he has in his possession . . . (b) any weapon of whatever description designed or adapted for the discharge of any noxious liquid, gas or other thing.

In **R** v **Deyemi** (2007) the defendants had been found in possession of an electrical stungun which they claimed to have mistaken for a torch. The offence was interpreted as a strict liability offence and so it was irrelevant if they had made a mistake. The harshness of this approach is highlighted by a statement by the trial judge:

> . . . [A]lthough it does offend one's sense of justice to exclude *mens rea* from an offence so a defendant can be guilty of being in possession of something when he knows he is in possession, if it is a prohibited article, albeit he thinks it is something different, and that view is not unreasonable, having regard to its appearance and usage, I am satisfied that that is the state of affairs Parliament intended to create in making the offence one of strict liability.

The conviction was therefore upheld by the Court of Appeal.

'Knowingly'

Clearly use of this word tells the courts that *mens rea* is required, and tends to be used where Parliament wants to underline the fact that the presumption should be applied.

The smallness of the penalty

Strict liability is most often imposed for offences which carry a relatively small maximum penalty, and it appears that the higher the maximum penalty, the less likely it is that the courts will impose strict liability. However, the existence of severe penalties for an offence does not guarantee that strict liability will not be imposed. In **Gammon** Lord Scarman held that where regulations were put in place to protect public safety, it was quite appropriate to impose strict liability, despite potentially severe penalties.

Relevance of the four factors

Obviously these four factors overlap to a certain extent – regulatory offences usually do have small penalties, for example. And in **Alphacell** *v* **Woodward**, the House of Lords gave their decision the dual justification of applying the common-sense meaning of the term 'cause', and recognising that pollution was an issue of social concern.

It is important to note that all these categories are guidelines rather than clear rules. The courts are not always consistent in their application of strict liability, and social policy plays an important part in the decisions. During the 1960s, there was intense social concern about what appeared to be a widespread drug problem, and the courts imposed strict liability for many drugs offences. Ten years later, pollution of the environment had become one of the main topics of concern, hence the justification of the decision in **Alphacell** *v* **Woodward**. Today, there appears to be a general move away from strict liability, and some newer statutes imposing apparent strict liability contain a limited form of defence, by which an accused can escape conviction by proving that he or she took all reasonable precautions to prevent the offence being committed. However, the courts could begin to move back towards strict liability if it seemed that an area of social concern might require it.

Crimes of negligence

Following the decision of **Attorney-General's Reference (No. 2 of 1999)** – discussed on p. 25 – it is arguable that crimes of negligence, such as gross negligence manslaughter, are actually crimes of strict liability. This is because in that case the Court of Appeal stated

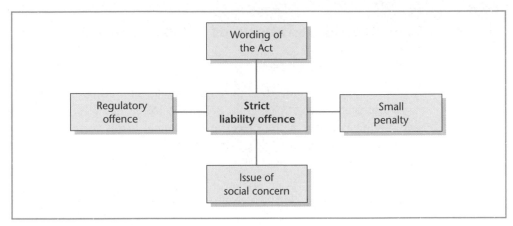

Figure 2.1 Strict liability

that gross negligence was not a form of *mens rea* and that a person could be found to have been grossly negligent without looking at their state of mind but simply by looking at the gross carelessness of their conduct.

The effect of mistake

Where strict liability applies, an accused cannot use the defence of mistake, even if the mistake was reasonable. The House of Lords judgment of **B (a minor)** *v* **DPP** is slightly misleading on this issue as it seems to blur the distinction between mistakes made in relation to strict liability offences and mistakes made in relation to offences requiring *mens rea*. This distinction is, however, fundamental. As the case was concerned with an offence that required *mens rea*, anything it stated in relation to strict liability offences was merely *obiter dicta* and therefore not binding on future courts.

The European Convention on Human Rights

TOPICAL ISSUE

The European Convention on Human Rights

Article 6(2) of the European Convention on Human Rights states:

Everyone charged with a criminal offence shall be presumed innocent until proved guilty according to law.

The decision of the European Court of Human Rights in **Hansen** *v* **Denmark** (1995) suggests that strict liability offences may breach Art.6(2) because once the prohibited act is proven, the defendant is 'presumed' to be liable. But the European Court stated in **Salabiaku** *v* **France** (1988):

the Contracting States may, under certain conditions, penalise a simple or objective fact as such, irrespective of whether it results from criminal intent or from negligence.

This has been interpreted by the English courts as allowing strict liability offences, most recently by the House of Lords in the case of **R** *v* **G** (2008).

Arguments in favour of strict liability

Promotion of care

By promoting high standards of care, strict liability, it is argued, protects the public from dangerous practices. Social scientist Barbara Wootton has defended strict liability on this basis, suggesting that if the objective of criminal law is to prevent socially damaging activities, it would be absurd to turn a blind eye to those who cause the harm due to carelessness, negligence or even an accident.

Deterrent value

Strict liability is said to provide a strong deterrent, which is considered especially important given the way in which regulatory offences tend to be dealt with. Many of them are handled not by the police and the Crown Prosecution Service (CPS), but by special Government bodies, such as the Health and Safety Inspectorate which checks that safety rules are observed in workplaces. These bodies tend to work by placing pressure on offenders to put right any breaches, with prosecution, or even threats of it, very much a last resort. It is suggested that strict liability allows enforcement agencies to strengthen their bargaining position, since potential offenders know that if a prosecution is brought, there is a very good chance of conviction.

Easier enforcement

Strict liability makes enforcing offences easier; in **Gammon** the Privy Council suggested that if the prosecution had to prove *mens rea* in even the smallest regulatory offence, the administration of justice might very quickly come to a complete standstill.

Difficulty of proving *mens rea*

In many strict liability offences, *mens rea* would be very difficult to prove, and without strict liability, guilty people might escape conviction. Obvious examples are those involving large corporations, where it may be difficult to prove that someone knew what was happening.

No threat to liberty

In many strict liability cases, the defendant is a business and the penalty is a fine, so individual liberty is not generally under threat. Even the fines are often small.

Profit from risk

Where an offence is concerned with business, those who commit it may well be saving themselves money, and thereby making extra profit by doing so – by, for example, saving the time that would be spent on observing safety regulations. If a person creates a risk and makes a profit by doing so, he or she ought to be liable if that risk causes or could cause harm, even if that was not the intention.

Arguments against strict liability

Injustice

Strict liability is criticised as unjust on a variety of different grounds. First, that it is not in the interests of justice that someone who has taken reasonable care, and could not possibly have avoided committing an offence, should be punished by the criminal law. This goes against the principle that the criminal law punishes fault.

Secondly, the argument that strict liability should be enforced because *mens rea* would be too difficult to prove is morally doubtful. The prosecution often find it difficult to prove *mens rea* on a rape charge, for example, but is that a reason for making rape a crime of strict liability? Although many strict liability offences are clearly far lesser crimes than these, some do impose severe penalties, as **Gammon** illustrates, and it may not be in the interests of justice if strict liability is imposed in these areas just because *mens rea* would make things too difficult for the prosecution. It is inconsistent with justice to convict someone who is not guilty, in the normal sense of the word, just because the penalty imposed will be small.

Even where penalties are small, in many cases conviction is a punishment in itself. Sentencing may be tailored to take account of mitigating factors, but that is little comfort to the reputable butcher who unknowingly sells bad meat, when the case is reported in local papers and customers go elsewhere. However slight the punishment, in practice there is some stigma attached to a criminal conviction (even though it may be less than that for a 'true crime') which should not be attached to a person who has taken all reasonable care.

In addition, as Smith and Hogan (2005) point out, in the case of a jury trial, strict liability takes crucial questions of fact away from juries, and allows them to be considered solely by the judge for the purposes of sentencing. In a magistrates' court, it removes those questions from the requirement of proof beyond reasonable doubt, and allows them to be decided according to the less strict principles which guide decisions on sentencing.

Strict liability also delegates a good deal of power to the discretion of the enforcement agency. Where strict liability makes it almost certain that a prosecution will lead to a conviction, the decision on whether or not to prosecute becomes critical, and there are few controls over those who make this decision.

Ineffective

It is debatable whether strict liability actually works. For a start, the deterrent value of strict liability may be overestimated. For the kinds of offences to which strict liability is usually applied, the important deterrent factor may not be the chances of being convicted, but the chances of being caught and charged. In the food and drinks business particularly, just being charged with an offence brings unwelcome publicity, and even if the company is not convicted, they are likely to see a fall in sales as customers apply the 'no smoke without fire' principle. The problem is that in many cases the chances of being caught and prosecuted are not high. In the first place, enforcement agencies frequently lack the resources to monitor the huge number of potential offenders. Even where offenders are caught, it appears that the usual response of enforcement agencies is a warning letter. The most serious or persistent offenders may be threatened with prosecution if they do not put matters right, but only a minority are actually prosecuted. Providing more resources for the enforcement agencies and bringing more prosecutions might have a stronger deterrent effect than imposing strict liability on the minority who are prosecuted.

In other areas too, it is the chance of getting caught which may be the strongest deterrent – if people think they are unlikely to get caught speeding, for example, the fact that strict liability will be imposed if they do is not much of a deterrent.

In fact in some areas, rather than ensuring a higher standard of care, strict liability may have quite the opposite effect: knowing that it is possible to be convicted of an offence regardless of having taken every reasonable precaution may reduce the incentive to take such precautions, rather than increase it.

As Professor Hall (1963) points out, the fact that strict liability is usually imposed only where the possible penalty is small means that unscrupulous companies can simply regard the criminal law as 'a nominal tax on illegal enterprise'. In areas of industry where the need to maintain a good reputation is not so strong as it is in food or drugs, for example, it may be cheaper to keep paying the fines than to change bad working practices, and therefore very little deterrent value can be seen. In these areas it might be more efficient, as Professor Hall says, 'to put real teeth in the law' by developing offences with more severe penalties, even if that means losing the expediency of strict liability.

Justifying strict liability in the interests of protecting the public can be seen as taking a sledgehammer to crack a nut. It is certainly true, for example, that bad meat causes food poisoning just the same whether or not the butcher knew it was bad, and that the public needs protection from butchers who sell bad meat. But while we might want to make sure of punishment for butchers who knowingly sell bad meat, and probably those who take no, or not enough, care to check the condition of their meat, how is the public protected by punishing a butcher who took all possible care (by using a normally reputable supplier for example) and could not possibly have avoided committing the offence?

The fact that it is not always possible to recognise crimes of strict liability before the courts have made a decision clearly further weakens any deterrent effect.

● Little administrative advantage

It is also open to debate whether strict liability really does contribute much to administrative expediency. Cases still have to be detected and brought to court, and in some cases selected elements of the *mens rea* still have to be proved. And although strict liability may make conviction easier, it leaves the problem of sentencing. This cannot be done fairly without taking the degree of negligence into account, so evidence of the accused's state of mind must be available. Given all this it is difficult to see how much time and manpower is actually saved.

Inconsistent application

The fact that whether or not strict liability will be imposed rests on the imprecise science of statutory interpretation means that there are discrepancies in both the offences to which it is applied, and what it actually means. The changes in the types of cases to which strict liability is applied over the years reflect social policy – the courts come down harder on areas which are causing social concern at a particular time. While this may be justified in the interests of society, it does little for certainty and the principle that like cases should be treated alike.

The courts are also inconsistent in their justifications for imposing or not imposing strict liability. In **Lim Chin Aik** v **R** (1963), the defendant was charged with remaining in Singapore despite a prohibition order against him. Lord Evershed stated that the subject matter of a statute was not sufficient grounds for inferring that strict liability was intended; it was also important to consider whether imposing strict liability would help to enforce the regulations, and it could only do this if there were some precautions the potential offender could take to prevent committing the offence. 'Unless this is so, there is no reason in penalising him and it cannot be inferred that the legislature imposed strict liability merely in order to find a luckless victim.'

In the case of **Lim Chin Aik**, the precaution to be taken would have been finding out whether there was a prohibition order against him, but Lord Evershed further explained that people could only be expected to take 'sensible' and 'practicable' precautions: Lim Chin Aik was not expected to 'make continuous enquiry to see whether an order had been made against him'.

Presumably then, our hypothetical butcher should only be expected to take reasonable and practicable precautions against selling bad meat, and not, for example, have to employ scientific analysts to test every pork chop. Yet just such extreme precautions appear to have been expected in **Smedleys** v **Breed** (1974). The defendants were convicted under the Food and Drugs Act 1955, after a very small caterpillar was found in one of three million tins of peas. Despite the fact that even individual inspection of each pea would probably not have prevented the offence being committed, Lord Hailsham defended the imposition of strict liability on the grounds that: 'To construe the Food and Drugs Act 1955 in a sense less strict than that which I have adopted would make a serious inroad on the legislation for consumer protection.' Clearly the subject areas of these cases are very different, but the contrast between them does give some indication of the shaky ground on which strict liability can rest – if the House of Lords had followed the reasoning of **Lim Chin Aik**, Smedleys would not have been liable, since they had taken all reasonable and practical precautions.

Better alternatives are available

There are alternatives to strict liability which would be less unjust and more effective in preventing harm, such as better inspection of business premises and the imposition of liability for negligence (see below).

2

Strict liability

Reform

The Law Commission's draft Bill

The Law Commission's draft Criminal Liability (Mental Element) Bill of 1977 requires that Parliament should specifically state if it is creating an offence of strict liability. Where this is not done the courts should assume *mens rea* is required. The practice of allowing the courts to decide when strict liability should be applied, under cover of the fiction that they are interpreting parliamentary intention, is not helpful, leading to a mass of litigation, with many of the cases irreconcilable with each other – as with **Lim Chin Aik** and **Smedleys v Breed**, above. If legislators knew that the courts would always assume *mens rea* unless specifically told not to, they would be more likely to adopt the habit of stating whether the offence was strict or not.

Restriction to public danger offences

Strict liability could perhaps be more easily justified if the tighter liability were balanced by real danger to the public in the offence – the case of **Gammon** can be justified on this ground.

Liability for negligence

Smith and Hogan suggest that strict liability should be replaced by liability for negligence. This would catch defendants who were simply thoughtless or inefficient, as well as those who deliberately broke the law, but would not punish people who were genuinely blameless.

Defence of all due care

In Australia a defence of all due care is available. Where a crime would otherwise impose strict liability, the defendant can avoid conviction by proving that he or she took all due care to avoid committing the offence.

Extending strict liability

Baroness Wootton advocates imposing strict liability for all crimes, so that *mens rea* would only be relevant for sentencing purposes.

? Answering questions

Strict liability tends to arise in essay rather than problem questions, because the offences to which it applies tend not to be included in course syllabuses. Given the large amount of theoretical discussion for and against strict liability, it should not be difficult to discuss critically, and is therefore a good choice for essay questions.

1 **Is it just to impose criminal liability where no *mens rea* has been proved?**

Avoid the natural temptation of using this question simply as a trigger for writing everything you know on the subject without applying that material to the specific question asked. Obviously you will want to learn off a lot of material before the exam, and it will probably help to follow the structure of this book when you do this, so that for this chapter, for example, you might learn the lists of arguments for and against strict liability. That material will provide the basis for answering many differently worded questions on strict liability, but, in the exam, you must angle that material to the actual question being asked. In this question, the key words are 'imposition' and 'justifiable' and these and their synonyms should be used at several points in the essay to show that you are answering the particular question asked. You could start by stating where strict liability is currently imposed, before discussing whether such impositions are justified – in this part you can describe the kind of offences to which strict liability applies, giving examples from case law. You should, however, devote the bulk of your essay to discussing when the imposition of strict liability is justified, if ever in your opinion, and when not, using the arguments for and against it to back up your points.

2 **How far does the imposition of criminal liability depend upon the existence of fault?**

This is a slightly more difficult question, but one for which it should be possible to get good marks if you plan your answer carefully. As well as strict liability discussed in this chapter, the question also raises issues discussed in the previous chapter on 'Elements of a crime'. A good answer could include such issues as an explanation of *actus reus* (including causation and voluntariness), and *mens rea* and the absence of defences (such as insanity and duress) giving rise to evidence of fault.

Summary

There are a small number of crimes which can be committed without any *mens rea*. These offences are known as strict liability crimes.

Which crimes are crimes of strict liability?

It is generally a question of statutory interpretation to determine whether an offence is one of strict liability. A leading case on how the courts decide this issue is **Gammon (Hong Kong) Ltd** *v* **Attorney-General** (1985). The starting point for the courts is a presumption that *mens rea* is required. There are certain factors which can, on their own or combined, displace this presumption. These can be grouped into four categories:

- regulatory offences
- issues of social concern
- the wording of the Act
- the smallness of the penalty.

Crimes of negligence

Following the decision of **Attorney-General's Reference (No. 2 of 1999)**, it is arguable that crimes of negligence, such as gross negligence manslaughter, are actually crimes of strict liability.

The effect of mistake

Where strict liability applies, an accused cannot use the defence of mistake, even if the mistake was reasonable.

The European Convention on Human Rights

There has been some debate as to whether strict liability offences breach the European Convention on Human Rights.

Arguments in favour of strict liability

A range of arguments have been put forward in support of strict liability offences:

- promotion of care
- deterrent value
- easier enforcement
- difficulty of proving *mens rea*
- no threat to liberty
- prevent profit from risk.

Arguments against strict liability

A range of arguments have been put forward against strict liability offences:

- injustice
- ineffective
- little administrative advantage
- inconsistent application
- better alternatives are available.

Reform

A number of reform proposals have been put forward. These range from the Law Commission's draft Criminal Liability (Mental Element) Bill of 1977 which would require Parliament to specifically state if it is creating an offence of strict liability, to Baroness Wootton's suggestion that all crimes should be strict liability offences.

Reading list

Carson, D. (1970) 'Some sociological aspects of strict liability' [1970] *Modern Law Review* 225.

Hogan, B. (1978) 'The mental element in crime; strict liability' [1978] *Criminal Law Review* 74.

Jackson, B. (1982) 'Storkwain: a case study in strict liability and self-regulation' [1991] *Criminal Law Review* 892.

Simester, A. (ed.) (2005) *Appraising Strict Liability*, Oxford: OUP.

Wootton, B. (1981) *Crime and the Criminal Law: Reflections of a Magistrate and Social Scientist*, London: Stevens.

Reading on the internet

The website of the Health and Safety Executive, responsible for the enforcement of a range of strict liability offences, can be found at:

http://www.hse.gov.uk

Visit **www.mylawchamber.co.uk/elliottcriminal** to access multiple-choice questions, flashcards and practice exam questions to test yourself on this chapter.

3 Murder

This chapter discusses:

- the common elements of all homicide offences: the death of a human being caused by the accused to the victim;

- how the requirement of causation can be analysed as requiring both factual and legal causation;

- that murder is committed when a person causes the death of a human being with the intention to kill or to cause grievous bodily harm;

- that intention is defined subjectively and can be divided into direct and indirect intention; and

- problems with the offence of murder.

Introduction

Offences against the person fall into two main categories: fatal (unlawful homicide) and non-fatal offences. Homicide means the killing of a human being, and in some circumstances it may be lawful – for example, in self-defence, or during a military operation in wartime. We are concerned here with unlawful homicides.

The common elements of homicide offences

To be liable for any homicide offence the defendant must cause the death of a human being. We will look at each of these three elements in turn, which hereafter will be referred to as the common elements.

A human being

For the purposes of the homicide offences, a person is a human being when capable of having an existence independent of a mother. Killing an unborn child (a foetus) can still be an offence, but not a homicide. In **Attorney-General's Reference (No. 3 of 1994)**, where a man stabbed his pregnant girlfriend, the Court of Appeal stated that there was no requirement that the person who died had to be a person in being when the act causing the death was perpetrated. Thus, if a man injured a foetus and the baby was then born alive but subsequently died from the injuries, the concept of a 'human being' would be satisfied for the purposes of a homicide offence. This aspect of the Court of Appeal judgment was approved by the House of Lords.

Death

There is no single legal definition of 'death'. In the past, absence of a heartbeat, pulse or breathing meant that a person could safely be pronounced dead, but medical advances mean that a person may now be kept on a life-support machine for many years. As a result, the courts have had to consider whether such a person is alive or dead and, if dead, at what point death can be said to have occurred. In **R** v **Malcherek and Steel** (1981) the court appeared to favour the approach that death occurs when the victim is brain-dead, but this did not form part of the *ratio decidendi* of the decision. Because there is no fixed legal definition of 'death', the point at which a person dies will be a question of fact for the court to decide in each case.

In considering this issue, the courts are likely to be influenced by the Code of Practice for the Diagnosis and Confirmation of Death which lays down guidelines for doctors in determining when a patient is dead. The code defines death as entailing 'the irreversible loss of those essential characteristics which are necessary to the existence of a living person and, thus, the definition of death should be regarded as the irreversible loss of the capacity for consciousness, combined with irreversible loss of the capacity to breathe'.

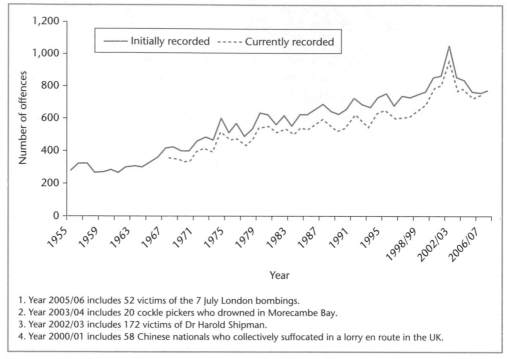

1. Year 2005/06 includes 52 victims of the 7 July London bombings.
2. Year 2003/04 includes 20 cockle pickers who drowned in Morecambe Bay.
3. Year 2002/03 includes 172 victims of Dr Harold Shipman.
4. Year 2000/01 includes 58 Chinese nationals who collectively suffocated in a lorry en route in the UK.

Figure 3.1 Offences recorded by the police as homicide in England and Wales 1955 to 2007/08

Source: 'Crime in England and Wales 2007/08 – Supplementary Volume 2: Homicide, Firearm Offences and Intimate Violence', p. 10.

The capacity of consciousness is the ability to feel, to be aware or to do anything. There may be some residual reflex movement of the limbs after a person is diagnosed as dead as this movement is not controlled by the brain but by the spinal cord and does not indicate a capacity for consciousness.

The code confirms that patients in the persistent vegetative state, such as Tony Bland (discussed on p. 14) who have permanently lost the capacity for consciousness, are not legally dead, by virtue of their ability to breathe unaided, without artificial respiratory support. Their brain stem is functioning, but not their cortex (the higher brain).

● Causation

The prosecution must prove that the death was caused by the defendant's act. In many cases this will be obvious: for example, where the defendant shoots or stabs someone, and the victim dies immediately of the wounds. Difficulties may arise where there is more than one cause of death. This might be the act or omission of a third party which occurs after the defendant's act, and before the death, or some characteristic of the victim which means that the victim dies of the injury when a fitter person would have survived.

Defendants can only be held responsible for a death where their acts are both a 'factual' and a 'legal' cause of the victim's death.

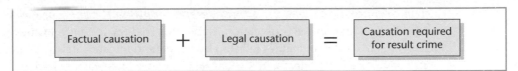

Figure 3.2 Causation (1)

Factual causation

In order to establish factual causation, the prosecution must prove two things:

- That *but for* the conduct of the accused the victim would not have died as and when he or she did.

    The defendant will not be liable for the death if the victim would have died at the same time regardless of the defendant's act (or omission): in **White** (1910), the defendant gave his mother poison but, before it had a chance to take effect, she died of a heart attack which was not caused by the poison. He was not liable for her death.
- That the original injury arising from the defendant's conduct was *more than a minimal cause* of the victim's death.

    This is known as the *de minimis* rule, and it refers to the fact that when we say a person kills someone, what we actually mean is that they make the person's death occur earlier than it otherwise would, since we are all dying anyway. The acceleration of death caused by the defendant's conduct must be more than merely trivial; pricking the thumb of a woman bleeding to death would hasten her death, for example, but not enough to be the real cause of it.

Legal causation

Even if factual causation is established, the judge must direct the jury as to whether the defendant's acts are sufficient to amount in law to a cause of the victim's death. Legal causation can be proven in one of two ways: where the thin skull test applies and where the original injury was an operative and significant cause of death.

The 'thin skull' test

Where the intervening cause is some existing weakness of the victim, the defendant must take the victim as he or she finds him. Known as the 'thin skull' rule, this means that if, for example, a defendant hits a person over the head with the kind of blow which would not usually kill, but the victim has an unusually thin skull which makes the blow fatal, the defendant will be liable for the subsequent death. The principle has been extended to mental conditions and beliefs, as well as physical characteristics.

KEY CASE

In **R v Blaue** (1975), the victim of a stabbing was a Jehovah's Witness, a church which, among other things, forbids its members to have blood transfusions. As a result of her refusal to accept a transfusion, the victim died of her wounds. The Court of Appeal rejected the defendant's argument that her refusal broke the chain of causation, on the ground that the accused had to take his victim as he found her.

Unusual characteristics of the victim do not break the chain of causation.

The original injury was an operative and significant cause of death

Under this criterion the prosecution must show that, at the time of the victim's death, the original wound or injuries inflicted by the defendant were still an 'operative and substantial' cause of that death. In **R** v **Smith** (1959), a soldier was stabbed in a barrack-room brawl. He was dropped twice as he was being taken to the medical officer, and then there was a long delay before he was seen by a doctor, as the doctor mistakenly thought that his case was not urgent. When he did eventually receive treatment it was inappropriate for the injuries he was suffering from and harmful. Nonetheless the court took the view that these intervening factors had not broken the chain of causation so that the original wound was still an operative cause and the accused was liable for murder.

The same principle was followed in **R** v **Malcherek and Steel**. The victims of two separate attacks had been kept on life-support machines; these were switched off in accordance with established medical practice when tests showed that they were brain-dead. The two defendants argued that when the hospital switched off the machines the chain of causation was broken, thereby relieving the defendants of liability for murder. The court rejected this argument on the grounds that the original injuries were still an operative cause of their victims' deaths.

In **R** v **Cheshire** (1991), a dispute developed in a fish and chip shop, ending with the defendant shooting his victim in the leg and stomach, and seriously wounding him. The victim was taken to hospital, where his injuries were operated on, and he was placed in intensive care. As a result of negligent treatment by the medical staff, he developed complications affecting his breathing, and eventually died. His leg and stomach wounds were no longer life-threatening at the time of his death. The court stated that the critical question for the jury to answer was: 'Has the Crown proved that the injuries inflicted by the defendant were a significant cause of death?' Negligent medical treatment could only break the chain of causation if it was so independent of the accused's acts, and such a powerful cause of death in itself, that the contribution made by the defendant's conduct was insignificant. This means that medical treatment can only break the chain of causation in the most extraordinary cases; incompetent or even grossly abnormal treatment will not suffice if the original injury is still an operative cause of death.

An example of such an extraordinary case might be **R** v **Jordan** (1956). The defendant was convicted of murder after stabbing the victim, but the conviction was quashed by the Court of Criminal Appeal when it heard new evidence that, at the time of the death, the original wound had almost healed, and the victim's death was brought on by the hospital giving him a drug to which he was known to be allergic – treatment that was described as 'palpably wrong'. It was held that the wound was no longer an operative cause of death. **Jordan** was described in the later case of **R** v **Smith** (1959) as a very particular case dependent upon its exact facts, and in **Malcherek** as an exceptional case, and is therefore unlikely to be used as a precedent. It seems that the law still requires very extraordinary circumstances for medical treatment to break the chain of causation.

It was pointed out in **R** v **Mellor** (1996) that the burden of proof is on the prosecution, so the defence do not have to prove that there was, for example, medical negligence in order to avoid liability. In that case the accused attacked a 71-year-old man breaking his ribs and facial bones. The victim died two weeks later of broncho-pneumonia, which would probably not have been fatal if, on the day of his death, he had been given oxygen.

This failure may have constituted medical negligence. Certain passages in the judge's summing-up implied that there was a burden on the defence to prove medical negligence. Citing with approval the vital question on causation laid down in **Cheshire**, it was accepted that the jury had been misdirected. Nevertheless the conviction was upheld as the evidence against the appellant was overwhelming, so that a correctly directed jury would have convicted.

Where the 'operative and significant' test applies the courts might well conclude that both the defendant's original act and the intervening act are in law the causes of the relevant result so that both parties can potentially be criminally liable. In **R v Cheshire** (1991) the Court of Appeal observed:

> Even though negligence in the treatment of the victim was the immediate cause of his death, the jury should not regard it as excluding the responsibility of the accused unless the negligent treatment was so independent of his acts, and in itself so potent in causing death, that they regard the contribution made by his acts as insignificant.

Under the traditional principles of causation, the free voluntary conduct of the victim (or a third party) breaks the chain of causation. This general principle was confirmed by the House of Lords in **R v Kennedy (No. 2)** (2007). The respected criminal law academic, Glanville Williams, wrote in his *Textbook of Criminal Law* (1983):

> Underlying this rule [that the victim's voluntary conduct breaks the chain of causation] is, undoubtedly, a philosophical attitude. Moralists and lawyers regard the individual's will as the autonomous prime cause of his behaviour. What a person does (if he reaches adult years, is of sound mind and is not acting under mistake, intimidation or similar pressure) is his own responsibility, and is not regarded as having been caused by other people. An intervening act of this kind, therefore, breaks the causal connection that would otherwise have been perceived between previous acts and the forbidden consequences.

Foresight and causation

There is some confusion in the case law on the relevance of an intervening event being foreseeable. Traditionally the approach taken has been that if an intervening event is so extraordinary that it is unforeseeable then this will break the chain of causation. There are a number of cases, known as the 'fright and flight' cases or the 'escape' cases which take this approach.

KEY CASE

The leading case is **R v Roberts** (1971) where the defendant had given a lift to a young woman and had touched her clothes. She panicked, thinking that he was about to sexually assault her and jumped out of the moving car injuring herself. He was found to have caused her injuries as her reaction was foreseeable and not so daft as to be extraordinary. In the words of the Court of Appeal:

> The victim's conduct will break the chain of causation if it was so daft as to be unforeseeable.

> Was [the victim's reaction] the natural result of what the alleged assailant said or did, in the sense that it was something that could reasonably have been foreseen as the consequence of what he was saying or doing? If the victim does something so 'daft' or so unexpected that no reasonable man could be expected to foresee it, then it is only in a very remote and unreal sense a consequence of his assault.

In **R** v **Corbett** (1996) a mentally handicapped man had been drinking heavily all day with the defendant. An argument ensued and the defendant started to hit and head-butt the victim, who ran away. The victim fell into a gutter and was struck and killed by a car. At Corbett's trial for manslaughter the judge directed that he was the cause of the victim's death if the victim's conduct of running away was within the range of foreseeable responses to the defendant's behaviour. An appeal against this direction was rejected. Thus in these cases the reaction of the victim was a natural consequence of the defendant's acts, it was not so daft as to be unforeseeable and break the chain of causation.

While these cases are still considered to be good law, there seems to be a tension between their approach to foresight and the approach of the House of Lords in **R** v **Kennedy (No. 2)**. In that case the defendant had supplied the victim with heroin. The victim had injected himself and died of an overdose. The House of Lords held that the chain of causation had been broken because of the free and voluntary conduct of the victim which had intervened between the act of supply and the death of the victim. The chain of causation was broken despite the fact that the victim's intervening conduct was completely foreseeable.

In addition, the thin skull test has always ignored the issue of foreseeability in tackling the question of causation because it could not really be said that it was foreseeable that the victim would be, for example, a Jehovah's witness and reject a blood transfusion. There appears to be a conflict in the legal reasoning in these cases and in particular the relevance of foreseeability which one hopes will be resolved by the courts in future.

The intervening act was a natural result

An intervening act which is a natural result will not break the chain of legal causation. For example, if the defendant knocks the victim unconscious, and leaves him or her lying on a beach, it is a natural result of the defendant's acts that when the tide comes in, the victim will drown, and the defendant will have caused that death. However, the defendant would not be liable for homicide if the victim was left unconscious on the seashore and run over by a car careering out of control off a nearby road as this is not a natural result of the defendant's act. In **R** v **Pagett** (1983), the defendant was attempting to escape being captured by armed police, using his girlfriend as a human shield. He shot at the police and his girlfriend was killed by shots fired at him in self-defence by the policemen. The defendant was found liable for the girl's death as it was a natural result of the defendant's behaviour that the police shot back and hit her in response to his shots. This is despite the fact that the police appear to have been negligent; as the mother of the girl subsequently succeeded in a claim for negligence in respect of the police operation in which her daughter was killed.

Joint enterprise

It is easier to find defendants to have caused a result where they are part of a joint enterprise. A joint enterprise exists where two or more people act together with a common

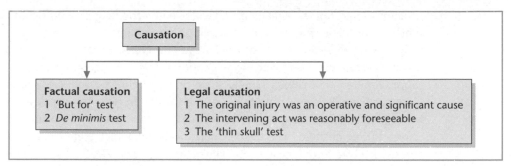

Figure 3.3 Causation (2)

intention that they have communicated to each other (see p. 290). For example, there is a joint enterprise where two men decide to attack a woman, and one hits her and the other kicks her. If the woman is killed as a result of a kick to the head both defendants will be found to have caused the death because the relevant injuries were inflicted as part of a joint enterprise (this will be considered in more detail when we look at accomplice liability and the case of **R v O'Flaherty** (2004) at p. 297).

Failure to prove causation

If the prosecution fail to prove both factual and legal causation of the death, the defendant will escape liability for murder (or any other unlawful homicide), on the ground that the original injury was not in law the cause of death. However, the defendant may still be liable for the original act, for example under a charge for a non-fatal offence against the person.

In practice, an area that has caused particular problems is where very young children have died, and it is unclear whether the death is a result of natural causes or due to criminal conduct of a parent or carer. This is because of serious disagreements within the medical profession as to whether, in certain types of case, a child has died accidentally or non-accidentally in cases categorised as cot death, and where there may have been shaken baby syndrome.

In 2003 the Court of Appeal cleared Sally Clark, Tripti Patel and Angela Canning of murdering their children. Angela Canning had been convicted in 2002 of killing her 7-week-old son, Jason, in 1991 and her 18-month-old child, Matthew, in 1999. The prosecution had relied on the fact that there were three unexplained deaths in one family which, according to expert evidence, made these deaths suspicious. She claimed that her children had died of sudden infant death syndrome (frequently called 'cot death') and the Court of Appeal allowed her appeal. The Court of Appeal ruled that where there was a dispute between experts as to the cause of the death, and there was no other evidence to support a finding of murder, a prosecution should not be brought. This was because the experts simply did not know what were the causes of cot death and it would therefore be impossible to have a safe conviction for murder of a child, when there was a possibility that the death of the child may have been caused by natural circumstances. The Court of Appeal stated: 'Unless we are sure of guilt, the dreadful possibility always

3

Murder

remains that a mother, already brutally scarred by the unexplained deaths of her babies, may find herself in prison for life for killing them when she should not be there at all.'

Following this case the Attorney-General announced that a review would be carried out of all criminal cases involving the sudden death of a child in the previous ten years (approximately 250 cases). Only a small number were subsequently referred on to the Criminal Cases Review Commission to re-examine in detail to check whether there had been a miscarriage of justice. The Criminal Cases Review Commission subsequently referred three of these cases to the Court of Appeal, which were the subject of an appeal along with one further case in **R** v **Harris and others** (2005). These appeals concerned 'shaken baby' cases, which relied upon medical evidence surrounding the sudden death of children. In all cases the prosecution relied upon medical evidence that the existence of three injuries together was consistent with non-accidental death caused by baby-shaking – swelling of the brain, bleeding around the brain and bleeding into the back of the eye, but with no external marks. On appeal the defence lawyers argued that actually this medical evidence was not conclusive that the child had died as a result of criminal violence, though they would certainly have been shaken. Such injuries could not have been caused by an accidental fall, for example. The Court of Appeal concluded that the existence of three injuries remained strong evidence of non-accidental death caused by the defendants, though their existence did not automatically lead to this conclusion. Each case had to be considered on its particular facts. As a result one conviction was reduced from murder to manslaughter, one appeal was dismissed and two appeals were allowed.

Murder

There are three types of unlawful homicide: murder, voluntary manslaughter and involuntary manslaughter. The degree of seriousness applied to each offence is essentially a reflection of the defendant's state of mind with regard to the killing. Murder is the most serious category of unlawful homicide, and is designed to apply to those killings which society regards as most abhorrent.

The definition of murder is traditionally traced back to Sir Edward Coke who was a highly influential writer on criminal law in the eighteenth century. His definition referred to the killing being 'under the King's peace' which during the reign of Queen Elizabeth II is today referred to as 'under the Queen's peace'. The academic Michael Hirst (2008) has pointed out that it is not really clear whether this adds anything to the definition of the offence. It may be a reminder that the offence is not committed when an enemy soldier is killed at war, or simply a reminder that the killing is only murder if it is unlawful, in other words if the defendant does not have a defence, such as that he was acting in self-defence.

Definition

The offence of murder is not defined in any statute. It is committed under common law where a person causes the death of a human being, with malice aforethought. Thus the *actus reus* comprises the common elements of all homicide offences discussed above, and the *mens rea* is malice aforethought.

Mens rea

The *mens rea* for murder is defined as malice aforethought, which has come to mean either an intention to kill or an intention to cause grievous bodily harm. 'Grievous' simply means 'really serious' – **DPP** *v* **Smith** (1961). When directing a jury, the judge can sometimes miss out the word 'really' and simply talk about the requirement that the defendant intended 'serious bodily harm'. In **R** *v* **Janjua and Choudury** (1998) a young man was stabbed to death with the five-and-a-half-inch blade of a knife. The trial judge merely referred to a requirement that the defendants needed to have intended 'serious bodily harm' in order to be liable for murder. They were convicted and appealed on the basis of a misdirection because the word 'really' had been omitted. The Court of Appeal dismissed the appeal stating that, given the nature of the weapon and the injuries caused, the use of the word 'really' in this case was not required. It was a matter for the trial judges in the light of the factual situations with which they were confronted to decide whether or not to use the word 'really' before the word 'serious'.

The term 'malice aforethought' is actually deceptive: the defendant's motives need not be malicious, and are in fact irrelevant; deliberate euthanasia prompted by motives of compassion satisfies the *mens rea* requirement just as well as shooting someone because you hate them. Nor, despite the word 'aforethought', is premeditation a necessary requirement; so long as the required intention is there, it is perfectly possible for a murder to be committed on the spur of the moment. For these reasons, the *mens rea* of murder is best thought of as intention to kill or cause grievous bodily harm. In Chapter 1 it was observed that there are actually two types of intention, direct and indirect, both of which are sufficient for the purposes of the criminal law.

Intention is purely subjective
The test of what the defendant foresaw and intended is always a subjective one, based on what the jury believes the defendant actually foresaw and intended, and not what he or she should have foreseen or intended, or what anyone else might have foreseen or intended in the same situation.

In **DPP** *v* **Smith**, a police officer tried to stop a car that had been involved in a robbery, by clinging to its bonnet as the car drove off, and was killed. The defendant said he did not want to kill the police officer; he had simply wanted to get away. The House of Lords appeared to say that a person intended death or grievous bodily harm if a reasonable person would have foreseen that death or grievous bodily harm would result from the act of the defendant, even if the defendant did not actually foresee this. However, this objective test was considered bad law and s. 8 of the Criminal Justice Act 1967 was passed to change it. This provides that a person is not to be regarded as having intended or foreseen the natural and probable consequences of an act simply because they were natural and probable, although this may be evidence from which the jury may infer that it was intended. The crucial issue is what the defendant actually foresaw and intended, not what he or she *should* have foreseen or intended.

Direct intention
Direct intention corresponds with the everyday definition of intention, and applies where the accused actually wants the result that occurs, and sets out to achieve it. An obvious

example of direct intention to kill would be deliberately pointing a gun at someone you want to kill and shooting them.

Indirect intention

Indirect intention (sometimes known as oblique intention) is less straightforward. It applies where the accused did not desire a particular result but in acting as he or she did, realised that it might occur. For example, a mother wishes to frighten her children and so starts a fire in the house. She does not want to kill her children, but she realises that there is a risk that they may die as a result of the fire. The courts are now quite clear that oblique intention can be sufficient for murder: people can intend deaths that they do not necessarily want. But in a line of important cases, they have tried to specify the necessary degree of foresight required in order to provide evidence of intention.

In **R** v **Moloney** (1985) the defendant was a soldier who was on leave at the time of the incident that gave rise to his prosecution. He was staying with his mother and step-father, with whom he was apparently on very good terms. The family held a dinner party, during which the appellant and his stepfather drank rather a lot of alcohol. They stayed up after everyone else had left or gone to bed; shortly after 4.00 a.m. a shot was fired and the appellant was heard to say, 'I have shot my father'.

The court was told that Moloney and his stepfather had had a contest to see who could load his gun and be ready to fire first. Moloney had been quicker, and stood point-ing the gun at his stepfather, who teased him that he would not dare to fire a live bullet; at that point Moloney, by his own admission, pulled the trigger. In evidence he said, 'I never conceived that what I was doing might cause injury to anybody. It was just a lark.' Clearly he did not want to kill his stepfather, but could he be said to have intended to do so? Lord Bridge pointed out that it was quite possible to intend a result which you do not actually want. He gave the example of a man who, in an attempt to escape pursuit, boards a plane to Manchester. Even though he may have no desire to go to Manchester – he may even hate the place for some reason – that is clearly where he intends to go.

Foresight is merely evidence of intention

Moloney established that a person can have intention where they did not want the result but merely foresaw it, yet the courts are not saying that foresight is intention. Foresight is merely evidence from which intention can be found.

Before **Moloney,** in the case of **Hyam** v DPP (1975), it had looked as though foresight was actually intention, though the judgment in that case was not very clear. The defendant, Pearl Hyam, put blazing newspaper through the letterbox of the house of a Mrs Booth, who was going on holiday with Pearl Hyam's boyfriend; Mrs Booth's two children were killed in the fire. On the facts it appeared that Pearl Hyam did not want to kill the two children; she wanted to set fire to the house and to frighten Mrs Booth. The court held that she must have foreseen that death or grievous bodily harm were highly likely to result from her conduct, and that this was sufficient *mens rea* for murder. In **Moloney,** the House of Lords held that **Hyam** had been wrongly decided, and that nothing less than intention to kill or cause grievous bodily harm would constitute malice afore-thought: merely foreseeing the victim's death as probable was not intention, though it could be evidence of it.

Lord Bridge suggested that juries might be asked to consider two questions: was death or really serious injury a 'natural consequence' of the defendant's act, and did the defendant foresee that one or the other was a natural consequence of their act? If the answer was 'Yes' the jury might infer from this evidence that the death was intended.

This guidance for juries in turn proved to be problematic. In **R** v **Hancock and Shankland** (1986), the defendants were striking miners who knew that a taxi, carrying men breaking the strike to work, would pass along a particular road. They waited on a bridge above it, and dropped a concrete block which hit the taxi as it passed underneath, killing the driver. At their trial the judge had given the direction suggested by Lord Bridge in **Moloney** and they were convicted of murder. On appeal, the House of Lords held that this had been incorrect, and a verdict of manslaughter was substituted. Their Lordships agreed with Lord Bridge that conviction for murder could result only from proof of intention, and that foresight of consequences was not in itself intention; but they were concerned that the question of whether the death was a 'natural consequence' of the defendants' act might suggest to juries that they need not consider the degree of probability. The fact that there might be a ten-million-to-one chance that death would result from the defendants' act might still mean that death was a natural consequence of it, in the sense that it had happened without any interference, but, with this degree of likelihood, there would seem to be little evidence of intention.

Lord Scarman suggested that the jury should be directed that: '. . . the greater the probability of a consequence, the more likely it is that the consequence was foreseen and that if that consequence was foreseen the greater the probability is that that consequence was also intended . . . But juries also need to be reminded that the decision is theirs to be reached upon a consideration of all the evidence.'

Thus if a person stabs another in the chest, it is highly likely this will lead to death or grievous bodily harm, and since most people would be well aware of that, it is likely that they would foresee death or serious injury when they acted. If they did foresee this then that is evidence of intention, from which a jury might conclude that the death was intended. But if you cut someone's finger, that person could die as a result – from blood poisoning for example – but since this is highly unlikely, the chances are that you would not have foreseen that they might die when you cut the finger, and your lack of foresight would be evidence that you did not intend the death.

KEY CASE

The concept of indirect intention was clarified in **R** v **Nedrick** (1986) which established what has become known as the 'virtual certainty' test. The defendant had a grudge against a woman, and poured paraffin through the letterbox of her house and set it alight. The woman's child died in the fire. Lord Lane C.J. said:

> A jury is entitled to conclude that a defendant intended something if it was virtually certain to happen and the defendant realised this.

Where the charge is murder and in the rare cases where the simple direction is not enough, the jury should be directed that they are not entitled to infer the necessary intention unless they feel sure that death or serious bodily harm was a virtual certainty (barring some unforeseen intervention) as a result of the defendant's actions and that the defendant appreciated that such was the case.

Where a man realises that it is for all practical purposes inevitable that his actions will result in death or serious harm, the inference may be irresistible that he intended that result, however little he may have desired or wished it to happen . . . The decision is one for the jury to be reached on a consideration of all the evidence.

In other words, Lord Lane considered that even if death or grievous bodily harm is not the defendant's aim or wish, the jury may infer intention if they decide that death or grievous bodily harm were virtually certain to result from what the defendant did, and the defendant foresaw that that was the case. Such foresight was still only evidence from which they might infer intent, and not intent itself, although it would be difficult not to infer intent where the defendant foresaw that death or grievous bodily harm was practically inevitable as a result of his or her acts.

The virtual certainty test in **Nedrick** became the key test on indirect intention. Then confusion was thrown into this area of the law by the Court of Appeal judgment in **R v Woollin** in 1996. Having given various explanations for his three-month-old son's injuries in the ambulance and in the first two police interviews, Woollin eventually admitted that he had 'lost his cool' when his son had choked on his food. He had picked him up, shaken him and thrown him across the room with considerable force towards a pram standing next to a wall about five feet away. He stated that he had not intended or thought that he would kill the child and had not wanted the child to die. The judge directed the jury that it was open to them to convict Woollin of murder if satisfied that he was aware there was a 'substantial risk' he would cause serious injury. On appeal the defence argued that the judge had misdirected the jury by using the term 'a substantial risk' which was the test for recklessness and failing to use the phrase 'virtual certainty' derived from **Nedrick** for indirect intention. The appeal was rejected by the Court of Appeal which held that in directing a jury a judge was obliged to use the phrase 'virtual certainty' if the only evidence of intention was the actions of the accused constituting the *actus reus* of the offence and their consequences on the victim. Where other evidence was available, the judge was neither obliged to use that phrase, nor a phrase that meant the same thing. The Court of Appeal felt that otherwise the jury function as laid down in s. 8 of the Criminal Justice Act 1967 would be undermined. This section (discussed at p. 28) states:

A court or jury in determining whether a person has committed an offence,
(a) shall not be bound in law to infer that he intended or foresaw a result of his actions by reason only of its being a natural and probable consequence of those actions; but
(b) shall decide whether he did intend or foresee that result by reference to all the evidence, drawing such inferences from the evidence as appear proper in the circumstances.

Thus Parliament had recognised in that provision that a court or jury could infer that a defendant intended a result of their actions by reason of its being a natural and probable result of those actions. In deciding whether the defendant intended the natural and probable result of their actions, s. 8 stated that the court or jury was to take into account all the evidence, drawing such inferences as appeared proper. Section 8 contained no restrictive provision about the result being a 'virtual certainty'. The facts of **Woollin** fell within the category of cases where there was more evidence of intention than purely the conduct of the defendant constituting the *actus reus* of the offence and the result of the conduct, for in addition there was the conduct of the defendant in the first two interviews and his description of events to the ambulance controller.

KEY CASE

A jury is entitled to find intention when the defendant foresaw a result as virtually certain.

A further appeal was made in the **Woollin** case to the House of Lords. This ruled that the Court of Appeal and the trial judge had been mistaken. It said that the **Nedrick** direction was always required in the context of indirect intention. Otherwise there would be no clear distinction between intention and recklessness as both would be concerned simply with the foresight of a risk. The **Nedrick** direction distinguishes the two concepts by stating that intention will only exist when the risk is foreseen as a virtual certainty. Accordingly, a conviction for manslaughter was substituted.

Thus the **Nedrick** 'virtual certainty' direction was approved, though two amendments were made to it. First, the original **Nedrick** direction told the jury that 'they are not entitled to *infer* the necessary intention, unless they feel sure that death or serious bodily harm was a virtual certainty'. The House of Lords substituted the word 'find' for the word 'infer'. This change was to deal with the criticism that the jury were told in the past that they could 'infer' intention from the existence of the foresight and this suggested that intention was something different from the foresight itself, but did not specify what it was. But the difficulties are not completely resolved by the change from 'infer' to 'find' as the jury are still only 'entitled' to make this finding, and it is still a question of evidence for the jury – it is not clear when this finding should be made. It might be more logical to oblige a jury to conclude that there is intention where a person foresaw a result as a virtual certainty. The change of wording from 'infer' to 'find' was expressly followed by the Court of Appeal in **R v Matthews and Alleyne** (2003).

The second amendment was that the majority of the House of Lords felt that the first sentence of the second paragraph of Lord Lane's statement in **Nedrick** quoted above ('Where a man realises . . .') did not form part of the model direction. So the jury will not normally be pressurised into finding intention by being told that a finding of intention 'may be irresistible'. Thus the model direction now reads as follows:

> Where the charge is murder and in the rare cases where the simple direction is not enough, the jury should be directed that they are not entitled to find the necessary intention unless they feel sure that death or serious bodily harm was a virtual certainty (barring some unforeseen intervention) as a result of the defendant's actions and that the defendant appreciated that such was the case. The decision is one for the jury to be reached on a consideration of all the evidence.

The House of Lords wanted less pressure to be put on the jury to find intention.

Despite the House of Lords' amendments to the **Nedrick** direction, in **R** v **Matthews and Alleyne** the Court of Appeal still stated that a finding of indirect intention was 'irresistible' on the facts of the case. An 18-year-old A-level student had been robbed and then thrown over a bridge. He had told his attackers that he did not know how to swim and he drowned. The two appellants appealed against their conviction for murder on the basis that the jury had been misdirected on the law of intent. The guidance on indirect intention had been presented as a rule of law (the jury was told they *must find* intention when foresight as a virtual certainty was established) rather than as a rule of evidence (the jury should have been told that they were *entitled to find* intention where foresight as a virtual certainty was established). The Court of Appeal stated 'there is very little to choose between a rule of evidence and one of substantive law' and that on the facts a finding of intention was 'irresistible'.

It is also slightly puzzling that in the high-profile case of **Re A (Children)** (2000), concerning the legality of an operation to separate Siamese twins, the Court of Appeal included as part of the direction on intention that should be given to a jury the statement from **Nedrick** which the majority of the House of Lords had said no longer formed part of the model direction. The decision of the Court of Appeal had to be given under significant time constraints due to the urgent need to carry out the operation and, with due respect, it is suggested that this part of the Court of Appeal judgment is misleading.

It is wrong to give a **Woollin/Nedrick** direction if the prosecution case is that the defendant's purpose was to achieve the relevant result. In **R** v **MD** (2004) the defendant was the victim's mother. The prosecution alleged that over a number of years she had pretended that her children suffered from serious illnesses in order to attract attention and sympathy. On the day her younger child died, she had dangerously administered medication through a tube. She was initially prosecuted for murder, but as the prosecution could not prove that her actions caused the death, this was changed to attempted murder and the jury were given a direction on intention in accordance with **R** v **Woollin**. This was found to be a misdirection because on the facts of the case, the prosecution were arguing that she had direct not indirect intention – that the purpose of her actions was to kill.

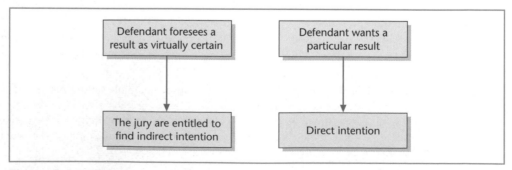

Figure 3.4 Intention

Table 3.1 Chronology of cases on indirect intention

Case	Legal principle
Hyam v **DPP** (1975)	May have wrongly decided that foresight was intention.
R v **Moloney** (1985)	Overturned **Hyam** v **DPP**, as foresight is not intention, it is merely evidence of intention.
R v **Hancock and Shankland** (1986)	Lord Scarman suggested that the jury should be directed that: 'the greater the probability of a consequence, the more likely it is that the consequence was foreseen and that if that consequence was foreseen the greater the probability is that the consequence was also intended . . . But juries also need to be reminded that the decision is theirs to be reached upon a consideration of all the evidence.'
R v **Nedrick** (1986)	Indirect intention can exist where the defendant foresaw a result as a virtual certainty.
R v **Woollin** (1998)	The **Nedrick** test of virtual certainty was confirmed.

Doctors and euthanasia

Technically in England the act of euthanasia can give rise to liability for murder if the doctor is found to have committed, with the intention of causing death, an act that caused the death of a human being. This can place doctors in a delicate position when treating terminally ill patients. In relation to the *mens rea* of murder, the law has in this context developed a concept of 'double effect'. This seeks to distinguish between the primary and secondary consequences of an action or course of treatment. An act which causes a death will not be treated as criminal if the action is good in itself. The doctors are merely viewed as having intended the good effect where there is sufficient reason to permit the bad effect. The doctrine of double effect was first formulated by Devlin J. in 1957 in the case of Dr John Adams. This doctor had been tried for the murder of an 84-year-old woman whom he had injected with a fatal dose of narcotics when she was terminally ill. In his summing-up, Devlin J. stated:

> If the first purpose of medicine, the restoration of health, can no longer be achieved there is still much for a doctor to do, and he is entitled to do all that is proper and necessary to relieve pain and suffering, even if the measures he takes may incidentally shorten human life.

After 42 minutes deliberating, the jury returned a 'not guilty' verdict. Thus liability for murder can be avoided if beneficial medication is given, despite the certain knowledge that death will occur as a side effect.

Davies in his *Textbook on Medical Law* (1998) has argued that, although one can sympathise with judicial reluctance to see competent and highly regarded medical practitioners convicted of murder, the doctrine of dual effect is both illogical and inconsistent with English criminal law. If a doctor injects a severely ill patient with a powerful painkiller in the certain knowledge that the drug will cause death within a matter of minutes, under the ordinary principles of criminal law (laid down in the cases of **Woollin** and **Nedrick**) this doctor intended to kill. English law has traditionally excluded any considerations of motive in determining criminal responsibility.

KEY CASE

The doctrine of 'double effect' was considered in the high-profile case of **Re A (Children)** which was concerned with Jodie and Mary who were conjoined twins. They each had their own vital organs, arms and legs. The weaker twin, Mary, had a poorly developed brain, an abnormal heart and virtually no lung tissue. She had only survived birth because

> The double effect doctrine cannot apply when a different person receives the benefit of the act, to the person who suffers the harm.

a common artery enabled her sister to circulate oxygenated blood for both of them. An operation to separate the twins required the cutting of that common artery. Mary would die within minutes because her lungs and heart were not sufficient to pump blood through her body. The doctors believed that Jodie had between a 94 and 99 per cent chance of surviving the separation and would have only limited disabilities and would be able to lead a relatively normal life. If the doctors waited until Mary died naturally and then carried out an emergency separation operation, Jodie would only have a 36 per cent chance of survival. If no operation was performed, they were both likely to die within three to six months because Jodie's heart would eventually fail.

The question to be determined by the Court of Appeal was whether the operation would constitute a criminal offence, and in particular, the murder of Mary who would be killed by the operation. Looking at whether the doctors carrying out the operation would have the *mens rea* of murder, submissions were made to the Court of Appeal that the doctrine of double effect should relieve the surgeons of criminal responsibility. It was argued before the Court of Appeal that the surgeons' 'primary purpose' in this case would be to save Jodie, and the fact that Mary's death would be accelerated was a secondary effect which would not justify a conviction for murder. But the majority of the Court of Appeal felt the doctrine of double effect could not apply to these facts, where the side effect to the good cure for Jodie was another patient's death for whom the act in question provided no benefit. They therefore found that the doctors would have 'murderous intent' if they carried out the operation, though they would avoid liability due to the defence of necessity (discussed at p. 368).

Sentence

Murder carries a mandatory sentence of life imprisonment under s. 1(1) of the Murder (Abolition of the Death Penalty) Act 1965. In practice, most murderers are not required to stay in prison for the rest of their life but are released on licence after spending some time in custody. They can then be returned to prison if their behaviour upon release gives rise to concern.

In the recent past, the final decision as to when murderers should be released on licence lay with a politician, the Home Secretary. This was found to be in breach of the European Convention on Human Rights in the case of **R** v **Anderson** (2002). The Home Secretary, however, seems anxious to retain some control in this area. Provisions were added to the Criminal Justice Act 2003 under which the Home Secretary, through Parliament, lays down an appropriate sentence for different types of murderer. The aim is to achieve consistency in the sentencing of murderers. Under these provisions, judges are required to slot offenders into one of three categories according to the severity of their crime. For the first category, actual life will be served by those convicted of the most serious and heinous crimes: multiple murderers, child killers and terrorist murderers. For the second category, there is a starting point of 30 years. This category will include murders of police and prison officers and murders with sexual, racial or religious motives. For the third category, the starting point is 15 years. In addition, there are 14 mitigating and aggravating factors which can affect the sentence imposed.

There are presently 22 people serving whole-life tariffs in England and Wales, none in Europe and 25,000 in America (along with 3,500 people under sentence of death).

Criticism

The mandatory sentence

The mandatory life sentence has been criticised as too rigid and harsh so that the judge is obliged to impose a severe sentence where leniency would have been more appropriate. For example, a man may have helped to kill his terminally ill wife because she begged him to put an end to her pain. The court may feel considerable sympathy for the husband who carried out a mercy killing, but would still be obliged to impose a life sentence. The mandatory life sentence for murder means that once convicted of the offence, defendants face the same penalty whether they are serial killers, terrorists or mercy killers. This inflexibility prevents the court from taking into account motive or circumstances, both of which can make a significant difference to the way in which society would view the individual offence.

In **R** v **Lichniak** (2002) the defendants argued that the life sentence was disproportionate to the offence, in breach of Art. 3 of the European Convention on Human Rights, and arbitrary, in breach of Art. 5 of the Convention. These arguments were rejected by the House of Lords.

Definition of death

The lack of a precise definition of death creates uncertainty in the law, but the courts are reluctant to clarify the issue because it is such an emotive subject. In many other comparable jurisdictions, legislation has been passed to provide a definition of death, with most countries accepting that for legal purposes death occurs when the brain stem is dead and the victim's brain cannot function spontaneously. However, when the Criminal Law Revision Committee considered the issue in 1980, it concluded that statute should not intervene.

The year and a day rule

For centuries, in order for a defendant to be liable for a homicide offence, the victim had to die within 366 days of the last act (or omission) done to the victim by the defendant. The rule traditionally acted as a rather primitive test of causation; if the victim survived for longer than a year and a day, it could be reasonably assumed that death was caused by something other than the defendant's act. In **R** v **Dyson** (1908), a father physically abused his baby daughter Lily on 13 November 1906 and then again on 29 December 1907. She died on 5 March 1908. On appeal, Dyson's conviction for murder was quashed, because the judge had wrongly directed at the original trial that he could be convicted even if she had died solely as a result of the first assault. This was incorrect because that act had taken place over a year and a day before her death.

Over the years this rule had attracted considerable criticism. Advances in medical science – particularly life-support technology – mean that victims can be kept alive for longer than a year and a day, even though the original injuries remain the actual cause of death. The Law Reform (Year and a Day Rule) Act 1996 has therefore abolished the old common law rule.

In order to prevent oppressive prosecutions, proceedings for a fatal offence require the consent of the Attorney-General if the victim dies over three years after the infliction of an injury which is alleged to have caused the death, or the accused has previously been convicted of an offence for the original injury.

Intention to cause grievous bodily harm
Murder is the most serious homicide offence and associated in the public's mind with deliberate killing, yet defendants may be convicted of it without intending to kill, or even foreseeing that death was a possible result of their acts, if they intended to cause grievous bodily harm. The rule has been questioned by several judges, notably in **Hyam**, but it was confirmed by the House of Lords in **Moloney**.

There has been a lengthy campaign to reduce the forms of malice aforethought to one, the intent to kill, on the grounds that the term murder should be reserved for the most blameworthy type of behaviour. A House of Lords Select Committee recommended replacing intent to cause grievous bodily harm with intent to cause serious personal harm, being aware that death may result from that harm. This is contained in the draft Criminal Code. 'Being aware' would imply subjective knowledge; it would not be sufficient that a reasonable person would have known if the accused did not.

Problems with intention
The criminal law as laid down in **Moloney** and subsequent cases does not define intent, it only gives guidelines on how a jury might tell when it is present; so the same facts might equally produce a conviction or acquittal depending on the make-up of the jury.

Smith and Hogan argue that the requirement that the consequences should actually be virtually certain is illogical, since the person who wrongly thinks that death is likely to result is as morally guilty as the one who is correct in his assumption. If you point a gun at someone with the intention of killing him, that intention is not lessened by the fact that unknown to you he is wearing a bulletproof vest.

It has been argued persuasively (A. Pedain (2003)) that the current law on indirect intention places undue emphasis on the degree of foresight of the harm by the defendant. The law should focus instead on whether the defendant had 'endorsed the harm', that is to say accepted that the harm might occur. The degree of foresight should merely be viewed as evidence of such an endorsement. This analysis potentially gives intention a wider meaning.

Euthanasia
For a discussion of the issues surrounding euthanasia see p. 378.

● Proposals for reform

Review of murder

Concerns were expressed by the Law Commission in 2004 that the law on murder was 'in a mess' and that there was a 'pressing need for a review of the whole law of murder rather than merely some of the partial defences'. As a result, the Government has announced that a major review of murder will be carried out jointly by the Home Office and the Law Commission. This is the first such review for 50 years. It is expected to take up to two years and will examine the overall framework of murder and the partial defences, to ensure that the law provides coherent and clear offences which protect the public and enable those convicted to be appropriately punished. The Government is particularly concerned about the law on provocation, where the provocation is due to sexual jealousy or infidelity. It has stated that the consultation will not lead to the abolition of the mandatory life sentence or any changes to the sentencing guidelines for murder set out in the Criminal Justice Act 2003. The Law Commission published a consultation paper at the end of 2005, *A New Homicide Act for England and Wales?* Its final report, *Murder, manslaughter and infanticide* (2006) is currently being considered by the Home Office.

At the moment, English law only recognises two types of homicide: murder and manslaughter. In its final report, the Law Commission has proposed that there should be three tiers of homicide:

1 **First degree murder** where there is an intention to kill, or an intention to cause serious injury, with an awareness that the conduct involved a serious risk of causing death. The mandatory life sentence would apply.

2 **Second degree murder** where the defendant killed with:
   - an intention to cause serious harm (but not to kill). This currently falls within the offence of murder. 'Serious harm' would be narrowly defined as 'harm of such a nature as to endanger life or to cause, or to be likely to cause, permanent or long term damage to a significant aspect of physical integrity or mental functioning';
   - an intention to cause some injury or a fear or risk of injury while being aware of a serious risk of causing death;
   - an intention to kill but the proposed revised partial defences of provocation, diminished responsibility and duress apply. The defences of provocation and diminished responsibility currently reduce liability to manslaughter, while duress does not provide a defence at all to a charge of murder.

The maximum sentence that could be applied would be a discretionary life sentence.

3 **Manslaughter** where the defendant killed and:
   - was grossly negligent;
   - the act causing the death was itself criminal and the defendant intended to cause harm but not serious harm, or foresaw a serious risk of causing injury.

In its consultation paper, the Law Commission had provisionally recommended that first degree murder should be restricted to where the defendant had an *intention* to kill. This

Table 3.2 Law Commission reform recommendations

First degree murder	Second degree murder	Manslaughter
• Defendant had an intention to kill; or • defendant had an intention to cause serious injury, with an awareness that the conduct involved a serious risk of causing death.	• Defendant had an intention to cause serious harm. • Defendant had an intention to cause some injury or a fear or risk of injury while being aware of a serious risk of causing death. • Defendant had an intention to kill along with a partial defence of provocation, diminished responsibility or duress.	• Defendant was grossly negligent. • The act causing the death was criminal and the defendant intended to cause harm but not serious harm or foresaw a serious risk of causing injury.
Mandatory life sentence	Discretionary life sentence	Discretionary life sentence

was perceived by some organisations representing victims and their families as too lenient on murderers, with the mandatory life sentence applying to fewer people. The Law Commission changed this recommendation in its final report, extending first degree murder to where the defendant had an intention to cause serious injury, being aware that the conduct involved a serious risk of causing death.

Under the Law Commission's proposals, manslaughter would be more narrowly defined than it is currently. Gross negligence manslaughter would continue to impose an objective standard on defendants, but they would only be liable if they had the capacity to appreciate the risk.

Abolish mandatory life sentence

The Law Commission, in its paper on the partial defences to murder published in 2004, suggested that the mandatory sentence should be reconsidered because it forces the courts in practice to artificially stretch the defences available to murder, in an attempt to avoid imposing a harsh life sentence where a lighter sentence would be more appropriate. The Government has, however, made it clear that it is opposed to the abolition of the mandatory life sentence.

A House of Lords Select Committee that reported in 1989 recommended that the mandatory sentence of life imprisonment for murder be abolished, and the sentence left at the discretion of the court.

Abolish murder and manslaughter distinction

A very different reform would be to abolish the distinction between murder and manslaughter altogether, creating a single offence of homicide, or unlawful killing. The offence would be the same, regardless of the accused's state of mind and the circumstances, but these would be taken into account in order to determine the appropriate level of punishment. One criticism of this suggestion is that it would take important elements of the decision-making process out of the hands of the jury, applying the standard of proof beyond reasonable doubt, and give them to the judge, who would decide them on the basis of the less strict criteria used in sentencing.

Domestic abuse causing suicide

In **R** v **D** (2006) the Crown Prosecution Service brought a test prosecution for manslaughter following the suicide of a woman after a lengthy period of domestic abuse. Mrs D committed suicide by hanging herself. On the evening of the suicide, her husband had struck her on the forehead, causing a cut from the bracelet he was wearing. He was subsequently prosecuted for manslaughter and inflicting grievous bodily harm under s. 20 of the Offences Against the Person Act 1861. In the Crown Court, the trial judge had ruled that the case should not proceed to trial as there was no basis on which a reasonable jury could convict the defendant of either offence. The Crown Prosecution Service appealed unsuccessfully against this ruling.

In the Crown Court the trial judge suggested that where a 'decision to commit suicide has been triggered by a physical assault which represents the culmination of a course of abusive conduct', it would be possible for the Crown to argue that that final assault played a significant part in causing the victim's death. The prosecution, however, chose not to pursue this argument. In reality there is a clear causal connection between domestic abuse and female suicides. Research carried out by Stark and Flitcraft *Killing the beast within: Woman battering and female suicidality* (1995) concluded that domestic abuse could be the single most important cause of women committing suicide. It has been calculated that each year 188 suicides by women in the UK can be linked to domestic abuse: Sylvia Walby *The Cost of Domestic Violence* (2004). This social reality should not be ignored by the criminal law.

A statutory definition of intention

In its consultation paper *A New Homicide Act for England and Wales?* (2005), the Law Commission has suggested that the common law approach to intention could be replaced by a statutory definition. It suggested that this definition could be in the following terms:

> A person acts intentionally with respect to a result when he or she acts either:
> (i) in order to bring it about; or
> (ii) knowing that it will be virtually certain to occur; or
> (iii) knowing that it would be virtually certain to occur if he or she were to succeed in his or her purpose of causing some other result.

People would not be deemed to have intended any result which it was their purpose to avoid. It was hoped that this statutory definition could provide clarity and certainty while achieving justice. Foresight of a virtual certainty would have amounted to intention, so foresight would again have formed part of the substantive law, not merely part of the evidence. At present, a person who kills foreseeing death or grievous bodily harm as virtually certain *may* be a murderer; if the proposed definition of intention applied they *would* be a murderer. The House of Lords' judgment in **Woollin** only goes halfway to achieving this reform, as the jury are still only 'entitled' to find intention and the matter remains a question of evidence. Lord Bridge in **R** v **Moloney** had not wanted to treat foresight as intention in law because he was anxious to draw a distinction between intention and recklessness. Thus, foresight amounted to recklessness in law, while foresight was only evidence of intention. But this problem is now avoided by drawing the distinction between the two forms of *mens rea* on the basis that only foresight of a virtual certainty will suffice for intention, while a lesser degree of foresight will suffice for recklessness.

Following the consultation process, the Law Commission changed its final recommendation, concluding that a statutory definition of intention should simply codify the existing common law and continue to leave a discretion to the jury.

? Answering questions

1 Simon wants to kill his girlfriend Polly and, in order to do so, puts rat poison in her coffee. This would normally only be sufficient to make an ordinary person sick, but Polly is unusually sensitive to rat poison. She is taken to hospital where the doctor diagnoses her illness as appendicitis. She is kept in hospital and dies a few days later from poisoning. Discuss Simon's liability for Polly's death.

Note that you are only asked to discuss Simon's liability, so you are not concerned with any possible liability of the doctors. The starting point in looking at Simon's liability is the offence of murder. Work your way through the elements of liability in the same order discussed in this chapter. Look first at the *actus reus*. Quite a lot of your time will be spent on discussing the issue of causation. Two factors might have broken the chain of causation – the abnormal sensitivity of Polly to the poison and the doctor's misdiagnosis – and you need to apply the tests of both factual and legal causation. As far as the doctor's misdiagnosis is concerned, relevant cases include **Cheshire** and **Smith**. You need to consider whether the original acts of Simon are still an operative cause of Polly's death, and whether the misdiagnosis falls into the 'normal band of competence' and was therefore reasonably foreseeable. Polly's abnormal sensitivity to rat poison is covered by **Blaue** and the 'thin skull' test.

Some students get confused and think that if one person, such as the doctor, is the cause of death nobody else (such as Simon) can be, but this is not the case: more than one person can be the cause of death.

If the chain of causation has been broken (unlikely) Simon could not be liable for any other homicide offence, but he could be liable for a non-fatal offence. You then need to consider the *mens rea* of murder: we know that Simon intended to kill which, if it can be proved, is sufficient *mens rea*. Simon's knowledge, or lack of it, concerning Polly's sensitivity to rat poison will be important evidence from which the jury may infer intent. Cite the relevant authorities such as **Moloney, Nedrick** and **Woollin** to support your argument.

2 Critically evaluate the *mens rea* of murder.

Your introduction should define the *mens rea* of murder, pointing out that it is a subjective test, covers both intention to kill and to cause grievous bodily harm, and includes both direct and indirect intention. On indirect intention, cases such as **Moloney, Hancock and Shankland, Nedrick,** and the important case of **R v Woollin**, should be looked at in detail. Then go through the criticism that applies to the current law on *mens rea* and some of the proposed reforms (see p. 69). Your conclusion might highlight the fact that *mens rea* is the factor that makes murder our most serious offence, and that it is therefore important that problems with it should be ironed out.

Make sure you stick to answering the question: you are asked only about the *mens rea* of murder, so you cannot discuss the *actus reus* of the offence. Nothing will be gained by analysing the law on, for example, causation. As the *mens rea* of murder is intention no marks would be gained for discussing recklessness. Avoid making the classic error of stating that the offence of murder is defined in s. 1 of the Homicide Act 1957. It is not. Murder is a common law offence and is therefore not defined in a statute.

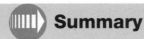 ## Summary

The common elements of homicide offences

To be liable for any homicide offence the defendant must cause the death of a human being.

A human being

For the purposes of the homicide offences, a person is a human being when capable of having an existence independent of a mother.

Death

There is no single legal definition of 'death'. In **R** v **Malcherek and Steel** (1981) the court appeared to favour the approach that death occurs when the victim is brain-dead, but this did not form part of the *ratio decidendi* of the decision.

Causation

The prosecution must prove that the death was caused by the defendant's act. Defendants can only be held responsible for a death where their acts are both a 'factual' and a 'legal' cause of the victim's death.

Factual causation

In order to establish factual causation, the prosecution must prove two things:

- That *but for* the conduct of the accused the victim would not have died as and when he or she did.
- That the original injury arising from the defendant's conduct was *more than a minimal cause* of the victim's death.

Legal causation

Even if factual causation is established, the judge must direct the jury as to whether the defendant's acts are sufficient to amount in law to a cause of the victim's death. Legal causation can be proven in one of two ways:

- The 'thin skull' test;
- The original injury was an operative and significant cause of death.

Murder

The offence of murder is not defined in any statute. It is committed under common law where a person causes the death of a human being, with malice aforethought. Thus the *actus reus* comprises the common elements of all homicide offences discussed above, and the *mens rea* is malice aforethought.

Malice aforethought has come to mean either an intention to kill or an intention to cause grievous bodily harm. 'Grievous' simply means 'really serious' – **DPP** *v* **Smith** (1961). The test of what the defendant foresaw and intended is always a subjective one, based on what the jury believes the defendant actually foresaw and intended. Intention can be divided between direct and indirect intention.

Direct intention

Direct intention exists where the accused actually wants the result that occurs, and sets out to achieve it.

Indirect intention

Indirect intention applies where the accused did not desire a particular result but, in acting as he or she did, realised that it might occur. Foresight is merely evidence of intention. In **R** *v* **Nedrick** (1986) the Court of Appeal stated that the jury may infer intent if they decide that death or grievous bodily harm were virtually certain to result from what the defendant did, and the defendant foresaw that that was the case.

Doctors and euthanasia

In relation to the *mens rea* of murder, the law has developed for doctors a concept of 'double effect'. This seeks to distinguish between the primary and secondary consequences of an action or course of treatment.

Criticism

A range of criticisms have been made of the law of murder, including the fact that there is no clear definition of a death, and the law is applied differently to doctors compared to other members of society.

Proposals for reform

There have been suggestions that the mandatory life sentence should be abolished and it is possible that we may see a major reform of the homicide offences in the near future. The Law Commission has recommended that the homicide offences should be divided into first degree murder, second degree murder and manslaughter.

 # Reading list

Burns, S. (2009) 'How certain is death' 159 *New Law Journal* 459.

Gardner, S. (2001) 'Compassion without respect? Nine fallacies in *R v Smith*' [2001] *Criminal Law Review* 623.

Hirst, M. (2008) 'Murder under the Queen's Peace' [2008] *Criminal Law Review* 541.

Norrie, A. (1999) 'After Woollin' [1999] *Criminal Law Review* 532.

Pedain, A. (2003) 'Intention and the terrorist example' [2003] *Criminal Law Review* 579.

Reading on the internet

The Law Commission report *Murder, manslaughter and infanticide* (2006, Law Com. No. 304) is available on the Law Commission's website at:
  http://www.lawcom.gov.uk/docs/lc304.pdf

The Law Commission's consultation paper *A New Homicide Act for England and Wales?* (2005, Consultation Paper No. 177) is available on the Law Commission's website at:
  http://www.lawcom.gov.uk/docs/cp177_web.pdf

Visit **www.mylawchamber.co.uk/elliottcriminal** to access multiple choice questions, flashcards and practice exam questions to test yourself on this chapter.

Use **Case Navigator** to read in full some of the key cases referenced in this chapter:

- R *v* Blaue [1975] 3 All ER 446
- Kennedy (No 2) [2005] EWCA Crim 685
- R *v* Pagett (1983) 76 Cr. App. R 279
- R *v* White [1910] 2 KB 124
- R *v* Woollin – [1998] 4 All ER 103

3

Murder

4 Voluntary manslaughter

This chapter explains that:

- people can be liable for voluntary manslaughter when their conduct satisfies all the elements of murder but they have one of three partial defences: loss of control, diminished responsibility or participation in a suicide pact;

- the defence of loss of control is contained in ss. 54 and 55 of the Coroners and Justice Act 2009;

- the defence of diminished responsibility is contained in s. 2 of the Homicide Act 1957, as amended by s. 52 of the Coroners and Justice Act 2009 and is available when defendants kill because they are suffering from an abnormality of mental functioning; and

- the defence of participating in a suicide pact is contained in s. 4 of the Homicide Act 1957 and is available when defendants were also trying to commit suicide alongside the victim, but happened to survive when the victim died.

Introduction

Most unlawful homicides which are not classified as murder are manslaughter. There are two kinds of manslaughter: voluntary, which is considered here; and involuntary, which will form the subject of the next chapter. The basic difference between these two types of manslaughter is that for voluntary manslaughter the *mens rea* for murder exists, whereas for involuntary manslaughter it does not.

Voluntary manslaughter occurs where the accused has the necessary *actus reus* and *mens rea* for murder, but there are mitigating circumstances which allow a partial defence, and so reduce liability to that of manslaughter (we call this a partial defence to distinguish it from other defences which remove liability completely). It is not therefore possible to charge someone with voluntary manslaughter; they will be charged with murder, and must then put their defence during the trial.

The three partial defences available are loss of control, diminished responsibility, and suicide pacts. Successful pleading of one of the three means that on conviction the sentence is at the discretion of the judge, and can be anything from life imprisonment to an absolute discharge, depending on the circumstances of the case; unlike murder, which carries a mandatory sentence of life imprisonment.

This area of law has been the subject of a major legislative reform in the Coroners and Justice Act 2009. The Act has abolished the old defence of provocation and replaced it with a new defence of loss of control; it has also replaced the old definition of the defence of diminished responsibility with a new definition.

The relevant provisions of the 2009 Act had not been brought into force at the time of writing (January 2010), but it is expected that they will be brought into force within the next few months when the book is published and therefore this chapter has been written on the assumption that the provisions have been brought into force. You can check the companion website to this book to see when the provisions have been brought into force. Alternatively, if you have access to the LexisNexis database, you can check whether the provisions have been brought into force by going to the legislation database and searching for 'Coroners and Justice Act 2009'. You can then click on the section numbers on the table of contents for the Act. At the bottom of where the section is set out there is a statement saying whether the provision is currently in force.

In looking at the new defence of loss of control, we will at each stage compare it with the old defence of provocation. The observations regarding the old defence of provocation will be placed in grey tinted boxes entitled 'Provocation' so that the reader can see clearly what the current law is and what the current law used to be on each aspect of the defence. This is a useful exercise both to highlight differences between the new and old defences and to consider how the new legislation might be interpreted in the future.

Loss of control

The Homicide Act 1957 s. 3 contained a statutory partial defence of provocation. This defence was the subject of considerable criticism and, as a result, the Government

4

Voluntary manslaughter

decided this area of law was in need of reform. Research was carried out by both the Law Commission and the Ministry of Justice and the following reports were published:

- Law Commission Report (2004), *Partial Defences to Murder*
- Law Commission Consultation Paper (2005), *A new Homicide Act for England and Wales?*
- Law Commission Report (2006), *Murder, Manslaughter and Infanticide*
- Ministry of Justice Consultation Paper (2008), *Murder, Manslaughter and Infanticide: proposals for reform of the law.*

These reports all concluded that the judges alone could not cure the defects in the defence of provocation and legislation was required. While the Law Commission put forward proposals for reforming the provocation defence, it did not feel that this reform could be successful while there was a mandatory life sentence for murder. This mandatory sentence means that judges have no discretion in the choice of sentence following a murder conviction. Where judges felt sympathy for the defendant and considered that a life sentence was not appropriate they would in practice try to stretch the definitions of the partial defences to try to bring the defendant within them, so that they then had a sentencing discretion. Thus, the Law Commission considered that any reform to the partial defences would be unsuccessful in practice until the mandatory life sentence for murder had been abolished. The Government, however, decided to push ahead with reform while retaining the mandatory life sentence. It considered that the old defence of provocation was too generous to those who killed out of anger and too hard on those who killed out of fear of serious violence. While the old defence of provocation was based on anger the new defence of loss of control prioritises the emotion of fear as justifying the killing, for example killings following domestic abuse. The Government was particularly concerned that the defence of provocation treated men and women differently in cases of domestic violence. It considered that it was too easy for men to rely on the defence of provocation, saying they killed their female partner because of sexual infidelity (how far this had actually been a problem in practice is open to debate) while women with abusive partners found it hard to mount a defence.

The Law Commission's recommendation would have amended the existing defence of provocation, whereas the Coroners and Justice Act 2009 has abolished the defence of provocation altogether and replaced it with a new defence of loss of self-control.

The defence of loss of control is defined in the following terms:

S. 54 (1) Where a person ("D") kills or is a party to the killing of another ("V"), D is not to be convicted of murder if—
  (a) D's acts and omissions in doing or being a party to the killing resulted from D's loss of self-control,
  (b) the loss of self-control had a qualifying trigger, and
  (c) a person of D's sex and age, with a normal degree of tolerance and self restraint and in the circumstances of D, might have reacted in the same or in a similar way to D.

(2) For the purposes of subsection (1)(a), it does not matter whether or not the loss of control was sudden.

(3) In subsection (1)(c) the reference to "the circumstances of D" is a reference to all of D's circumstances other than those whose only relevance to D's conduct is that they bear on D's general capacity for tolerance or self-restraint.

(4) Subsection (1) does not apply if, in doing or being a party to the killing, D acted in a considered desire for revenge.

(5) On a charge of murder, if sufficient evidence is adduced to raise an issue with respect to the defence under subsection (1), the jury must assume that the defence is satisfied unless the prosecution proves beyond reasonable doubt that it is not.

(6) For the purposes of subsection (5), sufficient evidence is adduced to raise an issue with respect to the defence if evidence is adduced on which, in the opinion of the trial judge, a jury, properly directed, could conclude that the defence might apply.

(7) A person who, but for this section, would be liable to be convicted of murder is liable instead to be convicted of manslaughter.

(8) The fact that one party to a killing is by virtue of this section not liable to be convicted of murder does not affect the question whether the killing amounted to murder in the case of any other party to it.

There are three key elements to the new defence which will be considered in turn: loss of control, a qualifying trigger (which can be linked together as a subjective test) and an objective test considering whether a reasonable person would have reacted in the way the defendant did.

Provocation: definition

The old defence of provocation was contained in section 3 of the Homicide Act 1957:

S. 3 Where on a charge of murder there is evidence on which the jury can find that the person charged was provoked (whether by things done or by things said or by both together) to lose his self-control, the question whether the provocation was enough to make a reasonable man do as he did shall be left to be determined by the jury; and in determining that question the jury shall take into account everything both done and said according to the effect which, in their opinion, it would have on a reasonable man.

The defence of provocation was interpreted by the courts as containing a two-part test:

1. Was the defendant provoked to have a sudden and temporary loss of self-control?
2. Would a reasonable person have been provoked to react in this way?

The first test was subjective, focusing on whether the defendant lost their self-control. The second test was objective, looking at whether a reasonable person would have reacted in this way. A loss of self-control occurred when someone lost their temper, so the defence was concerned with reducing a person's criminal liability for murder when they lost their temper and had a violent outburst.

 1. Loss of self-control

For the new defence under the Coroners and Justice Act 2009 the defendant must have lost their self-control at the time of the killing. Section 54(2) expressly states that the loss of self-control need not be sudden. This provision was included to try and avoid discriminating against women who might lose their self-control more slowly than men (known as a 'slow burn' reaction), though the explanatory notes to the Act state that delay could be evidence as to whether defendants had actually lost their self-control, so in practice women may still find that the defence discriminates against them. Where there is delay then there is a greater possibility that the defendant acted out of calculated revenge and s. 54(4) expressly states that the defence is not available if the defendant 'acted in a considered desire for revenge'.

The Law Commission had recommended that the idea of loss of self-control should be dropped altogether, but instead it is at the heart of the redrafted partial defence.

Provocation: a sudden and temporary loss of self-control

For the old defence of provocation, the loss of self-control had to be due to a loss of temper and the case of **R** v **Cocker** (1989) showed that this could produce harsh results. The accused suffocated his wife, who was suffering from a painful terminal illness, and had repeatedly begged him to end her life. The judge withdrew the issue of provocation from the jury, who then felt they had no alternative but to convict of murder, but wrote a letter of protest to the judge, stating that they felt the decision they had been forced to make was unfair. The Court of Appeal held that the judge had acted correctly: loss of self-control meant loss of temper and the appellant on these facts had not lost his temper but merely succumbed to his wife's requests. For the new defence of loss of control a different interpretation of 'loss of control' is likely, with the emphasis very literally on whether the defendant had lost control of him or herself, without a search for any loss of temper, since the loss of control need no longer be the result of provocation and could be due to fear.

Regarding the timing issue, for the old defence of provocation the defendant had to have had a sudden and temporary loss of control following the case of **R** v **Duffy** (1949). In **R** v **Ibrams** (1982) it was held that the existence of a 'cooling-off period' between the act of provocation and the killing was evidence that the loss of self-control was not 'sudden and temporary'. The defendants and a young woman had been severely bullied by a man called Monk, over a period up to and including Sunday 7 October, and had tried and failed to obtain effective police protection. On Wednesday 10 October, they discussed the fact that Monk was likely to terrorise them again on Sunday 14 October, and made a plan. On Sunday, they would get Monk drunk, and encourage him to take to his bed. The woman would leave a signal for the defendants, who would then enter and attack him, with the aim of breaking his arms and legs. All this they did, with the result that Monk was in fact killed. The appellants were convicted of murder and appealed on the ground that the judge had wrongly withdrawn the defence of provocation from the jury. The appeal was rejected; although it was possible that provocation might extend over a long period of time, it must culminate in a sudden explosion of temper, which did not seem to be apparent in the carefully planned killing.

The requirement for a 'sudden and temporary' loss of control, with the implication against a 'cooling-off period' as raised in **Ibrams**, was controversial because it was said to discriminate against women, an issue discussed in more detail below. Recent cases gave a more generous

Sara Thornton celebrating her release
Source: Rex Features

interpretation of the time factor. In **R** v **Thornton** (1992) Sara Thornton had at one point declared her intention of killing her husband, who had for years been beating her. Later, after a fresh provocation, she went to the kitchen, took and sharpened a carving knife and returned to another room where she stabbed him. The original trial judge considered that, despite the time lapse, the issue of provocation should be left to the jury; nevertheless the jury convicted Sara Thornton of murder. At her appeal the Court of Appeal confirmed that the issue of whether or not there had been a sudden and temporary loss of self-control was one for the jury. It should be remembered though that the existence of a cooling-off period was not a matter of law, but a piece of evidence which the jury could use to decide whether at the time of the killing the defendant was deprived of self-control. This was emphasised in the case of **Ahluwalia** (1993). The approach in practice taken to the issue of time delay may not prove so different therefore for the new loss of control defence, even though the statute expressly states that the loss of control need not be sudden.

The Law Commission (2004) was concerned that the defence of provocation could be relied upon by defendants who acted in revenge. It was particularly critical of the case of **Baille** (1995) where the defendant was incensed that the victim was supplying his three teenage sons with drugs. He had armed himself with a sawn-off shotgun and cut-throat razor, driven to the victim's home and shot him. The Court of Appeal ruled that the issue of provocation should have been left to the jury. The Law Commission comments:

> If on facts such as those in **Baille**, a jury accepted the defence of provocation, that would break the moral plank on which the defence of provocation has, at least since Victorian times, rested. Namely, that due to the loss of self-control, the defendant was not master of his or her own mind, and, in one way, lacked the full *mens rea* of the offence.

The new loss of control defence now expressly states that the defence is not available if the defendant acted out of revenge.

2. Resulting from a qualifying trigger

The loss of self-control must have been caused by a qualifying trigger, defined in section 55 of the 2009 Act:

55(1) This section applies for the purposes of section 54.
(2) A loss of self-control had a qualifying trigger if subsection (3), (4) or (5) applies.
(3) This subsection applies if D's loss of self-control was attributable to D's fear of serious violence from V against D or another identified person.
(4) This subsection applies if D's loss of self-control was attributable to a thing or things done or said (or both) which—
   (a) constituted circumstances of an extremely grave character, and
   (b) caused D to have a justifiable sense of being seriously wronged.
(5) This subsection applies if D's loss of self-control was attributable to a combination of the matters mentioned in subsections (3) and (4).
(6) In determining whether a loss of self-control had a qualifying trigger—
   (a) D's fear of serious violence is to be disregarded to the extent that it was caused by a thing which D incited to be done or said for the purpose of providing an excuse to use violence;
   (b) a sense of being seriously wronged by a thing done or said is not justified if D incited the thing to be done or said for the purpose of providing an excuse to use violence;
   (c) the fact that a thing done or said constituted sexual infidelity is to be disregarded.
(7) In this section references to "D" and "V" are to be construed in accordance with section 54.

So the qualifying trigger exists when the defendant has a loss of self-control attributable to:

- a fear of serious violence from the victim; or
- things said or done.

The qualifying trigger can also be a combination of both of these. Thus the defence will be available both where there is fear and where there is anger. The Law Commission partly justified this by pointing out that there is psychiatric evidence that fear and anger are not distinct emotions but are frequently present together in violent action.

A fear of serious violence from the victim

This form of the defence might be used by a woman who has been subjected to domestic violence and who reacts by killing her abusive partner. It could also be used by a homeowner who kills a burglar. The defence could be available where self-defence is not available because there was no imminent threat or their reaction was considered disproportionate for the purposes of self-defence. Thus it avoids the 'all or nothing' approach, by allowing a partial defence where the complete defence of self-defence cannot succeed, but there is still some justification for the killing. The reformed defence might be fairer on, for example, battered women who kill their abusive partners after a relatively minor attack, but in a context where they fear a more significant attack in the future.

Where the qualifying trigger is a fear of serious violence from the victim, this is a subjective test and the fear need not be reasonable. The fear of serious violence needs to be in respect of violence against the defendant or against another identified person. The explanatory notes to the Act state that the relevant fear could be in respect of a child or other relative of the defendant, but it could not be against an unidentified group of people (for example a political group).

When the defendant's fear of serious violence was caused by something that the defendant incited for the purpose of providing an excuse to use violence, it is to be disregarded (s. 55(6)(a)).

The defence would only succeed where the victim is the source of the violence feared by the defendant. This is slightly ironic because campaigners on behalf of domestic violence victims were unhappy that they could be blamed for their own deaths when a defence of provocation had been relied on, but in the context of the killing of an abusive partner the new defence effectively does blame (male) victims for their own death. Mackay and Mitchell (2005) have therefore argued that by defining the defence to require the defendant to have feared serious violence from the victim, instead of the other possible reformulation of 'emotional disturbance' the proposed reform places an undesirable focus on the victim's conduct rather than the defendant's.

Things said or done

Things said or done can only amount to a qualifying trigger if they amount to circumstances of an extremely grave character and cause the defendant to have a justifiable sense of being seriously wronged (s. 55(4)). The requirement that the circumstances must be of an extremely grave character may mean that this form of the defence will have a narrower application than the old provocation defence. The defendant must have a sense of being seriously wronged (a subjective test) but the defence will only be allowed if the sense of being wronged was justifiable (an objective test to be determined by the jury). An example given by the Law Commission was of a parent who arrives home to find his or her child has just been raped, and in response the parent loses self-control and kills the offender as he tries to escape. The wording suggests that the defendant should have some moral right on their side in relation to the victim rather than their conduct simply being an example of human frailty.

When the defendant's sense of being seriously wronged relates to something the defendant incited for the purpose of providing an excuse to use violence, it is to be disregarded (s. 55(6)(b)). Where something done or said related to sexual infidelity (on the part of the victim or anyone else) it also has to be disregarded (s. 55(6)(c)). So if a man kills a woman because she has been unfaithful, he will not be able to claim the partial defence. The senior judge, Lord Phillips, has stated he is:

> uneasy about a law which so diminishes the significance of sexual infidelity as expressly to exclude it from even the possibility of amounting to provocation.

Provocation: provocative conduct

Under the Homicide Act 1957, the old defence of provocation could be 'by things done or by things said or by both together', so, like the new defence of loss of control, words alone could suffice.

For the defence of provocation, the provocative act did not need to be illegal or even wrongful: in **Doughty** (1986), it was held that the persistent crying of a baby could amount to provocation. This case would be decided differently under the loss of control defence because a baby crying does not constitute circumstances of an extremely grave character which could give the defendant a justifiable sense of being seriously wronged. It is also worth noting that the loss of control defence extends the trigger from the concept of provocation to where the defendant had a fear of serious violence.

Mere circumstances could not constitute provocation, so a novelist discovering that his or her manuscript has been eaten by a dog, or a farmer finding a crop ruined by flooding, would not have had a defence if they consequently lost control and struck out and killed the nearest person. Given that the new defence of loss of control also refers to 'a thing or things done or said' circumstances will probably still not be sufficient to trigger this defence.

For the old defence of provocation, the provocative acts need not have been directed at the defendant. In **R v Pearson** (1992), two brothers killed their violent, tyrannical father with a sledgehammer. It was held that the father's violent treatment of the younger brother, during the eight years when his older brother was away from home, was relevant to the older boy's defence, especially as he had returned home to protect his brother. Under the new loss of control defence, the defendant must fear violence from the victim either against him or herself or another identified person (s. 55(3)), so there is a clarification as to whom the victim's conduct needs to be targeting.

Under the old common law before the 1957 Act, provocation had to be something 'done by the dead man to the accused' (**Duffy** (1949)), but the 1957 Act removed this requirement. In **R v Davies** (1975), it was held that the acts of the lover of Davies's wife could be taken into account as provoking Davies to kill his wife. For the new defence of loss of control, the acts of third parties are irrelevant if the trigger for the defence is fear of serious violence, because it has to be fear of serious violence from the victim (s. 55(3)), but are potentially relevant if the trigger is things said or done.

The fact that the provocation was incited by the defendant in the first place did not prevent the defence of provocation being made out. In **R v Johnson** (1989), Johnson and a friend, R, had been drinking at a nightclub. Johnson threatened violence towards R's female friend and to R himself, and a struggle developed between Johnson and R. Johnson was carrying a flick knife, and stabbed R, killing him. He was convicted of murder and appealed on the ground that the judge should have directed the jury on provocation, the provocation being R's reaction to Johnson's own aggressive behaviour. His appeal was allowed and a conviction for manslaughter was substituted. In such cases the provocation of the defendant had to be extreme by comparison with the defendant's original act. The defendant in **Edwards v R** (1973) tried to blackmail his victim, who attacked him with a knife. A fight ensued, during which Edwards grabbed the knife and fatally stabbed his attacker. The Privy Council held that the defendant could only rely on provocation as a defence if the victim's reaction to the blackmail had been extreme, compared to the blackmail itself. In this case they felt that it was, but said there could be cases where provocation should not be left to the jury because it was incited by the defendant. The new loss of control defence is never available where the defendant incited the potential trigger for his or her loss of control.

A defendant who was provoked as the result of a mistake of fact was entitled to be treated as if the facts were as that defendant mistakenly supposed them to be. In **R v Brown** (1972), the defendant, a soldier, struck his victim with a sword and killed him, because he wrongly, but apparently reasonably, supposed that his victim was a member of a gang attacking him. His defence of provocation was successful. The 2009 Act does not tackle the issue of mistakes by the defendant and this will have to be resolved by the courts.

3. The objective test

The new defence of loss of control is only available if a person of the defendant's sex and age with an ordinary level of tolerance and self-restraint and in the circumstances of the defendant might have acted in the same or similar way to the defendant (s. 54(1)(c)).

The reference to the defendant's 'circumstances' includes all circumstances except those that are only relevant to the defendant's general level of tolerance and self restraint (s. 54(3)). The explanatory notes to the Act state that a defendant's history of abuse at the hands of the victim could be taken into account in deciding whether an ordinary person might have acted as he or she did, whereas the defendant's short temper cannot.

The Law Commission considered that in most cases where the defendant argued he had killed due to a justifiable sense of being seriously wronged the judge would withdraw the defence from the jury. This is because the Law Commission considered there would be no evidence that a person of ordinary tolerance and self-restraint would react by killing with the *mens rea* of murder.

Provocation: the objective test

The objective test had proved very problematic for the defence of provocation. The problem for the courts is that reasonable people would almost never react to provocation by killing, so if a strict objective test was applied the defence would almost never succeed. The courts had therefore considered whether the reasonable person could be adapted to take into account some of the defendant's actual characteristics. The problem with this approach is that if all the defendant's characteristics are taken into account then the objective test ceases to really be objective as defendants are just being judged by their own standards and clearly by their own standards the evidence shows that they would react to the provocation by killing.

A serious conflict on the interpretation of this area of the law arose between the Privy Council and the House of Lords. The House of Lords binds the English courts and therefore the House of Lords case of **Smith (Morgan)** (2000) ought normally to have been followed. But the Privy Council's opinion laid down in **Attorney-General for Jersey v Holley** (2005) was treated as binding by the Court of Appeal in **R v James and Karimi** (2006), despite established rules of precedent.

In **DPP v Camplin** (1978), the House of Lords defined the reasonable person as a person with the power of self-control to be expected from an ordinary person of the defendant's age and sex. Camplin was a 15-year-old boy. At the time of the offence he had been drinking, and claimed that he had been homosexually assaulted by his victim and that afterwards the man had laughed at him. Camplin lost control, hit his victim over the head with a chapatti pan and killed him. The House of Lords said that the question the jury should ask themselves was whether the provocation would have caused a reasonable boy of Camplin's age to act as he did.

Much of the subsequent judicial and academic debate focused on determining the legal implications of **Camplin** – did it mean that only the sex and age of the defendant could be taken into account when applying the objective test, or did it mean that where appropriate a much wider range of characteristics could be considered, such as depression? The important House of Lords judgment of **R v Smith (Morgan)** (2000) was expected to be the last word on this issue. One evening in November 1996 Morgan Smith received a visit from an old friend, James McCullagh. They were both alcoholics and spent the evening drinking and arguing. Smith had grievances against McCullagh, some of which went back many years. The most recent was his belief that McCullagh had stolen the tools of his trade as a carpenter and sold them to buy drink. At the end of the evening, Smith took a kitchen knife and fatally stabbed McCullagh several times.

Smith claimed that he had been provoked to lose his self-control and kill his victim. Psychiatrists called by the defence said that he was suffering from depression, which made him less able to control his reactions and more likely to be violent. The focus of the proceedings was on the objective test and whether the reasonable person could be given certain characteristics of the accused, in this case the characteristic of having a severe depressive illness.

In his summing-up the trial judge told the jury that they could not take into account the depression when considering the objective test. The defendant was convicted of murder and appealed. The Court of Appeal allowed the appeal on the basis that the jury had been misdirected on the issue of provocation. It ruled that the trial judge ought to have directed the jury that the medical evidence of Smith's depression was relevant to the objective requirement of provocation. A subsequent appeal to the House of Lords was dismissed, as the Court of Appeal was found to have correctly interpreted the law. The House of Lords ruled that characteristics of the defendant beyond simply his age and sex could be taken into account when applying the objective test. The House treated the standard of the reasonable person as flexible, taking into account abnormalities of the actual defendant. The jury should apply the standard of control to be expected of the particular individual. Lord Hoffmann stated:

> The general principle is that the same standards of behaviour are expected of everyone, regardless of their individual psychological make-up. In most cases, nothing more will need to be said. But the jury should in any appropriate case be told, in whatever language will best convey the distinction, that this is a principle and not a rigid rule. It may sometimes have to yield to a more important principle, which is to do justice in the particular case. So the jury may think that there was some characteristic of the accused, whether temporary or permanent, which affected the degree of control which society could reasonably have expected of him and which it would be unjust not to take into account. If the jury take this view, they are at liberty to give effect to it.

4

Voluntary manslaughter

The House of Lords' starting point was that the jury should be sovereign in determining which characteristics to take into account. Lord Hoffmann stated:

> This is entirely a question for the jury. In deciding what should count as a sufficient excuse, they have to apply what they consider to be appropriate standards of behaviour; on the one hand making allowance for human nature and the power of the emotions but, on the other hand, not allowing someone to rely upon his own violent disposition.

It would only be in very exceptional cases that a judge should tell a jury to exclude a characteristic from their consideration.

In **Attorney-General for Jersey** v **Holley** (2005), however, the Privy Council directly refused to follow **Smith (Morgan)**, stating that the case wrongly interpreted Parliament's legislation:

> 'On this short ground their Lordships, respectfully but firmly, consider the majority view expressed in the **Morgan Smith** case is erroneous.'

An enlarged Board of nine judges sat in the Privy Council to hear the case of **Attorney-General for Jersey** v **Holley** (2005) and a majority of six refused to follow **Smith (Morgan)**. After an argument, the defendant's girlfriend had told him that she had just slept with another man. The defendant had been drinking heavily. When he picked up an axe that he had been using to chop wood, his girlfriend had said that he would not dare use it. He had then killed his girlfriend with the axe. There was expert evidence that the defendant was a chronic alcoholic, had a depressive and anxious personality, and was dependent on alcohol and female partners. The trial judge in Jersey had told the jury that the fact a person is drunk or under the influence of alcohol at the time of the killing, and as a result he is provoked more easily than if he were sober, was not something to be taken into account in his favour. The Court of Appeal held that this was a misdirection because following **Smith (Morgan)** the trial judge should have drawn a distinction between being drunk, which gives rise to no arguable ground of provocation, and suffering from the disease of alcoholism, which could be taken into account.

The Privy Council accepted that the Court of Appeal had correctly interpreted **Smith (Morgan)**, but that **Smith (Morgan)** itself was wrong. According to the Privy Council, evidence that the defendant was suffering from chronic alcoholism was not a matter to be taken into account by the jury when considering whether, in their opinion, having regard to the actual provocation, a person having ordinary powers of self-control would have done what the defendant did. The Attorney-General's appeal was allowed, though for procedural reasons the earlier decision to reduce the defendant's liability from murder to manslaughter was permitted to stand.

The Privy Council considered that the standard of a reasonable person had to be a constant, objective standard in all cases. If a defendant suffered from a mental abnormality this could not be taken into account for the defence of provocation (instead justice would be achieved by taking this into account for the defence of diminished responsibility). The statutory reasonable person had the power of self-control to be expected of an ordinary person of like sex and age. In other respects the reasonable person only shared such characteristics of the defendant as the jury thought would affect the gravity of the provocation to the defendant.

Although a House of Lords' judgment such as **Smith (Morgan)** should bind the Court of Appeal, and a Privy Council decision should only be persuasive, the Court of Appeal in **R** v **James and Karimi** (2006) chose to follow the Privy Council judgment of **Holley** rather than the House of Lords' judgment. The Court of Appeal decided that the Privy Council decision of **Holley** reasserted the correct law in England and not **Smith (Morgan)**. Accordingly, the reasonable person was given the defendant's age and sex, but not other characteristics that simply affected their general ability to exercise self-control.

The existence of the objective test enables the criminal law to impose a threshold of acceptable behaviour. The Coroners and Justice Act 2009 has put into statutory form the Privy Council judgment of **Attorney-General for Jersey** v **Holley**. When reviewing this area of law, the Law Commission (2004) considered that some form of objective standard was required, otherwise killings such as road rage could fall within the defence. It concluded that the House of Lords went too far in **Smith (Morgan)**. It was of the view that leaving the decision to the essentially subjective judgement of individual jurors was wrong because it was likely to lead to inconsistency. The Law Commission appears to have agreed with the Privy Council and to have accepted the arguments of the criminal law academic, Andrew Ashworth (1976). He has argued that the defence of provocation is 'for those who are in a broad sense mentally normal' but who snap under the weight of very grave provocation. Where the defendants are abnormal they should rely on the defence of diminished responsibility (discussed at p. 90) which requires an abnormality of mental functioning. Russell Heaton (2001) has commented that:

> The provocation excuse should be a concession to extraordinary external circumstances not to the extra-ordinary internal make-up of the accused. The moral foundation for the extenuation is the necessity for very serious provocation . . . If the reaction is essentially due to the internal character of the accused, his or her excusatory claim, if any, should sound in diminished responsibility. That is the proper defence for the abnormal.

But the academic Alan Norrie (2001) has rejected this distinction between characteristics relevant to why the defendant was triggered to lose their self-control and characteristics relevant to the ability to exercise self-control, arguing that 'it separates the inseparable'. If age (and perhaps sex) can justify different levels of self-control the same should be true of other characteristics which, through no fault of the individual, affect the ability to regulate his or her response to things said or done.

● Burden of proof

If sufficient evidence of the partial defence is raised, the burden of disproving the defence of loss of control beyond reasonable doubt rests with the prosecution (s. 54(5)). The evidence will be sufficient where a reasonable jury, properly directed, could conclude that the partial defence might apply. It will be a matter of law, and therefore for a judge to decide, whether sufficient evidence has been raised to leave the partial defence to the jury (s. 54(6)). Where there is sufficient evidence for the issue to be considered by the jury, the burden will be on the prosecution to disprove it. This is the same burden of proof as most other defences.

Provocation: burden of proof

For the old defence of provocation, if there was evidence that a person was provoked to lose his or her self-control, the judge was required by s. 3 of the Homicide Act 1957 to leave the partial defence to the jury even where no reasonable jury could conclude that a reasonable person would have reacted as the defendant did.

● Criticism

Loss of control

The loss of control defence aims to tackle some of the criticisms that had been made of the old provocation defence, but it is questionable whether the law goes far enough. It keeps at its heart the idea of loss of control and so excludes individuals who might have a moral justification for their conduct, such as arguably a 'mercy killer' who helps a terminally ill relative to die, because they have not lost control when they make a rational decision at their relative's request.

The old defence of provocation appeared to lack a sound moral justification for its existence because it was difficult to see why a person who had killed because they had lost their temper should have this defence. Why should a bad-tempered man be entitled to a verdict of manslaughter where a good-tempered one would be convicted of murder? Why should a person have a partial defence to murder when they kill out of anger, but someone who kills with a more creditable emotion, such as compassion, have no defence? There is an attempt to give the defence of loss of control a stronger moral foundation by requiring that the things said or done that made the defendant lose control constitute circumstances of an extremely grave character causing the defendant to have a justifiable sense of being seriously wronged.

By extending the defence to include where the defendant feared serious violence the defence does now recognise that it is not just anger that can effect a person's ability to exercise control. The new defence of loss control now recognises fear as a ground for the defence, but still ignores the compassion and empathy of the mercy killer.

Blaming the victim

The loss of control defence, like the defence of provocation, encourages a culture of blaming the victim for their own murder. Where the issue of loss of control is raised, a trial risks focusing on the deceased's behaviour rather than the defendant's. Inevitably, the deceased is not able to answer these accusations and the whole process can be extremely distressing to the deceased's family and friends. In the past this was particularly insensitive and inappropriate in a modern society, where the relevant provocation was the victim's purported sexual infidelity, but this ground for the defence of loss of control has been completely excluded.

Discrimination against women

The partial defence of provocation was originally found in the common law. Research by Dr Horder (1992) has shown that although the defence had much earlier roots, it emerged in its recognisably modern form in the late seventeenth and early eighteenth centuries. It came from a world of Restoration gallantry in which gentlemen habitually carried lethal weapons and acted in accordance with a code of honour, which required insult to be personally avenged by instant angry retaliation. The defence of provocation was developed to make allowance for the possibility that the man of honour might overreact and kill when a lesser retaliation would have been appropriate. Provided that he did not grossly overreact, liability would be reduced to manslaughter and the death penalty thereby avoided.

As society changed, the defence of provocation also had to change to reflect the different culture and values of modern society. While during the Restoration the defendant's behaviour was seen as rational, by the nineteenth century the defence could only be satisfied if the defendant was found to have lost their self-control.

The harsh stance of the law towards battered women who killed their abusive partners before the Homicide Act 1957, is illustrated by the case of Ruth Ellis. Ruth Ellis was the last woman to be hanged in England for murder. She had killed her boyfriend. Her sister campaigned after her death to have

Ruth Ellis with her boyfriend
Source: © Bettman/Corbis

her conviction reduced from murder to manslaughter on the basis that she had been the victim of domestic violence and suffered from 'battered woman's syndrome'. Her case was referred by the Criminal Cases Review Commission to the Court of Appeal and the court held that, on the law as it stood at the time of her conviction in 1955, the defence of provocation was not available to her.

It is arguable that the sexist foundations of the defence influenced the modern law of provocation. It may have discriminated against women both as victim and as defendant. Looking first at the risk of discrimination against female victims, every year 120 women and 30 men are killed by a current or former partner. The Government was concerned about the operation of the partial defences to murder. It considered that recent developments in the law had led to an extension of the scope and availability of the partial defence of provocation beyond what was envisaged by s. 3 of the Homicide Act 1957, and that the partial defence was often used in circumstances where the degree of provocation was minimal. It was particularly worried about domestic homicides where the provocation relied on was sexual jealousy or infidelity. In such cases, raising the partial defence of provocation involved an attack on the victim's reputation. This could be extremely traumatic for the family, who would perceive that the success of the defence of provocation in such circumstances meant the law was blaming the victim for their own death. The new defence of loss of control now expressly excludes sexual infidelity as serving as a trigger for the defence.

Looking, secondly, at the risk of discrimination against female defendants, a significant campaign in support of women who kill their partners after having being battered developed in the light of the cases of Kiranjit Ahluwalia and Sara Thornton. The much publicised cases of **Thornton** and **Ahluwalia** both involved women killing husbands who had subjected them to extreme violence – for over ten years in Kiranjit Ahluwalia's case – and in both there appeared to be evidence of a cooling-off period. In Sara Thornton's original trial the prosecution stressed she had deliberately gone into the kitchen and sharpened the knife she used to kill her husband; Kiranjit Ahluwalia waited for her husband to fall asleep before attacking him. At their original trials, the prosecution claimed that this meant there had been no sudden and temporary loss of self-control, and both were convicted of murder.

Campaigners suggested that the requirement for 'a sudden and temporary loss of self-control' discriminated against women. In their view the lashing out in a moment of temper is a male way of reacting, and takes no account of the fact that women, partly because they lack physical strength, may react to gross provocation quite differently, yet lose self-control just as powerfully. This is supported by American research which has developed the theory of the 'battered woman syndrome'. Walker's research (1999) shows that women who kill their abusers may not react suddenly to provocation. As Sara Thornton's counsel, Lord Gifford, put it at her original appeal in 1992, 'the slow burning emotion of a woman at the end of her tether . . . may be a loss of self-control in just the same way as a sudden rage'. Helena Kennedy QC describes the classic female reaction to provocation as 'a snapping in slow motion, the final surrender of frayed elastic'. A former Lord Chief Justice, Lord Lane, has suggested that 'sometimes there is not a time for cooling down but a time for realising what happened and heating up'.

The courts appeared to make some effort to appease their critics. Ahluwalia's final appeal was eventually granted on the grounds of diminished responsibility, but it was pointed out that just because there had been a time gap between the last provocative act and the lashing out, this did not automatically rule out provocation because the defendant could have lost control at the last minute. In Thornton's appeal in 1995 it was recognised that the concept of 'battered woman's syndrome' could be taken into account when deciding whether there had been a sudden and temporary loss of control. Another woman who had killed the partner who abused her for years, Emma Humphreys, successfully won an appeal against conviction for murder, and in her case the court accepted that the cumulative effects of years of abuse were relevant to provocation.

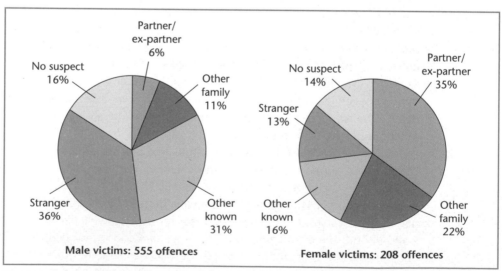

Figure 4.1 All victims by relationship of victim to principal suspect

Source: Crime in England and Wales 2007/08 – Supplementary Volume 2: Homicide, Firearm Offences and Intimate Violence, p. 10.

The new loss of control defence now expressly states that the loss of control need not be sudden, though the explanatory notes suggest that a time delay will still be relevant in determining whether the defendant actually had a loss of self-control. The defence will also be available where the defendant fears serious violence which may well be the case where a woman has been abused in the past. However, the defence of loss of control may still not be available to abused women who kill, because they may not have lost their self-control at all. Instead, the killing may have been planned and deliberate. Walker's research could in fact be interpreted as showing that the defence of loss of control is not suitable for abused women who kill. His research suggests that an abused woman may be calm rather than enraged during and after the killing of her abusive partner. Research by Susan Edwards (2004) has shown significant differences between the way men and women kill. Men who kill their female partners tend to do so by the use of bodily force while women who kill their male partners use knives in 83 per cent of cases. Where knives are used a conviction for murder is more likely.

Diminished responsibility

The defence of diminished responsibility was created by s. 2 of the Homicide Act 1957. This defence was introduced because of problems with the very narrow definition of insanity under the M'Naghten Rules (see p. 326), and had been given quite a broad interpretation. The Law Commission recommended in its report *Murder, Manslaughter and Infanticide* (2006) that the defence of diminished responsibility should be modernised to work more closely with the medical understanding of mental health problems. The Government accepted the Law Commission's recommendations and the definition of the defence was changed by s. 52 of the Coroners and Justice Act 2009 which has substituted a new definition of the defence. The aim is to bring the terminology up-to-date in a way that will accommodate future medical developments and encourage defences to be grounded in a valid medical diagnosis. By doing this, however, the defence may lose some of its flexibility which had been its strength in practice, allowing courts to do justice in the individual case, such as reducing liability from murder to manslaughter for a mercy killing by a relative of a person who was terminally ill and in pain.

The new definition of the defence is still found in s. 2 of the Homicide Act 1957 but that provision has been completely changed by s. 52 of the Coroners and Justice Act 2009. Section 2 of the Homicide Act 1957 now states:

(1) A person ("D") who kills or is a party to the killing of another is not to be convicted of murder if D was suffering from an abnormality of mental functioning which—
  (a) arose from a recognised medical condition,
  (b) substantially impaired D's ability to do one or more of the things mentioned in sub-section (1A), and
  (c) provides an explanation for D's acts and omissions in doing or being a party to the killing.
(1A) Those things are—
  (a) to understand the nature of D's conduct;
  (b) to form a rational judgment;
  (c) to exercise self-control.

(1B) For the purposes of subsection (1)(c), an abnormality of mental functioning provides an explanation for D's conduct if it causes, or is a significant contributory factor in causing, D to carry out that conduct.

● An abnormality of mental functioning

Before 2009 the defence referred to an abnormality of mind, now it refers to an abnormality of mental functioning. To come within the defence, the defendant must have been suffering from an abnormality of mental functioning which satisfies the three requirements discussed below.

(1) A recognised medical condition

The abnormality of mental functioning must have arisen from a recognised medical condition. The main aim of this reform is to modernise the defence to bring it into line with medical understanding of mental ill health. Thus, the defence will only be available if the defendant was suffering from a condition recognised by medical professionals.

The government has not adopted the Law Commission's recommendation to include developmental immaturity as a possible basis for reducing murder to manslaughter so the defence provides no special protection for children accused of murder.

KEY CASE

A high-profile case that raised the issue of diminished responsibility is that of **Anthony Martin** (2001). Martin lived in a ramshackle farmhouse, called Bleak House, in a remote part of Norfolk. He had been the victim of burglaries in the past and had been dissatisfied with the police response. He owned, without a licence, a powerful

> The defence of diminished responsibility can apply where a defendant has a paranoid personality disorder and depression.

Winchester pump-action shotgun. In 1999 his house was broken into by three men. Martin shot one of the intruders, a 16-year-old boy called Barras, three times, including once in the back. Barras died from his injuries. Another intruder was seriously injured. Martin was convicted of murder and causing grievous bodily harm and sentenced to life imprisonment. On appeal before the Court of Appeal in 2001, new expert evidence was produced that Martin was suffering from a paranoid personality disorder and depression. The court accepted that this evidence should have been considered by the jury and, as it had not been available to the jury, his conviction for murder was quashed and replaced by a conviction for voluntary manslaughter on the basis of diminished responsibility. This case is pre-2009 but it is likely that the defence would also have succeeded under the Coroners and Justice Act 2009 as the 'paranoid personality disorder' could probably be described as a recognised medical condition which amounted to an abnormality of mental functioning.

Anthony Martin
Source: Reuters/HO Old

Anthony Martin's victim, Fred Barras
Source: Rex Features

Under the old definition of diminished responsibility, there was considerable case law considering the relevance of drink or drugs to the availability of this defence. A mental abnormality caused by drink or drugs was not usually sufficient to ground the defence (**Fenton** (1975)). Following the case of **Tandy** (1989), alcohol would, however, be a valid cause of an abnormality if long-term alcoholism had caused brain damage or produced an irresistible craving so that consumption of the first drink of the day was involuntary (described sometimes as 'alcohol dependence syndrome'). The same principle also applied to drugs. It is not clear whether the courts will take the same approach to drink and drugs in the context of the new definition of diminished responsibility.

> **KEY CASE**
>
> In **R v Dietschmann** (2003) the appellant killed his victim in a savage attack. At the time of the killing he was very drunk and was also suffering from an abnormality of mind (a form of depression following the death of his aunt, with whom he had been in a relationship). At his trial for murder, D relied on a defence of diminished responsibility. The House of Lords found that the defence of diminished responsibility could be successful even if the defendant would not have killed if he had been sober. The abnormality of mind could still have been a substantial cause of the killing, which impaired his mental responsibility for what had happened. If the same facts were to be considered under the new definition of diminished responsibility, careful attention would have to be given as to whether Dietschmann's depression amounted to a recognised medical condition for the purposes of an abnormality of mental functioning.
>
> *For the defence of diminished responsibility, the abnormality must have been a substantial cause of the killing, but need not be the sole cause.*

(2) A substantial impairment of the defendant's ability

The abnormality of mental functioning must have substantially impaired the defendant's ability to do one of three things:

(a) understand the nature of their conduct;
(b) form a rational judgment; or
(c) exercise self-control.

The previous definition of the defence simply required a person's mental responsibility to have been diminished, but did not specify in what way. Thus, the new definition spells out more clearly than before what aspects of a defendant's mental functioning must be affected in order for the partial defence to succeed.

(3) A significant contributory factor to the killing

The abnormality of mental functioning must provide an explanation for the defendant's involvement in the killing. Section 2(1B) clarifies that this will be the case where the abnormality was at least a significant contributory factor in causing the defendant to carry out the conduct. Thus it is clear that the abnormality should cause, or be a significant contributory factor in causing, the defendant to kill.

Under the old definition of the defence, there was case law looking at the issue of drink and causation. This case law concluded that drink consumed voluntarily could not be taken into account as a cause of the killing that could reduce the defendant's mental responsibility (**R** v **Wood** (2008)). Sometimes the defendant's mental abnormality and drink both play a part in causing the defendant to kill. As long as the abnormality was a substantial cause of the killing, it did not matter that the drink was also a cause of the killing. But the defendant had to go on to satisfy the next aspect of the defence, that the mental abnormality substantially impaired his or her mental responsibility for the fatal acts. In practice it will be very difficult for a jury to determine whether an alcoholic consumed a particular drink voluntarily or involuntarily (due to an irresistible alcoholic craving).

If the defendant would not have killed if he or she had not taken drink, the mental abnormality could still have been a cause of the defendant's acts. In **Fenton** the defendant would not have killed if he had not taken drink, but nevertheless the trial judge was found to have correctly left the issue of diminished responsibility to the jury. The emphasis under the 2009 Act will be whether the abnormality of mental functioning (rather than the drink) was a significant contributory factor to the killing.

● Burden of proof

The defence must prove diminished responsibility on a balance of probabilities, calling evidence from at least two medical experts. The Court of Appeal has ruled in **R** v **Lambert** (2000) that this burden of proof is not in breach of the European Convention on Human Rights.

● Criticism

Comparison with the old definition of diminished responsibility
The defence of diminished responsibility was originally defined as follows:

> Where a person kills or is party to the killing of another, he shall not be convicted of murder if he was suffering from such abnormality of mind (whether arising from a condition of arrested or retarded development of mind or any inherent causes or induced by disease or injury) as substantially impaired his mental responsibility for his acts and omissions in doing or being a party to the killing

In order for the defence of diminished responsibility to succeed the court had to be satisfied that:

● the defendant suffered from an abnormality of mind;
● the abnormality was caused in one of three ways;
● the abnormality was a substantial cause of the defendant's act of killing; and
● the abnormality substantially impaired the defendant's mental responsibility for their acts.

Under this old definition, the required abnormality of mind was held to cover severe shock or depression, including cases of 'mercy killing', and pre-menstrual syndrome. In 1997 in **R** v **Hobson** the Court of Appeal accepted that 'battered woman's syndrome' was a mental disease and could cause an abnormality of mind. An abnormality of mental functioning for the purposes of the new definition of diminished responsibility is likely to be interpreted more narrowly than an abnormality of mind was interpreted, as it will need to result from a recognised medical condition.

When the Law Commission reviewed this area of the law in 2004, it concluded that the defence had worked quite well since it had been established. The courts had taken a practical approach and applied the defence in order to achieve justice where people killed in an abnormal mental state. As a result the defence had only needed to be considered by the House of Lords on one occasion in almost 50 years, compared with the regular appearance of the defence of provocation in the House of Lords. Diminished responsibility was being used on occasion pragmatically, where the court felt sympathy for the defendant and the requirements of the defence of provocation were not satisfied. For example, in **Ahluwalia** the defence was applied to an abused woman who killed her abusive partner.

In a recent case, Bernard Heginbotham killed his wife because she had been moved between different care homes and he did not want her to go through the stress of being moved again. The trial judge described the killing as 'an act of love'. The defendant was a 100-year-old man whom the judge considered had been suffering from a mental disorder at the time. His defence of diminished responsibility succeeded. He was given a 12-month community rehabilitation order.

Cases involving mercy killing put a strain on the law of diminished responsibility because strictly speaking the requirements for this defence may not have been satisfied. The Law Commission observed in its consultation paper (2003):

> There appears to be some inconsistency in the willingness of psychiatrists to testify on the diagnosis of the defendant's mental health. Some experts may be uncomfortable with classifying as an 'abnormality of mind' what essentially may be ordinary reactions to a highly stressful situation such as an abusive and violent relationship. This element of arbitrariness is far from ideal.

By reducing the defendant's conviction to manslaughter, this allowed the court to take into account the defendant's motivation when sentencing, and to treat a deserving case sympathetically. While this was often a misuse of the defence, it did achieve justice on the particular facts of a case, which may no longer be possible now that a 'recognised medical condition' is required. The risk of injustice is real while murder continues to carry a mandatory life sentence.

Ahluwalia leaving the high court in London celebrates as the court accepts her plea of manslaughter
Source: Rebecca Naden/Press Association Images

Prosecution's right to argue insanity in response

In some cases, once diminished responsibility is put forward as a defence, the prosecution may respond by arguing that the defendant is legally insane, leading to a situation where the prosecution is trying to get the defendant acquitted (by reason of insanity) while the defendant is arguing that he or she should be found guilty of manslaughter. The reason behind this apparently bizarre situation is that acquittal from a murder

4

Voluntary manslaughter

charge on the grounds of insanity inevitably leads to committal to a mental institution for an indeterminate length of time, which the prosecution may consider desirable if it feels the defendant is dangerous.

Negative stereotype of women

In **Ahluwalia** the defence of diminished responsibility was applied to an abused woman who killed her abusive partner. Labelling such women as mentally ill plays up to negative stereotypes of vulnerable women. The Law Commission has observed (2003):

> This, in effect, pathologises a woman's actions and implies that had her mental faculties not been impaired she would have continued to be a 'happy punch bag'. There is the further irony that the more robust the defendant is the less likely it is that she will succeed on a defence of diminished responsibility.

Reliance on diminished responsibility in this context places the focus of the defence on the woman's state of mind, when it would have been more appropriate to emphasise the abuse she had suffered.

If a woman is imprisoned for manslaughter following a finding of diminished responsibility, she may find that upon her release the social services are unwilling to allow her custody of her children because she has been diagnosed as mentally ill.

Harsh on the mentally ill

Research by Professor Mitchell (2000) may suggest that the current law is too harsh on mentally ill offenders, as his research has found that public opinion is against the criminal prosecution of those who kill when they are mentally ill. If this does accurately reflect public opinion, then the way forward would seem to be a reform of the defences of being unfit to plead and insanity, as these defences are available to all offences, and not just a charge of murder. There is no reason why the law should be lenient to the mentally ill who have killed and not when they have committed more minor offences.

By contrast, it appears the defence may also be wrongfully refused on policy grounds. In **R** v **Sutcliffe** (1981) – the trial of the 'Yorkshire Ripper' – both the defence and prosecution wanted the trial to proceed on the basis of diminished responsibility, and were backed by well-respected psychiatric experts. But the judge refused and Sutcliffe was eventually convicted of murder. Since Sutcliffe has spent his sentence in solitary confinement in a mental hospital, it looks as though the lawyers and psychiatrists were right, but, as Helena Kennedy QC has pointed out, it appears that public policy demanded that a man accused of such a notorious string of crimes should, if guilty, bear the label of murderer.

It has been suggested that qualified defences should be created to take account of the sort of mitigating circumstances involved in cases of mercy killing. While this does have considerable problems of its own, it might be preferable to the current bending of the rules to fit circumstances for which they were never designed.

Combined defence

Mackay and Mitchell (2003) have argued that following the case of **Smith (Morgan)** (discussed on p. 85) there was considerable overlap between the defences of diminished

responsibility and provocation. This is because under that case, in applyi[ng the]
test for provocation the court could take into account the defendant's [charac-]
teristics which would also be relevant to the abnormality of mental fun[ction]
for diminished responsibility. They therefore argued that it had be[come]
unnecessarily complicated to have two separate defences, and that instead th[ere]
be a single, merged defence which would arise where the defendant was acting under
an extreme emotional disturbance. As a stricter objective test is now being applied to the
defence of loss of control, so the distinction between diminished responsibility and the
defence of loss of control is relatively clear.

Abolition of the mandatory life sentence for murder

This would make a formal defence of diminished responsibility unnecessary, because the
circumstances and state of mind of the defendant could be taken into account for sentencing. However, as stated in the section on murder, this would remove an important
aspect of the decision from the jury.

Change to burden of proof

Under the draft Criminal Code, the burden of proof would be on the prosecution.

Suicide pacts

Section 4 of the Homicide Act 1957 states that:

> It shall be manslaughter and shall not be murder for a person acting in pursuance of a suicide
> pact between him and another to kill the other or be party to the other being killed by a third
> person.

Suicide was once a crime. This is no longer the case, but when that offence was abolished, the crime of aiding and abetting suicide remained, on the ground that helping
someone to take their own life might well be done with an ulterior motive – by a bene-
ficiary of the deceased's will, for example. Where someone dies due to acts of another
and that person intended to cause the death, he or she could be liable for murder.

Where the person can show that the death was a suicide and was part of a pact in
which that person too intended to die, liability will be reduced to manslaughter. It is
for the defence to prove this, on a balance of probabilities. The legality of this reverse
burden of proof was confirmed by the Court of Appeal in **R** v **H** (2003). The prosecution
accused the defendant of injecting his wife with a huge dose of insulin, thus killing her.
He took a minor dose of insulin which did not kill him. He said that he was the survivor
of a suicide pact. The Court held that the defendant had the burden of proving the
existence of a suicide pact on the balance of probabilities. This reverse burden of proof
was necessary to protect vulnerable members of society from being murdered and the
offender disguising his conduct as a suicide pact.

❓ Answering questions

1 **Does the defence of loss of control avoid the problems that had plagued the defence of provocation?**

This question required a detailed comparision between the old defence of provocation and the new defence of loss of control. You could start by pointing out that there are certain similarities between the two defences, including the fact that both can be divided into subjective and objective tests. Looking first at the subjective tests both defences focused on the requirement of loss of control. However, the causes of this loss of control are slightly different. The old defence of provocation restricted the defence to where things were said or done that made the defendant lose their self control. The new defence includes things said or done, though only where they amount to circumstances of an extremely grave character and where the defendant has a justifiable sense of being seriously wronged. In addition, the new defence is also available when the defendant feared serious violence. This might provide a partial defence to people using excessive force to protect their homes where they fear they might themselves be attacked during the burglary (consider the facts of the Anthony Martin case discussed on p. 92).

Under the new defence the loss of self control need not be sudden and this may help the defence succeed for battered women who kill, though a time delay will still probably be relevant in determining whether the defendant actually lost control. Sexual infidelity will not be taken into account, which was a concern of the Government under the old defence of provocation, though how far this had been a problem in practice is open to debate.

The objective test that applies to both offences seems to be the same: the test that applied in **Attorney-General for Jersey** v **Holley** appears to have been put into statutory form by the Coroners and Justice Act 2009. You could consider whether this form of the objective test achieves the right balance: the benefit of consistency and setting a basic standard of behaviour expected of individuals, or does it unfairly ignore the particular characteristics of the actual defendant who may be far from normal.

2 **Peter and Mary had been married for two years. Peter shouted at Mary that he hated her, he said that she was big and fat and did nothing all day apart from watch television. Mary was suffering from post traumatic stress disorder, having recently returned as a soldier from fighting a war where she had seen many horrific events. She shouted at Peter that she hated him, that she knew he was having an affair and she never wanted to see him again. She stormed out of the house, but ten minutes later she returned carrying a bayonet and stabbed Peter in the chest. Peter was dead when he arrived at hospital. Consider the criminal liability of Mary.**

You could start by pointing out that all the elements of the offence of murder exist on these facts: Mary has caused the death of a human being and when she stabbed Peter in the chest she must have at least intended to cause him grievous bodily harm.

You would then need to consider whether Mary would have a partial defence to murder. Looking first at the defence of loss of control under s. 54 of the Coroners and Justice Act 2009, on the facts it is arguable that she lost control. Her reaction does not appear to have been sudden, but this is not a requirement for this defence, though the time delay of ten minutes would probably be taken into account in determining whether she had actually lost control, or whether this was a calculated act of revenge which could not be the basis for this defence.

You then need to consider whether there is a qualifying trigger for the defence of loss of control. On the facts, there is nothing to suggest that she feared serious violence from Peter. You would therefore need to consider whether she was reacting to things said or done which constituted circumstances of an extremely grave character and caused a justifiable sense of being seriously wronged. She accuses Peter of having had an affair, but we are told in s. 55 (6)(c) that sexual infidelity must be disregarded, so even if this was true it must be ignored. It is difficult to see how the court could view what Peter said as amounting to things of an extremely grave character so this could be a problem in satisfying the defence.

As regards the objective test for the loss of control defence, the court could not take into account her post traumatic stress disorder, it will simply take into account her age and sex. Section 54(1)(c) states that the court has to consider whether 'a person of D's sex and age, with a normal degree of tolerance and self-restraint and in the circumstances of D, might have reacted in the same or in a similar way to D'. Thus, it might be arguable that a court could not take into account the post traumatic stress disorder as this would effect Mary's level of tolerance and self-restraint, but a court might take into account her circumstances, that she had just returned from war, in applying the objective test.

As regards the defence of diminished responsibility, the court would have to consider whether the new definition set out by the Coroners and Justice Act 2009 had been satisfied. A court would have to determine whether the post traumatic stress disorder was a recognised medical condition that had caused an abnormality of mental functioning and was a subsantial reason for the killing.

4
Voluntary manslaughter

Summary

Voluntary manslaughter occurs where the accused has the necessary *actus reus* and *mens rea* for murder, but there are mitigating circumstances which allow a partial defence, and so reduce liability to that of manslaughter. The three partial defences available are loss of control, diminished responsibility and suicide pacts.

Loss of control
The defence of loss of control is contained in s. 54 of the Coroners and Justice Act 2009. It can be analysed as requiring a three-part test:

1 Did the defendant have a loss of self control?
2 Was the loss of control caused by a qualifying trigger?
3 Would a reasonable person have reacted in this way?

The loss of control need not be sudden, but it must not have been an act of revenge. The qualifying trigger exists when the defendant has a loss of self-control attributable to a fear of serious violence from the victim; things said or done or a combination of these. Things said or done can only amount to a qualifying trigger if they amount to circumstances of an extremely grave character and cause the defendant to have a justifiable sense of being seriously wronged.

The objective test

The new defence of loss of control is only available if a person of the defendant's sex and age with an ordinary level of tolerance and self-restraint and in the circumstances of the defendant might have acted in the same or similar way to the defendant (s. 54(1(c)).

Criticism

The loss of control defence aims to tackle some of the criticism that had been made of the old provocation defence, but it is questionable whether the law goes far enough. It keeps at its heart the idea of loss of control and so excludes individuals who might have a moral justification for their conduct but remained in control at the time of the killing.

Diminished responsibility

The defence of diminished responsibility was created by s. 2 of the Homicide Act 1957, though its definition has been modernised by s. 52 of the Coroners and Justice Act 2009. To come within this defence the defendant must have been suffering from an abnormality of mental functioning which had arisen from a recognised medical condition. This must have substantially impaired the defendant's ability to do one of three things:

(a) understand the nature of their conduct;
(b) form a rational judgement; or
(c) exercise self-control.

The abnormality of mental functioning must have been at least a significant contributory factor in causing the defendant to carry out the conduct. The burden of proof is on the defendant to prove the existence of the defence on a balance of probabilities.

Suicide pacts

Section 4 of the Homicide Act 1957 provides a partial defence where a defendant can show that the victim's death was a suicide and was part of a pact in which the defendant also intended to die.

Reading list

Ashworth, A.J. (1976) 'The doctrine of provocation' [1976] *Criminal Law Journal* 292.

Edwards, S. (2004) 'Abolishing provocation and reframing self defence: The Law Commission's options for reform' [2004] *Criminal Law Review* 181.

Elliott, C. (2004) 'What future for voluntary manslaughter?' 68 *Journal of Criminal Law* 253.

Home Office (2003) Safety and Justice: The Government's Proposals on Domestic Violence, Cm. 5847, London: Home Office.

Horder, J. (1992) *Provocation and Responsibility*, Oxford: Clarendon Press.

Law Commission (2003) Partial Defences to Murder: A Consultation Paper, No. 173, London: HMSO.

Law Commission (2004) *Partial Defences to Murder*, No. 290, London: Stationery Office.

Mackay, R.D. and Mitchell, B.J. (2003) 'Provoking diminished responsibility: Two pleas merging into one?' [2003] *Criminal Law Review* 745.

Mackay, R.D. and Mitchell, B.J. (2005) 'But is this provocation? Some thoughts on the Law Commission's Report on Partial defences to murder' [2005] *Criminal Law Review* 44.

Mitchell, B. (2000) 'Further evidence of the relationship between legal and public opinion on the law of homicide' [2000] *Criminal Law Review* 814.

Mitchell, B., Mackay, R. and Brookbanks, W. (2008) 'Pleading for provoked killers: in defence of Morgan Smith' [2008] *Law Quarterly Review* 675.

Norrie, A. (2001) 'The structure of provocation' [2001] *Current Legal Problems* 307.

Power, H. (2006) 'Provocation and culture' [2006] *Criminal Law Review* 871.

Reading on the internet

The Law Commission Report, *Partial Defences to Murder* (2004, Law Com No. 290) is available on the Law Commission's website at:

   http://www.lawcom.gov.uk/docs/lc290(2).pdf

The House of Lords' judgment **R** *v* **Smith (Morgan)** (2001) on provocation is available on parliament's website at:

   http://www.publications.parliament.uk/pa/ld200102/ldjudgmt/jd011213/smith-1.htm

The Privy Council's judgment **Attorney-General for Jersey** *v* **Holley** (2005) is available on the Privy Council's website at:

   http://www.privy-council.org.uk/files/other/holley.rtf

Visit **www.mylawchamber.co.uk/elliottquinn** to access the property law glossary, weblinks and live updates, to test yourself on this chapter.

Use **Case Navigator** to read in full some of the key cases referenced in this chapter:

- AG for Jersey *v* Holley [2005] 2 A.C. 580

5 Involuntary manslaughter

This chapter explains that:

- involuntary manslaughter occurs where the defendant has committed the *actus reus* of murder but does not have the *mens rea* of murder;

- there are two forms of involuntary manslaughter: unlawful and dangerous act manslaughter and gross negligence manslaughter;

- Parliament has also created some road traffic homicide offences contained in the Road Traffic Act 1988; and

- the Domestic Violence, Crime and Victims Act 2004 establishes a new offence of causing or allowing the death of a child or vulnerable adult.

Introduction

Involuntary manslaughter is the name given to an unlawful homicide where the *actus* of murder has taken place, but without the *mens rea* for that offence. This area of the law has undergone significant case law development in recent years, leaving a considerable amount of uncertainty. It appears that now there are two kinds of involuntary manslaughter under common law: manslaughter by an unlawful and dangerous act (sometimes known as constructive manslaughter), and gross negligence manslaughter.

Manslaughter by an unlawful and dangerous act

Unlawful and dangerous act manslaughter arises where a criminal has set out to commit a less serious offence but has, in the process, killed a person. A classic example would be where the planned offence was a bank robbery, but a bank employee was killed. For public policy reasons, the law imposes liability for manslaughter on such criminals, even where they had no specific *mens rea* for the killing, only *mens rea* as to the lesser offence (in our example, robbery).

Actus reus

Common elements
The prosecution must prove that the common elements of a homicide offence exist, discussed at p. 51.

An unlawful act
Unlike other unlawful homicides death must be caused by an act; an omission is not sufficient. In **R v Lowe** (1973), the accused committed the offence of neglecting his child so as to cause unnecessary suffering or injury to health (under s. 1(1) of the Children and Young Persons Act 1933). This neglect caused the child's death. The Court of Appeal held that, for the purposes of constructive manslaughter, there should be a difference between omission and commission, and that neglecting to do something should not be grounds for constructive manslaughter, even if the omission is deliberate.

The act which causes the death must be a criminal offence; unlawfulness in the sense of a tort or a breach of contract (both civil wrongs) would not be sufficient. At one time it was thought that an act could be considered unlawful for this purpose if it was a tort, but the case of **Franklin** (1883) established that this was incorrect. The defendant was on the West Pier at Brighton. He picked up a large box from a refreshment stall and threw it into the sea. The box hit someone who was swimming underneath and caused their death. The prosecution argued that throwing the box into the sea comprised the tort of trespass to the stallkeeper's property and so therefore an unlawful act, making the defendant liable for manslaughter. However, the trial judge concluded that a mere tort was not sufficient to give rise to liability for constructive manslaughter; the unlawful act had to be a crime. The accused was in fact convicted of gross negligence manslaughter.

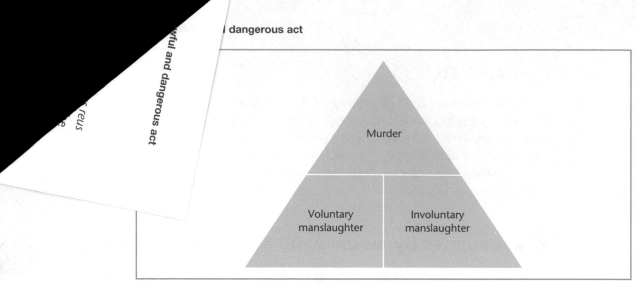

Figure 5.1 The homicide offences

In **R** *v* **D** (2006) the Crown Prosecution Service brought a test prosecution for manslaughter following the suicide of a woman after a lengthy period of domestic abuse. Mrs D committed suicide by hanging herself. There was clear evidence that, over a number of years, she had been the victim of serious domestic abuse at the hands of her husband. On the evening of the suicide, he had struck her on the forehead, causing a cut from the bracelet which he was wearing. He was subsequently prosecuted for constructive manslaughter with the unlawful act identified by the prosecution being grievous bodily harm, in breach of s. 20 of the Offences Against the Person Act 1861. The Court of Appeal rejected an appeal to proceed with the trial as it considered that there was insufficient evidence to support the existence of a s. 20 offence that had caused the death of the victim.

A dangerous act
The defendant must have been behaving dangerously.

KEY CASE

In **R** *v* **Church** (1966) the Court of Appeal held that an act could be considered dangerous if there was an objective risk of some harm resulting from it. The accused and a woman went to his van to have sexual intercourse, but he was unable to satisfy her and she became angry and slapped his

> An act is dangerous if a reasonable person would realise it creates a risk of some harm.

face. During the ensuing fight, the woman was knocked unconscious. Thinking she was dead, the accused panicked, dragged her out of the van and dumped her in a nearby river. In fact she was alive at the time, but then drowned in the river.

The Court of Appeal said that an act was dangerous if it was such as: 'all sober and reasonable people would inevitably recognise must subject the other person to, at least, the risk of some harm resulting therefrom, albeit not serious harm'. As this is a purely objective test, it did not matter that the accused himself had not realised that there was a risk of harm from throwing the woman in the river (because he thought she was already dead), as sober and reasonable people would have realised there was such a risk. Though there had been a misdirection on unlawful and dangerous act manslaughter by the court of first instance, the conviction for gross negligence manslaughter was upheld.

In **R** *v* **Dawson** (1985) the judge stated that when applying the objective test laid down in **Church**, 'sober and reasonable people' could be assumed to have the same knowledge as the actual defendant and no more. The defendants had attempted to rob a garage, wearing masks and carrying an imitation firearm and a pickaxe handle. Their plan went wrong when the 60-year-old garage attendant pressed an alarm button, and the robbers fled. Unfortunately the attendant had a severe heart condition and, shortly after the police arrived, he died of a heart attack. The robbers were found and charged with his manslaughter, but the conviction was quashed on the grounds that they did not know about their victim's weak heart, and therefore their unlawful act was not dangerous within the meaning of **Church**.

Dawson was distinguished in **R** *v* **Watson** (1989), where the accused burgled the house of a frail 87-year-old man, who died of a heart attack as a result. The courts held that the accused's unlawful act became a dangerous one for the purposes of the **Church** test as soon as the old man's frailty and old age would have been obvious to a reasonable observer; at that point the unlawful act was one which a reasonable person would recognise as likely to carry some risk of harm. The result of **Watson** is that where there are peculiarities of the victim which make an act dangerous when it might otherwise not be (such as the old man's frailty), they will only be treated as dangerous for the purpose of the *actus reus* of constructive manslaughter if they would have been apparent to a reasonable observer. In the event Watson's conviction was quashed because it was not proved that the shock of the burglary caused the heart attack and the old man's death.

In order to be considered 'dangerous' in this context, the unlawful act must be sufficient to cause actual physical injury. Emotional or mental shock are not enough on their own, though they will be relevant if they cause physical injury – by bringing on a heart attack, for example.

In **R** *v* **Ball** (1989), it was confirmed that whether an act was dangerous or not should be decided on a reasonable person's assessment of the facts, and not on what the defendant knew. Therefore a defendant who makes an unreasonable mistake is not entitled to be judged on the facts as he or she believes them to be. Ball had argued with some neighbours, who then came over to his house. Ball owned a gun, and frequently kept live and blank cartridges together in a pocket of his overall. He testified that he had been frightened by the arrival of the neighbours, and, intending to scare them, had grabbed a handful of cartridges from his pocket, and, thinking one was a blank cartridge, loaded it into the gun. In fact the cartridge was a live one, and just as one of the neighbours was climbing over a wall, he shot and killed her. He was acquitted of murder but convicted of manslaughter by an unlawful and dangerous act.

In **R** *v* **Carey** (2006) the defendants were charged with manslaughter. The victim and her friends had come across the defendants, and the defendants had started to make fun of them. The victim's group tried to get away, but the defendants followed them. The first defendant hit one of the victim's group and the second defendant stood on another's shoe. The second defendant attacked the victim by pulling her head back and punching her in the face, causing her to cower on the ground. The attack on the group lasted about one minute, until some boys came over and told them to stop. The victim ran 109 metres to get away. She collapsed and died later that evening. The immediate cause of her death was a ventricular fibrillation. She might not have died if she had not run so far and the most likely precipitating factor leading to her death was the running. She had not been aware of her physical vulnerability. The physical injuries she suffered during the attack itself were relatively slight. The defendants were convicted of constructive manslaughter and appealed. Their appeal was allowed.

The only dangerous act committed by the second defendant on the victim was the punch, but this had not caused her death. The defendants' other acts were not dangerous in the relevant sense to the victim. If the attack had not taken place, the victim would not have died, but that was not sufficient to make the defendants liable for manslaughter because the unlawful act was not dangerous in the sense that it was recognised by sober and reasonable persons as subjecting the victim to the risk of some physical harm, albeit not serious harm, which in turn caused death. The reasonable person is deemed to possess that 'knowledge gained by the sober and reasonable person as though he were present at the scene of and watched the unlawful act being performed' (**R v Dawson** (1985)). This includes any knowledge of the circumstances and of the victim's vulnerabilities gained during the commission of the crime (**R v Watson** (1989)). The only act committed against the victim which was dangerous in that sense was the second defendant's punch, but this had not caused her death. On the facts of the case, the Court of Appeal concluded that there was no real likelihood that a reasonable bystander would appreciate any risk of physical harm to an apparently healthy 15-year-old, which went on to cause her death.

Causation

The unlawful and dangerous act must cause the death – as **Watson** shows, the fact that the accused has done an unlawful and dangerous act and someone concerned in the events has died is not enough; there needs to be a proven causal link. This issue arose in **R v Johnstone** (2007) where the victim had been playing cricket with his son at a leisure centre. He was approached by a group of about 20 youths who started shouting abuse and spitting at him, and then throwing stones and pieces of wood at him, with at least one stone hitting him on the head. The spitting and shouting were not dangerous, but the throwing of wood and stones was dangerous. Shortly afterwards the victim walked away, collapsed and died of a heart attack. The medical evidence was that 'death resulted from the development of an abnormal rhythm in a diseased heart precipitated by being suddenly or unexpectedly attacked', in other words the attack caused an adrenaline rush which caused an irregular heart beat triggering the heart attack in a vulnerable heart. The youths had clearly caused the heart attack and therefore the death, but it was not clear whether the irregular heart beat which had been caused by the stress of the incident had been triggered purely by the spitting and shouting which were not dangerous acts, or whether it was triggered by the later dangerous acts of throwing wood and stones. On the evidence a jury could not, therefore, decide beyond reasonable doubt that an act which was both unlawful and dangerous had caused the death and the conviction was quashed by the Court of Appeal: insults and spitting cannot constitute an unlawful and dangerous act. This is rather an unsatisfactory judgment in practice because many deaths will result from a sequence of events which may start with some insults and progress into dangerous conduct, but it can be unrealistic to expect the medical experts to be able to separate these events and say which caused the death. The medical expert in the case commented:

> We are presented with what we are presented, and that is a sequence of events culminating in this man's collapse and death. I think it is academic to try and separate them out, and I do not think one can realistically.

This issue has been particularly important and problematic in a series of tragic cases involving the death of a drug user. How far can the drug dealer or friend who supplied the drug be liable for the death? Initially the courts took a harsh stance, imposing liability for manslaughter on such individuals. But in order to impose such liability the courts took a lax approach to finding an unlawful act that caused the death of the victim. The most authoritative case on the point is now **R v Kennedy (No. 2)** (2007).

KEY CASE

In **R v Kennedy (No. 2)** (2007) the House of Lords held that a drug dealer is never responsible for a drug user's death when the drug user is a fully informed and responsible adult who voluntarily chooses to self-administer the drug. If the defendant actually injected the victim who subsequently died then he can be liable for manslaughter: **R v Cato** (1976). The facts of **R v Kennedy (No. 2)** were that the victim had asked the defendant for something to make him sleep. The defendant had prepared a syringe filled with heroin and passed it to the victim. The victim had paid the defendant, injected himself and left immediately. He was dead within an hour. The defendant was convicted of manslaughter and appealed. He argued that he had not committed an unlawful act that caused the death of the victim. In the defendant's first appeal to the Court of Appeal, the Court dismissed the appeal, holding that as the defendant prepared the syringe, and handed it over for immediate use by the deceased, he had committed the unlawful act of assisting or encouraging the deceased to inject himself. In other words, it considered that the self-injection by the deceased was unlawful and the defendant was an accomplice to that offence. There was a fundamental problem with this judgment, as no offence is actually committed when a person injects him- or herself with a drug. Under the law of accomplices, an offence by the main offender is required before an accomplice can be liable (liability of accomplices is discussed in Chapter 11). There is an offence of possession, but the mere possession of the drug did not cause the death; the injection caused the death. The case could potentially have made many drug dealers liable for the death of the drug user that they supplied, provided an element of help or encouragement to use the drug could be found.

> Intervening, voluntary conduct of informed adult victims of sound mind breaks the chain of causation.

Following considerable academic and judicial criticism of the case, it was referred back to the Court of Appeal by the Criminal Cases Review Commission. This second appeal was again rejected, though the lax approach taken in the first appeal to the identification of an unlawful act that caused the death was held to be wrong. The prosecution had to identify the specific offence that had actually caused the death of the victim. On the facts of the case the victim had injected himself. In this second appeal, the Court of Appeal tried to interpret these facts to suggest that the defendant had been sufficiently involved with the injection process to be treated as having 'acted in concert' with the victim and therefore having jointly administered the drug.

In the final appeal to the House of Lords, Kennedy's appeal was at last successful. The House rejected the approaches taken by the Court of Appeal in the first and second appeals. The House took a very restrictive approach as to when a drug dealer could be liable for the death of a drug user. This would only be possible where the drug dealer had been genuinely involved in the administration of the drug. Where the victim was an informed adult who had voluntarily chosen to inject him- or herself then it would not be possible to impose liability on the drug dealer for the death. The Court of Appeal had asked the House of Lords:

> When is it appropriate to find someone guilty of manslaughter where that person has been involved in the supply of a class A controlled drug, which is then freely and voluntarily self-administered by the person to whom it was supplied, and the administration of the drug then causes his death?

The House of Lords answered this question in the following terms: 'In the case of a fully informed and responsible adult, never'. The judgment effectively reasserts the primacy in criminal law of free will, personal autonomy and informed voluntary choice. The House of Lords observes:

> The criminal law generally assumes the existence of free will. The law recognises certain exceptions, in the case of the young, those who for any reason are not fully responsible for their actions, and the vulnerable . . . But, generally speaking, informed adults of sound mind are treated as autonomous beings able to make their own decision how they will act . . .

There will therefore be a few limited circumstances where a drug dealer could be found liable for constructive manslaughter of a drug user who has self-administered a drug, in particular where the drug user was young or not fully informed about the nature of the drug (for example, they thought it was cocaine when it was actually heroin).

Following the case of **R** v **Evans** (2009), discussed on p. 14, liability might sometimes be imposed on a drug dealer for the death of a drug user on the basis of gross negligence manslaughter.

Mens rea

The *mens rea* of unlawful and dangerous act manslaughter is simply that of the crime constituting the unlawful act, which may be intention or recklessness, depending on the definition of the particular offence.

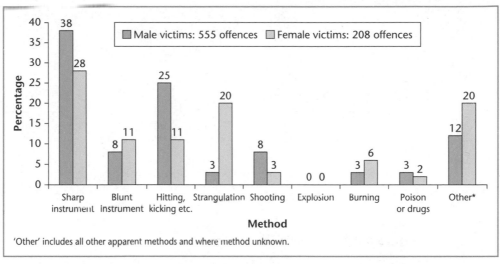

'Other' includes all other apparent methods and where method unknown.

Figure 5.2 Percentage of offences currently recorded as homicide, by apparent method of killing and sex of victim

Source: *Crime in England and Wales*, 2007/08 – Supplementary Volume 2: Homicide, Firearms Offences and Intimate Violence, p. 11.

KEY CASE

In **R** *v* **Lamb** (1967), the accused pointed a gun at his friend, as a joke and with no intention of harming him. As far as the accused knew, there were two bullets in the chambers of the gun, but neither was in the chamber opposite the barrel. He then pulled the trigger, which caused the barrel to rotate, putting a bullet opposite the firing pin. The gun went off and the friend was killed. The unlawful act in this case would have been assault and/or battery. The *mens rea* is intention or subjective recklessness in hitting the victim (battery) or in making the victim frightened that they were about to be hit (assault). As the accused viewed the whole incident as a joke, and did not know how a revolver worked, he neither intended nor saw the risk of hitting or frightening his victim. He therefore lacked the *mens rea* for either offence, and so did not have the *mens rea* of unlawful and dangerous act manslaughter either.

> The *mens rea* for constructive manslaughter is the *mens rea* of the unlawful act.

Rather surprisingly, in **R** *v* **Andrews** (2003) the Court of Appeal upheld a conviction for unlawful and dangerous act manslaughter, where the unlawful act was a strict liability offence. The prosecution were therefore not required to prove the existence of any *mens rea* in the case. This seems very unsatisfactory and runs counter to the view expressed in **R** *v* **Lamb** that *mens rea* is now 'an essential ingredient in manslaughter'.

Criticism

Causation

The courts have had considerable difficulties with the requirement of causation in the context of constructive manslaughter. The solution to the issue provided by the most

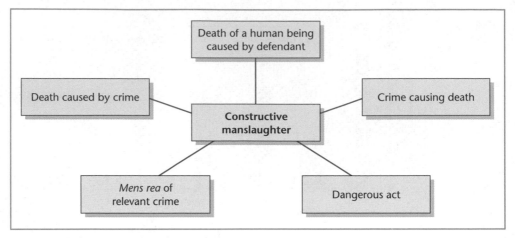

Figure 5.3 Constructive manslaughter

recent House of Lords judgment on the point, **R** v **Kennedy (No. 2)** (2007), is unsatis-factory because it absolves the drug dealer of all responsibility for the death of the drug user. It places a disproportionate emphasis on personal autonomy and informed volun-tary choice. A drug addict is assumed to be acting voluntarily when consuming drugs at a point when they are highly vulnerable and in need of the law's protection.

Prior to **Kennedy (No. 2)**, the Court of Appeal had been prepared to impose liability for the death of a drug user by extending the concept of causation. In **R** v **Finlay** (2003) the Court of Appeal had accepted that a person who simply handed the victim a drug caused their subsequent death. The Court of Appeal relied on the House of Lords judg-ment of **Environment Agency** v **Empress Car Company (Abertillery) Ltd** (1999) which took the view that the free, deliberate and informed act of another party can only break the chain of causation if it is something extraordinary as opposed to a matter of ordinary occurrence. The Court stated that the act of a victim choosing to consume the drug was not something which, as a matter of law, would normally be regarded as breaking the chain of causation. Where victims were habitual drug users it was foreseeable that they would consume the drug handed to them.

The **Finlay** decision was the subject of considerable criticism and the House of Lords in **Kennedy (No. 2)** held that **Finlay** was wrongly decided. The House stated that **Environment Agency** v **Empress Cars** should not be applied outside its statutory context, and that its application to constructive manslaughter was inappropriate. It is true that the imposition of liability in these circumstances runs counter to traditionally established legal principles based on the autonomy of the individual. Under this prin-ciple a person is presumed to have acted voluntarily rather than being caused to act by another and therefore each person should take responsibility for their own acts. In fact, the Court of Appeal's approach to the issue of causation in **Finlay** represents a common-sense approach and brushes aside any philosophical objections to such a finding. This approach represents more accurately the moral culpability of the defendant's acts. The defendant is culpable because he could foresee that his acts might lead to the death of the victim; there was nothing extraordinary in the victim subsequently consuming the drugs and dying as a result. Finding that the drug dealer did not cause the victim's death is artificial and ignores the factual reality.

Liability for omissions

The distinction between acts and omissions may be reasonable when applied to an omission which is simply negligent, but it is difficult to find grounds for excluding liability where an accused deliberately omits to do something and thereby causes death, and where that omission is clearly morally wrong.

Mens rea

The *mens rea* is very easy to satisfy, which can be seen as anomalous given the seriousness of the offence. The Law Commission (1996) has commented on unlawful and dangerous act manslaughter:

> [W]e consider that it is wrong in principle for the law to hold a person responsible for causing a result that he did not intend or foresee, and which would not even have been foreseeable by a reasonable person observing his conduct. Unlawful act manslaughter is therefore, we believe, unprincipled because it requires only that a foreseeable risk of causing some harm should have been inherent in the accused's conduct, whereas he is actually convicted of causing death, and also to some extent punished for doing so.

Gross negligence manslaughter

In civil law, an individual who fails to take the care a reasonable person would exercise in any given situation is described as negligent. Clearly there are degrees of negligence – if it is negligent for a nurse to leave a very sick patient alone for ten minutes, for example, it will be even more negligent to leave that patient alone for an hour. Where the death of a person is caused by another's negligence which is so severe as to deserve punishment under the criminal law, this is described as gross negligence and can give rise to liability for gross negligence manslaughter.

Until the summer of 1993 it was generally accepted that two forms of involuntary manslaughter existed: constructive manslaughter, described above, and **Caldwell** reckless manslaughter. However, that stance had to be reconsidered in the light of the House of Lords' decision in **R** v **Adomako** (1994), approving most of the Court of Appeal's judgment on the case in **R** v **Prentice** (1994).

KEY CASE

Lord Mackay LC gave the leading judgment in **R** v **Adomako** (1994), with which all the other Law Lords agreed. He stated that **Caldwell** reckless manslaughter does not exist but that instead there is gross negligence manslaughter.

> A person's conduct is grossly negligent if it falls below the standards of reasonable people to the extent that criminal liability should be imposed.

At the Court of Appeal level, several appeals had been heard together as they raised the same legal issues; one concerned Drs Prentice and Sulman, a second concerned Mr Adomako, and the third, Mr Holloway. Prentice and Sulman had injected a 16-year-old leukaemia patient in the base of her spine, unaware that the substance injected should have been administered intravenously, and that injecting it into the spine made it a virtual certainty that the patient would die. She did in fact die shortly afterwards. Adomako was an anaesthetist whose patient had died from lack of oxygen when the tube inserted into their mouth became detached from the ventilator; Adomako had not realised quickly enough why his patient was turning blue. Holloway was an electrician who had accidentally wired up a customer's mains supply to the kitchen sink, causing the death by electrocution of a man who touched the sink. All were convicted at first instance of manslaughter.

The appeals by Sulman, Prentice and Holloway were allowed by the Court of Appeal, but not that of Adomako. He, therefore, was the only one to appeal to the House of Lords, which is why the Court of Appeal judgment is known as **R** v **Prentice** and the House of Lords' judgment as **R** v **Adomako**. Adomako's appeal was dismissed and Lord Mackay gave the following analysis of the law:

> . . . in my opinion the ordinary principles of the law of negligence apply to ascertain whether or not the defendant has been in breach of a duty of care towards the victim who has died. If such breach of duty is established the next question is whether that breach of duty should be characterised as gross negligence and therefore as a crime. This will depend on the seriousness of the breach of duty committed by the defendant in all the circumstances in which the defendant was placed when it occurred. The jury will have to consider whether the extent to which the defendant's conduct departed from the proper standard of care incumbent upon him, involving as it must have done a risk of death to the patient, was such that it should be judged criminal.

The House of Lords stated that in order for liability for gross negligence manslaughter to arise there must be the common ingredients of all homicide offences, plus a risk of death, a duty of care, breach of that duty and gross negligence as regards that breach.

In **R** v **Watts** (1998), the appellant's daughter was born severely disabled. An operation was performed to assist the child with her breathing, and a tube was placed in her throat and held in place with tape. When the child was 14 months old she was admitted to hospital for a few days. Her mother spent the last night before the child was due to be discharged at the hospital. The following morning she took a suitcase to her car and was away from her child's bedside for three-and-a-half minutes. When the mother returned the breathing tube was out of her child's neck and she was still and grey. She shouted for help but very shortly thereafter the child died. The mother was charged with murder, with the prosecution alleging that she had removed the tube before she had gone to the car. She was convicted of manslaughter and appealed against her conviction on the grounds that the judge's direction on manslaughter was inadequate as it had indirectly referred to the possibility of a conviction for gross negligence manslaughter, but had failed to mention the ingredients of this offence.

The Court of Appeal allowed the appeal. It ruled that where gross negligence manslaughter might have been committed, the trial judge had to direct the jury in accordance with the passage from **Adomako** cited above. He had failed to do this, and therefore the conviction was quashed.

In **R** v **Willoughby** (2004) the Court of Appeal specified that the existence of a duty, breach and gross negligence was usually a matter to be decided by the jury. Once the

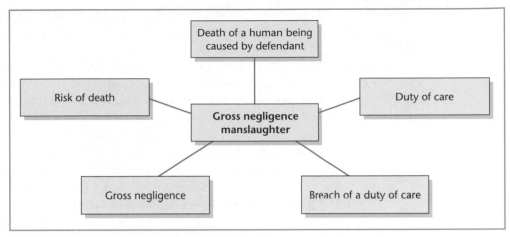

Figure 5.4 Gross negligence manslaughter

judge had accepted that some evidence existed to support their existence, the jury then had to decide whether they actually did exist. Each of these criteria will be considered in turn.

The common elements of homicide

The common elements of homicide offences need to be proved and are discussed at p. 51.

A duty of care

A duty of care in this context has exactly the same meaning as it has in the civil law of negligence. Lord Mackay stated in **Adomako**: '. . . in my opinion the ordinary principles of the law of negligence apply to ascertain whether or not the defendant has been in breach of a duty of care towards the victim who has died'. The classic statement of where a duty of care is owed in negligence is provided by Lord Atkin in **Donoghue** *v* **Stevenson** (1932), where he laid down what has been called the 'neighbour principle':

> You must take reasonable care to avoid acts or omissions which you can reasonably foresee would be likely to injure your neighbour. Who then, in law, is my neighbour? The answer seems to be – persons who are so closely and directly affected by my act that I ought reasonably to have them in contemplation as being so affected when I am directing my mind to the acts or omissions which are called in question.

This would suggest that, where a death occurs, the crucial test when deciding whether or not a duty is owed under the law of negligence – and also in relation to gross negligence manslaughter – is reasonable foresight that the claimant would be injured. In addition, following **Caparo Industries plc** *v* **Dickman** (1990), account will sometimes be taken of issues of public policy and whether the imposition of a duty would be just and reasonable. This was precisely the approach which was taken by the trial judge in **R** *v* **Singh** (1999), and the trial judge's approach was expressly approved by the Court of

Appeal. The issue as to whether there was a duty of care was treated as a question of law to be determined by the judge rather than the jury, which seems an appropriate approach as this is a technical area of civil law.

In **R v Wacker** (2003) the Court of Appeal accepted that the 'ordinary principles of the law of negligence apply' but excluded one specific aspect of these rules as being inappropriate in the criminal law context. The defendant was a lorry driver who had been involved in a criminal conspiracy to bring illegal immigrants into the United Kingdom. He was driving a lorry from Holland to the United Kingdom. The lorry was designed to carry refrigerated goods and was airtight, with a vent that could be opened to allow air to enter. Sixty Chinese citizens were hidden inside the lorry. The defendant shut the vent for over five hours to try and prevent detection during the Channel crossing. When the lorry was searched by Customs officials, 58 people were found to have died from suffocation. The defendant was convicted of manslaughter. At his appeal he argued that under one of the ordinary principles of negligence, a person did not owe a duty of care to another person when they were both carrying out a joint unlawful activity (known in Latin as the principle of *ex turpi causa*). In this case he and his victims were both carrying out the joint unlawful activity of smuggling illegal immigrants into the country. He argued that on the basis of the ordinary principles of negligence, and in particular the principle of *ex turpi causa*, he should not be criminally liable for the deaths of the illegal immigrants.

The Court of Appeal rejected this argument. While the ordinary principles of negligence applied, this did not extend to the principle of *ex turpi causa*. This was because the civil law and the criminal law had different roles and 'as a matter of public policy' it would not be appropriate to apply this principle to the criminal law. When Lord MacKay referred in **Adomako** to the 'ordinary principles of the law of negligence' he did not have in mind the principle of *ex turpi causa*, which was not relevant to the facts of the case before him. The duty of care for the people in the lorry arose the moment the vent was shut, and it was a continuing duty which continued until the vent was opened. The duty required the defendant to ensure that they had sufficient air to breathe. He had breached this duty and was liable for gross negligence manslaughter.

The approach taken in **Wacker** was approved and applied by the Court of Appeal in **R v Willoughby** (2004). In that case the defendant had recruited the victim to help him burn down a pub that he owned. He hoped to then claim the value of the pub from his insurers. They poured petrol over the building but this led to an explosion which both blew up the building and killed the victim. The defendant argued that he should not be liable because under the ordinary principles of negligence the defence of *ex turpi causa* would be available, but again this defence was rejected.

In **Willoughby** the Court of Appeal made it clear that the question of whether a duty of care was owed by the defendant to the victim was an issue that usually had to be decided by the jury. The judges accepted that there could not be a duty in law arising merely from the fact that the appellant was the owner of the premises. But the fact that the appellant was the owner, that his public house was to be destroyed for his financial benefit, he recruited the deceased to take part in this enterprise and that the deceased's role was to spread petrol inside were, together, factors which could in law give rise to a duty.

While the existence of a duty is usually a matter decided by the jury, the Court stated in **Willoughby** that there may be exceptional cases, for example where there is obviously a duty of care, when the judge can properly direct the jury that a duty exists. Such situations include the duty arising between doctor and patient and where Parliament has imposed a statutory duty.

In **R** v **Khan and Khan** (1998) the Court of Appeal appeared to take a different approach to the meaning a duty. It referred to cases where a duty will be imposed in the context of omissions (that were discussed at p. 12). However, the leading case of **Adomako** was itself a case involving an omission – the anaesthetist had failed to reconnect the patient's tube when it became disconnected – and the House of Lords made no reference to this line of cases in determining the issue of omission, nor have most subsequent cases done so. It is therefore unlikely that **Khan and Khan** will be followed on this point.

Breach of the duty of care

The defendant's conduct must have breached their duty of care to the victim.

Gross negligence

Traditionally, negligence lays down an objective test, in which a person is judged by the standards of reasonable and sober people. Lord Mackay in **Adomako** stated that he was not prepared to give a detailed definition of gross negligence and simply gave the key statement quoted at p. 112. He also quoted with approval a well-known statement on the issue made by Lord Hewart CJ in **R** v **Bateman** (1925):

> [I]n order to establish criminal liability the facts must be such that, in the opinion of the jury, the negligence of the accused went beyond a mere matter of compensation between subjects and showed such disregard for the life and safety of others as to amount to a crime against the State and conduct deserving punishment.

Lord Mackay did not provide a more detailed definition of gross negligence, as he was concerned that a jury would find such a definition incomprehensible. In **R** v **Misra and Srivastava** (2004) the defendant argued that the law on gross negligence manslaughter was, as a result, so uncertain that it breached Article 7 of the European Convention on Human Rights which requires the law to be certain, predictable and clear. The defence argued that the jury were being required to decide what the law was as well as what the facts were. The Court of Appeal rejected this argument, stating that the jury were not required to determine what would be sufficiently gross to amount to a crime (which would be a question of law), instead they were required to decide whether the conduct was grossly negligent (a question of fact). If it was, then an offence had been committed. In the words of the Court of Appeal:

> On proper analysis . . . the jury is not deciding whether the particular defendant ought to be convicted on some unprincipled basis. The question for the jury is not whether the defendant's negligence was gross, and whether, additionally, it was a crime, but whether his behaviour was grossly negligent and consequently criminal. This is not a question of law, but one of fact, for decision in the individual case.

In practice, without a definition that could limit the scope of gross negligence, the offence can potentially be given a very broad meaning by a jury, much broader than the previous test of **Caldwell** recklessness.

Following the judgment of the House of Lords in **Adomako**, the Court of Appeal has sought to clarify the legal implications of the case. In **R** v **Lidar** (1999) gross negligence was given a very broad meaning. A person would fall below the objective standard required, if they satisfied the old definition of **Caldwell** recklessness, but gross negligence was not limited to these states of mind. According to **Attorney-General's Reference (No. 2 of 1999)** a person can also be found to have been grossly negligent where a jury finds that their *conduct* has been sufficiently negligent – in this scenario there is no need for the jury to look at the defendant's state of mind at all; the focus is on the defendant's behaviour. Thus, where a company director has left railway tracks in a dangerous state of repair and allowed trains to run along them at full speed, this conduct could be found to be grossly negligent without looking at the director's state of mind.

The basic test for gross negligence is objective, asking whether a person's conduct has fallen below the standards of a reasonable person. In order to determine this question the courts are prepared to look at a range of factors:

- the defendant's thoughts
- a reasonable person's thoughts
- the defendant's acts or omissions.

Any of these three factors can be used to decide the basic question of whether the defendant's conduct has fallen below the standards of a reasonable person. Thus subjective criteria (the defendant's actual thoughts) as well as objective criteria (a reasonable person's thoughts and the defendant's conduct) can be used to determine whether the objective test has been satisfied. While for **Caldwell** recklessness the subjective limb amounted to a form of recklessness in itself, for gross negligence, such matters are merely evidence to decide whether the objective test has been satisfied.

In **Attorney-General's Reference (No. 2 of 1999)** the Court of Appeal stated that gross negligence was not a form of *mens rea* as it could be proved without the jury having to look at the state of mind of the defendant. This case arose from the unsuccessful prosecution of Great Western Trains following the Southall train crash in 1997. While the Court of Appeal accepted that gross negligence was not a form of *mens rea*, a person's state of mind could still be relevant to proving gross negligence. It could be relevant because **Adomako** requires the jury, when deciding whether gross negligence exists, to consider all the circumstances of the case. But the jury were not required always to look at the mental state of the defendant; they might find that their physical conduct alone fell so far below the standards of the reasonable person that it justified criminal liability.

In **R** v **Lidar** (1999) the trial judge gave a direction which looked very similar to **Caldwell** recklessness. The defendant appealed on the basis that this was a misdirection, and rather surprisingly the appeal was rejected. The Court of Appeal observed that the House of Lords in **Adomako** had held that juries might properly be directed in terms of recklessness although the House had stated that the precise definition laid down in **R** v **Seymour** (1983) (applying **Caldwell**) should no longer be used. Lord Mackay had observed in **Adomako**, 'I consider it perfectly appropriate that the word "reckless" be used in cases of involuntary manslaughter, but as Lord Atkin put it "in the ordinary connotation of the word".' From this dictum, the Court of Appeal concluded that 'Nothing here suggests that for the future "recklessness" could no longer be a basis of proving the offence of manslaughter: rather the opposite.'

This is a very unexpected judgment as the Court of Appeal appears to be reintroducing the old **Caldwell** test of recklessness for the purpose of involuntary manslaughter, but treating it as one aspect of the test for gross negligence, rather than the sole form of *mens rea* for the offence.

Risk of death

In **Adomako** Lord Mackay made a point of emphasising that there had to be a risk of death in order for a person to be liable for gross negligence manslaughter. He seemed to feel that this requirement imposed a significant restriction on liability. Yet logically, if a person has died then there clearly was a risk of death so this in itself would be very easy to prove. If he had required that there had been an 'obvious' or a 'foreseen' risk of death this requirement would have significantly narrowed the imposition of liability. The requirement of a risk of death was confirmed by the Court of Appeal in **R** *v* **Misra and Srivastava**. In that case the victim had undergone a routine operation to his knee. Two doctors responsible for his post-operative care had failed to diagnose a serious infection and as a result failed to prescribe the necessary antibiotics and the patient died a couple of days later. This failure to diagnose created a risk of death and the doctors were found to have been grossly negligent.

Application of constructive and gross negligence manslaughter

In **R** *v* **Willoughby** the Court of Appeal stated that the two forms of involuntary manslaughter – constructive manslaughter and gross negligence manslaughter – were not mutually exclusive. The same incident could potentially sometimes give rise to liability under both headings, and the prosecution could choose which offence to pursue. In **Willoughby** the prosecution had pursued the offence of gross negligence manslaughter and, while this was technically possible, the Court suggested that constructive manslaughter would have been easier to establish. This was because the jury had convicted the defendant of aggravated criminal damage and therefore to get a conviction for constructive manslaughter the prosecution would only have needed to prove that, in addition, the defendant had caused death.

⬤ Criticism

The rebirth of gross negligence manslaughter by the House of Lords was both unexpected and heavily criticised. By mixing concepts of civil law with the criminal law and potentially broadening liability, its reincarnation in its **Adomako** form has added to the confusion in this field of law.

The Court of Appeal in **R** *v* **Prentice** gave several reasons for preferring gross negligence manslaughter over **Caldwell** reckless manslaughter. They argued that the **Caldwell** reckless test was not satisfactory for situations in which a duty was owed. Their reasoning was that the 'obvious risk' of Lord Diplock's formulation in **Caldwell** meant

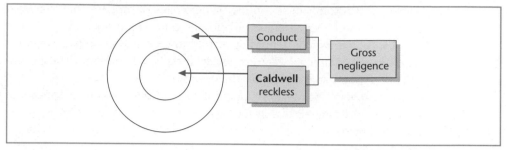

Figure 5.5 Gross negligence

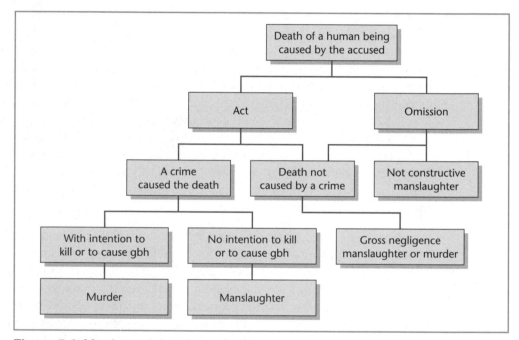

Figure 5.6 Murder and manslaughter

obvious to 'the ordinary prudent individual'. While most people know what can happen when you strike a match or drive the wrong way down a one-way street, an expert (such as an electrician or a doctor) who undertakes a task within their particular field would be expected to be aware of certain risks of which the 'ordinary prudent individual' might well know nothing.

The old **Caldwell** test for recklessness implied that the defendant actually created the risk, but in cases involving doctors, for example, the doctor might not have created the risk (for example, if a patient dies following a road accident), but might still reasonably be expected to be aware of it and deal with it competently.

The Court of Appeal was also concerned that **Caldwell** reckless manslaughter left a significant gap in the law because of the lacuna. However, this concern seemed to ignore the House of Lords' judgment in **R** v **Reid** (1990), where the scope of the lacuna was narrowed to where a person made an honest and reasonable mistake that there was no risk. Such a person would not be **Caldwell** reckless, but it is unlikely that he or she would be found grossly negligent either.

The main reason Lord Mackay in **Adomako** rejected the **Caldwell** model direction for involuntary manslaughter was because he was concerned that a jury would find such a definition incomprehensible. To achieve this goal of simplification for the jury, the House of Lords might have been wiser to follow their own advice in **R** v **Reid** that judges need not use the exact words of the Diplock direction, but could adapt them for the particular case.

The approach taken in **R** v **Bateman** (1925) can also be criticised. It is absurd simply to ask the jury to decide whether the negligence goes beyond a mere matter of compensation between parties. The negligence may go beyond that while still falling far short of what is required for manslaughter. The question should not be whether the negligence is bad enough to give rise to criminal liability, but whether it is bad enough to give rise to liability for the very serious offence of manslaughter.

The reintroduction of gross negligence has brought with it the concept of 'duty' to the law of involuntary manslaughter, which is regrettable. In the first place, no purpose is served by unnecessarily complicating this area of law by reference to civil law concepts. This occurs in other areas of criminal law, in particular in relation to issues of ownership in property offences, where it has caused considerable problems. It may nevertheless be necessary in that area of the law, due to the nature of the offences, but there is no such need for importing civil law concepts into the law of manslaughter. The complications that can result from incorporating civil law concepts into the criminal law are illustrated by the case of **R** v **Wacker**, concerning the deaths of 58 illegal immigrants, discussed at p. 114.

Secondly, in many factual situations, the concept of a duty merely duplicates issues concerning foresight of risk, which would often be considered anyway when deciding whether or not there was gross negligence. This overlap merely serves to complicate the law.

Thirdly, if the defendant actually does foresee the risk of harm to the victim, it should not matter whether a reasonable person would have foreseen it. A duty of care in negligence law is defined in objective terms as a result of the objective principle which applies to many areas of civil law – that external appearances matter more than the particular defendant's state of mind. However, such a criterion is wholly inappropriate to a criminal law offence – particularly of the gravity of manslaughter – where the defendant's subjective state of mind should be a key issue for deciding culpability and degrees of culpability.

Subjective reckless manslaughter?

The rather unexpected judgment in **Adomako** has produced considerable uncertainty as to the current forms of involuntary manslaughter. Before **Adomako**, the cases of **R** v **Seymour** (1983) and **Kong Cheuk Kwan** (1985) suggested that there was an offence of **Caldwell** reckless manslaughter. In **Seymour** the accused had argued with his girlfriend, and afterwards ran into her car with his lorry. She got out of the car, and he drove at her, crushing her between the car and the lorry. She died of her injuries. Seymour maintained that he had not seen her, and was merely trying to free his lorry from her vehicle. He was convicted of manslaughter and on appeal Lord Roskill approved the application of **Caldwell** recklessness as the relevant form of *mens rea*.

The subsequent case of **Kong Cheuk Kwan** was an appeal from the Hong Kong Court of Appeal to the Privy Council. It concerned a collision at sea on a clear sunny day between two hydrofoils carrying passengers from Hong Kong to the island of Macau. Two passengers died in the collision. The appellant was at the helm, in command of one of the vessels, and was convicted of manslaughter. Lord Roskill quashed his conviction on the ground that the judge should have directed the jury on the basis of the **Caldwell/Lawrence** test for recklessness.

Because **Caldwell** recklessness was so broad and included objective criteria, it was thought that there was no longer any need to have gross negligence manslaughter because this would completely overlap with **Caldwell** reckless manslaughter. However, **R v Seymour** was overruled by **R v Adomako** and **Kong Cheuk Kwan** was criticised, so it appears that **Caldwell** reckless manslaughter does not now exist.

Professor J.C. Smith has suggested that, alongside gross negligence manslaughter, there should also be a subjective reckless manslaughter, because there would otherwise be a gap in the law. A person would avoid liability if they caused a death having seen a risk that their conduct would cause this, despite the fact that the risk was not serious and obvious (unless they fell within constructive manslaughter). This conclusion seems to have been reached on the basis that gross negligence was a purely objective *mens rea*, whereas the discussion above (at pp. 115–117) suggests that in fact gross negligence takes into account both objective and subjective concepts, so on this particular basis there is no need to have a further subjective reckless manslaughter. In **R v Lidar** the comments in Professor J.C. Smith's textbook (2005) in favour of the existence of a form of subjective reckless manslaughter were quoted with approval by the Court of Appeal. But in their judgment they do not treat subjective reckless manslaughter as a separate form of manslaughter; instead it is treated as one aspect of gross negligence manslaughter.

Lord Mackay in **Adomako** does not himself appear to consider that it would be desirable to have any further type of involuntary manslaughter in existence beyond constructive manslaughter and gross negligence manslaughter. He considers that any exceptions to the general test of gross negligence would give rise to 'unnecessary complexity'.

One of the first Court of Appeal judgments to consider involuntary manslaughter following the **Adomako** ruling does not support the idea of a separate offence of subjective reckless manslaughter. In **R v Khan and Khan** the victim was a 15-year-old prostitute. The two defendants had supplied her with heroin in a flat. She consumed the drug by snorting it through her nose and eating it. It was probably the first time she had taken the drug, but the quantity she consumed was twice the amount likely to be taken by an experienced drug user. She began to cough and splutter and then went into a coma. The defendants left and when they returned the following day they found her dead. If the girl had received medical attention at any stage before she died she would probably have survived. The trial judge left the case to the jury on the basis of 'manslaughter by omission'. The defendants were convicted of manslaughter and appealed. The Court of Appeal ruled that there was no separate offence of manslaughter by omission and stated

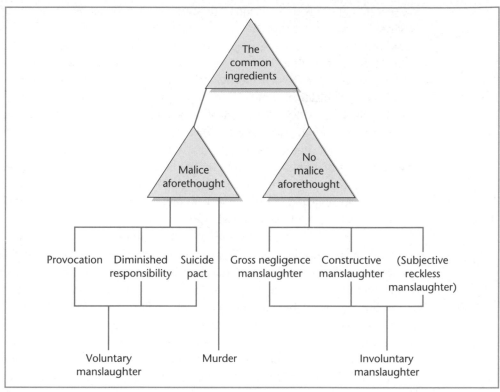

Figure 5.7 The structure of homicide offences

that there were only two forms of involuntary manslaughter: unlawful and dangerous act manslaughter; and gross negligence manslaughter. A retrial was ordered.

Causing death by dangerous driving

This offence is contained in s. 1 of the Road Traffic Act 1988, which provides: 'A person who causes the death of another person by driving a mechanically propelled vehicle dangerously on a road or other public place is guilty of an offence.'

No *mens rea* as regards the death needs to be proved for this offence. The prosecution merely have to prove that the defendant drove dangerously in a public place, and that this caused the death of the victim.

The primary issue will be whether the driving was dangerous. Section 2A(1) provides that a person was driving dangerously if:

(a) the way he drives falls far below what would be expected of a competent and careful driver, and

(b) it would be obvious to a competent and careful driver that driving in that way would be dangerous.

Subsection (2) states that '"dangerous" refers to danger either of injury to any person or of serious damage to property'.

In deciding whether the defendant's driving was dangerous, the courts will take account of the condition that the vehicle was in (including the way it was loaded) and any circumstances of which the defendant was aware. Apart from this final point, the issue is purely objective.

In **R** v **Skelton** (1995) the Court of Appeal upheld a conviction for causing death by dangerous driving. The appellant was a lorry driver who had taken his lorry on to a motorway despite being warned by another driver that his air pressure gauges were low. The effect of such a condition is for the handbrake system to be activated and expert evidence at his trial said that a competent driver would have been aware of this. When his handbrake activated, his lorry was left blocking the nearside lane and the victim drove his own lorry into the back of it and died.

The importance of the word 'obvious' in s. 2A(1)(b) was emphasised by the Court of Appeal in **R** v **Roberts and George** (1997). George had driven a truck owned and operated by his employer, Roberts. A rear wheel became detached from the truck and hit another vehicle, killing the driver. The prosecution case was that the truck was in a dangerous condition because of lack of proper maintenance which should have been obvious to both men. The defence case was that the design of the wheel was inherently dangerous and the wheel could come off without there being any indication that anything was wrong. In accordance with Roberts's instructions, George undertook a visual inspection of the wheels every day and physically checked the wheel nuts every week. They were both convicted but their appeals were allowed because the jury had been misdirected on the law. The Court of Appeal stated that, in determining liability for the offence, the jury had to decide whether the loose wheel bolt was obvious. Something was obvious to a driver if it could be 'seen or realised at first glance'. More might be expected of a professional driver than an ordinary motorist. Where a driver was an employee it would be important to consider the instructions given by the employer. Generally speaking it would be wrong to expect him to do more than he was instructed to do, provided that the instructions were apparently reasonable.

The focus was on the state of the driver rather than the state of the vehicle in **R** v **Marison** (1996). Marison was a diabetic who, while driving his car, veered on to the wrong side of the road and collided head-on with an oncoming vehicle, killing its driver. During the previous six months Marison had suffered several hypoglycaemic episodes (for an explanation of this term see p. 327), some of which involved losing consciousness without warning, and one of which had already led to a car accident. The trial judge ruled that the risk that he might have a hypoglycaemic attack while driving was obvious and fell within s. 2A. His conviction was upheld on appeal.

In **Milton** v **Crown Prosecution Service** (2007) a police officer had driven an unmarked police car at speeds of 148 m.p.h. on a motorway, 114 m.p.h. on a single carriageway, and 60 m.p.h. in a built-up area. He was charged with dangerous driving. The Administrative Court held that in determining whether he had driven dangerously a court should take into account the fact that he had specialist driving skills as a trained police driver who had completed the Grade 1 Advanced Police Driver's course. His case was referred back to a magistrates' court for a retrial.

In **Attorney-General's Reference (No. 4 of 2000)** the Court of Appeal held that a man could be liable for this offence if, due to a grossly negligent mistake, he put his foot on the accelerator instead of the brake. His mistake did not provide a defence.

A case that received a lot of media attention was **R** v **Hart** (2003). Hart had caused the Selby railway crash in 2001, in which ten people were killed. It seems that the night before he had been on the telephone to a woman he had met on the internet and had not slept at all. He had then been driving along a motorway early in the morning to go to work when (according to the prosecution case) he fell asleep at the wheel and went off the road and on to the railway track. A tragic rail accident resulted, and Hart was convicted of causing death by dangerous driving as it was dangerous to fall asleep at the wheel.

Sentence

The maximum sentence for this offence was increased from five years to 14 years partly due to public concern over deaths caused by joyriders. The Court of Appeal sentencing guidelines recommend that a person convicted of this offence should usually receive a prison sentence of at least 12 months. Aggravating features include speeding, racing, using a mobile phone or reading while driving.

Causing death by careless driving under the influence of drink or drugs

The Road Traffic Act 1988, s. 3A contains an offence of causing death by careless driving under the influence of drink or drugs. The section provides:

> (1) If a person causes the death of another person by driving a mechanically propelled vehicle on a road or other public place without due care and attention, or without reasonable consideration for other persons using the road or place, and –
> (a) he is, at the time when he is driving, unfit to drive through drink or drugs, or
> (b) he has consumed so much alcohol that the proportion of it in his breath, blood or urine at that time exceeds the prescribed limit, or
> (c) he is, within 18 hours after that time, required to provide a specimen in pursuance of section 7 of this Act, but without reasonable excuse fails to provide it,
> he is guilty of an offence.

Essentially the section is laying down an objective negligence test, which requires simply that the defendant's driving has fallen below the reasonable standard of care, and drink or drugs were involved. In **R** v **Millington** (1995) the defendant had killed a pedestrian while driving after drinking six vodkas and two pints of beer, taking the defendant to nearly twice the legal limit. In upholding his conviction, the Court of Appeal stated that the issue of drink was relevant to the question of whether he had been careless as well as to whether he was under the influence of drink.

Road Safety Act 2006

The Government set itself the target of reducing the number of fatal road traffic offences by 40 per cent before 2010. It issued a consultation paper entitled *Review of the Road*

Traffic Offences Involving Bad Driving (2005). Following this, the Road Safety Act 2006 has created two new driving offences. The first offence is causing death by careless, or inconsiderate, driving. This offence has been inserted into s. 2B of the Road Traffic Act 1988. It is defined in the following terms:

> A person who causes the death of another person by driving a mechanically propelled vehicle on a road or other public place without due care and attention, or without reasonable consideration for other persons using the road or place, is guilty of an offence.

Section 3Z of the Road Traffic Act 1988 states that:

> (2) A person is to be regarded as driving without due care and attention if (and only if) the way he drives falls below what would be expected of a competent and careful driver.
> (3) . . . in a particular case, regard shall be had not only to the circumstances of which he could be expected to be aware but also to any circumstances shown to have been within the knowledge of the accused.
> (4) A person is to be regarded as driving without reasonable consideration for other persons only if those persons are inconvenienced by his driving.

Thus an objective test will be imposed while taking account of the facts within the knowledge of the defendant. A person convicted of this offence can be subjected to a maximum of five years' imprisonment.

The second new offence created by the 2006 Act is committed where a person causes a death by driving and is, at the time of that act, driving either otherwise than in accordance with a licence or whilst disqualified or without insurance. This offence has been inserted into s. 3ZB of the Road Traffic Act 1988. A person convicted of this offence will be liable to a maximum of two years' imprisonment. The offence has been criticised for attaching liability to a person for a death, when the death does not occur as a result of the manner of driving. Professor Michael Hirst (2008) has commented:

> Lack of sympathy for disqualified or uninsured drivers should not however blind us to the fact that this new offence corrupts the usual principles governing causation. It appears that D may be convicted of 'causing' death without his actual driving being at fault.

 ## Criticism

TOPICAL ISSUE

Fatal road accidents

The Road Traffic Act 1991 amended the Road Traffic Act 1988 to replace the previous offence of causing death by reckless driving – with which such cases as **R v Reid** and **R v Lawrence** (1982) (discussed at p. 20) were concerned. The original statutory offence was created because juries were reluctant to convict a driver who caused death on a charge of manslaughter. Their attitude was often 'there but for the grace of God, go I'. However, evidence suggested that jurors continued to be reluctant to convict when the offence was defined as causing death by reckless driving. A joint report in 1988 for the Department of Transport and the Home Office concluded that part of the problem was that the test of recklessness still contained elements of subjectivity, and juries became reluctant to convict wherever they were asked to move on from the question of the standard of driving and consider the mental state of the defendant. The high rate of acquittals then led to reluctance to prosecute the offence at all, which meant that the law was simply not doing its job.

Even now that the law has been changed to focus on the standard of driving, there are over 3,000 deaths on the road each year, yet at most a few hundred prosecutions are brought under this section. The 1991 legislation has made it easier to prove a serious road traffic offence, but this has not been reflected in the conviction rates. Rather like accidents at work, accidents on the road seem to be seen as a risk we all have to take, even though a great many of them are not caused by chance or fate, but by human action or mechanical defect, and the risk is often one of serious injury or death. Perhaps if the Government, the police and the media made as much fuss about these as they do about the much less serious risk of street crime, the situation would change. The police are trying to alter the attitudes of the public to road deaths to reflect this. They are changing the terminology that is used in this area of law. Instead of the term 'accident', police documents frequently refer instead to a 'collision' or 'road death incident'. This is to reflect the fact that until the incident is investigated the cause of death cannot be assumed to be pure chance. It is hoped that the passing of the Road Safety Act 2006 will lead to more homicide convictions for road deaths, rather than the inadequate conviction for just careless driving.

While there has been a reluctance to prosecute individuals for these offences, research by Michael Hirst (2008) has found that if convicted the sentences imposed are quite heavy in practice. Motorists convicted of such offences are now punished more severely than most people convicted of manslaughter. He has also noted:

> By fixating on fatal offences, we have created a regime in which a motorist who makes one fatal error or misjudgement following a lifetime of exemplary driving can expect to be treated more severely (and in some cases many times more severely) than a serial traffic offender whose latest deliberate, prolonged and viciously irresponsible escapade miraculously leaves only damaged vehicles and traumatised road users in his wake. This makes no sense from a deterrence or road safety perspective. Human error cannot effectively be controlled or deterred by punishment.

What is dangerous?

Research has been carried out by the Transport Research Laboratory into the operation of the law on dangerous driving in practice (*Dangerous Driving and the Law* (2002)). This research has been analysed by an academic, Sally Cunningham, in an article published in the *Criminal Law Review* in 2002. The research identified problems in practice with the interpretation of the word 'dangerous'. The word 'dangerous' is not being interpreted by lawyers as purely objective. A range of people working within the criminal justice system were interviewed. They were asked whether the actions of driving through a red light and failing to observe a stop sign needed to be deliberate in order to prove dangerous driving. A quarter of those questioned thought deliberate actions were required, and some others thought it was 'sometimes' necessary. In fact, the legislation does not contain any such requirement. Whether or not the action was deliberate, it is prohibited because of the potential danger it creates.

In applying the current law, jurors will use their own driving as a yardstick against which to measure the actions of the defendant. The research report observed: 'The fact that "dangerous" is a word in common usage, which most adults feel they understand, may lead juries to apply their own, rather than a legal, interpretation of dangerous.' The standard of driving of the jurors will vary and therefore their approach to the word dangerous will also vary. Thus, the application of the offence would be improved if the public were educated to improve their own driving. One way the police are striving to achieve this is by sending offending motorists on driver improvement courses as an alternative to prosecution.

Causing or allowing the death of a child or vulnerable adult

Where non-accidental death or injury is caused by someone, but it is unclear which of two or more people actually caused the harm, and there is no evidence of secondary participation, then in the past nobody could be convicted (**Lane and Lane** (1986)). This had been a particular problem where children were injured or killed by a parent, but it was not clear which parent caused the death. When the child is very young they are particularly vulnerable because they are not able to speak and tell the authorities who caused them harm. The result appears to be that many non-fatal and fatal offences against children were going unpunished.

The NSPCC has found that every week three children under the age of 10 are killed or suffer serious injury (Plumstead (2002)). Children under the age of 3 are more at risk of being killed than any other age group in England and Wales (Home Office, 2006). Research carried out by Cardiff Family Studies Research Centre (Cathy Cobley and others (2003)) has found that the main suspects at the start of the police investigation are usually the natural parents of the child and occasionally other carers. In most cases it can be said with certainty that one of two identified people must have caused the serious injury, but it is often not possible to say which one. In this context, the rule in **Lane and Lane** applied, so that unless it could be proved that one carer failed to intervene to prevent the harm (and is thus liable as an accomplice, see p. 281), no conviction was possible. This difficulty in identifying which carer carried out the attack meant that only

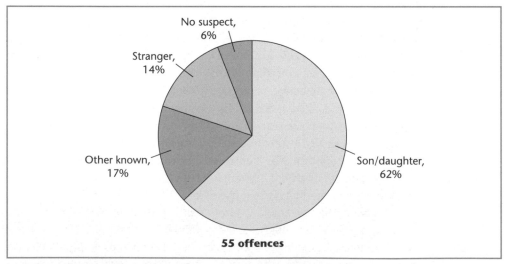

Figure 5.8 Victims under 16 years of age, by relationship of victim to suspect

Source: *Crime in England and Wales*, 2007/08 – Supplementary Volume 2: Homicide, Firearm Offences and Intimate Violence, p. 12.

a few cases of serious and fatal injury against children came to the criminal courts. As a result, sadly, a significant number of children were being killed or seriously injured each year, but only a relatively small number of those responsible were being convicted of any criminal offence. Where a conviction has been obtained, the charges and sentences did not reflect the gravity of the offence.

The Law Commission looked at the problem to see how the wrongdoers can be brought to justice. The Government has now passed a Domestic Violence, Crime and Victims Act 2004 which follows many of the Law Commission's proposals on the issue. Section 5 of the Act creates a new offence of causing or allowing the death of a child or vulnerable adult. The offence applies where a child or vulnerable person dies and:

- the death is the result of unlawful conduct;
- a member of the household with frequent contact with the victim caused the death;
- the death occurred in anticipated circumstances;
- the defendant was a member of the same household with frequent contact with the victim;
- the defendant either caused the death or was or should have been aware that the victim was at significant risk of serious, physical harm and failed to take reasonable steps to prevent the death.

People who do not live in the house can still be regarded as a member of the household, if they visit so often and for such periods of time that it is reasonable to regard them as a member of it. Only those who are 16 or over may be guilty of the offence, unless they are the mother or father of the victim. The existence of a risk to the victim is likely to be shown by a history of violence in the household. Thus, to impose liability, the prosecution will not have to show which member of the household actually caused the death and which failed to prevent the death. The fault element for this offence is only negligence and need not even be gross negligence. Defendants can be found negligent for failing to take steps to prevent a harm they should have foreseen. The offence puts legal responsibility on adult household members who have frequent contact with a child or vulnerable adult to take reasonable steps to protect that person if they knew or should have known they were at significant risk of serious physical harm. The offence carries a maximum sentence of 14 years. The Act also provides controversial procedural measures to help prosecutions for domestic homicides.

KEY CASE

The scope of the offence of allowing the death of a vulnerable adult was considered by the Court of Appeal in **R v Khan** (2009). The victim was a young woman from Pakistan who came to England to marry the defendant. She was subjected to domestic abuse and murdered by her husband.

The s. 5 offence is committed where the defendant ought to have foreseen the kind of acts that resulted in death.

Four adults who lived in the same household were convicted of committing the s. 5 offence of allowing the death of a vulnerable adult. The prosecution case was that the victim had been subjected to serious violence by her husband during the three weeks before her death and this must have been apparent to the other four adults in the household. The convictions were upheld by the Court of Appeal. The court emphasised that the definition of the offence included both where the defendant saw the risk of serious physical harm and foresaw the occurrence of the unlawful act which resulted in death, but also where the defendant was unaware of the risk but ought to have been aware of it. Thus it includes people who choose to close their eyes to a risk of which they ought to have been aware. The fatal attack occurred in the garage at night, when the appellants were asleep, and involved a degree of violence that was markedly more extreme than anything inflicted on the victim in the house itself during the previous three weeks. The appellants argued that the circumstances were utterly different and could not reasonably have been foreseen by them. The Court of Appeal rejected this argument:

> The act or conduct resulting in death must occur in circumstances of the kind which were foreseen or ought to have been foreseen by the defendants. They need not be identical. The violence to which [the victim] was subjected on the night she was killed was of the same kind but it was violence of an even more extreme degree than the violence to which her husband had subjected her on earlier occasions. The place where the fatal attack took place was irrelevant. Although ultimately a jury question, the circumstances would probably have been the same kind, if not identical, if the fatal attack had occurred while the couple were on holiday, away from their home.

The academic, Johnathan Herring (2007) has pointed out that often when there is child abuse there is also abuse against the mother. He has suggested that the s. 5 offence risks criminalising women who have been subjected to domestic abuse themselves and have made an effort to protect their children from abuse by, for example, trying to avoid leaving them on their own with their partner, but because of their experience as a victim they are not able to provide adequate protection for their child. He has argued persuasively that the offence is inappropriately judgemental of a woman's failure to prevent the killing of her child when she herself is also a victim of the killer. Because of the psychological damage caused to abused women they might fail to appreciate the extent of the risk to their child. Herring has commented:

> If the State is to impose obligations on victims of domestic violence to protect their children then the State needs to ensure that assistance is in place to enable them to do so. The provision of services for women seeking to escape violence is inadequate, especially given the vulnerable state they are in.

In **R** v **Khan** (2009) the Court of Appeal rejected these criticisms, pointing out that s. 5(1)(d)(ii) makes clear that the protective steps which could have been expected of the defendant depend on what could reasonably have been expected of him or her.

Reform of involuntary manslaughter

Home Office proposals

The Law Commission produced a report in 1996 called *Legislating the Criminal Code: Involuntary Manslaughter*. Initially the Government appeared to have accepted the Law Commission's main proposals. It produced a consultation document: *Reforming the Law of Involuntary Manslaughter: The Government's Proposals* (2000). The Government subsequently announced that it no longer intended to proceed with these reforms, but they are still of interest as they show how the law could potentially be improved. The suggestion was that the existing law on involuntary manslaughter would be replaced with five new homicide offences:

- reckless killing
- killing by gross carelessness
- killing with the intention to injure or being reckless as to whether injury was caused
- corporate killing
- substantially contributing to a corporate killing.

None of these offences would apply where there was a direct transmission of disease between one individual and another, unless a professional duty of care was owed. In other words, liability would not arise under these proposals where transmission occurs in the course of sexual activity, between mother and child during pregnancy, at birth or by breastfeeding. This exclusion of liability is justified in order to avoid deterring people from being tested, treated for or advised about the prevention of sexually transmitted diseases, such as AIDS. Also, the Government does not consider it appropriate for the criminal law to intervene in the private activities of individuals unless there is a deliberate intention to inflict bodily harm on another individual.

The first three proposed offences will be considered here and the latter two will be considered at p. 312 when looking at reform of the law on corporate liability.

Reckless killing
A person would commit the offence of reckless killing if:

- their conduct caused the death of another;
- they were aware of a risk that their conduct would cause death or serious injury; and
- it was unreasonable to take that risk having regard to the circumstances as they knew or believed them to be.

Here recklessness is given a purely subjective meaning. The Government accepted the Law Commission's recommendation that this offence should have a maximum sentence of life imprisonment.

Killing by gross carelessness
A person would commit the second offence of killing by gross carelessness if:

- their conduct caused the death of another;
- it would have been obvious to a reasonable person in their position that there was a risk that their conduct would cause death or serious injury;
- they were capable of appreciating that risk at the material time (but failed to do so);

and either:

- their conduct fell far below what could reasonably be expected in the circumstances; or
- they intended by their conduct to cause some injury, or were aware of, and unreasonably took the risk that it might do so, *and* the conduct causing (or intended to cause) the injury constituted an offence.

This offence would have a maximum sentence of ten years' imprisonment. It could apply where the defendant had not seen any risk of causing harm but 'their conduct fell far below what could reasonably be expected in the circumstances'. Under the current law on gross negligence manslaughter, the judgment of the **Attorney-General's Reference (No. 2 of 1999)**, which was concerned with the Southall rail crash, made it clear that the courts do not even have to look at the state of mind of the defendant to impose criminal liability. Under the proposed offence of killing by gross carelessness it would have to be shown that the defendant was capable of appreciating the risk of death or serious injury and had failed to do so. It was argued by the House of Lords in **R** v **Reid** that it was not appropriate to describe such inadvertent risk-taking as an objective test as the prosecution had to prove that the defendant gave no thought to the risk. While technically this may be true, the new offence still requires potentially a very low level of personal fault.

A marked improvement in the proposed offence is that there is no requirement to prove breach of a 'duty', as there has been much confusion under the common law as to the meaning of a duty in this context.

Killing with the intention to injure or being reckless as to whether injury was caused

At present a person who intends or is reckless as to causing a relatively minor offence can be liable for 'dangerous and unlawful act manslaughter' even though death was quite unforeseeable. If, for example, Ann entered into a fight with Ben causing him a small cut, not knowing that Ben suffered from haemophilia, then under the current law Ann would be liable for dangerous and unlawful act manslaughter. The Law Commission took the view that it was wrong in principle that a person should be convicted for causing death when the offender was only aware of a risk of some injury. Under the Law Commission's proposals, in the example above Ann would only be liable for a relatively minor non-fatal offence. The Government, however, was swayed by the argument that anyone who embarks on a course of illegal violence has to accept the consequences of their acts, even if the final consequences are unforeseeable. It therefore considered the possibility of a further homicide offence which would apply where:

- a person by their conduct caused the death of another;
- they intended or were reckless as to whether some injury was caused; and
- the conduct that caused the injury constituted an offence.

As for the offence of reckless killing, recklessness is given a subjective meaning. This offence would probably have a maximum sentence of seven years' imprisonment. This proposed maximum sentence looks uncomfortably low in a system which to date has allowed for a maximum of life.

Abolish gross negligence manslaughter

A leading criminal law academic, Glanville Williams (1983), has argued that neither negligence (even if gross) nor **Caldwell** recklessness is a sufficient base for a crime as serious as manslaughter. He feels that the *mens rea* for involuntary manslaughter should be intention to cause serious harm, or recklessness as to whether death or serious personal harm will be caused – recklessness being defined to mean subjective, **Cunningham** recklessness.

Williams argues that making subjective recklessness the minimum fault requirement would protect people from being charged with such a serious offence merely because their behaviour was inadequate. New, less serious offences could be created to deal with acts of gross but not deliberate negligence which caused death or injury and appeared to deserve punishment, though Williams believes that most such cases are already adequately covered by existing legislation, particularly the law on safety at work. In such circumstances, he suggests, vindictive punishment should be avoided.

However, these ideas can be criticised on the ground that abandoning gross negligence manslaughter in favour of what are really regulatory offences, usually punished only by fines, is an open invitation to companies to neglect safety standards, in an area where prosecution is already rare, and punishment, by the standards of large companies, very slight. While the kind of unthinking oversight that Williams is referring to might appear weak grounds for such a serious charge, gross negligence also covers states of mind that might be argued to be very much more blameworthy, yet still fall outside **Cunningham** recklessness.

In **R v G and another** (2003) the House of Lords suggested that all serious offences should require a subjective form of *mens rea*. It was subsequently argued before the Court of Appeal in **R v Misra and Srivastava** that subjective reckless manslaughter should replace gross negligence manslaughter. The Court of Appeal rejected this argument. An alternative solution might be to restrict the offence of gross negligence manslaughter to where the defendant had the capacity to foresee that they were subjecting the victim to a risk of death. Otherwise, there is a danger that people who lack the ability to realise that they are taking a risk due, for example, to their age and low intelligence could be treated too harshly by the criminal law.

Law Commission proposal

In its report *Murder, manslaughter and infanticide* (2006), the Law Commission suggests that gross negligence manslaughter should be retained but it should no longer include a requirement that the defendant owed a duty of care. Instead, the concept of a duty of care would be replaced by a requirement that 'it would have been obvious to a reasonable person in the defendant's shoes that the conduct involved a risk of death'. This would have the advantage of moving away from a tort test for the existence of a duty in the context of criminal law.

? Answering questions

When tackling a problem question concerned with homicide offences, a logical approach is to start by considering liability for murder. If the defendant has both the *actus reus* and *mens rea* of murder, then consider whether they have a complete defence or a partial defence. If they have the *actus reus* of murder but not the *mens rea*, then you can look at whether they could be liable for involuntary manslaughter. If they lack the *actus reus* of murder, then they can only be liable for a non-fatal offence.

1 'Negligence should never give rise to a criminal conviction.'

Discuss. *(London External LLB)*

The material you need to answer this question can be found in this chapter and in Chapter 1 where *mens rea* is discussed (pp. 25–26). Your answer might discuss four key issues:

● *mens rea* should be subjective;
● civil law concepts in criminal law;
● meaning of gross negligence;
● is negligence a form of *mens rea*?

You could use these four subjects as subheadings so that the reader can clearly see the structure of your essay.

Mens rea should be subjective
In the case of **R v G and another** (2003), the House of Lords stated that *mens rea* should require a subjective test to be satisfied. Negligence is currently only a minor form of *mens rea*, though gross negligence is the basis of liability for the important offence of manslaughter. Traditionally, the main forms of *mens rea* have been intention and recklessness. These are now both subjective forms of *mens rea*, since the abolition of **Caldwell** recklessness by **R v G and another**. Negligence has traditionally been an objective form of *mens rea*, where the emphasis has been on the defendant's conduct falling below the standard of a reasonable person. As an objective test, it is questionable whether negligence should give rise to criminal liability.

Civil law concepts in criminal law
In the context of gross negligence manslaughter the concept of negligence has introduced civil law issues. The difficulties with this can be seen in the case of **Wacker** (see pp. 114 and 119).

Meaning of gross negligence
You could discuss generally the problems the courts have had interpreting the meaning of 'gross negligence' (see pp. 115–117) and consider whether an alternative offence, of **Cunningham** reckless manslaughter, might be preferable.

Is negligence a form of *mens rea*?
There has also been some suggestion that negligence is not a form of *mens rea* at all (see p. 25), and again this raises questions as to whether it is a suitable basis for the imposition of criminal liability.

2 A, who is on bad terms with his neighbour B, hurls a petrol bomb through B's living-room window intending to destroy the house, but also being aware that the occupants of the house are highly likely to be severely injured. Mrs B and her baby are badly cut by flying glass but manage to escape from the ensuing fire. Both Mrs B and the baby are taken to hospital where doctors recommend blood transfusions. Mrs B refuses a transfusion because she is afraid of contracting the AIDS virus. She lapses into a coma and dies shortly afterwards. The baby is to receive a blood transfusion but C, a hospital technician, mistakenly identifies the baby's blood group. As a result, the baby receives incompatible blood and dies. Consider the liability of A for the deaths of Mrs B and the baby. *(OCR)*

As you are asked to consider the criminal liability of A for the deaths you should restrict yourself to looking at liability for homicide offences – a discussion of criminal damage, arson and non-fatal offences would be irrelevant because of this limitation. You should also not look at the liability of the hospital technician because you are asked only about the liability of A. You need to consider the death of each victim in turn as they raise slightly different factual issues.

On the issue of A's liability for a homicide offence, your starting point should again be murder. Causation needs to be looked at in depth with particular emphasis on the leading case of **Cheshire** and the blood transfusion case of **Blaue**.

As regards the *mens rea* of murder, A does not seem to have direct intention; the question will be whether he has indirect intention. We are told that he foresees severe injury as highly likely. You will have to consider whether this satisfies the **Nedrick/Woollin** criteria, and if it does this foresight will provide very strong evidence of intention, though it is not itself intention.

If A is found to have the *actus reus* and *mens rea* of murder you could consider quickly whether he might have a partial defence. On the facts we are given there is no basis for any such defence, though more facts might have revealed that he had been provoked by the neighbours or that he suffered diminished responsibility.

As we cannot say for certain that a jury would conclude that there was intention to cause grievous bodily harm you should consider in slightly less detail the issue of involuntary manslaughter. Unlawful and dangerous act manslaughter would be particularly relevant to these facts.

3 Whilst having a drink in a pub with his wife, Nina, Mark was subjected to a lot of rude comments from a very noisy and drunken group of women sitting nearby. Jane was particularly persistent in making sexual suggestions and, eventually, Nina went across to the group and threw a pint of beer over Jane. Mark and Nina then left.

Later that evening, Nina found herself in the toilets of a nightclub at the same time as Jane and called her a 'squint-eyed slut'. (Jane was, in fact, rather sensitive about the appearance of her eyes.) She immediately produced a small knife from her bag and stabbed Nina twice. One of the stab wounds pierced Nina's lung and she died a few days later.

Nina's death brought about a significant personality change in Mark. He found it difficult to concentrate, drank heavily and was treated for depression by his doctor. He worked in the service department of a garage and had been responsible for carrying out repairs on a car which had subsequently crashed into a bus shelter, resulting in injuries to a number of people in the queue and the death of a passer-by, Ian, from a heart attack. When examined, the car's steering was found to be seriously defective but, though the fault must have been present before the service, the service record made no mention of it.

When questioned, Mark was able only to say that he had felt 'very down' when he serviced the car, did not really know what he was doing at the time and had no recollection of it now.

(a) Discuss Jane's liability for the murder of Nina. *(15 marks)*

(b) Discuss Mark's liability for the manslaughter of Ian. *(15 marks)*

(c) Explain what assistance may be available to Jane and Mark to help them to pay for legal advice and representation. *(10 marks)*

(d) Discuss the aims pursued by the courts in the sentencing of offenders and indicate how they might be applied to Mark, were he to be convicted of manslaughter. *(10 marks) (Assessment and Qualifications Alliance)*

(a): this question raises no significant issues about the *actus reus* of murder and therefore this should be dealt with concisely. More time should be spent looking at whether Jane had the *mens rea* of murder. Having considered and applied cases such as **Moloney**, **Nedrick** and **Woollin** you should consider the defence of intoxication, which is discussed in Chapter 13. There is a possibility that a jury would find that the elements of murder existed. You could then consider whether Jane would have had any defence (other than intoxication) to murder. The defence to consider in the most detail is the partial defence of provocation. You need to consider the concept of cumulative provocation discussed in **R** *v* **Humphreys** and the attitude a court might take to alcohol consumption in the light of cases such as **R** *v* **Morhall** and the leading case of **Attorney-General for Jersey** *v* **Holley**.

(b): there was no evidence that Mark intended to cause death or serious injury to anyone. In answering this question you should therefore concentrate on involuntary manslaughter rather than voluntary manslaughter. Thus, despite the reference to depression, you cannot discuss diminished responsibility. Mark's conduct amounted to an omission and so there does not appear to be an unlawful act for the purposes of unlawful and dangerous act manslaughter. Having explained this, you need to concentrate on gross negligence manslaughter as defined by **Adomako**. Mark was clearly under a duty and his omission had created a risk of death. Ultimately it would be for the jury to decide whether Mark's conduct was sufficiently negligent to justify criminal liability. You also need to discuss the issue of causation, for while there was clearly factual causation there would only be legal causation if **Blaue** was strictly applied. The defences of insanity and, more briefly, non-insane automatism need to be looked at. These are discussed in Chapter 13.

For a discussion of the legal issues raised in parts (c) and (d), please see the authors' book, *English Legal System*.

4 Alice and Ben have been married for ten years, during five of which Ben has been addicted to heroin. In consequence, Alice has had to endure unpredictable behaviour from Ben, including verbal and physical abuse to herself and their children, unexplained absences, lack of money and loss of her possessions to Ben for the purchase of drugs. During the last two years, Alice has increasingly resorted to drink and her own behaviour has become unpredictable. In particular, she has become anxious, depressed and short-tempered, and has engaged in casual prostitution to supplement their income. In turn, this behaviour has led to further abuse from Ben and to two fights between them in which Alice suffered quite serious injuries.

Two days ago, Alice returned from seeing a 'client' and immediately drank half a bottle of whisky in front of Ben, whom she accused of being no use to her in any way at all. Ben punched her, called her a drunken whore and said that he would 'finish the job properly' after he had injected a dose of heroin. He then went off upstairs whilst Alice pushed the television set off its stand, broke a mirror and poured whisky over the furniture as well as drinking more of it. She then went into the kitchen and made and drank a cup of coffee.

About ten minutes after the incident with Ben, she armed herself with a knife and went upstairs. There, she found Ben unconscious and surmised that he had taken an excessively large or pure dose of heroin. She went back downstairs and paced around in an agitated manner, throwing pictures and other objects around the room from time to time until about an hour had gone by. She then telephoned for an ambulance. However, when the ambulance arrived, the medical emergency team failed to revive Ben and a doctor pronounced him dead.

(a) Explain the elements of the offence of murder and, ignoring Alice's anxiety and depression and Ben's behaviour towards her, apply them to determine whether Alice could be guilty of murdering Ben. *(10 marks)*

(b) Considering, especially, Alice's anxiety and depression and Ben's behaviour towards her, explain the elements of any defence(s) which Alice may raise to seek to reduce the crime to manslaughter and apply them to determine whether she would be successful in doing so. *(10 marks)*

(c) Explain the elements of unlawful act manslaughter and gross negligence manslaughter and consider whether, if a murder charge were to fail, Alice would be guilty of either. *(10 marks)*

(d) Alice might have difficulty in being able to pay for legal advice and representation. Explain what statutory provision is made to assist accused persons in her position. *(10 marks)*

(e) In answering parts (a)–(c) above, you have discussed rules of law concerning the offences of murder and manslaughter and related defences. Select either the offences or the defences and consider what criticisms may be made of the rules and what improvements might be suggested. *(10 marks) (Assessment and Qualifications Alliance)*

(a) You only needed to consider whether Alice satisfied all the elements of murder. Looking first at the *actus reus* of murder, on the facts we are concerned with an omission as Alice initially failed to call for medical assistance. While Alice did carry out various acts, such as going upstairs with a knife, it is only her initial failure to summon medical advice that could have caused the death. The law on omissions is discussed at p. 12. Murder is an offence that can potentially be committed by omission, and an example of this is **R v Gibbins and Proctor** (1918). She is likely to be found to have owed a duty to act as Ben was her husband and you would need to refer to cases concerning duties between close family members. The question of causation needs to be looked at in detail but, on the available facts, it is impossible to conclude definitely whether or not she would be found to have been the cause of Ben's death. It may be that he would have died even if the medical assistance had been summoned immediately and that medical workers would not have even been able to delay his death, in which case Alice would not be found to have been the cause of his death.

The *mens rea* of murder is malice aforethought, but it is not clear on the information given exactly what her state of mind was at the time. You would need to look at the line of authorities on the issue of intention and in particular **R v Woollin**. The issue of intoxication will be relevant here, which is discussed at p. 338.

(b) This question required a detailed discussion of both the partial defences of provocation and diminished responsibility. The defences of insanity and self-defence could not be considered on these facts because these are complete defences which would have given rise to an acquittal rather than a conviction for manslaughter. Looking first at provocation, you would need to give a systematic and detailed analysis of the law in this area. Particular consideration would need to be given to the issue of which characteristics of Alice could be taken into account for the objective test. The leading case on the subject is now **Attorney-General for Jersey v Holley**. On looking at the law on diminished responsibility the case of **R v Dietschmann** was particularly relevant.

(c) The offence of unlawful act manslaughter requires an act, and, therefore, while the question asks you to discuss this offence, you must conclude that Alice could not be liable under this heading. The most relevant offence to the facts was gross negligence manslaughter and the leading case of **Adomako** had to be discussed along with later Court of Appeal cases that have interpreted and applied this judgment, such as **Attorney-General's Reference (No. 2 of 1999)**. Ultimately, it would be for the jury to decide whether it felt that Alice's conduct constituted gross negligence. If a court found that she had not been the cause of death for the purposes of murder, then this finding would also prevent her being liable for gross negligence manslaughter.

(d) This question falls outside the scope of this book, but the relevant information can be found in the authors' book *English Legal System*.

(e) Criticisms of the law on murder can be found at p. 67, constructive manslaughter at p. 109 and gross negligence manslaughter at p. 117. In relation to the defences, you will find criticism of the law on provocation at p. 88, on diminished responsibility at p. 94, and on intoxication at p. 344. Make sure you follow the instructions of the examiner to discuss either the offences or the defences.

Summary

Involuntary manslaughter is the name given to an unlawful homicide where the *actus reus* of murder has taken place, but without the *mens rea* for that offence. There are two kinds of involuntary manslaughter under common law: manslaughter by an unlawful and dangerous act (sometimes known as constructive manslaughter), and gross negligence manslaughter.

Manslaughter by an unlawful and dangerous act
Unlawful and dangerous act manslaughter arises where a criminal has set out to commit a less serious offence but has, in the process, killed a person.

Actus reus
The prosecution must prove that the common elements of a homicide offence exist, but, unlike other unlawful homicides, death must be caused by an act; an omission is not sufficient.

An unlawful act
The act which causes the death must be a criminal offence; unlawfulness in the sense of a tort or a breach of contract (both civil wrongs) are not sufficient.

A dangerous act
The defendant must have been behaving dangerously.

Causation
The unlawful and dangerous act must cause the death. This has given rise to particular problems in determining whether a drug dealer can be liable for the subsequent death of a drug user. The leading case on the issue is now **R** *v* **Kennedy (No. 2)** (2007).

Mens rea
The *mens rea* of unlawful and dangerous act manslaughter is simply that of the crime constituting the unlawful act.

Gross negligence manslaughter
The leading case on this area of law is **Adomako**.

The common elements of homicide
The common elements of homicide offences need to be proved.

A duty of care
A duty of care in this context has the same meaning as it has in the civil law of negligence. Defendants owe a duty to anyone they could reasonably foresee would be affected by their conduct.

Breach of the duty of care
The defendant's conduct must have breached their duty of care to the victim.

Gross negligence
The basic test for gross negligence is objective, asking whether a person's conduct has fallen below the standards of a reasonable person.

Causing death by dangerous driving
This offence is contained in s. 1 of the Road Traffic Act 1988. The prosecution merely have to prove that the defendant drove dangerously in a public place, and that this caused the death of the victim.

Causing death by careless driving under the influence of drink or drugs
The Road Traffic Act 1988 s. 3A contains an offence of causing death by careless driving under the influence of drink or drugs. The section lays down an objective negligence test, which requires simply that the defendant's driving has fallen below the reasonable standard of care, and drink or drugs were involved.

Road Safety Act 2006
A number of additional road traffic offences for fatal accidents have been created by the 2006 Act.

Causing or allowing the death of a child or vulnerable adult
Section 5 of the Domestic Violence, Crime and Victims Act 2004 creates a new offence of causing or allowing the death of a child or vulnerable adult.

Home Office reform proposals

The Government had considered abolishing the existing law on involuntary manslaughter and replacing it with five new homicide offences:

- reckless killing
- killing by gross carelessness
- killing with the intention to injure or being reckless as to whether injury was caused
- corporate killing
- substantially contributing to a corporate killing.

The Government has subsequently decided not to change the law, apart from in relation to corporate manslaughter (see p. 312).

Reading list

Clarkson, C. and Cunningham, S. (2008) *Criminal Liability for Non-Aggressive Death, Aldershot:* Ashgate.

Cobley, C., Sanders, T. and Wheeler, P. (2003) 'Prosecuting cases of suspected "Shaken baby syndrome": A review of current issues' [2003] *Criminal Law Review* 93.

Cunningham, S. (2002) 'Dangerous driving a decade on' [2002] *Criminal Law Review* 945.

Elliott, C. and De Than, C. (2006) 'Prosecuting the drug dealer when a drug user dies: *R v Kennedy (No. 2)*', 69 *Modern Law Review* 986.

Herring, J. (2007) 'Familial Homicide, Failure to Protect and Domestic Violence: Who's the Victim' [2007] *Criminal Law Review* 923.

Herring, J. and Palser, E. (2007) 'The duty of care in gross negligence manslaughter' [2007] *Criminal Law Review* 24.

Hirst, M. (2008) 'Causing death by driving and other offences: a question of balance' [2008] *Criminal Law Review* 339.

Home Office (2000) *Reforming the Law of Involuntary Manslaughter: The Government's Proposals*, London: HMSO.

Horder, J. (ed.) (2007) *Homicide Law in Comparative Perspective,* Oxford: Hart Publishing.

Keating, H. (1996) 'The Law Commission Report on Involuntary Manslaughter (1) The restoration of a serious crime' [1996] *Criminal Law Review* 535.

Law Commission (1996) *Legislating the Criminal Code: Involuntary Manslaughter* (Law Com No. 237), London: HMSO.

Law Commission (2003) *Children: Their Non-accidental Death or Serious Injury (Criminal Trials)* (Law Com No. 279), London: HMSO.

Mitchell, B. (2009) 'More thoughts about unlawful and dangerous act manslaughter and the one-punch killer' [2009] Crim LR 502.

Rogers, J. (2006) 'The Law Commission's Proposed Restructuring of Homicide' [2006] *Journal of Criminal Law* 223.

Reading on the internet

The Home Office report, *Reforming the Law of Involuntary Manslaughter: The Government's Proposals* (2000) is available on the Home Office website at:

http://www.homeoffice.gov.uk/documents/cons-2005-corporate-manslaughter/
2000-cons-invol-manslaughter.pdf?view=Binary

The Domestic Violence, Crime and Victims Act 2004 is available on the website of the Office for Public Sector Information:

http://www.opsi.gov.uk/acts/acts2004/ukpga_20040028_en.pdf

The Law Commission report, *Children: Their non-accidental death or serious injury (criminal trials)* (2003, Law Com No. 282), which preceded the passing of the Domestic Violence, Crime and Victims Act 2004, is available on the Law Commission's website at:

http://www.lawcom.gov.uk/docs/lc282.pdf

Visit **www.mylawchamber.co.uk/elliottcriminal** to access multiple choice questions, flashcards and practice exam questions to test yourself on this chapter.

Use **Case Navigator** to read in full some of the key cases referenced in this chapter:

- R *v* Adomako [1995] AC 171
- AG for Jersey *v* Holley [2005] 2 A.C. 580
- R *v* Blaue – [1975] 3 All ER 446
- R *v* Cunningham [1957] 2 All ER 412
- R *v* G [2003] UKHL 50; [2004] 1 AC 1034
- Kennedy (No 2) [2005] EWCA Crim 685
- R *v* Woollin – [1998] 4 All ER 103

5

Involuntary manslaughter

6 Non-fatal offences against the person

This chapter explains that where a victim is hurt (physically or mentally) by the defendant a prosecution can be brought for a range of non-fatal offences depending on the gravity of the victim's injuries. The offences are:

- assault, where victims fear that they are about to be subjected to unlawful force;

- battery, where victims are subjected to unlawful force;

- assault occasioning actual bodily harm under s. 47 of the Offences Against the Person Act 1861;

- grievous bodily harm or wounding under s. 20 of the 1861 Act; and

- grievous bodily harm or wounding with intent under s. 18 of the 1861 Act.

Introduction

The previous chapters have studied offences against the person which result in death. This chapter considers, in order of seriousness, the remaining important offences against the person, where no death is caused.

Assault

The Criminal Justice Act 1988, s. 39 provides that assault is a summary offence with a maximum sentence on conviction of six months' imprisonment or a fine. It is a relatively common offence, with almost 12,000 adults convicted of this crime in 2003. The Act does not provide a definition of the offence; the relevant rules are found in the common law.

Actus reus

This consists of any act which makes the victim fear that unlawful force is about to be used against him or her. No force need actually be applied; creating the fear of it is sufficient, so assault can be committed by raising a fist at the victim, or pointing a gun. Nor does it matter that it may have been impossible for the defendant actually to inflict any force, for example if the gun was unloaded, so long as the victim is unaware of the impossibility of the threat being carried out.

Words alone can constitute an assault

Until the Court of Appeal decision in **R v Constanza** (1997) there was some uncertainty as to whether words alone could amount to an assault. **R v Constanza**, a case involving stalking, confirmed that they could. The House of Lords took this approach in **R v Ireland and Burstow** (1997) so that silent phone calls could amount to an assault. The offence would, for example, be committed if a man shouted to a stranger 'I'm going to kill you' – there is no need for an accompanying act, such as raising a fist or pointing a gun. The old case of **Meade and Belt** (1823) which had suggested the contrary, must now be viewed as bad law. Some people had gathered around another's house singing menacing songs with violent language and the judge had said 'no words or singing are equivalent to an assault'.

Words can also prevent a potential assault occurring – so, if a person shakes a fist at someone, but at the same time states that they will not harm that person, there will be no liability for this offence. This was the situation in **Tuberville v Savage** (1669). The defendant, annoyed by the comments someone had made to him, put his hand on his sword, which by itself could have been enough to constitute an assault, but also said, 'If it were not assize time I would not take such language', meaning that since judges were hearing criminal cases in the town at the time, he had no intention of using violence. His statement was held to negative the threat implied by putting his hand to his sword.

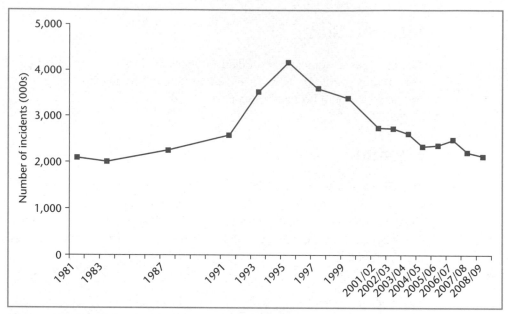

Figure 6.1 All violent crime, 1981 to 2008/09

Source: *Crime in England and Wales*, 2008/09, Home Office Statistical Bulletin, p. 45.

Fearing the immediate infliction of force

It has traditionally been said that the victim must fear the immediate infliction of force: fear that force might be applied at some time in the future would not be sufficient. The courts had often given a fairly generous interpretation of the concept of immediacy in this context. In **Smith *v* Chief Superintendent, Woking Police Station** (1983), the victim was at home in her ground-floor bedsit dressed only in her nightdress. She was terrified when she suddenly saw the defendant standing in her garden, staring at her through the window. He was found liable for assault, on the grounds that the victim feared the immediate infliction of force, even though she was safely locked inside. The Court of Appeal said:

> It was clearly a situation where the basis of the fear which was instilled in her was that she did not know what the defendant was going to do next, but that, whatever he might be going to do next, and sufficiently immediately for the purposes of the offence, was something of a violent nature. In effect, as it seems to me, it was wholly open to the justices to infer that her state of mind was not only that of terror, which they did find, but terror of some immediate violence.

However, the requirement that the victim must fear the immediate infliction of force was undermined by the House of Lords in **R *v* Ireland and Burstow** (1997).

KEY CASE

In **R *v* Ireland and Burstow** (1997) one of the defendants, Ireland, had made a large number of unwanted telephone calls to three different women, remaining silent when they answered the phone. All three victims suffered significant

For an assault the victim must be put in fear of immediate violence.

psychological symptoms such as palpitations, cold sweats, anxiety, inability to sleep, dizziness and stress as a result of the repeated calls. He was convicted under s. 47 of the Offences Against the Person Act 1861. This offence is discussed below, but what is important here is that for Ireland to have been liable there must have been an assault. Ireland appealed against his conviction on the basis that there was no assault since the requirement of immediacy had not been satisfied. His appeal was dismissed by the Court of Appeal. The court stated that the requirement of immediacy was in fact satisfied as, by using the telephone, the appellant had put himself in immediate contact with the victims, and when the victims lifted the telephone they were placed in immediate fear and suffered psychological damage. It was not necessary for there to be physical proximity between the defendant and the victim. A further appeal was taken to the House of Lords in 1997 and, while the initial conviction was upheld, the House of Lords refused to enter into a discussion of the requirement for immediacy. They said that this was not necessary on the facts of the case as the appellant had pleaded guilty and that, in any case, the existence of immediacy would depend upon the circumstances in each case. It is not sufficient that the victim is immediately put in fear, the fear must be of immediate violence.

In **R v Constanza**, another stalking case where the victim had been stalked over a prolonged period of time, the Court of Appeal stated that, in order to incur liability for assault, it is enough for the prosecution to prove a fear of violence at some time not excluding the immediate future. If the Court of Appeal in **Constanza** is followed, then there would be no need to fear the immediate infliction of force in the sense of a battery; the offence would include fearing some other type of injury, notably psychological damage. The concept of immediacy would also be considerably weakened.

Table 6.1 Location of violent incidents

Percentages									
		Violent offences				Violence typology			
	All violence[1]	Wounding	Assault with minor injury	Assault with no injury	Robbery	Domestic	Acquaintance	Stranger	Mugging
Around the home	25	35	30	19	17	82	22	5	14
Around work	7	3	8	10	1	0	13	5	1
Street	32	26	28	32	51	4	30	40	51
Pub or club	20	22	21	22	6	2	19	34	10
Transport	4	1	2	4	13	0	2	5	14
Other location	12	13	12	12	11	12	13	12	11

Source: Crime in England and Wales, 2007/08, Supplementary Tables 5.2.

Causation

Note that, as for all these offences against the person, the issue of causation may be relevant if there is any question that the defendant was not the cause of the relevant result – in the case of assault, if the victim was put in fear of immediate and unlawful force, but the defendant did not cause that fear. In such cases the discussion at p. 52 may be relevant.

● Mens rea

The *mens rea* of assault is either intention or subjective recklessness. The defendant must either have intended to cause the victim to fear the infliction of immediate and unlawful force, or have seen the risk that such fear would be created.

For all the non-fatal offences against the person discussed in this chapter where recklessness is relevant, it is subjective recklessness that is applied. This was confirmed in the case of **Savage and Parmenter** (1991) discussed below. As for the word 'intention', all the case law on oblique intention discussed in the context of murder is potentially relevant here.

Battery

By s. 39 of the Criminal Justice Act 1988, battery is a summary offence punishable with up to six months' imprisonment or a fine but, as with assault, it is left to the common law to define the offence.

● Actus reus

The *actus reus* of battery consists of the application of unlawful force on another. Any unlawful physical contact can amount to a battery; there is no need to prove harm or pain, and a mere touch can be sufficient. Often the force will be directly applied by one person to another, for example if one person slaps another across the face, but the force can also be applied indirectly. This was the case in **Fagan** *v* **Metropolitan Police Commissioner** (discussed at p. 12), where the force was applied by running over the police officer's foot in the car. A battery was also, therefore, committed in **Haystead** *v* **DPP** (2000). The defendant had punched a woman twice in the face while she was holding her three-month-old baby, causing her to drop her child. The baby hit his head on the floor. The defendant was convicted of the offence of battery against the child. He appealed the conviction, arguing that battery required a direct application of force, but this argument was rejected.

The force does not have to be applied to the victim's body; touching his or her clothes may be enough, even if the victim feels nothing at all as a result. In **Thomas** (1985), it was stated, *obiter*, that touching the bottom of a woman's skirt was equivalent to touching the woman herself.

Mens rea

Again either intention or recklessness is sufficient, but here it is intention or recklessness as to the application of unlawful force.

Offences Against the Person Act 1861, s. 47

According to s. 47:

> Whosoever shall be convicted upon an indictment of any assault occasioning actual bodily harm shall be liable . . . [to imprisonment for five years].

Section 47 of the Offences Against the Person Act 1861 provides that it is an offence to commit 'any assault occasioning actual bodily harm'. This offence is commonly known as ABH. The crime is triable either way and, if found guilty, the defendant is liable to a maximum sentence of five years' imprisonment.

Actus reus

Despite the fact that the Act uses the term 'assault' for this offence, s. 47 has been interpreted as being committed with either assault or battery. The first requirement is, therefore, to prove the *actus reus* of assault or battery, as defined above. In addition, the prosecution must show that the assault or battery caused ABH. Both **Ireland** and **Constanza**, discussed in the context of assault, were concerned with this offence as the issue of assault arose in the context of the *actus reus* of a s. 47 crime.

Actual bodily harm has been given a wide interpretation. In **Miller** (1954), the court stated: 'Actual bodily harm includes hurt or injury calculated to interfere with health or comfort.' Thus ABH can occur simply where discomfort to the person is caused. However, this was qualified slightly in **R v Chan-Fook** (1994), where Hobhouse LJ said in the Court of Appeal: 'The word "actual" indicates that the injury (although there is no need for it to be permanent) should not be so trivial as to be wholly insignificant.'

In **Donovan** (1934) the court stated that the injury had to be 'more than merely transient and trifling'. The defendant in **R v DPP** (2003) relied on this case to argue that he had not caused actual bodily harm because the victim had only momentarily lost consciousness following a kick to the head. He argued that this was only a transient harm and was not therefore sufficient. This argument was rejected by the court. **Donovan** merely required that the injury must not be both 'transient and trifling'; on these facts the injury was transient but it was not trifling.

In **DPP v Smith** (2006) the High Court held that cutting someone's hair can fall within the s. 47 offence. Mr Smith had cut off his ex-girlfriend's ponytail without her consent after she went into his bedroom and woke him up. He argued that he had not caused any actual bodily harm because hair could not be part of the body as it was dead tissue, he had not caused any bruising, bleeding or cutting of the skin and no expert evidence had been submitted regarding psychological harm. But the High Court rejected these arguments. It treated human hair as part of the body and it stated that the s. 47 offence was committed not just when there was injury, but also when there was harm or damage.

In **Miller**, it was also accepted that ABH included not just physical harm, but also psychological injury, such as shock. In later cases, the courts have made it clear that psychological injury will only count as ABH if it is a clinically recognisable condition.

KEY CASE

The defendant, in **R** v **Chan-Fook**, aggressively questioned a man he suspected of stealing his fiancée's jewellery. He then dragged him upstairs and locked him in a room. The victim, frightened of what the defendant would do on his return, tried to escape through the window, but injured himself when he fell to the ground. Charged with an offence under s. 47, the defendant denied striking the victim. The trial judge said, for liability to be incurred, it was sufficient if the victim suffered a hysterical or nervous condition at the time and the defendant was convicted at first instance. His appeal was allowed and Hobhouse LJ said: 'The phrase "actual bodily harm" is capable of including psychiatric injury. But it does not include mere emotions such as fear or distress or panic, nor does it include, as such, states of mind that are not themselves evidence of some identifiable clinical condition.'

> Actual bodily harm includes psychiatric injury which amounts to a medically recognised condition and not just mere emotions.

In **R** v **D** (2006) the victim had committed suicide following a long period of domestic abuse. On the evening of the suicide, her husband had struck her on the forehead, causing a cut from the bracelet which he was wearing. He was subsequently prosecuted for manslaughter and inflicting grievous bodily harm under s. 20 of the Offences Against the Person Act 1861. The defendant was not convicted. The Court of Appeal held that in order for there to be liability for a s. 20 offence the victim must have suffered bodily harm. This would include, following cases such as **Chan-Fook** (1994), medically recognisable psychiatric illnesses. From the evidence available to the court, while the victim had clearly suffered psychological harm, a jury could not be satisfied beyond reasonable doubt that she had suffered a clinically recognised psychiatric injury. Hobhouse LJ had stated in **Chan-Fook**:

> . . . the phrase 'actual bodily harm' is capable of including psychiatric injury, but it does not include mere emotions . . . nor does it include, as such, states of mind that are not themselves evidence of some identifiable clinical condition.

The Court of Appeal found that there was insufficient evidence of a clinically recognised psychiatric injury in the case. But in reaching this conclusion it took an extremely narrow interpretation of **Chan-Fook**. None of the experts was of the opinion that Mrs D was suffering from 'mere emotion'; each recorded some form of psychological condition. The court's conclusion on this issue amounted to an inappropriate belittling of the horrendous experience of domestic violence by refusing to acknowledge that its consequences amounted to bodily harm. It is regrettable that a court should be prepared to accept that cutting a person's hair (**DPP** v **Smith** (2006)) can constitute actual bodily harm, while years of cruel domestic abuse may not be deemed sufficient.

The offence of causing actual bodily harm has been applied in the context of stalking, but where the stalking consists of a course of conduct over a period of time it can be difficult to identify the actual assault that caused the actual bodily harm. In **R** v **Cox (Paul)** (1998) the Court of Appeal did not consider this problem insurmountable. The defendant's relationship with his girlfriend had ended. He started to make repeated telephone calls, some of which were silent, he prowled outside her flat, put through her letter-box a torn piece of a brochure showing details of a holiday she had booked, and, shortly before she was due to depart, he telephoned her to say that she was going to her death and he could smell burning. The complainant began to suffer from severe headaches and stress. The appellant was convicted of assault occasioning actual bodily harm and his conviction was upheld by the Court of Appeal even though it was difficult to identify an act that constituted the assault.

Mens rea

The *mens rea* of assault occasioning ABH is the same as for assault or battery. No additional *mens rea* is required in relation to the actual bodily harm, as the case of **R** v **Roberts** (1978) shows.

KEY CASE

The defendant in **R** v **Roberts** (1978) gave a lift in his car to a girl late at night. During the journey he made unwanted sexual advances, touching the girl's clothes. Frightened that he was going to rape her, she jumped out of the moving car, injuring herself. It was held that the defendant had committed the *actus reus* of a s. 47 offence by touching the girl's clothes – sufficient for the *actus reus* of battery – and this act had caused her to suffer actual bodily harm. The defendant argued that he lacked the *mens rea* of the offence, because he had neither intended to cause her actual bodily harm, nor seen any risk of her suffering actual bodily harm as a result of his advances. This argument was rejected: the court held that the *mens rea* for battery was sufficient in itself, and there was no need for any extra *mens rea* regarding the actual bodily harm.

> The *mens rea* for a s. 47 offence is the *mens rea* for assault or battery.

The point was confirmed in **Savage and Parmenter**. The defendant went into a local pub, where she spotted her husband's new girlfriend having a drink with some friends. She went up to the table where the group was sitting, intending to throw a pint of beer over the woman. On reaching the table, she said 'Nice to meet you darling' and threw the beer but, as she did so, she accidentally let go of the glass, which broke and cut the woman's wrist. The defendant argued that she lacked sufficient *mens rea* to be liable for a s. 47 offence, because her intention had only been to throw the beer, and she had not seen the risk that the glass might injure the girlfriend. This was rejected because she intended to apply unlawful force (the *mens rea* of battery) and there was no need to prove that she intended or was reckless as to causing actual bodily harm. The conflicting case of **Spratt** (1991) was overruled on this point.

Offences Against the Person Act 1861, s. 20

This section states:

> Whosoever shall unlawfully and maliciously wound or inflict any grievous bodily harm upon any other person either with or without any weapon or instrument shall be guilty of an offence triable either way, and being convicted thereof shall be liable to imprisonment for five years.

Actus reus

The prosecution has to prove that the defendant either inflicted grievous bodily harm or wounded the victim.

Inflicting grievous bodily harm

In **DPP** v **Smith** (1961) the House of Lords emphasised that grievous bodily harm (GBH) is a phrase that should be given its ordinary and natural meaning, which was simply 'really serious harm'. This was confirmed in **Saunders** (1985) where the Court of Appeal said that there was no real difference between the terms 'serious' and 'really serious'. The point was again made in **R** v **Brown and Stratton** (1998) where the Court of Appeal stated that trial judges should not attempt to give a definition of the concept to the jury. The victim was a transsexual who had undergone 'gender reassignment' treatment, and changed her name to Julie Ann. Stratton was the victim's son and he had felt humiliated when his father had come to the supermarket where he worked, dressed as a woman. With his cousin Stratton had gone round to Julie Ann's flat and attacked her with fists and part of a chair, resulting in a broken nose, three missing teeth, bruising, a laceration over one eye and concussion. These injuries were found by the Court of Appeal to amount to grievous bodily harm and the defendants were liable under s. 20. **R** v **Ireland and Burstow** recognises that a really serious psychiatric injury can amount to grievous bodily harm.

In determining whether grievous bodily harm has been inflicted, the courts can take into account the particular characteristics of the victim, such as their age and health. To gauge the severity of the injuries, an assessment had to be made of the effect of the harm on the particular victim. Thus, in **R** v **Bollom** (2003) the victim was a 17-month-old child who had bruises on her body. In determining whether these bruises amounted to grievous bodily harm the court could take into account the frailty of the child.

The difference between actual bodily harm under s. 47 and grievous bodily harm in this section is one of degree – grievous bodily harm is clearly the more serious injury.

The meaning of the word 'inflict' in this section has caused considerable difficulty. For many years it was held that 'inflict' implied the commission of an actual assault. Thus, in **Clarence** (1888), the Queen's Bench Division decided that a husband could not be said to have inflicted GBH on his wife by knowingly exposing her to the risk of contracting gonorrhoea through intercourse; the wife had not feared the infliction of lawful force at the time of the sexual intercourse. In **Wilson** (1984) the House of Lords stated that an assault is not necessary; the word 'inflict' simply required 'force being violently applied to the body of the victim, so that he suffers grievous bodily harm'. Thus it was thought that under s. 20 grievous bodily harm had to be caused by the direct application of force. This meant, for example, that it would cover hitting, kicking or stabbing a victim, but not digging a hole for them to fall into. In practice, the courts often gave a wide interpretation as to when force was direct. In **R** v **Martin** (1881), while a play was being performed at a theatre, the defendant placed an iron bar across the exit, turned off the staircase lights and shouted 'Fire! Fire!' The audience panicked and, in the rush to escape, people were seriously injured. The defendant was found liable under s. 20, even though strictly speaking it is difficult to view the application of force as truly direct on these facts.

A similarly wide interpretation was given in **Halliday** (1889). In that case, the defendant's behaviour frightened his wife so much that she jumped out of their bedroom window to get away from him. The injuries that she suffered as a result of the fall were found to have been directly applied, so that he could be liable under s. 20.

However, following the decisions in **R** v **Ireland and Burstow**, the word inflict no longer implies the direct application of force. Burstow had become obsessed with a female acquaintance. He started to stalk her, following her, damaging her car and breaking into her house. He was convicted for this conduct but after his release from prison he continued to stalk her, following her and subjecting her to further harassment, including silent telephone calls, sending hate mail, stealing clothes from her washing line and scattering condoms over her garden. His behaviour caused his victim to suffer severe depression, insomnia and panic attacks. For this subsequent behaviour he was charged with inflicting grievous bodily harm under s. 20 of the Offences Against the Person Act 1861. The trial court convicted, stating that there was no reason for 'inflict' to be given a restrictive meaning. On appeal against his conviction the appellant argued that the requirements of the term 'inflict' had not been satisfied. The appeal was dismissed by both the Court of Appeal and the House of Lords. The House stated that s. 20 could be committed where no physical force had been applied (directly or indirectly) on the body of the victim.

The offence can be committed when somebody infects another with HIV.

KEY CASE

A prosecution was brought under s. 20 in **R** v **Dica** (2004). The defendant knew that he was HIV positive and had unprotected sexual intercourse with two women (see p. 156). He was prosecuted under s. 20 of the Offences Against the Person Act 1861. His initial conviction was quashed on appeal and a retrial ordered because of a misdirection on the issue of consent, but the Court of Appeal accepted that a person could be liable under s. 20 for recklessly infecting another with HIV.

> A person can be liable under s. 20 for recklessly infecting another with HIV.

Wounding

Wounding requires a breaking of the skin, so there will normally be bleeding. This may seem odd given that for this serious offence the *actus reus* can be satisfied simply by pricking somebody's thumb with a pin.

KEY CASE

In **C (a minor)** v **Eisenhower** (1984), the defendant fired an air pistol, hitting the victim in the eye with a pellet. This ruptured a blood vessel in the eye, causing internal bleeding, but the injury was not sufficient to constitute a wounding, as the skin had not been broken.

Wounding requires breaking of the skin.

Mens rea

The *mens rea* for this offence is defined by the word 'maliciously'. In **R** v **Cunningham** it was stated that for the purpose of the 1861 Act maliciously meant 'intentionally or recklessly' and 'reckless' is used with a subjective meaning.

The case of **Mowatt** (1967) established that there is no need to intend or be reckless as to causing GBH or wounding. The defendant need only intend or be reckless that his or her acts could have caused some physical harm. As Lord Diplock said: 'It is quite unnecessary that the accused should have foreseen that his unlawful act might cause physical harm of the gravity described in the section, i.e. a wound or serious physical injury. It is enough that he should have foreseen that some physical harm to some person, albeit of a minor character, might result.' The leading case on the point is now the House of Lords judgment of **R** v **Savage; DPP** v **Parmenter** (1992).

In **R** v **Grimshaw** (1984), the defendant was in a pub when she heard someone insult her boyfriend. She pushed the glass he was holding into his face. She was found guilty of an offence under s. 20: she had inflicted grievous bodily harm and she had the *mens rea* because she had at least foreseen that he might suffer some harm.

The Divisional Court decision of **Director of Public Prosecutions** v **A** (2000) highlighted the fact that the defendant is only required to have foreseen that some harm *might* occur, not that it *would* occur. In that case the defendant was a 13-year-old boy who had been playing with two air pistols with his friend. He shot his friend in the eye, causing him to lose his sight in that eye. The defendant was charged with committing an offence under s. 20 of the Offences Against the Person Act 1861. He argued that he lacked the requisite *mens rea*. On the issue of *mens rea* the magistrates were referred by the court clerk to a passage in *Stone's Justices' Manual*, a book frequently used in the magistrates' courts. This passage stated: 'In order to establish an offence under s. 20 the prosecution must prove either that the defendant intended or that he foresaw that his act would cause some physical harm to some person, albeit of a minor nature.' The prosecution appealed against the defendant's acquittal and the appeal was allowed. The passage in *Stone's Justices' Manual* was wrong as it required too high a level of *mens rea*. It was only necessary for the prosecution to show that the defendant had foreseen that some harm *might* occur, not that it *would* have occurred. In fact, if the defendant had foreseen that the harm would have occurred the court could have found an intention to commit that harm under the **Nedrick** test for indirect intention, which exists where the harm is foreseen as a virtual certainty.

Where the offence is concerned with the infection of HIV, the defendant need not have known that he was actually infected, provided he was aware that there was a high risk that he was infected. In the Crown Court case of **R** v **Adaye** (2004), Mr Adaye had been informed by his wife that she was HIV positive. Shortly afterwards he started a new sexual relationship with another woman and failed to use condoms. His new partner contracted HIV and he was prosecuted for the s. 20 offence. Mr Adaye had not taken an HIV anti-body test and did not conclusively know of his HIV status at the time of transmission. However, the Crown Court held that knowledge of a higher level of risk of HIV infection was sufficient to hold that the defendant had acted recklessly.

Offences Against the Person Act 1861, s. 18

Section 18 provides:

> Whosoever shall unlawfully and maliciously by any means whatsoever wound or cause any griev-ous bodily harm to any person, with intent to do some grievous bodily harm to any person, or with intent to resist or prevent the lawful apprehension or detainer of any person, shall be guilty of an offence triable only on indictment, and being convicted thereof shall be liable to imprison-ment for life.

This is similar to the offence of s. 20, and, like that offence, requires proof of either griev-ous bodily harm or wounding. The crucial difference is in the *mens rea*: while recklessness can be sufficient for s. 20, intention is always required for s. 18. It is for this reason that s. 18 is punishable with a life sentence, while the maximum sentence for s. 20 is only five years' imprisonment – a person acting with intent is considered to have greater moral fault than a person merely acting recklessly.

Actus reus

Wounding and grievous bodily harm are given the same interpretation as for s. 20. In **R** v **Ireland and Burstow** Lord Steyn said that the word 'cause' in s. 18 and 'inflict' in s. 20 were not synonymous, but it is difficult to see how they differ in practice. Both refer to the need for causation.

Mens rea

As noted above, the prosecution must prove intention. The intent must be either to cause grievous bodily harm (by contrast with s. 20, where an intention to cause some harm is sufficient) or to avoid arrest.

In addition, the section states that the defendant must have acted 'maliciously'. This bears the same meaning as discussed for s. 20, so if the prosecution have already proved that the defendant intended to cause grievous bodily harm, 'maliciously' imposes no further requirement: a defendant who intends to cause grievous bodily harm obviously intends to cause some harm. If the prosecution have proved the other form of intent, the intent to avoid arrest, then the requirement that the defendant acts maliciously does

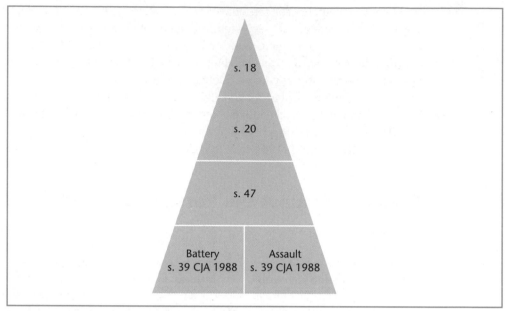

Figure 6.2 Non-fatal offences against the person

impose a further requirement: an intent to avoid arrest does not necessarily imply intention, or recklessness, as to whether you cause some harm. Therefore, where the prosecution prove intent to avoid arrest, they must also show that the defendant intended to cause some harm, or was reckless as to whether harm was caused.

Problems with offences against the person

Domestic violence

Domestic violence accounts for 16 per cent of all violent crime (*Crime in England and Wales 2003/04*, Home Office). This form of violence is defined by the Home Office as: 'Any violence between current and former partners in an intimate relationship, wherever and whenever the violence occurs. The violence may include physical, sexual, emotional and financial abuse.' One in four women and one in six men will be the victims of domestic violence at some point in their lives (Mirlees-Black (1999)). Every minute the police receive a 999 emergency telephone call reporting an incident of domestic violence (Stanko (2000)). Between one-quarter and one-third of victims of homicide are killed by a partner or former partner (Criminal Statistics (2000)). In 90 per cent of incidents where the couple have children, a child is present or in the next room. Domestic abuse occurs throughout the whole of our society, regardless of social class.

While the law itself does not distinguish between these victims and the person who gets attacked in the streets by a stranger, in practice the victims of domestic assaults rarely receive the law's protection. The first reason for this is simply that very few domestic assaults – research suggests around 2 per cent – are reported to the police. On average, a woman will be assaulted 35 times before she contacts the police (Yearnshire *et al.*

Table 6.2 Victim/offender relationship in violent incidents

Percentages									
	All violence	Wounding	Assault with minor injury	Assault with no injury	Robbery	Domestic	Acquaintance	Stranger	Mugging
Stranger	44	34	36	43	75	0	0	100	77
Known by sight or to speak to	26	22	27	29	21	1	62	0	19
Known well	30	45	37	28	5	99	38	0	4

Source: *Crime in England and Wales*, 2007/08, Supplementary Tables.

(1997)). If the offences are not reported, obviously they cannot be prosecuted, and the violent partner escapes punishment.

Research among battered wives suggests a variety of reasons for this underreporting. Women are embarrassed by what the violence says about their relationship, and often blame themselves – a feeling frequently supported by a violent partner's claims that he has been provoked into violence by the woman's behaviour. In the early stages, a woman may make excuses for a man's behaviour, and tell herself that it will not happen again; by the time the violence has been repeated over a long period, she may feel powerless and unable to escape or take any steps towards reporting the offence. This situation can lead to a recognised psychological state, often called 'battered woman's syndrome', in which the victim loses the ability to see beyond the situation or any means of changing it (discussed on p. 89).

Equally important is the fact that victims may fear that reporting the offence will simply lead to further beatings, given that even if charges are brought, the partner will usually be granted bail, and is highly likely to arrive home and attack her again in revenge for her making the complaint.

These problems are intensified by the traditional police approach to domestic violence which is to avoid involvement, leaving the partners to sort things out themselves. This is prompted partly by the emphasis on the privacy of the home and the family which has been a traditional part of British culture where 'an Englishman's home is his castle'. The expression 'rule of thumb' comes from a rule that a man was allowed to hit his wife with a stick if it was no thicker than his thumb. In addition there were concerns that the intervention of the legal system might lead to increased marriage breakdown. The assumption was that a couple might divorce if a prosecution were brought, but left alone, they would patch up their differences. The police also claimed that, where prosecutions were brought, by the time the case came to court wives and girlfriends were refusing to give evidence leading to cases collapsing.

In recent years some changes have been made in an attempt to address these problems. A spouse can now be compelled to give evidence against their partner in court proceedings, following the passing of s. 80 of the Police and Criminal Evidence Act 1984, and orders can be made prohibiting violence against a partner and even ousting the

6

Non-fatal offences against the person

violent person from the home, though the effect of such an order in practice may be minimal where the violent partner is really determined to get at the victim.

The Crown Prosecution Service has issued policy guidance on prosecuting cases of domestic violence. This encourages prosecutors to not just rely on the victim's evidence, but to also collect such evidence as medical reports and tape recordings of 999 calls. The prosecution can then proceed even where the victim no longer wishes to pursue the complaint. Special measures can be used during the trial to help the victim give evidence, such as allowing the victim to give evidence behind a screen. Bail conditions can be applied which order the defendant to keep away from the family home and the children's school.

In June 2003 the Government published a consultation paper, *Safety and Justice: The Government's Proposals on Domestic Violence*. This focuses on improving the legal protection available to the victims of domestic violence, using both the civil and criminal systems. It acknowledges that attitudes have changed towards domestic violence, but more needs to be done:

● to mark out domestic violence as unacceptable;
● to ensure effective prevention, detention and punishment; and
● to provide appropriate support for domestic violence victims.

This consultation process was followed by the Domestic Violence, Crime and Victims Act 2004 which introduces a range of practical reforms to try and improve the protection afforded to people who are the victims of domestic violence. The legislation brings closer the civil and criminal response to domestic violence.

The Government promised in its 2005 election manifesto to promote the use of 'advocates' in domestic violence, murder and rape cases. These advocates would be volunteers providing support to the victims during the criminal justice process. It also promised to develop specialist courts to deal with domestic violence.

The law and legal procedure alone cannot deal with this problem; a cultural change is required that would make domestic violence as unacceptable as any other kind of violent behaviour. Society tends to ignore domestic abuse or even consider it acceptable. One boy in five believes it is alright to hit a woman. One girl in ten agrees with this view.

● Definitions of the offences

Criticism is also often made of the way the offences themselves are defined. There is still no clear statutory definition of assault and battery, while the definitions of the more serious offences are contained in an Act passed back in 1861, with much of the vocabulary antiquated and even misleading, such as 'assault' in s. 47 and 'maliciously' in s. 18.

The requirement that the threat must be of immediate force in order to fall within an assault means that there is a gap in the law. Currently, if a person shouts that he or she is going to kill you, that may be an assault; but if the threat is to kill you tomorrow, it is not. The Law Commission has produced a draft Criminal Law Bill in the belief that prompt reform of this area is necessary, and creates an offence that would cover this example.

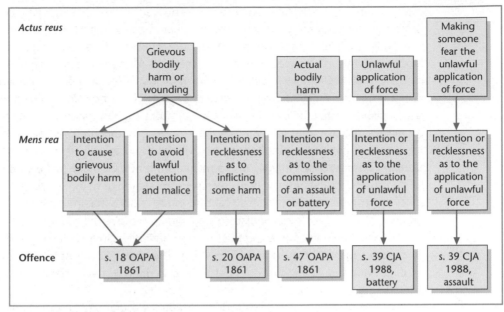

Figure 6.3 Distinguishing the non-fatal offences

6

Structure of the offences

The 1861 Act was merely a consolidating Act which gathered together a whole host of unrelated provisions from existing statutes. No attempt was made to rationalise the provisions. As a result the offences lack a clear structured hierarchy. First, while assault and battery can only be punished with a maximum of six months' imprisonment, and s. 47 can be punished by five years', the only real difference between them is that ABH is caused – yet ABH can mean as little as causing discomfort to the person. Secondly, the s. 20 offence is defined as a much more serious offence than s. 47, and yet they share the same maximum sentence of five years. A third problem is that the only significant difference between s. 20 and s. 18 is arguably a slightly more serious *mens rea*, and yet the maximum sentence leaps from five years to life. This can perhaps be justified by the fact that a defendant who intends to cause GBH within s. 18 has the *mens rea* of murder, and it is merely chance which dictates whether the victim survives, leading to a charge under s. 18, or dies, leading to a charge of murder and a mandatory life sentence if convicted.

Reform

Modernising the legislation

In 1980 the Criminal Law Revision Committee recommended that this area of the law should be reformed. Its proposals were incorporated into the draft code of the criminal law prepared by the Law Commission. The Law Commission again considered the matter at the beginning of the 1990s, producing a report and draft Criminal Law Bill on the issue in 1993. In February 1998, the Home Office produced a Consultation Document in furtherance of its commitment to modernise and improve the law. This presents a draft Offences Against the Person Bill modelled largely, but not entirely, on the Law Commission's 1993 Draft Criminal Law Bill. There now looks like a real possibility that legislation may follow. The draft Bill updates the language used for these offences by talking about serious injury rather than grievous bodily harm, and avoiding the words 'maliciously' and 'wounding' altogether. Under the draft Bill s. 18 is replaced by 'intentionally causing serious injury', with a maximum sentence of life (clause 1); s. 20 by 'recklessly causing serious injury', with a maximum sentence of seven years (clause 2); and s. 47 by 'intentionally or recklessly causing injury' with a maximum sentence of five years (clause 3). Thus the offence replacing s. 47 would remove the requirement of an 'assault', which would be tidier and avoid the problem of finding an assault where there is a course of conduct (see **R** v **Cox (Paul)** on p. 147). The draft Bill still proceeds to use the term 'assault' for conduct which would better be described as two separate offences of assault and battery (clause 4).

Statutory definitions are given for the mental elements of the offences which would continue to give recklessness a subjective meaning. Difficulties could arise as the statutory definitions differ from the common law definitions and if, for example, a jury was also faced with an accusation of murder, they would have to understand and apply two different tests for intention. The most serious offence in clause 1 could be committed by an omission but not the lesser offences. Injury is defined (clause 15) to include physical and mental injury, but 'anything caused by disease' is not an injury of either kind, except for the purpose of clause 1. So it would be an offence under clause 1 to intentionally infect another with AIDS but no offence to recklessly do so under clause 2.

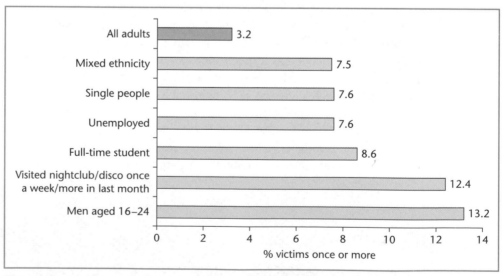

Figure 6.4 Adults most at risk of violence, 2008/09 British Crime Survey
Source: Crime in England and Wales, 2008/09, Home Office Statistical Bulletin, p. 48.

Spreading disease

In the case of **R** v **Dica** the Court of Appeal accepted that in principle a defendant could be liable under s. 20 of the Offences Against the Person Act 1861 for recklessly infecting another with AIDS. There is, however, much debate on whether criminal liability should be imposed for infecting another with a disease, particularly sexually transmitted diseases, such as AIDS. The World Health Report lists AIDS as the fourth biggest world killer, with an estimated 5,000 new infections every day, and the number of HIV patients in Britain is increasing. Clearly it is in everybody's interests to stop the spread of AIDS, but there is much controversy over whether the criminal law can help to achieve this. The United Nations has put forward a range of reasons why the criminal law should get involved in preventing the transmission of AIDS in a document entitled *Criminal Law, Public Health and HIV Transmission: A Policy Options Paper* (Elliott (2002)). However, there are concerns that criminalising this type of activity risks discriminating against the ill. Where the relevant disease is AIDS, many of those infected belong to some of the more vulnerable groups in society. Prior to the **Dica** case, the Home Office had rejected criminalising the reckless transmission of disease because 'the government is particularly concerned that the law should not seem to discriminate against those who are HIV positive, have AIDS or viral hepatitis or who carry any kind of disease'. A counter-argument to this is that the criminal law will only step in if an ill person behaves in a reprehensible manner, not simply because they are ill.

Another concern is that criminalising such conduct could prove to be counterproductive in terms of protecting public health. The involvement of the criminal law in the field may encourage secrecy and constitute an obstacle to educating the public about AIDS. If the reckless transmission of a disease is criminalised, people might avoid having health checks, so that they can claim that they were not reckless in having unprotected sexual intercourse, because they did not know that they were carrying an infection. It could also encourage those who know they are infected to engage in casual sexual intercourse after which they cannot be traced, rather than being in a long-term sexual relationship. Following a criminal conviction for HIV transmission in Scotland, two academics, Bird and Brown (2001) carried out research into the impact of the case on HIV transmission in Scotland. They suggested that after the conviction there was evidence of a 25 per cent reduction in HIV testing. They also found that even a modest fall in the uptake of HIV testing as a result of the judgment could produce a third increase in sexually transmitted HIV infections.

It may be appropriate to impose criminal liability where a person has intentionally infected another, but it will frequently be difficult to prove such an intention in this type of case, and it is much more controversial to impose liability for reckless infection. In 1993 the Law Commission proposed the creation of an offence of recklessly causing serious injury, which would have covered the reckless transmission of disease (*Legislating the Criminal Code: Offences Against the Person and General Principles*, Law Com No. 218, Home Office (1998)). Five years later, however the Home Office rejected this proposal (*Violence: Reforming the Offences Against the Person Act 1861*). It would have restricted liability for the transmission of a disease to where there was intention to cause serious injury. An intention to cause a lesser harm would not be sufficient and recklessness would not be sufficient. The Government considered that 'it would be wrong to criminalise the reckless transmission of normally minor illnesses such as measles or mumps'.

In the context of AIDS, its transmission can be prevented by the use of a condom, and it is not unreasonable to expect people to use a condom when they know that failure to do so risks giving their partners a disease that will ultimately kill them.

Stalking

The problems of stalking have attracted considerable media attention. 'Stalking', like 'shoplifting' and 'football hooliganism', is not a technical legal concept but one used in everyday language. It describes a campaign of harassment, usually with sexual undertones. Such conduct raises two important questions which have concerned Western legal systems in the late twentieth century: what are the boundaries of acceptable sexual behaviour and how far should psychiatric damage be recognised by the law? So any legal developments in this area are very sensitive.

In response to public concern the Protection from Harassment Act 1997 was passed. As well as enacting certain civil wrongs, it creates several new criminal offences. Section 1 prohibits a person from pursuing a course of conduct which they know or ought to know amounts to harassment of another. This is punishable by a maximum of six months' imprisonment. Section 4 contains the offence of aggravated harassment where, in addition, the defendant knows or ought to know that they placed the victim in fear of violence on at least two occasions. This is punishable with up to five years' imprisonment.

It is questionable whether this piece of legislation was necessary. The Act follows a pattern witnessed in other areas (for example, joyriding and dangerous dogs) of addressing a narrowly conceived social harm backed by a single issue pressure group campaign, with a widely drawn provision which overlaps with existing offences. The new offences in the 1997 Act are broadly defined and there is a danger that they could impinge upon other activities hitherto regarded as legitimate, such as investigative journalism and door-to-door selling. Cases such as **R** v **Ireland and Burstow** and **R** v **Constanza** show that the courts were prepared to adapt existing criminal law offences to include this type of harmful conduct. On the other hand, some people feel that these cases artificially distorted the existing law ignoring accepted authorities and that a fresh legislative approach was required with this specific problem in mind. In practice the value of the 1997 Act may be that it includes a power to make restraining orders forbidding the defendant from pursuing any conduct which amounts to harassment and a power of arrest to enforce these orders.

? Answering questions

1. Eric had recently been very unhappy because his wife had been having an affair with Greg. When he left work, carrying his toolbag with him, he went along to a beer festival being held in a small park. As Eric got his first pint of beer, he was suddenly aware that Harry, the person standing next to him but whom he did not know, had begun throwing bottles of full beer over his shoulder and high into the air. In trying to avoid being hit by one of the bottles, Imran stepped heavily onto Jane's foot and badly bruised it. Another bottle struck Kamran full in the face as he looked up. The blow knocked out one of his teeth, loosened others, and broke his cheekbone. When Harry was examined later, he was semi-conscious and was found to have drunk a lot of beer.

In the commotion that followed, everyone was angry and confused, and Eric was at first blamed for throwing the bottles. He was very frightened and ran out of the park, chased by a number of men. Eventually, they split up to try to find Eric, who by now was becoming very tired. Eric took a hammer out of his toolbag but then tried to hide. As he did so, Greg (who did not realise that the person whom he was chasing was Eric) came round the corner, and Eric immediately hit him a swinging blow with the hammer just above the ear. As Greg fell to the ground, Eric saw who he was, became instantly enraged and kicked his head viciously. Greg died from the effects of the two blows.

(a) Discuss Harry's criminal liability resulting from throwing the bottles.

(b) Discuss Eric's criminal liability for the death of Greg.

(c) How satisfactory is the current law on murder?
(AQA)

(a) By throwing the bottles, Harry caused harm to three individuals: Imran, Jane and Kamran. These three incidents will be considered in turn.

Imran
Looking first at the harm to Imran, Harry did not actually hit Imran with a bottle, but Imran seems to have feared that he might be hit by a bottle. You would therefore need to look at the offence of assault (see p. 141).

Jane
As regards Jane, the injuries that Jane suffered would be sufficient to amount to a battery or actual bodily harm under s. 47 of the Offences Against the Person Act 1861. Harry did not directly touch Jane; Imran stood on Jane's foot in trying to avoid a bottle. He could still be found criminally liable for Jane's injuries, even though it was Imran who physically touched Jane. Imran could be described as an innocent agent, and Harry could be viewed as the principal offender (see p. 282). Harry was the cause of Jane's injuries, and Imran's acts did not break the chain of causation. Note that for the purposes of a battery, force can be applied indirectly (see p. 144 and the case of **Haystead** *v* **DPP** (2000)).

Kamran
The third person who suffers harm from Harry's acts is Kamran. He suffers quite serious injuries so you would need to consider s. 47, s. 20 and s. 18 of the Offences Against the Person Act 1861. We are not told enough about Harry's state of mind, though it is more likely that he had the *mens rea* for s. 20 rather than s. 18, as he appears to have been reckless as to causing harm, rather than specifically intending grievous bodily harm.

When Harry was examined he was semi-conscious and had drunk a lot of beer. This raises the question of whether he could have a defence of intoxication. The defence is discussed at p. 338. It is not available if Harry had the *mens rea* of an offence (**R** *v* **Kingston**). If he lacked the *mens rea*, he was voluntarily intoxicated, so the defence would only be available for specific intent crimes, such as s. 18 of the Offences Against the Person Act 1861, but not for basic intent crimes, such as s. 20 of the 1861 Act.

(b) Eric might be liable for murder. He probably had both the *actus reus* and the *mens rea* of murder. If he lacked malice aforethought, then he could have been liable for unlawful and dangerous act manslaughter.

As regards defences, Eric might have a defence of provocation to a charge of murder. In relation to the subjective limb of the test, Eric does appear to have had a sudden and temporary loss of self-control. It would be difficult on these facts for Eric to satisfy the objective part of the test. Eric might have been able to rely on the self-defence and public defences (discussed on p. 346) when he initially hit Greg just above the ear with a hammer, though there would be an issue as to whether this was a proportionate level of violence. However, when he recognised Greg and went into a rage the public and private defences would have ceased to be available. If the initial hit was lawful on the basis of the public and private defences, but the subsequent acts were not, then the question of causation would need to be considered: did the unlawful acts cause the death? Given the tough approach that the courts are currently taking to causation, it is likely that causation will be found.

(c) To answer this question you could have relied on the material at pp. 67–68.

2 **Adrian became friendly with Bill, who had had treatment over the years for bouts of schizophrenia and often forgot to take the medication prescribed for him. They got into the habit of behaving in an antisocial manner. This included the making of a telephone call by Adrian to his 75-year-old neighbour, Connie, to tell her that he was coming to eat her cat. Connie was very frightened. Adrian convinced Bill that they should enter into a 'blood pact'. This involved Adrian carving his initials into Bill's arm. Bill made no attempt to cover the knife cuts or to get any treatment. When, eventually, he went to hospital, it was discovered that he had suffered a serious infection and that his arm was now partly paralysed.**

Subsequently, Bill's behaviour became even more outrageous. He told Adrian that he was going to walk along the balcony of his third floor flat, which overlooked a busy street, and would 'fly' if he overbalanced. After almost falling off twice, he suddenly overbalanced when halfway along, and fell onto Dan, a small child who was in a pushchair. Bill suffered only minor injuries but Dan was killed by the impact.

(a) **Discuss Adrian's criminal liability arising out of the incidents with Connie and Bill.**

(b) **Discuss Bill's criminal liability for the death of Dan.**

(c) **Select any two aspects of the law on offences against the person which you believe are unsatisfactory. Explain the reasons for your belief. (You may relate your answer to homicide, or to non-fatal offences, or to both.)**
(AQA)

(a) We look first at the incident involving Connie and then the incident involving Bill. The most relevant offence in relation to Connie is assault. The *actus reus* of an assault requires an act which makes the victim fear that unlawful force is about to be used against them. Adrian has threatened to eat the cat. This makes Connie very frightened, but Adrian's conduct could only amount to assault if the telephone call makes her fear that force will be used against her, not just the cat. In the light of cases such as **R v Constanza**, words alone can constitute an assault. It has traditionally been said that the victim must fear the immediate infliction of force. However, this requirement has been undermined by the Court of Appeal in **R v Ireland** (1996), a case that also involved unwanted telephone calls.

The *mens rea* of assault is either intention or subjective recklessness. The defendant must either have intended to cause the victim to fear the infliction of immediate and unlawful force, or have seen the risk that such fear would be caused. On the facts given, it is not certain that Adrian saw the risk that he would frighten Connie by making the calls, though it is likely that he did so realise.

Moving on to Adrian's liability for Bill's injury from the knife cuts, the most relevant offence on these facts was s. 20 of the Offences Against the Person Act 1861. As regards the *actus reus* of this offence, this can be either wounding or inflicting grievous bodily harm. The original cuts amounted to a wounding as the skin had been broken. The infection also led to paralysis which would amount to grievous bodily harm. The *mens rea* required under s. 20 is that Adrian intended or was reckless that his act would cause some harm. This would be satisfied on the facts. It is unlikely that he intended grievous bodily harm which would be the *mens rea* requirement for s. 18. Alternatively, the lesser offence of s. 47 of the Offences Against the Person Act 1861 would also have been committed on these facts.

Adrian's self-neglect would not have broken the chain of causation. On the issue of causation see p. 52, and the case of **R v Dear** would have been particularly relevant to these facts.

Adrian might be able to argue the defence of consent. This is discussed on p. 375. While, following **Brown**, the defence of consent is not usually available if actual bodily harm has been caused, there are certain exceptions where the offence can apply. One such exception is tattoos, which has certain similarities with a blood pact, and the case of **Wilson** (see p. 382) could be considered.

(b) Bill might be liable for involuntary manslaughter. He has not committed murder as there is no suggestion that he intended to kill or to cause grievous bodily harm. You would need to look at both gross negligence manslaughter and unlawful act manslaughter. As regards unlawful act manslaughter, it is difficult to identify an offence that led to the death. There would have been a battery if Bill realised there was a risk that someone might be hurt by his conduct.

Bill could raise the defence of insanity as he suffers from schizophrenia. In this context you needed to discuss the **M'Naghten Rules**, which are outlined at p. 326. Bill would find it difficult to show that he did not appreciate the nature and quality of his act, but he may be able to prove the alternative that he did not know that what he was doing was wrong. The defence of diminished responsibility was not relevant because the offence of murder could not be proved.

(c) Any of the critical material discussed at pp. 153–156 on non-fatal offences and in Chapter 5 on fatal offences could have been relied on here, though note you had to restrict yourself to two issues.

③ Is it time to repeal the Offences Against the Person Act 1861 and replace it with a new piece of legislation?

Criticisms of the drafting of the 1861 Act can be found at pp. 154–155 under the subheadings 'Definitions of the offences' and 'Structure of the offences'. You could develop these points by referring to the relevant case law in the first part of the chapter. You could also examine how the law is working in a modern context by discussing the continuing problem with domestic violence and with stalking. You could then examine proposals for reform, which are discussed at p. 155.

6

Non-fatal offences against the person

Summary

This chapter looked at offences against the person where no death is caused.

Assault

Actus reus

This consists of any act which makes the victim fear that unlawful force is about to be used against him or her. Words alone can constitute an assault.

It has traditionally been said that the victim must fear the immediate infliction of force: fear that force might be applied at some time in the future would not be sufficient. However, the requirement that the victim must fear the immediate infliction of force was undermined by the House of Lords in **R** *v* **Ireland and Burstow** (1997).

Mens rea

The defendant must either have intended to cause the victim to fear the infliction of immediate and unlawful force, or have seen the risk that such fear would be created.

Battery

Actus reus

The *actus reus* of battery consists of the application of unlawful force on another.

Mens rea

The defendant must have intended or been subjectively reckless as to the application of unlawful force.

Offences Against the Person Act 1861, s. 47

Actus reus

The prosecution must prove the existence of the *actus reus* of an assault or battery. Actual bodily harm has been given a wide interpretation. In **Miller** (1954), the court stated: 'Actual bodily harm includes hurt or injury calculated to interfere with health or comfort.' In **Miller**, it was also accepted that ABH included not just physical harm, but also psychological injury, though psychological injury will only count as ABH if it is a clinically recognisable condition.

Mens rea

The *mens rea* of assault occasioning ABH is the same as for assault or battery. No additional *mens rea* is required in relation to the actual bodily harm: **R** *v* **Roberts** (1978).

Offences Against the Person Act 1861, s. 20

Actus reus

The prosecution has to prove that the defendant either inflicted grievous bodily harm or wounded the victim. Wounding requires a breaking of the skin.

Mens rea

The defendant need only intend or be subjectively reckless that his or her acts could have caused some physical harm.

Offences Against the Person Act 1861, s. 18

Actus reus

This offence has the same *actus reus* as for s. 20: the defendant must have caused grievous bodily harm or have wounded the victim.

Mens rea

The defendant must have intended to cause grievous bodily harm or to avoid arrest while behaving maliciously.

Problems with offences against the person

The application of the law in this field has highlighted the problem of domestic violence in our society, and raised questions as to how far criminal liability should be applied following the transmission of a sexual disease. Problems with the definitions of these offences have led to a range of suggestions for reform.

Reading list

Bird, S. and Brown, A. (2001) 'Criminalisation of HIV transmission: implications for public health in Scotland' [2001] *British Medical Journal* 323, 1174.

Budd, T. and Mattinson, J. (2000) *The Extent and Nature of Stalking: Findings from the 1998 British Crime Survey*, Home Office Research Study 210, London: HMSO.

Criminal Law Revision Committee, Fourteenth Report (1980) *Offences Against the Person*, London: HMSO.

Finch, E. (2002) 'Stalking the Perfect Stalking Law: An evaluation of the efficacy of the Protection from Harassment Act 1997' [2002] *Criminal Law Review* 703.

Home Office (1998) *Reforming the Offences Against the Person Act 1861*, London: HMSO.

Home Office (2003) *Safety and Justice: The Government's Proposals on Domestic Violence*, Cm. 5847, London: Home Office.

Mirrlees-Black, C. (1999) *Domestic Violence: Findings from a New British Crime Survey Self-Completion Questionnaire*, Home Office Research Study No. 191, London: Home Office.

Wells, C. (1997) 'Stalking: The Criminal Law Response' [1997] *Criminal Law Review* 30.

Reading on the internet

The leading House of Lords judgment of **Ireland and Burstow** on the non-fatal offences is available on Parliament's website at:
    http://www.publications.parliament.uk/pa/ld199798/ldjudgmt/jd970724/irland01.htm

The Home Office report, *Violence: Reforming the Offences Against the Person Act 1861* (1998) is available on the Home Office website at:
    http://www.homeoffice.gov.uk/documents/cons-1998-violence-reforming-law/

6

Non-fatal offences against the person

The United Nations report, *Criminal Law, Public Health and HIV Transmission: A Policy Options Paper* (Elliott, 2002) is available on the United Nations' website at:

http://data.unaids.org/Publications/IRC-pub02/JC733-CriminalLaw_en.pdf

---

Visit **www.mylawchamber.co.uk/elliottcriminal** to access multiple choice questions, flashcards and practice exam questions to test yourself on this chapter.

Use **Case Navigator** to read in full some of the key cases referenced in this chapter:

- R v Brown [1993] 2 All ER 75
- R v Cunningham [1957] 2 All ER 412
- Dear [1996] Crim LR 595
- Fagan v MPC [1968] 3 All ER 442

---

7 Rape

This chapter explains that:

- the offence of rape is defined in s. 1 of the Sexual Offences Act 2003;

- the *actus reus* of this offence is committed when a male defendant penetrates the victim's vagina, anus or mouth with his penis without the victim's consent;

- the *mens rea* of the offence is that the defendant did not reasonably believe that the victim was consenting;

- an offence of rape of a child under 13 is contained in s. 5 of the 2003 Act which does not require proof of the absence of consent or the existence of *mens rea* beyond an intention to penetrate; and

- there are controversies surrounding how the law on rape works in practice.

Introduction

The Government has undertaken a major reform of the sex offences with the passing of the Sexual Offences Act 2003. The reforms were introduced because the old law was 'archaic, incoherent and discriminatory' (Home Office White Paper, *Protecting the Public* (2002)). The passing of the Human Rights Act 1998 had incorporated the European Convention on Human Rights into English law. There was concern that the law on sexual offences could be in breach of the Convention and it was therefore felt desirable to review and reform the law to avoid legal challenges through the courts. The Government's reform proposals were published in its report, *Setting the Boundaries: Reforming the Law on Sex Offences* (2000).

In the light of this report, the Sexual Offences Act 2003 has now been passed which has introduced radical reforms to the law on rape. Rape is the most serious of the non-fatal, sexual offences against the person. The definition of rape can now be found in s. 1 of the 2003 Act:

1(1) A person (A) commits an offence if –
   (a) he intentionally penetrates the vagina, anus or mouth of another person (B) with his penis,
   (b) B does not consent to the penetration, and
   (c) A does not reasonably believe that B consents.
(2) Whether a belief is reasonable is to be determined having regard to all the circumstances, including any steps A has taken to ascertain whether B consents.

Actus reus

The *actus reus* of rape is committed where a man has sexual intercourse with a man or a woman without that person's consent.

The defendant

Only a man can be a defendant to a charge of rape; in law a woman cannot commit rape. However, a woman may be charged with being an accomplice to rape: for example, Rosemary West, wife of the serial killer Frederick West, was initially charged on two counts of aiding and abetting the rape of a girl. In **DPP** *v* **K and C** (1997) two teenage girls were convicted as accomplices to a rape.

The victim

Until 1994, the offence of rape could only be committed against a woman. Situations where a man was forced to submit to buggery were sometimes described in the media as male rape, but in legal terms they could only be charged as indecent assault or buggery. This was changed by the Criminal Justice and Public Order Act 1994, so that now both women and men can be victims of rape.

Research by Michael King and Gillian Mezey (1992) looked into the issue of male sexual assault before this change in the law. Sexual offences are generally under-reported, which means that not only do we not know the true number which are committed, but also that if the offence is not reported, it cannot be prosecuted, so the offenders go unpunished. King and Mezey discovered that sexual assaults on males were even less likely to be reported than sexual offences generally, for a variety of reasons: victims feared that they would not be believed, or that people would assume they were gay, or they blamed themselves, thinking that as men they should have been able to fight off their attacker. Where the offence involved incest, the victims were often under considerable emotional and physical pressure not to report. Finally, in the past, male complainants were not guaranteed anonymity so they feared unwanted publicity. It may be that some of these fears will decrease with time now that male rape has received official recognition and anonymity is guaranteed to both male and female victims.

Campaigners on the issue of rape also hope that the extension of the offence to include men will signal a change in perception about rapes of women. As Susan Brownmiller argued in her book, *Against our Will,* 'Women are trained to be rape victims. To simply hear the word "rape" is to take instruction in the power relationship between males and females. . . . Girls get raped. Not boys. Rape is something awful that happens to females, and [the suggestion is] unless we watch our step it might become our destiny.' Once it is accepted that rape is not something that only happens to women, there may be less scope for the mistaken idea, still held by some judges, among others, that it is somehow women's responsibility to prevent it, by staying indoors at night, wearing 'respectable' clothing, and so on.

Sexual intercourse

For the purposes of rape, sexual intercourse was limited until 1994 to penetration of the vagina by the penis. This was amended by the Criminal Justice and Public Order Act 1994 and it now includes penetration of the anus by the penis. The Sexual Offences Act 2003 further extended the offence of rape to cover penetration of the mouth – oral intercourse.

Section 44 of the 1956 Act also provides that the man need not have ejaculated; the offence is committed simply on penetration: '. . . it shall not be necessary to prove the completion of intercourse by the emission of seed, but the intercourse shall be deemed complete upon proof of penetration only'.

 Sexual intercourse is treated as a continuing act, so that there can be liability for what might have appeared to be an omission, under the principle laid down in **Fagan v Metropolitan Police Commissioner**, discussed at p. 12. Thus in **Kaitamaki** (1985) it was stated by the Privy Council that if a victim consented to penetration, but after penetration they ceased to give their consent (in other words, the victim wanted to stop), a man would be committing the *actus reus* of rape if he did not withdraw.

Absence of victim's consent

Consent is defined by s. 74 of the Sexual Offences Act 2003:

> For the purposes of this Part, a person consents if he agrees by choice, and has the freedom and capacity to make that choice.

It is the absence of the victim's consent that transforms sexual intercourse into rape. Consent is perhaps one of the most difficult issues in a trial. Now that sophisticated forensic methods of investigation mean that denying sexual intercourse took place is less likely to be an option, consent, along with *mens rea*, naturally becomes the obvious line of defence.

The victim's consent must be real and not a mere submission given under pressure.

KEY CASE

In **R v Olugboja** (1981) the defendant threatened to keep a girl in his bungalow overnight. He made no explicit threat of violence and she did not resist sexual intercourse. The court said that on the evidence she had not given a genuine consent, but had merely submitted under pressure of his threat. In practice, the line between a mere submission and consent is not an easy one to draw.

A mere submission given under pressure is not a consent.

The case of **R v K and another** (2008) confirms that under the 2003 Act, a mere submission is still not a consent. In that case a young woman had sexual intercourse with a relative who had abused her in the past and who she had approached when she was hungry and homeless. The Court of Appeal stated the trial judge's direction on consent had correctly left open the possibility that the complainant 'submitted to sexual intercourse rather than consented to it'.

In **R v C** (2009) the House of Lords stated that where, due to a physical disability, a complainant is unable to communicate a choice not to consent it would be appropriate to prosecute the offence of rape. It also stated that if the complainant suffers from an irrational fear which prevents the exercise of choice, this can amount to a lack of capacity to choose.

In the past it had to be shown that the sexual intercourse had been obtained by force, but this is no longer a requirement: the sole question is whether the victim gave a genuine consent. The point was reiterated in **R v Larter and Castleton** (1995), in which the defendant had sexual intercourse with a woman while she was asleep. The Court of Appeal upheld his conviction for rape, emphasising that the key issue was whether or not the victim had consented to sexual intercourse; if not, the fact that no force was used would not prevent the act being rape. Evidence of force will be relevant to the issue of consent, but only as evidence – at least in theory. In practice, juries have a tendency not to believe victims where there is no evidence of force having been used.

A recent case that took the same approach as **R v Larter and Castleton** is **R v Malone** (1998). The victim was a 16-year-old girl and the appellant was a friend who lived near her home. She had gone out with some other friends one evening, but had drunk so much wine that she was unable to walk and her friends took her home by car. One of the friends went round to the appellant's house and asked him to help them carry the girl into her bedroom. While the others were downstairs, the appellant went back upstairs. The victim said she became aware of his presence, that he climbed on top of her and inserted his penis into her vagina, which caused considerable pain and she kicked out against the appellant's chest. The appellant was convicted of rape and appealed on the grounds that the judge had made a mistake on the issue of consent where no force, lies or threats had been used and the complainant had offered no resistance. The appeal was dismissed. The Court of Appeal stated that in order to obtain a conviction there had to be some evidence of lack of consent, but this could simply be the assertion of the complainant that he or she did not consent.

If a victim is drunk but has still consented to sexual intercourse, then the current position would appear to be that no offence of rape has been committed – a drunken consent is still a consent – provided the victim is treated as having had the 'capacity' to consent within the terms of the statutory definition. In **R** v **Dougal** (2005) the trial judge ordered a jury to deliver a not guilty verdict for a man accused of raping a 21-year-old university student. She had become unwell when she had drunk a number of vodkas at a university party and was escorted home by a part-time security guard. The security guard had sexual intercourse with the student in the corridor of her flat. The woman subsequently complained that she had been raped and a prosecution was brought. The security guard denied rape, stating that she had consented to sexual intercourse. The case was dropped when the student said in her evidence that she had been so drunk she had no memory of the incident and therefore could not be 100 per cent certain that she had not consented.

The Government consultation paper *Convicting Rapists and Protecting Victims – Justice for Victims of Rape* (2006) questioned whether the trial judge in such cases should draw the jury's attention to the issue of whether the victim had the capacity to consent at the time of the sexual intercourse. In **R** v **Hysa** (2007) the Court of Appeal expressly stated that just because a complainant cannot remember if she consented or not does not automatically prevent a conviction. The jury can still look at whether at the time of the alleged offence the complainant had the capacity to give a genuine consent. The Court stated that issues of consent and capacity to consent to intercourse in cases of alleged rape should normally be left to the jury to determine.

KEY CASE

The issue of whether a person has the capacity to consent when they have become voluntarily intoxicated was considered by the Court of Appeal in **R** v **Bree** (2007). The court held that this was a question of fact to be determined in the light of the evidence before the court. A young man and a 19-year-old student had gone out for the evening together. They had drunk heavily and returned to the student's flat. She was sick and the man helped wash her hair afterwards. Later they had sexual intercourse, but when the young man asked if she had a condom and she said 'no' they stopped. In court she said that she had not wanted sexual intercourse, but had not said 'no' because she had only been semi-conscious and had a sense of being outside her body observing events. When arrested, the young man argued that he had reasonably believed that the woman consented. He was initially convicted but his appeal was successful on the basis that the trial judge's direction to the jury had been inadequate. The jury should have been given careful guidance on s. 74 of the Sexual Offences Act 2003, looking at the issue of capacity. A drunken consent could still be consent; it was a question of fact whether the particular individual had the capacity to consent in the circumstances.

> It is a question of fact for the jury whether a drunk person had the capacity to give a genuine consent.

The inclusion of anal intercourse within the *actus reus* of rape raises a question that the legislation appears not to answer: if a woman consents to vaginal intercourse, and the man proceeds to penetrate her anus, could this be rape? We would suggest that it should be; to allow consent to one form of intercourse to imply consent to another would be to deny a woman's autonomy over her own body.

The burden of proof

The Government has been concerned at the low conviction rate for rape and the distress caused to the complainant by the trial process. A major obstacle in getting convictions has been that the prosecution has had to prove that the complainant did not consent to sexual intercourse. Frequently the purported attack will have taken place in private and the defendant will be a former sexual partner. The defendant will often argue in these circumstances that sexual intercourse took place, but that the complainant consented. It will then be the defendant's word against the complainant's. The focus of the trial will move from the defendant to the complainant to determine whether or not he or she consented. The trial has then become a gruelling experience for complainants, with their past sexual history being discussed in open court, and complainants feeling as if they have been put on trial rather than the defendant. At the end of such trials, the jury have been reluctant to convict.

In a radical reform introduced by the Sexual Offences Act 2003, the Government has tried to facilitate proving the absence of consent, by changing the burden of proof in certain circumstances. These changes to the burden of proof will be considered when we consider *mens rea* (see below), as the changes apply to both *mens rea* and consent.

Mens rea

The *mens rea* of rape has been changed significantly by the Sexual Offences Act 2003. Under the old law, s. 1(2)(b) of the Sexual Offences Act 1956 stated the *mens rea* required was that: 'at the time he knows that the person does not consent to the intercourse or is reckless as to whether that person consents to it'. Recklessness no longer forms part of the *mens rea* of rape. The Sexual Offences Act 2003 requires an intentional penetration and that the defendant did not reasonably believe that the victim was consenting. This latter *mens rea* can be broken down into two questions. Only if the answer to both these questions is yes, will the defendant be found not to have *mens rea*:

- Did the defendant believe that the victim was consenting?
- Was that belief reasonable?

Section 1(2) of the 2003 Act states:

> Whether a belief is reasonable is to be determined having regard to all the circumstances, including any steps [the defendant] has taken to ascertain whether [the victim] consents.

It is up to the future courts to interpret what is meant by the broad reference to 'all the circumstances'. Following the case of **R v TS** (2008) the Court of Appeal seems to be interpreting this as allowing the defendant's personal characteristics to be taken into account. In that case the wife accused her husband of raping her when, after they had separated, he had visited the family home to see their children. The wife said she had repeatedly told her husband she would not have sex with him and actually bit him in the mouth when he kissed her. The appellant alleged that she had effectively seduced him. After his trial a prison psychiatrist diagnosed the husband as suffering from Asperger's Syndrome. Some people suffering from this mental disorder are unable to understand how other people think, get intimate and social signals wrong, and can be so convinced of their own false beliefs that they have the nature of psychotic delusions. In the light of this new evidence a retrial was issued. The objective standard of reasonableness has thereby been softened. Temkin and Ashworth (2004) have raised the concern that an analysis of this issue could degenerate into a reliance on stereotypes about male and female relationships.

Burden of proof

The burden of proof is normally on the prosecution to prove the existence of the elements of an offence beyond reasonable doubt. However, because of the problems that there have been in the past with the prosecution of the offence of rape, the Sexual Offences Act 2003 has reversed the burden of proof in relation to the issue of consent and *mens rea* in certain circumstances. It does this by creating a rebuttable presumption, and, where particular lies were used, an irrebuttable presumption.

The rebuttable presumption

Section 75 of the Sexual Offences Act 2003 creates a rebuttable presumption that the complainant did not consent and the defendant had *mens rea* where:

- violence or the threat of violence was used against the complainant or a third person;
- the complainant was unlawfully detained;
- the complainant was asleep or otherwise unconscious when the offence was committed;
- due to a physical disability, the complainant was unable to communicate a consent; or
- the complainant had been given a substance which was capable of causing him or her to be stupefied or overpowered at the time of the attack.

In these circumstances an evidential burden of proof is on the defendant. He has to adduce sufficient evidence to raise an issue of consent and the absence of *mens rea*, in order for the burden of proof to pass back to the prosecution.

The last scenario where the rebuttable presumption applies is concerned primarily with situations where victims have been given powerful intoxicants, particularly the drug Rohypnol, to facilitate a sexual attack. Rohypnol is a colourless, odourless, tasteless drug that can be slipped into a victim's drink and then causes sedation or euphoria approximately 15 minutes afterwards. It is generally manufactured for the treatment of sleep disorders. People under the influence of the drug seem to be drunk, though awake and functioning, and subsequently may not remember what they had done while they were under the influence of the drug. The scope of the legislative provision could potentially include secretly adding alcohol to a victim's drink.

The irrebuttable presumption

The Sexual Offences Act 2003, s. 76 creates an irrebuttable presumption that the victim did not consent and the defendant had *mens rea*. This irrebuttable presumption applies where specific types of lies have been used to dupe the victim into having sexual intercourse. These lies are where:

(2)(a) the defendant intentionally deceived the complainant as to the nature or purpose of the relevant act;

   (b) the defendant intentionally induced the complainant to consent to the relevant act by impersonating a person known personally to the complainant.

Before the 2003 Act, lies as to the nature of the act of sexual intercourse would have effectively led to the imposition of an irrebuttable presumption that the victim did not consent, but the prosecution would still have had to prove the existence of *mens rea*. The earlier case law on the issue is of interest in illustrating the type of lies as to the nature of the relevant act that would be relevant under the 2003 Act. In **Flattery** (1877) the defendant told the victim that he was performing a surgical operation, when in fact he was having sexual intercourse with her. This was a lie as to the nature of sexual intercourse. In **Williams** (1923) the defendant was a singing teacher, who had a 16-year-old pupil. She consented to sexual intercourse when he said it was a method of improving her breathing. Again, this was a lie as to the nature of sexual intercourse.

The 2003 Act goes further than the old common law because it also imposes an irrebuttable presumption where the defendant has deceived the victim as to the purpose of the sexual intercourse. There has been some uncertainty as to whether this should be interpreted broadly, so that it could include a wide range of lies or whether it should be interpreted narrowly to only where there is a lie that the purpose of the act is not sexual (making it very similar to a lie as to the 'nature' of the sexual act).

KEY CASE

A narrow interpretation of s. 76 was given in the case of **R v Jheeta** (2007). In that case the defendant had entered into a sexual relationship with the victim at college. Being worried that the victim might end the relationship, he started sending her anonymous, threatening text messages including a threat that she would be kidnapped. When she told the defendant, he said 'Don't worry, I'll protect you', though in fact he was the person sending the texts. When she decided to go to the police to report the harassing text messages she was receiving he said he would do this for her. She then started getting text messages supposedly from the police but actually from her boyfriend, telling her she must have sexual intercourse with her boyfriend or she would be fined by the police. She continued in the relationship for another couple of years, but unwillingly and only because of the threats. Eventually her mother realised what was going on and the matter was referred to the police. At his trial, the defendant was convicted of rape on the basis that he had deceived the victim as to the purpose of the act under s. 76. On appeal, this was held to be a misdirection as there had been no deception as to the purpose of sexual intercourse which was for sexual gratification. The victim was sexually experienced and knew both the nature and

> S. 76 cannot apply if the victim knows the identity of the defendant and that the purpose of intercourse is sexual gratification.

purpose of intercourse and the identity of the person she was having sexual intercourse with. However, the conviction was upheld because on the facts the victim had not given a valid consent to sexual intercourse within the meaning of s. 74, as she had not been able to exercise a free choice when agreeing to sexual intercourse because of the threats and the lies.

In **R** *v* **Jheeta** the Court of Appeal approved the pre-2003 case of **R** *v* **Linekar** (1995) where a woman working as a prostitute was seeking clients outside a cinema in London. The defendant approached her and they agreed he would pay her £25 for sexual intercourse. They went to the balcony of some flats nearby and had sexual intercourse, but afterwards the defendant ran away without paying. He was eventually found and charged with rape but at the trial it was stated that, as she consented to the sexual intercourse, there was no rape. Although the defendant had lied that he would pay for sexual intercourse in order to gain her consent, he had not lied as to the nature and quality of the act. Commenting on the case, the Court of Appeal stated in **Jheeta**:

> Linekar deceived the prostitute about his intentions. He undoubtedly lied to her. However she was undeceived about either the nature or the purpose of the act, that is, intercourse. Accordingly the conclusive presumption in section 76 would have no application.

On this approach, s. 76 could apply to a case with the facts of **R** *v* **Tabassum** (2000). In that case three women had agreed to remove their bras to allow the appellant to examine their breasts, because they understood that he was medically qualified and was carrying out the procedure in order to put together a medical database on the subject. In fact the appellant was not medically qualified and was not putting together a medical database. The Court of Appeal took the view that on the facts there was consent to the nature of the acts but not to their quality, since they were not for a medical purpose. The appellant's conviction for sexual assault was therefore upheld.

In the case of **R** *v* **Devonald** (2008), the complainant had split with his girlfriend. The girlfriend's father was unhappy with how his daughter had been treated and decided to get his revenge by humiliating him. He established an online friendship with the complainant, pretending to be a girl. He then arranged for the complainant to mastur-bate in front of a webcam pretending that the girl was enjoying seeing this. The father was subsequently prosecuted for the sexual offence of causing a person to engage in a sexual activity without their consent which is contained in s. 4 Sexual Offences Act 2003 and to which s. 76 can also potentially apply. The Court of Appeal held that on the facts s. 76 applied because the father had deceived the complainant as to the purpose of the act – the purpose was to humiliate him and not for sexual gratification.

In the light of this case law it would seem that if the defendant's purpose is sexual gratification when he has represented that it is not (for example, he suggests that it is medical research or a clinical examination) or if the defendant suggests his purpose is for sexual gratification when it is not (for example, it is to humiliate) then s. 76 will apply. If the defendant simply lies about surrounding circumstances which do not represent the purpose of the act (for example, that he is wealthy, or single or in love with the victim) then s. 76 does not apply. These matters would simply be relevant in determining whether there is a genuine consent under s. 74. **Linekar** can then be explained by the fact that the defendant's purpose was to have sexual intercourse, the deception regarding payment was simply as to a surrounding circumstance.

There are likely to be arguments before the courts that ss. 75 and 76 violate the European Convention on Human Rights, and in particular the right to a fair trial and the presumption of innocence in Art. 6. In a different context, the House of Lords stated in **Sheldrake** *v* **DPP** (2004) that reverse burdens of proof do not breach the European Convention if they are a proportionate response to a social problem, taking into account the gravity of the offence. Should a future court conclude that s. 76 is not proportionate, it would be interpreted as merely imposing an evidential burden on the defence.

Only reasonable mistakes negative *mens rea*

Prior to the Sexual Offences Act 2003, the controversial case of **DPP** *v* **Morgan** (1976) ruled that an honest mistake that the victim was consenting could negative *mens rea*, even though the mistake was not reasonable. The facts of the case were that Morgan was a senior member of the air force and had been drinking with three junior members of that service. He invited the men to come back to his house to have sexual intercourse with his wife, telling them that his wife might appear to protest, but that they should ignore her as she did not mean it; this was her way of increasing her sexual pleasure. The three men accepted the invitation, and, on arriving in the house, Morgan woke up his wife, who was asleep in their child's bedroom, and dragged her into another room, where the men forced her to have sexual intercourse with them. She struggled and protested throughout, and afterwards she had to go to hospital.

The three men were charged with rape; unfortunately Morgan himself could not be charged with rape because at the time a husband could not in law rape his wife, though he was charged with being an accomplice. The three men argued that they lacked *mens rea* because Morgan's comments had led them to believe that his wife was consenting, despite her protests. The House of Lords accepted that, if this had been the case, they would not have been liable; their mistake did not need to be reasonable (which it clearly was not), provided it was genuine. However, the convictions were upheld on the grounds that a properly directed jury would not have accepted that the men honestly believed Mrs Morgan was consenting.

The law has now been changed by the Sexual Offences Act 2003. The defendant who makes a mistake and thinks that the victim was consenting will only lack *mens rea* if that mistake was reasonable. This is because the *mens rea* of rape is now defined in terms of reasonableness: the defendant will have *mens rea* if he 'does not reasonably believe' that the victim was consenting. So a defendant has *mens rea* where he honestly believes that a victim is consenting, but has not taken due care to discover that he or she was not actually consenting.

Sentence

The maximum sentence for rape is life imprisonment. In practice, the usual starting point is five years' imprisonment. This can be increased where the offence had any aggravating features.

Rape of a child under 13

Section 5 of the Sexual Offences Act 2003 has created a new offence of rape of a child under 13. For this offence the consent of the child is irrelevant; the offence is automatically committed by intentionally having sexual intercourse with a child under 13. The offence is defined in the following terms:

> 5(1) A person commits an offence if –
>   (a) he intentionally penetrates the vagina, anus or mouth of another person with his penis, and
>   (b) the other person is under 13.

The maximum sentence for this offence is life imprisonment.

KEY CASE

In **R v G** (2008) the House of Lords confirmed that the offence in s. 5 of the Sexual Offences Act 2003, is an offence of strict liability. The defendant was a 15-year-old boy who had sexual intercourse with a girl under 13 (the complainant was 12 at the time of the offence). He was charged with the s. 5 rape offence. The defendant claimed that he had believed the complainant to be 15 and she admitted she had told him on an earlier occasion she was 15, but this provided no defence to the charge because his mental state regarding her age was irrelevant as this was a strict liability offence. The House of Lords held that the strict liability offence did not breach the European Convention, including the presumption of innocence in article 6.

> The section 5, statutory rape offence is a strict liability offence.

Rules of evidence and procedure

There are special rules of evidence and procedure for rape trials, which have caused considerable controversy.

The corroboration rule

Until 1994, a mandatory corroboration ruling had to be given at a rape trial. This meant that the judge always had to warn the jury that it was unwise to convict on the woman's evidence alone. That did not mean there could be no conviction without evidence corroborating what the woman said, but clearly juries may place great weight on what the judge has to say, and the warning may well have raised doubts where none would have existed without it. The warning seemed to imply that women were liars by nature, and prone to make false allegations of rape.

In 1991 the Law Commission recommended that the corroboration rule should be abolished, as did the Royal Commission on Criminal Justice in 1993. In the light of these recommendations, and widespread criticisms of the warning, ss. 32 and 33 of the Criminal Justice and Public Order Act 1994 abolished the mandatory corroboration rule.

However, this does not necessarily solve the problem. Although it is no longer mandatory to give the warning, judges may still give it where they feel it is necessary, and, given the pronouncements which some of our judges have made on rape (discussed below), it is questionable whether this discretion is safe in their hands.

● The victim's sexual history

Evidence of a woman's past sexual experience is sometimes admissible as evidence in court. Such evidence has in the past been used to give the jury a bad impression of the victim and make it appear that she was not a credible witness – the insinuation being that a woman who has had an active sex life with men other than a husband is immoral and cannot be trusted generally. In addition, it plays up to the belief that only 'good' women deserve protection from rape.

Back in 1975, the Heilbron Committee concluded that urgent reform was necessary. It proposed that evidence of the woman's past sexual experiences should only be admitted if it concerned previous sexual intercourse with the defendant, or the past sexual experience was 'strikingly similar'. This approach was rejected by Parliament as too narrow. Instead, s. 2 of the Sexual Offences (Amendment) Act 1976 was passed. Under this section, past sexual experience with the particular defendant was always admissible, and evidence of such experience with someone else would also be admissible if the judge concluded that 'it would be unfair to that defendant to refuse to allow the evidence to be adduced or the question to be asked'.

Unfortunately this section was given a very broad interpretation by the courts. In **Lawrence** (1977) the Crown Court stated that the defence could question the complainant about past sexual relationships with other men if such questions 'might reasonably lead the jury, properly directed in the summing-up, to take a different view of the complainant's evidence from that which they might take if the question or series of questions was or were not allowed'. This seems to miss the point: the fact that juries often do take a different view after such evidence is given is precisely why defence lawyers seek to introduce it, but the question is whether such evidence should be the basis on which the jury changes its view. The Court of Appeal in **Viola** (1982) proceeded to approve this direction. In practice, 75 per cent of women who had been raped leading to court proceedings were questioned about their previous sexual encounters with men other than the defendant.

The Government concluded that rape victims were not being adequately protected in court proceedings and new legislation was passed on the matter. The Youth Justice and Criminal Evidence Act 1999, s. 41 replaced s. 2 of the Sexual Offences (Amendment) Act 1976. Under s. 41 of the 1999 Act, evidence of the complainant's past sexual behaviour can only be used in a trial with the leave of the court. Section 41(2)(b) states that leave can only be given if 'a refusal of leave might have the result of rendering unsafe a conclusion of the jury or . . . the court on any relevant issue in the case'. In addition, under s. 41(3) leave can only be granted:

> . . . if the evidence or question relates to a relevant issue in the case and either –
> (a) that issue is not an issue of consent; or

(b) it is an issue of consent and the sexual behaviour of the complainant to which the evidence or question relates is alleged to have taken place at or about the same time as the event which is the subject matter of the charge against the accused; or

(c) it is an issue of consent and the sexual behaviour of the complainant to which the evidence or question relates is alleged to have been, in any respect, so similar –

   (i) to any sexual behaviour of the complainant which . . . took place as part of the event which is the subject matter of the charge against the accused, or

   (ii) to any other sexual behaviour of the complainant which . . . took place at or about the same time as that event,

that the similarity cannot reasonably be explained as a coincidence.

(4) For the purposes of subsection (3) no evidence or question shall be regarded as relating to a relevant issue in the case if it appears to the court to be reasonable to assume that the purpose (or main purpose) for which it would be adduced or asked is to establish or elicit material for impugning the credibility of the complainant as a witness.

The clear intention of Parliament was to significantly restrict the use of past sexual history evidence in rape trials. Unfortunately, in the first case to reach the House of Lords concerning this section, **R v A** (2001), the House relied on the Human Rights Act 1998 in order to ignore the clear intention of Parliament.

KEY CASE

In **R v A** (2001) the House of Lords ruled that a defendant had to be given the opportunity to adduce evidence as to the complainant's past sexual behaviour with the defendant which had taken place over a week before the purported rape. It considered that otherwise the section would be in breach of Art. 6 of the European Convention on Human Rights guaranteeing a fair trial, which was incorporated into national law by the Human Rights Act 1998.

> Past sexual history evidence will be admissible if its exclusion would endanger the fairness of the trial.

The defendant claimed that he had sexual intercourse with the complainant on several occasions during three weeks prior to the purported rape, with the last instance being approximately one week before this. The purported rape occurred when the defendant and the complainant were walking along a towpath that ran by the side of the Thames in the early hours of the morning. As they walked along the towpath the defendant fell down. The complainant's account was that she tried to help him to his feet, whereupon he pulled her to the ground and had sexual intercourse with her without her consent. Later that day the complainant made a complaint of rape to the police. The defendant claimed that sexual intercourse had taken place with the complainant's consent and that this was part of a continuing sexual relationship. Alternatively, he intended to rely on the defence that he believed she consented. The complainant was at the time in a sexual relationship with the defendant's flatmate.

At a preparatory hearing the defendant applied for leave to cross-examine the complainant about the alleged previous sexual relationship. Relying on the provisions of s. 41 of the Youth Justice and Criminal Evidence Act 1999, the judge ruled that the complainant could not be questioned about her alleged sexual relationship with the defendant. Appeals were made to the Court of Appeal and then the House of Lords. The House found that, in interpreting s. 41, it had to take into account s. 3 of the Human Rights Act 1998. This requires that: 'So far as it is possible to do so, primary legislation . . .

must be read and given effect in a way which is compatible with the Convention rights.' The House concluded that: 'the test of admissibility is whether the evidence (and questioning in relation to it) is nevertheless so relevant to the issue of consent that to exclude it would endanger the fairness of the trial under Article 6 of the Convention'.

This decision constitutes an important early use of the Human Rights Act 1998 in the context of the criminal law. It is a significant ruling, which severely curtails the impact of the 1999 Act, and moves back towards the position prior to the passing of this legislation.

The academic Kibble (2005) has carried out research in this field, by questioning 78 judges about their approach to s. 41. The majority of the judges were critical of the legislation, considering it to be too victim orientated. They thought that evidence of a previous relationship between the defendant and the complainant should be admissible as it is 'essential background evidence, without which the jury would be approaching the case in a vacuum'. Kibble concluded that the legislation had not struck the right balance, judges could be trusted with some discretion on the admissibility of sexual history evidence and therefore the case of **R** v **A** was an appropriate response to the legislation because it allowed the judges discretion on the issue. He found that the judges took a consistent and thoughtful approach, and had significantly improved their treatment of rape complainants, particularly because of judicial training they received on the subject.

Research carried out for the Home Office has found that the rules laid down in s. 41 were frequently 'evaded, circumvented and resisted' and had produced 'no discernible effect' on reducing the number of failed prosecutions. Sexual history evidence was introduced in more than three-quarters of trials. The researchers observed:

> Findings from case files, trial observations and interviews raise the possibility that both prosecution and defence share stereotypical assumptions about 'appropriate' female behaviour and that these continue to play a part when issues of credibility are addressed in rape cases.

In the light of this research, the Government's lawyer, the Solicitor-General, has written to the Criminal Law Rules Procedure Committee asking it to tighten up the procedural rules for the admissibility of this evidence. Defence lawyers may be required to give prior written notice of their intention to raise previous sexual history so that the victim is not taken by surprise by such a request.

The legislation still gives judges a discretion to allow a victim to be questioned about sex with men other than the accused. The campaign group Women Against Rape (WAR) argues that the admission of such evidence gives juries the wrong message: they are being asked to decide, not whether a woman was raped, but whether she is entitled to the protection of the law. WAR would favour the banning of sexual history evidence completely.

● Questioning of rape victims by defendants

Until recently the experience of rape complainants during the trial could be made particularly traumatic due to their exposure to direct questioning by the defendant. In one case the complainant, Julia Mason, was subjected to six days of cross-examination by her attacker, Ralston Edwards. She subsequently waived her right to anonymity in order to call for a change in the law. Parliament has now intervened to deal with this problem, with the Youth Justice and Criminal Evidence Act 1999. Section 34 imposes an absolute prohibition on any person charged with a sexual offence from themselves asking any question of a complainant with regard to the offence charged or any other offence. Usually this is not a problem as the vast majority of defendants are represented by a lawyer and the cross-examination is carried out by their lawyer. The problem arises where defendants have chosen to act in person, rather than be represented by a lawyer. Under s. 38, a court-appointed defence representative can now conduct the cross-examination in this situation.

Criticism and reform

Consent

The Sexual Offences Act 2003 has reversed the burden of proof in relation to the issue of consent in certain circumstances. But there will remain problems with the law's focus on whether the victim consented.

The consultation paper *Convicting Rapists and Protecting Victims – Justice for Victims of Rape* (2006) considered allowing prosecutors and defendants to present general expert evidence concerning the psychological effects of sexual offences on victims, in order to overcome the problem of 'rape myths'. For example, expert evidence could be submitted where a complainant has delayed reporting a rape to the police. The expert evidence could explain to the jury that 'such apparently problematic features of a person's evidence are common and should not necessarily lead to the conclusion that the victim/witness is lying or unreliable'.

Following this consultation process, the Government appears to have rejected this idea, partly because if the prosecution were able to introduce expert evidence in this field, the defence should also be allowed to present expert evidence in order for there to be a fair trial and so the reform could be counterproductive.

The Heilbron Committee found that the issue of consent encouraged lawyers to bring up evidence of the victim's sexual history, in an effort to prove that she was likely to have consented to sex. As the feminist writer, Carol Smart, points out in *Feminism and the Power of Law*, the implication is that if a woman has consented to sex with various men in the past, she would probably consent to anyone, including the defendant in the case.

An American academic, D. Dripps (1992), has suggested that the emphasis on consent is harmful, because of the way it focuses on the victim's state of mind, rather than on the defendant, making it appear that the victim is on trial. To avoid this problem he suggests serious sexual offences should be defined without reference to consent at all; rape would be abolished, and a new sexual offence created, which would be defined as the defendant knowingly presenting the victim with the choice of sex or violence. A second, lesser offence would then be that of knowingly obtaining sexual intercourse with the victim in disregard of a verbally expressed refusal.

7

Rape

Temkin and Ashworth (2004), academics who have written extensively on the issue of rape, have questioned the way the 2003 Act has drawn distinctions between the different situations in which consent can be undermined. Obtaining compliance by deception seems no less objectionable than obtaining compliance through violence or the threat of violence, but in the former the Act creates a conclusive presumption and in the latter only a rebuttable presumption that the complainant did not consent. Temkin and Ashworth have also pointed out that the scenario currently falling within the rebuttable presumption in s. 75, where a person was administered a stupefying drug, might be more appropriate under s. 76 and the irrebuttable presumption. In these circumstances the complainant does not have 'the freedom and capacity' to make a choice within the definition of consent in s. 74.

An alternative approach would simply be to change the burden of proof in all cases, so that it always fell on the defendant to prove that the complainant consented. Temkin (1987), has argued that a man should have a legal duty to ask if a woman is consenting, though it is debatable how far this proposal is realistic.

Steven Box argues in *Power, Crime and Mystification* (1983) that coercion and not consent should be the central issue – where a man is in a position to impose sanctions for refusal, his ability to coerce should be the key question, not her consent. He points out that the law currently focuses on the man's physical superiority, but ignores his social, economic and organisational superiority.

TOPICAL ISSUE

Rape, drink and drugs

The Home Office issued a consultation paper, *Convicting Rapists and Protecting Victims – Justice for Victims of Rape* (2006). There was some public disquiet following the Crown Court case of **R** v **Dougal** (2005), when a student at Aberystwyth University had become extremely drunk and had been escorted home by a security guard. She subsequently alleged that he raped her but he claimed that they had consensual intercourse. At the trial she admitted she had been so drunk that she could not remember whether she had consented or not. The trial judge then directed the jury that they should acquit. The consultation paper considers whether in this type of case the trial judge should actually ask the jury to consider whether the complainant was so drunk that she did not have the capacity to give a genuine consent. To assist the trial process, the Government consultation paper considered introducing a legal definition of 'capacity' to consent to sexual activity to help courts and juries in cases where drink or drugs may have affected the complainant's ability to choose. However, the Government seems to be satisfied that the courts have resolved this problem effectively with the direction in **R** v **Bree** (2007) that the jury should be given clear guidance on capacity in such cases.

● Sexual intercourse

Before 1994, rape was restricted to vaginal intercourse. It was extended to anal intercourse by the Criminal Justice and Public Order Act 1994, so that men as well as women could be the victims of rape. The Sexual Offences Act 2003 has further extended the offence to cover oral intercourse, but penetration by objects other than the penis is not covered by the offence.

In a report in 1984 the Criminal Law Revision Committee (CLRC) favoured restricting rape to vaginal intercourse. It argued that rape was a specific form of conduct which the public recognised; to extend it would cause confusion, and might weaken the social stigma attached to the offence. The CLRC also pointed out that with other forms of penetration there was no risk of pregnancy.

TOPICAL ISSUE

Conviction rate

Very few rapes lead to the offender being convicted and punished. Obstacles to a successful prosecution exist at every stage of the criminal justice system. Many victims do not report the offence to the police, though the proportion of rapes reported has increased in recent years. In 2007, the proportion of reported rapes that resulted in a conviction fell to only 5.3 per cent of the 13,000 reported offences. The complainant withdraws their complaint in 25 per cent of cases (Harris and Grace (1999)). Of those cases that are brought to court, about 47 per cent result in a conviction.

A major reason for underreporting is fear of the criminal justice process itself, which can make the victim feel as though they are the one on trial. The thought of recounting intimate details in front of a court of strangers, and possibly having their sexual history dragged up by an aggressive defence barrister, is a significant barrier to reporting the offence.

Even where rape is reported, there is, in fact, little chance of the offender being tried. This is not just because some rapists are obviously never caught, but also, according to a 1995 report by the pressure groups Women Against Rape and Legal Action for Women, because the Crown Prosecution Service (CPS) has shown itself reluctant to prosecute in many cases of rape. They point out that during the early 1980s, about half of all reported rapes were prosecuted; by 1993, following the creation of the CPS in 1986, this had dropped to less than one-fifth. In 1977, 33 per cent of reported rapes resulted in a conviction, compared with only 5.3 per cent today. The gap between the number of recorded crimes and convictions is known as the 'attrition rate'. In cases studied in the report, the CPS had refused to prosecute on the grounds that evidence was insufficient, inconclusive or uncorroborated, though the pressure groups claim the evidence was actually stronger than in high-profile cases such as that of Austen Donellan (see p. 185). The CPS has denied that rape is treated differently from any other offence as regards the decision to prosecute. The raw statistics have to be treated with care. While the gap between reported crimes and convictions has increased significantly in recent years, we may not be comparing like with like. About 1,000 rapes were reported to the police in 1977 compared to 8,000 in 1999. The proportion of complainants who had previously had a sexual relationship with the suspect or were on a 'date' has increased. As social morals have changed with increased casual sex, promiscuity and heavy drinking among men and women, the task of the criminal justice system to establish the commission of a rape has become harder.

A fundamental problem in gaining a conviction is the credibility conflict that frequently arises between the complainant and the defendant: she says she did not consent to sexual intercourse and he says she did. There may be no other witnesses and no other evidence of any kind which could help the jury decide who is telling the truth. In an adversarial system where the prosecution have to prove guilt beyond reasonable doubt this conflict is always weighted in favour of the defendant. This reluctance to convict without corroborative evidence is combined with the jury's reluctance to convict where the facts of the case do not fit the popular stereotype of a violent rape by a stranger (HM Crown Prosecution Service Inspectorate (2002) *A Report on the Joint Inspection into the Investigation and Prosecution of Cases involving Allegations of Rape*).

7

Rape

● Anonymity of suspects

A person who complains to the police that they have been raped currently benefits from anonymity, to avoid unwanted publicity. There is no such protection for suspects. Certain celebrities have had their careers ruined by complaints being made against them which have received considerable media publicity, even though there has not been any subsequent trial. Some attempts were made to introduce into the Sexual Offences Act 2003 statutory anonymity for defendants in rape cases until the point of conviction, but these were not successful. Publicity can help the investigation, because it can lead to witnesses or further victims coming forward. A Home Office spokesman stated: 'We do understand the distress that is caused if people are wrongly accused of rape, but the British criminal justice service works on the principle of openness.'

● The trial

The ordeal of rape complainants is frequently made worse by their experience of the criminal trial process. In court it can often seem that it is the victim who is on trial, rather than the defendant. The Sexual Offences Act 2003 hopes to improve the experience of the victim at the trial, in particular by reversing the burden of proof in certain circumstances, but problems are likely to remain.

A major concern has been the way victims are cross-examined by defence lawyers. In a study conducted by Victim Support in 1996, complainants described their experiences of cross-examination as 'patronising', 'humiliating' and 'worse than the rape'. A number of women complained that they had been asked intrusive and inappropriate questions about their private lives. The personal lives of complainants are subjected to close scrutiny during cross-examination. Sue Lees carried out a study in 1996 on rape trials based upon the transcripts of 31 trials and 116 questionnaires completed by victims of rape. Seventy-two per cent of respondents complained that they had been asked irrelevant and unfair questions during cross-examination and 83 per cent felt that they were on trial and not the defendant. Lees reports that questioning routinely centred on a complainant's lifestyle and 'in more than half the cases where consent was in issue, questioning included whether the complainant was divorced, was an unmarried mother, had a habit of drinking with strangers or drank to excess'. According to Lees, such questioning was directed simply at discrediting the complainant in the eyes of the jury, rather than at eliciting relevant evidence. She argues that the question should not only be whether such evidence is relevant but whether it is of sufficient probative value to counter the potential dangers flowing from its admission. A number of studies suggest that juries are unduly swayed by character evidence. Research conducted by Kalvin and Zeisel (1996) found that there is a danger that juries may be distracted from the real issues in a case by lengthy investigation of a witness's character during cross-examination.

Louise Ellison (1998) has argued that the focus of debate on rape trials is too narrow. She considers that the bullying and browbeating of rape complainants in court is rooted in the adversarial trial process and therefore an inescapable feature of cross-examination. It may be that the assumption that rape complainants are treated differently from other complainants is mistaken. Paul Rock examined proceedings in Wood

Green Crown Court in 1993. He found that other crime victims, and prosecution witnesses in general, often feel humiliated, degraded and frustrated by the process of cross-examination. In one case, he observed, the complainant in an assault trial was described by defence counsel in his closing speech as 'a spiteful, bitchy woman with a drink problem'. In another trial the complainant was cast as a 'deceitful, conniving, drug-pushing, lesbian'.

Research conducted by Brereton in 1997 also challenges the assumption that rape complainants are treated differently during cross-examination. Brereton conducted a comparative study of rape and assault trials based upon the transcripts of 40 rape and 44 assault trials. He found substantial similarities in the cross-examination strategies employed by defence counsel in both types of proceedings. Complainants of assault were just as likely as rape complainants to be subjected to attacks upon their character and credibility and to be questioned about their drinking behaviour and their mental stability. He argued that the tactics employed by counsel during cross-examination were 'tools of the trade' rather than unique to rape trials.

● Sentencing

There have been concerns in the past that judges were too lenient when sentencing rapists. While the efforts of the Court of Appeal have generally led to higher sentences for rape, there are still occasional examples of leniency, which call into question the attitudes of the judges concerned to the offence and its victims. In a 1994 case, a trial judge imposed a three-year supervision order, along with a compensation order for £500, so that the 15-year-old victim 'could have a good holiday to get over it'. The prosecution made an appeal against this sentence under the procedures contained in s. 36 of the Criminal Justice Act 1988, and the sentence was subsequently increased to two years' detention.

Now that the offence has been extended to include male rape, there is concern that the judges may be inclined to pass heavier sentences where there has been a male victim rather than a female victim. The first conviction for attempted male rape occurred in the case of **Richards** (1995). Richards was sentenced to a term of life imprisonment for the attempted rape of an 18-year-old man and an additional six years' imprisonment for assault occasioning actual bodily harm. The sentence attracted a degree of criticism as it was claimed that the case indicated a willingness on the part of the judiciary to treat male rape more seriously than female rape. However, the academics Philip Rumney and Martin Morgan-Taylor (1998) argue that the sentence was entirely consistent with the sentencing guidelines developed in cases of female rape. In particular, they point out that Richards had previous convictions for sex offences and suffered from a 'psychopathic personality disorder'. In sentencing, the trial judge stated 'this personality defect is one that makes it probable he will commit similar offences in the future if he is not subject to . . . confinement for an indefinite period'. Under the existing sentencing guidelines, someone posing such a continuing threat may give rise to the imposition of a life sentence. They conclude that the trial judge adopted an approach to sentencing which gave primacy to the facts of the case rather than the sex of the victim, in accordance with Parliament's intentions.

Alternative offences

In Canada they have abolished the offence of rape altogether, and replaced it with a graded offence of sexual assault. Simple sexual assault carries a maximum sentence of ten years; sexual assault accompanied by bodily harm, the use of weapons or of third parties has a maximum sentence of 14 years' imprisonment; and finally, aggravated sexual assault with wounding, maiming or endangering life has a maximum sentence of life imprisonment. This reform shifts the emphasis away from the sexual element of the offence, to the aggression which it really represents, and puts the victim under less pressure because there is no need to prove such matters as penetration. The grading of the offence also gives more structure to sentences and one of the results has been that sentences have increased.

Changing attitudes

Many of the problems surrounding the law of rape arise from attitudes to women and sex, and misconceptions about the offence itself. It is often viewed as a sexual act, so that people express surprise when, for example, very old ladies are raped. But research suggests that in fact rape has little to do with sexual intercourse as understood in everyday life; it is a crime of violence, with the penis being used as a weapon in the same way as another attacker might use a knife. A 1976 study carried out for the Queen's Bench Foundation found that rapists were not primarily motivated by sexual desire: they wanted to dominate and humiliate their victim. As a result, physical attractiveness played little part in the selection of their victim; physical vulnerability was more important.

Another common myth is that rape is something that happens when a stranger jumps out on a woman walking alone in the dark. While it is certainly true that some rapes do happen in situations like this, they appear to be in the minority. Most rapes are committed by a man known to the complainant. A recent report shows that in 45 per cent of recorded rapes the suspect was a spouse or lover; in 13 per cent, a family member; and in only 8 per cent, a stranger (*A Report on the Joint Inspection into the Investigation and Prosecution of Cases Involving Allegations of Rape* (2002)).

It is when the victim is raped by someone they know that outdated attitudes to women and sex have most influence. In the past, these attitudes were responsible for holding back the law on marital rape; currently, they focus on so-called 'date rape' – rapes which occur when the victim has had some social contact with the rapist. This was the situation alleged in the case of the university student, Austen Donellan, who was acquitted, and that of the boxer Mike Tyson, who was convicted.

Research by Warshaw (1984) suggests that the incidence of rape and attempted rape in such situations may be high. She surveyed students at an American campus university. One in 12 undergraduate men admitted they had acted in ways that conformed to the legal definition of rape, while 26 per cent had attempted to force intercourse on a woman to the extent that she cried or fought back. Of women undergraduates who had been raped, 84 per cent of them knew their attacker and 57 per cent happened on dates. The psychological harm caused to a woman raped by an acquaintance can be greater than if they are raped by a stranger. One research study suggests that 'women raped by men they knew attribute more blame for the rape to themselves, see themselves in a less positive light, and tend to have higher levels of psychological stress' than women raped by strangers: Parrot and Bechhofer, *Acquaintance Rape* (1991).

In law, conduct which satisfies the definition of rape falls within the offence whether the rapist is a perfect stranger, a person the victim has met once, or someone she knows well. But whether or not a jury believes the defendant's conduct to fit within that definition may well depend on their own attitudes to the male–female relationship. For example, it is widely believed that, once aroused, a man cannot stop himself going on to have sex, and that therefore a woman who arouses a man has only herself to blame if he insists on having sex. Quite apart from the fact that this theory is biologically untrue, it assumes that a woman's rights over her own body are limited: she can say 'No', but only up to a point. In addition, the cultural stereotypes of aggressive men and docile women contribute to the idea that women say 'No' when they actually mean 'Yes', and that it is somehow a man's role in the game to overcome the woman's resistance.

The extent to which these views may be held by juries can be seen in the results of a survey carried out for Amnesty International in 2006. This found that more than a third of people believe women who flirt are partially or totally responsible for being raped. Twenty-two per cent thought the same if the woman had had a high number of sexual partners. One in three people questioned also thought a woman was partially or totally to blame for being raped if she was drunk. Twenty-six per cent of respondents said a woman was partially or totally responsible for being raped if she was wearing sexy or revealing clothes. It is hard to imagine the same response if people were asked if those who failed to fit security systems were responsible for their own burglaries, or those who chose to cross the street were responsible for the injuries suffered if they were run over.

The media coverage of the Austen Donellan case in 1994 revealed similar attitudes. While the evidence in that case was certainly weak, it was not that which caused the outcry, but the fact that the complainant had got drunk and got into bed with the defendant. The *Daily Mail* described the complainant as 'drunk and sexually shameless', while the *Today* newspaper wrote: 'This sort of drunken shenanigans should not be compared to a young girl walking alone in the dark who is raped by a stranger.' The idea seems to be that only two kinds of women deserve protection from rape: the innocent virgin, or those who know their place, accepting that their sexuality belongs not to them but is held on trust for their husband or future husband.

The sociologist Matza (1964) points out that this background culture allows rapists to use techniques of neutralisation – justifying their behaviour with claims that 'she asked for it', 'she enjoyed it', 'women are masochists', 'I have a strong sex drive', 'I was drunk', 'she's a prostitute/or promiscuous so it did not matter to her'. Unfortunately these ideas are all too often backed up by the comments of judges: examples include 'all she has to do is keep her legs shut, and she will not get it without force'; 'women who say "No" do not always mean "No"'; and, of a hitchhiker, 'she was "guilty of contributory negligence"'.

In 2006, the Government launched an advertising campaign to make men aware of the legal requirement of obtaining consent before sexual intercourse. The campaign targeted 18 to 24-year-old men through posters in pub toilets, magazine adverts and radio broadcasts. It aimed to remind men that, under the Sexual Offences Act 2003, defendants need to show they have reasonable grounds to believe the other person had given consent. For a long time, work to raise awareness of sexual violence has focused on the need for women to take responsibility for their personal safety, so this is an important development, as it places the onus on men.

Only when attitudes towards women change will there ever be any chance of bringing the majority of rapists to justice. Although, sadly, some of these attitudes are held by women as well as men, involving more women in making, interpreting and enforcing the law would be one way to make progress.

TOPICAL ISSUE

Paedophiles

The release from prison of paedophiles such as Sidney Cooke and his friend Robert Oliver produced serious concern amongst the public in general. There is a public perception of a growing threat of sexual abuse to children in society. A study was carried out by Don Grubin, Professor of Forensic Psychiatry at Newcastle University, entitled *Sex Offending Against Children: Understanding the Risk*. It looked at research and criminal statistics in the field, while acknowledging the serious limitations of official statistics, which invariably underestimate both the incidence and the severity of sexual offences. He remarked that 'any attempt to arrive at a realistic estimate of the actual rate of child abuse in England and Wales has to rely on assumptions, guesswork and a bit of putting one's finger in the wind'. The criminal statistics available, however, show that during the course of a year there are some 4,000 formal cautions or convictions for sexual offences against children, and that of these about one-half are for sexual assault of girls under 16. The figures do not confirm the public perception that this sort of crime is increasing. While he notes that the Home Office estimated that there were over 100,000 individuals with convictions for sexual offences against children in 1993, it also appears that the proportion has been declining over a 40-year period. The total number of known offenders represents a decline of some 30 per cent since 1985.

Sex offenders who target children represent an extremely diverse group and no clear picture of the 'child molester' emerges. What is certain, however, is that most of the offences do not involve strangers and that about 80 per cent take place within either the home of the victim or the offender. He notes that some research suggests that abusers have often also been the victims of abuse, but he considers a key factor in triggering deviant behaviour may simply be the amount of violence within the family.

Professor Grubin observes that sex offenders have relatively low reconviction rates and that where there is a reconviction it is usually for a non-sexual offence. A study that looked at offenders 21 years after their original conviction in 1973 found that the threat of reconviction for any indictable offence, such as offences against property, was around 50 per cent while only 16 per cent were reconvicted for sexual offences against children.

● Sex offenders and politics

Recent legislation suggests that sex offenders, particularly paedophiles, are being used as an emotive and vulnerable target to score political points. The large number of legislative measures that have resulted do not necessarily represent the most effective way for a society to be dealing with sexual deviance.

Sex offenders' details are now held on a register. These are similar to the registers kept in America, following what was known as 'Megan's law'. Megan was a seven-year-old girl who was raped and murdered by a convicted paedophile who lived on her street in New Jersey. The aim of such legislation is clearly to protect young people, but one has to wonder why a register is being kept purely of sex offenders and not other offenders. It encourages vigilante activity by local neighbourhoods. Efforts at rehabilitation are undermined by the publication of such information, as evidence in America suggests that sex offenders are being driven underground to avoid victimisation by their neighbours.

Lord Bingham CJ has commented in **R** v **Chief Constable of the North Wales Police, ex p. Thorpe** (1998):

> It is not acceptable that those who have undergone the lawful punishment imposed by the courts should be the subject of intimidation and private vengeance, harried from parish to parish like paupers under the old Poor Law. It is not only in their interests but in the interest of society as a whole that they should be enabled, and if need be helped, to live normal, lawful lives. While the risk of repeated offending may in some circumstances justify a very limited amount of official disclosure, a general policy of disclosure can never be justified, and the media should be slow to obstruct the rehabilitation of ex-offenders who have not offended again and who are seriously bent on reform.

Professor Grubin in his study discussed above concluded that there is a risk in concentrating too intensely on the minority of offenders known to the authorities. He felt that to be effective and coherent, a policy to tackle sex offences had to emphasise prevention through education, vetting procedures and the provision of services to encourage potential abusers to seek help.

Following the tragic murder of the young child, Sarah Payne, in 2000 there was a high-profile campaign to make the names of sex offenders on the Sex Offenders' Register available to the public at large. The *News of the World* led a 'name and shame' campaign which was linked to aggressive vigilante attacks with people being driven from their homes and demonstrations on the Paulsgrove housing estate in Portsmouth. The Government decided against making the names on the Sex Offenders' Register available to the public but instead proposed a series of measures to ensure stronger safeguards for children.

Sex offenders cause considerable harm to their victims and need to be rehabilitated. If they are simply used as targets for harsh legislation to gain political votes they will not receive the treatment they need and they will become the victims of unjust discrimination.

❓ Answering questions

1 Steven is a homosexual and is obsessed with Paul. He invites him for a drink one evening at a wine bar. After the drink Paul allows Steven to come back to his house for a coffee. By midnight Paul is very tired and asks Steven to leave but he refuses and starts to become very violent. He hits Paul across the face and then forces him to have anal intercourse. Paul screams out with the pain and when a neighbour arrives, having heard the noise, Steven runs off. He later claims to friends that Paul obviously fancied him and that while he was saying 'No' to anal intercourse he obviously meant 'Yes'. Discuss the criminal liability of Steven.

The most serious offence here is rape, as this has a maximum sentence of life imprisonment. When discussing the *actus reus*, you should point out that the definition of the offence has been amended to include male rape by anal intercourse. On the issue of consent, Steven's remarks to his friends suggest that he will claim he believed Paul consented. Following the Sexual Offences Act 2003, Steven's belief must have been reasonable. As Paul had asked Steven to leave, Steven had used force and Paul had screamed, it is unlikely that a court would find that Steven reasonably believed Paul had consented. The case of **Morgan** no longer applies. Because force has been used, the rebuttable presumption in s. 75 would apply. In addition, by hitting Paul across the face, he may have committed a non-fatal, non-sexual offence, such as that defined in s. 47 of the Offences Against the Person Act 1861. With regard to all these offences, you need to consider the defence of intoxication, as they had been out drinking before the incident occurred.

2 **Is the current definition of rape satisfactory?**

This is a fairly broad essay question, but so long as you remember to take a strongly critical approach, assessing what the law should be, as well as what it is, you can score high marks here. After briefly outlining the offence of rape, you should point out that this is an area where the law has been reformed recently, explaining the problems which the changes were designed to remedy, and stating to what extent these problems have in fact been solved. Then you can go on to point out the problems that still exist, and possible reforms. You could include some of the material on changing attitudes, pointing out that legal reform alone may not be enough to change the problems with rape.

3 **Commenting on the Sexual Offences Act 2003, Simester and Sullivan have observed:**

> What can be said at present is that, in certain particulars, there seem to be improvements over the old law. Yet, without indulging in pessimism, there are also a number of difficulties and obscurities that seem sure to engender appellate litigation (Simester and Sullivan (2004) *Criminal Law Theory and Doctrine*, Oxford: Hart Publishing, p. 408)

With regard to the reforms made to rape, do you agree?

You need to discuss the changes made to the offence of rape by the Sexual Offences Act 2003. In particular, you could discuss the broadening of the definition of the *actus reus* of rape to include oral intercourse, the change to the *mens rea* of rape, the rebuttable and irrebuttable presumptions, and the statutory definition of consent. Broader issues relating to the problem of underreporting, the low conviction rate and complainants' perception of the trial process could also be discussed.

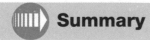 **Summary**

The definition of rape can now be found in s. 1 of the Sexual Offences Act 2003:

Actus reus

The *actus reus* of rape is committed where a man has sexual intercourse with a man or a woman without that person's consent. Sexual intercourse occurs where there is penetration by a penis of the victim's vagina, anus or mouth. Section 74 of the Sexual Offences

Act 2003 states that a person consents 'if he agrees by choice, and has the freedom and capacity to make that choice'.

Mens rea

The *mens rea* of rape is an intentional penetration and the defendant must not have reasonably believed that the victim was consenting.

Burden of proof

The burden of proof is normally on the prosecution to prove the existence of the elements of an offence beyond reasonable doubt. However, the Sexual Offences Act 2003 has reversed the burden of proof in relation to the issue of consent and *mens rea* in certain circumstances. Section 75 of the 2003 Act creates a rebuttable presumption that the complainant did not consent and the defendant had *mens rea* where:

- violence or the threat of violence was used against the complainant or a third person;
- the complainant was unlawfully detained;
- the complainant was asleep or otherwise unconscious when the offence was committed;
- due to a physical disability, the complainant was unable to communicate a consent; or
- the complainant had been given a substance which was capable of causing him or her to be stupefied or overpowered at the time of the attack.

In these circumstances an evidential burden of proof is on the defendant. Section 76 creates an irrebuttable presumption where the defendant intentionally deceived the complainant as to the nature or purpose of the relevant act; and where the defendant impersonated a person known personally to the complainant.

Rape of a child under 13

Under s. 5 the offence of rape is automatically committed when a person intentionally has sexual intercourse with a child under 13.

Rules of evidence and procedure

There are special rules of evidence and procedure for rape trials, which have caused considerable controversy. In particular, there have been problems in the way the past sexual history of the complainant has been used to undermine the credibility of the complainant.

Criticism and reform

The Sexual Offences Act 2003 introduced radical reforms to the offence of rape, but further reforms could be considered. These include removing the issue of consent from the definition of rape and re-defining the meaning of sexual intercourse for the purposes of the offence. There is an ongoing problem with the low conviction rate for this offence and a debate as to whether suspects should benefit from anonymity which would be lifted if they were subsequently convicted. The trial experience can be a terrible ordeal for the complainant, primarily because of the focus on whether the complainant consented. A controversial issue at the moment is how society should handle paedophiles and whether the handling of sex offenders is becoming too politicised.

Reading list

Brereton, D. (1997) 'How Different are Rape Trials? A Comparison of the Cross-Examination of Complainants in Rape and Assault Trials' 37 *British Journal of Criminology* 242.

Ellison, L. (1998) 'Cross-Examination in Rape Trials' [1998] *Criminal Law Review* 605.

Finch, E. and Munro, V.E. (2004) 'The Sexual Offences Act 2003: Intoxicated consent and drug assisted rape revisited' [2004] *Criminal Law Review* 789.

Finch, E. and Munro, V. (2005) 'Juror stereotypes and blame attribution in rape cases involving intoxicants' 45 *British Journal of Criminology* 25.

Gross, H. (2007) 'Rape, moralism and human rights' [2007] *Criminal Law Review* 220.

Grubin, D. (1999) Sex *Offending Against Children: Understanding the Risk*, Home Office, Police Research Series, Paper 99.

Harris, J. and Grace, G. (1999) *A Question of Evidence? Investigating and Prosecuting Rape in the 1990s*, Home Office Research Study 196, London: Home Office.

Herring, J. (2005) 'Mistaken sex' [2005] *Criminal Law Review* 519.

Herring, J. (2007) 'Human rights and rape: a reply to Hyman Gross' [2007] *Criminal Law Review* 228.

HM Crown Prosecution Service Inspectorate (2002) *A Report on the Joint Inspection into the Investigation and Prosecution of Cases Involving Allegations of Rape*, London: HMCPSI.

Home Office (2000) *Setting the Boundaries: Reforming the Law on Sex Offences*, London: Home Office.

Home Office (2002) *Protecting the Public: Strengthening Protection Against Sex Offenders and Reforming the Law on Sexual Offences*, London: HMSO.

Kibble, N. (2005) 'Judicial discretion and the admissibility of prior sexual history evidence under section 41 of the Youth Justice and Criminal Evidence Act 1999: Sometimes sticking to your guns means shooting yourself in the foot: Part 2' [2005] *Criminal Law Review* 263.

Kibble, N. (2005) 'Judicial perspectives on the operation of s. 41 and the relevance and admissibility of prior sexual history evidence: four scenarios: Part 1' [2005] *Criminal Law Review* 190.

Lees, S. (1996) *Carnal Knowledge Rape on Trial*, London: Hamish Hamilton.

Queen's Bench Foundation (1976) *Rape: Prevention and Resistance*, San Francisco.

Rodwell, D.A.H. (2005) 'Problems with the Sexual Offences Act 2003' [2005] *Criminal Law Review* 290.

Tadros, V. (2006) 'Rape without consent' 26 *Oxford Journal of Legal Studies* 449.

Temkin, J. and Ashworth, A. (2004) 'The Sexual Offences Act 2003 (1) Rape, sexual assaults and the problems of consent' [2004] *Criminal Law Review* 328.

Temkin, J. and Krahe, B. (2008) *Sexual Assault and the Justice Gap: A Question of Attitude*, Oxford: Hart Publishing.

Without Consent: Her Majesty's Crown Prosecution Service Inspectorate and Her Majesty's Inspectorate of Constabulary Thematic Report, London: Home Office.

Reading on the internet

The consultation paper *Convicting Rapists and Protecting Victims – Justice for Victims of Rape* (2006) is available on the Home Office website at:
> http://www.homeoffice.gov.uk/documents/cons 290306–justice-rape-victims

The Sexual Offences Act 2003 is available on the website of the Office of Public Sector Information at:
> http://www.opsi.gov.uk/acts/acts2003/20030042.htm

The explanatory notes for the Sexual Offences Act 2003 are available on the website of the Office of Public Sector Information at:
> http://www.opsi.gov.uk/acts/en2003/2003en42.htm

The report, *Sex Offending Against Children: Understanding the Risk* (D. Grubin, 1998, Police Research Series Paper 99) is available on the Home Office website at:
> http://www.homeoffice.gov.uk/rds/prgpdfs/fprs99.pdf

7

Rape

Visit **www.mylawchamber.co.uk/elliottcriminal** to access multiple choice questions, flashcards and practice exam questions to test yourself on this chapter.

Use **Case Navigator** to read in full the key cases referenced in this chapter:
- Fagan *v* MPC [1968] 3 All ER 442
- Morgan [1976] AC 182

8 Non-fraudulent property offences

This chapter discusses the main non-fraudulent property offences:

- theft, contained in s. 1 of the Theft Act 1968, consisting of the appropriation of property belonging to another, dishonestly and with the intention of permanently depriving;

- robbery, contained in s. 8 of the Theft Act 1968, committed where a person steals and immediately before or at the time of doing so and in order to do so, he uses force on any person or puts or seeks to put any person in fear of being then and there subjected to force;

- burglary, contained in s. 9 of the Theft Act 1968, committed where a person carries out a theft (or a range of other offences) when trespassing in a building;

- blackmail, contained in s. 21 of the Theft Act 1968 where a person makes an unwarranted demand with menaces;

- handling, contained in s. 22 of the Theft Act 1968, where a person dishonestly deals with stolen goods knowing or believing them to be stolen;

- taking without consent, contained in s. 12 of the Theft Act 1968, which is the offence used to prosecute joy riders; and

- criminal damage contained in the Criminal Damage Act 1971 which is the offence used to prosecute people who paint graffiti in public places.

Introduction

So far we have considered offences where the target of the wrongdoing is people; in this chapter we will look at offences concerned with property, such as theft and fraud. Until 1968 this area of the law was governed by the common law, and was extremely complex. The Criminal Law Revision Committee identified this field as one suitable for codification, and an attempt to do this was made in the form of the Theft Act 1968. This Act was described as a mini-code, since it covered only the key property offences; a full code would cover criminal law as a whole.

Despite the fact that the 1968 Act was designed to clarify the law, the courts encountered a series of problems with interpretation and application, so that ten years later part of the Act was repealed and the Theft Act 1978 was passed. In 1996 the House of Lords' judgment in **R** v **Preddy** drew attention to further problems with the law, leading to the passing of the Theft (Amendment) Act 1996 which amends the two earlier Theft Acts. The mini-code was therefore contained in the three Acts.

Property offences can be divided into two types: fraud offences and non-fraudulent property offences. Problems remained with the key fraud offences and so the Government decided to repeal these offences and replace them with a new piece of legislation, the Fraud Act 2006, which will be discussed in the next chapter. This chapter deals with non-fraudulent property offences. If fraud does exist there can still be liability for one of these non-fraudulent offences provided the essential ingredients of these offences are established.

Theft

Theft is the main non-fraudulent property offence, and is defined in s. 1 of the Theft Act 1968: 'A person is guilty of theft if he dishonestly appropriates property belonging to another with the intention of permanently depriving the other of it . . .'

Actus reus

The *actus reus* of theft has three elements: 'property', 'appropriation' and 'belonging to another'.

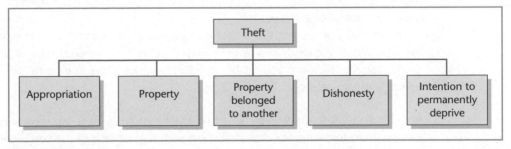

Figure 8.1 Theft

Property

The meaning of 'property' for the purposes of theft is considered in s. 4: 'Property includes money and all other property, real or personal, including things in action and other intangible property.' Intangible property means property that does not exist in a physical sense, and a 'thing in action' (also called a 'chose in action') is a technical term to describe property that does not physically exist but which gives the owner legal rights that are enforceable by a court action. For example, when a bank account is in credit, the bank owes the customer money, and if the bank refuses to pay the customer that money when asked, the customer can sue the bank for the amount in the account. This right is the 'thing in action'. Other examples of things in action are shares in a company and copyright.

The approach to be taken with cheques has caused particular problems. The balance of the account is reduced when the cheque is cashed and can be treated as a thing in action if the cheque was drawn on an account which was in credit or within an agreed overdraft facility (**R** v **Kohn** (1979)). If the account was overdrawn beyond any agreed overdraft facility then the account holder has no right to money held by the bank which could be treated as a thing in action. The case of **R** v **Duru** (1973) suggested that the piece of paper on which the cheque was written could be treated as the property, but this approach was disapproved of in **R** v **Preddy** (1996). Professor J.C. Smith (1997) has argued that cheques should be treated as property on the basis that they are a 'valuable security', rather than focusing on a thing in action or a piece of paper. This approach appeared to be followed by the Court of Appeal in **R** v **Arnold** (1997) but in **R** v **Clark** (2001) the Court of Appeal refused to take this stance, as it considered itself bound by **Preddy**. It said that such an interpretation would have to be accepted first by the House of Lords.

Information cannot be stolen: in **Oxford** v **Moss** (1979) a student who stole an exam paper was not liable for the theft of the information contained in it, though he could have been liable for theft of the piece of paper itself, assuming all other elements of the offence were present. This has implications for business, since it means that trade secrets, such as the recipe for Coca-Cola, cannot be stolen (though there are other legal means of dealing with this problem). This area of the law was reviewed by the Law Commission in its Consultation Paper, *Legislating the Criminal Code: Misuse of Trade Secrets*, of 1997. It noted that most trade secrets were actually taken in the briefcases of employees leaving to join a competitor or to set up their own business. In other countries such conduct tends to fall within theft. In England, such behaviour could give rise to civil remedies for breach of confidence, but the Law Commission considered this to be an inadequate deterrence and recommended that a separate offence should be created of 'unauthorised use or disclosure of a secret'.

Section 4(2) of the Act states that property does not normally include land or things forming part of the land, and severed from it, such as harvested crops or picked flowers. These cannot therefore usually be stolen. However, there are some circumstances in which land can be stolen:

(a) when the defendant is in certain positions of trust, and 'appropriates the land or anything forming part of it by dealing with it in breach of the confidence reposed in him or her';

(b) when the defendant is not in possession of the land and appropriates anything forming part of the land by severing it or causing it to be severed, or after it has been severed;

(c) when a defendant in possession of land under a tenancy appropriates the whole or part of any fixture or structure let to be used with the land.

An example of (b) would be knocking down your neighbour's brick wall and carrying away the bricks, or shaking apples off someone's tree and taking them, or even picking up fruit which has fallen to the ground. 'Severing' simply means that the item has been detached from the land. However – to complicate matters further – there is no theft if the thing severed is growing wild and it is not taken for commercial purposes. Section 4(3) provides: 'A person who picks mushrooms growing wild on any land, or who picks flowers, fruit or foliage from a plant growing wild on any land, does not (although not in possession of the land) steal what he picks, unless he does it for reward or for sale or other commercial purpose.' Under this subsection 'mushroom' includes any fungus, and 'plant' includes any shrub or tree.

Part (c) is aimed at people who rent premises; they may be committing theft if they remove something which is considered a fixture or structure, such as a fixed kitchen cupboard, and take it with them when they move.

Section 4(4) provides that wild animals cannot be stolen unless they have been tamed:

Wild creatures, tamed or untamed, shall be regarded as property, but a person cannot steal a wild creature not tamed nor ordinarily kept in captivity, or the carcase of any such creature, unless either it has been reduced into possession by or on behalf of another person and possession of it has not since been lost or abandoned, or another person is in the course of reducing it into possession.

The main implication of this is that poaching does not normally fall within the offence of theft.

The human body will only be treated as property if it has been altered for the purpose of medical or scientific examination and thereby acquired financial value. In **R** v **Kelly and Lindsay** (1998) the first defendant was an artist who had been granted access to the Royal College of Surgeons so that he could draw anatomical specimens. Aided by the second defendant, a junior technician at the College, he had removed approximately 35 human body parts from the Royal College of Surgeons. They were convicted of theft and their appeals were dismissed.

Appropriation

Section 3(1) defines appropriation: 'Any assumption by a person of the rights of an owner amounts to an appropriation, and this includes, where he has come by the property (innocently or not) without stealing it, any later assumption of a right to it by keeping or dealing with it as owner.'

Thus an 'appropriation' means doing something with the property that the owner has a right to do, but which no one else has the right to do without the owner's permission. This could include selling, keeping, damaging, destroying or extinguishing the property; it is not limited to physically taking the property. In **R** v **Morris** (1983) it was stated that assuming any one of the owner's rights is sufficient to amount to appropriation. This case has been overruled on another point of law, but is still good law on this issue.

8

Non-fraudulent property offences

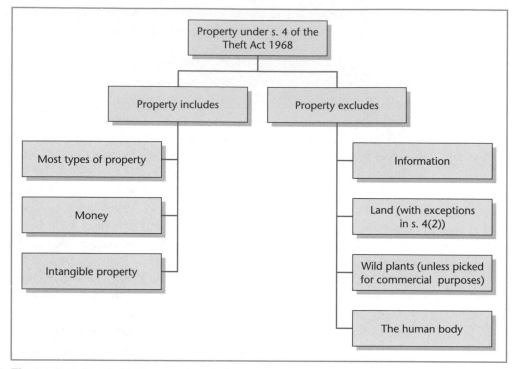

Figure 8.2 Property that can be stolen

The second half of s. 3(1) makes it clear that appropriation covers a situation in which someone gains possession of property without stealing it, but later assumes some right of the owner – for example, where a person is lent a book by a friend and then later refuses to return it. In this example the appropriation would occur at the moment of refusal.

Where someone buys something in good faith, but ownership does not pass because unknown to them the goods are stolen, they will not be treated as appropriating the goods. In the words of s. 3(2): 'Where property or a right or interest in property is or purports to be transferred for value to a person acting in good faith, no later assumption by him of rights which he believed himself to be acquiring shall, by reason of any defect in the transferor's title, amount to theft of the property.'

A situation which caused some problems for the courts was where a defendant assumed some right of the owner, but with the owner's permission. Was this an appropriation? At first glance, the common-sense answer might be 'No'; why should it be illegal to do something to property which the owner allows you to do? The case of **Lawrence v Metropolitan Police Commissioner** (1971) shows that the question is not as simple as that. The case concerned an Italian student, who spoke little English. On arrival in London, he climbed into a taxi at the airport, showing the driver a piece of paper bearing the address of the family with whom he was going to stay. This was not far from the airport, and the fare should have been about 50p. When they arrived, the student tendered a £1 note, but the taxi-driver said that it was not enough. Being unfamiliar with British currency, the student held out his wallet for the taxi-driver to take the correct fare, upon which the driver helped himself to a further £6. The driver was convicted of theft, and appealed on the basis that he had not appropriated the money because the student had consented to his taking it. This argument was rejected by the House of Lords and his conviction upheld.

However, when the question arose again, in **R v Morris** (1983), the House of Lords said that there could only be an appropriation where the acts of the defendant were 'unauthorised', in other words where the owner had not consented to the defendant's acts. The situation in that case was that Morris took goods from the shelves of a supermarket, and switched their price labels with those of cheaper products. He then took them to the checkout and was charged the lower price on the new labels, which he paid. Charged with theft, he argued that there had been no appropriation on the basis that he had not assumed all the rights of the owner. As pointed out above, the House of Lords held that it was not actually necessary to assume all the rights of an owner, so long as at least one was assumed, and they agreed that an appropriation had taken place. In pinpointing exactly when that appropriation occurred, they stated that it was not when the goods were removed from the shelves, since shoppers had implied permission to do that. Appropriation required some 'adverse interference' with the owner's rights which could not be satisfied if the owner's consent had been given. This appeared to be in direct conflict with the House of Lords' judgment in **Lawrence**. The problem was eventually resolved by the House of Lords in **R v Gomez** (1993).

KEY CASE

In **R v Gomez (1993)** the defendant (Gomez) was the assistant manager of a shop selling electrical goods. Ballay sought to buy £17,000 worth of electrical goods from the shop. In payment he tendered some Building Society cheques, which had in fact been stolen and were therefore

> Theft can occur even when the owner's consent to the defendant taking their property.

worthless. Gomez acted as Ballay's accomplice, and persuaded the shop manager to accept these cheques by pretending that the Building Society had confirmed the cheques were 'as good as cash', and not revealing that they were in fact stolen. Both Gomez and Ballay knew that the cheques were worthless. This would have been a fairly straightforward case of obtaining property by deception (an offence discussed in the next chapter), but for some reason Gomez was charged with theft instead. The question of whether appropriation could include an act permitted by the owner arose because Ballay had the owner's authority to take possession. If **Morris** was followed no appropriation would be treated as having occurred, and therefore no liability for theft imposed. The House of Lords decided to opt for the principle established in **Lawrence** instead; **Morris** was thereby overruled on this issue and an appropriation can take place even if the assumption of the owner's rights takes place with the owner's consent.

Gifts

Because the consent of the owner is irrelevant, a person who simply accepts a gift can be treated as appropriating it. This was the view of the House of Lords in **R v Hinks** (2000).

KEY CASE

The victim in **R** *v* **Hinks** (2000) was a 53-year-old man of limited intelligence who had been left money by his father. The defendant had befriended the man and was alleged by

Accepting a gift can amount to an appropriation.

the prosecution to have encouraged him to withdraw £60,000 from his building society account and deposit it in her account. The defence argued that this money was either a gift or a loan. The defendant was convicted of theft and her subsequent appeals were rejected. The majority in the House of Lords took the view that the leading House of Lords judgment of **R** *v* **Gomez** (1993) treated 'appropriation' as covering any assumption by a person of the rights of an owner. The fact that the owner consented to handing over their property was always irrelevant. Appropriation therefore included the acceptance of a valid gift of property. They refused to give a narrower definition of appropriation because they feared that this would 'place beyond the reach of the criminal law dishonest persons who should be found guilty of theft'. Though this approach led to a wide definition of the *actus reus* of theft, they thought that the mental requirements of theft provided an 'adequate protection against injustice'.

Lords Hutton and Hobhouse both gave powerful dissenting judgments. They were of the view that when looking at a potential gift the courts needed to consider whether it was in fact void or voidable under civil law. They criticised the majority decision for failing to draw a distinction between a fully effective gift and one which was vitiated by incapacity, fraud or some other feature. They favoured the approach that had been adopted on the issue in **R** *v* **Mazo** (1996), where such matters had been taken into account. In that case the Court of Appeal had been reluctant to apply **R** *v* **Gomez** where there was no deception. Mazo was working as a maid to Lady S. Over a period of two years Lady S had made out a number of cheques in her favour to the value of £37,000. On one occasion, when Lady S's bank had telephoned her to query the payments, she had abruptly reaffirmed her instructions. Mazo was subsequently charged and convicted of theft of the cheques on the basis that she had taken dishonest advantage of Lady S's mental incapacity. On appeal the conviction was quashed on the ground that there could be no theft if a valid gift had been made. Following the House of Lords' judgment of **R** *v* **Hinks**, **R** *v* **Mazo** is now bad law.

The decision in **Hinks** has the advantage of protecting the vulnerable in society (see on this issue Alan Blogg and John Stanton-Ife (2003) in the bibliography). On the other hand, in his dissenting judgment in **R** *v* **Hinks**, Lord Hobhouse argued very persuasively that the law on appropriation as laid down in **R** *v* **Lawrence** (1971), **R** *v* **Morris** (1983) and **R** *v* **Gomez** (1993) had been misinterpreted by the lower courts and the majority of the House of Lords in that case. In his view **Lawrence** and **Gomez** were not saying that the consent of the owner was never relevant to the issue of appropriation, but simply that on the facts of those particular cases it was not relevant. They did not apply where no fraud had been used to get the property.

The danger of the majority approach in **R** *v* **Hinks** is that there can be a conflict between the criminal law and the civil law, with a convicted thief in theory being able to bring a civil action to recover the stolen property from the alleged victim. The majority acknowledged that ideally civil and criminal law should be in perfect harmony, but they were prepared to accept an interpretation of the law that could lead to conflicts between the two.

The majority of the House of Lords in **R v Hinks** was understandably anxious to try and make the law on theft simple. It appears that they wanted to avoid the problems of **R v Preddy** (discussed in detail at p. 204) of creating technical loopholes by relying on civil law concepts through which morally guilty defendants could avoid criminal liability. While this desire is laudable, the danger is that by taking a firm stance in the context of gifts, where the moral boundaries can be very fine, this could lead to unjust convictions. As Lord Hobhouse points out in his dissenting judgment, the property offences inevitably rely on civil law concepts and it is dangerously artificial to try to ignore them in this type of case. The civil law niceties in **R v Preddy** could have been safely ignored by the House of Lords because they bore no link with the understanding of members of the public of that transaction. By contrast, members of the public are fully able to understand the concept of a gift and will have views on whether a gift should be treated as a valid gift due to the mental incapacity of the donor or the use of undue influence or coercion by the donee. Yet the House of Lords wants these issues to be ignored when considering the question of appropriation. It seems to be an oversimplification of the law to say that consent can never be relevant to appropriation and only relevant to the issue of dishonesty. Lord Hobhouse's interpretation of **Lawrence** and **Gomez** appears to be preferable, according to which these cases are merely stating that the existence of a consent does not always prevent the existence of an appropriation.

Remoteness

The act constituting the *actus reus* of the offence must not be too remote to amount to an appropriation. This point was emphasised in the case of **R v Briggs** (2003). In 1997 an elderly couple, Mr and Mrs Reid, decided to sell their home to move to a new house near to their great-niece. The sale was handled on their behalf by a firm of licensed conveyancers, Bentons. The solicitors acting for the sellers of the new house were called Metcalfs. On 6 October 1997 the appellant wrote to Bentons enclosing a letter of authority in the appellant's handwriting but which was signed by the Reids. In it, the Reids instructed Bentons to send by telegraphic transfer £49,950 of the sale proceeds to Metcalf's bank account and to remit the outstanding balance of the sale price to the bank account of Mr and Mrs Reid. The title in the new property was transferred to the appellant and subsequently registered in her and her father's name. At first instance, the appellant was convicted of theft of the £49,950.

On appeal to the Court of Appeal the central issue was whether there had been an appropriation. The trial judge had directed the jury that 'there may be an appropriation of the credit balance . . . notwithstanding that it was transferred with the Reids' consent, if that consent was induced by fraud'. The appellant submitted that such a payment did not amount to an appropriation, as it was made in accordance with, and as a result of, the Reids' instructions. The appeal was allowed. The Court of Appeal held that there had been no appropriation and therefore no theft. The trial judge had misdirected the jury. The Court of Appeal cited with approval the case of **Naviede** (1997) where Hutchison LJ stated:

> We are not satisfied that a misrepresentation which persuades the account holder to direct payment out of his account is an assumption of the rights of the account holder as owner, such as to amount to an appropriation of his rights within section 3(1) of the 1968 Act.

The Court of Appeal concluded in this case that: 'where a victim causes a payment to be made in reliance on deceptive conduct by the defendant, there is no appropriation by the defendant'. The key issue was that of remoteness. The Court of Appeal held that appropriation is a word which connotes a physical act which must not be a remote action triggering the payment which gives rise to the charge. It considered that an act of deceiving an owner to do something fell outside the meaning of appropriation.

Thus, in the light of this case, certain acts will be treated as too remote to amount to an appropriation. But the cut-off point between those acts which can amount to an appropriation and those which cannot because they are too remote is not sufficiently clear. The Court of Appeal is trying to draw a distinction between those acts which are 'the key' to the property and those which are not. If the defendant signs or forges a cheque or gives a bank instructions, those acts are treated as the key to the property and can amount to an appropriation. Acts which are further removed from the final transfer of the property or where the defendant has induced the victim to act as the key to the property, will not amount to an appropriation because the defendant's acts are treated as too remote.

The court seems anxious to develop the concept of remoteness in this context in order to draw some distinction between theft and the fraud offences. But the reason the boundaries between theft and fraud have broken down is because of the ruling that the consent of the owner to the taking of their property is irrelevant. This has been taken to its extreme in the case of **Hinks**. While this principle has become an established part of the criminal law, perhaps it is time to reconsider this approach and the case of **DPP** v **Gomez** (1993). Trying to draw a distinction between theft and fraud offences on the basis of remoteness is artificial. There is no moral difference between a case where the facts are found to be too remote and fall outside theft, such as the current one, and where they are not found to be too remote.

Belonging to another

The property appropriated must belong to another just before the appropriation takes place. Section 5 states: 'Property shall be regarded as belonging to any person having possession or control of it, or having in it any proprietary right or interest . . .' Thus if property is treated as belonging to someone under civil law it will also belong to that person for the purposes of theft.

In fact, the definition goes further than this, and includes mere possession without rights of ownership. So if, for example, someone takes a book you have borrowed from the library, they can be said to have appropriated property belonging to you, even though you do not actually own the book.

This means that owners can in some cases be liable for stealing their own goods. The point is illustrated by the case of **R** v **Turner** (1971). Turner had taken his car to a garage to be repaired. When the repairs were done, he saw the car parked outside the garage and drove it away without paying for the work that had been carried out. He was liable for stealing his own car, because the garage had possession of the car at the time he took it, and all the other elements of theft existed. In **R v Marshall** (1998) the defendants had obtained used tickets for the underground from members of the public and resold them. This activity was causing London Underground to lose revenue. The defendants were convicted of stealing the tickets from London Underground. They appealed on the basis that the tickets no longer belonged to London Underground as they had sold them to members of the public. Their appeals were dismissed as on the reverse of each ticket it was stated that the tickets remained the property of London Underground. Thus the company remained owners of the ticket for the purposes of theft after the sale transaction.

Lost property still belongs to the original owner and can be stolen. On the other hand, abandoned property cannot be the subject of a theft. In **R v Rostron** (2003) the defendant had gone to a golf course at night and collected golf balls from a lake without the golf course owner's permission. The Court of Appeal said it would be a question of fact for the jury to decide whether the golf balls had been lost or abandoned by their original owners, and upheld his conviction.

A problematic situation is where employees take advantage of their position to make an illegitimate profit. In the past, under civil law laid down in **Lister & Co v Stubbs** (1890), such a profit has been treated as belonging to the employee, which means that the employee could not be liable for theft, because of the absence of property belonging to another. This was the case in **Powell v McRae** (1977) where the defendant operated an entrance turnstile at Wembley Stadium. A person arrived who did not have a ticket and the defendant allowed the person in on payment of £2. He had no authority from his employer to do this and he pocketed the money himself. No liability for theft was incurred. However, the civil law may have changed on this point. In **Attorney-General for Hong Kong v Reid** (1993) the Privy Council suggested that if a person makes an illegal profit from his or her work that profit belongs to the employer. If this is followed there could be liability for theft.

TOPICAL ISSUE

Donations to charity

When money is collected for charity, there is a danger that the person who collected the money might keep it, instead of passing it on to the charity concerned. This happened in **R v Dyke and Munro** (2001), where the defendants arranged street collections claiming that the money was for the Hands of Hope Children's Cancer Fund. They raised substantial sums of money but did not hand this over to the charity. The defendants were charged with theft. The judge directed the jury that they could convict if the defendants 'stole money belonging to person or persons unknown' (meaning the members of the public who made the donations). The defendants were convicted but their appeal was successful because they should have been charged with stealing money from the charity, not from 'person or persons unknown'. When members of the public put money in the collection tin, they ceased to own it. The money was held on trust for the charity by the people who collected it. So, the charity immediately became the owners of the money for the purposes of theft.

Keeping property in one's possession

Subsections (3) and (4) of s. 5 deal with the specific problem of where the owner hands someone else their property for some reason, and this person proceeds to keep the property where there is a moral obligation to hand it back. According to s. 5(3), where property is handed over to another, but that other has a legal obligation to deal with the property in a particular way, the property is treated as still belonging to the original owner. The subsection states: 'Where a person received property from or on account of another, and is under an obligation to the other to retain and deal with that property or its proceeds in a particular way, the property or proceeds shall be regarded (as against him) as belonging to the other.' This covers situations such as a builder asking a client for money to buy materials; under s. 5(3), the money still belongs to the client, even though the builder has possession of it, and the builder is obliged to use it to buy bricks; any other use would be appropriation of property belonging to another. This is only the case where the money is clearly handed over for a particular purpose, and would not apply if the builder requested the £100 as a deposit or part-payment. In such a situation the builder would not be liable for theft even if the building work was never actually carried out, because by having possession of the money, he or she would be treated as its owner (on the other hand the builder may have committed a fraudulent offence, and in any case the client would have a civil remedy).

The obligation to treat the property in a particular way must be a legal obligation recognised under civil law. This was the view of the Court of Appeal in **R** v **Breaks and Huggan** (1998). The defendants worked for a company which placed insurance on behalf of clients with Lloyds of London through Lloyds' brokers. They were charged with theft in relation to premiums received from clients in respect of business negotiated with a firm of Lloyds' brokers but to whom no payments were made. The prosecution case was that the premiums received by the company remained the property of the clients, being destined for onward transmission to the brokers, and the company owed an obligation to the clients to use the payments for that purpose but did not do so, spending them in some other way. The trial judge had ruled that the purpose of s. 5(3) was to avoid provisions of the civil law and accordingly there was a case to go to the jury. The defendants were convicted and appealed against conviction on the grounds that the judge's ruling was wrong. Their appeal was allowed and the Court of Appeal stated that the civil law determined whether or not a duty to deal with property in a particular way existed. Judges in criminal cases are understandably reluctant to become involved with the civil law; but in cases of this kind they will have to do so.

R v **Hall** (1972) is an example of a case that fell outside s. 5(3). A client had paid a travel agent a deposit for a holiday. The money had been paid into the company's general account, but the agent went bust, leaving the client unable to recover the deposit. It was held that the travel agents had not stolen the deposit because, for the purposes of the Theft Act 1968, the money belonged to them, so they could not appropriate it. Section 5(3) did not apply as they had no legal obligation to spend the money in a particular way; it was simply security for them against the client cancelling.

In **Davidge** v **Bunnett** (1984), the defendant was one of a group of people sharing a flat. His flatmates gave him money to pay certain household bills, but he spent the money on himself, leaving the bills unpaid. He was held liable for theft; the money was given to him for the specific purpose of paying the bills, and since that meant it still belonged to his flatmates, his alternative use of it amounted to appropriation. This authority was applied by the Court of Appeal in **R v Wain** (1995). The appellant had raised almost £3,000 for a 'Telethon' organised by Yorkshire Television. He opened a separate bank account under the name 'Scarborough Telethon Appeal' and deposited the money into the account. With the permission of the telethon organisers, he was permitted to transfer the money from this account to his own and then wrote out a cheque to the organisers for the sum due. The cheque was dishonoured and he was convicted of theft. His appeal failed, and the court stated that Wain was under an obligation to retain at least the proceeds of the sums collected, if not the actual notes and coins: he had to keep in existence a fund sufficient to pay the bill. Therefore the sums credited to his own account remained property belonging to another because of s. 5(3).

In **R v Klineberg and Marsden** (1998) the Court of Appeal stated that s. 5(3) could be used to avoid the problems of **R v Preddy** in suitable cases. In **R v Preddy** s. 5(3) could not apply because the money had been lent for the purposes of a mortgage and it was used in this way. In **R v Klineberg and Marsden** the money was lent to buy timeshares in apartments in Lanzarote. The money was not used in this way and s. 5(3) could apply. J.C. Smith in his commentary on this case in the *Criminal Law Review* (1999) has argued that the reasoning of the Court of Appeal was wrong because s. 5(3) requires that the property has been 'received' and he considers that as there has not been an obtaining for the purposes of s. 15 (discussed in the next chapter) there has not been a receipt. However, with all due respect, his reasoning is flawed – there was an obtaining under s. 15 in **Preddy** but it was simply not of property belonging to another. Thus there is also a receipt, and s. 5(3) deems that the property shall be treated as having belonged to another.

Section 5(4) provides that if a person receives property by mistake and has a legal obligation to give it back, then for the purposes of the 1968 Act it will be treated as belonging to the original person who handed it over by mistake – so that failure to hand it back will count as appropriation. In **Attorney-General's Reference (No. 1 of 1983)** (1984), a police officer received an extra £74 in her wages, due to an accounting error by her employer, and failed to alert anyone or give it back. The Court of Appeal held that this amounted to appropriation.

Passage of ownership

The point at which appropriation occurs is important in situations where ownership will pass to the thief, since if appropriation happens after ownership has passed, the property appropriated does not belong to another. Prior to **Gomez**, this caused frequent problems. In **Dip Kaur v Chief Constable for Hampshire** (1981) the defendant was in a shoe shop where some of the shoes were £4.99 and some were £6.99. She noticed that one shoe which should have been priced at £6.99 bore a label saying £4.99. Carefully positioning this shoe on top, she went to the cash desk hoping that the cashier would not notice the incorrect price label. The cashier did not notice and sold the shoes at the lower price. When the mistake was discovered the defendant was charged with theft. Her conviction was quashed on appeal on the basis that by the time the appropriation took place at the cash till, the shoes already belonged to her because the cashier had authority to accept the lower price and did so.

Recent cases avoid this problem by interpreting appropriation as taking place at a very early stage – as soon as any right of an owner has been assumed, even if the owner consented to that assumption. **Dip Kaur** would probably be decided differently now since the decision in **Gomez** established that the shop's consent to the appropriation was irrelevant. In the light of **Gomez** it could be argued that the appropriation took place when the defendant assumed the right of the owner to have possession of the goods by taking them off the shelves, even though this is an action to which the shop had consented. At this earlier time it is clear that the goods still belonged to the shop, so today a conviction might be upheld if the same facts of **Dip Kaur** were to appear before a court.

The issue of passage of ownership can still be relevant in relation to goods which lose their own identity when supplied to another – such as food when consumed, or petrol when poured into the tank of a car. Because it is no longer possible to take back the original goods, they are treated in civil law as belonging to the receiver as soon as they lose their identity; while with other types of goods this usually occurs only at the time of payment. Therefore such items can only be stolen before they lose their identity; all the elements of theft must be present at this point. This was the ground for the decision in **R v McHugh** (1976), which concerned the theft of petrol. By contrast, in **Corcoran v Wheat** (1977) the defendant was not liable for theft when he ate a meal and only afterwards formed the dishonest intent not to pay. During the time when the property belonged to another he lacked the *mens rea* of theft, and when he did have the *mens rea* for theft, he could not commit the *actus reus* because by then the property belonged to him.

KEY CASE

An important House of Lords' judgment on the application of the property offences is **R v Preddy** (1996). This case concerned three appeals that had been joined together as they raised the same legal issues. The appellants had been involved in mortgage frauds, which means they had made applications for mortgages giving false information, for

> Property could not belong to another before it belonged to the defendant if it had never existed before the defendant owned it.

example about their income or the value of the property they were seeking to purchase. The mortgage advances were paid by the lenders to the appellants by cheque, telegraphic transfer and the Clearing House Automated Payment System (CHAPS) – a computerised electronic transfer of funds. The House of Lords allowed their appeals. Lord Goff concluded that the debiting of a bank account and the corresponding crediting of another's bank account did not amount to the obtaining of property belonging to another by deception. This fraud offence used to be contained in s. 15 of the Theft Act 1968 and though it has been repealed by the Fraud Act 2006, the legal analysis of banking transactions is still of interest. The House of Lords took the view that the initial bank balance in the lender's account was a thing in action. This initial thing in action did not simply pass to the borrower. Instead, it was extinguished and a completely new thing in action was created in the borrower's account that belonged to the borrower. The new property that the appellants had obtained was not the property that had belonged to the victim and therefore no property that had belonged to another had been obtained for the purposes of s. 15. This was true for all three modes of payment.

Initially it was thought that the reasoning in **Preddy** would apply to theft and mean that not only was there no fraud offence under s. 15, but also no theft. The Court of Appeal in **R** v **Graham** (1997) had commented that where the reasoning in **Preddy** was fatal to a conviction of obtaining property by deception, it was likely to be fatal on a conviction of theft as well. However, the Court of Appeal appears to have significantly revised its view of the law in **R** v **Williams (Roy)** (2000). In that case the Court of Appeal found that an appropriation took place when the credit balance in the victim's account was reduced and the equivalent sum was transferred into the defendant's account. The appellant ran a building business, and the prosecution alleged that between 1992 and 1997 he used the business to target and cheat vulnerable elderly householders. Having gained their trust, he would charge them excessive prices for building work. In ten cases he was paid in cash and in the rest he was paid by cheque. The appellant was convicted of theft and appealed. His appeal was rejected as the Court of Appeal found that the appellant had appropriated property belonging to another. It found that the act of effecting the reduction of the credit balance in the victim's account, and the transfer of a like sum to the defendant's account, amounted to an appropriation within the meaning of s. 1 of the Theft Act 1968. The defendant had exercised the victim's right as the owner of the credit balance to dispose of it; and this was an appropriation of the victim's property. The Court of Appeal cited with approval the case of **R** v **Kohn** (1979), where a company director was authorised to sign cheques on behalf of the company. In fact he signed some cheques for his own benefit and the signing of the cheques amounted to an appropriation.

In **R** v **Williams (Roy)**, the case of **R** v **Preddy** was distinguished. It was stated that that case was concerned with the offence of obtaining property by deception under (the now repealed) s. 15 of the Theft Act 1968 and not with the appropriation of property. While property was only obtained once the defendant's account was credited, an appropriation took place at an earlier stage. The Court of Appeal appears to have been anxious to find a workable solution to this type of case. **Preddy** had created real problems for the prosecution and unnecessary loopholes for defendants to avoid criminal liability, even where they had clearly done something which was immoral and which the general public would describe as criminal.

Another way of avoiding the problems in **Preddy** was put forward, *obiter*, in **Re Holmes** (2004). It was suggested that the money credited to the new account would be held on a constructive trust for the rightful owners. Thus, when it was subsequently taken out of the account that transaction would amount to an appropriation of property belonging to another.

Mens rea

The *mens rea* of theft has two elements: intention permanently to deprive, and dishonesty.

Intention permanently to deprive

The defendant must have the intention of permanently depriving the other of the property. The victim need not actually be deprived permanently of the property, so long as the prosecution can prove that the defendant intended permanent deprivation.

Merely borrowing without permission does not amount to theft. For this reason, although cars count as property which can be stolen, there are a number of specific property offences dealing with the taking of cars, because cars are so frequently taken with the intention of driving them for a while and then dumping them, otherwise known as 'joyriding'.

Section 6 contains certain exceptions where a mere borrowing will be sufficient to constitute a theft. The Court of Appeal observed in **R** v **Fernandes** (1996) that the critical notion in s. 6 is whether a defendant intended 'to treat the thing as his own to dispose of regardless of the other's rights'. Everything else in the section is merely specific illustrations of this point, rather than restrictions on where s. 6 applies. Section 6(1) provides:

> A person appropriating property belonging to another without meaning the other permanently to lose the thing itself is nevertheless to be regarded as having the intention of permanently depriving the other of it if his intention is to treat the thing as his own to dispose of regardless of the other's rights; and a borrowing or lending of it may amount to so treating it if, but only if, the borrowing or lending is for a period and in circumstances making it equivalent to an outright taking or disposal.

This section was applied in **Chan Man-sin** v **Attorney-General for Hong Kong** (1988). The defendant was a company accountant. He drew a forged cheque on the company's account knowing that the company would not be permanently deprived of their money because the bank would have a legal obligation to reimburse them for any money paid out as a result of such a trick. This knowledge, he argued, meant he lacked any intention permanently to deprive the company of its property. The Privy Council held that his situation fell within s. 6(1); he intended to treat the company's property as his own to dispose of regardless of the company's rights.

If the defendant takes the victim's property and says he will return it upon payment then, even though the defendant intends to return the property to the victim, under s. 6 the defendant will be deemed to have an intention to permanently deprive. This was the position in **R** v **Raphael** (2008) where two defendants assaulted the victim and drove away with his car. They then telephoned the victim and said they would return his car to him if he paid them £500. They were prosecuted for conspiracy to rob (note that robbery includes in its definition the commission of theft – see p. 209) and the Court of Appeal upheld their conviction. On the issue of *mens rea*, the Court stated that this was exactly the type of scenario where s. 6 was meant to apply as the defendants had an intention to treat the car as their own to dispose of regardless of the owner's rights.

The specific illustration of where s. 6(1) can arise, that is where a defendant borrows property for a period and in circumstances making it equivalent to an outright taking or disposal, was the focus of **R** v **Lloyd** (1985). The defendant removed films from a cinema for a few hours, made illegal copies of them, and then returned them. He argued that since he intended all along to return the films, he had no intention permanently to deprive; nor had he borrowed the films in circumstances making the borrowing equivalent to an outright taking or disposal. The Court of Appeal accepted that he was not liable for theft. Lord Lane CJ felt that to fall within this part of s. 6(1) there must be an intention 'to return the "thing" in such a changed state that it can truly be said that all its goodness or virtue is gone'. Just what this situation would cover is still unclear: would it, for example, include borrowing someone's season ticket without permission and returning it when it has almost – but not quite – expired?

In **R** v **Mitchell** (2008) the defendant had abandoned a person's car. The Court of Appeal stated that this could not amount to theft because there was no intention to permanently deprive as the defendant intended the car to be returned to the owner and when it was returned it would not have lost all its value for the purposes of the second limb of s. 6(1).

Section 6(2) states:

> Without prejudice to the generality of subsection (1) above, where a person, having possession or control (lawfully or not) of property belonging to another, parts with the property under a condition as to its return which he may not be able to perform, this (if done for purposes of his own and without the other's authority) amounts to treating the property as his own to dispose of regardless of the other's rights.

This subsection is most likely to apply where someone has pawned another's property without their permission and is uncertain whether they will be able to satisfy the condition for the property's return.

Conditional intent

A person has conditional intent where he or she intends to do something if certain conditions are satisfied. In **R** v **Easom** (1971), it was held that such an intent was not sufficient for theft; the person will only start to intend permanently to deprive when the condition is satisfied and they go on to carry out their intention. The defendant was in a cinema, where the victim had placed her handbag on the floor. He picked up the bag, intending to steal if there was anything worth taking in it. In fact there were only a few tissues and aspirins inside, so he put the bag back. Unknown to him, the owner of the bag was a policewoman in plain clothes; the bag was attached to her wrist by a piece of thread and she was fully aware of what was happening. The defendant was charged with theft, but his conviction was quashed on the ground that he had no intention permanently to deprive the victim of any property. This may be considered to be a rather lenient interpretation of the law.

Intention to return similar property

By contrast, the courts have taken a very harsh view of defendants who take property, intending to return similar property in the future: for example, a cashier who takes £5 out of the till, intending to pay it back later. Even if the person actually replaces the money, they can be treated as intending to deprive the shop permanently of the specific banknote that was removed – **R** v **Velumyl** (1989). In such cases the defendant may plead that they lack the other element of the *mens rea*: dishonesty.

Dishonesty

The 1968 Act only provides a partial definition of dishonesty, leaving some discretion to the courts. Unusually, the statutory definition, contained in s. 2(1), makes use of examples, stating three situations in which a defendant should not be deemed dishonest:

(a) if he appropriates property in the belief that he has in law the right to deprive the other of it, on behalf of himself or of a third person; or

(b) if he appropriates the property in the belief that he would have the other's consent if the other knew of the appropriation and the circumstances of it; or

(c) (except where the property came to him as trustee or personal representative) if he appropriates the property in the belief that the person to whom the property belongs cannot be discovered by taking reasonable steps.

If the facts of a particular case do not fall within any of these examples, the courts have to look to the common law to decide whether the defendant has been dishonest.

KEY CASE

Following a period of uncertainty, the Court of Appeal laid down a test for dishonesty in **R v Ghosh** (1982). Lord Lane said:

> Under common law a person is dishonest if they behave dishonestly by the standards of reasonable people and the defendant realised this.

In determining whether the prosecution has proved that the defendant was acting dishonestly, a jury must first of all decide whether according to the ordinary standards of reasonable and honest people what was done was dishonest. If it was not dishonest by those standards, that is the end of the matter and the prosecution fails. If it was dishonest by those standards, then the jury must consider whether the defendant himself must have realised that what he was doing was by those standards dishonest.

Thus, the court should first ask whether the defendant had been dishonest by the ordinary standards of reasonable and honest people. If the answer was 'Yes', the court should then ask whether the defendant realised that he or she had been dishonest by those standards. If the answer to this second question was also 'Yes', there was dishonesty.

Where a court feels it necessary to give a **Ghosh** direction, it was stated in **Hyam v DPP** (1974) that it was preferable, though not compulsory, for that court to use Lord Lane's precise words.

 Sentence

The maximum sentence for theft is seven years' imprisonment.

TOPICAL ISSUE

Shoplifting

One of the most common forms of theft in practice is shoplifting. In 2004/5 there were 280,461 recorded offences of theft from shops. However, it is estimated that this figure actually represents only 3 per cent of such incidents because most shoplifting offences are not reported to the police. Only 1 per cent of shoplifting incidents result in a conviction but, because of the scale of the problem of shoplifting, shoplifters still represent the largest single group of offenders sentenced in British courts each year. A third of all women given custodial sentences by the court are being sentenced for shoplifting. Custodial sentences rather than fines are increasingly being given for shoplifting: in 1994 custody was used in 5 per cent of cases, in 2004, custody was used in 21 per cent of cases.

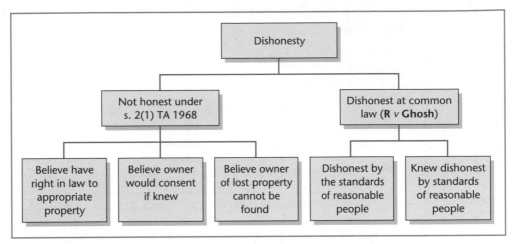

Figure 8.3 Dishonesty

Robbery

This offence is defined by s. 8 of the Theft Act 1968: 'A person is guilty of robbery if he steals, and immediately before or at the time of doing so and in order to do so, he uses force on any person or puts or seeks to put any person in fear of being then and there subjected to force.'

Robbery is most simply described as aggravated theft, as it usually involves theft accompanied by force or a threat of force. This can cover anything from a mugging in the street to a big bank robbery with guns.

Actus reus

The *actus reus* of robbery is the *actus reus* of theft, plus one of three things:

- he uses force in order to steal; or
- he puts a person in fear of force in order to steal; or
- he seeks to put a person in fear of force in order to steal.

Force is not defined in the Act. In **R v Dawson and James** (1978) it was said that it was an ordinary English word and its meaning should be left to a jury. A mere nudge so that someone lost their balance could be sufficient. So in practice a relatively low level of physical contact can amount to force for the purposes of robbery.

The force or threat of force must be used in order to steal, so there is no robbery if the force is only used when trying to escape after the theft, or if the force was accidental. The force or threat of force must also be used immediately before or at the time of the theft. The theft occurs at the time of the appropriation, but again the courts have taken a very flexible approach to this rule. In **R v Hale** (1979) the two defendants broke into a house. While the first defendant went upstairs and stole a jewellery box, the second stayed downstairs and tied up the owner of the house. It was impossible to say whether these activities took place at precisely the same moment or whether the jewellery box was taken

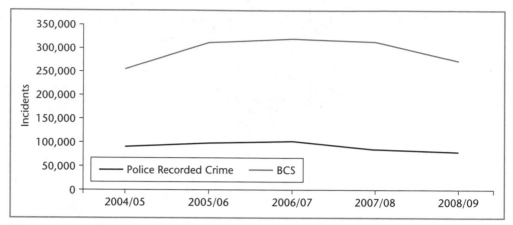

Figure 8.4 Police recorded and British Crime Survey robbery, 2004/05 to 2008/09

Source: Crime in England and Wales, 2008/09, Home Office Statistical Bulletin, p. 27 and p. 31.

after the force was applied. Despite this, the Court of Appeal upheld the convictions on the basis that appropriation was a continuing act, and it was open to the jury to conclude on these facts that it was still continuing at the time the force was applied.

The case of **Hale** was confirmed in **R** *v* **Lockley** (1995). The appellant and two others took cans of beer from an off-licence and when the shopkeeper approached they used violence. It was submitted on appeal in the light of **Gomez** that the theft was complete before the force was used and the robbery charge should not have been left to the jury. Their appeal was dismissed because actually **Gomez** was irrelevant to this point and **Hale** was still good law that appropriation was a continuing act.

In the case of a threat, the threat must be of force 'then and there', rather than at some time in the future. If the defendant sought to make someone fear being subjected to force, it does not matter that the person was not actually put in fear of the use of force because, for example, he or she was very brave. In **R and B** *v* **DPP** (2007) the appellants were among a group of teenagers who surrounded a 16-year-old boy and demanded that he hand over his mobile phone and money. When he refused, B held the victim's arms and went through his pockets while R stood in front of the victim. B took the victim's money, watch and travel card. The victim stated afterwards that he had not felt threatened or scared but had merely been a bit shocked. On upholding the convictions for robbery, the High Court stated that it is the intention of the perpetrator rather than the fortitude of the victim which is key to determining whether a defendant sought to make a victim fear force and transform an incident from a basic theft into the more serious offence of robbery.

Mens rea

The defendant must have the *mens rea* of theft. This requirement led to surprising results in **R** *v* **Robinson** (1977). The defendant threatened his victim with a knife in order to obtain payment of money he was owed. He was convicted of robbery, but the conviction was quashed by the Court of Appeal because the defendant lacked dishonesty according to the Theft Act; he fell within s. 2(1)(a) of the Act because he honestly believed he had a legal right to the money, even though he may have known that his mode of seeking repayment was dishonest.

Completion of the offence

The question has arisen as to when the offence of robbery is completed; in other words when a person is liable for the full offence and not just its attempt. It was held in **Corcoran** v **Anderton** (1980) that the full offence takes place when the appropriation is complete. In that case, two defendants tried to take a woman's handbag by force. They managed to grab hold of the bag, but then dropped it and ran off. The court held that the appropriation was complete when the defendants got hold of the handbag, and therefore they were liable for robbery and not just attempted robbery, regardless of the fact that they had failed to run off with the bag.

Sentence

The maximum sentence for robbery is life imprisonment. In 2001, most robbers aged 18 and over received a custodial sentence. More than half of those under 18 received a community sentence, though the number has gone down following Lord Woolf's sentencing guidelines for mobile phone robberies. The frequent use of custody for young offenders has been heavily criticised by the chairperson of the Youth Justice Board.

In 2006 the Sentencing Guidelines Council issued sentencing guidelines for the offence of robbery. A sentence of imprisonment will usually be imposed, unless there are exceptional circumstances. A community order may be appropriate for a young offender where only a minimal level of force was used. A non-custodial sentence will be appropriate for minor robberies or where there are mitigating factors, particularly when the offence is carried out by a young person.

Criticism

The number of robberies recorded by the police doubled during the 1990s, primarily because of the growing problem of young people robbing mobile phones from other young people. Research by Morrison and O'Donnell (1994) found that threats of force were used more often than actual force in robbery cases. Injuries were caused in 7 per cent of armed robberies, not usually by firing the gun, but by punching, kicking, or using the firearm as a blunt instrument. The clear-up rate for robbery is low, with only 3 per cent of all robberies leading to an offender being sentenced by a court, and robbers are broadly aware of this.

Andrew Ashworth (2002) has carried out a study of how the law on robbery is working in practice. He observes that the offence of robbery is extremely broad, drawing no distinction between minor street muggings where a teenager pushes their victim to grab a mobile phone, and organised bank robberies by professionals. A well-known example of a robbery by professional criminals is the Great Train Robbery (**Wilson** (1964)) where £2.6 million was stolen, and the train driver was injured. Professional, organised robberies are becoming less common because of increased preventative measures and more lucrative criminal activity with lower risks. Today, most robberies are street muggings.

Non-fraudulent property offences

The breadth of the offence of robbery carries the danger that relatively minor criminal conduct can incur unduly harsh sentences, with the offence of robbery potentially carrying a life sentence. The dividing line between robbery and theft is often a very fine one. 'Force' for the purposes of robbery has been interpreted to include minor violence, such as pulling on a handbag, or barging into someone. But the impact of a finding of force is significant because it raises the maximum possible sentence from seven years' to life imprisonment.

Andrew Ashworth argues persuasively that the law should distinguish between the different degrees of force currently falling within robbery. He recommends that the current single offence should be divided into two separate offences, which would depend on the gravity of harm used or threatened. A practical consequence would be efficiencies in procedure. At the moment all robberies have to be tried in the Crown Court. A more minor offence reflecting the gravity of the criminal conduct could be tried in the cheaper magistrates' court.

Burglary

Burglary is generally associated with someone breaking into a private home and stealing from it. In law, burglary covers this situation, but it also goes further. Section 9 of the Theft Act 1968 defines the offence:

(1) A person is guilty of burglary if—
   (a) he enters any building or part of a building as a trespasser and with intent to commit any such offence as is mentioned in subsection (2) below; or
   (b) having entered any building or part of a building as a trespasser he steals or attempts to steal anything in the building or that part of it or inflicts or attempts to inflict on any person therein any grievous bodily harm.
(2) The offences referred to in subsection (1)(a) above are offences of stealing anything in the building or part of a building in question, of inflicting on any person therein any grievous bodily harm, and of doing unlawful damage to the building or anything therein.

As there is a higher maximum sentence available if the property burgled was a dwelling, s. 9 technically creates four offences:

- s. 9(1)(a) of a dwelling
- s. 9(1)(a) of a non-dwelling
- s. 9(1)(b) of a dwelling
- s. 9(1)(b) of a non-dwelling.

The offences in ss. 9(1)(a) and 9(1)(b) will be considered in turn.

Burglary under s. 9(1)(a)

The s. 9(1)(a) offences are committed by entering any building or part of a building as a trespasser, and with intent to commit theft, grievous bodily harm or criminal damage. In the past the offence could also be committed where there was an intention to rape, but this form of the offence was removed by Schedule 7 to the Sexual Offences Act 2003.

Actus reus

There are three elements: trespass, entry, and a building or part of a building.

Trespass

Trespass is a civil law concept which essentially means being on someone else's property without authority. A person who has authority to be on land is not a trespasser there, but someone who has authority to enter the land for a particular purpose will become a trespasser if they enter it for some other purpose.

KEY CASE

In **R v Jones and Smith** (1976) the defendant had left home, but had his father's permission to visit whenever he liked. One night the son came home and stole the television. The Court of Appeal upheld his conviction for burglary because, while he had permission to enter the house, in stealing the television he had gone beyond what he had permission to do, and was therefore a trespasser at the time of the theft.

> For the purposes of burglary, a person is a trespasser if they exceed the scope of the owner's permission to be in the building.

Entry

In order for there to be a burglary the defendant must enter property. This may seem a straightforward concept, but the question of exactly what entering entails has caused quite a lot of judicial debate. In **R v Collins** (1972) the defendant had been out drinking, and at the end of the evening decided to find a woman with whom he could have sex, without her consent if necessary. Seeing an upstairs light on in a house, he climbed up a ladder and saw a girl asleep naked on her bed. He went back down the ladder and took off all his clothes, except for his socks, then climbed back up the ladder and stood on the windowsill, intending to climb inside. At this point the girl woke up, and mistaking him for her boyfriend, invited him in. She then consented to sexual intercourse and it was only afterwards that she realised her mistake. In order for the defendant to be liable for burglary under s. 9(1)(a), he had to have entered the house as a trespasser with the intention to rape. Once the girl invited him in, he was no longer a trespasser, so he could be liable only if he had entered before that invitation was made. The court stated that for there to be an entry it must be 'substantial' and 'effective'. The appeal was allowed as there had been a misdirection at the trial.

However, two subsequent cases suggest that the entry need be neither substantial nor effective. First, in **R v Brown** (1985) a shop window had been broken and the defendant was found standing on the pavement, with the top half of his body inside the shop, rummaging among the goods inside. According to the Court of Appeal in that case the critical question was whether the entry had been 'effective'; it considered the word 'substantial' an unhelpful addition. On the facts, the jury was entitled to conclude that there was an effective entry and the defendant's appeal against conviction was rejected.

Secondly, in **R v Ryan** (1996) the appellant was found with his head and right arm trapped in a downstairs window in the middle of the night. He was subsequently convicted of burglary. He appealed on the ground that there had not in law been an entry. His appeal was rejected on the basis that his partial entry was sufficient, and that it was

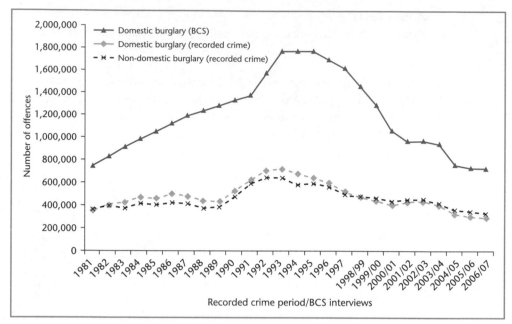

Figure 8.5 Trends in British Crime Survey and police recorded burglary, 1981 to 2006/07

Source: Crime in England and Wales, 2006/07, p. 75.

irrelevant whether he was capable of stealing anything, which raises doubts as to whether the entry must be 'effective'.

Building or part of a building

The place which the defendant enters as a trespasser must be a building or part of a building. A building is not defined, but s. 9(3) states that it includes inhabited vehicles or vessels (for example, caravans and houseboats).

The term 'part of a building' was considered in **R v Walkington** (1979). The accused entered a department store during opening hours. This was not a trespass, since everyone has implied permission to enter open shops (although if it could be proved that the defendant was entering with the intention to steal, he may have been entering as a trespasser as he would have been exceeding his authority to enter – **Jones and Smith** (1976)). The defendant then went behind a counter – an area where customers did not have permission to go – and took money from a till. The court held that the counter area was part of a building and, having entered this area as a trespasser, the defendant was liable for burglary.

Coincidence in time

The defendant must be a trespasser *at the time of entry* into the building or part of the building. In **R v Laing** (1995) the defendant had been found in the stockroom of a department store after the store had been closed. Initially he was convicted of burglary but on appeal his conviction was quashed because the prosecution had relied on his entry into the shop and had failed to provide evidence that at that time he was a trespasser. There was no doubt he was a trespasser when he was found, but he needed to have been a trespasser when he entered. This problem could have been avoided if the prosecution had relied on his entry into the stockroom as they had relied on the 'entry' into the area behind the counter in **R** v **Walkington**.

Mens rea

There are two elements: intention or recklessness as to the trespass, and intention to commit the ulterior offence.

Intention/recklessness as to the trespass

In civil law there is no need for *mens rea* to be proved in relation to a civil trespass, but in criminal law it is necessary in the context of burglary. The relevant form of *mens rea* is intention or subjective recklessness. In the case of **Collins** the defendant probably lacked intention or recklessness to trespass if he entered the house after the girl had invited him in.

Intention to commit the ulterior offence

The defendant must intend to commit one of the offences listed in s. 9(2), known as the ulterior offences: theft; inflicting grievous bodily harm; unlawful damage to the building or anything in it. The intention must exist at the time of entry. Provided the defendant enters with the relevant intention, the full offence of burglary is committed at the point of entry; the defendant need not actually proceed to commit the ulterior offence.

Conditional intent

It was observed above that conditional intention is probably not enough for theft. However, for burglary, conditional intention can be sufficient; so if, for example, a defendant breaks into a house intending to steal if he or she finds anything worth taking, or to commit grievous bodily harm to a particular person if that person is in the house, then that intention may be sufficient for burglary.

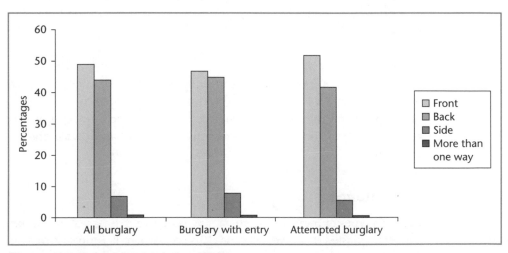

Figure 8.6 Point of entry in burglaries

Source: Crime in England and Wales, 2007/08 – Supplementary Tables.

Some confusion over this issue was caused by the case of **R** v **Husseyn** (1977). The defendants opened the door of a van in which there was a holdall containing valuable sub-aqua equipment. They were charged with attempted theft of that equipment, and the indictment specified that they had opened the van door with the intention of stealing the equipment. The Court of Appeal allowed their appeal, saying: 'It cannot be said that one who has it in mind to steal only if what he finds is worth stealing has a present intention to steal.' As a result, it was thought for a time that conditional intention was not sufficient for burglary, despite the fact that this would cause serious practical problems for prosecutors, since it is quite common for burglars to intend stealing only if they find something worth the trouble once they have broken in. The issue was reconsidered in **Attorney-General's References (Nos 1 and 2 of 1979)**, and the Court of Appeal made it clear that the remark in **Husseyn** quoted above should be understood as a criticism of the indictment in that case, which had been inaccurate: the defendants could not have opened the van door intending to steal the equipment since they did not know it existed. Had the indictment simply stated that the defendants opened the van door with the intention of stealing the contents of the van, the problem could have been avoided. The outcome is that there can be a conviction where the defendant only has conditional intent, so long as the indictment is appropriately worded.

Burglary under s. 9(1)(b)

The s. 9(1)(b) burglary offences are committed where the defendant enters any building or part of the building as a trespasser, and then steals, attempts to steal, inflicts or attempts to inflict grievous bodily harm.

Actus reus

The prosecution must prove all the elements of the *actus reus* of a s. 9(1)(a) offence, and in addition prove that the *actus reus* of the ulterior offence (in this case stealing, attempting to steal, inflicting or attempting to inflict grievous bodily harm) has been carried out. This offence is committed not at the time of entry but at the time of committing the ulterior offence.

Mens rea

As for the s. 9(1)(a) offence, the prosecution must prove intention or recklessness as to the trespass. In addition, they must prove the *mens rea* of the ulterior offence (in grievous bodily harm this includes recklessness). The defendant need not have the *mens rea* of this ulterior offence at the time of entry, but must have it when the ulterior offence is committed.

Sentence

For both types of burglary, the maximum sentence is 14 years' imprisonment where the property burgled is a dwelling, and 10 years' where it is not a dwelling. The Court of Appeal has laid down sentencing guidelines for burglaries in **R** v **Saw** (2009) which place an emphasis on the impact of the burglary on the victim, rather than the cash value of

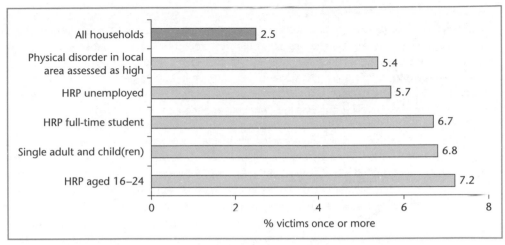

Figure 8.7 Households most at risk of burglary, 2008/09, British Crime Survey

Source: *Crime in England and Wales*, 2008/09, Home Office Statistical Bulletin, p. 77.

the burglary. These guidelines replace earlier Court of Appeal guidance in **R** *v* **McInerney and Keating** (2002) which had been criticised as too lenient partly because they emphasised the use of community sentences for first time burglars. The Powers of Criminal Courts (Sentencing) Act 2000 provides for the imposition of a minimum sentence of three years for repeat burglars. How effective this provision will be is a matter of debate. Research suggests the level of property crime is more likely to be reduced through methods of prevention and by tackling drug addiction rather than the use of heavier sentences, particularly as Home Office statistics show that only 2 per cent of offences lead to a conviction. For example, in the 1990s security was tightened up for the use of credit cards, with better card design and card distribution. This reduced credit card fraud by almost half, from £166 million in 1991 to £97 million in 1996.

TOPICAL ISSUE

Burglary in society

According to the British Crime Survey (2003), domestic burglaries had fallen by 45 per cent in the previous ten years. There are likely to be a number of reasons for this. These include improved home security (for example, more homes are protected by burglar alarms) and low unemployment. In addition, in the past burglars frequently targeted expensive electrical equipment, such as videos and music centres, but the value of this equipment has significantly decreased. Today burglars are more likely to take smaller items, such as money, credit cards, cheque books and mobile phones. People tend to carry these things with them on the street, which may be why alongside the reduction in burglaries, there has been an increase in street robberies.

   Research into house burglaries has been carried out for the Home Office by Hearnden and Magill in 2004. They found that the main reasons given for carrying out a burglary was the need for money to buy drugs. In choosing which property to target the burglars' first consideration was where they might find high value goods to steal. Some burglars said they would not burgle flats because there were fewer escape routes out of the property, there was more chance of being observed by other residents in the block and

8

Non-fraudulent property offences

flats were often inhabited by old people (a group whom many declared they were unwilling to victimise). Others preferred burgling flats to any other type of property because of the large number of potential victims available once past the main entrance to the building. They generally burgled a place near to their own home due to laziness, wanting to get money quickly to buy drugs, needing to avoid walking far with heavy goods, and the benefits of knowing the area in detail. Over half of the sample knew who lived in the property they were burgling because they were either a friend, associate in crime or neighbour.

Over two-thirds of the burglars questioned said they had returned to a property they had burgled before and taken items from it on a second occasion, frequently within a month of the first burglary. This was often due to the fact that they knew there were still goods worth taking because they had been told this by an associate, they had left the goods the last time as they were too big to carry, they had seen goods being delivered or they had seen empty boxes being placed outside for dustmen to collect.

Burglars generally entered from the back of the property. They either used force or prised open a window or door using a screwdriver or other similar tool. Sometimes they did not need to break in because the window or door was already open. Once they had entered, over one-third of burglars searched for specific goods because they had a likely buyer or because they thought these goods would be in the house and they would be able to remove them. They generally spent less than ten minutes inside the property.

Aggravated burglary

Aggravated burglary is defined in the Theft Act 1968, s. 10:

A person is guilty of aggravated burglary if he commits any burglary and at the time has with him any firearm or imitation firearm, any weapon of offence, or any explosive; and for this purpose—

(a) 'firearm' includes an air gun or air pistol, and 'imitation firearm' means anything which has the appearance of being a firearm, whether capable of being discharged or not; and

(b) 'weapon of offence' means any article made or adapted for use for causing injury to or incapacitating a person, or intended by the person having it with him for such use; and

(c) 'explosive' means any article manufactured for the purpose of producing a practical effect by explosion, or intended by the person having it with him for that purpose.

Actus reus

Aggravated burglary essentially involves committing a burglary when equipped with a weapon. The defendant must be in possession of the weapon at the time of the burglary (as was noted above, the moment at which the burglary occurs depends on whether it is a s. 9(1)(a) or s. 9(1)(b) offence).

So long as the defendant was in possession of the weapon when the offence was committed, it does not matter that they only armed themselves seconds before. This point was made in **R** v **O'Leary** (1986). The accused entered a house as a trespasser, then took a knife from the kitchen and went upstairs. He proceeded to use the knife to force the victim to hand over some of his property. Liability was incurred for aggravated burglary, because the accused fell within the aggravated form of a s. 9(1)(b) offence, which is committed at the time the ulterior offence is committed, by which point he was equipped with the knife.

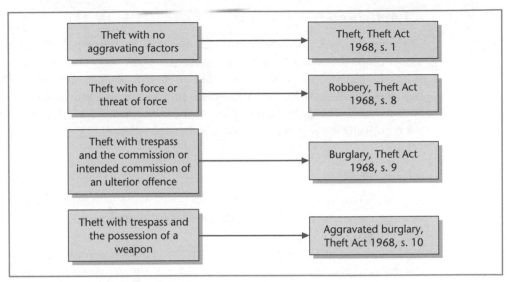

Figure 8.8 Theft and aggravated forms of theft

Mens rea

The defendant must have the *mens rea* of burglary and also know that he or she has the weapon. In **R** *v* **Russell** (1984), the defendant had known he had a weapon, but by the time of the burglary had forgotten it was there. He was liable for the burglary only and not for aggravated burglary.

There is no need to prove that the defendant had any intention to use the weapon. In **R** *v* **Stones** (1989) the defendant was equipped with a kitchen knife at the time of committing the burglary, but argued in his defence that he had no intention to use the knife during the burglary; he said he was carrying it because he feared being attacked by a gang. Nevertheless, he was held liable for the aggravated offence.

Sentence

The maximum sentence for aggravated burglary is life imprisonment.

Blackmail

Blackmail is defined in s. 21 of the Theft Act 1968:

> A person is guilty of blackmail if with a view to gain for himself or another or with intent to cause loss to another, he makes any unwarranted demand with menaces, and for this purpose a demand with menaces is unwarranted unless the person making it does so in the belief—
> (a) that he has reasonable grounds for making the demand; and
> (b) that the use of the menaces is a proper means of reinforcing the demand.

Actus reus

There must be a demand supported by menaces. In **Harry** (1974), the organisers of a student rag week wrote to shopkeepers requesting donations to charity, and stating that shopkeepers who gave donations would be given immunity from the inconvenience of rag week activities. These activities included throwing flour and water and tickling people with feathers. The court held that while there was a demand, the activities threatened were not sufficiently grave to be classified as menaces.

Mens rea

The defendant must intend to make his or her demand with menaces, and s. 34(2) specifies that this demand must be made with a view to making a financial gain or causing a financial loss.

Section 21 contains a statutory defence that a person will not be liable for blackmail if the demand was warranted. A demand will only be warranted if the defendant believes that he or she has reasonable grounds for making the demand *and* that the means used to reinforce the demand are proper. The scope of this defence has been narrowed by the case of **R** *v* **Harvey** (1981). The appellant had paid £20,000 to the victim who promised to supply him with cannabis. In fact the victim had no intention to supply any cannabis, and simply pocketed the money. When the appellant realised this, he threatened to kill, maim and rape unless he was repaid. The appellant claimed that his demand for repayment was warranted, but the court held that the means used to make the demand were clearly not proper, since it could not be proper to threaten to do something that was known to be unlawful or morally wrong.

Sentence

The maximum sentence for blackmail is 14 years' imprisonment.

Handling

The definition of handling can be found in s. 22 of the Theft Act 1968:

> A person handles stolen goods if (otherwise than in the course of the stealing) knowing or believing them to be stolen goods he dishonestly receives the goods, or dishonestly undertakes or assists in their retention, removal, disposal or realisation by or for the benefit of another person, or if he arranges to do so.

The most obvious type of handling is where someone receives stolen goods, but the offence actually covers a much wider range of activities. While there is only one offence of handling, there are 18 different potential ways that it can be committed, and in practice almost anything a person does with stolen goods may be classified as handling, provided it takes place after the original theft ('otherwise than in the course of stealing'). Thieves can be liable for handling the goods they have stolen, provided that they are dealing with those goods in a totally separate incident from the original theft (for example, selling them on to someone else).

Actus reus

The *actus reus* may be committed in any of the following ways: (a) receiving stolen goods; (b) arranging to receive them; (c) undertaking the keeping, removing, disposing of or realising of stolen goods by or for the benefit of another person, or helping with any of those things; (d) arranging to do any of the things in (c).

Stolen goods are very broadly defined in s. 24 of the Act. They include goods obtained not just by theft but also by blackmail or under the fraud offence defined in s. 15 of the Theft Act 1968 (discussed in the next chapter).

In **R** *v* **Kanwar** (1982) a wife was held liable for handling because she lied to the police in order to protect her husband who had brought stolen goods into the house. She was held to be assisting in the retention of those goods.

Mens rea

The handler must know or believe the goods to be stolen and have behaved dishonestly. The concept of 'dishonestly' for these purposes has the common law meaning laid down in **Ghosh** and s. 2(1) of the Theft Act 1968 does not apply.

Sentence

The maximum sentence for this offence is 14 years' imprisonment.

Taking without consent

Section 12 of the Theft Act 1968 is the most appropriate offence for joyriders. Such offenders are not normally liable for theft of the car as they have no intention to permanently deprive. Section 12(1) states:

> . . . a person shall be guilty of an offence if, without having the consent of the owner or other lawful authority, he takes any conveyance for his own or another's use or knowing that any conveyance has been taken without such authority, drives it or allows himself to be carried in or on it.

Any passengers as well as the driver can be liable for this offence. The vehicle must have been taken; simply using it, for example, to sleep does not suffice. The vehicle must move, but it need not be driven. Thus in **Bow** (1977) there was a 'taking' when the defendant had released the handbrake of the car and coasted some 200 yards down a hill. But in **Stokes** (1982) the defendant had not 'used' the car when for a joke he pushed a car round a corner in order to create the impression that it had been stolen.

In relation to the *mens rea* of the offence there is no requirement to prove dishonesty, nor an intention to permanently deprive. Section 12A of the 1968 Act contains an aggravated form of this offence which arises when a person commits the s. 12 offence in various aggravating circumstances such as driving dangerously, injuring someone or

8

Non-fraudulent property offences

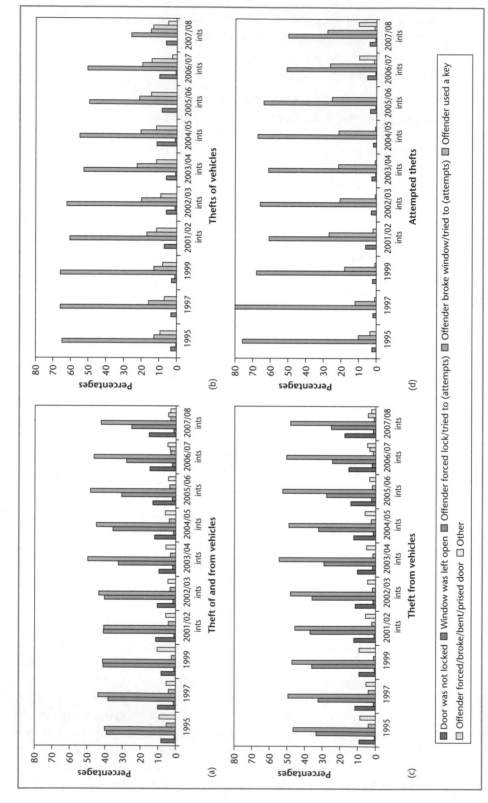

Figure 8.9 Method of entry in vehicle-related thefts 1995 to 2007/08

Source: Crime in England and Wales, 2007/08: Supplementary Tables.

damaging property, including the vehicle. In **Marsh** (1997) the accused had taken a car and was driving it when a woman stepped out in front of the car and was knocked down. The accused was guilty of the aggravated offence despite not being at fault for the accident.

Retaining a wrongful credit

The Theft (Amendment) Act 1996 inserts a new offence of retaining a wrongful credit under s. 24A of the Theft Act 1968. This offence occurs when a person's bank account is wrongfully credited and, knowing or believing this to be the case, they dishonestly fail to take reasonable steps to secure that the credit is cancelled. A credit is 'wrongful' if it derives from any of the following offences: theft, blackmail, fraud (contrary to s. 1 of the Fraud Act 2006, discussed in the next chapter) or stolen goods. This offence is very similar to the offence of handling and was introduced to criminalise people who benefited from the proceeds of fraud.

Criminal damage

The offence of criminal damage is contained in the Criminal Damage Act 1971. The basic offence of criminal damage is contained in s. 1(1) of that Act: 'A person who without lawful excuse destroys or damages any property belonging to another intending to destroy or damage any such property or being reckless as to whether any such property would be destroyed or damaged shall be guilty of an offence.'

Actus reus

This consists of destroying or damaging property that belongs to another. The definition of property is different from that in theft, in that it includes land, but does not include intangible property – so you can cause criminal damage to a field but not to a company share. The question of whether the property belonged to another is essentially the same as for the law of theft.

The damage caused must not be purely nominal. In **A (a juvenile) v R** (1978), the defendant spat on a policeman's raincoat. The spit was easy to remove from the coat by wiping it with a damp cloth and so the damage was considered insufficient to amount to criminal damage. Similarly, in **Morphitis v Salmon** (1990), a scratch on a scaffolding bar was held not to be criminal damage because it did not affect the value or usefulness of the scaffolding. By contrast, in **Hardman v Chief Constable of Avon and Somerset Constabulary** (1986) the defendant had drawn a large painting with water soluble paints. If it had been left in place, rain would eventually have washed it away, but the local authority incurred expense by washing it off. Due to this expenditure, the painting was held to constitute criminal damage. In **Lloyd v DPP** (1991) the defendant's car had been clamped for illegal parking and in trying to remove it he damaged the clamp, which amounted to criminal damage.

8

Non-fraudulent property offences

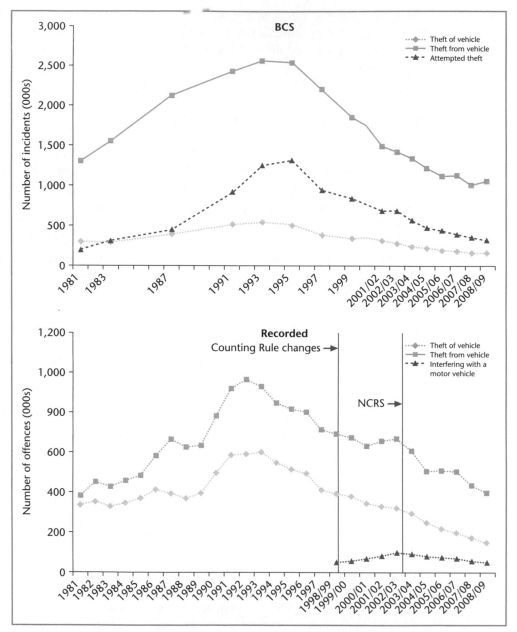

Figure 8.10 Trends in BCS and police recorded vehicle-related theft, 1981 to 2008/09

Source: Crime in England and Wales, 2008/09, Home Office Statistical Bulletin, p. 79.

Mens rea

Section 1(1) of the 1968 Act, quoted above, requires that the defendant must have either intended or been reckless as to the criminal damage. In the past **Caldwell** recklessness applied in this context, since that case was itself concerned with an offence contained in the Criminal Damage Act 1971. Subjective recklessness now applies, following the case of **R v G and another** (2003).

Defence

Section 1(1) provides that the defendant is only liable if the damage was done 'without lawful excuse'. A defendant will have a lawful excuse if they can prove some general defence (such as self-defence) or if their conduct falls within one of the categories of behaviour listed in s. 5(2) of the Act, which states that a person has a lawful excuse:

(a) if at the time of the act or acts alleged to constitute the offence he believed that the person or persons whom he believed to be entitled to consent to the destruction of or damage to the property in question had so consented, or would have consented to it if he or they had known of the destruction or damage and its circumstances; or

(b) if he destroyed or damaged . . . the property in question . . . in order to protect property belonging to himself or another . . . and at the time of the act or acts alleged to constitute the offence he believed—

(i) that the property, right or interest was in immediate need of protection; and

(ii) that the means of protection adopted or proposed to be adopted were or would be reasonable having regard to all the circumstances.

Section 5(3) states that, for the purposes of this statutory defence, it is immaterial whether the relevant belief is justified or not, so long as it is honestly held.

While (a) is a purely subjective test, the courts have introduced an objective element to (b), despite the subjective wording of that subsection.

KEY CASE

In **R v Jones** (2004) the defendants had caused damage to property at military bases in the UK. They were charged with a range of offences and argued in their defence that they were trying to prevent the impending military attack on Iraq, which they claimed was illegal. The House of Lords held that the defendants would have a lawful excuse within s. 5(2)(b) if:

> The statutory defence to criminal damage contains both a subjective and objective element.

- they acted to prevent damage to property (this did not need to be unlawful damage to property, so that the court did not need to rule on whether the war in Iraq was lawful);
- they believed that property in Iraq was in immediate need of protection; and
- they believed the property damage was reasonable having regard to all the circumstances.

The first issue contained an objective test, while the second and third issues were subjective tests. On the facts the defence was unsuccessful.

In **Hill and Hall** (1989) the appellants had been involved in the longstanding demonstrations against the presence of American weapons in the UK, best known by the activities of the Greenham Common women. They were convicted of an offence under the Criminal Damage Act because they had equipped themselves to cut the perimeter fence of the military base, so that they could stage a demonstration on the site. In their defence it had been submitted that they had a lawful excuse within the meaning of s. 5(2)(b), as they had acted in order to protect the property of those living nearby, which would be destroyed in the event of the kind of attack which they felt the presence of the weapons rendered highly likely. By encouraging the authorities to remove the military equipment such a threat would be removed. This argument was rejected both by the trial court and the Court of Appeal. The Court of Appeal said that in relation to the property damage, two questions had to be asked: first, whether the defendants did think they were protecting property; and secondly, whether as a matter of law they were protecting homes in the vicinity. The court concluded that the answer to the second question was 'No', because the threat of harm to the property concerned was too remote. This result has been criticised by some as distorting the clear wording of the Act for political ends.

The defendant in **R v Kelleher** (2003) had entered an art gallery and decapitated a statue of Margaret Thatcher. He was charged with criminal damage, and sought to rely on the defence in s. 5(2)(b). He argued that his aim was to draw attention to his opposition to Margaret Thatcher's policies, which continued to influence English society and which he considered made the world a more dangerous place to live, and would eventually lead to the destruction of the planet. The trial judge rejected his defence because the defendant's primary purpose had been to attract publicity for his views, and this motive did not fall within the defence. There was no evidence that he genuinely believed that his action was necessary in order to protect property, a right or interest.

Criminal damage endangering life

Section 1(2) of the Criminal Damage Act 1971 defines an aggravated offence of criminal damage, which contains all the elements of ordinary criminal damage, with an additional requirement that the defendant intended or was reckless as to the endangering of life. This offence has a maximum sentence of life imprisonment.

There is no need to prove that life was in fact endangered, so long as it is proved that the defendant intended such danger, or was reckless as to whether it occurred. There must be a connection between the destruction of or damage to property and the intention or recklessness to destroy life. This link was not proved in **R v Steer** (1987). The defendant fired a gun at someone, intending to hurt them, but missed. The bullet ricocheted off the window, damaging it. He was held not liable under s. 1(2); the shooting had both endangered life and caused criminal damage, but the danger to life was not caused by the criminal damage.

Arson

Arson is another form of aggravated criminal damage, committed where all the elements of s. 1(1) of the 1971 Act are proved but in addition the destruction or damage was caused by fire. Again the maximum sentence is life imprisonment as fire is seen to be an unusually dangerous weapon, given its tendency to get out of control very quickly. **Caldwell, Elliott** and **R v G and another**, discussed at pp. 18 and 24, were all concerned with this offence.

In **Hunt** (1977) the defendant was charged with arson and he argued that he fell within the statutory defence of having a lawful excuse. He was a deputy warden in an old people's home, and had been concerned about the fire risks posed by the building. Unable to persuade the fire officer to improve the conditions, he decided to set fire to the property to show the authorities what the risks were, in the hope of prompting them to take action. He was held to fall outside the defence under s. 5 as he was not acting to protect property.

? Answering questions

As a general comment make sure you do not make the mistake of talking about offences under, for example, s. 2 or s. 6 of the Theft Act 1968. These sections are not offences in their own right, they are merely elements that may need to be proved for the offence of theft.

1 **What offences, if any, have been committed as a result of the following occurrences in the Heaton department store?**

(a) D, who works in the electrical department, borrows an electric drill, without telling his supervisor, for the weekend. When he returns the drill its motor has burnt out. *(10 marks)*

(b) E, a cleaner of low intelligence, finds a diamond ring in the ladies' cloakroom. She keeps the ring. When this is discovered she says she did not realise it would be possible to find the owner. *(10 marks)*

(c) F, the flower department manager, picks daffodils growing wild in nearby woods. He sells them in the store and keeps the proceeds. *(10 marks)*

(d) G, a customer in the self-service food department, takes a number of items from a shelf and places them into the wire basket provided by the store. G then takes a tin of salmon from the shelf and places it into his coat pocket. G is detained by a store detective before he leaves the food department. G admits it was his intention to take the salmon and the other items in the basket from the store without payment. *(20 marks) (OCR)*

(a): the most relevant offence here is theft. While all the elements of this offence would need to be mentioned – the dishonest appropriation of property belonging to another with the intention of permanently depriving – the issues of intention and dishonesty would need particular consideration on these facts. Section 6 should be looked at closely. You could also discuss liability for criminal damage.

No other property offences would appear to have been committed. There is no fraud offence because nobody has been deceived; D simply fails to tell his supervisor anything about borrowing the drill. Nor are there any of the aggravating factors to bring the incident within burglary (no trespass) or robbery (no force or threat of force).

(b): this is also concerned with theft. Given the cleaner's low intelligence, and her belief that the owner could not be found, dishonesty is a key issue here, and in particular its definition in s. 2(1)(c). Note that it is the defendant's actual belief that is important for s. 2(1)(c): it is a subjective and not an objective criterion.

(c): the first question is whether there has been a theft of the daffodils, and the crucial issue is whether the daffodils constitute property, as defined by s. 4(3). Because they were picked for commercial purposes they are treated as property. F may also be liable for theft of the illegal profit, if **Attorney-General for Hong Kong** v **Reid** is preferred over **Lister** v **Stubbs**. The fact that customers consented to handing over the money will not prevent there being an appropriation: **Gomez**.

F might also be liable for obtaining property by deception (discussed in the next chapter), the deception being the implied representation that he had authority to sell the daffodils. A crucial question will be whether the obtaining was by the deception (**Laverty**) as it may be that the customers did not care whether he had authority or not; all they may have been interested in was the quality of the flowers.

(d): here we are again concerned with theft. Your answer will be clearer if you deal with the items in the basket and the tin of salmon separately. The critical issue in both cases will be whether G's conduct is sufficient to constitute an appropriation. In the light of **Gomez**, both acts are likely to suffice, because G only needs to have assumed a right of an owner, and here he has done that by taking possession. The old idea that theft could only be committed if the person had left the store or gone past the point of payment is no longer true. Before **Gomez**, only the salmon would have been appropriated because putting the other items in the basket was authorised conduct – **R** v **Morris**. As a result of **Gomez**, it no longer matters that the owner had impliedly consented to these actions.

2 Bill and Tim go to their local hypermarket. On an earlier visit, the hypermarket manager told Tim he was not to return again as he suspected him of being connected with a spate of thefts which his store had recently suffered. As they are about to enter the hypermarket, Bill and Tim agree that they will unplug all the freezers in the store, thus spoiling the frozen foods which they contain. They each enter the store, Bill heading for the freezers in the meat department and Tim heading for the freezers in the dairy produce department. Bill unplugs several freezers and spoils £1,000 worth of meat. On his way out, he enters a room marked 'Staff only' and takes £25 from an unattended handbag. As he is leaving the room, a store detective challenges him, whereupon Bill strikes him on the nose and makes good his escape. As Tim is about to unplug a freezer full of cheeses, he is challenged by Mary, a shop assistant. Knowing that Mary is having a secret affair with the manager, Tim threatens to reveal this fact to Mary's husband if she stops him. He then unplugs the freezer, spoiling its contents, Mary being too frightened to intervene.

Consider the criminal liability of
(a) **Bill** (*25 marks*) and
(b) **Tim** (*25 marks*)
ignoring any possible offences of conspiracy and secondary participation. (*OCR*)

The key offences here are criminal damage and burglary, along with the blackmail of Mary and a non-fatal offence against the storekeeper. Take them one at a time, working through the ingredients for liability in the order you find them in this chapter. Notice that you are not required to discuss conspiracy or secondary participation – this means you will get no marks for comments on these points, so do not waste your time, even if you are dying to show off your knowledge in the field!

In discussing burglary it is important to discuss s. 9(1)(a) and s. 9(1)(b) burglary; both are relevant on these facts. You should also consider whether the defendants are trespassers and both **Collins** and **Jones and Smith** can be analysed on this point.

3 **Is the concept of appropriation too broadly defined?**

The concept of appropriation is discussed at pp. 195–200. Appropriation has undoubtedly been given an extremely broad meaning by the courts. Its basic definition can be found in s. 3 of the Theft Act 1968. In **Morris** they stated that there only needs to be an appropriation of one of the rights of the owner, not all of the rights of the owner. **Gomez** confirmed **Lawrence** and stated that there could be an appropriation even where the owner had consented to the defendant taking their property. This was taken to an extreme in the case of **Hinks**, because the court concluded that there could be an appropriation where the defendant simply accepts a gift. By giving appropriation a very wide meaning, the key issue in determining liability for theft moves to the requirement of dishonesty. It also means that there is a considerable overlap between theft and the fraud offences. In addition, there can be a conflict between the civil and the criminal law (see p. 198).

4 **Professor J.C. Smith has observed that 'anyone doing anything whatever to property belonging to another, with or without the authority or consent of the owner, appropriates it; and if he does so dishonestly and with intent, by that act or any subsequent act, permanently to deprive, he commits theft'** (J.C. Smith (1997) *The Law of Theft*, London: Butterworths, p. 2)
Is the law of theft too harsh?

This question requires an examination of the scope of theft. In particular, it raised the issue of the definition of appropriation following cases such as **Gomez** and **Hinks** and whether an appropriation now includes any dealings with another's property, placing all the emphasis on the issue of *mens rea*. Can this approach be justified on the basis that vulnerable people need the protection of the criminal law, and is there a risk of a conflict with the civil law? Given the wording of the question, you could critically analyse other aspects of the definition of theft, such as the way that 'dishonesty' has been interpreted.

Summary

Theft

Theft is defined in s. 1 of the Theft Act 1968: 'A person is guilty of theft if he dishonestly appropriates property belonging to another with the intention of permanently depriving the other of it . . .'

Actus reus

The *actus reus* of theft has three elements: 'property', 'appropriation' and 'belonging to another'.

Property

Under s. 4: 'Property includes money and all other property, real or personal, including things in action and other intangible property.' Information cannot be stolen: **Oxford** v **Moss** (1979). Section 4(2) of the Act states that property does not normally include land or things forming part of the land, and severed from it, such as harvested crops or picked flowers.

Appropriation

Section 3(1) states: 'Any assumption by a person of the rights of an owner amounts to an appropriation.' The consent of the owner is irrelevant: **R** v **Gomez** (1993). As a result, a person who simply accepts a gift can be treated as appropriating it: **R** v **Hinks** (2000).

Belonging to another

Section 5 lays down that: 'Property shall be regarded as belonging to any person having possession or control of it, or having in it any proprietary right or interest . . .' Subsections (3) and (4) of s. 5 deal with the specific problem of where the owner hands someone else their property for some reason, and this person proceeds to keep the property despite a moral obligation to hand it back. According to s. 5(3), where property is handed over to another, but that other has a legal obligation to deal with the property in a particular way, the property is treated as still belonging to the original owner. Under s. 5(4) if a person receives property by mistake and has a legal obligation to give it back, then for the purposes of the 1968 Act it will be treated as belonging to the original person who handed it over by mistake – so that failure to hand it back will count as appropriation.

Mens rea

The *mens rea* of theft has two elements: intention permanently to deprive, and dishonesty. Section 6 contains certain exceptions where a mere borrowing will be sufficient to constitute a theft. The critical notion in s. 6 is whether a defendant intended 'to treat the thing as his own to dispose of regardless of the other's rights'. As regards the issue of dishonesty, s. 2(1) gives a partial definition. Where this does not resolve the matter the courts will have resort to the common law definition of dishonesty contained in **R** v **Ghosh** (1982).

Robbery

This offence is defined by s. 8 of the Theft Act 1968: 'A person is guilty of robbery if he steals, and immediately before or at the time of doing so and in order to do so, he uses force on any person or puts or seeks to put any person in fear of being then and there subjected to force.'

Actus reus

The *actus reus* of robbery is the *actus reus* of theft, plus using force against a person or seeking to put him or her in fear of being subjected to force.

Mens rea

The defendant must have the *mens rea* of theft.

Burglary

There are two main forms of burglary defined in s. 9(1)(a) and (b) of the Theft Act 1968.

Burglary under s. 9(1)(a)

The s. 9(1)(a) offences are committed by entering any building or part of a building as a trespasser, and with intent to commit theft, grievous bodily harm or criminal damage. Trespass is a civil law concept which essentially means being on someone else's property without authority. The defendant must have intended to be a trespasser or been reckless about the issue.

Burglary under s. 9(1)(b)

The s. 9(1)(b) burglary offences are committed where the defendant enters any building or part of the building as a trespasser, and then steals, attempts to steal, inflicts or attempts to inflict grievous bodily harm. This offence is committed not at the time of entry but at the time of committing the ulterior offence. The prosecution must prove intention or recklessness as to the trespass. In addition, they must prove the *mens rea* of the ulterior offence.

Aggravated burglary

Aggravated burglary is defined in the Theft Act 1968, s. 10. People are guilty of aggravated burglary if they commit any burglary and at the time they have with them any firearm or imitation firearm, a weapon, or any explosive. Defendants must have the *mens rea* of burglary and also know that they have the weapon.

Blackmail

Blackmail is defined in s. 21 of the Theft Act 1968. People are guilty of blackmail if, with a view to gain for themselves or another or with intent to cause loss to another, they make any unwarranted demand with menaces. Defendants must intend to make their demand with menaces.

Handling

The definition of handling can be found in s. 22 of the Theft Act 1968. People handle stolen goods if (otherwise than in the course of the stealing) knowing or believing them to be stolen goods they dishonestly receive the goods, or dishonestly undertake or assist in their retention, removal, disposal or realisation by or for the benefit of another person, or if they arrange to do so.

Taking without consent

Section 12 of the Theft Act 1968 criminalises joyriders and their passengers. In relation to the *mens rea* of the offence there is no requirement to prove dishonesty, nor an intention to permanently deprive.

Retaining a wrongful credit

Section 24A of the Theft Act 1968 provides that an offence is committed when a person's bank account is wrongfully credited, and knowing or believing this to be the case they dishonestly fail to take reasonable steps to secure that the credit is cancelled.

Criminal damage

Under s. 1(1) of the Criminal Damage Act 1971 an offence is committed where a person without lawful excuse destroys or damages any property belonging to another intending to destroy or damage any such property or being reckless as to whether any such property would be destroyed or damaged.

8

Non-fraudulent property offences

Criminal damage endangering life

Section 1(2) of the Criminal Damage Act 1971 defines an aggravated offence of criminal damage, which contains all the elements of ordinary criminal damage, with an additional requirement that the defendant intended or was reckless as to the endangering of life.

Arson

Arson is another form of aggravated criminal damage, committed where all the elements of s. 1(1) of the 1971 Act are proved but in addition the destruction or damage was caused by fire.

Reading list

Ashworth, A. (2002) 'Robbery re-assessed' [2002] *Criminal Law Review* 851.

Blogg, A. and Stanton-Ife, J. (2003) 'Protecting the vulnerable: legality, harm and theft', 23(3) *Legal Studies* 402.

Griew, E.J. (1985) 'Dishonesty – the objections to Feely and Ghosh' [1985] *Criminal Law Review* 341.

Heaton, R. (2001) 'Deceiving without thieving' [2001] *Criminal Law Review* 712.

Reading on the internet

The report *Crime in England and Wales 2005/06* is available on the website of the Home Office at:

http://www.homeoffice.gov.uk/rds/crimeew0506.html

The report *Decision-making by house burglars: offenders' perspectives* (I. Hearnden and C. Magill, 2004, Home Office Findings 249) is available on the website of the Home Office at:

http://www.homeoffice.gov.uk/rds/pdfs04/r249.pdf

Visit **www.mylawchamber.co.uk/elliottcriminal** to access multiple choice questions, flashcards and practice exam questions to test yourself on this chapter.

Use **Case Navigator** to read in full some of the key cases referenced in this chapter:

- DPP *v* Gomez (Edwin) [1993] AC 442
- Ghosh [1982] QB 1053; [1982] 3 WLR 110
- R *v* G [2003] UKHL 50; [2004] 1 AC 1034

9 Fraudulent property offences

This chapter explains that:

- the key fraud offences are contained in the Fraud Act 2006;

- a general fraud offence is contained in s. 1 of the 2006 Act;

- section 11 of the 2006 Act contains an offence of obtaining services dishonestly; and

- the offence of making off without payment is contained in s. 3(1) of the Theft Act 1978.

Introduction

The fraudulent property offences have been the subject of a major legislative reform. The Fraud Act 2006 has been passed and was brought into force on 15 January 2007. This Act has replaced most of the old fraud offences with a new general fraud offence.

Until 2007, the key fraud offences were contained in the Theft Act 1968, the Theft Act 1978 and the Theft (Amendment) Act 1996. The central concept of these offences was the existence of a deception which amounted to lying – either expressly or impliedly. The basic fraud offence was obtaining property by deception contained in s. 15 of the Theft Act 1968, which stated that:

> A person who by any deception dishonestly obtains property belonging to another with the intention of permanently depriving the other of it, shall on conviction on indictment be liable to imprisonment for a term not exceeding ten years.

Most of the elements of this offence were given the same or a similar meaning to that for theft, which we have discussed in the previous chapter. Other offences included obtaining a money transfer by deception (s. 15A of the Theft Act 1968, introduced by the Theft (Amendment) Act 1996); obtaining a pecuniary advantage by deception (s. 16 of the Theft Act 1978); obtaining services by deception (s. 1 of the Theft Act 1978) and evasion of liability by deception under s. 2 of the Theft Act 1978.

Problems with the pre-2007 fraud offences

As was observed at the start of Chapter 8, the Theft Act 1968 was created because the previous law on the property offences was complex and confused. It had developed in a piecemeal way, and in many cases the law was stretched to fit behaviour which the

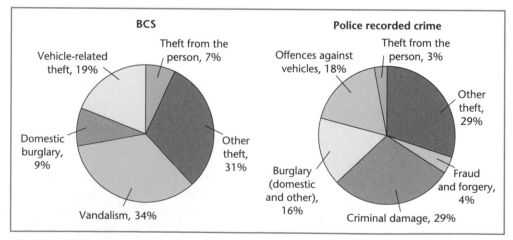

Figure 9.1 Police recorded and British Crime Survey property crime by offence, 2007/08

Source: Crime in England and Wales, 2007/08, Home Office Statistical Bulletin, p. 90.

courts perceived as dishonest, leading to a mass of fine distinctions and overlapping offences. The 1968 Act was designed to be a completely new start, bringing together all the relevant law in a clear, accessible mini-code. Unfortunately this ambitious aim was not fulfilled.

Complex and confused

The old fraud offences had become complex and confused. One provision of the Theft Act 1968, s. 16, containing certain deception offences, was so obscure and difficult to use that just four years after the Act was passed, the Criminal Law Revision Committee was asked to look at amending it. There were also gaps in the coverage of the 1968 Act. The 1978 legislation was passed to remedy both problems, repealing the troublesome part of s. 16 and creating deception offences of obtaining services by deception, evasion of liability by deception and making off without payment.

More recently, problems with the legislation were highlighted by the House of Lords' judgment in **R** v **Preddy** (1996). While some of the difficulties arising from the case were dealt with by the Theft (Amendment) Act 1996 and subsequent case law, some problems still remained.

Fraudsters could avoid liability

The fact that conduct was fraudulent would not necessarily mean that it was an offence. The current law gave fraudsters the opportunity to avoid liability by relying on the detail of the individual offences.

Poor prosecuting decisions

The difficulties with the pre-2006 legislation were partly due to poor prosecuting decisions, and, in particular, to charging defendants with theft when a s. 15 offence would have been more appropriate. Compounding the problem was the reluctance of the courts in such cases to acquit a person who had acted dishonestly, even though the facts did not fit the legal pigeonhole establishing liability. One result of this has been the problems with appropriation, where the courts have tended to adopt whatever interpretation would lead to the conviction of the dishonest defendant, even though that might lead to difficult precedents. This problem has been particularly acute where the owner of property has consented to the conduct of the accused, as seen in **Lawrence**, **Morris** and **Gomez**. In all three cases, a deception offence would have been a more appropriate charge, and the decision to charge theft instead left the courts with the unpalatable choice of acquitting defendants who were clearly guilty of dishonest behaviour, or stretching the concept of appropriation to fit the facts, and creating problematic precedents in the process.

Jury discretion

In interpreting the Acts, the courts tried to give words their ordinary, everyday meaning, in order to steer clear of unnecessary technicality. This was not a problem in itself – in fact it seemed sensible – but it led in practice to a tendency to leave the interpretation of terms used in the Acts to juries, which could lead to a lack of consistency. It was hard to ensure that like cases were treated alike when juries were given such a large degree of discretion.

● Civil law concepts

Professor Smith (1997) pointed out a difficulty with the property offences, which might be unavoidable, however carefully legislation is drafted: legislation delimiting the property offences is necessarily concerned with the civil law of property. The civil law in the field is complicated, not because it is badly drawn, but because the issues themselves are complex. It is this type of difficulty which was highlighted in the case of **Preddy**.

● Breadth of the criminal law

Some conduct could give rise to criminal liability where civil liability would be sufficient. For example, the offence of evasion of liability by deception was concerned with unpaid debts. Given the mass of civil law powers in the area of debt, it was questionable whether it was necessary for the criminal law to intervene.

● Conspiracy to defraud

The offence of conspiracy to defraud (discussed at p. 267) was frequently used by prosecutors as a general fraud offence, based primarily on dishonesty, but it was the subject of considerable criticism. A major concern is that this offence is committed when two or more people agree to do something which, if done by one person alone, would not be an offence.

● Codification

The implications of these problems extend further than just the Theft Acts. For some time, there has been an intention to codify the whole of the criminal law, though little progress has been made (see Chapter 14). Given the difficulties which existed after the limited codification of the Theft Acts, it might be concluded that the criminal law may simply be unsuitable for such a process.

Reform process

The Law Commission published a report in 2002, entitled simply *Fraud*, which proposed a radical reform of the fraud offences. The Commission had been working on the law of fraud intermittently since the 1970s. It was keen to reform the law so that the fraud offences were wide enough to convict fraudsters, without being too vague or so wide as to impose unacceptable restrictions on personal freedom and amount to a breach of the European Convention on Human Rights.

In the past, the Law Commission had rejected the idea of a general deception offence as it feared its breadth might breach the rule of law and the European Convention. However, its report in 2002 recommended that a general fraud offence should be created. The common law offence of conspiracy to defraud would be abolished.

The Home Office subsequently issued a consultation paper, *Fraud Law Reform* (2004) and accepted most of the Law Commission's proposals, though it decided to retain the offence of conspiracy to defraud to avoid any gaps in the law.

Fraud offences today

All of the old fraud offences have been repealed by the Fraud Act 2006 and replaced with a new general offence of fraud, a new offence of obtaining services dishonestly, and a number of additional related offences. The offence of conspiracy to defraud and making off without payment under s. 3(1) of the Theft Act 1978 have both been retained. The most important aspect of this reform is the creation of a single, general fraud offence. This general offence of fraud seeks to encompass fraud in all its main forms. The aim of the reform was to simplify the law to facilitate successful prosecutions. It achieves this partly by emphasising the concept of dishonesty and moving away from the issue of deception and the victim's state of mind. It is hoped that by having a general fraud offence the law will be more comprehensible to juries. There should be practical advantages for the prosecution as it should be possible to use a single, simple charge of fraud for a large scale criminal operation, rather than divide it for technical reasons into separate complex offences. As a result, more evidence should be usable for a single charge of fraud rather than only some evidence being relevant for each single smaller fraud offence.

The offence of obtaining services dishonestly has been included to try to avoid any gaps in the law.

General offence of fraud

The Fraud Act 2006 has created a new general offence of fraud, with a maximum sentence of ten years' imprisonment. This offence can be committed in one of three ways:

- false representation;
- failure to disclose information;
- abuse of position.

For the offence to have been committed, the person must have behaved dishonestly, and this concept will continue to be given the common law Ghosh meaning (see p. 208). Before 2006, the deception offences were result offences but, after 2006, the fraud offences are conduct offences. This means that a fraud offence today will be committed when the defendant acts in the relevant way, regardless of whether the result is, for example, that the defendant obtains property. This is an important change in the law. Under the old law, the defendant's conduct had to deceive the victim so that it caused the victim to do whatever act was appropriate to charge, such as transfer property. Under

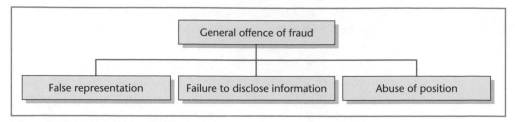

Figure 9.2 General offence of fraud

the new general fraud offence there is no need to prove any result was caused by the defendant.

We will look in turn at the three different ways of committing this new fraud offence.

False representation

Section 2 explains the meaning of a false representation:

> 2(1) A person is in breach of this section if he –
>   (a) dishonestly makes a false representation, and
>   (b) intends, by making the representation –
>   (i)   to make a gain for himself or another, or
>   (ii) to cause loss to another or to expose another to a risk of loss.
> (2) A representation is false if –
>   (a) it is untrue or misleading, and
>   (b) the person making it knows that it is, or might be, untrue or misleading.
> (3) 'Representation' means any representation as to fact or law, including a representation as to the state of mind of –
>   (a) the person making the representation, or
>   (b) any other person.
> (4) A representation may be express or implied.
> (5) For the purposes of this section a representation may be regarded as made if it (or anything implying it) is submitted in any form to any system or device designed to receive, convey or respond to communications (with or without human intervention).

The *actus reus* of this form of the offence requires proof that the accused made a false representation. A false representation looks very similar to the old concept of deception, though sub-s. (5) now makes it clear that a machine can be the victim of this offence. Subsection (2)(a) also explicitly states that a false representation includes a 'misleading' representation. In addition, as noted above, this offence is now a conduct crime and not a result crime. Thus, unlike the old offence of obtaining property by deception, there is no need to prove that the false representation caused anything to occur. The law is now purely criminalising the simple act of dishonest lying, regardless of whether anybody's property interests have actually been affected. As a consequence, the offence is completed at the time the false representation is made.

The *mens rea* requires proof that the accused knew the representation was or might be false and acted dishonestly, with intent to make a gain or cause loss. The type of conduct which would fall within this offence is false representations on mortgage application forms and life insurance forms.

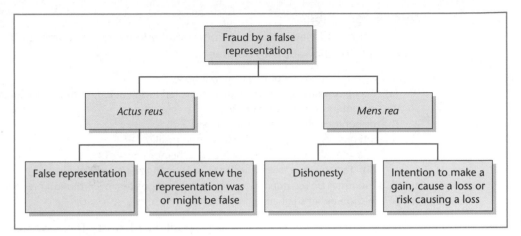

Figure 9.3a False representation

Failure to disclose information

Turning now to the second way in which the new fraud offence can be committed, s. 3 explains when there is a fraud by failing to disclose information:

> 3. A person is in breach of this section if he –
>   (a) dishonestly fails to disclose to another person information which he is under a legal duty to disclose, and
>   (b) intends, by failing to disclose the information –
>   (i) to make a gain for himself or another, or
>   (ii) to cause loss to another or to expose another to a risk of loss.

The *actus reus* for this form of the offence requires a failure to disclose information which the defendant is under a legal duty to disclose. A person may have a duty to disclose information in a company prospectus or when entering into an insurance contract. The *mens rea* requires dishonesty and an intention to make a gain or to cause a loss. Thus, an offence would be committed under this section if a person intentionally failed to disclose information relating to his or her heart condition when making an application for life insurance.

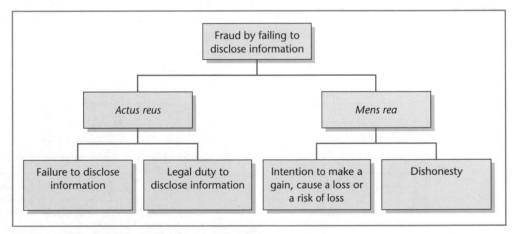

Figure 9.3b Failure to disclose information

Abuse of position

As regards the third way in which the new fraud offence can be committed, s. 4 explains the concept 'fraud by abuse of position':

> 4(1) A person is in breach of this section if he –
>   (a) occupies a position in which he is expected to safeguard, or not to act against, the financial interests of another person,
>   (b) dishonestly abuses that position, and
>   (c) intends, by means of the abuse of that position –
>   (i) to make a gain for himself or another, or
>   (ii) to cause loss to another or to expose another to a risk of loss.
> (2) A person may be regarded as having abused his position even though his conduct consisted of an omission rather than an act.

The *actus reus* requires the abuse of a position of trust. The Law Commission has explained that a wide range of people could hold a relevant position for the purposes of this form of the offence: 'The necessary relationship will be present between . . . director and company, professional person and client, agent and principal, employee and employer or between partners.' The concept of 'abuse' is not defined because it is intended to cover a very wide range of conduct or even omission. The *mens rea* requires dishonesty and an intention by the abuser to make a gain or cause a loss. An example of this offence would be an employee who fails to sign a contract so that a rival company can have the contract instead. Another example is where a person employed to care for an elderly person abuses their position to get access to the elderly person's bank account and transfer funds from that account for their own benefit. A waiter who makes a secret profit by selling his own bottle of wine would fall within this offence as having abused his position as a waiter.

● Obtaining services dishonestly

Section 11 of the Fraud Act 2006 replaces the old offence of obtaining services by deception with a new offence of obtaining services dishonestly. The main differences between

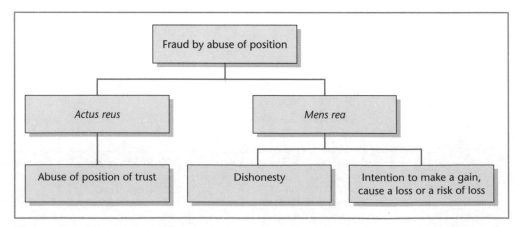

Figure 9.4 Abuse of position

the two offences is that the new offence does not require proof of deception and the offence can be committed through a machine, such as a cashpoint or a computer. Thus theatre tickets bought dishonestly over the internet could fall within this offence, as could the act of downloading music from the internet without paying where payment is required. Using a cloned satellite decoder to watch Sky TV will be caught by this offence. Section 11 provides:

11(1) A person is guilty of an offence under this section if he obtains services for himself or another –
    (a) by a dishonest act, and
    (b) in breach of subsection (2).
(2) A person obtains services in breach of this subsection if –
    (a) they are made available on the basis that payment has been, is being or will be made for or in respect of them,
    (b) he obtains them without any payment having been made for or in respect of them or without payment having been made in full, and
    (c) when he obtains them, he knows –
        (i) that they are being made available on the basis described in paragraph (a), or
        (ii) that they might be,
    but intends that payment will not be made, or will not be made in full.

The *actus reus* requires obtaining services for which payment is or will become due and failing to pay in whole or in part. Thus, unlike the general fraud offence, this offence is a result crime, because in order for this offence to be committed, defendants must have produced a result – they must have obtained a service. Therefore, the requirement of causation must also be satisfied; the defendant's dishonesty must have caused the property to be obtained.

The *mens rea* requires knowledge that the services are to be paid for or knowledge that they might have to be paid for with the dishonest intent to avoid payment in whole or in part. The person must know that the services are made available on the basis that they are chargeable, or that they might be. It is not possible to commit the offence by omission alone. This offence would be committed where a person used a stolen credit card to try to pay for software on the internet (provided the card payment does not go through – see 11(2)(b)); or where a person climbed over a wall to watch a football match without buying a ticket. The maximum sentence for this offence is five years' imprisonment.

● Additional related offences

A number of less important offences are also created by the 2006 Act. Section 6 creates a new offence for a person to possess or have under his or her control any article for use in the course of, or in connection with, any fraud. The maximum sentence for this offence is five years. This offence could be committed, for example, if a person is found to have at their home a credit-card cloning device.

Section 7 makes it an offence to make, adapt, supply or offer to supply any article knowing that it is designed or adapted for use in the course of, or in connection with, fraud, or intending it to be used to commit or facilitate fraud. The offence has a maximum sentence of ten years. An example of when this offence is committed is where

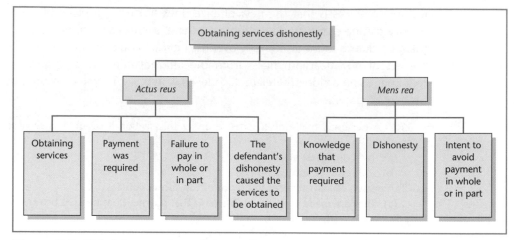

Figure 9.5 Obtaining services dishonestly

someone makes devices to attach to electric meters so that the meter does not work properly and the person does not have to pay for their electricity.

Section 9 creates an offence of fraudulent trading. The offence is committed where a person is knowingly a party to the carrying on of fraudulent business, where the business is not carried on by a company or corporate body. If the fraudulent business is carried on by a company or corporate body, the relevant offence is already contained in s. 458 of the Companies Act 1985. The maximum sentence is ten years' imprisonment.

● Making off without payment

This crime is defined in s. 3(1) of the Theft Act 1978:

> Subject to subsection (3) below, a person who, knowing that payment on the spot for any goods supplied or service done is required or expected from him, dishonestly makes off without having paid as required or expected and with intent to avoid payment of the amount due shall be guilty of an offence.

An obvious example of this offence occurs where a defendant sits down to a restaurant meal and then leaves without paying the bill, but it could also cover, among other things, putting petrol in a car and then driving off without paying, or even having a haircut and refusing to pay afterwards. It is a useful offence for prosecutors because there is no need to prove deception nor that property belonged to another at the time that it was obtained.

Actus reus

There are three elements: goods supplied or service done, making off from the spot and failure to pay as required or expected.

Goods supplied or service done

The Act does not define either of these, and they are therefore to be given their ordinary, everyday meaning where possible.

Makes off from the spot

R v **Brooks and Brooks** (1983) observes that 'to make off' simply means 'to depart'; there is no need for the person to have run away. Where exactly 'the spot' is will depend on the particular facts of the case. In **R** v **McDavitt** (1981), where the defendant left a restaurant without paying, 'the spot' was regarded as being the restaurant itself, so the defendant was only liable for an attempt to make off without payment, because he was stopped as he reached the door. On the other hand, in **Brooks and Brooks**, 'the spot' was treated as being the 'spot where payment is required', which would normally be the cash register. It is not clear which authority will be preferred in the future.

Fails to pay on the spot as required or expected

The offence can only take place if the defendant makes off at or after the point where payment is required or expected. In **Troughton** v **Metropolitan Police** (1987), the defendant was drunk. He got into a taxi and asked the driver to take him home, which he said was somewhere in Highbury. When the taxi reached Highbury, the defendant failed to give more precise directions so the driver drove to the police station. The man then tried to leave and he was charged with making off without payment. His conviction was quashed by the Court of Appeal on the basis that as the driver had not completed his part of the contract by taking the man home, payment was not yet required at the point when the defendant tried to make off.

The offence is not committed if payment is no longer expected, even if it is no longer expected because the defendant lied to the victim. In **R** v **Vincent** (2001) the defendant left two hotels in which he had stayed without paying the bill. He was charged with offences of making off without payment, contrary to s. 3 of the Theft Act 1978. At his trial it was accepted that there had been discussions between the defendant and the hotel owners about whether the defendant could pay his bill after he had left. The defendant contended that an agreement to this effect had been made with each owner so that there was no longer an expectation that he would pay before departure. The trial judge directed the jury that if such an agreement had been obtained dishonestly it could be ignored and there would still be an expectation that payment on the spot would be made. The defendant was convicted and appealed. The Court of Appeal found that the judge had misdirected the jury. Section 3(1) was intended to create a simple and straightforward offence. Where an agreement had been made some time before payment would normally be expected, that agreement was capable of defeating the expectation. While the offence under s. 3 was not committed, there could be an offence of obtaining services dishonestly under s. 11 of the Fraud Act 2006 if the customer continued to stay at the hotel with a dishonest intention of avoiding payment.

Mens rea

There are three elements: knowing that payment on the spot was required or expected, dishonesty and intention permanently to avoid payment.

Knowledge that payment on the spot is required or expected

There must be some obvious indication that payment on the spot is required or expected – either a specific statement, or a well-known practice, such as the tradition of paying for

9

Fraudulent property offences

taxi rides, haircuts and restaurant meals once those services are finished. In **Troughton** *v* **The Metropolitan Police** it could also have been argued that the defendant did not know that payment on the spot was required, since this would usually only be the case when the destination was reached.

Intention to avoid payment permanently

KEY CASE

Section 3 does not state that there must be an intention to avoid payment permanently, but this requirement was implied by the House of Lords in **R** *v* **Allen** (1985). In that case the appellant left a hotel without paying his bill. He argued that he was prevented from paying by temporary financial difficulties, and intended to pay as soon as he received the proceeds from a certain business venture. The trial judge said that this argument was in law irrelevant, but the House of Lords accepted that it was relevant, because the prosecution had to prove an intention to avoid payment permanently. The issue should therefore have been left to the jury and the conviction was quashed.

> The defendant must have intended to avoid payment permanently to be liable for making off without payment.

Dishonesty
This is defined by the common law test laid down in **Ghosh**.

Sentence
Being regarded as a relatively minor offence, it carries a maximum sentence of only two years' imprisonment.

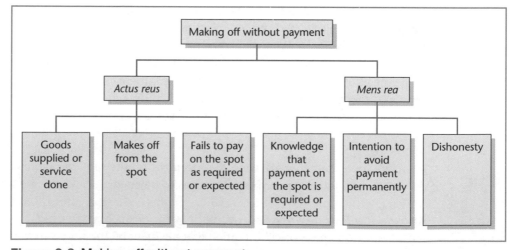

Figure 9.6 Making off without payment

Criticism of the Fraud Act 2006

The Fraud Act 2006 provides a response to some of the problems that existed with the legislation in force before 2006, identified above (at p. 234). But some of these problems remain and there are concerns that the Fraud Act 2006 will generate new problems. Inevitably with a new piece of legislation there will be scope for parties to dispute how the legislation should be interpreted. This problem will be aggravated by the fact that many of the key terms have been left undefined. Thus, for example, as s. 4 dealing with the abuse of a position leaves both the concepts of abuse and position undefined, this offence could be dangerously broad in scope. Green (2006) has commented on the danger of over-criminalisation in the context of the fraud offences:

> if fraud really were to encompass not just stealing by deceit, but also deceptive and non-deceptive breaches of trust, conflicts of interest, non-disclosure of material facts, exploitation, taking unfair advantage, non-performance of contractual obligations, and misuse of corporate assets, it would be virtually impossible to distinguish between different offences in terms of their nature and seriousness, and even to know whether and when one had committed a crime.

Some of the problems with the old fraud offences cannot be avoided by a new general fraud offence because it was actually the complexity of the facts, rather than the complexities of the law, which were giving rise to difficulties for the prosecution.

Many people wanted to see the abolition of conspiracy to defraud, on the basis that it is too broadly defined and includes criminalising people for getting together to do something which, if they did it on their own, would not be a criminal offence. But the legislation retains conspiracy to defraud for the time being, with a promise from the Government that the continued existence of the offence will be reviewed in the future.

The new general fraud offence places considerable emphasis on the concept of dishonesty, but dishonesty is left to the jury to define following **Ghosh**. The Law Commission was concerned in its initial consultation paper on the fraud offences that this reliance on dishonesty in the definition of a general fraud offence would leave it in breach of Article 7 of the European Convention on Human Rights. Article 7 bans retrospective criminalisation – a criminal offence being defined after an offence has been committed. In its final report, the Law Commission concluded that its proposed general offence of fraud was sufficiently defined by other elements of the offence that there was no dangerous reliance on the undefined concept of dishonesty. It is arguable, however, that the other elements of the fraud offence are so broadly defined that the dependence on dishonesty remains. The joint parliamentary committee which scrutinised the Fraud Act 2006 as it passed through Parliament, concluded:

> the new general offence of fraud is not a general dishonesty offence. Rather, it embeds as an element in the definition of the offence some identifiable morally dubious conduct to which the test of dishonesty may be applied . . .

However, an over-dependence on the concept of dishonesty is already a problem in the context of theft where the *actus reus* has been very broadly interpreted by the courts. As with the old deception offences, there will continue to be a considerable overlap between the fraud offences and theft where the false representation enables the defendant to appropriate the victim's property.

9

Fraudulent property offences

The new Fraud Act 2006 will only have a limited impact on the level of fraud being committed in society because of the major problem of under-reporting. Businesses reported only 15 per cent of fraud to the police in 2006, despite a 40 per cent rise in the number of cases. Companies often fail to report fraud to the police because they lack confidence in the criminal justice system. It often takes two years for a fraud case to get to a criminal court. Companies have little chance of recovering money through the criminal courts, so they prefer to sue the fraudster in the civil courts.

White-collar crime

Fraud offences have given rise to some controversy because of the different response to the problem of fraud compared with non-fraudulent property offences. Some have argued that fraud is a 'white-collar crime', that it tends to be carried out by middle or upper class professionals and is therefore dealt with more leniently than other property offences, despite the huge sums that are often involved. The Fraud Advisory Panel, set up by the private sector to assist the government in dealing with fraud, has observed that fraud often takes place within commercial businesses and these companies tend to prefer not to report this conduct to the police. The reasons for this are varied. The company may simply be embarrassed and prefer to deal with the issue behind the scenes. It may fear damaging the company's reputation and a resulting loss of clients and profit. It may not have a clear idea as to what constitutes criminal fraud. The management may feel there is no benefit for the company of reporting the fraud as the amount of employee time and effort required to establish that a crime has been committed would be disproportionate to the perceived benefits. Or the senior management might themselves have been involved in the fraud and it may not have been detected.

Because much of this fraud is unreported it is difficult to assess the extent of the problem in the UK. Police and private sector estimates vary from £400 million to £20 billion a year. The Association of British Insurers puts the total at nearer £16 billion. As the Fraud Advisory Panel notes: 'It is difficult to know what level of resources to devote to fighting the problem of fraud, without some sense of the scale and nature of the problem.' As much of the offending activity does not come to the attention of the police the deterrent effect of any existing legislation, or proposed changes, may be lost or at least not well targeted.

The largest type of fraud in terms of financial loss is fraud against Her Majesty's Revenue and Customs (HMRC) where people fraudulently evade paying income tax, VAT and taxes for importing goods (known as excise duty). Carousel fraud exploits the VAT free status of imports between EU countries, with criminal organisations requesting to be paid back VAT from the UK Treasury when they are not genuinely entitled to this. Alarmingly fraudsters are obtaining about £3bn a year of taxpayers' money in this way.

The losses caused by identity fraud are smaller but directly affect a large number of individuals (80,000 people in 2006) causing them considerable stress and anxiety. Even more people are the victims of confidence frauds involving fake lotteries, prize draws and e-mails that money can be made abroad (according to the Office of Fair Trading 500,000 people were the victim of a confidence fraud in 2006).

Two hundred thousand fraud and forgery offences were reported to the police in 2006–07, though these figures have to be treated with care as many offences are not reported to the police and benefit frauds and frauds against HMRC are prosecuted by the relevant government departments. Of the offences reported to the police, 12 per cent result in a prosecution and 9 per cent lead to a conviction.

		2003/04	2004/05	2005/06	2006/07	2007/08	2008/09
51	Fraud by company director	80	51	626	101	198	818
52	False accounting	721	541	487	462	249	145
53A	Cheque and credit card fraud (pre-Fraud Act 2006)	131,022	121,376	87,860	59,011		
53B	Preserved other fraud and repealed fraud offences (pre-Fraud Act 2006)	171,002	141,667	128,182	127,854		
53C	Fraud by false representation: cheque, plastic card and online bank accounts					23,289	26,613
53D	Fraud by false representation: other frauds					118,400	122,569
53E	Fraud by failing to disclose information					265	305
53F	Fraud by abuse of position					672	917
53G	Obtaining services dishonestly					1,882	1,156
53H	Making or supplying articles for use in fraud					183	600
53J	Possession of articles for use in fraud					1,109	1,456
55	Bankruptcy and insolvency offences	9	11	93	14	31	15
60	Forgery or use of false drug prescription	805	747	693	593	439	448
61	Other forgery	7,992	10,249	10,627	8,479	4,200	4,243
61A	Possession of false documents					2,301	2,621
814	Vehicle/driver document fraud	8,016	5,420	4,206	3,138	2,160	1,377
	Total fraud and forgery offences	319,647	280,062	232,774	199,652	155,378	163,283

Figure 9.7 Recorded fraud offences, 2003/04–2008/09

Source: *Crime in England and Wales*, 2008/09, Home Office Statistical Bulletin, p. 32.

? Answering questions

Property offences are popular subjects for problem questions and, when answering these, you should note that a lot of these offences now overlap. That means it is not sufficient to pull out the most obvious offence that has been committed; you need to discuss the whole range of possible offences, while allocating more time to the ones that fit the facts most closely. In particular, if you believe that a fraud offence has been committed, in the light of **Gomez** it is also likely that theft has been committed.

1 P stole some cheques from a building society where he worked. He went into Q's shop where he agreed to buy £2,000 worth of electrical goods. He said he would return with a building society cheque for £2,000. Twenty minutes later he returned with a stolen building society cheque made out for £2,000 drawn in favour of Q. P took away the goods and sold them to R for £1,800 cash after P had said that he had been given them by an aunt and, as he had similar equipment, he wanted 'to get shot of them'. When the facts came to light R refused to give the goods back to Q or to repay the building society.

P paid a stolen cheque drawn in favour of X, P's wife, for £300,000 into a building society account which X had opened for her own savings. Before P's conduct had come to light X discovered the large balance. Without telling P, she closed her account and took the £300,000 before disappearing with S, her lover.

9

Fraudulent property offences

Advise the parties of their criminal liability. What difference, if any, would it make to your advice if X thought that there had been merely an accounting mistake and this was 'tough on the building society who should have known better'. *(London External LLB)*

We are told that P 'stole' some cheques from a building society where he worked. It is therefore clear that he has committed the offence of theft, contrary to s. 1 of the Theft Act 1968.

He then used one of the cheques to pay for electrical goods from Q's shop. This would appear to be the general fraud offence in the Fraud Act 2006 committed by a false representation under s. 2. In the light of **Gomez** it could also have been an offence of theft, as the consent of the owner is irrelevant.

P then sold the goods to R for £1,800. R does not appear to have the *mens rea* to be liable for handling under s. 22 of the Theft Act. P has again committed the general fraud offence through a false representation under s. 2 of the Fraud Act 2006, as he has made a false representation that he had been given the electrical equipment by his aunt.

It would depend on the civil law whether R would be allowed to keep the goods. The refusal to return the goods could amount to theft. In particular, in relation to the requirement of appropriation, s. 5(4) would apply, which is concerned with property that has been received by mistake (see p. 203).

P proceeded to pay £300,000 into his wife's account, using one of the stolen building society cheques. This would appear to be a theft in the light of the case of **R** *v* **Williams (Roy)** (2000). When X withdrew the money from her account she presumably believed that it belonged to her husband. This would amount to a theft.

If X had believed that the building society had made an accounting mistake, then she would still have had the *actus reus* of theft, but she could have argued that she lacked the *mens rea*. She would have been under an obligation to return the money and her failure to do so would have amounted to an appropriation under s. 5(4). She could have argued that she lacked the *mens rea* of dishonesty under s. 2(1) of the Theft Act 1968.

2 C entered D store intending to steal bottles of Pong, her favourite perfume. She went to the perfume counter and found that Pong was no longer stocked by D store. C went to the clock department of the store and, while the assistant's attention was elsewhere, C went behind the counter and took a cheap Zip watch and put it in her pocket. C bought batteries from the electrical department and, by mistake, C was given too much change, though C did not find this out until C arrived home. C put a foreign coin in a coffee vending machine but the machine delivered the coffee before it returned the coin.

Advise C of her criminal liability. What difference, if any, would it make to your advice if Zip watches were being given free to any shoppers who required one? *(London External LLB)*

When C enters D store with the intent to steal, she is guilty of burglary under s. 9(1)(a) of the Theft Act 1968. She is liable regardless of the fact that the store did not have any of the perfume in stock; her entry as a trespasser with intent to commit the crime is sufficient to give rise to liability.

When she goes to the perfume counter and discovers that the perfume is not in stock she may be liable for an attempted theft, depending on whether what she has done is found to have been more than merely preparatory. There is no doubt that she has the *mens rea* for an attempted theft.

C went behind the counter in the clock department. This could be another offence of burglary contrary to s. 9(1)(a) of the Theft Act 1968, as she had entered another part of the building as a trespasser.

C took a Zip watch, which constituted theft. It was also a burglary under s. 9(1)(b) of the Theft Act 1968.

The cashier gave C too much change. When she was given the excess change C did not realise the cashier's mistake and therefore lacked the *mens rea* of theft. Even though she would have become in civil law the owner of the money, if she had an obligation to return the money then, under s. 5(4) of the Theft Act 1968, the excess change would still be treated as the shop's money for the purposes of theft (see p. 203). The appropriation would have been committed when she kept the money – see s. 3(1) on p. 196.

C put a foreign coin into the vending machine. She may then have committed theft of the coffee. She would also be liable for the general fraud offence through a false representation as under s. 2(5) the offence can be committed through deceiving a machine. This incident could also amount to making off without payment under s. 3 of the Theft Act 1978.

It would not have made any difference if the Zip watches were being given as free gifts. Following **Gomez**, the fact that an owner has consented to the taking of property does not prevent the occurrence of an appropriation. The cases of **Hinks** and **Mazo** (see p. 198) could have been discussed in this context.

③ **Elaine and Felicity were friends but they had recently fallen out because Elaine owed Felicity £500. Elaine had delayed repaying the money by telling Felicity that she urgently needed an operation for which she would have to pay privately. The true reason, however, was that Elaine was frightened of her new partner, Gerry, a drug addict. He had threatened to injure Elaine's children and smash up her house if she did not get money for him. Consequently, she had told the lies to Felicity to avoid repaying the loan. She had also punched an old woman, Helen, whom she met in the street, and had taken her purse.**

Felicity discovered that Elaine's excuse was untrue, though she did not learn of Elaine's true reason for not repaying the money. Being very angry, she went to Elaine's house and let herself in with a key which Elaine had given her some time ago. Once inside, she looked around for any money that she could take. Finding none, she threw one of Elaine's favourite books across the room. The book hit a wall light and broke the fitting, exposing live wires.

(a) Discuss Elaine's criminal liability in connection with her avoiding repayment of the money to Felicity, and with the incident involving Helen. *(25 marks)*

(b) Discuss Felicity's criminal liability in connection with her visit to Elaine's house and her actions once inside. *(25 marks)*

(c) Select one of the property offences you have discussed in your answers to (a) and (b) above, and critically analyse its elements. *(25 marks)*
(AQA)

(a) You are asked to discuss two incidents and you should discuss each in turn. Looking first at Elaine's criminal liability for avoiding repaying the money to Felicity, this might be the general fraud offence under s. 2 of the Fraud Act 2006. It is not certain whether a court would find Elaine's conduct dishonest within the meaning of **Ghosh**, given her specific circumstances.

Elaine's attack on Helen amounted to a robbery (see p. 209).

For both these offences, Elaine may have had a defence of duress (see p. 358). You needed to consider whether the threat from Gerry was sufficiently specific, serious and immediate to fall within this defence; in particular, there might have been an opportunity to inform the police about the threat.

(b) Felicity could have been liable for burglary and criminal damage. Looking first at the burglary, both s. 9(1)(a) and s. 9(1)(b) burglary needed to be considered. Felicity could argue that she lacked dishonesty, on the basis that she believed she was entitled to the money: s. 2(1)(a) of the Theft Act 1968. As regards criminal damage, Elaine may have committed the aggravated criminal damage offence under s. 1(2) of the Criminal Damage Act 1971, because the exposed electricity cables could have endangered life.

(c) To answer this question you could have critically analysed one of the following offences: the general fraud offence in the Fraud Act 2006, robbery, burglary or criminal damage. A discussion of robbery or burglary would inevitably have entitled you to discuss theft as this forms part of the elements of the aggravated offences.

4 T orders a taxi to take him to the railway station. What offences, if any, does T commit in the following separate situations:

(a) T resolves not to pay before ordering the taxi. The journey is completed and T does not pay; *(10 marks)*

(b) T falsely tells the driver during the journey that he is unemployed and homeless. The driver feels sorry for him and does not require payment; *(15 marks)*

(c) at the end of the journey T threatens to assault the driver and takes £50 from the driver's wallet; *(10 marks)*

(d) at the end of the journey T discovers he has left his money at home. Too embarrassed to explain, he runs away from the taxi intending to trace and pay the driver later. *(15 marks) (OCR)*

(a): the main offence here is obtaining services dishonestly under s. 11 of the Fraud Act 2006. Making off without payment under s. 3 of the 1978 Act could be discussed more briefly. Theft and the general fraud offence through a false representation under s. 2 of the Fraud Act 2006 are only relevant if you can pinpoint some property that has been the subject of the offence; the only possible property here would be the petrol the taxi-driver uses, and given the existence of a deception, the Crown Prosecution Service are unlikely to pursue this approach.

(b): the most relevant offence is s. 2 of the Fraud Act 2006, as the driver knew that a debt was owing but agreed because of the false representation to let T off. Section 11 of the Fraud Act 2006 was relevant in relation to the driving (services) after the false hard-luck story had been told. Following the case of **R** *v* **Vincent** (2001) no offence of making off without payment has been committed.

(c): the main offence to consider is robbery because of the threat of force. You could also discuss assault and theft.

(d): the most appropriate offence on these facts is making off without payment. On the issue of T's intention to pay later, the case of **Allen** is particularly important.

◉ Summary

Introduction
The Fraud Act 2006 has been passed and was brought into force on 15 January 2007. This Act has replaced most of the old fraud offences with a new general fraud offence.

Problems with the pre-2007 fraud offences
The fraud offences before 2007 were unsatisfactory for the following reasons:

- The offences were complex and confused.
- Fraudsters could avoid liability.
- Poor prosecuting decisions were made.
- Broad jury discretion existed.
- Complicated civil law concepts applied.
- Inappropriate criminalisation.
- The overuse of conspiracy to defraud.
- Difficulties with codification.

Fraud offences today
All of the old fraud offences have been repealed by the Fraud Act 2006 and replaced with a new general offence of fraud, a new offence of obtaining services dishonestly and a number of additional related offences. The offences of conspiracy to defraud and making off without payment have been retained.

General offence of fraud
The most important aspect of the Fraud Act 2006 is the creation of a general fraud offence. This offence has a maximum sentence of ten years' imprisonment. It can be committed in one of three ways:

- false representation;
- failure to disclose information;
- abuse of position.

Obtaining services dishonestly
Section 11 of the Fraud Act 2006 replaces the old offence of obtaining services by deception with a new offence of obtaining services dishonestly. The main differences between the two offences are that the new offence does not require proof of deception and the offence can be committed through a machine, such as a cashpoint or a computer.

Additional related offences
A number of less important offences are also created by the 2006 Act. Section 6 creates a new offence for a person to possess or have under his or her control any article for use in the course of, or in connection with, any fraud. Section 7 makes it an offence to make, adapt, supply or offer to supply any article knowing that it is designed or adapted for use in the course of, or in connection with, fraud, or intending it to be used to commit or facilitate fraud. Section 9 creates an offence of fraudulent trading.

Making off without payment

Under s. 3(1) of the Theft Act 1978:

> a person who, knowing that payment on the spot for any goods supplied or service done is required or expected from him, dishonestly makes off without having paid as required or expected and with intent to avoid payment of the amount due shall be guilty of an offence.

Reading list

Law Commission (2002) *Fraud* (Law Com No. 276, Cm 5560), London: HMSO.

Levi, M. and Handley, J. (1998) *The Prevention of Plastic and Cheque Fraud Revisited*, Home Office Research Study No. 182, London: HMSO.

Ormerod, D. (2007) 'The Fraud Act 2006 – Criminalising Lying' [2007] *Criminal Law Review* 193.

Smith, J.C. (1997) 'Obtaining cheques by deception or theft' [1997] *Criminal Law Review* 396.

Reading on the internet

The Fraud Act 2006 is available on the website of the Office of Public Sector Information at:
http://www.opsi.gov.uk/acts/acts2006/20060035.htm

The explanatory notes to the Fraud Act 2006 are available on the website of the Office of Public Sector Information at:
http://www.opsi.gov.uk/acts/en2006/2006en35.htm

The Home Office consultation paper, *Fraud Law Reform* is available on the Home Office website at:
http://www.homeoffice.gov.uk/documents/cons-fraud-law-reform/fraud_law_reform.pdf?view=Binary

The Law Commission report, *Fraud* (2002, Law Com No. 276) is available on the Law Commission's website at:
http://www.lawcom.gov.uk/docs/lc276.pdf

Visit **www.mylawchamber.co.uk/elliottcriminal** to access multiple choice questions, flashcards and practice exam questions to test yourself on this chapter.

Use **Case Navigator** to read in full the key case referenced in this chapter:

- DPP *v* Gomez (Edwin) [1993] AC 442
- Ghosh [1982] QB 1053; [1982] 3 WLR 110

10 Inchoate offences

This chapter explains that:

- the inchoate offences are concerned with the preparatory stages of other criminal offences which may never actually have been committed;

- the inchoate offences are attempting, conspiring, encouraging and assisting the commission of a criminal offence;

- attempts are defined by the Criminal Attempts Act 1981 s. 1, where a person has done an act which is more than merely preparatory to the commission of the full offence;

- a conspiracy is an agreement between two or more people to commit an offence; and

- assisting or encouraging the commission of a crime are criminalised by the Serious Crime Act 2007 and replace the old common law on incitement.

Introduction

The inchoate offences – attempt, conspiracy and encouraging or assisting – are concerned with the preparatory stages of other criminal offences. A person may be convicted of an inchoate offence even if the main offence was never actually committed: in some circumstances he or she may be guilty of an inchoate offence even if it would for some reason have been impossible to commit the complete offence. Where a person is convicted of an inchoate offence and the full offence has actually been committed, they may also be liable as a principal or a secondary party to the full crime. In practice, the courts encourage the prosecution to pursue a defendant for secondary party liability where the principal offence has been committed rather than prosecuting the inchoate offence.

One of the reasons for the existence of inchoate offences is that without them the police would often have to choose between preventing an offence being committed, and prosecuting the offender – it would be ridiculous, for example, if they knew a bank robbery was being planned, and had to stand by and wait until it was finished before the robbers could be punished for any offence. In addition, the person would have had the *mens rea* for the commission of the offence, and it may often merely be bad luck that he or she did not complete the crime – for example, if a planned bank robbery did not take place because the robbers' car broke down on the way to it.

All the inchoate offences are offences in their own right, but they can only be charged in connection with another offence (which from now on we shall call the main offence), so a person would be charged with incitement to rob, or attempted murder, or conspiracy to blackmail, but not with 'attempt', 'conspiracy' or 'encouragement' alone.

The Serious Crime Act 2007 (discussed at p. 272) contains a major reform to this area of law. Section 59 of the Act has abolished incitement and replaced it with two new offences of assisting or encouraging a criminal act under ss. 44, 45 and 46 of the Act.

Attempt

The criminal law does not punish people just for intending to commit a crime, but it recognises that conduct aimed at committing an offence may be just as blameworthy if it fails to achieve its purpose as if it had been successful – the person who tries to kill someone but for some reason fails is as morally guilty as someone who succeeds in killing, and possibly just as dangerous.

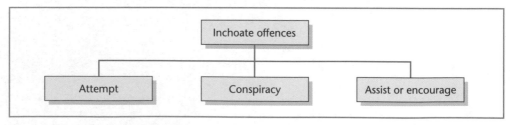

Figure 10.1 Inchoate offences

The difficulty for the law on attempts is to determine where to draw the line – how far does someone have to go towards committing an offence before his or her acts become criminal? Over the years the common law proposed various tests to answer this question, but all have been problematic. Consequently, much of the common law was replaced by the Criminal Attempts Act 1981, which laid down statutory rules instead.

● *Actus reus*

Section 1(1) of the Criminal Attempts Act 1981 provides that: 'If with intent to commit an offence to which this section applies, a person does an act which is more than merely preparatory to the commission of the offence, he is guilty of attempting to commit the offence.'

The question of whether an act is 'more than merely preparatory' is a matter of fact and, in a trial on indictment, will be for the jury to decide. The judge must consider whether there is enough evidence to leave this question to the jury, but s. 4(3) of the Act states that, the judge having concluded that there is, the issue should be left completely to the jury.

What the jury have to ask themselves is whether the accused was simply preparing to commit the offence or whether the accused had done something that was more than merely preparatory to the commission of the offence. The courts have interpreted the legislation narrowly, requiring the defendant to have 'embarked upon the crime proper'. Thus, Lord Bingham stated in **Geddes** (1996) that an accurate paraphrase of the statutory test was to ask whether the defendant 'has actually tried to commit the offence in question'. This will frequently only be the case if the defendant has done the last possible act before the commission of the actual offence itself. Thus a criminal attempt will often only occur when the criminal plan has gone wrong (for example, the bullet missed the victim). Clearly, there will be many cases where it is difficult to prove that the accused has crossed this line.

KEY CASE

In **R** *v* **Campbell** (1991) the accused was arrested by police within a yard of the door of a post office, carrying a threatening note and a fake gun. He admitted that he had originally planned to rob the post office, but said he had changed his mind and was going back to his motorbike when he was arrested. His conviction for attempted robbery was quashed because, rather surprisingly, it was held that there was no evidence on which a jury could safely find that his acts were more than merely preparatory to committing the offence.

> A person standing outside a building intending to rob a person inside the building has not committed an attempted robbery.

Similarly, in **Gullefer** (1987), the accused had backed a greyhound and, once the race was started, it became clear that the dog would probably lose. The accused thought that by disrupting the race, so that it would be declared null and void, he would get his stake money back, so he ran on to the track. The Court of Appeal held that there was no evidence that this act was more than merely preparatory, as the accused had clearly not

10

Inchoate offences

started on 'the crime proper' – the offence consisted not of stopping the race, but of using that disruption to get his money back, and he had not yet started to get that money back. In **R** v **Geddes** (1996) a man was found in the boys' toilets at a school equipped with a knife, tape and rope. He was found not to have committed an attempted false imprisonment because he had not approached a child before he was apprehended.

There is some inconsistency in the case law and in **R** v **Dagnall** (2003) the Court of Appeal found an attempted rape where the defendant could not accurately be described as having actually tried to commit the offence but the court emphasised the fact that the victim had been convinced by the defendant's conduct that she was going to be raped. It seems that the victim had spoken to the defendant at a bus stop. When she started to walk away he had followed her and put his arms around her. He told her that he wanted to have sexual intercourse with her, and said that no one would hear if he took her into a dark road and raped her. The victim started to run away screaming, but the defendant ran after her and pulled her backwards by the hair. He held her in an arm lock, covered her mouth and dragged her to another bus stop. At that point a police car arrived and the defendant was arrested. The defendant was convicted of attempted rape and appealed. At his appeal he argued that his acts had not been more than merely preparatory, as he had not touched the victim in a sexual way. The appeal was rejected and the Court of Appeal pointed to the fact that the victim had been convinced that she was going to be raped.

Attempting the impossible

Before the Criminal Attempts Act 1981, impossibility was a defence to a charge of attempts – **Haughton** v **Smith** (1975) – which effectively meant that if an accused reached into someone's bag, intending to steal a purse, but found no purse in there, they were not guilty of attempted theft. Many commentators found this ridiculous, and now s. 1(2) of the Act states: 'A person may be guilty of attempting to commit an offence to which this section applies even though the facts are such that the commission of the offence is impossible.'

Though generally viewed as more sensible than the position prior to the Act, this concept has caused some problems for the courts. In **Anderton** v **Ryan** (1985), the defendant bought what she thought was a stolen video recorder, and then went and confessed as much to the police. She was charged with, among other things, attempted handling of stolen goods, but when the evidence was examined, there was no proof that the video

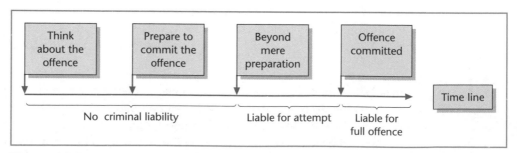

Figure 10.2 Attempt

recorder had in fact been stolen. The Divisional Court held that the Act indicated that although the facts meant it was impossible for the full offence to have been committed, this was not a defence to the charge of attempted handling. The House of Lords reversed the decision, which they considered absurd, and the conviction was quashed, thus rendering impossibility a defence despite the apparently clear wording of the Act.

However, their Lordships swiftly (by legal standards) overruled their own decision. In **Shivpuri** (1987), the accused was arrested by customs officers and confessed that there was heroin in his luggage. After forensic analysis, it transpired that in fact the substance was only harmless ground vegetable leaves, but Shivpuri was nevertheless convicted of attempting to be knowingly concerned in dealing with a controlled drug. The House of Lords held that on an accurate construction of s. 1(1) of the Criminal Attempts Act 1981 Shivpuri was guilty. Lord Bridge, who had also been a judge in **Anderton** v **Ryan**, admitted that he had got the law wrong in that case. He said that if the accused intended to commit the offence he was charged with attempting, and had done an act that was more than merely preparatory to committing the intended offence, he was guilty of attempt, even if the offence would be factually or legally impossible for any reason. It was stated that **Anderton** v **Ryan** had been wrongly decided.

As a result of **Shivpuri** a criminal attempt would be committed if Ann put her hand into a pocket intending to steal whatever was in there, but found it empty; or when Ben stabbed Chris intending to kill him not knowing that he had already died of a heart attack.

The only case in which impossibility can now be a defence is where the accused attempts to commit what they think is an offence, but which actually is not against the law. In **Taaffe** (1984), the accused imported foreign currency into the UK, believing it to be a crime. In fact it is not against the law, so although Taaffe was in his own mind attempting to commit an offence, he could not be liable. This case was recently confirmed by the House of Lords in **R** v **Forbes** (2001).

Mens rea

The Criminal Attempts Act 1981 specifies that intention is required to commit this offence. Case law has made it clear that an accused can only be liable for an attempt if they act with the intention of committing the complete offence – recklessness as to the consequences of the act is not enough. This means that, even if the offence attempted can be committed recklessly, there will be no liability for attempt unless intent is established – for example, for most non-fatal offences against the person, recklessness is sufficient *mens rea*, but it is not enough for a charge of attempting to commit any of them.

In attempted murder, the only intention that suffices for liability is an intent to kill; despite the fact that intention to cause grievous bodily harm is a sufficient *mens rea* for the full offence of murder, for an attempt you must intend to commit the complete offence, and the complete offence of murder requires the killing of a human being. In **Whybrow** (1951), the accused was convicted of the attempted murder of his wife. He had wired up a soap dish to the mains electricity supply, with the result that she received an electric shock while in the bath. Whybrow claimed that in fact that wiring arrangement

10

Inchoate offences

had been designed to provide an earth for a wireless set he kept in his bedroom, so any electric shock received by his wife had been purely accidental. The Court of Appeal reaffirmed that to be liable for attempted murder, the accused must have intended to kill. On the facts the conviction was upheld, as the jury had clearly not believed his explanation.

Where the definition of the main offence includes circumstances, and recklessness as to these circumstances is sufficient for that aspect of the *mens rea*, then it will also be sufficient for an attempt to commit that offence (though intention will still be required for the rest of the *mens rea*). For example, liability for the main offence of rape is imposed if a man intends to have sexual intercourse with a man or a woman knowing that they are not consenting, or being reckless as to whether or not they are consenting. With attempted rape the absence of the victim's consent is viewed as a circumstance of the offence; so long as the accused intends to have unlawful intercourse, it will suffice that he is reckless as to the fact that the victim may not be consenting – he does not have to know for certain that there is no consent. Thus in **Khan and others** (1990), a 16-year-old girl left a disco with five youths, going with them in a car to a house, where they were joined by other youths. Three of them had sexual intercourse with the girl without her consent, and four others, the appellants, tried to do so but failed. The four were convicted of attempted rape, and appealed, contending that the judge had misdirected the jury by telling them that a man who intended to have sexual intercourse with a woman (the result of the crime) and did not know she was not consenting, but was reckless about whether she was or not, and nevertheless attempted to have intercourse with her, was guilty of attempted rape. The Court of Appeal held that this direction was correct, and the convictions were upheld.

The point was confirmed in the case of **Attorney-General's Reference (No. 3 of 1992)**. The defendant had been charged with attempting to commit aggravated arson. This offence essentially consists of intentionally or recklessly causing damage to property by fire with the intention of endangering life or being reckless as to whether life was endangered. The Court of Appeal stated that to attempt this offence the defendant must have intended the criminal damage by fire, but endangering life was merely a circumstance of this crime and so recklessness as to that issue was sufficient. A problem with this concept is that it is difficult to predict what elements of an offence will be treated as a mere circumstance, and in fact s. 1(1) of the 1981 Act makes no reference to recklessness, referring only to an 'intent to commit an offence'. The *actus reus* of an inchoate offence will be limited as the main offence was never carried out, so *mens rea* is fundamental to the imposition of criminal liability. It is therefore questionable whether the *mens rea* requirement should have been lowered in this way.

Conditional intention

The concept of conditional intention has caused the courts problems in the past. Conditional intention arises where a person intends to do something if a certain condition is satisfied, for example they intend to steal a wristwatch from a woman if it is a genuine Rolex. The question is, will this intent be sufficient to be the *mens rea* of an attempt? Doubt was raised by the case of **R v Husseyn** (1977). The defendants had seen a parked van and decided to break into it, intending to steal if there was anything worth stealing inside. In fact the van contained a bag full of sub-aqua equipment, which the defendants did not steal. At their trial the indictment said that they had attempted to steal the sub-aqua equipment. On appeal Lord Scarman said in the Court of Appeal that 'it cannot be said that one who has it in mind to steal only if what he finds is worth stealing has a present intention to steal'; their conditional intention was found to have been inadequate to impose liability.

This case caused considerable concern, because it seemed to leave a significant gap in the law. However, in **Attorney-General's References (Nos 1 and 2 of 1979)** it was said that the judgment in **Husseyn** could be explained by the fact that the indictment had specified that the attempted theft was theft of the sub-aqua equipment. If it had simply said, for example, that they intended to steal anything of value in the van then they could have been convicted. In conclusion, conditional intention is sufficient to impose liability for an attempt provided the indictment is carefully worded.

Offences which may not be attempted

There are some offences for which liability for attempts cannot be imposed. The Criminal Attempts Act covers all indictable offences, and either way offences when they are tried on indictment, but for summary offences there is no liability for attempts unless Parliament creates a specific statutory provision stating that there should be – for the offence of drink-driving, for example, the Road Traffic Act 1988 provides that it is an offence to 'drive or attempt to drive' after drinking more than the prescribed limit.

There is no liability for attempting to be a secondary party to a crime – so there is no offence of attempting to aid, abet, counsel or procure the commission of an offence. Nor is it an offence to attempt to conspire, though it is possible to attempt to incite (one exception to this rule is aiding and abetting suicide, as charged in **Reed** (1982) – below – as this is a full offence in its own right rather than an inchoate offence, and therefore can be attempted).

Some offences cannot be attempted because of their *mens rea*. The most obvious example is manslaughter. An attempt requires intention to commit the full offence; if the accused has the intention to kill, the attempted offence would be attempted murder, and not attempted manslaughter.

Section 1(1) of the Criminal Attempts Act 1981 describes an attempt with the words 'does an act', and it is therefore not possible to commit an attempt by an omission. This point was confirmed by the Court of Appeal in **R** *v* **Nevard** (2006) though the application of this legal principal was rather unsatisfactory on the facts. A husband had attacked his wife with an axe and knife. She tried to dial 999, but he forced her to end the call. When the emergency services were suspicious and dialled back he said that children in the house must have been playing with the phone. She survived the attack and he was prosecuted for both causing grievous bodily harm with intent and attempted murder. The Court of Appeal upheld his conviction for attempted murder, but it stated that the jury should have been given clear directions that only the axe and knife attack could have been taken into account when considering the issue of attempt and not the failure to get emergency services as the latter was a mere omission. However, it might be unduly favourable to the husband to describe his conduct with regard to the emergency services

10

Inchoate offences

as an omission, as he took positive steps to try to prevent the emergency services from coming.

It is possible for an act done in another country to amount to an attempt to commit a crime in England. In **DPP** *v* **Stonehouse** (1978) the accused went to Miami, and there falsely staged his own death, so that his wife in England (who knew nothing of the plan) could claim on his life insurance policies. He was convicted of attempting to enable his wife to obtain property by deception.

● Sentence

Under s. 4(1) of the 1981 Act the maximum sentence that can be imposed for an attempt is usually the same as that for the main offence.

● Criticism and reform

The narrow interpretation of the *actus reus*

The limited approach taken to the meaning of 'more than merely preparatory' has unfortunate implications for efforts at crime prevention and protecting the public. The police can still lawfully arrest anyone behaving as the defendant did in **Campbell**, for example, on the basis that they have reasonable grounds for believing that he or she is about to commit an arrestable offence, but it appears that, in order to secure a conviction for attempt in such circumstances, they would have to hold back until that person has actually entered the post office and approached the counter before arresting him or her. Clearly this may mean putting post office and other staff, the general public and police officers at unnecessary risk.

The dangers of this approach are highlighted in **R** *v* **Geddes** (1996). The accused had entered some school premises including the boys' toilets. On being discovered he ran away discarding a rucksack which was found to contain rope, masking tape and a large kitchen knife. He was charged with attempted false imprisonment and the trial judge ruled that there was a case fit for the jury's consideration. The accused was convicted but his appeal was allowed. While there was no doubt about the appellant's intention, there was no evidence of the *actus reus* of the offence. The evidence showed that he had made preparation, got himself ready and put himself in a position to commit the offence of false imprisonment, but he had not made contact with any pupil. He had not moved from the role of preparation and planning into the area of execution or implementation.

The Law Commission has issued a consultation paper *Conspiracy and Attempt* (2007). The Commission considers that the courts have been inconsistent in applying the more than merely preparatory test, creating doubt as to whether a person is criminally liable when commonsense suggests they are guilty. It has recommended that s. 1(1) of the Criminal Attempts Act 1981 should be repealed and replaced by two separate inchoate offences. The first would keep the label 'attempt' but would be restricted to 'the last acts needed to commit the intended offence'. The second would be an offence of 'criminal preparation', consisting of acts of preparation which are part of the execution of the plan to commit the intended offence. It suggests that specific examples of acts that should constitute more than mere preparation should be included in the legislation. These examples could include:

> D, with a view to committing the intended offence there and then or as soon as an opportunity presents itself:
> (a) approaches the intended victim or the object of the intended offence, or
> (b) lies in wait for an intended victim, or
> (c) follows the intended victim.

Such examples would provide some real substance to a test which currently does no more than state in theoretical rather than practical terms that a line has to be drawn where a criminal attempt begins. The two offences would have the same maximum sentence, that is to say the maximum sentence of the offence that has been attempted/ prepared.

Under this scheme, therefore, a criminal attempt would be concerned with last acts and criminal preparation with preparatory acts. A person would be liable for criminally preparing the offence of murder when they hid and waited for the victim armed with a gun. He or she would be liable for attempted murder upon firing a bullet at the victim and missing its target. At this point the last act necessary for the commission of the full offence would have been carried out and this offence will often be limited in practice to situations where the plan to commit an offence has gone wrong.

The Law Commission states that its aim is not to extend the scope of the offence of attempt (though in practice the offence of criminal preparation would appear to extend the law). Instead it suggests that cases such as **Campbell** (1991) and **Geddes** (1996) reflect the popular understanding of an 'attempt', capturing a core idea of the defendant *trying* to commit the substantive offence. This would be the limit of the attempt offence and other acts which are less proximate, but still part of the execution of the plan, can then be caught by the criminal preparation offence. The *mens rea* for the offences would remain unchanged.

The decision in *Shivpuri*

This case has been criticised on the ground that it allows the law to punish people merely on account of their intentions. However, it should be remembered that, to incur liability, the accused must have done something which is more than merely preparatory to committing the offence, and may in fact have tried very hard to commit an offence, failing to do so only through carelessness, chance or the intervention of the police. In such cases incurring no liability would simply give potential offenders the opportunity to try harder next time.

Sentencing

Some have argued that the maximum sentence for an attempt is too harsh. In certain US states, for example, the maximum that can be imposed is usually only half that for the main offence. Arguments in favour of the English position include the fact that the defendant had the *mens rea* for the complete offence, and may be equally dangerous. The academic Becker (1974) argues that whether an offence is actually committed or merely attempted, the same type of harm can be caused: disruption to social stability. On the other hand another academic, James Brady (1980), has suggested that the harm is

10

Inchoate offences

not the same and so it does not justify the same sentence. In practice the judge still has a discretion and most of the time judges choose to impose a lower sentence if the offence was not completed.

Attempts by omission

The draft Criminal Code proposes that it should be possible to attempt offences where the *actus reus* is an omission.

A defence of withdrawal

In the US, a defence of withdrawal is widely accepted. This allows a defendant to avoid liability if he or she voluntarily chooses not to go on and carry out the offence. At the moment in England this defence is available to accomplices, but not to those charged with attempts. This means that, once a person has done something that is more than merely preparatory to the commission of the offence, they might just as well carry on and finish the job, since stopping at that point will not necessarily reduce their liability.

The Law Commission is opposed to the idea of a defence of withdrawal, arguing that this issue can be left to mitigation in sentencing.

Conspiracy

Conspiracy covers agreements between two or more people, usually to commit a crime. Until 1977, conspiracy was a purely common law crime, but there were difficulties with the definition of the offence. One of the problems was that its definition was extremely broad and included situations where two or more people had simply agreed to commit a tort. Thus, in **Kamara v DPP** (1974), where the defendants had reached an accord to commit the tort of trespass to land together, they were liable for the criminal offence of conspiracy. This was felt to be extremely harsh and consequently the Criminal Law Act 1977 abolished most of the common law offences of conspiracy, and created a new statutory offence of conspiring, which is limited to an agreement between two or more people to commit a crime.

But Parliament was not prepared to abolish the whole of the common law of conspiracy because it was concerned that this might leave a gap in the law, where people had not agreed to commit a crime but their agreement was of a type that still required criminal liability to be imposed. Therefore they chose specifically to preserve two small areas of the old common law of conspiracy. The result is that there are now two categories of conspiracy: statutory conspiracy and common law conspiracy.

With one exception, statutory and common law conspiracy are mutually exclusive, and statutory conspiracy takes priority; if the act the conspirators agree to do is an offence, the charge will necessarily be statutory conspiracy. The exception is conspiracy to defraud.

Statutory conspiracy

Statutory conspiracy is an agreement by two or more people to do something that will amount to a crime.

Actus reus

The Criminal Law Act 1977, s. 1(1) provides:

> Subject to the following provisions of this Part of this Act, if a person agrees with any other person or persons that a course of conduct shall be pursued which, if the agreement is carried out in accordance with their intentions, either:
> (a) will necessarily amount to or involve the commission of any offence or offences by one or more of the parties to the agreement, or
> (b) would do so but for the existence of facts which render the commission of the offence or any of the offences impossible,
> he is guilty of conspiracy to commit the offence or offences in question.

There must be an agreement that the planned actions will be committed by one or more parties to that agreement; so long as this is the case, the conspirators will be liable even if they never act upon their plan. It can be argued that there should be liability only when the agreement is carried out, as is largely the case in US law, because there is no real threat to society until the conspirators start acting on the agreement. In practice, though, it will be rare for conspirators who have not taken any action to be convicted, simply because it would be difficult to prove the agreement existed.

The fact that a conspirator has second thoughts and withdraws does not provide a defence. If the main offence is carried out, the defendants will not usually be charged with conspiracy as well, unless the additional charge is felt necessary to show the seriousness of what they have done.

Who can conspire?

Section 2 of the 1977 Act provides:

> (1) A person shall not by virtue of section 1 above be guilty of conspiracy to commit any offence if he is an intended victim of that offence.
> (2) A person shall not by virtue of section 1 above be guilty of conspiracy to commit any offence or offences if the only other person or persons with whom he agrees are (both initially and at all times during the currency of the agreement) persons of any one or more of the following descriptions, this is to say:
> (a) his spouse or civil partner;
> (b) a person under the age of criminal responsibility; and
> (c) an intended victim of that offence or of each of those offences.

Married couples and civil partners cannot therefore be liable for conspiring with each other, though they may both be liable for a conspiracy involving one or more people besides the two of them. Nor is there a conspiracy where two people agree to commit a crime for which one has a defence; there must be more than one person who has no defence.

Where an offence is designed to protect certain groups of people, such as minors or the mentally ill, members of those groups cannot be convicted of conspiring to commit those offences against themselves – so a girl under 16 cannot be liable for conspiring with her boyfriend to have under-age sex, even though she planned it with him, and he was guilty of the main offence.

Conspiracy to do the impossible

Section 1(1)(b) of the Criminal Law Act 1977 (quoted above) makes it clear that the fact that the crime agreed on turns out to be impossible to commit does not prevent a conviction for conspiracy.

Mens rea

The parties must intend that the agreement will be carried out and the crime committed by one or more of the conspirators. In **Edwards** (1991), the accused had agreed to supply amphetamine but appeared to have intended to supply a different drug, ephedrine, which was not a controlled drug. According to the Court of Appeal, the judge had rightly directed the jury that they could only convict of conspiracy to supply amphetamine if it was proved he had agreed to supply amphetamine and he intended to supply that drug – merely agreeing with no intention of actually supplying the controlled substance was not enough. His conviction was upheld.

KEY CASE

The requirement of an intention was reiterated by the House of Lords in **R v Saik** (2006) which is now the leading case on the *mens rea* of conspiracy. Recklessness will not be sufficient to impose liability. The defendant had operated a currency exchange office in London. In the course of the business he had converted a substantial amount of pounds sterling provided by others in the form of cash into foreign currency. The cash was the proceeds of drug trafficking or other criminal activity. He was subsequently prosecuted for being involved in a money laundering conspiracy. At his trial he admitted that he suspected the money was the proceeds of crime, but had not known that fact for certain. His appeal against conviction was successful. The House of Lords held that the defendant did not have sufficient *mens rea* for the commission of the offence. In order to impose liability for conspiracy he must have known that the money was actually the proceeds of crime in order for him then to have the intention to commit the offence. Recklessness would have been sufficient for the imposition of liability for the substantive offence of money laundering but it was not sufficient for the conspiracy.

> The *mens rea* for conspiracy is intention.

The issue had been somewhat confused by the House of Lords' judgment in **Anderson** (1985) which seemed to suggest that defendants must personally intend to play some part in carrying out the agreement, but that also they did not need to intend that the crime would actually be committed. The accused had been in prison with Andaloussi, a man who was awaiting trial for serious drug offences. Anderson, who was expecting to be released on bail quite quickly, agreed to take part in a plan to free Andaloussi. His part in the scheme was to supply diamond wire, to be used to cut through bars in the prison, for which he was given a downpayment of £2,000, to be followed by another £10,000 on delivery of the wire. Anderson gave evidence that he had never believed that the escape plan would actually work, and that after supplying the wire he had intended simply to take the money and leave the country for Spain, playing no further part in helping Andaloussi to escape. Nevertheless, his conviction was upheld on appeal. Lord Bridge said:

> The appellant, in agreeing that a course of conduct be pursued that would, if successful, necessarily involve the offence of effecting Andaloussi's escape from lawful custody, clearly intended, by providing diamond wire to be smuggled into the prison, to play a part in the agreed course of conduct in furtherance of that criminal objective. Neither the fact that he intended to play no further part in attempting to effect the escape, nor that he believed the escape to be impossible, would, if the jury had supposed they might be true, have afforded him any defence.

While this approach gave a satisfactory outcome in the particular case, it could cause difficulties in some situations. Conspiracy charges are extremely useful with regard to organised crime. For example, in a Mafia-style organisation, there is often a 'Mr Big', who may initiate the whole criminal enterprise, but never actually become involved in committing the criminal acts himself – he will pay others to smuggle drugs or kill his enemies rather than risk doing it himself. The approach in **Edwards** would ensure that such a person could still be liable for conspiracy as he had been party to the agreement, and intended it to be carried out and the crime committed, but under the apparent *ratio* of **Anderson** he would avoid liability because he would intend to play no part himself. However, in **R** v **Siracusa** (1990) the court said that **Anderson**, despite its fairly clear *dicta*, did not mean that the defendant had to intend to play any part in the carrying out of the agreement; and in **Yip Chiu-Cheung** v **R** (1994) the Privy Council assumed that the defendant only needed to intend that the crime be committed by someone. On the whole it makes most sense to view **Anderson** as an aberration, and regard the *mens rea* of statutory conspiracy as that laid down in **Edwards**.

We saw that, in relation to attempts, recklessness as regards the circumstances of the main offence is sometimes sufficient. This is not the case with conspiracy. Section 1(2) of the Criminal Law Act 1977 states:

> Where liability for an offence may be incurred without knowledge on the part of the person committing it of any particular fact or circumstance necessary for the commission of the offence, a person shall not be guilty of conspiracy to commit that offence . . . unless he and at least one other party to the agreement intend or know that fact or circumstance shall or will exist at the time when the conduct constituting the offence is to take place.

It can be seen from this section that only intention or knowledge concerning all the circumstances of the *actus reus* will be satisfactory for a charge of conspiracy. This is the case even if the agreement involves committing a crime for which recklessness is sufficient *mens rea*. For example, in relation to the offence of rape, recklessness as to whether the woman was consenting to sexual intercourse is sufficient *mens rea*, but to be liable for a conspiracy to rape, the accused must have known that the woman was not consenting. Even where an offence imposes strict liability, intention or knowledge will be required for conspiracy to commit that offence.

Both parties to a conspiracy (or, if there are more than two, at least two of them) must have *mens rea* – so if A and B agree to take C's car, but B believes that A has C's permission to do so, there is no liability for conspiracy for stealing the car. Interestingly, in **Yip Chiu-Cheung** v **R**, the conspiracy concerned the importation of controlled drugs, and the co-conspirator was an undercover drug enforcement officer, participating in the offence in order to detect and report the crime. The operation never progressed further than a conspiracy because on the morning that the officer was supposed to undertake the actual smuggling, he overslept and missed the plane. Despite the fact that he was an honest police officer doing his job, he was treated as having the *mens rea* of the offence, on the grounds that his motive was irrelevant, which meant that the co-conspirator could be liable. Theoretically, the law enforcement officer could have been prosecuted and convicted as well, but his protection would be that the prosecution authorities would exercise their discretion and not proceed in such situations.

Where a conspiracy involves more than two people, it is not necessary for everyone to know what all the others are doing, but each defendant will only be liable for conspiracy to commit those crimes which he or she knows about – so if A, B and C conspire to steal from D, but A and B also agree to kill D, C is liable for conspiracy to steal but not for conspiracy to murder.

Conditional intention

In some cases two or more people may agree to do something that would amount to a crime, but decide that they will only carry out the plan on condition that certain circumstances exist – this is the idea of conditional intention already discussed in the context of the property offences. In **Reed** (1982), the defendants had agreed that one of them would visit individuals who they knew were thinking about committing suicide and, after assessing the circumstances in each case, would either try to persuade them out of it, or actively help them to kill themselves. It was held that they were guilty of conspiring to aid and abet suicide.

In explaining the decision, the court drew a distinction between situations where the intention to commit the offence if necessary is only incidental to the plan, and where it could be said to be the whole object of the exercise. They gave the example of a pair of motorists who agree to drive from London to Edinburgh within a specified time. This journey can only be achieved without speeding if the traffic is exceptionally light, and the two have therefore agreed that if the traffic conditions are not sufficiently favourable, they will drive above the speed limit, committing an offence. Their main purpose, the court said, would not be to break the speed limit, but to get to Edinburgh. By contrast, for the defendants in **Reed**, aiding and abetting suicide, where they thought the circumstances warranted it, could be said to be their main purpose, and so conditional intent would suffice for conspiracy.

Acquittal of the alleged conspirators

Section 5(8) of the Criminal Law Act 1977 provides that a person can be convicted of conspiracy even if his or her alleged co-conspirators have been acquitted, unless such a conviction is inconsistent with the fact that the others have been acquitted. This protects against guilty conspirators going free because another party has been acquitted due to evidential problems or procedural irregularities at trial.

Conspiracy and secondary parties

In **R** v **Kenning** (2008) the Court of Appeal stated that there was no such offence as conspiring to be a secondary party. The defendants ran a shop selling cannabis seeds and provided information and equipment used for growing cannabis plants. They were prosecuted for conspiring to aid and abet the production of a controlled drug, contrary to s. 1(1) of the Criminal Law Act 1977. The defendants were convicted but their appeal was successful because no offence of conspiring to aid and abet exists. This type of conduct might in future be prosecuted for assisting or encouraging the commission of a crime under ss. 44–46 of the Serious Crime Act 2007.

Sentencing

The sentence for a statutory conspiracy may not exceed the maximum penalty for the crime that the conspirators agreed to commit.

● Common law conspiracy

Actus reus

The main principles discussed in relation to the *actus reus* of statutory conspiracy also apply here. The only difference is that instead of agreeing to commit a crime, the defendants agree to do one of the two things laid down in s. 5 of the Criminal Law Act 1977. This provides:

> (1) Subject to the following provisions of this section, the offence of conspiracy at common law is hereby abolished.
>
> (2) Subsection (1) above shall not affect the offence of conspiracy at common law so far as relates to conspiracy to defraud.
>
> (3) Subsection (1) above shall not affect the offence of conspiracy at common law if and in so far as it may be committed by entering into an agreement to engage in conduct which:
>
>   (a) tends to corrupt public morals or outrages public decency; but
>
>   (b) would not amount to or involve the commission of an offence if carried out by a single person otherwise than in pursuance of an agreement.

Thus s. 5 makes two exceptions to the abolition of common law conspiracies. We will look at each of these in turn.

Conspiracy to defraud

This is a property offence, mainly used to deal with the situation where a person dishonestly obtains someone else's property, but his or her behaviour is not covered by the Theft Acts. It therefore helps the courts to keep pace with ever-increasing methods of fraud, which may develop too quickly to fall within the existing legislation. For example, conspiracy to defraud was the charge used against the Maxwell brothers, inheritors of their father's publishing empire, with regard to their transactions concerning the Maxwell pension funds. It is a popular charge with the Serious Fraud Office because it avoids some of the complexities of the Theft Acts.

KEY CASE

In **Scott** v **Metropolitan Police Commissioner** (1974), the defendants copied films without securing the consent of the copyright owners. They planned to make money by charging others to watch them, and therefore clearly intended to cheat the copyright owners out of funds that should rightfully have been paid to them. They could not be charged under the Theft

Conspiracy to defraud is committed when there is an agreement to deprive another dishonestly of something.

10

Inchoate offences

Acts, because they had stolen nothing, nor had there been any deception. Because they had only conspired to commit a civil wrong and not a criminal offence, they could not be liable for statutory conspiracy either. However, the House of Lords held that an agreement by two or more people to deprive another dishonestly of something to which that person would normally be entitled could constitute the common law offence of conspiracy to defraud.

The House of Lords held in **Norris** v **USA** (2008) that where companies fix prices in breach of competition law this can only amount to an offence of conspiracy to defraud if the conduct of price fixing is combined with other wrongful conduct, such as deliberate misrepresentation. This case was applied by the House of Lords in **R** v **GG plc** (2008). That case involved allegations of price-fixing by pharmaceutical companies at the expense of the Department of Health. The House of Lords criticised the wording of the indictment:

> It goes on the incorrect assumption that price fixing, when carried out in circumstances of secretive and deceptive behaviour, is dishonest in itself and is a sufficient basis for conspiracy to defraud. It does not isolate and charge any specific aggravating elements which would elevate price fixing into an indictable conspiracy to defraud.

As a result, the prosecution for conspiracy to defraud was not allowed to proceed.

In **Adams** v **R** (1995) the Privy Council said that the offence could only be committed where the victim had some right or interest capable of being prejudiced. The case involved a complicated fraud on a large company. As the company had a legal right to recover secret profits made by its directors they had a sufficient interest for these purposes.

When the 1977 Act was first passed, defendants could not be charged with the common law offence of conspiracy to defraud if they could be charged with statutory conspiracy. So, for example, a couple of defendants who conspired to do something which would amount to burglary would have had to be charged with the statutory offence of conspiracy to burgle under s. 1 of the 1977 Act, rather than the common law offence of conspiracy to defraud. This caused problems in practice, because defendants were being acquitted on the technical basis that they should have been charged with statutory conspiracy rather than common law conspiracy to defraud. So, in 1987, the law was changed. Statutory conspiracy and conspiracy to defraud are no longer mutually exclusive; a conspiracy to commit an offence such as theft may be covered by either offence, and the prosecution may choose which to charge.

Conspiracy to corrupt public morals or outrage public decency
The Act provides that there is still a common law offence of conspiracy to do an act which is likely to corrupt public morals or outrage public decency, where that act would not in itself be a criminal offence. For some time after the legislation was passed, it was not clear whether these activities were offences in their own right or whether criminal liability could only be imposed if there was a conspiracy to do them. Recent cases make it clear that outraging public decency is an offence in itself, and a conviction for this was upheld by

the House of Lords in **R** v **Gibson** (1990), where the defendant exhibited earrings made from freeze-dried human foetuses of three or four months' gestation.

As a result of **Gibson**, outraging public decency is itself an offence, which means that, in the light of the terms of s. 5(3)(b) above, this should be charged as a statutory conspiracy and not a common law conspiracy. This appears to mean that only conspiracy to corrupt public morals is left as a common law offence. This approach is supported by the Court of Appeal in **R** v **Walker** (1995) where no objection was raised to the conviction of an individual defendant for outraging public decency on his own, though the appeal was allowed on a different ground.

The kind of behaviour required for liability for these two conspiracies has rarely been defined. As regards conspiracy to outrage public decency. In the case of **R** v **Walker** the defendant was accused of having committed the offence of outraging public decency in his own home. The complainant was a 10-year-old girl. The Court of Appeal allowed his appeal on the basis that this offence must be carried out in a public place, the defendant's conduct must have been obscene or disgusting and that two or more persons must have been able to see the incident.

In **R** v **Hamilton** (2007) a barrister had carried a hidden camera in a rucksack and placed it strategically on the floor in public places, such as supermarket checkout queues, to film up ladies' skirts (known as 'upskirting'). Nobody had actually seen him do this but the Court of Appeal stated that for the purposes of the offence of outraging public decency it was sufficient that two or more people were capable of having seen the conduct, and it did not matter whether they actually had seen the relevant conduct.

In **Shaw** v **DPP** (1962), the publication of a directory listing the names, addresses and photographs of prostitutes, with details of any unusual sexual practices they were willing to pursue, was held to be conduct liable to corrupt public morals, and in **Knuller** (1973) the same view was taken of an agreement to publish advertisements designed to secure sexual partners for homosexual men.

In **Knuller**, Lord Simon suggested that conduct tending to corrupt public morals had to be more than just behaviour which might 'lead morally astray'; it should be conduct which a jury 'might find to be destructive of the very fabric of society'. He also defined conduct likely to outrage public decency, stating that it would have to 'go beyond offending the susceptibilities of, or even shocking, reasonable people', and that, in deciding what kind of conduct fitted the definition, juries should remember that they lived in a society which aimed to tolerate minorities.

Impossibility

Section 1(1)(b) of the 1977 Act does not apply to common law conspiracies, so this issue is still governed by case law. It is therefore likely, in the light of the cases on impossibility and incitement discussed below, that impossibility can still be a defence.

Mens rea

The *mens rea* for statutory and common law conspiracy is the same, except that conspiracy to defraud requires an extra element of *mens rea*: dishonesty (**Scott**, above). Dishonesty for the purposes of the Theft Acts was defined in **Ghosh** (1982) and it has been held that the same test should be applied in cases of conspiracy to defraud. Defendants are therefore dishonest if their conduct would be considered dishonest by ordinary decent people, and the defendants realise that it would be so regarded.

Sentence

Conspiracy to defraud has a maximum sentence of ten years' imprisonment. There is no set maximum for the other form of common law conspiracy; it is left to the discretion of the judge.

Criticism and reform

Evidential rules

Special evidential rules can be used in conspiracy charges, which allow evidence against one party to be put forward against the others – this would not be permitted if they were charged for separate offences. These rules mean that a conspiracy charge can be brought where there is not enough evidence to charge one or more of the parties individually with the main offence, and, while this may be a useful way of ensuring that guilty conspirators do not go free due to evidential problems, it is open to abuse by the prosecution.

Conspiracies not put into action

It is questionable whether there is a need for the crime of conspiracy to cover cases where the conspirators take no action to put their agreement into practice, since this appears to pose no threat to anyone. On the other hand, one of the principal reasons for the offence is the state's fear of criminals getting together, as they are seen as a greater threat to society when they co-ordinate their activities.

Conspiracy and attempts

In many cases, a conspiracy will be committed prior to an attempt: it is the agreement that precedes the conduct. As a result it can be argued that if the law of attempts is broadly defined there is no need for the offence of conspiracy. On the other hand, this

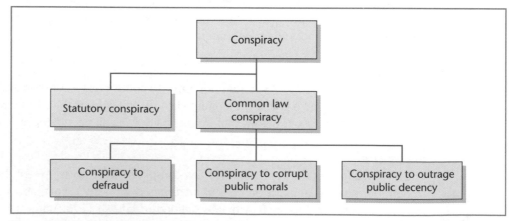

Figure 10.3 Conspiracy

would leave a gap as regards 'Mr Big' who does not himself become involved in the criminal activity. In addition, where there is some degree of organised crime, the actual offences may be quite minor – shoplifting by gangs, for example – but the profit to be made by the person running the operation can be enormous. The charge of conspiracy enables the judge to see the whole picture and appreciate the seriousness of their conduct.

One benefit of the conspiracy charge is that an agreement is more concrete than such concepts as 'more than merely preparatory'.

Outraging public decency and corrupting public morals

The desirability of maintaining the offences of conspiracy to corrupt public morals or outrage public decency is debatable. Both are potentially extremely wide and the Law Commission favours their abolition.

Conspiracy to defraud

Conspiracy to defraud is very broadly defined, and, while this is clearly useful for the prosecution, it may cause injustice to the defendant. However, the Law Commission has concluded that the offence bridges important gaps and should be retained.

Sentencing

The wide sentencing discretion has been criticised, particularly in the context of the common law conspiracies.

Mens rea of conspiracy

The Law Commission has issued a consultation paper *Conspiracy and Attempt* (2007). It considers that conspiracy needs to be reformed to tackle the growing problem of organised crime. At the moment people can only be liable for conspiracy if the prosecution can prove that they knew the planned crime would be committed. A man who brings a locked suitcase into this country realising that it probably contains drugs or guns cannot be convicted of conspiracy because he is unsure what is in the case. It recommends that s. 1(2) should be repealed because it considers that knowledge as to circumstances should no longer be a necessary element of the *mens rea* for conspiracy. It suggests that where a substantive offence requires proof of a circumstance element, a person conspiring to commit that offence must be shown to have been reckless as to the possible existence of that element at the time when the substantive offence was to be committed (which is the current position for attempts). If a higher degree of fault (such as intention or knowledge) regarding that circumstance is required for the full offence then it should be required for conspiracy as well. It also proposes that there should no longer be a defence for married couples and civil partners.

Assisting or encouraging a crime

Following recommendations of the Law Commission in its report *Inchoate Liability for Assisting and Encouraging Crime* (2006) the common law offence of incitement has been abolished and replaced by the offences of assisting or encouraging a crime contained in the Serious Crime Act 2007. While the old offence of incitement included the idea of encouragement, the main change brought about by the legislation is that the inchoate offences now include assisting. In the past assisting had only been criminalised when a person was acting as an accomplice (discussed in Chapter 11). The potential gap that had existed before 2007 was illustrated by the Law Commission with an example of the defendant lending his van to someone believing that person would use the van to carry out a robbery. If the robbery was not committed the defendant would be liable for no offence, but if he had uttered words encouraging the person to commit a robbery, then he would have been liable.

The Serious Crime Act 2007 is an extremely complex piece of legislation but in summary three new offences are established by ss. 44, 45 and 46 of the Act. The s. 44 offence is committed when the defendant had intended the relevant offence to be committed, s. 45 is committed when the defendant believed it would be committed and s. 46 is committed when the defendant believed that one or more offences would be committed. The statutory provisions are as follows:

> **s. 44** (1) A person commits an offence if –
>   (a) he does an act capable of encouraging or assisting the commission of an offence; and
>   (b) he intends to encourage or assist its commission.
> (2) But he is not to be taken to have intended to encourage or assist the commission of an offence merely because such encouragement or assistance was a foreseeable consequence of his act.
>
> **s. 45** A person commits an offence if –
>   (a) he does an act capable of encouraging or assisting the commission of an offence; and
>   (b) he believes –
>   (i)   that the offence will be committed; and
>   (ii) that his act will encourage or assist its commission.
>
> **s. 46** (1) A person commits an offence if –
>   (a) he does an act capable of encouraging or assisting the commission of one or more of a number of offences; and
>   (b) he believes –
>   (i)   that one or more of those offences will be committed (but has no belief as to which); and
>   (ii) that his act will encourage or assist the commission of one or more of them.
> (2) It is immaterial for the purposes of subsection (1)(b)(ii) whether the person has any belief as to which offence will be encouraged or assisted.

● *Actus reus*

These are inchoate offences and there is therefore no need for the actual crime being encouraged or assisted to be committed (s. 49). The acts must simply be capable of providing assistance or encouragement, they need not have actually provided any assistance or encouragement (unlike accomplice liability, discussed in the next chapter). Encouragement includes threats and putting pressure on another person to commit a crime (s. 65(1)). The person encouraged or assisted need not be aware of this, unlike the common law offence of incitement where communication was required. The offence can also be committed by taking steps to reduce the possibility of criminal proceedings being brought in respect of the relevant offence (s. 65(2)). The offence cannot be committed by omission, a positive act is required. Where the prosecution is based on the provision of assistance it must simply be proved that the conduct was capable of assisting, it is not necessary to show that assistance was actually provided.

Section 65 states that encouraging or assisting will include omissions to act where the omission is a failure to take reasonable steps to discharge a duty. Section 66 extends liability to individuals who arrange for another to do the encouraging or assisting, – for example, a gang leader who orders a gang member to encourage a woman to kill someone will be regarded as having encouraged or assisted the woman.

The old common law is also likely to be of assistance in interpreting the concept of encouragement. The case of **Invicta Plastics Ltd** v **Clare** (1976) held that the encouragement may not be explicit but can be implied from the relevant circumstances. The defendants manufactured a device called a Radatec which could detect wireless transmissions, including those used by police radar traps designed to catch speeding motorists. They advertised the product in a motoring magazine, the advertisement showed a road with a speed limit sign, seen through a car windscreen. The court held that this was an implied encouragement to use the device without a licence, constituting an offence under the Wireless Telegraphy Act 1949. The fact that the company's advertisement did point out that using the device without a licence would be an offence did not prevent liability being incurred. In **R** v **Goldman** (2001) the defendant had seen an advertisement in a magazine for the sale of pornographic videos of children. The defendant ordered a video and on the facts he was found to be encouraging another person to distribute indecent photographs of children below the age of 16.

Under the old common law offence of incitement the courts stated that the defendant did not need to be encouraging any particular person, the encouragement could be addressed to a group, or to people in general. In **R** v **Most** (1881) it was held that an article in a revolutionary newspaper encouraging revolutionaries all over the world to assassinate their heads of state was an offence of incitement to murder.

Impossibility is no defence (s. 47(6)), so defendants can be liable even if the offence which they helped or encouraged could not be committed.

Under s. 56, if the anticipated offence had been committed and it cannot be proved whether the defendant has either encouraged or assisted the offence or committed it as a principal, he or she can be convicted of an offence under s. 44, s. 45 or s. 46 of this Act.

Mens rea

The *mens rea* for s. 44 is an intention to encourage or assist and intention in this context is restricted to direct intention and does not include indirect intention (s. 44(2)). The *mens rea* for s. 45 is a belief that a crime will be committed and that your conduct will provide encouragement or assistance for its commission. The *mens rea* for s. 46 is a belief that one or more crimes will be committed and that your conduct will provide encouragement or assistance for the commission of one or more crimes. For both sections 45 and 46 a belief that an offence *might* be committed will not be sufficient. No definition of 'belief' is provided, but in **R** v **Hall** (1985) the Court of Appeal stated that it was something short of knowledge, but more than a suspicion.

Where the anticipated crime requires *mens rea*, defendants must believe or be reckless as to whether the person encouraged or assisted would act with the *mens rea* for the anticipated offence, or if the defendants had themselves carried out the anticipated crime they would have had sufficient *mens rea* for that offence (s. 47(5)). For all the offences recklessness is sufficient as to the particular circumstances or consequences of the offence and as to the principal offender's state of mind (s. 47(5)). To explain the concept of a circumstance, for the offence of driving while disqualified, the relevant circumstance is the fact that the person was disqualified from driving. For example, if the defendant gives a woman a knife intending the woman to use it to inflict minor injuries on the victim, but the woman kills the victim, the defendant will not be liable for encouraging or assisting murder because he did not intend or believe that this offence would be committed.

Where defendants have encouraged the commission of a strict liability offence, they will only be liable if they themselves have *mens rea*. For example, if a defendant encourages a person to drive their car home unaware that the person is disqualified from driving, the defendant will not be liable for encouraging or assisting the crime due to lack of *mens rea*, the driver will, however, be liable for the strict liability offence of driving while disqualified if he or she goes ahead and drives home.

When s. 44 is being prosecuted, s. 44(2) states that a person is not to be taken to have intended to encourage or assist the commission of an offence merely because such encouragement or assistance was a foreseeable consequence of his act.

Defence

Section 50 of the 2007 Act contains a statutory defence that the defendant acted reasonably in the circumstances that he or she knew, or reasonably believed, to exist. This defence aims to protect people acting in a normal way from criminal liability. For example, if a person is driving a car at 70 miles per hour on a motorway and moves over into the slow lane to allow a speeding car to overtake, he has technically assisted that driver to commit the speeding offence, but his conduct would be considered reasonable. In determining reasonableness, the courts will take into account the seriousness of the anticipated offence or offences, any purpose for which the defendants claim to have been acting and any authority by which they claim to have been acting (s. 50(3)).

There is also an exemption from liability where the offence encouraged or assisted was created in order to protect a category of people and the person doing the encouragement or assistance falls into that category (s. 51). The explanatory notes to the 2007 Act give the following example:

> D is a 12 year old girl and encourages P, a 40 year old man to have sex with her. P does not attempt to have sex with D. D cannot be liable for encouraging or assisting child rape despite the fact it is her intent that P have sexual intercourse with a child under 13 (child rape) because she would be considered the 'victim' of that offence had it taken place and the offence of child rape was enacted to protect children under the age of 13.

Sentence

A person convicted for one of these offences can be subject to the same maximum sentence as for the full offence, except for murder where the maximum sentence is a discretionary life sentence rather than a mandatory life sentence.

Criticism

The Government appears to have been concerned to introduce legislation which could tackle effectively career criminals and terrorist support networks in particular. This desire was understandable but it is questionable whether legislation to achieve this goal was actually needed and the new offences of assisting and encouraging are unnecessarily complex. The common law incitement offence was simple for a jury to understand and caused few problems in practice. An inchoate offence involving assistance could have been added by a few lines in a statute rather than the lengthy and confused provisions in the Serious Crime Act 2007. While the legislation contains long explanations of the core offences, key concepts such as 'encouraging', 'assisting' and 'belief' are left undefined. At the same time it is unsatisfactory that in this context 'intention' is restricted to direct intention, when in other contexts in criminal law it includes indirect intention.

10

Inchoate offences

TOPICAL ISSUE

Incitement in the community

In 2006, there were two high-profile incitement cases before the courts. These two cases had very different outcomes and raised questions about the way the law is applied in practice. The first involved a prosecution of Nick Griffin, the leader of the British National Party. Mr Griffin was charged with four counts of inciting racial hatred under the Public Order Act 1986, following a TV documentary in which he was shown making derogatory comments about Muslims. He was acquitted on two counts but the jury failed to reach a verdict on the other two.

The second case involved a prosecution of Abu Hamza, an Islamic cleric. He was convicted of 15 charges of inciting racial hatred and murder after secret recordings had been made of his sermons in a London mosque.

Reform

In 1993, the Law Commission issued a consultation paper entitled *Assisting and Encouraging Crime* which recommended the establishment of two new inchoate offences of assisting and encouraging crime, but these offences were intended to replace the law on accomplice liability (see Chapter 11) whereas the offences contained in the Serious Crime Act 2007 have left accomplice liability intact.

? Answering questions

Inchoate offences can arise as part of a problem question – obviously they cannot form problem questions on their own, because by their nature they must be linked with another complete offence. Part of the skill in answering problem questions which give rise to such issues is simply recognising that this set of facts gives rise to the issue, and if you spend some time looking at past papers, you should soon begin to pick up the key situations which suggest that the examiners want you to consider inchoate offences. For example, where you are told that a person tries to commit an offence but fails, you will usually be required, among other things, to consider that person's liability for an attempt. On the other hand, if the problem question only mentions the activities of one individual then it is unlikely to raise issues of incitement or conspiracy. For example: 'David walked into a bank with a gun and asked the cashier to hand over the money in the till. She refused to do so and set off the emergency alarm. He panicked, shot her dead and ran off.' Among other offences, David can be liable for attempted robbery, as what he did would amount to something more than merely preparatory to the commission of the complete offence of robbery and he intended to steal by seeking to put someone in fear that force would be used.

Similarly, if you spot someone encouraging or asking someone else to commit an offence, you should consider the offence of encouragement under the Serious Crime Act 2007. If, in the above example, David had gone to rob the bank after being asked to by someone else, or if David himself had tried to persuade a friend to join him in committing the robbery, the offence of encouragement should be discussed. If more than one person is involved in an offence, you should also be aware of the possibility of conspiracy.

1 **A, who lived on the 20th floor of a high-rise building, saw his former girlfriend, B, passing below. He picked up a large plant pot and dropped it from his balcony. The plant pot missed B and, instead, hit C who was severely injured. When B realised what had happened she developed severe depression and as a result was admitted to hospital. There she received inappropriate medical treatment and as a result died.**

Advise A of his criminal liability. What difference, if any, would it make to your advice if the plant pot would have hit B but for a freak gust of wind? *(London External LLB)*

When A threw the plant pot he may have been attempting to hit his former girlfriend. He missed her, and therefore we first need to consider his liability for an attempt. The offence that he was attempting will depend on his state of mind. If he intended to kill his girlfriend, then we would be looking at attempted murder. A mere intent to cause grievous bodily harm rather than death will not be sufficient for attempted murder. If he wanted to cause harm but not death then we would be looking at an attempted non-fatal offence. The action of dropping the pot was more than merely preparatory to the commission of the full offence (whether murder or a non-fatal offence).

The pot struck C who was severely injured. The doctrine of transferred malice could be applied here (see p. 26), so that any *mens rea* that A had in relation to harming B could be transferred to his actual victim, C. There would certainly be liability for a s. 20 offence under the Offences Against the Person Act 1861. If A intended to cause grievous bodily harm there would be liability for a s. 18 offence.

A's conduct made B so depressed that she needed hospital treatment. In the light of **Ireland and Burstowe** and **Chan-Fook**, psychological harm is sufficient to give rise to liability for a non-fatal offence. A critical issue would be the question of causation. Did A cause B's depression (see **Cheshire** and **Jordan** on p. 54)?

B received inappropriate medical treatment and died. Medical negligence does not normally break the chain of causation, but this is an extreme case as depression in itself does not kill, so there could be a convincing argument that the medical treatment had broken the chain of causation. If causation were satisfied, liability for murder and manslaughter would need to be considered and again the question of *mens rea* would be important. For liability for murder to be imposed, an intention to kill or to cause grievous bodily harm would need to be found. The law in **Nedrick** and **Woollin** had to be considered. If there was no direct intention (a desire to kill) then indirect intention would need to be found. For indirect intention, the death or grievous bodily harm would need to have been both virtually certain, and foreseen as virtually certain. This is unlikely to be the case.

The fact that a freak gust of wind caused the pot to miss B raises the issue of whether the death or grievous bodily harm was virtually certain for the purposes of indirect intention.

2 **'The criminal law does not punish people for their guilty thoughts alone but only for overt conduct accompanied by those guilty thoughts.' Assess the validity of this statement with reference to the offence of attempt.** *(OCR)*

Again, this should not be used as an opportunity to write all you know about attempts – or anything else for that matter! As always, there is no right or wrong answer, but one approach might be to divide the essay into the following three parts. First, consider whether the law of attempt requires 'overt conduct'. This will be a matter of looking at the 'more than merely preparatory' test. Secondly, discuss the fact that you do need guilty thoughts by looking at the *mens rea* of the offence. Finally, consider whether the current law gets the right balance, pointing, for example, to the fact that you can be liable for attempting the impossible, and looking at some of the relevant criticisms of the law. Errors to avoid are writing purely about the issue of impossibility when the question was intended to be much broader than this; and discussing conspiracy when the question was limited to attempts.

3 **Should there be criminal offences of encouragement or assisting and conspiracy?**

To keep your essay clear, it would be wise to divide it into two halves, considering encouragement or assisting separately from conspiracy – make it clear in your introduction that this is what you will be doing. To tackle this question, you need a clear statement of the current law, and some critical material.

When explaining what the law is, link your points to the question, pointing out the public policy reason why these are types of conduct which the state currently feels should be penalised with criminal liability. You can also show how the boundaries of the offences have changed – for example, the abolition of most of common law conspiracy and the extension of conspiracy to include conspiracy to do the impossible. Some time could be spent considering the particular uses of conspiracy to defraud and the uncertain role of the other forms of common law conspiracy. The criticism and reform sections in this chapter will be of particular use in answering this question.

4 **David and Ian agree that they want to beat up their neighbour, Faro, because he makes too much noise at night, and the police have failed to do anything about this disturbance. David says he wants to put Faro in hospital for a month. Ian tells David 'Be careful, if he ends up in hospital the police will be on to us, let's just scare him, push him about a bit, and make him understand that the noise has got to stop.' That night, David and Ian march round to Faro's house. They bang on the door and Faro's wife, Meg, answers. They try to push past Meg but the family dog runs towards the two men and they run away.**

The next day David sees Faro in the street. He takes out a knife and plunges towards him. Faro moves out of the way and David slips and cuts the hand of a child who is nearby.

Advise David and Ian as to their criminal liability. *(LLB)*

This problem question raises issues about liability for inchoate offences. There appears to have been a conspiracy to commit a non-fatal offence. A discussion of the relevant non-fatal offence was required. When Ian and David go round to Faro's house, they fail to enter and therefore this appears to be only an attempt to commit a non-fatal offence, or an attempted burglary. Relevant case law on attempts must be examined in detail and the facts of these cases compared with the facts in the problem question.

The second scenario in relation to the injury to the child raised an issue of transferred malice and wounding under s. 20 and s. 18 of the Offences Against the Person Act 1861.

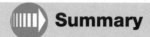 ## Summary

The inchoate offences – attempt, conspiracy and encouraging or assisting – are concerned with the preparatory stages of other criminal offences. The common law offence of incitement has been abolished by the Serious Crime Act 2007. A person may be convicted of an inchoate offence even if the main offence was never actually committed.

Attempt

Actus reus
Section 1(1) of the Criminal Attempts Act 1981 provides that: 'If with intent to commit an offence to which this section applies, a person does an act which is more than merely preparatory to the commission of the offence, he is guilty of attempting to commit the offence.' The question of whether an act is 'more than merely preparatory' is a matter of fact and, in a trial on indictment, will be for the jury to decide. Under s. 1(2) of the Act, people can be guilty of this offence even if the main offence they were attempting to commit was impossible.

Mens rea
Defendants can only be liable for an attempt if they act with the intention of committing the complete offence – recklessness as to the consequences of the act is not enough. Where the definition of the main offence includes circumstances, and recklessness as to these circumstances is sufficient for that aspect of the *mens rea*, then it will also be sufficient for an attempt to commit that offence (though intention will still be required for the rest of the *mens rea*).

Conspiracy
Conspiracy covers agreements between two or more people, usually to commit a crime. There are now two categories of conspiracy: statutory conspiracy and common law conspiracy.

Statutory conspiracy
Under s. 1 of the Criminal Law Act 1977, statutory conspiracy is an agreement by two or more people to do something that will amount to a crime. Section 1(1)(b) of the

Criminal Law Act 1977 makes it clear that where the crime agreed on turns out to be impossible to commit there can still be a conviction for conspiracy. The parties must intend that the agreement will be carried out and the crime committed by one or more of the conspirators.

Common law conspiracy

Under s. 5 of the Criminal Law Act 1977, a common law conspiracy is committed where two or more people agree to defraud, or to corrupt public morals or outrage public decency. A conspiracy to defraud is a property offence, mainly used to deal with the situation where a person dishonestly obtains someone else's property, but his or her behaviour is not covered by the Theft Acts. It does not necessarily involve deceiving anyone.

Assisting or encouraging a crime

The common law offence of incitement has been abolished and replaced by the offences of assisting or encouraging a crime contained in the Serious Crime Act 2007. Three new offences are created by ss. 44, 45 and 46 of the Act. The s. 44 offence is committed when the defendant had intended the relevant offence to be committed, s. 45 is committed when the defendant believed it would be committed and s. 46 is committed when the defendant believed that one or more offences would be committed.

Reading list

Becker, B.C. (1974) 'Criminal attempts and the law of crimes', 3 *Philosophy and Public Affairs* 262.

Brady, J. (1980) 'Punishing attempts' 63 *The Monist* 246.

Glazebrook, P. (1969) 'Should we have a law of attempted crime?' 85 *Law Quarterly Review* 28.

Law Commission (2007) *Conspiracy and Attempts*, Consultation Paper No. 183, London: Law Commission.

Law Commission (2006) *Inchoate Liability for Assisting and Encouraging Crime*, Law Com. No. 300, London: Law Commission.

Ormerod, D. and Fortson, R. (2009) *Serious Crime Act 2007: the Part 2 offences* [2009] Crim LR 389.

Rogers, J. (2008) 'The codification of attempts and the case for "preparation"' [2008] *Criminal Law Review* 937.

Williams, G. (1983) 'The problems of reckless attempts' [1983] *Criminal Law Review* 365.

Reading on the internet

The Law Commission Report *Inchoate Liability for Assisting and Encouraging Crime* (2006) is available on the Law Commission's website at:
   http://www.lawcom.gov.uk/lc_reports.htm

The House of Lords' judgment in **R** v **Saik** (2006) is available on Parliament's website:
http://www.publications.parliament.uk/pa/ld200506/ldjudgmt/jd060503/saik-1.htm

Visit **www.mylawchamber.co.uk/elliottcriminal** to access multiple choice questions, flashcards and practice exam questions to test yourself on this chapter.

Use **Case Navigator** to read in full the key cases referenced in this chapter:

- Ghosh [1982] QB 1053; [1982] 3 WLR 110
- R v Woollin – [1998] 4 All ER 103

11 Accomplices

This chapter explains:

- the different roles that people can play in the commission of a criminal offence: the principal offender, the joint principals, the innocent agents and the secondary parties (also known as accomplices);

- to be a secondary party a person must have aided, abetted, counselled or procured the commission of a principal offence;

- where a person was part of a joint enterprise then the courts are more willing to impose criminal liability; and

- a defence of withdrawal is available in limited circumstances.

Introduction

The person who actually commits the *actus reus* of an offence may not be the only one who is liable for it. If other people play a part in the crime, they too may incur liability as secondary parties – so, for example, a woman who hires a contract killer to murder her husband cannot escape liability merely because she did not physically take part in the killing.

The principal offender

The principal is the main perpetrator of the offence, and usually the person who commits the *actus reus*. Where more than one person is directly responsible for the *actus reus*, there may be more than one principal; they are known as joint principals. The test of whether someone is a joint principal or a secondary party is whether they contribute to the *actus reus* by their own independent act, rather than simply playing a supporting role.

Innocent agents

In some circumstances the principal may not directly carry out the *actus reus*, but instead use what is called an innocent agent. There are two situations in which the person committing the *actus reus* may be considered an innocent agent.

Where someone lacks the *mens rea* for the offence

If, for example, Ann wants to kill Ben, Ann might give Chris a poisonous drug, telling Chris it is an aspirin and asking Chris to give it to Ben. If Chris does so, Chris will be committing the *actus reus*, but as an innocent agent – because Chris, with no idea that the drug is poison, has no *mens rea*. He therefore incurs no criminal liability. Ann is the principal offender since she brought about the innocent agent's act. Similarly, a terrorist who sends a letter bomb which kills the recipient will be the principal, and the postman who unknowingly delivers the parcel is merely an innocent agent.

Where someone has a defence

If Ann persuades Ben to shoot and kill Chris, by convincing Ben that the target is a bear rather than a human being, Ben is an innocent agent and can rely on the defence of mistake; Ann will be the principal offender. The same applies if the principal uses someone below the age of criminal responsibility to bring about the *actus reus*.

Offences to which the concept of an innocent agent cannot apply

It has been suggested that there are some crimes which, by their nature, need to be carried out personally and to which the idea of an innocent agent cannot apply. This is because, for that offence, it would be wrong in logic to describe a person who did not carry out the *actus reus* of the offence as the principal offender. Murder is not such a crime, so in the poisoning example above there is no problem in saying that Ann killed Ben, even though Ann did not actually give Ben the poison. On the other hand, if we take bigamy, for which the *actus reus* is marrying while still married to someone else, it would seem inappropriate to rely on the doctrine of an innocent agent. If Mary persuades Peter to marry Kate, when Mary knows such a marriage would be bigamous because Peter's wife is alive though Peter does not know that, Peter cannot be liable as a principal offender because he lacks the *mens rea* of the offence. It has been argued by academics that Peter should not be treated as an innocent agent nor Mary as the principal, because it is not possible to say that Mary had married Kate while she was married to someone else. She may, however, still be a secondary party.

This problem was ignored in the case of **R v Cogan and Leak** (1976). The case concerned the offence of rape which, like bigamy, one would have expected to be an offence that had to be committed in person. Leak made his wife have sexual intercourse with Cogan. Mrs Leak did not consent to this, but Cogan thought she did. Cogan's mistake meant he lacked the *mens rea* of rape, so he was not liable for the offence. But he was treated as an innocent agent and Leak was liable as the principal offender in the rape of his wife. The case has been heavily criticised but the philosophy behind the case is supported by the decision in **DPP v K and C** (1997) which is discussed below.

Secondary parties

This chapter is primarily concerned with looking at the liability of secondary parties – often described as accomplices or accessories. The key provision for indictable offences is s. 8 of the Accessories and Abettors Act 1861. This states: 'Whosoever shall aid, abet, counsel or procure the commission of any indictable offence, whether the same be an offence at common law or by virtue of any Act passed or to be passed, shall be liable to be tried, indicted and punished as a principal offender.' Section 44 of the Magistrates' Courts Act 1980 lays down a similar provision with respect to summary offences. As the provisions are so similar, we will concentrate on the 1861 Act.

A secondary party is essentially a person who helps or encourages the principal offender before the offence is committed, or at the time when it is committed. Help or encouragement given after the principal has committed the offence – to enable the principal to escape or to sell stolen goods, for example – does not amount to secondary participation, though it might amount to some other offence.

Under s. 8 such a person can generally incur the same liability as the principal offender, for the section states that he 'shall be tried, indicted and punished as a principal offender'. The extent of each party's involvement in a crime will usually be taken into account for sentencing purposes (except where the penalty is fixed, as in murder), but, technically, helping or encouraging someone else to commit a crime can attract the same punishment as actually committing the crime.

The implications of this principle can be seen in the controversial case of **R v Craig and Bentley** (1952), the story of which was made into the film *Let Him Have It*. Bentley was caught and arrested after the pair were chased across rooftops by police. Craig had a gun, and Bentley is alleged to have said to Craig, 'Let him have it.' Craig then shot and killed a policeman. Craig was charged with murdering a police officer (at that time a hanging offence) and Bentley was charged as his accomplice. In court Bentley argued that when he shouted 'Let him have it', he was telling Craig to hand over his gun, rather than, as the prosecution claimed, encouraging him to shoot the police officer. Nevertheless, both were convicted. Craig was under the minimum age for the death sentence, and was given life imprisonment. Bentley, who was older, was hanged. The conviction was subsequently overturned by the Court of Appeal in July 1998, following a long campaign by his family. But the error by the trial judge had simply been that his summing-up was too harsh to the defendant and the legal principle in relation to equal liability for secondary parties as for the principal still stands.

Because the secondary party 'shall be tried, indicted and punished as a principal offender' the prosecution do not have to establish whether the accused was the principal offender or a secondary party, provided it is proven that he was definitely one or the other. In **R** v **Galliano** (1996) the accused was charged with the murder of his wife. There was evidence that either he carried out the killing himself or a killer carried it out on his behalf. The accused's appeal against his conviction was dismissed.

Actus reus

A principal offence

Unlike a person who incurs liability for an inchoate offence, a secondary party cannot (with one exception) be liable if the principal offence is not committed. So if Ranjit encourages Jill to kill Lisa, Ranjit will be immediately liable for inciting murder but will only be liable as a secondary party to the murder if Jill goes ahead and kills Lisa.

In **Thornton** v **Mitchell** (1940) a bus driver was charged with careless driving after an accident. The conductor of the bus had been giving directions to help the driver reverse when the accident occurred, and was charged as a secondary party. The driver was acquitted on the basis that he had not been careless; this meant that the *actus reus* of the offence had not been committed, and so the conductor could not be liable either.

Provided that the prosecution prove that the offence was carried out by someone, a secondary party may be convicted even if the principal is unknown, or has not been caught. Secondary parties can also be convicted where the principal is acquitted. This is because an acquittal does not necessarily mean that the principal has not committed the offence; they may be acquitted because there is a lack of evidence against them, or some procedural defect occurred in the trial (assuming the parties are not tried together), or because they have a defence which accepts the offence was committed but excuses the conduct in the circumstances. In **R** v **Bourne** (1952), the accused forced his wife to commit buggery with a dog. Because the wife had acted under duress (see p. 358), she was not liable as a principal offender, but as an *actus reus* had been committed Bourne was liable as a secondary party.

The exception to the rule that the secondary party can only be liable if the principal offence is committed applies to the particular type of secondary party conduct known as 'procuring', which is discussed in more detail in the next section. Where the secondary party procured the principal offence, only the *actus reus* and not the *mens rea* of the principal offender need be proved. In **R** v **Millward** (1994) the appellant instructed an employee to drive a vehicle on a public road. The appellant knew that the vehicle was in a dangerous condition but the employee did not. Driving the vehicle caused a collision which resulted in a death. The employee was acquitted of causing death by reckless driving (an offence that has since been repealed) since he lacked the *mens rea* of the offence; the appellant was convicted as a secondary party as it was sufficient that he had procured the *actus reus* of the principal offence.

This approach was approved in **DPP** *v* **K and C** (1997). Two girls aged 14 and 11 were charged with procuring the offence of rape of a young girl by an unidentified boy. The two girls had imprisoned and robbed the victim when they were joined by the boy. They ordered the victim to remove her clothes and have sexual intercourse with the boy who partially penetrated her. The magistrates found that the boy could have been under 14 and might have lacked the *mens rea* of the principal offence, so the girls were acquitted. On appeal by way of case stated, it was held that it did not matter if the principal lacked *mens rea*; the girls could still be liable for procuring the principal offence.

Aid, abet, counsel or procure

Section 8 of the Accessories and Abettors Act 1861 provides that liability as a secondary party lies on 'Whosoever shall aid, abet, counsel or procure'. Thus there are four types of secondary liability: aiding, abetting, counselling and procuring.

Up until 1975, it was generally assumed that these particular words had no specific meaning and were interchangeable. This interpretation had to be reconsidered following the case of **Attorney-General's Reference (No. 1 of 1975)**. This stated that these four words describe four different types of behaviour, though their meanings may overlap, and each word should be given its ordinary and natural meaning. In summary, aiding means helping at the time of the principal offence; abetting means encouraging at the time; counselling means encouraging prior to the commission of the principal offence; and procuring means helping prior to its commission.

In practice, the courts often fail to draw this distinction. For example, in **Gillick** *v* **West Norfolk and Wisbech Area Health Authority** (1986) the House of Lords considered the issue of doctors providing contraceptives to girls under the age of 16. It is an offence for a man to have sexual intercourse with a girl under that age, and the judges considered whether, in giving contraceptives to girls under 16, doctors were aiding and abetting this offence. It has since been pointed out that in the light of **Attorney-General's Reference (No. 1 of 1975)**, aiding or abetting means providing help or encouragement at the time the offence is committed, and it is highly unlikely that doctors would be present when sexual intercourse actually took place. It would have been more appropriate to talk about counselling or procuring, which take place prior to the commission of the offence.

An accused may often have committed more than one of these offences, and can be charged with more than one in the same proceedings, the most obvious example being aiding and abetting. We will now look in detail at the meanings of the different words, whether the accomplice must have caused the commission of the main offence, and whether the principal offender needs to have been aware of the accomplice's conduct.

Aiding

Aiding signifies helping the principal at the time when the offence is committed. Providing that some help is given, the prosecution do not have to prove that the help caused the principal to commit the offence, nor that the principal even knew about it.

11

Accomplices

Abetting

Abetting comprises encouragement to commit the crime, which is given at the time that the crime is committed. The principal probably needs to be aware of this encouragement, though the encouragement need not have caused the principal to go ahead and commit the principal offence.

Simply being present at the scene of a crime and failing to stop it or report it to the police is not usually sufficient to constitute aiding the principal, but can it constitute encouragement at the time of the offence and thus abetting? The conclusion from the authorities seems to be that mere presence is not enough; the prosecution must prove something more in order for a court to conclude that this conduct amounted to encouragement. In **R** *v* **Clarkson** (1971), the defendants were soldiers who stood and watched a girl being raped by another soldier in their barracks. It was held that this did not amount to abetting the rapist; in order for it to do so the soldiers must have intended that their presence should encourage the rapist to continue, and it must have in fact encouraged him.

In **Allan** (1963), the accused was present when some of his friends got into a fight. He stayed at the scene and decided that he would help his friends if it became necessary, but in the event his assistance was not needed. The court held that presence at the scene combined with a secret intention to participate was not abetting, provided nothing was done to show that intention.

The defendant in **Coney** (1882) attended an illegal prize fight (a fight that is not carried out in accordance with the Queensberry Rules) and the court said that, while without the spectators there would be no fight, there was insufficient evidence to constitute an abetting.

By contrast, in **Wilcox** *v* **Jeffrey** (1951), a well-known saxophone player came into the UK from the US on a tourist visa. This visa prohibited him from working in England, but he breached its terms by taking part in a musical performance. The defendant not only attended the performance, but also met the saxophonist at the airport, and wrote a favourable review of the performance afterwards. It was held that these things together were sufficient to make him liable for abetting the commission of the offence.

Where an accused has a right to control someone else's actions and deliberately fails to do so, that failure may be a positive encouragement to the other to commit an illegal act, and therefore amount to an abetting. In **Tuck** *v* **Robson** (1970), the defendant was the licensee of a public house who let his customers commit the offence of drinking after hours. Because he was in a position of authority and control, the fact that he did not prevent his clientele from consuming drinks after hours was held to have abetted the offence.

Counselling

This encompasses encouraging the principal to commit the crime. Since encouraging someone at the scene of the crime is abetting, counselling covers giving such encouragement before the crime takes place. The principal must at least be aware that they have the encouragement or approval of the secondary party to commit the offence, and there must be some connection between the encouragement and the commission of the offence though not full causation. On the other hand, it is not necessary to prove that without the counselling the offence would not have been committed.

In **R** v **Calhaem** (1985) the defendant was charged with murder. She had been infatuated with her solicitor and hired another person, Zajac, to kill the solicitor's girlfriend. At her trial, she was alleged to have counselled Zajac to commit murder. In his evidence, Zajac said that, although Ms Calhaem had indeed told him to carry out the killing, he had never had any intention of doing so – he was simply intending to go to her home and pretend that he meant to kill her, so that Ms Calhaem would think he had tried to carry out the plan and pay him his money. However, the victim had screamed a great deal, and he had gone 'berserk' and killed her. On appeal, the court held that it was not necessary to prove that the counselling caused the offence; a less direct connection would suffice, and here that was satisfied by the fact that Zajac would never have gone to the girlfriend's flat if Ms Calhaem had not asked him to do so. Ms Calhaem's conviction was upheld.

Procuring

In **Attorney-General's Reference (No. 1 of 1975)** the Court of Appeal specified that to procure means 'to produce by endeavour'. This suggests that procuring an offence means causing it, or bringing it about, and this does not necessarily require the agreement or knowledge of the principal. In the case, the principal offender was caught driving with a blood-alcohol level over the prescribed limit. The secondary party had 'spiked' the principal's drink with alcohol, knowing that the principal would be driving, and was held to be guilty as a secondary party, even though the principal was not aware of what the secondary party had done.

Mens rea

Once the prosecution have established that the secondary party did an act or acts which could help or encourage the principal to commit the crime, they must prove that the accomplice had the *mens rea* to be liable as a secondary party. It has to be shown that the defendant knew that acts and circumstances constituting a crime would exist (they do not need to know that these acts or circumstances would be a crime, because ignorance of the law is no defence). For example, a woman who tells a man to have sexual intercourse with another woman, knowing that he may have sexual intercourse with that

	Encourage	Help
Before	Counsel	Procure
At the time	Abet	Aid

Figure 11.1 Liability of secondary parties

287

woman, and aware of the circumstance that that woman might not be consenting at the time, could be liable for counselling the offence of rape.

The level of *mens rea* required is very low, because there is no need to prove that the defendant intended to help or encourage the principal. While the courts sometimes talk of 'intending' the help or encouragement, all this appears to mean in this context is that the person acted voluntarily – that they intended to do what they did, rather than that they intended its effect on the principal. Thus, for example, if Peter sells Beatrice a gun, knowing that she intends to kill Jane but not wanting her to do so, and Beatrice proceeds to kill Jane, then Beatrice will be liable for murder and Peter will be liable as a secondary party. The prosecution do not need to prove that Peter intended to help Beatrice, simply that he intended to sell the gun.

If a person acts in complete ignorance of a principal offender's plan to commit a crime they will not be liable as an accomplice. For example, if Bill tells Mohammed that he has locked himself out of his house, and Mohammed helps Bill break into the house, Mohammed will not be liable as a secondary party to the burglary if it later transpires that Bill was breaking into his neighbour's house. This approach was laid down in the leading case of **National Coal Board** v **Gamble** (1959).

KEY CASE

In **National Coal Board** v **Gamble** (1959) an employee of the National Coal Board operated a weighbridge at a colliery. His job included checking the loaded weights of lorries leaving the colliery, since it was an offence to take on to the road a lorry which was overloaded. On seeing that one lorry was over the weight limit, he informed the driver, but the

> An accomplice, when helping or encouraging, must have known that acts and circumstances constituting a crime would exist.

driver replied that he was prepared to take the risk. The weighbridge operator proceeded to give him the ticket with which he was able to leave the colliery. Under the principle of corporate liability and, more specifically, vicarious responsibility (discussed in Chapter 12), the Board were liable for their employees' acts, and were thus secondary parties to the offence committed by the lorry driver. The employee may not have intended to help the driver commit the offence but this did not need to be proved. He had committed the *actus reus* of the crime and all that had to be proved in addition was his awareness of the risk that the acts and circumstances constituting the offence existed.

An example of a secondary party lacking *mens rea* because he was unaware of the circumstances that constituted the offence occurred in **Ferguson** v **Weaving** (1951). The defendant was the licensee of a pub, and had been charged with aiding and abetting customers to commit the offence of consuming intoxicating liquor on licensed premises outside permitted hours. As he did not know that the customers were drinking after closing time he was not liable.

While defendants need not intend the help or encouragement, they must know that their acts were capable of assisting or encouraging. This point was confirmed in **R** v **JF Alford Transport Ltd** (1997). A company, its managing director and its transport manager were charged with aiding and abetting lorry drivers employed by them in the making of false entries on tachograph record sheets. The prosecution claimed that the defendants, as managers of the company, must have known and accepted, if not actively encouraged, what the drivers did. They were convicted and appealed arguing that the trial judge's summing-up suggested to the jury that passive acquiescence would suffice for the purpose of secondary party liability. The Court of Appeal held that, to impose liability on a secondary party, it had to be proved that the particular defendant intended to do the acts which he knew to be capable of assisting or encouraging the commission of the principal offence. He did not need to intend that the crime be committed. A defence that the management turned a blind eye in order to keep the drivers happy rather than to encourage them to produce false tachograph records would therefore fail. Where the defendant knew of the offence the prosecution had to show in addition that the defendant had made a deliberate decision not to prevent its commission. On the facts there was insufficient evidence of knowledge so the appeal was allowed.

The secondary party does not have to want the crime to be committed, and may in fact be very much against it, and yet still be liable. In **DPP for Northern Ireland** v **Lynch** (1975), Lynch was ordered by a man called Meehan to drive him and some others to a place where they planned to kill a policeman. Meehan was known to be ruthless and extremely violent, and apparently made it clear to Lynch that it would be extremely dangerous for him to disobey – in fact Lynch testified that he believed he would himself have been shot if he refused to drive. Lynch did as he was told, staying in the car during the shooting, and driving the killers away afterwards. The court held that although he might not have condoned the plan, and may even have been horrified by it, the fact that he drove the principal to the appointed place, knowing of the relevant circumstances that constituted the offence, meant he could be liable for aiding and abetting (the appeal against his conviction as a secondary party to murder was, however, allowed on a different point).

Merely knowing that some kind of illegal activity is being planned is not sufficient to impose liability as a secondary party. In **Bainbridge** (1960), the accused purchased some cutting equipment for a man called Shakeshaft which was later used in a bank robbery. Bainbridge admitted that he suspected Shakeshaft wanted the equipment for some illegal act, but said he thought it would be breaking up stolen goods rather than a bank robbery. It was held that, for the defendant to be liable as a secondary party to the robbery, he would at least have to know that the equipment was for some form of robbery, though he need not know which bank was going to be robbed and when. In fact, Bainbridge's story was not believed and his conviction was upheld.

In a situation like the one presented in **Bainbridge**, a secondary party will not escape liability by practising 'wilful blindness' – if someone sells a sawn-off shotgun to a person he knows to be a bank robber, and the gun is used in such a robbery, he or she will not escape liability as a secondary party to the crime on the grounds that the buyer did not actually say that the gun was to be used in a bank robbery, and the seller did not ask.

The Court of Appeal in **Bainbridge** talked about the defendant needing to foresee the risk that that 'type' of offence would be committed. But, there are difficulties in trying to divide offences into types. Is burglary the same type of offence as robbery? Is grievous bodily harm the same type of offence as murder? While not overruling this *dictum*, in **DPP for Northern Ireland** v **Maxwell** (1978) the court talked about the offence

11

Accomplices

committed having to fall within the range of offences contemplated by the defendant. The accused was a member of a terrorist organisation which ordered him to drive some men to a public house. He realised that he was being asked to take the men there for some illegal and probably violent purpose, but did not know the specific details of what they planned to do. The men in fact planted a bomb, and Maxwell was convicted of abetting an act done with intent to cause an unlawful explosion. The House of Lords held that Maxwell's knowledge that the men were terrorists and would intend to endanger life or property was sufficient for liability as a secondary party; he did not need to know precisely what kinds of weapons or methods the terrorists planned to use. The offence committed was within the range of offences that he must have contemplated the men were likely to commit.

TOPICAL ISSUE

Teenage suicides

The public has become concerned that some websites and chat rooms on the internet might be encouraging young people to commit suicide. After 17 suicides of young people in the Welsh town of Brigend within the space of 2 years, there was concern that these were 'copycat' suicides which were being encouraged by internet websites. Within hours of the death of a 17 year old teenager called Natasha Randall, a site dedicated to her name appeared on the web, with poems, photographs and tributes. Within a few days the site had nearly 3,000 hits. Does this apparent glorification of teenage suicide amount to an internet suicide cult which could encourage others to follow suit? Teenagers increasingly use social networking sites and chat rooms to discuss their problems and there is a lot of information on the internet about suicides, all of which is almost unregulated. Is the current law adequate to respond to this modern day risk posed by the internet? At the moment under s. 2 of the Suicide Act 1961, it is an offence to encourage or assist a suicide or suicide attempt. In its report *Inchoate Liability for Assisting and Encouraging Crime* (2006), the Law Commission said there was a 'strong case' for updating the language of section 2. The Commission said the problems posed by suicide websites could be tackled without reforming the substance of the law. The Government therefore updated the definition of the offence in section 2 with the passing of the Coroners and Justice Act 2009. The aim of these new legislative provisions is not to change the scope of the current law but to clarify the law by using clearer, modern language in order to improve understanding. The new provisions state that it is an offence to intentionally do something, or arrange for someone to do something, that is capable of encouraging or assisting suicide or attempted suicide of any person, whether known personally to the defendant or not. The offence is committed regardless of whether someone commits suicide as a result of the defendant's conduct. The offence could therefore be committed online, though it would cover more than just websites encouraging teenage suicides. For example, it might include the distribution of information about the Swiss Dignitas Clinic which assists people to commit suicide.

Joint enterprise

The courts have shown themselves more willing to impose criminal liability on secondary parties where they feel that the defendants were involved in a joint enterprise, sometimes described as a joint plan. So what is a joint enterprise? The simplest form of a joint enterprise is where two or more people plan to commit an offence, and go ahead and commit that offence. If all participated in carrying out the plan, all are liable. It does not matter who actually carried out the *actus reus* of the offence. For example, if there was a joint plan between two men to commit a murder, and both men go to the victim, one carrying a stick, the other a gun, and it is a gun wound that kills the victim, both will be liable for murder.

The issue of a joint enterprise can also arise when two or more people plan to commit an offence, but one participant commits a separate offence which goes beyond the original plan. The most common example is a planned robbery, in which the participants hope to be able to get what they want without killing anyone, but one of them does in fact kill. In such a case, the other participants may still be guilty of murder, provided that they had the necessary state of mind.

In **Petters and Parfitt** (1995) the Court of Appeal said that for a joint enterprise to exist, the defendants must have a common purpose or intention. It is not sufficient that they both separately intend the same thing; they must have made it clear to each other, by their actions or words, that they have this common intention, though this might not be communicated until just before or at the point of committing the offence. The two defendants in the case had arrived separately at a car park, where they proceeded to attack the victim. The victim died as a result of a kick in the head, but it was not clear which one of the defendants had given the fatal kick, since they both admitted punching the victim, but denied kicking him at all. An appeal against their convictions was allowed on the ground that it had not been made clear to the jury that, in order for there to be a joint enterprise, the two defendants had to have communicated their common intention to each other.

The significance of the existence of a joint enterprise for liability has caused some debate. **R v Stewart and Schofield** (1995) concerned a robbery that went badly wrong. Stewart had suggested to Schofield and a third man that they should rob a shop. Stewart went armed with a knife and the third man with a scaffolding pole, while Schofield played the role of lookout. During the robbery, the owner of the shop was killed by a blow from the scaffolding pole. The third man was found liable for murder, and the other two were convicted for manslaughter. On appeal, while rejecting their applications, Hobhouse LJ suggested that the law on joint enterprise was separate to the law on secondary participation:

> The allegation that a defendant took part in the execution of a crime as a joint enterprise is not the same as an allegation that he aided, abetted, counselled or procured the commission of that crime. A person who is a mere aider or abettor etc, is truly a secondary party to the commission of whatever crime it is that the principal has committed although he may be charged as a principal. If the principal has committed the crime of murder, the liability of the secondary party can only be a liability for aiding and abetting murder. In contrast, where the allegation is joint enterprise, the allegation is that one defendant participated in the criminal act of another.

The Court of Appeal also appeared to support this distinction in **R v O'Brien** (1995), which concerned a secondary party to the attempted murder of a policeman. The Law Commission took a similar approach, suggesting that the law of secondary parties could be abolished while retaining the law on joint enterprises. However, leading criminal law academics have severely criticised this analysis, arguing that joint enterprise is clearly part of the law on secondary participation, the only distinction being that, where a joint enterprise exists, it will usually be easier to find the elements of helping or encouraging and the relevant *mens rea*. The leading authority on joint enterprises is now **R** *v* **Powell and English** (1997), which gave no support to the suggestion that liability for participation in a joint enterprise was separate to liability as a secondary party. Thus the preferred approach is that the law on joint enterprises is part of the law on secondary party liability, and **Stewart and Schofield** should now be seen as bad law on this point. The main significance of the presence of a joint enterprise is simply to lower the threshold of *mens rea* required by a secondary party.

We have seen that under the principle laid down in **National Coal Board** *v* **Gamble** (1959) you normally need to prove knowledge to impose liability on a secondary party. The existence of a joint enterprise means that liability can be imposed where there is mere foresight rather than knowledge. Where there is a joint enterprise and someone commits an offence that goes beyond the scope of the joint enterprise, the others will be liable as secondary parties to that offence if they foresaw it might be committed. If Pat and Jill have agreed to rob a bank and in the process Pat goes outside their plan and kills a member of the public, Jill will be liable not only for the robbery but also as a secondary party to the murder if she foresaw the risk that Pat might commit murder.

If the perpetrator's acts were fundamentally different from those foreseen by a member of the joint enterprise, then that member will not be liable for them (**R** *v* **Powell and English**). If the *mens rea* of the perpetrator is fundamentally different from that foreseen by the member of the joint enterprise, that difference will be irrelevant and he or she will still be liable (**R** *v* **Rahman**).

KEY CASE

In **R** *v* **Powell and English** two separate appeals were heard together before the House of Lords. On the issue of the *mens rea* required to be liable as part of a joint enterprise, Lord Hutton stated: 'It is sufficient to found a conviction for murder for a secondary party to have realised that in the course of the joint enterprise the primary party might kill with intent to do so or with intent to cause grievous bodily harm.'

> To be liable for murder as part of a joint enterprise a person must have realised that the principal offender might kill with the *mens rea* of murder.

In the first appeal, three men visited a drug dealer and the dealer was shot. The prosecution was unable to prove which of the three shot the victim, but agreed that all three participants were guilty because the two who did not fire the gun nevertheless knew that the third man had a gun and realised he might use it to kill or cause serious injury. Their appeal against conviction was rejected.

In the second case, English was involved in a joint enterprise to attack a police officer with wooden posts. The principal offender went beyond the joint enterprise by stabbing the officer to death with a knife. English's appeal was allowed, as the House of Lords stated that, where the lethal act by the primary party was fundamentally different from the acts foreseen by the secondary party, the latter would only be liable for a homicide if the weapon used was as dangerous as the one contemplated.

The law on joint enterprises was considered by the House of Lords in 2008 in **R v Rahman**. An Asian gang of up to 20 youths carrying wooden and metal poles had chased a bi-racial teenager through the streets of Leeds. The victim was killed when he was stabbed in the back with a knife,

> To be liable under a joint enterprise a person only needs to foresee the acts, not the *mens rea*, of the principal offender.

and the injury was probably caused with an intention to kill. Four men were convicted of murder having been part of the joint criminal enterprise and having acted as secondary parties to the killing. There was no evidence that they had themselves inflicted the fatal stab wound. They argued in their defence that they were not carrying a knife and did not know or foresee that anyone else was carrying a knife; the principal offender was acting beyond the scope of any joint enterprise. Both the prosecution and the defence accepted that the key form of *mens rea* required was foresight, but the defence argued that the defendants could only be liable if they had foreseen that the principal offender would intend to kill (arguing that foreseeing an intention to cause serious bodily harm should not be sufficient), while the prosecution argued that all that was required was for the defendants to have foreseen what the principal might do. The House of Lords unanimously agreed with the prosecution. It looked at the 'fundamental difference' rule and held that the difference in mental intention between the principal offender and the defendants could not amount to a fundamental difference. The House considered that the men intended to cause serious physical harm and knew weapons such as baseball bats, a scaffolding pole and a knife might be used:

> Given the fluid, fast-moving course of events in incidents such as that which culminated in the killing of the deceased, incidents which are unhappily not rare, it must often be very hard for jurors to make a reliable assessment of what a particular defendant foresaw as likely or possible acts on the part of his associates. It would be even harder, and would border on speculation, to judge what a particular defendant foresaw as the intention with which his associates might perform such acts. It is safer to focus on the defendant's foresight of what an associate might do, an issue to which knowledge of the associate's possession of an obviously lethal weapon such as a gun or a knife would usually be very relevant.

The House suggested that the fundamental difference rule could be qualified as follows:

> If B realises (without agreeing to such conduct being used) that A may kill or intentionally inflict serious injury, but nevertheless continues to participate with A in the venture, that will amount to a sufficient mental element for B to be guilty of murder if A, with the requisite intent, kills in the course of the venture unless (i) A suddenly produces and uses a weapon of which B knows nothing and which is more lethal than any weapon which B contemplates that A or any other participant may be carrying and (ii) for that reason A's act is to be regarded as fundamentally different from anything foreseen by B.

Therefore, following **R v Rahman** the foresight required for liability as part of a joint enterprise is foresight with respect to the actions of the principal offender. No foresight is required with regard to the *mens rea* of the principal offender. On the facts the appellants intended grievous bodily harm, they did not intend to kill and they did not foresee that anybody in the joint enterprise intended to kill. The actual killer appeared to have an intention to kill but this was irrelevant to the issue of liability of those in the joint enterprise. All that mattered was that they had foreseen the acts of the killer, it did not matter that they had not foreseen the *mens rea* of the killer. The intention to kill of the killer does not make the killer's fatal acts fundamentally different. Before **Rahman** it had been thought that the defendant who had a lesser *mens rea* than the principal would be liable for the offence which reflected his own level of *mens rea*, but following **Rahman** this is not the case. An accomplice may foresee that the principal offender will commit manslaughter, but the principal offender carries out the expected stabbing with sufficient *mens rea* for murder. Both the accomplice and the principal offender will be liable for murder.

An example of a defendant who lacked the *mens rea* to be liable in a joint enterprise is **R v Rafferty** (2008). The defendant had been involved in attacking the victim on a beach. He had then left the group carrying out the attack to try and withdraw money from the victim's account using the victim's cash point card. When he returned to the group he discovered they had drowned the victim in the sea. The Court of Appeal allowed his appeal against conviction for being a secondary party to murder on the basis that he had not foreseen the victim would be drowned.

Saunders and Archer (1573) is a very old case in this field. Saunders wanted to kill his wife, and Archer supplied him with poison for this purpose. Saunders, who was presumably an avid reader of fairy tales, put the poison into an apple and gave the apple to his wife. She took a bite from it, but then passed it to their daughter, who finished off the apple and died as a result. Saunders was found liable for the murder of the daughter, but Archer was acquitted as a secondary party, because he could not have foreseen that Saunders would fail to intervene. If the same facts were to occur today, the doctrine of transferred malice would probably mean that Archer would be liable.

In **Davies v DPP** (1954) two gangs of boys were involved in a brawl on Clapham Common. One of them, E, had a knife, and ended up stabbing and killing someone. Davies was charged as a secondary party to the murder but it was held that, as there was no evidence that he knew E had a knife, he could not have contemplated the risk that E might use it. Therefore he was not a party to the murder, though he was guilty of common assault. A similar conclusion was reached, on different facts, in **Mahmood** (1994). The defendant was 'joyriding' with a friend, who was driving the car. The police spotted the car and pursued it, and the friend drove recklessly in order to get away. Finally the two boys jumped out of the car, leaving it in gear. The car mounted the pavement, killing a baby in its pram. The defendant was charged as a secondary party to manslaughter. On appeal, the Court of Appeal concluded that he would have been liable if death had occurred while the car was being driven recklessly, but there was no evidence that he had foreseen that the friend might abandon the car while it was still in gear.

While a defendant can be liable on the basis of foresight that someone else would behave in a certain way, it needs to be decided what degree of foresight is required. Sir Robin Cooke commented in **Chan Wing-Siu** (1985): 'Various formulae have been suggested – including a substantial risk, a real risk, a risk that something might well happen. No one formula is exclusively preferable.' However, he said, risks that the defendant had merely considered 'fleetingly or even causing him some deliberation' were not sufficient. The three defendants in the case were charged with murder. They had gone to the victim's flat in order to enforce payment of a debt, and the victim had been stabbed during the ensuing fight. One of the three said he had not realised the other two had knives. The Privy Council held that, where the principal was convicted of murder, secondary parties could be liable for the same offence, if they foresaw that it was more probable than not that the principal might kill or cause grievous bodily harm. Therefore, all the parties in the case were liable if they foresaw a substantial risk that one of their accomplices might have a knife and use it with the intention of inflicting serious injury, even though they did not intend or want this to happen.

The Court of Appeal upheld the conviction of the defendant in **R** v **O'Brien** (1995) as a secondary party for the attempted murder of a policeman. He had been the driver in the car when the policeman had been shot by his co-defendant. As regards his *mens rea* it only had to be proved he knew that in the course of committing the agreed crime the principal offender *might* act with an intent to kill. It was not necessary for him to know that the principal offender *would* act with such an intent.

Liability of a secondary party for a different offence

Until 1986 the courts took the approach that a secondary party could not be convicted of a more serious offence than the principal. In **R** v **Richards** (1974) the defendant hired two men to attack her husband, telling them to 'put him in hospital for a month'. She was convicted as a secondary party to wounding with intent under s. 18 of the Offences Against the Person Act 1861, but the two men were acquitted of that offence, and instead convicted of unlawful wounding, a lesser offence. The Court of Appeal quashed Mrs Richards's original conviction and substituted a conviction for unlawful wounding, holding that, as a secondary party, she should not be liable for a more serious offence than the two principals.

However, Lord Mackay pointed out in **R** v **Howe** (1986) that sometimes this would cause the law to be unduly lenient on a secondary party. As an example of this, consider a situation in which Ann hands Ben a gun, telling him that it is loaded only with blank cartridges, and asking him to fire it at Clare, just to scare her. Ann actually knows that the gun is loaded with live ammunition, and wants Ben to kill Clare. When Ben fires the gun at Clare she dies instantly. Ben, as the principal offender, can only be liable for manslaughter, because he did not intend to kill nor to cause grievous bodily harm to Clare. If the *ratio* of **Richards** were applied, Ann would also only be liable for manslaughter, even though she did intend to kill Clare. Because of this anomaly, the case of **Richards** was overruled by **R** v **Howe**.

Strict liability offences

In strict liability crimes the secondary party must have *mens rea*, even though the principal can be convicted without it. In **Callow** v **Tillstone** (1900) a butcher was liable as a principal offender for exposing unfit meat for sale, which is a strict liability offence. The defendant was a vet who had examined the carcasses at the butcher's request and

11

Accomplices

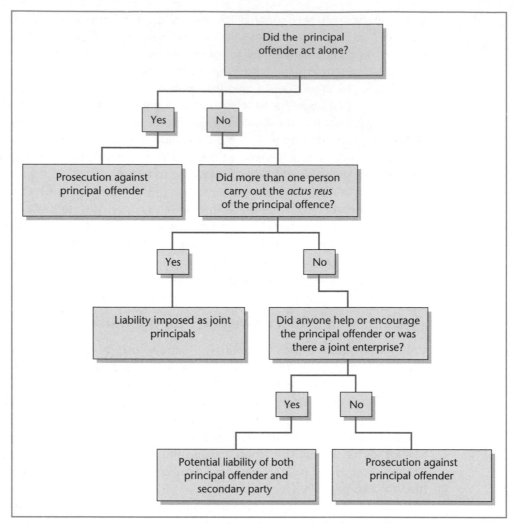

Figure 11.2 Accomplices

certified that the meat was sound. He was convicted of aiding and abetting the offence, but this verdict was quashed on appeal, because he had not known the meat was unfit.

The offence of causing death by dangerous driving is an offence of strict liability. In **R v Webster** (2006) the defendant owned a car and allowed Westbrook, who he knew to have been drinking, to drive the car. Westbrook drove the car erratically and at excessive speed. As a result, one of the passengers was thrown out of the car and died. The defendant was charged with aiding and abetting Westbrook to cause death by dangerous driving. His initial conviction was quashed by the Court of Appeal because the trial judge had not made clear that in order for the defendant to be liable he would need *mens rea* as a secondary party. The trial judge should have directed the jury that he would only be liable if he had foreseen that Westbrook was likely to drive dangerously. Knowing that Westbrook had been drinking was strong evidence that he had this *mens rea*, but did not constitute the *mens rea* itself.

Withdrawal

An alleged secondary party who withdraws from a joint enterprise before the offence is committed and decides not to take part (or take any further part) may escape liability. Where the criminal conduct is spontaneous they can withdraw, and thereby avoid liability, without communicating it to the principal offender, for example by simply walking away. In **R** v **Mitchell and King** (1999) there had been some trouble inside an Indian restaurant. A fight ensued between staff and three customers outside the restaurant. One member of staff was killed and all three customers, including Mitchell, were charged with his murder. There was some evidence that after the deceased had been repeatedly kicked and hit, the three accused had walked away from the deceased leaving him on the ground. Mitchell had then turned back, picked up a stick and hit the victim several more times. It was possible that these constituted the fatal blows. In their defence the other two defendants argued that they had withdrawn from the joint enterprise by the time the fatal blows were struck. The trial judge directed the jury that someone participating in a joint enterprise could only withdraw by communicating his withdrawal to the principal offender. They were convicted and appealed. The Court of Appeal held that for an effective withdrawal from the criminal conduct communication was not required where the criminal enterprise was spontaneous rather than pre-planned. The appeals were allowed and a retrial ordered, as it was possible that the death had resulted from the injuries incurred before Mitchell returned with the stick.

Mitchell and King was followed in **R** v **O'Flaherty** (2004). The Court of Appeal stated that the question of whether people had done enough to demonstrate that they were withdrawing from a joint enterprise was ultimately a question of fact and degree for the jury. In that case there was an effective withdrawal from a spontaneous fight, where the defendants did not actually walk away, but where they did not follow the fight when it moved to the next street.

If the criminal conduct is planned, a person can only withdraw from the plan and avoid criminal liability if their withdrawal happens at a sufficiently early stage and the secondary party communicates their withdrawal to the principal offender and does everything they reasonably can to prevent the crime from going ahead. What constitutes sufficient withdrawal depends on the facts of each case and is for the jury to decide. In **R** v **Becerra** (1975), the accused took part in a burglary, armed with a knife. He and his accomplice had agreed that if they were caught in the act, Becerra should use the knife, but when they saw someone approach, Becerra changed his mind, said 'Let's go' and ran away. The other burglar used the knife, killing the victim. The court held that Becerra's words were not enough in themselves to constitute a withdrawal from the crime. At such a late stage only more definite action, such as attempting to take away the knife, could have amounted to repentance.

The defendant in **Rook** (1993) was involved in a plan to murder. He later changed his mind and decided not to take part; so on the day that the murder was to take place he made sure that he was not at home when the other parties to the plan came round to collect him. This conduct was held to be insufficient to constitute an unequivocal communication of his withdrawal, and so he was still liable as a secondary party to the murder.

11

Accomplices

Defendants who change their minds and do not take part in a planned crime may still be liable for incitement or conspiracy, as already discussed in Chapter 10.

Who did it?

Sometimes the prosecution can establish that a victim died as a result of a wound, and that a group of people were involved in the attack, but it cannot be established which person caused the fatal blow. In this situation they can be convicted of murder if the prosecution can show that they foresaw that the fatal blow would be carried out by one of them. It does not matter that the prosecution cannot identify precisely who administered the fatal blow, as under s. 8 of the Accessories and Abettors Act 1861 they are all treated as if they are the principal offender.

Where, however, non-accidental death or injury is caused by someone, but it is unclear which of two or more people actually caused the harm, and there is no evidence of secondary participation, then nobody can be convicted (**Lane and Lane** (1986)). This has been a particular problem where children have been injured or killed by a parent, but it is not clear which parent caused the death. When the child is very young they are particularly vulnerable because they are not able to speak and tell the authorities who caused them harm. The result appears to be that many non-fatal and fatal offences against children are going unpunished.

The NSPCC has found that every week three children under the age of 10 are killed or suffer serious injury (Plumstead (2002)). Research carried out by Cardiff Family Studies Research Centre (Cathy Cobley *et al.* (2003)) has found that the main suspects at the start of the police investigation are usually the natural parents of the child and occasionally other carers. In most cases it can be said with certainty that one of two identified people must have caused the serious injury, but it is often not possible to say which one. In this context, the rule in **Lane and Lane** applies, so that unless it can be proved that one carer failed to intervene to prevent the harm (and is thus liable for aiding and abetting the assault), no conviction has historically been possible. This difficulty in identifying which carer carried out the attack meant that only a few cases of serious and fatal injury against children were being brought to the criminal courts. As a result, sadly, a significant number of children were being killed or seriously injured each year, but only a relatively small number of those responsible were being convicted of any criminal offence. Where a conviction has been obtained, the charges and sentences do not reflect the gravity of the offence. The Law Commission looked at this problem to see how the wrongdoers could be brought to justice. Parliament has now passed the Domestic Violence, Crime and Victims Act 2004. This contains the offence of causing or allowing the death of a child or vulnerable adult, which aims to tackle this problem (discussed on p. 126).

● Victims as secondary participants

Some statutes are passed specifically to protect a particular group of people, such as minors. People who fall within such groups cannot be held liable as participants in the criminal offence created by the statute. In **Tyrell** (1894), the defendant was a girl under 16 years old. It was stated that she could not be held guilty of aiding or abetting a male to commit the offence of having unlawful sexual intercourse with her, or of inciting him to commit that offence, however willing she might have been for the offence to be committed.

Gangs

One of the aims of the inchoate and accomplice offences is to try and tackle the problem of criminal gangs. Therefore, to evaluate the effectiveness of these offences it is worth considering how criminal gangs operate in the UK. In a study of criminals in the 1960s, Downes concluded that there were no criminal gangs in the East End of London that matched the American stereotype. Instead there were small 'cliques' of four or five members who sometimes committed crimes together.

Bennett and Holloway (2004) have carried out an interesting review of the gang problem in modern English society. Newspaper articles have suggested that gang membership is increasing, and have linked this with the problem of gun crime and drugs. Gangs have been described in the media as 'Asian gangs', 'Turkish gangs', 'Albanian gangs', 'Black gangs', 'Drug gangs' and 'Girl gangs'. The National Criminal Investigation Service has also reported an increase in gun possession among gangs.

A report by Manchester City Council estimated that over 1,000 young people in Greater Manchester were involved in gangs. Bullock and Tilley (2002) found that in south Manchester there were four major street gangs, with between 26 and 67 members. The gang members were all male and typically heavily involved in criminal behaviour with, on average, 12 prior arrests and two convictions. They committed a wide range of offences, including both serious violent offences and property crime. Each gang had a core group of main players and a number of additional and associate members. Weapon carrying was common among gang members.

Mares (2001) also looked at gangs in Manchester. He described the heavy involvement of gangs in drug trading, including heroin, crack and cocaine. The gangs in the city centre had about 90 members in each gang and the large majority were Afro-Caribbean in origin. The gangs were only loosely organised and there were no formal leaders. Outside the city centre the gangs were different. Gangs in Salford were all white, most gang members were under 25 years old and some were as young as 10. Gangs in Wythenshawe were smaller, with an average of 25 members and were mixed in terms of gender (about a quarter were women) and ethnicity (about 10 per cent were black).

11

Accomplices

Criticism

Joint enterprises

The simple requirement of foresight where there is a joint enterprise seems hard to reconcile with **Moloney**, which stressed that liability for murder requires an intent to kill or cause grievous bodily harm and that foresight was only evidence of intention. Since secondary parties may be punished as if they were a principal, it seems unjust that they should be convicted without the same *mens rea* as that required for the principal. Despite this, the approach was approved in **R v Powell**, **R v English** (1997) due to the need to protect the public from criminals operating in gangs.

The law was challenged in **R v Concannon** (2001) as being unfair contrary to Art. 6 of the European Convention on Human Rights. However, this argument was rejected as it was an attack on the substantive law, while Art. 6 is concerned only with procedural fairness.

The law on joint enterprises is extremely complex and arguably unfair in penalising people who had only a remote connection with the commission of a criminal offence and did not directly participate in that offence. Now that the inchoate offences have been extended to include assisting the commission of a criminal offence under the Serious Crime Act 2007 it is questionable whether we need to criminalise people purely on the basis of their involvement in a criminal enterprise. Professor Sullivan (2008) has observed:

> . . . a person who is party to a joint criminal venture may be guilty of a criminal offence despite a lack of intent to commit the offence, a lack of agreement to commit the offence, a lack of any involvement in the commission of the offence and a lack of any assistance or encouragement to those involved in its commission.

There is some uncertainty whether joint enterprises should be analysed in law as a branch of secondary party liability, or whether it is a totally separate area of law. In **R v Stewart and Scholfield** (1995) the Court of Appeal treated joint enterprises and secondary participation as two separate areas of law:

> The allegation that a defendant took part in the execution of a crime as a joint enterprise is not the same as an allegation that he aided, abetted, counselled or procured the commission of that crime. A person who is a mere aider or abettor etc, is truly a secondary party to the commission of whatever crime it is that the principal has committed although he may be charged as a principal. If the principal has committed the crime of murder, the liability of the secondary party can only be a liability for aiding and abetting murder. In contrast, where the allegation is joint enterprise, the allegation is that one defendant participated in the criminal act of another.

The Law Commission also considers that secondary party liability and joint enterprise liability are separate areas of law. It considers that offences committed pursuant to a joint criminal venture can be committed without any actual assistance or encouragement by the defendant. As a result it has suggested that the law of secondary parties could be abolished while retaining the law on joint enterprises. However, Professor Smith has argued persuasively that joint enterprise is part of the law on secondary participation, the only distinction being that where a joint enterprise exists, it will usually be easier to find the elements of helping or encouraging and the relevant *mens rea*. Recent case law appears to support Professor Smith's analysis, including dicta in the House of Lords' judgment of **Rahman** (2008).

Deviations from the plan

The distinction highlighted in **R v Bamborough** (1996), between those who foresaw the harm but contemplated it would be committed in a different way and would be secondary parties, and those who avoid liability because the principal offender went beyond the agreement, is a very fine distinction which will be difficult to apply in practice.

Sentencing

The current law treats the secondary party as if he committed the actual crime. This is very harsh and can be seen as lowering the threshold of criminal liability. Under German law the accessory has a lower maximum sentence than the principal.

Reform

The draft Criminal Code would abolish secondary party liability and replace it with inchoate offences where the defendant 'procures, assists or encourages'. Inchoate offences do not require the final offence to be committed and liability would arise as soon as the procuring, assisting or encouraging took place. This would avoid problems of deciding what the relationship should be between the accomplice's conduct and the final offence. The Serious Crime Act 2007 has introduced the inchoate offences of assisting or encouraging, but left the secondary party offences intact.

In its most recent report on the subject, *Participating in Crime* (2007) the Law Commission has recommended that s. 8 of the Accessories and Abettors Act 1861 should be repealed and replaced with legislation that uses the words 'assisting or encouraging'. The reformed offences would still constitute secondary party liability, rather than inchoate offences, as they would only apply if the principal offence was committed.

The Commission is concerned that the current law is both complex and uncertain leading to numerous appeals to the higher courts. Secondary party liability for murder is particularly sensitive because a conviction gives rise to a mandatory life sentence. The Government initially appeared to accept the core recommendations of the Law Commission on this subject. It issued a consultation paper entitled *Murder, manslaughter and infanticide: proposals for reform of the law* (2008). The consultation paper considered reforming the law on secondary party liability for a homicide offence with a view to reforming accomplice liability more generally at a later stage, guided by the same principles. The paper is less radical than the draft criminal code as secondary party liability would be retained and reformed, rather than replaced by inchoate offences. The consultation paper suggested that the current law on secondary liability in the Accessories and Abettors Act 1861 should be repealed in so far as it applies to homicide offences. However, following consultation, the Government has concluded that it would be better to reform all of secondary liability at the same time rather than trying to focus purely on secondary parties to homicide. As the proposed reforms would effectively be bolted onto an existing common law framework, the resulting proposals were extremely complex and would be difficult for any jury to understand. These reforms have therefore been put on hold until further consideration can be given to the general law of secondary parties.

? Answering questions

① **Using cases to illustrate your answer, critically consider whether the words 'aid, abet, counsel and procure' each have a separate meaning.** *(OCR)*

An answer to this question might start by pointing out that these words come from s. 8 of the Accessories and Abettors Act 1861 and point to the leading case of **Attorney-General's Reference (No. 1 of 1975)**. Most of the material discussed under the subheading 'Aid, abet, counsel or procure' is of relevance to this essay, including the fact that the *mens rea* in relation to those words is much the same, apart from perhaps for procuring. You are asked to

11

Accomplices

consider the law 'critically', so you need to draw out some of the confusion that still exists, illustrated by the case of **Gillick** and the problems with joint enterprises. You should also discuss the reform proposals in the draft Criminal Code.

2 '. . . if four words are employed here, "aid", "abet", "counsel" or "procure", the probability is that there is a difference between each of those four words . . .' (Lord Widgery CJ, in Attorney-General's Reference (No. 1 of 1975)).

Do you agree that each of the four words should have a separate meaning? *(10 marks)*

Do the four words together satisfactorily summarise the law relating to secondary participation? *(15 marks) (OCR)*

This is a situation where it would have been tempting to talk generally on the subject without really answering the question.

In fact, this question can be answered quite precisely, if you plan your answer carefully. For the first part, you can say what the law is on the meaning of the four words, but you must also say whether you think there should be a separate meaning. You are free to answer in favour or against, but you should point to confusion from the cases, intricate distinctions which merely complicate the law without adding much of substance, problems for the jury and so forth. Again, the draft Criminal Code will be relevant.

For the second part (which you should spend slightly longer on as it is worth more marks), you are free to take any approach you want, but one line of argument would be that the words are misleading, old-fashioned and give little clue as to the intricate distinctions that are drawn between them. For example, there seems no linguistic reason why aiding should not require any causal connection while abetting does.

3 David and Shirley are members of the Animals Have Rights organisation. In order to draw attention to their demands they decide to blow up a farm house. They persuade Neil, a former member of the organisation who had not participated in its affairs for a year, to supply bomb-making equipment, by threatening to kill his girlfriend and son if he refused. They persuaded Ian, a timorous taxi-driver, to take them to the farm. David and Shirley planted the explosive device with a three-minute time fuse and shouted a warning that the occupants had three minutes to get out. The bomb exploded prematurely, killing Liz and seriously injuring Tony.
Consider the criminal liability of David, Shirley, Neil and Ian.

In this question David and Shirley do exactly the same things, so they can be dealt with together. As they are principal offenders, it is probably best to deal with them first, and to start with their liability for complete offences before looking at their liability for inchoate offences.

The most serious complete offence they could be liable for is the murder of Liz. They have committed the *actus reus* of murder (causation is not an issue on these facts as there is no intervening event), so the only debate will be whether they had the *mens rea* of murder. As they shout a warning and the bomb goes off prematurely, the key question will be whether they foresaw that death or personal injury were virtually certain to result from their conduct (though remember to point out that the *mens rea* required is intention, and foresight will only be evidence of this intention). The key cases of **Moloney**, **Nedrick** and **Woollin** will need to be discussed. Remember that in discussing *mens rea*, motive (such as helping animals) is irrelevant.

If David and Shirley are found to have the *mens rea* of murder, there is nothing to suggest that they would fall within the defences of provocation or diminished responsibility (or any other defence), so voluntary manslaughter is not an issue. Although murder is the likely offence, it would also be worth considering involuntary manslaughter as a fall-back position in case a jury found that they did not have the *mens rea* of murder.

Next, you should consider the non-fatal injury to Tony. We are told that he is seriously injured, but it is not clear whether this would be sufficiently serious to fall within s. 18 of the Offences Against the Person Act 1861. If it does, David and Shirley can only be liable for this if they were also liable for murder, since if they lacked the *mens rea* for murder, they would also lack the *mens rea* for s. 18 of the 1861 Act. They might have the *mens rea* of a s. 20 offence, if they foresaw the risk that they might cause some physical harm to a person. If Tony's injuries are not sufficient to constitute GBH then David and Shirley are likely to be liable under s. 47.

David and Shirley will also be liable for criminal damage and aggravated criminal damage, as they were reckless as to the endangering of life. Note that the relevant form of recklessness used to be **Caldwell** recklessness, but is now subjective recklessness following the decision of **R v G and another**. This should be easy to prove on the facts.

As for inchoate offences discussed in Chapter 10, David and Shirley will be liable for conspiring to commit at least criminal damage. They will also incur liability for inciting the commission of criminal damage in relation to their behaviour towards Neil and Ian.

Moving on to Neil, he is obviously not the principal offender, as he does not personally carry out the *actus reus* of the principal offences, so his potential liability is that of a secondary party. He provides assistance prior to the time of the commission of the main offence, so his role would be that of a procurer. Procurers are thought to require knowledge of the acts and circumstances of the crime. He would probably have the *mens rea* of a secondary party to the criminal damage, but would he have the *mens rea* of a secondary party to murder? The fact that he provided a three-minute time fuse may be relevant here. Neil is also likely to argue that he acted under duress (see p. 358). Note that following **Re A (Children)** (2000) the defence of duress may be available to murder as well as to the lesser offences. You need to consider the fact that he did originally join the organisation.

Ian is potentially liable as a secondary party. His role was to provide help at the time of the *actus reus*, so he might be labelled an abettor. On the issue of *mens rea*, foresight of the acts and circumstances of the offence would be sufficient. The case of **Lynch** makes it clear that the fact that Ian does not want the bombing to happen may not help him. Like Neil, he will also seek to rely on the defence of duress, and in this case it is not self-induced. Note that in applying the second limb of the **Graham** test of duress, the court could not take into account that Ian was timorous, because the reasonable person must be treated as someone of reasonable firmness.

Summary

The principal offender

The principal is the main perpetrator of the offence, and usually the person who commits the *actus reus*. Where more than one person is directly responsible for the *actus reus*, there may be more than one principal; they are known as joint principals.

Innocent agents

In some circumstances the principal may not directly carry out the *actus reus*, but instead use what is called an innocent agent, who is a person lacking the *mens rea* of the offence or having a valid defence.

Secondary parties

The key provision relating to the liability of accomplices for indictable offences is s. 8 of the Accessories and Abettors Act 1861. This states: 'Whosoever shall aid, abet, counsel or procure the commission of any indictable offence, whether the same be an offence at common law or by virtue of any Act passed or to be passed, shall be liable to be tried, indicted and punished as a principal offender.' Section 44 of the Magistrates' Courts Act 1980 lays down a similar provision with respect to summary offences.

A secondary party is essentially a person who helps or encourages the principal offender before the offence is committed, or at the time when it is committed.

Actus reus

A secondary party cannot usually be liable if the principal offence is not committed. There are four types of secondary liability: aiding, abetting, counselling, and procuring. Aiding means helping at the time of the principal offence; abetting means encouraging at the time; counselling means encouraging prior to the commission of the principal offence; and procuring means helping prior to its commission.

Mens rea

It has to be shown that the defendant knew that acts and circumstances constituting a crime would exist (they do not need to know that these acts or circumstances would be a crime, because ignorance of the law is no defence). The level of *mens rea* required is very low, because there is no need to prove that the defendant intended to help or encourage the principal. This approach was laid down in the leading case of **National Coal Board** *v* **Gamble** (1959).

Joint enterprise

The courts have shown themselves more willing to impose criminal liability on secondary parties where they feel that the defendants were involved in a joint enterprise, sometimes described as a joint plan. Where defendants are part of a joint enterprise they will be liable for any offence which they foresaw might occur.

Liability of a secondary party for a different offence

The secondary party can be liable for a different offence than the principal offender, even if this offence is more serious.

Strict liability offences

In strict liability crimes the secondary party must have *mens rea*, even though the principal can be convicted without it.

Withdrawal

An alleged secondary party who withdraws from a joint enterprise before the offence is committed and decides not to take part (or take any further part) may escape liability. Where the criminal conduct is spontaneous they can withdraw, and thereby avoid liability, without communicating this fact to the principal offender, for example by simply walking away. Where the criminal conduct is planned, a person can only withdraw from the plan and avoid criminal liability if their withdrawal happens at a sufficiently early stage and the secondary party communicates their withdrawal to the principal offender and does everything they reasonably can to prevent the crime from going ahead. What constitutes sufficient withdrawal depends on the facts of each case and is for the jury to decide.

Who did it?

Sometimes the prosecution can establish that a victim died as a result of a wound, and that a group of people were involved in the attack, but it cannot be established which person caused the fatal blow. In this situation they can be convicted of murder if the prosecution can show that they foresaw that the fatal blow would be carried out by one of them. It does not matter that the prosecution cannot identify precisely who administered the fatal blow.

Reading list

Clarkson, C.M.V. (1998) 'Complicity, *Powell* and manslaughter' [1998] *Criminal Law Review* 556.

Heaton, R. (2004), 'Principals? No principles!' [2004] *Criminal Law Review* 463.

Law Commission (1993) *Assisting and Encouraging Crime* (Consultation Paper No. 131), London: Law Commission.

Law Commission (2007) *Participating in Crime* (Law Commission No. 305), London: Law Commission.

Smith, J.C. (2001) 'Withdrawal in complicity: a restatement of principles' [2001] *Criminal Law Review* 769.

Smith, K.J.M. (1994) 'The Law Commission consultation paper on complicity (1) A blue print for rationalism' [1994] *Criminal Law Review* 239.

Sullivan, G.R. (2008) 'Participating in crime: Law Com No. 305 – joint criminal ventures' [2008] *Criminal Law Review* 19.

Taylor, R. (2008) 'Procuring, causation, innocent agency and the Law Commission' [2008] *Criminal Law Review* 32.

Wilson, W. (2008) 'A rational scheme of liability for participating in crime' [2008] *Criminal Law Review* 3.

Reading on the internet

The House of Lords' judgment of **R** v **Powell and English** (1997) is available on Parliament's website at:

   http://www.publications.parliament.uk/pa/ld199798/ldjudgmt/jd971030/ powell01.htm

Visit **www.mylawchamber.co.uk/elliottcriminal** to access multiple choice questions, flashcards and practice exam questions to test yourself on this chapter.

Use **Case Navigator** to read in full the key cases referenced in this chapter:

- R *v* English [1997] 4 All ER 545
- R *v* G [2003] UKHL 50; [2004] 1 AC 1034
- R *v* Woollin [1998] 4 All ER 103

12 Corporate liability

This chapter explains that:

- corporations as well as individuals can be liable for criminal offences;

- the common law has developed two devices by which criminal liability can be imposed on a corporation: vicarious liability and the doctrine of identification; and

- under the Corporate Manslaughter and Corporate Homicide Act 2007 a corporation can be found liable for manslaughter.

Introduction

Criminal offences may not only be committed by individual people, but also by companies. A corporation can only be held liable for an offence which may be punished by a fine – so, for example, a corporation cannot be liable for murder, since the mandatory sentence is life imprisonment. In **R** v **Coroner for East Kent, ex p. Spooner** (1987), an application for judicial review arising from a coroner's inquest into the deaths caused by *The Herald of Free Enterprise* ferry disaster, it was accepted that a corporation could be convicted of manslaughter, though the consequent prosecution was dropped due to lack of evidence.

It is unlikely that corporate liability would ever be imposed for more personal crimes, such as rape or bigamy.

There are several reasons for the imposition of corporate liability.

- Without it, companies might escape regulation by the criminal law, and individuals could be prosecuted for offences which were really the fault of company practices.
- In some cases it is more convenient for procedural purposes to prosecute a company rather than its employee(s).
- Where an offence is serious, a company may be more likely to be able to pay the required level of fine than an individual employee would be.
- The threat of criminal prosecution may encourage shareholders to exercise control over the activities of companies in which they invest.
- If a company has made a profit through an illegal practice, it should be the one to pay the price, not an employee.
- Corporate liability can discourage companies from putting pressure on employees, directly or indirectly, to raise profits by acting illegally – for example, if a haulage firm sets its drivers targets for delivery times that those drivers could not meet without speeding, imposing corporate or vicarious liability would be a way of ensuring that the company does not get off scot-free if the driver is charged with speeding.
- Adverse publicity and fines may act as a deterrent against acting illegally – this might not be the case if an individual was prosecuted.

The imposition of corporate liability raises obvious problems regarding the existence of *mens rea* – how do you define the state of mind of a company? Consequently the common law has developed two devices by which criminal liability can be imposed on a corporation: vicarious liability and the doctrine of identification. In addition, the Corporate Manslaughter and Corporate Homicide Act 2007 has been passed to deal with the specific issue of corporate liability for manslaughter, as the old common law on the subject was considered unsatisfactory in practice.

Vicarious liability

This type of liability tends to be applied where the law is faced with a regulatory offence. Vicarious liability means the liability of one legal person for the acts of another (a 'legal person' may be a company or a group, as well as an individual human being). The law rarely imposes liability on one person for acts done by someone else, but there are three types of situation where vicarious criminal liability can arise.

- In strict liability offences, where the statutory description of the *actus reus* can be interpreted in such a way as to cover someone other than the actual perpetrator. An example might be where the offence involves 'selling' goods – when shop assistants 'sell' food, it can reasonably be said that at the same time their employer is also selling it, even if the owner of the shop is not present. By contrast, if a lorry driver was charged with an offence using the word 'driving' – driving a lorry with worn tyres perhaps, or driving over the speed limit – liability could not be shifted to the driver's employer, because the term used is not capable of this extended meaning; in normal language we would not say the employer 'drove' the lorry.

- Where the possibility of vicarious liability is expressed or implied in a statute. An example of vicarious liability being expressly allowed for in a statute is the Licensing Act 1964 which states that 'A person shall not, in pursuance of a sale by him of intoxicating liquor, deliver that liquor, either himself or by his servant or agent.'

- In cases of delegated management. If an employer is under a statutory duty, and delegates that duty to one of his or her employees, the employer will be vicariously liable for any criminal offence which the employee commits while carrying out the delegated duty, even one which requires *mens rea*. In **Allen** *v* **Whitehead** (1929), the owner of a café was charged with knowingly permitting prostitutes to meet together and remain in a place where refreshments were sold. The café was run by a manager who knew about the prostitutes; the accused had no knowledge of them. The court held that the café owner had delegated his statutory duty, and was therefore vicariously liable, so that his manager's *actus reus* and *mens rea* could be assigned to him.

The doctrine of identification

This doctrine of identification applies to all offences to which vicarious liability does not attach. It allows certain senior people within a company, usually company directors, to be recognised for legal purposes as being the company, so that any criminal liability they incur while going about the company's business can be assigned to the company.

KEY CASE

The House of Lords in **Tesco Supermarkets** *v* **Nattrass** (1972) adopted a rather narrow attitude towards the kind of employee who could be identified with the company, known as the 'controlling mind'. It stated that only individuals who had some power of control within the organisation, including some discretion over the activity with which the offence is concerned, would fall within this doctrine.

> The doctrine of identification for the purposes of corporate liability applies to individuals who have some power of control within an organisation.

This would only include 'the board of directors, the managing director and perhaps the superior officers of a company carrying out the functions of management and speaking and acting as the company'. It would not normally cover a sales assistant. As a result, the larger a company, the more difficult it would be to convict it of an offence, unless the offence was one where vicarious liability applied.

In the case, Tesco were charged with an offence under the Trade Descriptions Act 1968. The company had advertised that they were selling a particular soap powder at a specified (reduced) price. An old-age pensioner had tried to buy a packet at the advertised price, but in his local branch the packets were all marked at the full price. The shop refused to sell him the soap powder at less than the full cost. It appeared that the failure to display the goods at the reduced price was the fault of the branch manager, so the issue in the case was whether he could be considered to be representing the company by his acts – if he was not, Tesco were not liable. The House of Lords found that Tesco exercised strict controls over its branch managers, allowing them no power of control over pricing policy, and therefore the branch manager could not be identified as the company, and Tesco were not liable.

This restrictive approach to identification liability has been challenged by the Privy Council in **Meridian Global Funds Management Asia Ltd** v **Securities Commission** (1995). Two men were employed in New Zealand by Meridian as investment managers. Under New Zealand legislation any person becoming a substantial security holder in a public company had to give notice of the fact. The employees used Meridian's funds to acquire such an interest and failed to give the relevant notice. The Court of Appeal in New Zealand ruled that the knowledge of the employees could be attributed to Meridian, and so Meridian were liable for breaching the legislation. An appeal to the Privy Council was rejected. Lord Hoffmann suggested that in attributing knowledge, a court should not take too literal an approach to the concept of a 'directing mind'. It was relevant to examine the language of the particular statute, its content and underlying policy to decide how it was meant to apply to a company. Since, in this case, the policy was to compel disclosure of a substantial security holder, the knowledge should be that of the person who acquired the relevant interest, in other words the person who was actually in charge of the matter. This would include people who fell outside the nerve centre of command who could be taken into account under **Tesco** v **Nattrass**.

Privy Council judgments are not binding on the domestic courts but are only persuasive. Following the Southall train crash in 1997, in which seven people were killed, the prosecution sought to rely on the case of **Meridian Global Funds Management** to argue that it had given rise to a change in the law. In **Attorney-General's Reference (No. 2 of 1999)** the Court of Appeal was asked to consider the following question by the Attorney-General:

> Can a non-human defendant be convicted of the crime of manslaughter by gross negligence in the absence of evidence establishing the guilt of an identified human individual for the same crime?

The trial judge had ruled that the answer to this question was 'No'. The Attorney-General submitted that the trial judge was wrong. Relying on **Meridian**, the Attorney-General's barrister, Mr Lissack QC, argued that there were three theories of corporate criminal liability, namely vicarious liability, identification liability and personal liability, and that personal liability should be relied on in this case. According to his view, personal liability would exist if the jury were satisfied that the deaths occurred by reason of a gross breach by the defendant of its personal duty to have a safe system of train operation in place. Under this approach a court would be able to aggregate the minds of the different people involved to find the relevant fault – known as the aggregation principle.

The Court of Appeal rejected this argument. Instead it concluded that **Meridian** was interpreting a statutory offence according to Parliament's intention so that the statutory offence applied to companies without the need to identify any *mens rea* in a directing mind of the company. But such an exception could not be applied to common law offences. In the words of the Court of Appeal:

> None of the authorities since **Tesco** *v* **Nattrass** relied on by Mr Lissack supports the demise of the doctrine of identification: all are concerned with statutory construction of different substantive offences and the appropriate rule of attribution was decided having regard to the legislative intent, namely whether Parliament intended companies to be liable. There is a sound reason for a special rule of attribution in relation to statutory offences rather than common law offences, namely there is, subject to a defence of reasonable practicability, an absolute duty imposed by the statutes.
>
> There is, as it seems to us, no sound basis for suggesting that, by their recent decisions, the courts have started a process of moving from identification to personal liability as a basis for corporate liability for manslaughter . . .
>
> None of the authorities relied on by Mr Lissack as pointing to personal liability for manslaughter by a company supports that contention . . . In each case it was held that the concept of directing mind and will had no application when construing the statute. But it was not suggested or implied that the concept of identification is dead or moribund in relation to common law offences.

The court is, in effect, treating these statutory offences as imposing vicarious liability.

Corporate manslaughter

The most controversial form of corporate liability is corporate manslaughter. The offence of corporate manslaughter might be committed when an employee is killed at work. Until recently, this area of law was governed by the common law. Under the common law a prosecution for corporate manslaughter would normally be based on the offence of gross negligence manslaughter (see p. 111). Because of the common law requirement to identify a directing mind, this meant in practice that two prosecutions would be brought at the same time against the company and a senior employee of the company. Liability would be imposed on the company using the principle of a directing mind and the employee would be personally liable for manslaughter.

Following considerable criticism of the application of this law in practice the Corporate Manslaughter and Corporate Homicide Act 2007 has been passed.

TOPICAL ISSUE

Corporate manslaughter in society

In 2004/05 there were 581 deaths at work. Over the last 40 years 22,000 people have been killed at work or through business-related disasters. The Health and Safety Executive considers that 70 per cent of work-related deaths are preventable. But, between 1992 and 2000 there have only been 34 prosecutions for work-related manslaughter and only six of these have been successful, all where the defendant was a small organisation making it easier to identify a 'directing mind'. The best-known successful prosecution is the case of **Kite v OLL Ltd** (1994), which was concerned with a canoeing disaster on a school trip that killed several school children.

It is often very difficult, particularly with larger companies, to identify an individual who is the embodiment of the company for the purposes of the identification doctrine. P&O were indicted for manslaughter following the drowning of 188 people in 1987 when their ferry, the *Herald of Free Enterprise*, capsized. This tragedy occurred because the bow doors were left open when leaving Zeebrugge harbour. The employee responsible for shutting the doors had fallen asleep. An inquiry set up following the disaster (the Sheen Inquiry) found that the company's own regulations made no reference to the closing of the doors and this was not the first occasion on which the company's ships had gone to sea with their doors open. The inquiry concluded that the company's management shared responsibility for the failure in their safety system, but the criminal case against the company collapsed. The prosecution had been unable to satisfy the doctrine of identification.

Railtrack and the privatised train operators have been the focus of considerable public anger after three fatal rail accidents in four years. In 1997 there was the Southall railway disaster. A high-speed train travelling from Swansea to London was racing at 125 mph about ten minutes from Paddington when it passed a red light. Soon afterwards it collided with a freight train. Seven people were killed and 151 injured. The train was being operated with its automatic warning system switched off because it did not work, and the automatic train protective system was also inoperative. Furthermore, there was no second driver in the cab. Despite these failings, the prosecution against Great Western Train Company collapsed. In 1999 there was the Ladbroke Grove train accident, where a train driver with only limited training and experience may have driven through a red light at a very complex rail junction. Thirty-one people were killed. Then in 2000, there was the Hatfield railway accident, where a badly maintained piece of track had broken. The public anger following these tragedies highlighted the need for the criminal law to provide effective deterrence, so that companies are not tempted to make savings through safety cuts. Six railway managers of Network Rail and Balfour Beatty were charged with corporate manslaughter in connection with the Hatfield railway accident, but the prosecution was not successful.

In practice, the Health and Safety Executive brings a prosecution for only 18 per cent of workplace deaths. Seventy-five per cent of these are brought for statutory health and safety offences before the magistrates' court, rather than for corporate manslaughter before the Crown Court. The maximum fine that the magistrates' court can impose is £20,000. A company sentenced in the Crown Court can be fined an unlimited amount.

● Corporate Manslaughter and Corporate Homicide Act 2007

The Corporate Manslaughter and Corporate Homicide Act 2007 has been passed with a view to tackling some of the problems with the common law identified above. The Law Commission had produced a report in 1996 called *Legislating the Criminal Code: Involuntary Manslaughter*. This included proposals to reform corporate manslaughter to facilitate convictions. Initially, the Government appeared to have accepted the Law Commission's main proposals. It produced a consultation document: *Reforming the Law of Involuntary Manslaughter: The Government's Proposals*. These proposed reforms would have introduced two new offences:

- corporate killing; and
- substantially contributing to a corporate killing.

The Government subsequently announced that it no longer intended to proceed with these reforms, and issued a further consultation paper. The Corporate Manslaughter and Corporate Homicide Act 2007 has now been passed. This Act contains a single offence of corporate manslaughter. The Act is disappointing, as it significantly waters down the original proposals to the point that the new offence looks very similar to the old common law, and will be almost as difficult to prosecute. The Home Office has stated that the 2007 Act will allow easier prosecution of big companies, but this is far from certain.

Section 1 of the Act states:

(1) An organisation to which this section applies is guilty of an offence if the way in which its activities are managed or organised –
 (a) causes a person's death, and
 (b) amounts to a gross breach of a relevant duty of care owed by the organisation to the deceased.

This offence is called corporate manslaughter in England and Wales and corporate homicide in Scotland to reflect each region's legal culture. Conviction could give rise to a fine (with no maximum limit) and a remedial order instructing the offending company to remedy any breach of the health and safety legislation.

Under s. 1(3), an organisation is guilty of this offence if 'the way in which its activities are managed or organised by its senior management is a substantial element' in the gross breach of a duty of care.

The offence only applies where the organisation owed a relevant duty of care to the victim. Section 2 states:

2(1) A 'relevant duty of care', in relation to an organisation, means any of the following duties owed by it under the law of negligence –
 (a) a duty owed to its employees or to other persons working for the organisation or performing services for it;
 (b) a duty owed as occupier of premises;
 (c) a duty owed in connection with –
  (i) the supply by the organisation of goods or services (whether for consideration or not),
  (ii) the carrying on by the organisation of any construction or maintenance operations,
  (iii) the carrying on by the organisation of any other activity on a commercial basis, or
  (iv) the use or keeping by the organisation of any plant, vehicle or other thing.

Under s. 1(4), a duty is also owed to a person detained in custody, including police custody.

The earlier proposals simply referred to a management failure. The Act refers to senior managers. Section 2 states that 'senior management' means:

the persons who play significant roles in –
 (i) the making of decisions about how the whole or a substantial part of its activities are to be managed or organised, or
 (ii) the actual managing or organising of the whole or a substantial part of those activities.

This will make it significantly more difficult for the prosecution to establish their case than under the earlier proposals for reform. It gives rise to some of the problems that the earlier requirement to establish a 'directing mind' has caused. One advantage of the new law is that the prosecution does not need to point to a single individual; instead, it can point to a group of senior managers (not necessarily directors) to establish a gross breach of duty. In 2004 Barrow Borough Council was prosecuted for corporate manslaughter. A middle-ranking council manager was prosecuted for manslaughter. The manager had stopped a maintenance contract to clean an air-conditioning unit in an arts centre run by the council. This had led to the growth of bacteria in the system, leading to an outbreak of Legionnaires' Disease which killed seven people and made 150 others very ill. It is questionable whether, under the 2007 Act, this manager would be sufficiently senior for the purposes of the new statutory offence.

Two parliamentary committees have expressed concern that by limiting liability to senior managers, a company might be tempted to delegate health and safety responsibility further down to junior managers to avoid criminal liability, which would be counterproductive.

It will be necessary to show that the management failure caused the victims' death. The ordinary rules of causation will apply to determine this question. The Law Commission was concerned that these rules meant that it would be very difficult to establish that a management failure had caused death, as opposed to the more immediate conduct of the employee. Under the earlier recommendations, management failure would therefore have been viewed as a cause of death even if the immediate cause is the act or omission of an individual. The Home Office suggest that causation is no longer a problem because of a change in the case law. They are not specific as to which case, but one presumes they are referring to **R** v **Finlay**. Unfortunately, the approach of the Court of Appeal in that case was recently criticised by the House of Lords in **R** v **Kennedy (No. 2)** and the House said it should not be followed. Thus, causation is likely to remain a problem, as it is under the current law of corporate manslaughter, and should be reconsidered.

The offence could be applied to public and private corporations. In addition, government departments and Crown bodies could be found liable, which is an extension of the current law, though the legislation significantly restricts when they can be liable. The offence would only apply where an organisation owes a duty of care as:

- an employer
- an occupier of land
- a supplier of goods or services
- an organisation engaged in a commercial activity (for example, mining or fishing).

The Government has put forward rather weak justifications for these limitations, arguing that other remedies, such as public inquiries, are available and thus there would be overlapping remedies if the criminal law was applied more widely. While it is true that other remedies are available, such as civil claims and public inquiries, the problem is that the public have not felt that these were adequate and there is no reason why the public would feel differently in relation to the government. Deaths in custody have been included, but the death of a soldier in his barracks is excluded. The previous recommendations of the Government would not have imposed any liability at all on government bodies but such an exclusion might well have breached the Human Rights Act 1998.

Under its earlier proposals, the Home Office had concluded that many unincorporated bodies are in practice indistinguishable from corporations and that therefore their liability for fatal accidents should be the same. It would have applied the new legislation to 'undertakings' which are defined in the Local Employment Act 1960 as 'any trade or business or other activity providing employment'. This would have greatly broadened the scope of the offence. The final Act does not use the word 'undertaking' but does extend to some unincorporated organisations, including Government departments, partnerships and trade unions.

The Law Commission considered it would be inappropriate to impose punitive sanctions on company officers where a company was found liable for corporate killing, as the latter offence stressed the liability of the company rather than of the individual. But the Government initially feared that without punishing the individual, the offence would not act as a sufficient deterrent, and culpable individuals could continue to work in management positions, exposing the public to similar risks. It therefore initially proposed that, following a conviction of the company, disqualification proceedings could be brought against certain individuals. If it could be shown that an individual had had some influence on, or responsibility for, the circumstances in which a management failure had caused a person's death, they could be disqualified from acting in a management role in any undertaking carrying on a business or activity in Great Britain. The ground for disqualification would not be that of causing the death but of contributing to the management failure resulting in the death. This recommendation was dropped, but the justification for it still seems very valid.

Under its original proposals, the Home Office considered imposing criminal liability on an individual who contributed to the corporate offence, leading to the death. This offence would be relied on in circumstances where, although the corporate offence has been committed by a company or organisation, it is not (for whatever reason) possible to secure a conviction against any individuals for manslaughter. Again, this recommendation has been dropped. Individual liability will remain possible under the common law offence of gross negligence manslaughter, though the common law offence can no longer apply to corporations (s. 20).

Criticism

A range of criticisms have been made in relation to corporate liability for criminal offences.

Punishment

The courts do not usually set fines in proportion to the profit a company may have made as a result of their illegal practice – ignoring health and safety regulations, or anti-pollution laws, can save companies a great deal of money. Guidance on sentencing is set out in the Court of Appeal case **R v F Howe and Son (Engineers) Ltd** (1999). The court said that any fine should reflect the gravity of the offence, and also the means of the defendant. Since this decision, some large fines have been imposed. Thames Trains was fined £2 million for its involvement in the Paddington train crash in 1999. In **R v Network Rail** (2005) Network Rail was fined £3.5 million and Balfour Beatty £10 million for breaching health and safety regulations, leading to the Hatfield train crash. Despite this, in 2003, the director of the Health and Safety Executive (HSE) complained that fines were still too low. He said:

> It is incomprehensible that fines for especially serious big company breaches in health and safety are only a small percentage of those fines handed down for breaches of financial services in similarly large firms. I understand that financial service breaches can affect people's wealth and well-being, but breaches in health and safety can, and do, result in loss of limbs, livelihoods and lives.

Fines themselves may only deter companies from offending if they are higher than the profits to be made from illegal activities – so if, for example, it is cheaper for a company to pay fines for polluting the environment than to improve their waste disposal processes, the fines may be regarded as no more than a business expense.

The fact that corporate liability can only be punished by fines can mean that the guilty company simply shifts the financial burden on to the consumer. By charging higher prices, the company can make up the cost of the fine, so that the only penalty it really suffers is bad publicity and a slight dent in its competitiveness – though even this is ineffective where the company has a monopoly on the supply of particular goods or services.

There was a joint public inquiry into the Southall and Ladbroke Grove rail accidents, but this will not lead to any punishment of the wrongdoers.

Lack of deterrence

In large companies shareholders are very rarely able to exercise control over firms with regard to the kinds of issues likely to come before the courts, so corporate liability may have little effect in promoting better standards.

As with strict liability, the success of corporate liability in encouraging companies to ensure that their employees maintain high standards depends largely on the possibility of being caught; unless there is a good chance of illegal activity being discovered and prosecuted, the fact that corporate liability will be imposed if it is may carry little weight. More resources should be given to the Health and Safety Executive, which currently investigates about 1,000 workplace accidents per year – just 5.6 per cent of cases. Without more resources, the aim of the Corporate Manslaughter and Corporate Homicide Act 2007 to reduce deaths at work will not succeed.

Individual responsibility

Where serious offences such as manslaughter are concerned, bringing a prosecution against a company may allow the individual responsible to go free. For example, the owner of a company who deliberately neglects safety precautions in order to maximise profits is just as morally guilty of the resulting death of an employee as the careless driver who kills a pedestrian. In practice, the driver is likely to end up in prison convicted of dangerous driving, while the owner of the company may only suffer the prosecution of their company for a health and safety offence with a fine imposed, rather than being prosecuted personally for manslaughter and possibly imprisoned.

Reform

Statutory vicarious liability

The draft Criminal Code retains the principle of vicarious liability but would apply it only where specifically written into a statute. It abolishes the principle of delegated authority, and provides that a company would not be liable where the controlling officer was acting against the interests of the company.

Civil liability

It has been suggested that some of the offences for which companies are likely to incur responsibility should be taken out of the criminal system, with companies being sued through the civil courts for damages, rather than being fined under the criminal law. Civil awards of damages could be made to reflect the harm caused more easily than fines, which often have a statutory maximum.

Alternative punishments

Where a fine does not reflect the harm done, nor appear to offer a sufficiently strong deterrent, companies could be punished with sanctions other than fines. Steven Box, in his book *Power, Crime and Mystification* (1983), suggests the following:

- Requiring companies to advertise the details of their convictions, at their own expense. This has been tried in the US, but large corporations got round the punishments by advertising only in publications which were unlikely to be read by their target consumers; consequently strict supervision would be needed.
- Nationalising the company for a specific period, so that all its profits during that time would go to the state, or forcing it to sell a proportion of its products at cost price (meaning without making a profit) to underprivileged sections of the community.
- Putting companies 'on probation' by appointing teams of accountants, lawyers, managers and technical staff (depending on the nature of the company) who would monitor any of the company's working practices which might be relevant to the offence committed, and then make recommendations for improvement. If these recommendations were not followed, the company would be returned to court for resentencing. The 'probation officers' would be paid for (but not chosen) by the offending company.
- Imposing a community service order. Just as individual offenders can be ordered to take part in work for the community, companies could be required to undertake

12

Corporate liability

projects of social importance, such as building a new hospital, or paying for a new school or library, at their own expense.

- Preventing corporate crime, by means of training in health and safety for example, may be more useful than criminal charges in relevant cases.
- Increasing a company's chances of being caught acting illegally, for example by increasing the number of Health and Safety Inspectors, and requiring offences resulting in death or serious injury to be investigated by the police, would strengthen the deterrent effect.

 ## Answering questions

Is the current law on corporate liability for criminal offences inadequate?

This is a straightforward question which you could answer in much the same order as this chapter. A logical approach would be to say first what the law is, then look at some of the criticisms of this to decide whether or not the law is 'inadequate'. Then if you had time you could look quickly at possible reforms that might make the law more satisfactory.

 ## Summary

The law has developed two devices by which criminal liability can be imposed on a corporation: vicarious liability and the doctrine of identification.

Vicarious liability

In practice this type of liability tends to be applied where the law is faced with a regulatory offence. There are three types of situation where vicarious criminal liability can arise.

- In strict liability offences, where the statutory description of the *actus reus* can be interpreted in such a way as to cover someone other than the actual perpetrator.
- Where the possibility of vicarious liability is expressed or implied in a statute.
- In cases of delegated management. If an employer is under a statutory duty, and delegates that duty to one of his or her employees, the employer will be vicariously liable for any criminal offence which the employee commits while carrying out the delegated duty, even one which requires *mens rea*.

The doctrine of identification

The doctrine of identification allows certain senior people within a company to be recognised for legal purposes as being the company, so that any criminal liability they incur while going about the company's business can be assigned to the company. The House of Lords in **Tesco Supermarkets** *v* **Nattrass** (1972) adopted a rather narrow attitude towards the kind of employee who could be identified with the company. It stated that only individuals who had some power of control within the organisation, including some discretion over the activity with which the offence was concerned, would fall within this doctrine.

Offences for which corporations are never liable

A corporation can only be held liable for an offence which may be punished by a fine – so, for example, a corporation cannot be liable for murder, since the mandatory sentence is life imprisonment. It is unlikely that corporate liability would ever be imposed for more personal crimes, such as rape or bigamy.

Criticisms and reform

The failings of the law of corporate liability have been highlighted in the context of corporate manslaughter, where only a small number of prosecutions have succeeded despite a high number of workplace deaths each year. There has also been concern that the punishments imposed even where a company is convicted of a criminal offence are inadequate and, as a result, provide only a limited deterrence to further criminal conduct. In the light of these concerns the Government has introduced new legislation which created a statutory offence of corporate manslaughter. Unfortunately, the new statutory offence looks inadequate to tackle the problems.

Reading list

Gobert, J. (2008) 'The Corporate Manslaughter and Corporate Homicide Act 2007 – Thirteen years in the making but was it worth the wait?' (2008) 71 *Modern Law Review* 413.

Jefferson, M. (2001) 'Corporate criminal liability: the problem of sanctions' [2001] *Journal of Criminal Law* 235.

Nash, S. and Furse, M. (1995) 'Companies' human rights' [1995] *Business Law Review* 248.

Ormerod, D. and Taylor, R. (2007) 'The Corporate Manslaughter and Corporate Homicide Act 2007' [2007] *Criminal Law Review* 589.

Sullivan, B. (2001) 'Corporate killing – some government proposals' [2001] *Criminal Law Review* 31.

Wells, C. (1996) 'The corporate manslaughter proposals: pragmatism, paradox and peninsularity' [1996] *Criminal Law Review* 545.

Reading on the internet

The Corporate Manslaughter and Corporate Homicide Act 2007 is available on the website of the Office for Public Sector Information at:
   http://www.opsi.gov.uk/acts/acts2007/20070019.htm

The explanatory notes to the Corporate Manslaughter and Corporate Homicide Act 2007 are available on the website of the Office for Public Sector Information at:
   http://www.opsi.gov.uk/acts/en2007/2007en19.htm

12

Corporate liability

The House of Commons Library Research Paper 06/46, *The Corporate Manslaughter and Corporate Homicide Bill*, is available on Parliament's website at:

http://www.parliament.uk/commons/lib/research/rp2006/rp06-046.pdf

---

Visit **www.mylawchamber.co.uk/elliottcriminal** to access multiple choice questions, flashcards and practice exam questions to test yourself on this chapter.

Use **Case Navigator** to read in full the key case referenced in this chapter:

- Kennedy (No. 2) [2005] EWCA Crim 685

13 General defences

This chapter discusses a wide range of defences which can be put forward by a defendant prosecuted for a criminal offence:

- the defence of being a minor;

- insanity;

- automatism;

- mistake;

- intoxication;

- self-defence and the public defence;

- duress;

- necessity;

- consent; and

- lawful chastisement.

Introduction

There are several ways in which accused persons may try to prevent themselves from being found guilty of a crime, reduce their liability for the alleged offence, or lower their sentence if convicted. When pleading not guilty, they may challenge the evidence on matters of fact – by arguing that they have an alibi for the time of the offence, or that witnesses who have identified them are mistaken. Alternatively, defendants may admit the offence, but argue that there is some reason why they should be leniently sentenced – this is an argument that there are mitigating circumstances. Finally, they may raise a substantive defence, such as self-defence, duress or necessity. The effect of a substantive defence is usually to assert that although the accused may have committed the *actus reus* with *mens rea*, there is a legal reason why he or she should not be liable.

Complete and partial defences

Some defences, such as self-defence, may result in an acquittal; they are described as complete defences. Others result in conviction for a lesser offence – for example, successfully pleading diminished responsibility or provocation on a charge of murder leads to a conviction of manslaughter. These are sometimes known as partial defences.

General and specific defences

Substantive defences may be either general or specific. Specific defences are linked to particular crimes, and cannot be applied to other offences – for example, provocation is a defence only to murder. General defences can be used for a range of different crimes.

The burden of proof

In a criminal case, the burden of proof always lies with the prosecution: they must prove beyond all reasonable doubt that the defendant committed the offence, rather than defendants having to prove themselves innocent. On the other hand, defendants who claim they have a substantive defence will be required to provide some proof of it – they cannot simply claim to have acted in self-defence, or under duress, and expect the court to leave it at that.

The precise nature of the burden of proof depends on the defence which is put forward. Where it is self-defence, provocation, duress, necessity, automatism or intoxication, defendants bear an evidential burden, which means that they must produce some evidence to support the claim. Once this evidence is produced, the burden of proof passes back to the prosecution, who have to disprove the defence in order to prove their case. Where the defence put forward is either insanity or diminished responsibility, defendants bear not only an evidential but also a legal burden: as well as producing evidence of this defence, they also have to prove to the jury that it was more likely than not that factors amounting to such a defence existed (this is called proving on a balance of probabilities, a standard of proof usually associated with civil actions).

Infancy

Children under 10 cannot be criminally liable. When they appear to have committed an offence, the social services can be informed but they cannot be prosecuted.

If the young person is aged 10 or over, but under 14, there used to be a presumption that they could not form *mens rea* (known in Latin as *doli incapax*). This presumption could be rebutted if the prosecution proved that the young person knew that what they had done was seriously wrong – a young person with this knowledge was described as having mischievous discretion. The Divisional Court had suggested, in **C (a minor)** *v* **DPP** (1995), that the presumption against criminal liability for the under-14s no longer existed, on the grounds that with compulsory education young people matured much more quickly than in the past. On appeal the House of Lords rejected this approach, stating that there was a line of cases dating back many years making it clear that the presumption did exist; if such an important and drastic change in the law were to be made it should come from Parliament, not the courts. The House observed that, while the Law Commission had proposed abolishing the presumption in 1985, the Government chose not to adopt this proposal in its 1990 review of the law. The defendant's appeal was allowed because, on the facts, the prosecution had failed to provide clear and positive evidence that the child in the case knew what he was doing was wrong.

However, in 1998 Parliament enacted s. 34 of the Crime and Disorder Act which abolished the presumption of *doli incapax*, as part of the Government's fight against youth crime. Section 34 states:

> The rebuttable presumption of criminal law that a child aged 10 or over is incapable of committing an offence is hereby abolished.

This would appear to be short and simple but in fact there was some confusion as to whether the abolition of the presumption implied with it the abolition of the defence, or whether the defence was separate from the presumption and survived after its abolition. Nigel Walker (1998) argued that all that was abolished was the common law presumption, and that the defence remained. Thus it would still be open to the defence to prove that a child lacked mischievous discretion. If this approach had been accepted then the only change made by the legislation would have been a change in the burden of proof, from the prosecution to the defence.

KEY CASE

The House of Lords has now ruled in **R** *v* **T** (2009) that the Crime and Disorder Act 1998 has abolished the defence of *doli incapax* altogether and not just changed the burden of proof. The case involved a 12 year-old boy accused of causing or inciting other boys under 13 to engage in sexual activity contrary to the Sexual Offences Act 2003. When interviewed by the police the boy admitted the sexual activity but claimed he did not think what he was doing was wrong. The House reached its interpretation of the Act by looking at the government

> The doctrine of *doli incapax* has been abolished by the Crime and Disorder Act 1998.

reports that preceded the introduction of the legislation and the parliamentary debates and concluded that abolition was the clear intention of Parliament:

> Parliament was in no doubt as to the meaning of the clause, in part perhaps because in the consultation paper and the White Paper that preceded the legislation the Home Office had made it quite clear what was meant by abolition of the presumption of doli incapax.

Criticism

In favour of the abolition of the presumption of *doli incapax* is the fact that the children who avoided criminal liability under the test – those who did not know right from wrong – might be those who were most in need of control. Glanville Williams had argued (1983) that the test was also out of line with current sentencing practice. In the past, when conviction was likely to lead to severe punishments, it was right to save children who, through no fault of their own, did not know right from wrong; but these days, such a test only kept them from probation officers or foster parents who might be able to help them. On the other hand, there is evidence that juvenile offenders diverted from the criminal justice system at an early stage are less likely to reoffend. Also, when a child of 10 commits a criminal offence this might be more a reflection of the failings of their parents than any fault of their own. The Youth Justice Board found that parenting programmes aimed at giving parents support and advice in raising children reduced reoffending of children by one-third.

Some judges seem very unhappy with the way the criminal process is applying to young children. In **DPP v R** (2007) a mentally handicapped boy of 13 was acquitted of a relatively minor sexual assault against a handicapped girl of the same age. The judge in the case commented:

> . . . where very young, or very handicapped, children are concerned there may often be better ways of dealing with inappropriate behaviour than the full panoply of a criminal trial. Even where the complaint is of sexual misbehaviour it ought not to be thought that it is invariably in the public interest for it to be investigated by means of a criminal trial, rather than by inter-disciplinary action and cooperation between those who are experienced in dealing with children of this age and handicap.

The United Nations' Committee on the Rights of the Child has condemned the UK for imposing criminal liability on very young children. In a report in 2002, it criticised the 'high and increasing numbers of children being held in custody at earlier ages for lesser offences and for longer custodial sentences'. It has called on the Government to raise the age of criminal responsibility to 14 or higher, to bring it into line with most other European countries.

Insanity

The defence of insanity, also known as insane automatism, actually has little to do with madness, or with any medical definition of insanity; the concept is given a purely legal definition. As a result, it has been held to include conditions such as sleep-walking and epilepsy, despite the fact that doctors would never label such conditions as forms of insanity. Where the defence of insanity is successful a special verdict will be given of 'not guilty by reason of insanity'. In order for this verdict to be given the prosecution must have proved the *actus reus* of the offence but not the existence of the *mens rea*. The defendant's state of mind will only be relevant to the issue of insanity – **Attorney-General's Reference No. 3 of 1998** (1999).

As well as being put forward by the accused, a defence of insanity may be raised by the prosecution if the defendant makes their mental state an issue in the case, for example by raising a defence of automatism or diminished responsibility. In such situations the prosecution can then try to prove that the defendant was insane when the offence was committed, rather than suffering from diminished responsibility or automatism. A judge may raise the issue of insanity in very exceptional circumstances. In **Dickie** (1984), the accused was charged with arson and introduced evidence of extreme hyperactivity. The judge decided that this evidence required a direction to the jury on insanity. The Court of Appeal allowed an appeal against the verdict, saying that the judge should only interfere if all the medical evidence suggested insanity and the defence were deliberately evading the issue.

The case of **R v Horseferry Road Magistrates' Court, ex p. K** (1996) made it clear that the defence is available to summary as well as indictable offences. The defence of insanity is not available for strict liability offences. Thus, in **DPP v H** (1997) the defendant was charged with drink driving. He suffered from manic depressive psychosis, but he had no defence of insanity as drink driving is a strict liability offence.

In the past, successfully pleading insanity meant only one possible result: a hospital order under which the accused could be detained for an indefinite period of time. Consequently, once the death penalty was abolished, most defendants preferred to plead guilty to an offence rather than raise the defence of insanity, on the grounds that the punishment was unlikely to be worse than being locked away in a mental hospital with no fixed date for their release. When the defence of diminished responsibility was introduced for murder in 1957, this defence could be raised instead of pleading insanity, and insanity is now successfully put forward in only two or three cases a year.

The Criminal Procedure (Insanity and Unfitness to Plead) Act 1991 has altered the situation by introducing various sentencing options. Where the offence is murder, the court *must* still make a hospital order, under which the accused can be detained for an indefinite period. For any other crime, the court *may* make:

- a hospital order and an order restricting discharge either for a specified time or for an indefinite period;
- a guardianship order under the Mental Health Act 1983;
- a supervision and treatment order under Schedule 2 to the 1991 Act;
- an order for absolute discharge.

These changes are likely to encourage defendants to put forward the defence of insanity in the future.

13

General defences

The M'Naghten rules

KEY CASE

The rules on the defence of insanity were laid down in the **M'Naghten** case back in 1843. Daniel M'Naghten was obsessed with the then Prime Minister, Sir Robert Peel, and tried to kill him. He actually killed Peel's secretary instead, and was charged with the secretary's murder. He was found not guilty by reason of insanity, and this verdict produced enormous public disapproval. One result of the outcry was

> A person is insane if they suffer from a disease of the mind causing a defect of reason so they did not know the nature and quality of their act or that it was wrong in law.

that the judges outlined their reasoning on insanity as a defence, producing what became known as the M'Naghten Rules.

The starting point of the rules is that everyone is presumed sane. In order to rebut this presumption the accused must prove, on a balance of probabilities, that, when the offence was committed, they were suffering from a defect of reason, caused by a disease of the mind, so that either: (a) they did not know the nature and quality of their act; or (b) they did not know that what they were doing was wrong in law. In essence, this is saying that the defendant did not know what they were doing.

Defect of reason

A defect of reason means being deprived of the power to reason, rather than just failing to use it. In **Clarke** (1972), Mrs Clarke was accused of shoplifting, and argued that she had been acting absentmindedly because she was suffering from depression. The court ruled that this evidence meant she was denying *mens rea*, rather than raising the defence of insanity.

It does not matter whether the defect of reason was temporary or permanent. Thus, in **R** v **Sullivan** (1984), the defendant was treated as suffering from a defect of reason when he suffered from an epileptic fit which is inevitably a temporary state.

Disease of the mind

This is a legal definition, not a medical one, and covers states of mind which doctors would be highly unlikely to characterise as diseases of the mind. In legal terms it means a malfunctioning of the mind, and this has been held to include a hardening of the arteries, which is called arteriosclerosis – **R** v **Kemp** (1957); epilepsy – **R** v **Sullivan** (1984); diabetes – **R** v **Hennessy** (1989); and sleep-walking – **R** v **Burgess** (1991).

In **Kemp**, the defendant hit his wife with a hammer, causing her grievous bodily harm. He was suffering from arteriosclerosis, which caused temporary blackouts. Evidence showed he was devoted to his wife, and could not remember picking up the hammer or attacking her. In medical terms, arteriosclerosis is not considered to be a disease that affects the brain, but the court held that for the defence of insanity, the 'mind' meant 'the ordinary mental faculties of reason, memory and understanding', rather than the brain in the physical sense.

The courts are now drawing a distinction between a disease of the mind caused by an internal factor and one caused by an external factor. In the former the relevant defence is insane automatism; in the latter it is automatism. An example of a situation in which a disease of the mind is caused by some external factor is where someone is knocked on the head or undergoes hypnotism. This distinction was drawn in **Sullivan**. The appellant kicked and injured a friend during an epileptic fit, and was charged with inflicting grievous bodily harm. Medical evidence suggested that he would not have been aware, during the fit, that he was kicking anyone. The House of Lords held that epilepsy was a disease of the mind, because during a fit mental faculties could be impaired to the extent of causing a defect of reason. The internal/external divide was applied strictly in **R v Burgess** (1991). Burgess and a friend, Miss Curtis, had spent the evening watching videos at her flat. She fell asleep and while sleeping Burgess hit her over the head with a bottle and the video recorder and then grasped her throat. She cried out and he seemed to come to his senses, showing considerable distress at what he had done. Having been charged with wounding with intent under s. 18 of the Offences Against the Person Act 1861, he argued that he fell within the defence of automatism. The judge said the appropriate defence on the facts was insanity. Burgess was found not guilty by reason of insanity and ordered to be detained in a secure hospital. His appeal was dismissed on the grounds that as his sleep-walking was caused by an internal factor, the judge had given the correct direction.

Even diabetes, a disease which is in no medical sense a disease of the brain, has been treated as legal insanity. Diabetes is a disease which affects the body's ability to use sugar. It is usually controlled by injections of insulin, the substance which the body uses to break down sugar. Problems can arise where diabetics either fail to take their insulin, causing high blood sugar and what is known as a hyperglycaemic episode, or take the insulin and then drink alcohol, or fail to eat when they should; this causes low blood sugar and is known as a hypoglycaemic episode. Either situation may lead the diabetic to behave aggressively, which is why the problem has been brought to the attention of the courts. The result has been a rather odd approach, in which hyperglycaemic episodes are regarded as insanity, because they are caused by an internal factor – the action of the diabetes when insulin is not taken – while hypoglycaemic episodes are regarded as non-insane automatism, because they are caused by an external factor, the insulin.

In **R v Hennessy** (1989), the accused was a diabetic, charged with taking a vehicle and driving while disqualified. He gave evidence that at the time of the offence he had failed to take his usual dose of insulin due to stress and depression, and as a result was suffering from hyperglycaemia, which it was argued put him in a state of automatism. The trial judge ruled that since this state had been caused by diabetes, a disease, the proper defence was one of insanity under the M'Naghten rules. Hennessy then pleaded guilty (since successfully pleading insanity would have led to committal to a mental institution), and then appealed against his conviction. His appeal was dismissed.

By contrast, in **Quick** (1973), the diabetic defendant was a nurse at a psychiatric hospital, who attacked a patient. He claimed that due to hypoglycaemia, brought on by not eating after taking insulin, he had acted without knowing what he was doing. The judge directed that this was a plea of insanity, upon which Quick changed his plea to guilty. On appeal, it was held that the alleged mental condition was not caused by diabetes, but by the insulin used to treat it, and his appeal was allowed.

The disease of the mind may need to manifest itself in violence. In **Bratty** v **Attorney-General for Northern Ireland** (1963) Lord Denning said, 'Any mental disorder which has manifested itself in violence and is prone to recur is a disease of the mind.' Thus some mental disorders which do not manifest themselves in violence, such as kleptomania (a compulsion to steal) are not diseases of the mind for the purposes of the defence of insanity. On the other hand, Lord Denning's statement that the mental disorder must be 'prone to recur' was not followed by Lord Lane in **Burgess**. The expert evidence in that case was that there was no reported incident of a sleep-walker being repeatedly violent. As Lord Lane concluded that the mental disorder need not be 'prone to recur' the defendant still fell within the defence of insanity.

Once a suitable disease of the mind has been proved, the defence must also prove that the disease of the mind meant that the defendant lacked knowledge as to the nature and quality of the act, or that the act was wrong.

The nature and quality of the act
In **Codere** (1916) this was held to mean the physical, rather than the moral, nature of the act. A classic example of not knowing the nature and quality of an act is where the defendant cuts the victim's throat under the delusion of slicing a loaf of bread – it is not that they do not realise cutting someone's throat is wrong, but that they do not know they are cutting someone's throat.

Knowledge that the act was wrong
This has been held to mean legally rather than morally wrong. In **Windle** (1952) the accused killed his suicidal wife with an overdose of aspirin. When giving himself up to the police, he said, 'I suppose they will hang me for this.' There was medical evidence that although he was suffering from a mental illness, he knew that poisoning his wife was legally wrong. The Court of Appeal upheld his conviction and he was hanged.

This interpretation of the law was confirmed in **R** v **Johnson** (2007). The defendant had stabbed the victim. He was suffering from paranoid schizophrenia, but the medical evidence stated that while he thought he had a moral right to do as he did, he still knew that what he had done was legally wrong. The Court of Appeal held that in those circumstances the defence of insanity was not available to him.

Criticism

Medical irrelevance
The legal definition of insanity stems from an 1843 case, and has not developed to take account of medical and legal progress since then. As long ago as 1953, medical evidence given to the Royal Commission on Capital Punishment showed that even then the rules were considered by doctors to be based on 'an entirely obsolete and misleading conception of the nature of insanity'. In the Victorian period when the test was developed, insanity was associated with a failure of the power to reason. But doctors now recognise that insanity does not just affect the power to reason and understand, but the whole personality, including the will and the emotions. A medically insane person may well know the

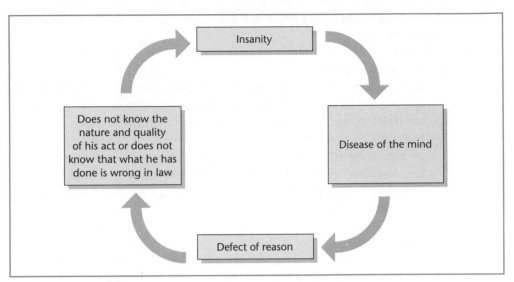

Figure 13.1 Insanity

nature and quality of his or her act, and know that it is wrong, but commit the offence all the same because of the mental illness.

Though the courts maintain that the legal definition of insanity can reasonably remain separate from medical definitions, it is difficult to uphold this distinction without absurdity. The most striking anomaly is that the courts claim a purely legal definition suffices, yet still impose mandatory committal to a mental institution in cases of murder; if a defendant is not medically insane, or even mentally ill, there is little point in imposing medical treatment. The current law may well be in breach of the European Convention on Human Rights. Article 5 of the Convention, which protects the right to liberty, states that a person of unsound mind can only be detained where proper account of objective medical expertise has been taken. This may be brought to the attention of the British courts under the Human Rights Act 1998.

The fact that diabetes has been held to give rise to a defence of insanity when it causes hyperglycaemia, but not when it causes hypoglycaemia, shows how absurd the application of the defence can be. The charitable organisation MIND has criticised the link being drawn between epilepsy and insanity, saying that it encourages a dangerous and outdated approach to epileptics, who form 0.5 per cent of the population and, for the most part, lead lives which bear no relation to the cases in which epilepsy has featured.

The narrow interpretation given to the defence of insanity is highlighted by the House of Lords' judgment of **R** v **G and J** (2008). The defendant G had been prosecuted under the Terrorism Act 2000 for collecting information likely to be useful to a person committing an act of terrorism. While in prison for another offence the defendant had collected plans for making bombs and made his own hand-drawn map of an army base. There was medical evidence that he was psychotic, hearing voices which made him think that the prison guards were whispering about him. He said he had prepared this terrorist material to 'wind up' the prison staff. The medical experts said he had collected the terrorist material as a direct consequence of his illness. The House of Lords held that on these facts the defence of insanity was not available to the defendant because he was not in law 'insane'.

Burden of proof

The fact that the defence must prove insanity, even though only on a balance of probabilities, conflicts with the principle that the burden of proof should always be on the prosecution, and the accused be innocent until proven guilty. It could be argued that the question of whether the accused knew what they were doing, and knew that it was wrong, is part of *mens rea* and should therefore be for the prosecution to prove. The Criminal Law Revision Committee and the Committee on Mentally Abnormal Offenders of 1975 (the Butler Committee) have recommended that the burden of proof should be on the prosecution.

Ineffective

The purpose of the test for insanity is to distinguish between the accused who is a danger to society and to themself, and one who is not, but the rules appear not to be an effective way of doing this. They are so narrow that they rule out those whose mental illness makes them behave in ways that they know are wrong, yet wide enough to include people such as diabetics and epileptics, who are rarely likely to be a recurring danger to others. The divisions made by the rules seem to bear little relation to the purpose of the test: why should a diabetic with high blood sugar be more dangerous than one with low blood sugar, when the results are medically similar? Why should a 'defect of reason' be more dangerous when caused by a disease than when caused by a blow to the head? Diseases such as diabetes and most forms of epilepsy can be controlled by modern drugs. If the reason for the rules is to catch those defendants whose illnesses mean that unlawful behaviour is likely to recur, then as far as diabetes and other controllable diseases are concerned, the relevant issue is whether the accused has failed to take medication through some isolated lapse (in which case it is clearly less likely to recur), or through unwillingness or inability to accept the need for medication, in which case some help may be needed. The M'Naghten rules take no account of this kind of issue.

Wrong in law

Following **R** v **Windle**, the courts apply the defence when the defendant does not know his conduct is wrong in law, but reject the defence when he does not know his conduct is morally wrong. This can be harsh on those who are so mentally ill that they think they have, for example, a divine right to commit the offence which they still know to be legally wrong. The Butler Committee (1975) observed that:

> Knowledge of the law is hardly an appropriate test on which to base ascription of responsibility to the mentally disordered. It is a very narrow ground of exemption since even persons who are grossly disturbed generally know that murder and arson are crimes.

Most common law jurisdictions incorporate moral wrongness within the test for insanity.

Sentencing for murder

The standard penalty for a successful plea of insanity where the charge is murder greatly limits use of the defence. Even though the sentence for murder is life imprisonment, most defendants would prefer this to an unlimited time in a mental institution (especially as in practice they will usually only serve around 12 years in prison), and so may plead guilty to an offence which they have not committed rather than raise the plea. This has two undesirable results: defendants who are neither morally liable for their actions nor medically insane are forced to plead guilty rather than be found legally insane; and defendants who know what they are doing and know that it is wrong, but cannot stop themselves, might really need the help that could be given by a mental institution, yet fall outside the legal definition of insanity (though they may come into the definition of diminished responsibility if the charge is murder).

Proposals for reform

Abolition of the rules

The British Medical Association recommended to the Royal Commission on Capital Punishment 1953 that the M'Naghten rules ought to be abolished or, at least, amended so that they were more in line with current medical knowledge. This was not done, though the creation of the defence of diminished responsibility for murder has gone some way towards meeting their criticisms.

Despite this evidence the Royal Commission concluded that the issue of whether a person was suffering from a disease of the mind should be determined neither by medicine nor the law, but was a moral question to be decided by the jury. Alternatively, they proposed an extension of the definition of insanity to include where the defendant 'was incapable of preventing [themself] from committing it'.

A new defence of mental disorder

The Butler Committee recommended a new defence, leading to a verdict of 'not guilty on evidence of mental disorder'. This terminology would avoid the stigma of being labelled insane. The new defence would apply where:

- evidence of mental disorder was put forward, and the jury find that the accused has committed the *actus reus* but without *mens rea*; and
- at the time of the act the accused was suffering from one of a range of severe mental illnesses or abnormalities, which are defined in line with medical knowledge.

No causal link would have to be proved between the mental illness and the act, as the illnesses covered by the defence would be sufficiently serious to make it reasonable to presume such a link. The draft Criminal Code substantially adopted the Butler Committee's proposals though it does require a causal connection to be proved.

Extending automatism

In cases of diseases which can be controlled by drugs, and/or by following certain rules about eating and drinking, attacks brought on by those diseases could all be treated under the defence of automatism, with liability imposed in cases where the attack has been brought on by the defendant's own carelessness, but not where it has happened through no fault of their own. This may seem rather harsh on those who suffer from such diseases, but is actually no different from the fact that the law expects people who know they become violent when drunk to prevent themselves from getting drunk, rather than making allowances for them when they do.

Abolish the defence

In the US, there have been claims that defences referring to insanity should be abolished completely. The issue hit the headlines after the attempted assassination of the then President, Ronald Reagan, by John Hinckley. At his trial, Hinckley claimed that he was obsessed by the actress Jodie Foster, and in carrying out the killing he had been under the delusion of acting out a movie script. He was found not guilty by reason of insanity, and critics argued that this was simply because he was able to pay for a very good psychiatrist. They have also pointed out that insanity defences cause procedural problems, with expert evidence often conflicting, making the trials very lengthy, and that the criminal justice system is not the ideal place to determine mental health. Perhaps not surprisingly, President Reagan himself gave his support to restrictions being placed on the defence.

One suggestion is that a mental disorder should be purely relevant to the issue of *mens rea*, and could be taken into account as mitigation in sentencing. However, the proposal ignores the fact that, where defendants have mental problems, there may be little to gain by punishing them.

The attempted assassination of Ronald Reagan
Source: Ron Edmonds/AP/Press Association Images

Automatism

Sometimes known as sane automatism, this arises where the crime was committed by an involuntary act caused by an external factor.

Involuntary act

As was noted in Chapter 1, a basic requirement for criminal liability is that the *actus reus* of an offence must have been committed voluntarily (p. 10). Therefore defendants will have a complete defence if they can show that, at the time of the alleged offence, they were not in control of their bodily movements, rendering their conduct involuntary.

The defence was discussed by the Court of Appeal in **Bratty** *v* **Attorney-General for Northern Ireland** (1963):

> No act is punishable if it is done involuntarily and an involuntary act in this context – some people nowadays prefer to speak of it as 'automatism' – means an act which is done by the muscles without any control by the mind such as a spasm, a reflex action or a convulsion; or an act done by a person who is not conscious of what he is doing . . . [However] to prevent confusion it is to be observed that in the criminal law an act is not to be regarded as an involuntary act simply because the actor does not remember it . . . Nor is an act to be regarded as an involuntary act simply because the doer could not control his impulse to do it.

The law gives the defence a very narrow interpretation, emphasising that there must be a total loss of voluntary control. The case of **Broome** *v* **Perkins** (1987) shows the limited scope of the defence. The accused got into a hypoglycaemic state and, during this period, drove home very erratically from work, hitting another car at one point. Afterwards he could remember nothing about the journey but, seeing the damage to his car, reported himself to the police. Medical evidence suggested that it was possible for someone in his state to complete a familiar journey without being conscious of doing so, and that although his awareness of what was going on around him would be imperfect, he would be able to react sufficiently to steer and operate the car, even though not very well. The court held that since the accused was able to exercise some voluntary control over his movements, he had not been acting in an entirely involuntary manner, and therefore the defence of automatism was not available.

This decision was heavily criticised as being too harsh, but it was nevertheless followed in **Attorney-General's Reference (No. 2 of 1992)**. When driving a lorry down a motorway, the accused crashed into a car parked on the hard shoulder, killing two people. Expert evidence showed that while he had not fallen asleep at the wheel, he had been put into a trance-like state by the repetitive vision of the long flat road which reduced, but did not eliminate, awareness of what he was doing. On acquittal the prosecution raised the case as an issue of law in the Court of Appeal. That court concluded that his state did not amount to automatism, again implying that reduced awareness cannot amount to the defence. Thus, the trial court got the law wrong and the defendant should probably not have been acquitted.

External cause

A distinction is drawn between sane automatism and insane automatism (the latter is the defence of insanity). Sane automatism is caused by an external factor (such as being banged on the head by a hammer or stung by a bee). Insane automatism is caused by an internal factor (a disease of the mind).

It was on this basis that the courts distinguished between **Quick** and **Hennessy** (see above), stating that Hennessy's hyperglycaemia was triggered by an internal factor (his diabetes) and was therefore within the legal definition of insanity, but the causes of Quick's hypoglycaemia were the insulin he had taken and the fact that he had drunk alcohol and not eaten, all external factors, and so he could successfully raise the defence of automatism.

Hennessy's counsel had argued that the hyperglycaemia was caused by the defendant's failure to take insulin, which in turn was caused by stress and depression, which, it was suggested, were external factors. But in the Court of Appeal Lord Lane stated: 'In our judgment, stress, anxiety and depression can no doubt be the result of the operation of external factors, but they are not, it seems to us, in themselves separately or together external factors of the kind capable in law of causing or contributing to a state of automatism.' The Court of Appeal pointed out that they were prone to recur and lacked the feature of novelty or accident. The kind of external factors the law required would be something like a blow to the head, or an anaesthetic.

Since the Criminal Procedure (Insanity and Unfitness to Plead) Act 1991, the difference between a finding of sane automatism and a finding of insane automatism has lost some of its importance.

Self-induced automatism

The defence of automatism may not be available if the automatism was caused by the accused's own fault. Where someone loses control of their actions through drinking too much, or taking illegal drugs, the defence is unavailable, for obvious reasons of policy. Where the accused brings about the automatism in some other way, the availability of the defence will depend on whether they knew there was a risk of getting into such a state.

In **Bailey** (1983) the defendant was a diabetic, who attacked and injured his ex-girlfriend's new boyfriend during a bout of hypoglycaemia. Feeling unwell beforehand, he had eaten some sugar but no other food. The Court of Appeal held that self-induced automatism (other than that caused by drink or drugs) can provide a defence if the accused's conduct does not amount to recklessness, taking into account his knowledge of the likely results of anything he has done or failed to do. In Bailey's case this meant that he would have a defence if he did not realise that failing to eat would put him into a state in which he might attack someone without realising it. If he was aware of this, and still failed to eat, he was reckless and the defence ought not to be available.

Should a defendant take drugs which normally have a soporific or sedative effect, and then commit a crime involuntarily, the defence of automatism may be available, if their reaction to the drug was unexpected. In **Hardie** (1984), a person whose condition of automatism was due to taking Valium (a tranquilliser) could rely on the defence, even though the drug had not been prescribed by a doctor.

Criticism

Irrational distinctions

Distinguishing between internal and external causes has been criticised as leading to absurd and irrational distinctions – such as that drawn between **Hennessy** and **Quick** above. The main reason given for the difference in treatment is that automatism caused by an internal factor, namely a disease, is more likely to recur than such a state caused by an external factor. This may be true of a comparison between an automatic state caused by a long-term mental illness, and one caused by a blow to the head, but, as the cases on diabetes show, the distinction can be tenuous, to say the least.

Possibility of wilful action

Criminal law writers Clarkson and Keating (2003) have drawn attention to the fact that some psychiatrists believe that, even when unconscious, people can act voluntarily. For example, Robert White recorded an incident during the Second World War, in which a soldier set off to take a message to a place where there was a lot of fighting and enormous danger. Some hours later, he found himself pushing his motorcycle through a coastal town nearly a hundred miles away, but had no idea how he had got there. Thoroughly confused, he gave himself up to the military police, who used hypnotism to try to discover what had happened. Under hypnosis, the soldier recalled that he had been knocked over by an explosion, got back on his bike and headed straight for the coastal town, asking directions and studying road signs in order to get there. Despite his genuine amnesia, he had acted rationally throughout; the amnesia had simply enabled him to do what he wanted to do, which was to escape without having to face up mentally to the consequences of being a deserter.

The implication of this argument is that perhaps automatism should not give rise to a complete acquittal. Automatism rests on the idea that the person acts without thought, but if it is the case that many everyday actions are carried out automatically without there

Table 13.1 Comparison of insanity, automatism and diminished responsibility

	Diminished responsibility	Insanity	Automatism
Availability of defence	Murder only	All offences	All offences
Type of impairment	Abnormality of the mind	Disease of the mind	Inability to control one's acts
Degree of impairment	Substantial	Total	Total
Cause	Internal or external	Internal	External
Burden of proof on defence	On the balance of probabilities	On the balance of probabilities	Evidential burden
Verdict	Voluntary manslaughter	Special verdict	Acquittal

being any distinctive thinking process involved, this situation is not as exceptional as the defence suggests.

Reform

The draft Criminal Code

The draft Criminal Code proposes maintaining the law on automatism as it stands, on the grounds that the public interest is best served by the complete acquittal of anyone who acts while in a condition of non-insane automatism. While this may be reasonable for the one-off offender, it offers no public protection against someone who is prone to recurring states of automatism through some external factor – though in this case the accused's own awareness of the dangers might lead to liability being imposed, on the grounds that he or she has behaved recklessly.

Abolition of the external/internal distinction

The distinction between internal and external causes could be abolished. Reform of the insanity defence to bring it in line with medical thinking would go some way towards this; behaviour which was allegedly automatic but clearly did not fall within medical definitions of insanity could then be considered solely in the light of the danger of recurrence, and the element of recklessness in the accused's behaviour.

Mistake

The issue of mistake is relevant in two contexts: it may mean that the accused could not have had *mens rea*, or it may be relevant in deciding whether a person has another defence such as self-defence.

Mistake and *mens rea*

In some cases, a defendant's mistake may mean that they lack the *mens rea* of the offence. For example, the *mens rea* of murder requires that the defendant intends to kill or cause grievous bodily harm to a person. If the defendant makes a mistake and thinks that the victim is already dead before they bury their body, then they would not have the *mens rea*, because when they buried what they thought was a dead person they could not have intended to kill or cause grievous bodily harm to that person.

The mistake must be one of fact, not of law, and a mistaken belief that your conduct is not illegal will not suffice as a defence. In **R v Reid** (1973) a motorist had been asked to take a breathalyser test. Mistakenly believing that the police officer had no legal right to ask him to take such a test in the particular circumstances, he refused to provide a specimen. The courts held that his mistake as to the law was no defence against a charge of refusing to provide the specimen.

The *mens rea* must be negatived by the mistake; a mistake which simply alters the circumstances of the offence is not enough. If a defendant thinks that they are stealing a silver bangle, but in fact it is made from platinum, for example, they still have the *mens rea* of theft and so the mistake is irrelevant. If, however, they mistakenly thought that the bangle was their own, or that the owner had given permission to take it, the required *mens rea* is not present, and the mistake will provide a complete defence.

For offences of strict liability, there is no *mens rea* to negative, so mistake will be irrelevant in this context and not serve as a defence. Thus, if it is a strict liability offence to sell bad meat, and a butcher sells infected meat under the mistaken impression that it is perfectly all right, that mistake will be no defence because no *mens rea* is needed.

Some offences provide that liability will be incurred where there was either intention or recklessness, and in these cases, an accused will be able to rely on mistake as a defence only if it meant that they had neither type of *mens rea* – so if a mistake meant that there was no intention, but the accused could still be considered reckless, mistake will not be a defence.

An honest mistake

For many years it was considered that a mistake could only be relied on as a defence if it was a reasonable mistake to make. Thus, in **Tolson** (1889) a woman who reasonably believed that her first husband was dead, remarried, only to discover later that the first husband was in fact alive. She was accused of bigamy, but acquitted because her mistake had been both honest and reasonable. Recently, in the case of **B (a minor)** v **DPP** (2000) the House of Lords have ruled that **Tolson** was bad law and that it was not necessary for a mistake to have been reasonable; what mattered was whether the mistake prevented the defendant from having the *mens rea* of the offence. This will be the case where the *mens rea* of the offence is subjective, but where it is objective then a mistake is only likely to prevent the existence of the *mens rea* if it was reasonable. Following the case of **R** v **G and another** (2003), *mens rea* will normally be subjective.

In the case of **DPP** v **Morgan** (discussed at p. 174), the House of Lords looked at the issue of mistake in relation to the offence of rape. The House stated that if the accused honestly believed the complainant was consenting, they did not have the *mens rea* for rape, even though they were mistaken in that belief and their mistake could not even be said to be a reasonable one. The law in the context of rape has now been changed by the Sexual Offences Act 2003. The *mens rea* of rape is defined by s. 1 of the 2003 Act as existing where the defendant intended to penetrate the victim with his penis and he did not have reasonable grounds to believe that the victim was consenting. An unreasonable mistake will therefore no longer be sufficient to negative the existence of *mens rea* for the offence of rape, and the decision of **DPP** v **Morgan** no longer reflects the current law.

Since proving *mens rea* is the responsibility of the prosecution, the defendant does not legally have to introduce evidence to support a claim of mistake which negatives *mens rea*, though in practice it is obviously sensible to do so, since without such evidence the jury are more likely to believe the prosecution.

Mistake and other defences

The issue of mistake can also arise in the context of other defences, and these situations are considered in the discussion of the relevant defences.

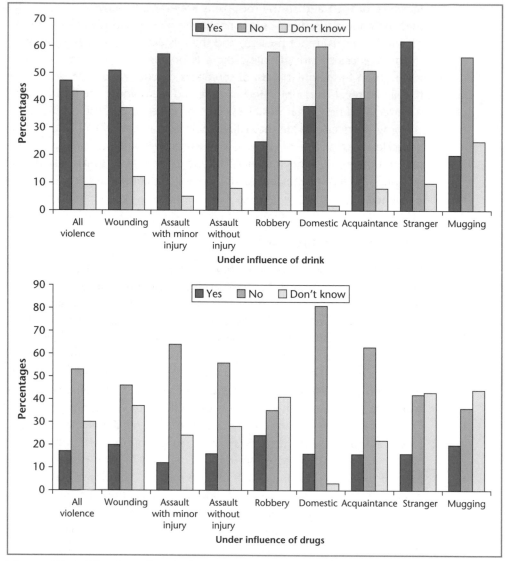

Figure 13.2 Whether offender/s under the influence of drink or drugs in violent incidents

Source: *Crime in England and Wales*, 2008/09, Home Office Statistical Bulletin, p. 71.

Intoxication

Intoxication can be caused by alcohol or drugs or a combination of the two; the same legal principles apply whichever the cause. The defence of intoxication poses something of a problem for the law. On the one hand, it can be argued that intoxicated people are not in full control of themselves, and do not think rationally, so they should not be held as liable for their actions as when they know exactly what they are doing. On the other hand, there are obvious policy reasons for not allowing people to use intoxication to excuse their criminal behaviour, not least the sheer number of crimes, particularly crimes of violence against the person, which occur as a result of intoxication. For this reason, the defence of intoxication is allowed only in a limited number of circumstances, and only where it means that the defendant lacked the *mens rea* of the offence.

Absence of *mens rea*

In some respects it is quite misleading to describe intoxication as a defence, because intoxication can actually be a reason to impose criminal liability where, in the absence of intoxication, criminal liability would not have been imposed. Thus, the starting point is that if the defendant did actually have the *mens rea* of the crime, then intoxication cannot be a defence. This was made very clear by the House of Lords in **R** v **Kingston** (1994), overturning an unexpected decision in the case by the Court of Appeal.

KEY CASE

In **R** v **Kingston** (1994) the defendant was attracted to young boys, but he normally managed to control these tendencies and prevent himself from acting on them.

> An intoxicated intent is still an intent.

Unfortunately, his business associates decided to set him up so that he could be photographed in a compromising situation with a young boy, which could then be used to blackmail him. The defendant was invited with a 15-year-old boy to a flat, where their drinks were laced with drugs; when they were both intoxicated, the defendant indecently assaulted the child. Kingston admitted that, at the time of committing the assault, he intended it, but argued he would not have committed the offence if he had been sober. The House of Lords held that an intoxicated intent was still an intent, and the fact that the intoxication was not voluntary made no difference to that. He had the *mens rea*, and so the intoxication was no defence and he was liable.

If defendants lack *mens rea*, criminal liability can still be imposed if they were intoxicated and would have had *mens rea* if they had been sober. In **R** v **Richardson and Irwin** (1999) a group of university students had got very drunk and had thrown one of their fellow students over the balcony, seriously injuring him. The Court of Appeal ruled that when recklessness forms part of an offence, if defendants lacked *mens rea* because they were intoxicated, and would have had *mens rea* if they had been sober, they can be found liable.

Specific and basic intent crimes

Even where intoxication means that the accused lacks the *mens rea* of a crime, in some circumstances they can still be found liable, forming an exception to the rule that both *mens rea* and *actus reus* are required. In determining whether a defence of intoxication applies the court must first establish that the defendant lacked *mens rea*, and then, secondly, the court looks at what type of offence the defendant has been charged with. In

13

General defences

this respect, the courts distinguish between crimes of basic intent and crimes of specific intent; intoxication will usually be a defence to crimes of specific intent where the defendant lacked *mens rea*, but not usually to crimes of basic intent.

KEY CASE

The leading case on the defence of intoxication is **DPP v Majewski** (1977). The accused had spent 24 hours getting drunk and taking drugs, and then smashed windows and attacked a police officer. Majewski argued that he had been so intoxicated that he could not remember the incidents at all, and therefore could not have formed the necessary *mens rea*. The trial judge ruled that intoxication was only a defence to crimes of specific intent, and that, since the accused was charged with offences of basic intent, his intoxication gave him no defence.

> Voluntary intoxication is only a defence to specific intent crimes.

In deciding whether the defence of intoxication is available, we therefore need to know which crimes are classified by the courts as ones of basic intent and which of specific intent. This sounds straightforward, but unfortunately the courts have been far from clear about which crimes fall into which category, and why.

In **Majewski** the House of Lords attempted to explain the concepts but there now seem to be two possible approaches. The first is that if the offence can only be committed intentionally, it is a crime of specific intent, but if it can be committed with some other form of *mens rea* such as recklessness, it will be a crime of basic intent.

The second possible approach is slightly more complex. On this analysis specific intent offences are those where the required *mens rea* includes the purpose of the defendant's acts which may go beyond the *actus reus*. A simple example of the distinction can be made by contrasting assault and assault with intent to resist arrest. The *actus reus* of assault is the doing of an act which causes another to apprehend immediate and unlawful violence, and the *mens rea* is intention to cause another to apprehend immediate and unlawful violence, or recklessness as to whether the other would be caused to apprehend immediate and unlawful violence. Clearly the two correspond exactly and there is no mention of the purpose of the defendant's acts and on this analysis would be treated as a crime of basic intent. In assault with intent to resist arrest, however, the *actus reus* remains the same, but the *mens rea* has the additional element of intention to resist arrest. This is therefore an offence of specific intent.

Obviously these two tests are quite different, and will not always produce the same result, so that certain crimes may be offences of basic intent under one test, and specific intent under the other. For example, take the offence of criminal damage with intent to endanger life. The *mens rea* is intention or recklessness, so under the first test this should be an offence of basic intent. Yet the *mens rea* – intention or recklessness as to the damaging or destroying of property and as to endangering life – extends beyond the *actus reus*, damaging or destroying property, making this an offence of specific intent under the second test.

In the most recent Court of Appeal case on intoxication, **R v Heard** (2007), the Court appeared to reject the first test in favour of the second. At the same time, it stated that it was difficult to categorise some offences as either basic intent crimes or specific intent crimes because different elements of the offence required different forms of *mens rea*. The Court of Appeal acknowledged that there is 'a great deal of policy in the decision whether voluntary intoxication can or cannot be relied upon' and that the rule is 'firmly grounded on common sense, whether purely logical or not'.

In practice the only reliable method of classifying an offence seems to be to see how offences have been defined when cases have come before the courts. The following list details some of the more important offences, and the case (or one of several cases) in which the distinction was made.

Offences of basic intent include:

- Involuntary manslaughter – **Lipman** (1970);
- Maliciously wounding or inflicting grievous bodily harm, Offences Against the Person Act 1861, s. 20 – **Majewski**;
- Assault occasioning actual bodily harm, Offences Against the Person Act 1861, s. 47 – **Majewski**;
- Common assault, Criminal Justice Act 1988, s. 39 – **Majewski**;
- Rape, Sexual Offences Act 2003, s. 1 – **Heard** (2007).

Offences of specific intent include:

- Murder – **DPP** v **Beard** (1920);
- Wounding or causing grievous bodily harm with intent, Offences Against the Person Act 1861, s. 18 – **Bratty** (1963);
- Theft, Theft Act 1968, s. 1 – **Majewski**;
- Burglary with intent to steal, Theft Act 1968, s. 9 – **Durante** (1972).

An example of the application of the rules on intoxication is **Lipman** (1970). The accused and his girlfriend had taken LSD at his flat. The effects of this drug include hallucinations and, while under its influence, the accused attacked the girl under the illusion that he was descending to the core of the earth and being attacked by snakes. He stuffed a sheet into her throat, with the result that she suffocated. At his trial for murder, the accused said that he had no intention of harming his victim, for he had not known what he was doing while under the influence of LSD. It was accepted that this gave him a defence against murder, since this was a crime of specific intent and he clearly had not formed the intention to kill or to cause GBH, but his intoxication was not allowed as a defence against manslaughter, which was a crime of basic intent. The Court of Appeal said that if a person deliberately takes alcohol or drugs in order to escape from reality – to 'go on a trip' – they cannot plead that self-induced disability as a defence to a criminal offence of basic intent.

Liability for lesser offences

For most offences of specific intent there is a similar crime for which basic intent suffices, providing a fall-back position – so that if, for example, intoxication means that an accused cannot be convicted of the specific intent crime of murder, they can be charged with the basic intent offence of manslaughter (as in **Lipman**). However, where there is no appropriate basic intent offence, intoxication can become a complete defence. This approach was confirmed in **Majewski**.

● Involuntary intoxication

If the defendant is treated as being involuntarily intoxicated, then intoxication may be a defence to any crime, whether one of basic or specific intent, provided the defendant lacks *mens rea*. There are three situations where a person will be treated as involuntarily intoxicated.

Prescribed drugs

Taking drugs on prescription from a doctor is not regarded by the courts as reckless, so intoxication as a result of taking them will be a defence.

Soporific drugs

Where the accused has taken drugs that normally have a soporific effect, making the user relaxed or sleepy, they will be treated as involuntarily intoxicated. In **Hardie** (1985), the accused had been living with a woman at her flat, but the relationship broke down and she wanted him to leave. Very upset, the accused tried to calm his nerves by taking Valium, a tranquilliser which had been prescribed for the woman. He then started a fire in a bedroom, while the woman and her daughter were in the living-room. He was prosecuted for damaging property with intent to endanger the life of another or being reckless whether another life would be endangered, contrary to s. 1(2) of the Criminal Damage Act 1971. On appeal, the Court of Appeal confirmed that, as a general rule, self-induced intoxication from alcohol or a dangerous drug could not be a defence to ordinary crimes involving recklessness, since the taking of the alcohol or drug was itself reckless behaviour. However, the court stated that where the normal effect of a drug was merely sedative, different rules applied. The issue, according to the court, was whether the taking of Valium had itself been reckless, taking into account the fact that the drug was not unlawful in prescribed quantities; that the accused did not know the drug was likely to make him behave as he did; that he had been told it would do him no harm; and that the normal effect of the drug was soporific or sedative. In this case Hardie was held to have a defence.

Laced drinks

Involuntary intoxication also arises where the defendant was unaware that they were consuming the intoxicant, for example because drinks were laced (in **Kingston**, above, the defendant's drinks were laced, but he could still not rely on the defence because he had the *mens rea* of the offence). The provision is quite tightly interpreted; in **Allen** (1988), the defendant voluntarily drank wine, but was unaware that the wine he was drinking had a high alcohol content. It was held that simply not knowing the precise strength of the alcohol did not make his intoxication involuntary.

● 'Dutch courage'

There is one circumstance where intoxication will not even be a defence to an offence of specific intent. This is where a person gets intoxicated in order to summon up the courage to commit a crime – often called getting 'Dutch courage'. In **Attorney-General**

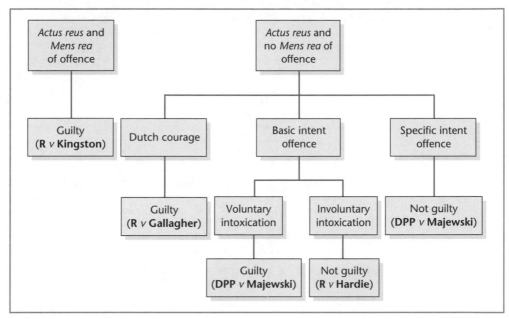

Figure 13.3 The defence of intoxication

for Northern Ireland *v* **Gallagher** (1963), Gallagher wanted to kill his wife. He bought a knife and a bottle of whisky, which it seems he drank to give himself Dutch courage. He got so drunk that he would have been incapable of forming the *mens rea* for murder (possibly because the drink also brought on a mental condition from which he already suffered). In this state he killed his wife with the knife. The House of Lords held that drunkenness is no defence for a sane and sober person who, being capable of forming an intention to kill, and knowing it would be legally wrong to do so, forms the intention to kill and then gets so drunk that when he does carry out the attack he is incapable of forming that intention.

● Intoxication and automatism

An accused who appears to have acted involuntarily, and was intoxicated at the time, is in legal terms considered to be acting voluntarily (assuming that the intoxication was voluntary), and the defence of automatism will not be available. Such a person may, however, have the defence of intoxication.

● Mistake and intoxication

Mistake will not be a defence if it was made as a result of intoxication. In **O'Grady** (1987), the accused had drunk a considerable amount of cider. In his drunken state, he killed his friend, believing (apparently mistakenly) that the friend was trying to kill him. If he had been sober, this mistake could have allowed him a defence, but because he had voluntarily got drunk, the courts held that he should be found liable.

13

General defences

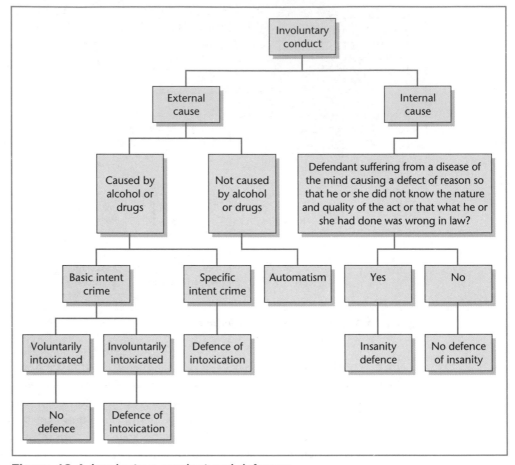

Figure 13.4 Involuntary conduct and defences

● Criticism

The basic/specific intent distinction

As we have seen, the distinction between basic and specific intent appears neither logical nor consistently applied. It can be said that drunkenness should either be relevant or irrelevant, but not arbitrarily relevant for some aspects of some crimes.

In theory, the issue in all crimes is: did the accused have the required mental state to constitute the *mens rea* of the offence? One approach would be to acquit all defendants who were unable to form the *mens rea* because they were so intoxicated. However, from the point of view of policy, this approach has obvious drawbacks. Would we really want a rapist to be acquitted if he deliberately got himself so drunk that he could not know that his victim was not consenting? Or if a drunken brawl results in someone's death, would we want to allow the participants to go free because they were too drunk to realise that they might kill someone?

Most people would agree that this would not be a desirable state of affairs. But the problem is not solved by pretending that logical distinctions can be drawn on the basis of types of *mens rea*; by trying to avoid openly discussing policy considerations, the courts have created a series of anomalies (just one example is that intoxication can be a defence to attempted rape, but not to rape itself), and made the law on this important issue uncertain. One suggested solution is to recognise that policy issues are involved, and leave the question of when intoxication should be a defence to the facts of each case and the common sense of juries.

Accused's attitude to intoxication

No distinction is drawn between the person who intends to lose all self-control, and one who intends no more than social drinking but in the event ends up very drunk. On the normal principles of criminal liability, the first would seem more blameworthy than the second.

Difficulties for juries

The state of the law at the moment can require juries to enter the world of fantasy and guess what might have happened if the person had not been intoxicated. Where an accused is charged with a crime of basic intent, a jury may have to disregard their intoxication when deciding whether they committed the offence. In **Lipman**, for example, the jury were asked to decide whether the accused would have realised that what he was doing was dangerous if he had not been under the influence of LSD; yet if the accused had not been so heavily drugged, it seems highly unlikely that he would have tried to stuff a bedsheet down his girlfriend's throat anyway.

Inconsistency

The fall-back position which allows an intoxicated offender to be convicted of a similar, lesser offence can act as a reasonable compromise, but for some specific intent offences there is no corresponding crime of basic intent – for example, theft. This leads to a situation in which intoxication is a complete defence to some crimes but not to others, apparently with no logical reason for the distinction.

 ## Reform

Codification

The Law Commission has issued a report entitled *Intoxication and Criminal Liability* (2009) in which it proposes to put into legislative form most of the current common law rules on intoxication to provide greater clarity on this subject. Unfortunately the draft Bill produced by the Law Commission is itself extremely complicated. The substance of the distinction between specific and basic intent offences is to be retained, although the terminology is changed.

A full defence of intoxication

In Australia intoxication is a full defence on the basis that the accused lacks the necessary *mens rea*; there are obvious policy objections to this approach.

An intoxication offence

The Law Commission recommended back in 1993 the creation of a new offence of dangerous intoxication. Where the jury found that the accused had committed the *actus reus* of the offence charged, but was so intoxicated as to be unable to form *mens rea*, they could find the accused guilty of dangerous intoxication. Whatever the offence originally charged, the maximum sentence for dangerous intoxication would be one year for a first offence, and three for subsequent convictions.

A special verdict

In the Criminal Law Revision Committee's Fourteenth Report, a minority of its members recommended the introduction of a special verdict that the offence was committed while the defendant was intoxicated. The defendant would then be liable to the same potential penalty as if they had been convicted in the normal way (except where the charge was murder, where the penalty would be that for manslaughter). Sentencing could then both reflect the harm done, and take the intoxication into account where appropriate.

Miscellaneous proposals

Other proposals have included the introduction of a crime of negligently causing injury; retaining the current law on specific and basic intent but creating some new offences to ensure every specific intent offence has a corresponding 'fall-back' offence of basic intent; and treating persistent drunken offenders outside the criminal law system, on the basis that treating their drinking problems would be more helpful in preventing crime than repeatedly punishing them.

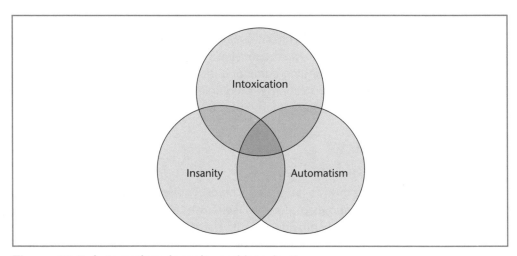

Figure 13.5 Automatism, insanity and intoxication

Self-defence and public defence

Where a person uses violence in order to protect themselves or another they may be able to argue that they acted under common law in self-defence. Under the Criminal Law Act 1967 s. 3(1) a person can also use reasonable force to prevent the commission of a crime or effect or assist in the lawful arrest of a person. In practice the common law defence of self-defence and the statutory defence in the Criminal Law Act 1967 overlap because if a victim takes out a knife and approaches the defendant, when the defendant reacts by slapping the victim's hand to make him or her drop the knife, the defendant is both acting in self-defence and acting to prevent a crime. Section 3(2) states that the statutory defence should be applied in preference to the common law defence when there is this potential overlap:

> S. 3(2). Subsection (1) above shall replace the rules of the common law on the question when force used for a purpose mentioned in the subsection is justified by that purpose.

Following public concern after the criminal prosecution of Anthony Martin (the reclusive Norfolk farmer who shot and killed an intruder), and confusion as to how far people are allowed to use force to protect their homes against burglars, s. 76 of the Criminal Justice and Immigration Act 2008 was passed. This aims to clarify the common law on self-defence and the defences provided by s. 3(1) of the Criminal Law Act 1967 relating to the use of force in the prevention of crime or making an arrest. It does not aim to change the law in any way, instead the explanatory notes to the Act describe the provision as providing 'a gloss' on these defences. The hope is that the statutory provision will improve understanding of the practical application of this area of law by putting into legislative form some of the legal principles established in the case law. Section 76 provides:

(1) This section applies where in proceedings for an offence—
   (a) an issue arises as to whether a person charged with the offence ('D') is entitled to rely on a defence within subsection (2), and
   (b) the question arises whether the degree of force used by D against a person ('V') was reasonable in the circumstances.
(2) The defences are—
   (a) the common law defence of self-defence; and
   (b) the defences provided by section 3(1) of the Criminal Law Act 1967 (c. 58) or section 3(1) of the Criminal Law Act (Northern Ireland) 1967 (c. 18 (N.I.)) (use of force in prevention of crime or making arrest).
(3) The question whether the degree of force used by D was reasonable in the circumstances is to be decided by reference to the circumstances as D believed them to be, and subsections (4) to (8) also apply in connection with deciding that question.
(4) If D claims to have held a particular belief as regards the existence of any circumstances—
   (a) the reasonableness or otherwise of that belief is relevant to the question whether D genuinely held it; but
   (b) if it is determined that D did genuinely hold it, D is entitled to rely on it for the purposes of subsection (3), whether or not—
      (i)   it was mistaken, or
      (ii) (if it was mistaken) the mistake was a reasonable one to have made.
(5) But subsection (4)(b) does not enable D to rely on any mistaken belief attributable to intoxication that was voluntarily induced.
(6) The degree of force used by D is not to be regarded as having been reasonable in the circumstances as D believed them to be if it was disproportionate in those circumstances.
(7) In deciding the question mentioned in subsection (3) the following considerations are to be taken into account (so far as relevant in the circumstances of the case)—
   (a) that a person acting for a legitimate purpose may not be able to weigh to a nicety the exact measure of any necessary action; and

(b) that evidence of a person's having only done what the person honestly and instinctively thought was necessary for a legitimate purpose constitutes strong evidence that only reasonable action was taken by that person for that purpose.

(8) Subsection (7) is not to be read as preventing other matters from being taken into account where they are relevant to deciding the question mentioned in subsection (3).

(9) This section is intended to clarify the operation of the existing defences mentioned in subsection (2).

(10) In this section—
  (a) 'legitimate purpose' means—
    (i) the purpose of self-defence under the common law, or
    (ii) the prevention of crime or effecting or assisting in the lawful arrest of persons mentioned in the provisions referred to in subsection (2)(b);
  (b) references to self-defence include acting in defence of another person; and
  (c) references to the degree of force used are to the type and amount of force used.

This legislative provision puts into statutory words the existing common law and the individual subsections will be considered as we look at the requirements for these defences.

Public defence

This is a statutory defence contained in s. 3 of the Criminal Law Act 1967. This section states:

> S. 3(1) A person may use such force as is reasonable in the circumstances in the prevention of crime, or in effecting or assisting in the lawful arrest of offenders or suspected offenders or of persons unlawfully at large.

Thus, this defence is available to any person who uses such force as is reasonable in the circumstances to prevent crime, or lawfully to arrest or assist the lawful arrest of offenders, suspected offenders or persons unlawfully at large (such as escaped prisoners). For example, if you saw someone snatch a bag, chased that person and then caught them with a rugby tackle, your action would normally be an assault, but because you were attempting to make a lawful arrest, the public defence would probably allow you to avoid liability.

In **R v Jones** (2004) the defendants were anti-war protesters who had trespassed and caused damage to a number of military bases in the United Kingdom as a protest against the war in Iraq. At their trial for a range of criminal offences, they argued that they had a defence under s. 3 of the Criminal Law Act 1967. They said that they were trying to prevent an international crime of aggression being committed against Iraq. The House of Lords rejected this defence, pointing out that aggression was not a crime under national law and therefore this requirement of the defence under s. 3 had not been satisfied.

Self-defence

This term covers the common law defences of self-defence or defence of another, again using such force as is reasonable in the circumstances. Situations where this defence might be appropriate include hitting someone who seems about to attack you or another person.

In the past it was generally accepted that self-defence was only available where a crime had been or was going to be committed against the person seeking to rely on the defence. In **Re A (Children)** (2000) the weaker Siamese twin, Mary, was committing no offence as she was under the age of 10 and lacked any *mens rea*. Despite this, Lord Justice Ward stated *obiter* (in other words this did not form part of the reasoning of the majority of the court and does not form part of a binding precedent) that the defence should still be available. On the facts of the case, the weaker twin Mary was, by sharing Jodie's heart, killing Jodie. Thus Lord Justice Ward concluded:

> The availability of such a plea of quasi self-defence, modified to meet the quite exceptional circumstances nature has inflicted on the twins, makes intervention by the doctors lawful.

Despite this, the High Court has recently confirmed that the defendant must be acting to prevent a crime. The defendants in **DPP v Bayer** (2003) had attached themselves to tractors to prevent the planting of genetically modified maize. They genuinely believed that the crops would damage neighbouring property. In their defence they sought to rely on self-defence. This defence was rejected because they were not seeking to prevent the commission of a crime, as the crops were going to be planted legally.

The same basic principles apply to the statutory and common law defences which are discussed below.

Necessity for action

Defendants can only rely on these defences if their action was necessary because of a threat of unjustified harm to themselves, to someone else, or because of a need to prevent crime in one of the ways listed above. In deciding whether or not the behaviour was necessary, the courts will take into account three key issues: whether the person could have retreated from the situation; whether the threat was imminent; and whether the defendant made some mistake which caused them to think the action was justified.

Possibility of retreat

At one time it was believed that in order for these defences to apply, the accused must have retreated as far as possible from the situation before using force – so that a person who had a chance to run away from an attacker but instead chose to fight back might not have a defence. But in **McInnes** (1971), it was stated that failure to make use of a chance to retreat is simply evidence which the jury can use to decide whether it was necessary to use force, and whether the force used was reasonable. The Court of Appeal said that the jury should have been directed that, in order for force to be considered reasonable in the circumstances, the defendant's behaviour should certainly have demonstrated that he did not want to fight, but simply failing to take an opportunity to run away did not in itself make the defence unavailable.

Imminent threat

A defendant will only be justified in reacting to a threat which is imminent. This does not mean that defendants have to wait until they are hit, for example, before hitting back, but it does mean there must be some immediacy about the threat. The balance which the courts have sought to establish in this area can be seen from the following two cases. In **Attorney-General's Reference (No. 2 of 1983)** the defendant owned a shop in an area where there had been extensive rioting. He made up some petrol bombs, and kept them ready to defend his property if required. The court found that a defence was available to him as the threat was sufficiently imminent. By contrast, in **Malnik** v **DPP** (1989) the defendant went to visit a man who was believed to have stolen some valuable cars belonging to an acquaintance of the defendant. The suspected thief was known to be violent, so the defendant took with him a rice flail – a martial arts weapon consisting of two pieces of wood joined together by a chain. He was arrested while approaching the man's house, and the court rejected the argument that carrying the weapon was justified because he was in imminent danger of attack, pointing out that he had himself created the dangerous situation by choosing to go to the man's house.

Mistake

If a defendant makes a mistake which leads him or her to believe there are circumstances making defensive action necessary, the courts will assess the necessity of the defendant's conduct on the basis of the facts as the defendant believed them to be, even if the mistake was not a reasonable one to make. This is the position laid down in s. 76(4) of the Criminal Justice and Immigration Act 2008:

> S. 76(4) If D claims to have held a particular belief as regards the existence of any circumstances—
> - (a) the reasonableness or otherwise of that belief is relevant to the question whether D genuinely held it; but
> - (b) if it is determined that D did genuinely hold it, D is entitled to rely on it for the purposes of subsection (3), whether or not—
>   - (i) it was mistaken, or
>   - (ii) (if it was mistaken) the mistake was a reasonable one to have made.

This is a statutory confirmation of the established position in common law.

KEY CASE

In **R** v **Williams (Gladstone)** (1987) a man saw a youth rob a woman in the street. He grabbed the youth and a struggle ensued, at which point the defendant arrived on the scene, and, not having seen the robbery, attempted to help the youth. The first man claimed to be a police officer, and told

> When considering self-defence, the courts treat the facts as the defendant honestly thought them to be.

the defendant that he was arresting the youth for a mugging. In fact he was not a policeman, so, when the defendant asked to see some police identification, he was unable to produce it. As a result, the defendant concluded that the man was simply attacking the youth without justification and, in an attempt to defend the youth, he punched the man in the face. He was charged with occasioning actual bodily harm under s. 47 of the Offences Against the Person Act 1861. The court held that, in deciding whether or not he had a defence, the facts should be treated as he honestly thought them to be; if the man had been attacking the youth, the defendant would have had a defence, so he was not liable.

Jean Charles de Menezes was fatally shot at Stockwell tube station in the summer of 2005 when the police mistook him for a suicide bomber. No individual police officers have been prosecuted for a criminal offence despite a jury disbelieving police evidence about the shooting at his inquest. The Crown Prosecution Service have taken the view a court would not convict the police partly because they would seek to rely on the public defence as they shot Jean Charles to prevent a crime. They were mistaken as to the facts but the court would, under the current law, take into account the facts as the police believed them to be. However, this interpretation of the defence might violate the European Convention on Human Rights under which mistakes made by agents of the state should be based on reasonable grounds: **Caraher** v **United Kingdom** (1994).

Under s. 76(5) of the Criminal Justice and Immigration Act 2008, if a mistake is induced by intoxication then the mistake has to be ignored in relation to the defence:

S. 76(5) But subsection (4)(b) does not enable D to rely on any mistaken belief attributable to intoxication that was voluntarily induced.

This principle was established in the case of **O'Grady** in 1987 (discussed on p. 343) and confirmed by the Court of Appeal in 2006 in **R** v **Hatton**. In **O'Connor** (1991) the defendant got drunk in a pub, and started arguing with the victim. Mistakenly believing that he was about to be attacked, he head-butted the victim three times. The victim died from his injuries and the defendant was convicted of murder, but appealed. The Court of Appeal stated that because his mistake was produced by intoxication, it could not be taken into account when considering self-defence, though it was relevant to the defence of intoxication and the issue of whether he had *mens rea* (discussed above). In fact the appeal was allowed because the trial judge had made a mistake.

Up to this point, we have been looking at mistakes where the mistaken facts suggest there is a defence when the true facts suggest there is not. We now need to consider the reverse situation, where the true facts suggest there is a defence but the mistaken facts suggest there is not. In the former situation the mistake will be taken into account, in the reverse situation it will not. Thus, in both situations the most favourable interpretation is given for the defendant. In **R** v **McKoy** (2002) a policeman restrained the defendant by holding his arm but without arresting him. The defendant may have mistakenly believed that he was being arrested. He pushed the policeman, who fell through a window, and was prosecuted for an assault occasioning actual bodily harm and for causing criminal damage. Usually people are entitled to use reasonable force against a police officer who is not carrying out a lawful arrest, in order to free themselves. But the trial judge directed the jury that this defence would not be available to the defendant if he mistakenly thought the police officer was carrying out a lawful arrest. This was found to be a misdirection. The defendant had the right to use reasonable force to free himself, regardless of whether he had a mistaken belief that he was under a lawful arrest.

Reasonable force

Self-defence and the public defence can only succeed if the defendant used reasonable force. Section 76(6) of the Criminal Justice and Immigration Act 2008 provides:

S. 76(6) The degree of force used by D is not to be regarded as having been reasonable in the circumstances as D believed them to be if it was disproportionate in those circumstances.

What constitutes reasonable force is a matter for the jury to decide, balancing the amount of force used against the harm the accused sought to prevent – so that, for example, force considered reasonable for protecting a person might be considered excessive if used to prevent a crime against property.

The Civil Division of the Court of Appeal stated in **Cross** v **Kirkby** (2000) that a defence could still be available where 25 per cent more force was used than was necessary. In that case Cross had seen the defendant, a farmer, attempting to walk his partner off private land during an anti-hunt demonstration. Cross took a baseball bat from his vehicle and hit the farmer on the hand and arm. The farmer grappled the baseball bat from him and hit him back across the head, fracturing his skull and causing permanent damage. In civil proceedings in which Cross sought financial compensation for his injuries, the farmer's defence of self-defence was allowed.

Strictly speaking, the defence is all or nothing: if the accused used reasonable force, they are not guilty; if the force was unreasonable, often described as excessive, the defence is unavailable. However, in considering this issue, the courts place great emphasis on the fact that defendants are not expected to perform precise calculations in the heat of the moment. In **Attorney-General for Northern Ireland's Reference (No. 1 of 1975)** (1977) a soldier in Northern Ireland stopped a man, who started to run away. Mistakenly thinking that the man was a member of the IRA, the soldier shot and killed him. He was charged with murder and argued that he had both the statutory and common law defences. The House of Lords said it was a question for the jury whether the force used by the soldier was reasonable or excessive, and in deciding this they had to take into account the limited time for reflection in these types of circumstances. In this case, they would have to balance the high risk of death or serious injury to the man running away, against the harm which could be avoided by preventing the man's escape if he were a terrorist:

> [I]t would not be unreasonable to assess the level of harm to be averted by preventing the accused's escape as even graver – the killing or wounding of members of the patrol by terrorists in ambush and the effect of this success by members of the Provisional IRA in encouraging the continuance of the armed insurrection and all the misery and destruction of life and property that terrorist activity in Northern Ireland has entailed.

The law recognises that in the kind of situations where the defence is used, there is rarely much time to consider what should be done. As Lord Morris put it in **Palmer** (1971):

> A person defending himself cannot weigh to a nicety the exact measure of his necessary defensive action.

Professor J.C. Smith (2002) has argued that where a mistake has been made and a person has been killed, the defendant may have a defence to murder, but they may still incur liability for manslaughter. He argues that if the defendant has made a grossly negligent mistake then liability could be imposed for gross negligence manslaughter.

Mistake as to the degree of force

In the case of **R** v **Anthony Martin** (2001) the defendant had been entitled to use force, but on the facts he had made a mistake about the amount of force he was entitled to use.

The law imposes an objective test, so it does not matter if the defendant thought they were using a reasonable amount of force, what matters is whether objectively they have used a reasonable amount of force. The Criminal Justice and Immigration Act 2008 provides:

> S. 76(3) The question whether the degree of force used by D was reasonable in the circumstances is to be decided by reference to the circumstances as D believed them to be, and subsections (4) to (8) also apply in connection with deciding that question.
>
> . . .
>
> (7) In deciding the question mentioned in subsection (3) the following considerations are to be taken into account (so far as relevant in the circumstances of the case)—
> > (a) that a person acting for a legitimate purpose may not be able to weigh to a nicety the exact measure of any necessary action; and
> > (b) that evidence of a person's having only done what the person honestly and instinctively thought was necessary for a legitimate purpose constitutes strong evidence that only reasonable action was taken by that person for that purpose.
>
> (8) Subsection (7) is not to be read as preventing other matters from being taken into account where they are relevant to deciding the question mentioned in subsection (3).

Again the legislation is confirming the case law on this point. In the leading case of **Williams (Gladstone)** (1987) it was decided that the matter had to be decided objectively and the mistake of the defendant could not be taken into account in deciding whether reasonable force had been used.

KEY CASE

The objective test was confirmed in the high-profile case of **R v Anthony Martin** (2001), although it was watered down slightly as the Court of Appeal left open the possibility of sometimes taking into account specific characteristics of the

> A person must only use reasonable force when acting in self-defence.

defendant when applying this test. Martin lived in a remote farmhouse which was broken into by three intruders, who were probably intending to carry out a burglary. He used a pump-action shotgun to shoot one of the intruders three times, including once in the back, and seriously injured another. There was some dispute as to whether Martin was on the stairs or downstairs waiting for the intruders when he fired the first shot. The issue of self-defence was left to the jury and rejected. He was convicted of murder and wounding with intent contrary to s. 18 of the Offences Against the Person Act 1861. His conviction was reduced to that of manslaughter on appeal because the defence of diminished responsibility had not been left to the jury, but the defence of self-defence was rejected by the Court of Appeal as Martin had used excessive force. The defence barrister submitted that in determining the question of reasonable force the courts should take the same approach as the House of Lords laid down in **Smith** (2001) for the objective test in provocation. This would allow the defendant's characteristics to be taken into account when determining whether his response had been reasonable, which in this case would include the fact that Martin suffered from a paranoid personality disorder. The Court of Appeal accepted that the jury was entitled to take into account the physical characteristics of the defendant. They also said that, in exceptional circumstances which made the evidence especially probative, the court could take into account the fact that the defendant was suffering from a psychiatric condition. But this was not such an exceptional case, and the court concluded that on the facts reasonable force had not been used.

Following public concern at the case of Anthony Martin, the Government, the Crown Prosecution Service and the Association of Chief Police Officers, jointly published guidance on the subject to make the law clear to the public. This leaflet was entitled *Householders and the Use of Force Against Intruders*. It stated:

> So long as you only do what you honestly and instinctively believe is necessary in the heat of the moment, that would be the strongest evidence of you acting lawfully and in self-defence. This is still the case if you use something to hand as a weapon.

Even if the intruder is killed, the homeowner will have acted lawfully if the force used was reasonable. Conduct which would be viewed as excessive and might lead to prosecution includes continuing to hurt someone after they are unconscious, and setting a trap.

In practice, cases where a householder is prosecuted for using excessive force are rare. According to the Crown Prosecution Service, only 11 prosecutions have been brought against people defending their home or commercial premises from burglars, and these included a case where a man laid in wait for a burglar, beat him, tied him up, threw him into a pit and set fire to him, and one where a man repeatedly shot poachers in the back as they fled his land.

● Criticism

The 'all or nothing' approach

The 'all or nothing' approach to the defence can work harshly in murder cases. For other offences, if the accused cannot be acquitted because they have used excessive force, but it is obvious that some force was justified, this can be taken into account as a mitigating factor in sentencing. The mandatory sentence for murder means that there can be no such mitigation. It has been suggested that more flexibility in sentencing could be gained by allowing juries to convict of manslaughter rather than murder in such circumstances (as is done, for example, when an accused successfully raises the defence of provocation). This was the law in Australia for a time, but was later rejected as being too difficult for juries to understand. The reform of the partial defences to murder contained in the Coroners and Justice Act 2009 will effectively provide a partial defence to murder where excessive force has been used (see p. 77).

The case of the soldier, Sergeant Lee Clegg, has highlighted such concerns over the current law of self-defence. In **R** v **Clegg** (1995), Clegg was on duty at a Northern Ireland checkpoint when a car containing joyriders failed to stop. Although Clegg admitted he did not think the car contained terrorists, he shot at the car four times, killing one of the passengers. He was convicted of murder. At his trial he said he had shot at the car, three times from the front and once from the side, because it was driving towards a soldier and he thought that the soldier's life needed protecting. The soldier in question was found to have an injured foot after the incident, and the suggestion was that the car had driven over it. In fact, the soldier's injury was later discovered to have been caused by someone stamping on his foot, in an attempt to fabricate evidence to support Clegg's defence. Forensic examination of the bullet holes in the car showed that the fourth shot had not been fired from the side, but from behind, after the car had passed and when there could have been no danger to the other soldier. Clegg admitted in court that he did not believe there was any justification for shooting at the car from behind. In the light of this evidence, the logical conclusion of the House of Lords was that Clegg had used excessive force in shooting from behind, and, because he realised this, he could not rely on **Scarlett** as it was then understood. His conviction for murder was upheld with its mandatory life sentence, but, after a campaign by tabloid newspapers in England, he was released after serving only four years' imprisonment. The case caused enormous political controversy, to which Clegg's release added. Sympathisers with Clegg argued that British soldiers should not be locked up for 'doing their duty' when IRA terrorists were causing much more harm, while those who opposed Clegg's release stated that the family of the girl who died were denied justice.

In the light of the controversy the case aroused, the Home Secretary announced the Home Office would carry out a review of the law of the public defence and self-defence. This review was criticised by the academic Andrew Ashworth in an editorial comment to the 1995 *Criminal Law Review*. His criticism was that the review had been confined to cases where police officers or members of the armed forces use excessive force in situations where some force would be allowed. He pointed out that the law should be neutral as to the status of the individual, and that there are grave dangers in having one law for private individuals and another for representatives of the state. Certainly the Lee Clegg campaign itself reflected the attitude which lay behind the problem Ashworth highlighted. It was noticeable that the same British newspapers which campaigned for the release of Clegg, who had definitely killed somebody whatever one thought of the circumstances, took little interest in campaigns for the release of the Guildford Four, the Birmingham Six and other Irish victims of miscarriages of justice. These people were guilty of nothing at all – yet when they were released, several papers asked where was the justice for the bomb victims, as though releasing those who had nothing to do with the bombings in some way increased the injustice for the victims. It is hard not to conclude that the complaints about the law arising from **Clegg** had less to do with problems in the law than they did with political interests in Northern Ireland.

European Convention on Human Rights

A defence can be successful where a defendant honestly but mistakenly believes that force was necessary. This means, for example, that the police can avoid liability where they have shot members of the public mistakenly and unreasonably believing that they were armed and dangerous. In 1999, Harry Stanley was shot dead by police officers who believed that he was a dangerous armed terrorist about to shoot them with a sawn-off shotgun. Their belief was based on a telephone call from a member of the public who thought Mr Stanley had an Irish accent and had left the pub carrying something that looked like a gun. In fact he was Scottish and was carrying a plastic bag containing a wooden table leg. No member of the police force has been prosecuted for his death as such a prosecution is unlikely to be successful given the current state of the law.

Fiona Leverick (2002) has argued that the law on this subject may be in breach of the right to life, protected by Art. 2 of the European Convention on Human Rights. In her view, Art. 2 requires a criminal sanction to be imposed where a person kills on the basis of an erroneous and unreasonable belief. The European Court has consistently stated that any exception to Art. 2 based on a mistaken belief, must be held for good reasons. Professor J.C. Smith (2002) has, however, counter-argued that there is no such violation of the European Convention. He has pointed to the decision of **Re A (Children)** – the case concerned with the conjoined twins, which is discussed at p. 66. There the Court of Appeal took the view that Art. 2 was only concerned with intentional killing, with 'intention' being given a narrower meaning under the Convention than under English law. Under the Convention it was limited to where the killing was the purpose of the defendant's acts. J.C. Smith interprets **Re A (Children)** as deciding that Art. 2 has no application to a person acting honestly in self-defence. This argument is dubious, as Fiona Leverick has pointed out, since the European Court of Human Rights has ruled that Art. 2 does not only apply to intentional killing, but also places an obligation on the state to protect the individual from any unjust deprivation of life, intentional or not: **LCB** v **UK** (1999).

Both Professor J.C. Smith and Fiona Leverick agree that for this type of case, the most appropriate label might be manslaughter rather than murder. J.C. Smith suggests that if the defendant has made a grossly negligent mistake then they could avoid liability for murder but could still be liable for gross negligence manslaughter.

Mistake and intoxication

Section 76(5) of the Criminal Justice and Immigration Act 2008 and the case of **O'Grady** create an exception to the rule in **Williams (Gladstone)** that a person has a defence if they are acting under a mistake of fact. This creates an anomaly in that, on the one hand, an accused who is so drunk that they cannot form *mens rea* will be acquitted of murder, since it is an offence of specific intent; on the other hand, if the accused was drunk and this caused them to believe they were being attacked by the victim, they cannot rely on self-defence. Section 76(5) and **O'Grady** are thus out of line with cases which allow a defence of intoxication to offences of specific intent.

Sex discrimination

It is arguable that the public defence and self-defence are more likely to succeed for male as opposed to female defendants. The defences are usually raised in the context of offences against the person, and most reported violent crime is between young males, typically when they are out drinking in the evening. While there is probably just as much violence against women – if not more – most of it takes place in the domestic setting, and often goes unreported. Because of this, the cases which have developed the rules for these defences have been concerned primarily with male defendants, which means that, as with the defence of provocation, there is a danger that they have been shaped with male responses to danger in mind, when female responses may be quite different. In particular, the lesser strength of a woman may mean she has to use a weapon to defend herself even if her attacker is unarmed, whereas a man can usually fight fists with fists, so making his response proportionate to the attack.

As with provocation, this type of difference has caused problems with the use of the defences by battered women. Ewing studied 100 cases of battered women who killed their partners, and found a number of common features: they had been the victims of violence for many years; had received insufficient help from the community and the police; felt unable to leave the situation though they had often made unsuccessful attempts to do so; and the killing was committed in anticipation of further violence in the future. In the past, the mere fact that they did not leave the situation could make the defence unavailable. **McInnes** should change this, but there are still problems: if a woman acts in anticipation of further violence, it may be held that the threat cannot be described as 'imminent'; and if she uses a weapon when her partner is unarmed, the force may be considered excessive.

 Reform

TOPICAL ISSUE

Increase the rights of home owners

Following the case of **Anthony Martin** (discussed on p. 352) there was considerable discussion as to whether the law needed to be reformed to increase the rights of home owners to tackle intruders discovered in their houses. The Conservative Party claimed that the law was unclear and suggested that it should be reformed so that householders would be allowed to use any force necessary unless it was 'grossly disproportionate'. However, the academic Ian Dennis (2000) has commented on the dangers of extending the right to use force in self-defence too far:

> If an Englishman should be allowed to kill in defence of his castle – as some appear to claim – then the aggressive armed burglar can be safely despatched, but so also can the ten-year-old boy found stealing apples from the kitchen.

The Government considered whether reform was necessary and concluded that it was not because the law already provides an element of flexibility because it takes into account the fact that the homeowner is being forced to react in the heat of the moment. The Home Secretary said:

> I have come to the conclusion that guidance and clarification will ensure that the current law is properly understood and implemented; and that therefore no change in the law is required.

A leaflet to explain the law was therefore published, which is discussed on p. 353. However, the reformed partial defences to murder contained in the Coroners and Justice Act 2009 may provide a partial defence to home owners who use excessive force (see p. 76).

The draft Criminal Code, in line with the approach recommended by the Law Commission and the Criminal Law Revision Committee, provides that where excessive force is used in self-defence, this should reduce murder to manslaughter, a proposal also put forward by the House of Lords Select Committee on Murder and Life Imprisonment in 1989.

Duress

Duress is the defence that applies where a person commits a crime because they were acting under a threat of death or serious personal injury to themselves or another. By allowing the defence the criminal law is recognising that the defendant had been faced with a terrible dilemma. In **R** *v* **Symonds** (1998) it was observed that the same facts could fall within both the defence of duress and self-defence. It felt that self-defence should be preferred for offences against the person and duress for other offences (such as dangerous driving). At one time the defence of duress only covered acts done as a result of an express threat to the effect of 'do this or else', but modern cases have introduced the concept of duress of circumstances, which arises from the situation that the person was in at the time. There are thus now two forms of this defence: duress by threats and duress of circumstances.

Duress by threats

This traditional defence of duress covers situations where defendants have been forced by someone else to break the law under a direct threat of death or serious personal injury to themselves or someone else. The most important recent case on duress is now the House of Lords judgment of **R** *v* **Hasan** (2005). The House was concerned that the defence of duress was increasingly being relied upon, particularly by people who had been involved with organised crime and drugs. To put a stop to this growth, the judges in **Hasan** have severely restricted where this defence can be successfully relied upon.

Two-part test

In order to try to find the balance between the seriousness of the harm threatened to the accused and the seriousness of the consequent illegal behaviour, a two-part test was laid down in **Graham** (1982). The test is similar to that used in the defence of provocation as it involves both a subjective and an objective criterion:

1 Was the defendant forced to act as he or she did because he or she feared that otherwise death or serious personal injury would result to the defendant, an immediate relative or someone for whom the defendant reasonably regarded him or herself as responsible?
2 Would a sober person of reasonable firmness, sharing the defendant's characteristics, have reacted to that situation by behaving as the defendant did?

Graham was a homosexual who lived with his wife and his lover, King. In the past King had behaved violently, for example tipping Graham and his wife off the settee when he found them cuddling. Threatened by King, Graham took part in the strangling of his wife with an electric flex. On the facts the Court of Appeal did not consider duress existed, as the threats were not sufficiently grave.

The first part of the test

Seriousness of the threats

The defence will only be available where there has been a threat of death or serious personal harm. In **R** v **Valderrama-Vega** (1985), the accused was charged with taking part in the illegal importation of cocaine from Colombia. He argued that he was acting under duress, in that a Mafia-type organisation in Colombia had threatened to kill or injure him or his family, and to expose his homosexuality; he was also under great pressure financially, facing ruin if he did not take part in the smuggling. The courts held that only the threats of death or personal injury could constitute duress, although it was not necessary that those threats should be the only reason for the accused's behaviour.

Threats to property will not usually be sufficient for duress to be treated as a defence to a serious crime; it may still be possible to argue that an extremely serious threat to property might excuse a very minor crime, but there is no authority on the point.

The House of Lords stated in **R** v **Hasan** that the threat must be of death or serious personal harm to the defendant, the defendant's immediate family or someone for whom the defendant reasonably regarded himself as responsible.

An unavoidable threat

The defendant must have had no opportunity to avoid the threat, except by complying with it. If there is time for defendants to report the threat to the police, or to escape without harming themselves or others, then the defence cannot apply. Therefore, evidence that the threat is unavoidable will be that the threat is imminent. In **Gill** (1963) the defendant was told to steal his employer's lorry, and threatened with violence if he failed to do so. At his trial for theft, the court stated, *obiter*, that he probably would not have been able to rely on the defence of duress: between the time of the threat and his carrying out the crime he had the opportunity to inform the police of the threat, so the threat was not sufficiently immediate to justify his conduct.

Following the case of **R** v **Hasan**, this rule is likely to be strictly applied. The House of Lords stated that it should be made clear to juries that:

> . . . if the retribution threatened against the defendant or his family or a person for whom he feels responsible is not such as he reasonably expects to follow immediately or almost immediately on his failure to comply with the threat, there may be little if any room for doubt that he could have taken evasive action, whether by going to the police or in some other way, to avoid committing the crime with which he is charged.

The House criticised the earlier case of **R** v **Hudson and Taylor** which had given a lenient interpretation to this requirement. That case had stated that a threat would be counted as imminent if, at the time of the crime, it was operating on the accused's mind, even though it could not have been carried out there and then. The defendants were two teenage girls who had been the main witnesses for the prosecution at the trial of a man charged with wounding. In court, neither identified the accused as the attacker, and both falsely testified that they did not recognise him. On being charged with perjury, they explained that before the trial they had been threatened with serious injury if they told the truth, and during the trial they had noticed in the public gallery a member of the gang who had made those threats. The threat to injure was held to have been immediate, even though it obviously could not have been carried out there and then in the courtroom. In light of the criticism of this case in **R** v **Hasan**, it is unlikely that it will be followed in the future. Commenting on the case, the House stated in **R** v **Hasan**: 'I cannot, consistently with principle, accept that a witness testifying in the Crown Court at Manchester has no opportunity to avoid complying with a threat incapable of execution then or there.'

Following **Hasan**, the earlier case of **R** v **Abdul-Hussain** (1999) would also probably be decided differently today. The defendants were Shia Muslims from southern Iraq who were fugitives from the Iraqi regime. For a while they lived in Sudan but they feared that they and their families would be deported to Iraq where they would almost certainly have been executed. In desperation, using fake weapons made of plastic, they hijacked a plane that was going to Jordan, which, after negotiations, landed in Stansted airport. After eight hours the hostages were released and the defendants gave themselves up. At their trial, the judge ruled that the defence of duress (duress of circumstances on these facts) should not be left to the jury because the threat was insufficiently close and immediate to give rise to a virtually spontaneous reaction to the physical risk arising. They were all convicted of the statutory offence of hijacking. The defendants appealed against their convictions on the ground that the judge had made a mistake in withdrawing the defence of duress from the jury's consideration. Their appeal was allowed. The Court of Appeal stated that the trial judge had interpreted the law too strictly in seeking a virtually spontaneous reaction. However, the House of Lords in **Hasan** now seems closer to the trial judge's approach, than that of the Court of Appeal.

Mistake

There may not be any actual imminent threat. If there is no such threat, but the defendant makes a mistake and honestly and reasonably believes there is an imminent threat, the defence of duress can be available. In earlier cases such as **R** v **Martin**, the Court of Appeal had suggested that a subjective test should be applied and that the defence could be available if the defendant made an honest mistake, even if it was not a reasonable mistake. This has now been rejected by the House of Lords in **R** v **Hasan** – the mistaken belief must be both honest and reasonable in order for the defence to apply.

In **R** v **Safi and others** (2003) the appellants had been convicted of hijacking an Afghan aircraft. In February 2000, the appellants had hijacked the plane, armed with guns and grenades. They had forced the pilot to fly from Afghanistan to Stansted where they threatened to blow up the plane. They eventually surrendered to the British authorities after a three-day siege.

In their defence, the appellants said they acted under duress of circumstances. They were members of an Afghan organisation opposed to the Taliban regime. As four members of the organisation had been arrested and tortured, the appellants believed that their names were known to the regime. This would have exposed them and their families to the risk of capture, torture and death. They argued that the duress continued on landing at Stansted, as there then arose an imminent threat of being returned to Afghanistan.

At the first trial the jury failed to reach a verdict. At their retrial the trial judge ruled that, for the defence of duress to apply, there had to be an imminent peril. Following their conviction, the defendants appealed to the Court of Appeal. The Court of Appeal held that the judge had made an error of law. There did not need to be an imminent peril. What was required was that the appellants reasonably believed that there was an imminent peril. The appeal was allowed.

The acquittal of the defendants in this high-profile hijacking case led to suggestions in the media that the law amounts to a 'hijackers' charter' and that Britain had become a 'soft touch' for hijackers. However, it should be borne in mind that the appeals were allowed only because the trial judges had made an error of law. If the trial judges had got the law right the juries might still have been prepared to convict on the basis that the objective part of the test for duress had not been satisfied, if the defendants' conduct was disproportionate to their perceived danger. The law has also been tightened up by the House of Lords in **Hasan**.

Voluntary exposure to duress

Following the House of Lords case of **R** v **Hasan** (2005) the defence of duress is not available when: 'as a result of the accused's voluntary association with others engaged in criminal activity, he foresaw or ought reasonably to have foreseen the risk of being subjected to any compulsion by threats of violence'. This is sometimes described as self-induced duress. An objective test on this issue is applied, despite the general move in criminal case law towards subjective tests.

13

General defences

KEY CASE

In **R** v **Hasan** (2005) the defendant had become involved with a violent drug dealer. The drug dealer was the boyfriend of a woman who was involved in prostitution and for whom the defendant acted as driver and minder. The

> The House of Lords limited the availability of the defence of duress.

drug dealer ordered the defendant to burgle a house, saying that if he failed to do so he and his family would be harmed. The defendant was caught trying to burgle the house armed with a knife and was prosecuted for aggravated burglary. He raised the defence of duress. He was convicted at his trial, his appeal to the Court of Appeal was allowed, but the prosecution's appeal to the House of Lords was successful so his conviction was reinstated. The House held that the defence of duress was excluded where the defendant voluntarily exposed himself to the risk of threats and the defence of duress could not therefore succeed. In considering whether the duress was self-induced the House stated that it was not necessary for the defendant to have personally foreseen that he would be threatened to commit that particular offence. All that was required was that, when associating with criminals, he had foreseen or ought to have foreseen that he might be subjected to threats. Where this is the case the defence is excluded.

In the earlier case of **R** v **Baker and Ward** (1999), the Court of Appeal had suggested that the defence would only be disallowed if defendants had voluntarily associated with criminals knowing that they were likely to be subjected to threats to commit a crime of the type of which they were charged. This no longer represents the current law. There is now no requirement that the anticipated coercion be to commit crimes, let alone crimes of the type ultimately committed. The courts are therefore more likely to conclude that the duress is self-induced and therefore the defence excluded.

The second part of the test

In applying the second, objective limb of the **Graham** test, the reasonable person can be given some of the characteristics of the defendant but not all. The defendant in **R v Martin** (2000) claimed that he had committed a robbery under duress consisting of threats from two men. Medical evidence established that the defendant was schizoid and more likely than others to interpret what was said and done as a threat, and act upon this. The Court of Appeal held that any personal characteristics relevant to the defendant's interpretation of the threat should be attributed to the reasonable person. In **R v Bowen** (1996) the defendant was accused of obtaining services by deception, having dishonestly obtained electrical goods on credit. In his defence he argued that throughout he had been acting under duress, as two men had threatened to attack him and his family with petrol bombs if he did not obtain the goods for them. The trial judge directed the jury members that, in applying the objective limb of the **Graham** test, they could take into account the age and sex of the defendant. On appeal it was argued that the jury should also have been directed to take into account his very low IQ. The appeal was rejected. The Court of Appeal stated that the mere fact that an accused is pliable, vulnerable, timid or susceptible to threats does not mean these are characteristics which can be invested in the reasonable person. On the other hand, if a defendant is within a category of persons whom the jury might think less able to resist pressure than people not within that category – such as being of a certain age or sex or suffering from a serious physical disability, recognised mental illness or psychiatric condition (including a post-traumatic stress disorder) – then this could be treated as a characteristic of the reasonable person. A low IQ, short of mental impairment or mental defectiveness, cannot be treated as such a characteristic. In **R v Hurst** (1995) expert evidence was inadmissible on the issue that the defendant had suffered sexual abuse as a child, resulting in lack of firmness in their personality, though not amounting to a psychiatric disorder. The court said, 'we find it hard to see how the person of reasonable firmness can be invested with the characteristics of a personality which lacks reasonable firmness'.

The Court of Appeal stated in **R v Flatt** (1996) that a self-induced characteristic of the defendant would not be given to the reasonable person. Flatt was charged with possession of a prohibited drug with intent to supply. He argued in his defence that he was acting under duress. As an addict to crack cocaine, he owed his supplier £1,500. Seventeen hours before the police searched his flat, his drug dealer ordered him to look after the drugs subsequently found in his possession, saying that, if Flatt refused, he would shoot Flatt's mother, grandmother and girlfriend.

On appeal it was argued that the judge had misdirected the jury. In assessing the response of the hypothetical reasonable person to the threats, the judge had not told the jury to consider how the reasonable drug addict would have responded to the threats. His appeal was dismissed as drug addiction was a self-induced condition and not a characteristic. Also there was no reason to think that a drug addict would show less fortitude than any other member of the public when faced with such threats.

A complication in **Graham** (see p. 358) was that the accused had been drinking alcohol and taking Valium before the killing took place; the court held that the fact that a defendant's will to resist threats had been reduced by the voluntary consumption of drink or drugs or both could not be taken into account when assessing whether he had behaved as a reasonable person would have done. In other words, he had to be assessed on the basis of how a reasonable person who was sober would have behaved.

To which crimes does duress allow a defence?

In **R** v **Hasan** the House of Lords confirmed its earlier decision of **Howe** (1986) that the defence of duress is not available for murder. The exclusion of this defence was accepted by the Court of Appeal in **R** v **W** (2007). The defendant was a 13-year-old boy who claimed that pressure had been placed on him by his father to kill the victim. The court held that the defence of duress was not available to a charge of murder, whatever the age of the defendant. Nor is it available to attempted murder and probably not to treason. The principle that duress should never be a defence to murder was laid down as far back as the sixteenth century, with the legal writer Blackstone stating that a person under duress should die him- or herself rather than escape by means of murdering an innocent person. Thus in **Howe** (1986) the defendant had fallen under the evil influence of a man called Murray and, as a result, had assaulted one person who had been killed by another, and then actually killed a man on Murray's orders. It was held by the House of Lords that the defence of duress was available to neither the murder that he had carried out as a principal, nor the murder where he was merely a secondary participant.

In **Gotts** (1992) the House of Lords specified that duress was also unavailable as a defence to attempted murder. In that case the accused, aged 16, seriously injured his mother with a knife. He argued that he was acting under duress because his father had threatened to shoot him unless he killed his mother, but his defence was rejected.

An old case that has been relied on to support the argument that duress was not available as a defence to murder is **R** v **Dudley and Stephens** (1884). This is a classic case on the defence of necessity (discussed at p. 368), and duress can be seen as a specific form of the necessity defence.

● Duress of circumstances

The basic rules for this defence are the same as for duress by threats, except that it applies where there is no express threat of 'do this or else' but the circumstances threatened death or serious personal injury unless the crime were committed.

The defence is relatively new, originating in **R** v **Willer** (1986). Willer was charged with reckless driving, and pleaded that he had to drive in such a way in order to escape from a gang of youths who appeared to be about to attack him. Driving up a narrow road, he had been confronted by the gang, which was 20 to 30 strong, and heard shouts of 'I'll kill you Willer', and threats to kill his passenger. With the gang surrounding the car, the only means of escape was to drive along the pavement and into the front of a shopping precinct. After the trial judge ruled that the defence of necessity was not available, Willer changed his plea to guilty and appealed. On appeal it was held that the issue of duress should have been left to the jury, and Willer's conviction was quashed. The Court of

Appeal did not use the term 'duress of circumstances', but clearly the case was different from the 'do this or else' scenario previously associated with the defence: Willer was threatened, but he was not told that the threats would be carried out unless he drove on the pavement.

This extension of the defence was subsequently considered in **R** v **Conway** (1989) where the label 'duress of circumstances' was introduced. After being followed in his car by an unmarked vehicle, Conway had driven off in a reckless manner when two men, who were police officers in plain clothes, got out of the car and started to approach him. Conway's passenger, Tonna, had earlier been in a car in which someone had been shot, and, when he saw the two men running towards the car (not knowing that they were policemen), believed that he was about to be attacked. Consequently he yelled 'Drive off' and Conway, also failing to realise the men were police officers, responded accordingly, believing that Tonna was indeed about to be attacked. Conway's conviction for reckless driving was quashed on appeal because the defence of duress of circumstances should have been put to the jury. It was said that this defence was available only if, from an objective viewpoint, the defendant could be said to be acting in order to avoid a threat of death or serious injury to himself or someone else.

The defence was discussed in **R** v **Martin** (1989) where Martin had been disqualified from driving. One morning, while the driving ban was still in force, his stepson was late for work and Martin's wife, who had been suicidal in the past, started to bang her head against a wall and threatened to kill herself unless he drove the boy to work. Martin was charged with driving while disqualified, and argued that he had reasonably believed that his wife might carry out her threat. The trial judge refused to allow the defence of duress, but the Court of Appeal held that the defence of duress of circumstances should have been put before the jury, who should have been asked two questions. First, was the accused, or may he have been, compelled to act as he did because what he reasonably believed to be the situation gave him good reason to fear that otherwise death or serious physical injury would result? Secondly, if so, would a sober person of reasonable firmness, sharing the characteristics of the accused, have responded to that situation by behaving as the accused did? If the answer to both of these questions was 'Yes', the defence was proved and the jury should acquit.

All the cases discussed so far have been concerned with road traffic offences. But in **R** v **Pommell** (1995) the Court of Appeal explicitly stated that the defence did not just apply to road traffic cases, but applied throughout the criminal law. The police obtained a search warrant and burst into the defendant's London flat at 8 a.m. They found him in bed holding a loaded gun and he was charged and convicted of possessing a prohibited weapon without a licence. Defence counsel argued that the night before someone had visited Pommell with the gun, intending to go and shoot some people who had killed a friend. Pommell had persuaded the man to leave the weapon with him to avoid further bloodshed. This happened at 1 a.m., so he had decided not to take the gun straight to the police, but to sleep and take it in the morning. The police had arrived before he was able to do so. His conviction was set aside on appeal as the defence of duress of circumstances would technically be available in these circumstances. In the case of **R** v **Abdul-Hussain** (1999) the Court of Appeal found that the defence could be available for the offence of hijacking.

As with duress by threats, duress of circumstances usually applies only where death or serious bodily harm is feared. In **R** *v* **Baker and Wilkins** (1997) the Court of Appeal stated that the defence of duress of circumstances could not be extended to cover situations where serious psychological injury was feared. The father of a child had refused to return the girl at the end of a contact visit. Her mother, along with her husband, had gone round to the father's house and, hearing a child crying, they feared for the girl's psychological health and proceeded to pound on the front door. The mother and her husband were convicted of criminal damage and their appeals were rejected, as the defence of duress of circumstances applied only where there was a fear of an imminent death or serious physical injury.

● Criticism

Too narrow

In the leading case of **R** *v* **Hasan** the House of Lords was concerned that the defence of duress was increasingly being relied upon by defendants who had been involved in organised crime, including the illegal drug trade. The House felt that the scope of the defence needed to be narrowed, so that it would succeed less often, but it is possible that the House went too far, so that people who genuinely have an excuse for their behaviour can be convicted of a criminal offence. Aspects of the defence which may be too harsh include:

- the narrow range of threats that will suffice;
- the objective requirement where a mistake has been made, despite the fact that the criminal case law has made a general move away from objective tests; and
- the wide exception that defendants voluntarily exposed themselves to the risk of harm.

By including an objective test in deciding whether defendants voluntarily exposed themselves to the risk, the law is being too harsh. It essentially penalises anybody who associates with a criminal, even though they thought there was no risk in doing so. Taken to its limit, convicted criminals who have completed their sentence could become equivalent to social outcasts within our society.

In her dissenting judgment in **R** *v* **Hasan**, Baroness Hale expressed concern that the restrictions relating to self-induced duress could mean that a woman subjected to domestic abuse who is bullied into committing a crime might be denied the defence:

> The battered wife knows very well that she may be compelled to cook the dinner, wash the dishes, iron the shirts and submit to sexual intercourse. That should not deprive her of the defence of **duress** if she is obliged by the same threats to herself or her children to commit perjury or shoplift food.

Baroness Hale would have preferred this limitation to apply only where defendants had foreseen or ought to have foreseen the risk that they would be pressurised to commit crimes.

Duress and murder

The refusal to allow duress as a defence to murder is very harsh, notably where terrorist organisations have coerced individuals into committing crimes for them by threatening to harm their families. The policy argument for such severity is that, without it, the terrorists' job would be made easier, but in practice this seems unlikely; where a person's family is seriously threatened, the possibility of prosecution is unlikely to be an issue in that person's decision whether or not to help those making the threats.

In **Howe** the House of Lords put forward four grounds for its decision that duress should not be a defence for secondary parties to murder.

1 An ordinary person of reasonable fortitude was expected to lay down their own life rather than take that of someone else.
2 In choosing to kill an innocent person rather than die themselves, defendants could not be said to be choosing the lesser of two evils.
3 Parliament had not chosen to make duress a defence to murder when recommendations had been made that this should be done.
4 Difficult cases could be dealt with by applying a discretion not to prosecute.

Smith and Hogan (2005) refute all four points.

1 The criminal law should not expect heroism, and in any case the defence is only available on the basis of what the reasonable person would do.
2 There are circumstances in which murder could be seen as the lesser of two evils. One example might be committing an act (such as planting a bomb) which causes death rather than having your family killed, where there is a chance that your act may not cause death, and little or no chance that your family will be spared if you fail to do it.
3 We should not assume lack of action by Parliament to represent its intention that the law should not be changed – it might, for example, be that reform was put off because of pressures on parliamentary time.
4 Leaving the issue to administrative discretion is not a satisfactory substitute for clear and just legal provisions.

The House of Lords in **Hasan** itself notes that the Law Commission had recommended that the defence should be available to all offences, including murder (*Report on Defences of General Application*, Law Com No. 83, 1977). Despite stating that 'the logic of this argument is irresistible' the House continued to limit the defence in this way. The reasoning in **Re A (Children)** (2000) – discussed in detail at p. 348 – would seem to provide a basis upon which the defence could be extended, but instead the courts have preferred to interpret this case as restricted to the defence of necessity. This attitude is difficult to justify when there is so much similarity between the two defences and where the Court of Appeal drew no distinction between its use of the terms duress and necessity.

Psychiatric illness

In applying the objective test the courts will only take into account 'recognised' psychiatric illnesses. This is a move that has also been seen in the case of **R v ChanFook** (1994) in the context of non-fatal offences against the person. An interesting discussion on this matter has been provided by Alec Buchanan and Graham Virgo in an article published in the *Criminal Law Review* in 1999 entitled 'Duress and mental abnormality'. They observed that the requirement for the psychiatric illness to be a 'recognised' illness demonstrates a scepticism on the part of the courts – no one talks about recognised heart attacks or recognised broken legs. This scepticism may reflect the widespread perception that psychiatric illnesses are less 'real' than other illnesses, and that their victims are better able to help themselves. The judges may also have been concerned that psychiatric symptoms are less amenable to verification: a heart attack can be diagnosed by blood tests and a broken bone by an X-ray, but the diagnosis of a psychiatric condition depends partly on observation but largely on listening to what the patient says. The danger is that people could avail themselves of the defence of duress simply by describing symptoms that did not exist. Buchanan and Virgo state that developments in psychiatry mean that the diagnosis of a psychiatric illness by a psychiatrist is often primarily based on the description of symptoms by the patient, thus increasing this danger. They also point out that the labelling of a psychiatric illness by a medical professional is aimed at treatment and not at the needs of the criminal law.

 ## Reform

The Law Commission

The Law Commission has recommended in its report *Murder, Manslaughter and Infanticide* (2006) that the defence of duress should be available as a full (not just a partial) defence to all three of its proposed forms of homicide: first degree murder, second degree murder and manslaughter. The legal burden of proving on the balance of probabilities the existence of the defence would be on the defendant. This fits with its earlier report in 1977, *Report on Defences of General Application*, where the Law Commission had recommended that duress should be a general defence and applicable to all crimes including murder. An alternative reform which the Law Commission had considered in its 2005 consultation paper, A *New Homicide Act for England and Wales?*, would be for duress to act as a partial defence to murder, in the same way as provocation and diminished responsibility currently reduce liability from murder to manslaughter.

Abolish the defence

Remarks made *obiter* in **Howe** and **Gotts** suggest that the defence of duress should be abolished, and the circumstances of the offence taken into account as mitigation when sentencing. But this would take an important issue away from juries and the standard of proof beyond reasonable doubt.

In their 1977 report, the Law Commission recognised the following arguments against duress as a broad general defence:

- doing wrong can never be justified;
- it should not be up to individuals to weigh up the harm caused by their wrongful conduct against the harm avoided to themselves or others;
- duress could be classified as merely the motive for committing a crime, and the criminal law does not take motive into consideration for the purposes of conviction;
- the criminal law is itself a system of threats (if you commit a crime you will be punished), and that structure would be weakened if some other system of threats was permitted to play a part;
- allowing the defence helps such criminals as terrorists and kidnappers.

Despite recognising these points, the Law Commission did not recommend that the defence should be abolished.

Necessity

This defence essentially applies to situations in which defendants are faced with the choice of committing a crime, or allowing themselves or someone else to suffer or be deprived in some way. Public and private defence and duress can be seen as specific forms of the necessity defence. The courts, in the past, have been reluctant to recognise a general defence of necessity. The judiciary have frequently expressed their concern that a broad, generally available defence of necessity might be seen as going too far towards providing excuses for law-breaking. This fear can be seen in the case of **R** v **Dudley and Stephens** (1884).

KEY CASE

In **R** v **Dudley and Stephens** (1884) three sailors and a cabin boy were shipwrecked and cast adrift in an open boat, 1,000 miles from land, with only a small amount of food. After 20 days, the last eight with no food, two of the

> The defence of necessity is not available to a charge of murder.

sailors killed the cabin boy, the smallest and weakest among them, and the three ate him. After four more days, they were rescued by a passing ship. Once the story was revealed, they were tried for murder, but the jury refused to convict, returning instead a statement of the facts which they found had been proved: there was little chance that the four could survive for much longer without killing and eating one of them; the cabin boy was the weakest, and least likely to survive; he was killed and eaten by the defendants; without eating him they would probably not have survived. The Divisional Court found that, on these facts, the accused were guilty of murder. The judges acknowledged the defendants had been in a truly desperate situation, but stated that even these circumstances could not afford them a defence. Although the court felt that the defence of necessity could not be allowed, it did alter the usually mandatory death sentence to six months' imprisonment.

This restrictive approach to a defence of necessity can also be seen in the case of **Southwark London Borough Council** v **Williams** (1971) which involved a homeless family who had squatted in an empty council flat. Mr and Mrs Williams and their children had been forced to leave the boarding house in Kent where they lived when the landlady died. Unable to find local accommodation they could afford, they had gone to London, where they thought accommodation might be easier to find. After a couple of nights spent with friends, and one with a kind stranger, they found themselves on the streets, the local council having been unable to help. Scared that their homelessness would mean their children being taken from them by social services, they approached a squatters' association, which helped them make an orderly entry into a council house that neighbours said had been empty for years. The court heard that hundreds of other council homes in the borough were also standing empty, awaiting repairs, yet the council had a waiting list of around 9,000 people.

The council applied for an order for immediate possession, which would allow them to eject the squatters. Mr Williams gave evidence that he did not want to squat, but saw no other way to find a home for his family. The Williams family contended that the council was in breach of its statutory duty to provide accommodation for people in emergency situations. While expressing sympathy, the court granted the council the order it required. Lord Denning explained that, while a defence of necessity had always been available 'in case of imminent danger in order to preserve life', such a defence had to be carefully circumscribed. Otherwise, he said:

> Necessity would open a door which no man could shut . . . If hunger were once allowed to be an excuse for stealing it would open a way through which all kinds of disorder and lawlessness would pass. If homelessness were admitted as a defence to trespass, no man's house would be safe . . . The pleas would be an excuse for all sorts of wrongdoing. So the courts must, for the sake of law and order, take a firm stand. They must refuse to admit the plea of necessity to the hungry and the homeless and trust that their distress will be relieved by the charitable and the good.

Thus, in the past some legal academics have asserted that English law did not recognise a defence of necessity at all, largely on the ground that if it was not allowed as a defence to a crime in the desperate circumstances of **Dudley and Stephens** the court would be unlikely to allow it in any other circumstances. However, in **Richards** (1986) Lord Goff commented that there was no doubt that a defence of necessity existed, even though its scope was not well established. In **R v Jones** (2004) the House of Lords stated that the defence of necessity was potentially a defence to a crime but it restricted the defence to where a defendant has acted to avoid an imminent peril of danger to life or serious injury to himself or towards people for whom he reasonably regards himself as being responsible.

In the high-profile case of **Re A (Children)** (2000), involving the medical separation of Siamese twins, which is discussed in detail at p. 348, the Court of Appeal paved the way for an established, general defence of necessity. It expressly stated that a defence of necessity existed at common law. Lord Justice Brooke said that there were three requirements for the application of the defence of necessity:

1 the act was needed to avoid inevitable and irreparable evil;
2 no more was done than was reasonably necessary for the purpose to be achieved;
3 the evil inflicted was not disproportionate to the evil avoided.

As these criteria were satisfied in the case, he, along with Robert Walker LJ, relied on the defence of necessity to rule that the operation to separate the Siamese twins would not constitute the offence of murdering Mary.

To these three criteria listed above, a fourth criterion should be added following the decision of **R v Quayle** (discussed at p. 374):

4 the necessity must have arisen as a result of extraneous circumstances.

In other words, the situation must not have arisen from a human threat because this would fall under the defence of duress of threats.

A fifth criterion was added in the case of **R** v **Shayler** (2001):

5 the evil must be directed towards the defendant or a person or persons for whom he or she had responsibility.

Mr Shayler had been a member of MI5 and was prosecuted for disclosing confidential information without lawful authority in breach of the Official Secrets Act 1989. He claimed that his disclosures revealed that MI5 had in the past acted incompetently and that he needed to reveal this information so MI5 would be forced to improve their working practices so that they would effectively protect the public in the future. Mr Shayler subsequently fled to France, but had chosen to return to England to face charges. In his defence he argued that he had acted out of necessity, in order to prevent death or serious injury to others. The Court of Appeal ruled that the defence was available when a defendant committed an otherwise criminal act to avoid an imminent peril of danger to life or serious injury to himself or towards somebody for whom he was responsible. The person for whom he was responsible might not be ascertained and might not be identifiable. However, if it was not possible to name the individuals beforehand, it had at least to be possible to describe the individuals by reference to the action which it was threatened would be taken that would make them victims unless preventive action was taken by the defendant.

In order to determine the scope of the defence, it was therefore necessary to determine the people for whom the defendant was responsible. The defendant was responsible for those people who would be injured if he did not take preventive action. Thus, if the threat was to explode a bomb in a building if the defendant did not accede to what was demanded, the defendant owed responsibility to those who would be in the building if the bomb exploded.

On the facts of the case, Mr Shayler could not identify any potential imminent danger to members of the public as a result of the security service's alleged abuses and blunders. He could therefore not describe the people for whom he was responsible and so the defence of necessity did not apply.

The court contrasted two scenarios. At one end of the spectrum was the example of a spy who was kidnapped and was told his wife or child would be murdered if he did not disclose top-secret information. At the other end of the spectrum was the disillusioned agent who claimed that someone, somewhere, might one day suffer if he did not make certain disclosures and that he had responsibility for all such persons, which amounted to the general public as a whole. The first was a situation where almost certainly a defendant would be able to rely on the defence of necessity. The second position was one where a defendant could not possibly rely on the defence. The court considered that Mr Shayler fell squarely within the second position.

Necessity and murder

The case of **Dudley and Stephens**, discussed at p. 368, has been treated as authority for the view that the defence of necessity is not available to a charge of murder. However, that case and the case of **Howe** (discussed at p. 363) were reinterpreted by the Court of Appeal in **Re A (Children)** (2000). This case appeared to suggest that, in appropriate cases, the defence of duress would be available to murder, and therefore logically also to secondary parties to murder and attempted murder. **Re A (Children)** was a high-profile case heard by the Court of Appeal, looking at the legality of an operation to separate Siamese twins, where the operation would automatically lead to the death of the weaker twin. The Court of Appeal acknowledged that **Dudley and Stephens** and **Howe** were frequently interpreted as authority for the proposition that necessity could never under any circumstances provide a legal justification for murder. However, they proceeded to distinguish those cases on their facts and interpreted them as only laying down that necessity would not be a defence to murder in the type of factual scenario which shared the same policy considerations as those cases.

There were two key policy considerations behind the decisions of **Dudley and Stephens** and **Howe**, neither of which applied to the present case. There was the policy consideration that a person should not be the judge in their own cause of the value of their life over another's. Lord Justice Ward pointed out that the doctors have a right and duty to choose whether or not to operate. As there is a conflict between their duty to Mary and their duty to Jodie, they were in the same position as the court in having to resolve that conflict by putting into the scales the benefits to each child of the operation taking place or not taking place.

In considering this policy consideration, Lord Justice Brooke referred to the 1989 Hamlyn Lecture 'Necessity and Excuse' given by Professor J.C. Smith. In that lecture Professor Smith discussed the situation where, at the coroner's inquest conducted in October 1987 into the Zeebrugge ferry disaster, an army corporal gave evidence that he and many other people were near the foot of a rope ladder. They were all in the water and in danger of drowning. Their route to safety, however, was blocked for at least ten minutes by a young man who was petrified by cold or fear (or both) and was unable to move up or down. Eventually the corporal gave instructions that the man should be pushed off the ladder, and he was never seen again. The corporal and many others were then able to climb up the ladder to safety. Professor Smith suggested that if such a case ever did come to court a judge would be able to distinguish **Dudley and Stephens**. There was no question of choosing who had to die, which had concerned Lord Coleridge in **Dudley and Stephens**, because the unfortunate young man on the ladder had chosen himself by blocking the exit for the others.

The second policy consideration that lay behind **Dudley and Stephens** and **Howe** was that the availability of a defence on the facts of those cases would mark an absolute divorce of law from morality. But in the present case Mary was endangering Jodie's life. As Professor Smith pointed out in his analysis of the Zeebrugge case, unlike the cabin boy, the young man on the ladder, although in no way at fault, was preventing others from going where they had a right and a most urgent need to go, and was thereby endangering the lives of others. Thus, to permit such a defence in these circumstances would not mark an absolute divorce of law from morality. While some people thought that it would be immoral to operate when this would hasten Mary's death, others felt that it would be immoral not to operate to save Jodie's life:

> All that a court can say is that it is not at all obvious that this is the sort of clear-cut case, marking an absolute divorce from law and morality, which was of such concern to Lord Coleridge and his fellow judges.

This case only reached the Court of Appeal, but the reasoning of the court is convincing and it would seem likely that the House of Lords would accept this restrictive interpretation of its earlier authorities.

● Should there be a general defence of necessity?

There are arguments both for and against a general defence of necessity.

Arguments against

An excuse for wrongdoing

The argument most often offered against a defence of necessity is that it would simply be an excuse for crime, and that there would be no end to its use; see, for example, **Southwark London Borough Council** v **Williams** (p. 368).

The reasoning in Dudley and Stephens

We have seen at p. 371 that various policy arguments were put forward in **Dudley and Stephens** as to why necessity should not afford a defence in a case involving murder.

Discretion over prosecution

In **Buckoke** v **GLC** (1971), Lord Denning said, *obiter*, that if the driver of a fire engine, who could see a person in a burning building 200 yards down the road, was faced with a red traffic light between them and the building, it would be an offence not to stop at the light, even though not stopping would clearly be the right thing to do. Lord Denning's solution to the problem was that the driver should simply not be prosecuted for the offence, and in fact it appears that this is one way in which the harshness of the law is evaded.

Duress of circumstances

In recent years the courts have developed a defence of duress of circumstances, which bears a strong similarity to the traditional idea of necessity. In some cases this has met the need for a general defence of necessity, but it is limited to situations in which there has been a threat to life, or one of personal injury. In **R** v **Shayler** the Court of Appeal considered that there was no significant distinction to be drawn between the two defences.

Arguments for

Relevance of motive

The law accepts that people should incur criminal liability for only those acts which they do of their own free will, but critical legal theorists argue that, by ignoring the motive behind the act, the law's view of free will is too narrow. Alan Norrie, writing in *The Critical Lawyer's Handbook*, points out that the defence of necessity tends to be raised in cases where the accused's motive for acting as they did is the result of social or natural circumstances beyond their control (such as the homelessness suffered by the Williams family), and therefore it is difficult to argue that they acted of their own free will.

Impossible standards

The lack of a defence of necessity in a case as desperate as **Dudley and Stephens** suggests that the law requires people to behave heroically – in that case the court appears to have felt that all four people should simply have allowed themselves to die. This seems a strangely high standard to set in a legal system that on the other hand recognises no general duty of care, and would not, for example, impose liability on a healthy adult who fails to help a child drowning in shallow water (see p. 12).

Discretion on prosecution insufficient

It is argued above that the possibility of not prosecuting those who have acted from necessity, or of allowing their circumstances to act as mitigating factors in sentencing, means there is no need for a defence of necessity. There are, however, several arguments against this view.

First, it is against the interests of justice to convict people of a criminal offence, no matter how lightly they are eventually sentenced, when by normal standards they have done nothing wrong, and may even have acted in the interests of others, or of the general public. Where the offence is murder the sentence is mandatory, so the circumstances in which the accused acted cannot be used to lessen the sentence anyway.

Secondly, it is absurd to make rules (or not to allow exceptions to rules) which discourage people in difficult situations from taking actions which are in the public interest – such as Lord Denning's hypothetical firefighter ignoring the red light in order to save people from a burning house.

Finally, leaving the issue to the discretion of prosecuting authorities seems an undesirably vague and subjective way of dealing with the matter – while deciding not to prosecute in such cases may be the best outcome for all concerned, there is no way of ensuring that such decisions are made in every appropriate case, and so the need for a defence may remain.

Reform

A single, broad defence

Professor Clarkson (2004) has argued that the current defences of duress, necessity and public and private defence should be replaced by one single defence of necessary action. He has argued that the present separation between the different defences is primarily for historical reasons and that the differences in their rules are not necessarily rational. The proposed new defence of necessary action would apply where the defendant's conduct was, taking into account all the relevant circumstances, reasonable and proportionate to the specific danger faced by the defendant. Under the current law on duress, for example, there must be a threat of death or grievous bodily harm. Under the proposed reform any threat could suffice to give rise to a defence of necessary action. Even minor threats to the person or property could suffice because the focus would be shifted to the reasonableness and proportionality of the response to that threat. The new defence would also be available to any crime, including murder. Such a reform would greatly simplify this area of law.

A general defence of necessity

A general defence of necessity is recognised in many other parts of the world, apparently without the results envisaged by Lord Denning in **Williams (Gladstone)**. For example, many American states have adopted the American Model Penal Code, which provides that conduct which the defendants believe to be necessary to prevent harm to themselves or another is justified, providing that the harm they are aiming to prevent is greater than that which the law seeks to prevent by prohibiting the act committed (though it has to be said that even this is not entirely satisfactory – how would it apply, for example, where defendants have been told to kill someone else, or be killed themselves?).

No necessity defence

In 1977 the Law Commission stated its opposition to a defence of necessity, and proposed that any common law defence of this kind should be abolished. This proposal was subsequently severely criticised, and the draft Criminal Law Bill 1993, drawn up by the Law Commission, explicitly retains any defence of necessity that currently exists at common law.

Euthanasia

Suzanne Ost (2005) has argued that the defence of necessity should be available to doctors who help terminally ill people who are suffering extreme pain to die. At the moment doctors can only avoid liability for murder if they satisfy the requirements of the double effect doctrine (discussed on p. 65). Suzanne Ost considers this to be unsatisfactory as it ignores what may actually be the real intent of the doctor and the reality of the situation in which the doctor is working. A study has been carried out involving 683 Australian surgeons. Two hundred and forty-seven of these surgeons stated that, when administering drugs in order to relieve a patient's suffering, they had administered a greater dosage than they felt necessary to relieve symptoms with the intention of hastening death (Douglas *et al.* (2001)).

TOPICAL ISSUE

Cannabis for medicinal purposes

There has been some debate as to whether it should be legal to use cannabis for medicinal purposes, for example to soothe the pain of arthritis sufferers. Judges could do this through accepting a defence of necessity in these circumstances, but in **R v Quayle** (2005) the Court of Appeal stated that the defence of necessity is not available to offences involving cannabis, except in the context of ongoing trials for official medical research purposes. Before that case there was growing evidence that juries were prepared to accept a defence of necessity in these circumstances. Alan Blythe supplied cannabis to his suicidal wife to reduce the pain and discomfort she experienced as a result of multiple sclerosis. He was prosecuted in April 1998 for several drug offences. At his trial, expert evidence was given that cannabis can relieve the symptoms of this disease and the jury acquitted. Another man was acquitted by a jury in Manchester who admitted cultivating cannabis to relieve his back pain.

A working party on the therapeutic uses of cannabis has been established by the Royal Pharmaceutical Society of Great Britain and the Home Office has granted limited permission for experiments involving cannabis and related substances. It may be that in the future cannabis will be made available to patients on prescription, as was the case until 1971.

Consent

A victim's consent to the defendant's behaviour can exempt the defendant from liability. The issue normally arises in relation to non-fatal offences against the person, and has already been touched upon in the context of rape where, instead of being viewed as a defence, it is treated as part of the definition of the offence.

Historically consent had the same meaning in whatever context it was applied. Now, following the Sexual Offences Act 2003, in the context of the sex offences consent now has a statutory definition (see p. 167), but in other contexts the meaning of consent remains an issue for the common law. There is therefore a risk that the concept of consent may develop differently depending on its context (see Elliott and de Than (2007)) and our primary focus here is on the common law concept of consent.

By recognising a defence of consent, the courts are acknowledging that individuals should be independent and free to control their own lives, but there are limitations to this principle, which seem to depend on the nature and degree of harm to which the victim has consented.

An informed consent

For the defence to be allowed the defendant must know what they are consenting to – you cannot consent to something of which you are not aware. This was not a requirement in the past. Thus, in **R** v **Clarence** (1888) a husband had not informed his wife that he was infected with gonorrhoea (which was, at the time, an incurable and fatal disease). He was prosecuted with infecting his wife with the disease under s. 20 of the Offences Against the Person Act 1861. He argued that he had the defence of consent and the High Court accepted his defence. The court considered that consent to sex also involved consent to any incidental risk of injury or illness of which the victim may be unaware.

However, in **R** v **Dica** (2004) the Court of Appeal ruled that the old case of **Clarence** no longer reflects the current law. A person consenting to sexual intercourse was not also automatically consenting to any incidental risk of injury or infection. In order for a person to consent, they must know the nature and quality of what they are accepting.

KEY CASE

In **R** v **Dica** the defendant knew that he was HIV positive. He had unprotected sexual intercourse with two women. He claimed that they knew that he was HIV positive and had

> A valid consent must be an informed consent.

impliedly consented to the risk of becoming HIV positive themselves by agreeing to have unprotected sexual intercourse. They denied this. The defendant was convicted, sentenced to eight years' imprisonment, and appealed. The Court of Appeal ruled that **Clarence** no longer reflected the current law on consent. In **Dica** the victims had consented to sexual intercourse and therefore the defendant was not liable for rape. However, the victims had not automatically consented to the risk of incidental HIV infection, because they did not know that the defendant was carrying an infection. Implied consent to a risk must presuppose knowledge of it. There was therefore an informed consent with regard to sexual intercourse and no offence of rape, but no informed consent with regard to HIV transmission and therefore possible liability for inflicting grievous bodily harm. A retrial was ordered where he was again convicted.

In **R** *v* **Konzani** (2005) the Court of Appeal again pointed to the requirement of an informed consent. Just because a person consents to sexual intercourse without a condom, this does not automatically mean that the person has consented to the risk of contracting HIV. For a valid defence, there had to be an informed consent to the specific risk of contracting HIV. Consent could be implied for certain minor risks, but not to a fatal disease. In that case the defendant had unprotected sexual intercourse with three women. He did not reveal to them that he was HIV positive and they subsequently caught the disease. He was convicted of inflicting grievous bodily harm under s. 20 of the Offences Against the Person Act 1861. A person who is HIV positive therefore has a duty to disclose their status, and gain the willing consent of their sexual partner to the risk of HIV transmission.

Consent obtained by fraud

In the past, where a consent was obtained by fraud, the consent would not be valid if the defendant had lied about the nature or quality of their act. The case of **R** *v* **Tabassum** (2000) interpreted this requirement. In that case three women had agreed to remove their bras to allow the appellant to examine their breasts, because they understood that he was medically qualified and was carrying out the procedure in order to put together a medical database on the subject. In fact the appellant was not medically qualified and was not putting together a medical database. The appellant submitted that he was not liable for indecent assault because the women had all consented to their breasts being examined. The defendant claimed that his absence of medical qualifications did not change the nature and quality of his acts to which the women had consented. The Court of Appeal took the view that on the facts there was consent to the nature of the acts but not to their quality, since they were not for a medical purpose. The appellant's conviction for indecent assault was therefore upheld.

Now that **Dica** has laid down a requirement of informed consent, any fraud which means that the victim lacked relevant information about what they were consenting to should nullify the victim's apparent consent.

A genuine consent

In **R** *v* **Olugboja** (see p. 168) it was pointed out that a mere submission is not a consent.

Capacity to consent

Certain people do not have the capacity to consent to the use of physical force over their body. They may lack this capacity due to, for example, their youth or mental ill-health.

Sometimes parents or the court can give consent on behalf of a child or an incompetent adult, particularly in relation to surgery which is needed in an emergency. The law on capacity was set out in the judgment of Butler-Sloss LJ in **Re MB** (1997). She stated that every person is presumed to have the capacity to consent to medical treatment; that presumption can be rebutted. A person lacks capacity if some impairment or disturbance of mental functioning renders the person unable to make a decision whether to consent. Such inability to make a decision will occur when the person is unable to:

- comprehend and retain information which is material to the decision, especially as to the likely consequences of having or not having medical treatment;
- use the information and weigh it in the balance as part of the process of arriving at a decision.

In **Gillick** *v* **West Norfolk and Wisbech Area Health Authority** (1986) the House of Lords said that a parent continues to be able to give consent on behalf of their child until 'the child achieves a sufficient understanding and intelligence to enable them to understand fully what is proposed', a situation now known as being 'Gillick competent'. The case concerned the question of whether doctors could give girls under the age of 16 contraceptives if the girls consented, without having also to seek their parents' consent. The answer was that doctors could if the girls were 'Gillick competent'.

The scope of the Gillick competence test has since been restricted to situations where the child gives a positive consent; if a Gillick competent child refuses treatment then a parent's consent can override that refusal. In **Re W** (1992) a 16-year-old girl was suffering from anorexia nervosa, and refused medical treatment which would have saved her life. The court was prepared to override her refusal even though she was regarded as being Gillick competent.

The nature and degree of harm

Following the leading case of **Brown** (1993), in deciding whether to allow the defence of consent the courts will look at the nature and degree of harm consented to by the defendant. This is primarily a question of public policy, and the courts seek to strike a balance between the seriousness of the harm consented to, and the social usefulness, if any, of the conduct. The defence of consent is generally available to very minor harms of assault and battery. It is not available to more serious harms, unless the conduct involved falls within a recognised exception.

 There is some confusion as to whether the general prohibition on causing consensual actual bodily harm applies only in respect of harm intentionally caused. Dicta in **Brown** (1993) and the recent decisions of **Dica** (2004) and **Barnes** (2004) suggest that the law treats the victim's factual consent as invalid only in respect of intentionally inflicted harms. On this reasoning the defence of consent can still be available for more serious harms which have only been caused recklessly. Therefore, in **Dica** the Court of Appeal would not have allowed the defence of consent to be left to the jury if the defendant had intentionally passed on his HIV infection to the victims.

13

General defences

● Euthanasia

Suicide is no longer a criminal offence in England. A person can choose to take their own life. But it is unlawful to do a positive act to assist a person to commit suicide (known as euthanasia or mercy killing). The person providing the assistance could be liable for the offence of assisting suicide (s. 2 of the Suicide Act 1961), murder or manslaughter. The victim's consent to their own death does not provide a defence.

In the light of **Airedale National Health Service Trust** v **Bland** (1993) (discussed on p. 14) a distinction has to be drawn between active euthanasia and passive euthanasia. Passive euthanasia is lawful. In that case it was held that hospital authorities could legally terminate the treatment which was keeping Tony Bland alive. The courts did not acknowledge that the Trust had the defence of consent, but justified their conclusion on the basis that it was in the best interests of the patient and that switching off the life-support machine constituted only an omission to act. In similar situations in the US, courts admit that they are substituting their judgment for that of the patient, and therefore consenting on behalf of that person.

The English law on euthanasia conforms with the European Convention on Human Rights. In **Pretty** v **UK** (2002), Diane Pretty was terminally ill with motor neurone disease. She was physically incapable of killing herself. She wished instead to commit suicide with help from her husband, so that she could die with dignity at a time of her choosing. The Director of Public Prosecutions (DPP) refused to undertake not to prosecute her husband if he assisted her suicide. Diane Pretty applied for judicial review of this refusal, claiming that the law violated the European Convention on Human Rights. The case went up to the European Court of Human Rights where she argued that the criminalisation of the acts of assisting suicide amounted to a violation of Art. 8, which protects the right to a private life. Article 8 provides:

> (1) Everyone has the right to respect for his private and family life . . .
> (2) There shall be no interference by a public authority with the exercise of this right except such as is in accordance with the law and is necessary in a democratic society in the interests of national security, public safety or the economic well-being of the country, for the prevention of disorder or crime, for the protection of health or morals, or for the protection of the rights and freedoms of others.

Diane Pretty said this gave her a right to self-determination, including a right to decide how to live and a right to decide when and how to die.

The European Court of Human Rights accepted that the English law did intrude on a person's private life, but considered that this was allowed under Art. 8. States are entitled to regulate, through the operation of the general criminal law, activities which are detrimental to the life and safety of other individuals. Many terminally ill people are vulnerable and the law seeks to protect them from abuse.

If a person is physically capable of taking their own life, then the issue of consent need not arise, because they can carry out the suicide themselves without any criminal sanction. The issue of consent arises more frequently where the person is physically incapable of taking their own life and therefore wants to give their consent to someone else taking their life for them. Diane Pretty argued that the law discriminated between those who were physically able to take their own lives and who could commit suicide without any criminal sanction being imposed, and those who were not physically able to do so and who required assistance from someone else on whom a criminal sanction could subsequently be imposed. She argued that this constituted a breach of Art. 14 of the European Convention on Human Rights, which provides for the right to enjoy Convention rights without discrimination. This argument was rejected by the European Court of Human Rights.

Note, however, that competent adults are entitled to refuse medical treatment, even if the absence of treatment will inevitably lead to their death. A decision to refuse medical treatment by a patient capable of making the decision does not have to be sensible, rational or well considered. This situation is viewed by the courts as simply allowing nature to take its natural course, so that no individual is treated as being responsible for the patient's death. It is not technically euthanasia. The issue arose in **Ms B v An NHS Trust** (2002). Following a rare illness, Ms B was left paralysed from the neck down and was dependent on a mechanical ventilator to breathe. She remained conscious, intelligent and highly articulate. Having given much thought to the subject, she decided that she wanted her ventilator switched off, which would cause her to die from suffocation shortly afterwards. Her doctors did not wish to carry out her instructions and she went to court for an order telling them to follow her wishes to stop medical treatment. The order was granted and she was allowed to die shortly afterwards.

The right to refuse medical treatment will be reinforced by the Mental Capacity Act 2005 when it is brought into force. This will allow a person aged 18 and over to make an advanced decision to refuse treatment.

● Exceptions

A victim cannot consent to injury (other than assault and battery) unless the activity causing that injury falls into certain exceptions which are considered to have some social usefulness, in which case the defendant can consent to conduct which might otherwise constitute a serious offence. In **Leach** (1969) the victim had arranged to be crucified on Hampstead Heath. The defendants, at his request, nailed him to a wooden cross, piercing his hands with six-inch nails. They were found liable under s. 18 of the Offences Against the Person Act 1861 and were not allowed to rely on the victim's consent as a defence. This was because he had suffered serious injury and there was no social benefit from the activity.

KEY CASE

Considerable controversy has been caused by the case of **R v Brown** (1993) which is now the leading House of Lords judgment on the law of consent. The case arose when police officers by chance came across a private party in the home of one of the defendants. The guests were homosexuals who enjoyed sadomasochistic experiences, and the party had involved activities such as whipping, caning, branding, applying stinging nettles to the genital area and inserting sharp objects into the penis. The whole event

A victim cannot consent to injuries above an assault or battery unless the defendant's conduct falls within a recognised exception.

took place in private, with the consent of everyone there; none of the men had suffered permanent injury or infection as a result of these practices, nor sought any medical treatment, and no complaint had been made to the police. Despite this, the men were charged with offences under ss. 47 and 20 of the Offences Against the Person Act 1861. They were convicted, the defence of consent being rejected. Lord Templeman said:

> In principle there is a difference between violence which is incidental and violence which is inflicted for the indulgence of cruelty. The violence of sado-masochistic encounters involves the indulgence of cruelty by sadists and the degradation of victims. Such violence is injurious to the participants and unpredictably dangerous. I am not prepared to invent a defence of consent for sado-masochistic encounters which breed and glorify cruelty and result in offences under sections 47 and 20 of the Act of 1861.

The House of Lords concluded that defendants can only rely on a victim's consent to serious injury if the activity falls within certain recognised exceptions, but the exact *ratio* of the judgment is unclear. The academic J.C. Smith (1993) has argued that the *ratio* could be limited to cases where the harm is intentionally imposed, so that situations where the *mens rea* was recklessness would not be excluded from the defence. Alternatively, it might be further limited to its facts, and so only affect sado-masochistic encounters, though this seems unlikely.

An appeal against the House of Lords' judgment was taken to the European Court of Human Rights in **Laskey** *v* **Jaggard** and **Brown** *v* **United Kingdom** (1997). The European Court of Human Rights concluded that the law as laid down in the House of Lords judgment did not breach the European Convention on Human Rights. Article 8 of the Convention provides for the right to respect for a person's private life, though this right can be restricted where it is 'necessary in a democratic society'. The court found that Art. 8 had not been breached as interference by a public authority in the consensual activities of a sado-masochistic group was necessary in a democratic society for the protection of health. The state authorities were entitled to rely on the criminal law in regulating the infliction of physical harm; the authorities could consider the potential for serious harm that might result from the extreme activities of the men. Such conduct could not be viewed as purely a matter of their own private morality. The level of the sentences given and the degree of organisation involved in the group meant that the interference in the men's private lives could not be viewed as disproportionate.

The extent of the exceptions where the defence of consent will be allowed for serious harms mentioned by the House of Lords in **R** *v* **Brown** (1993) is not clear, despite the fact that the House described them as 'recognised' exceptions. The exceptions include:

- sports
- rough horseplay
- tattooing
- non-violent sexual relations
- surgery

- ear-piercing, and
- male circumcision.

Some of these exceptions are considered in more detail below.

Sports

Sports activities are viewed as having social usefulness, and so defendants are treated as having consented to even serious injuries provided they occurred when the players were acting within the rules of the game or resulted from conduct which the players could reasonably be regarded as having consented to. The most important recent case on this issue is **R** v **Barnes** (2004). This accepted that many injuries caused during a sport will have been implicitly consented to. Those taking part in sports impliedly agree to physical injury that is an inevitable risk. The Court of Appeal emphasised that criminal proceedings should be reserved for those situations where conduct is sufficiently grave as to be properly categorised as criminal. An instinctive error, reaction or misjudgement in the heat of a game should not be treated as criminal. The facts of the case were that during the course of an amateur football match, the defendant seriously injured the leg of another player in a tackle. He was prosecuted for inflicting grievous bodily harm contrary to s. 20 of the Offences Against the Person Act 1861. At his trial the prosecution argued that this was a late, unnecessary, reckless and high tackle. The defendant claimed that it was a fair challenge in the course of play and the resulting injuries were accidental.

The defendant's appeal against conviction was allowed. The Court of Appeal stated that the fact that the rules of the game are broken or that there is a foul which justifies a warning by the referee or a sending-off does not necessarily take the conduct outside what a player can reasonably be regarded as having consented to. Even if the offending contact had been a foul, it was still necessary for a jury to determine whether it might be anticipated in a normal game of football. The defence of consent will be excluded only if the defendant's conduct went outside what could be expected to occur in the course of a football game. In highly competitive sports, conduct outside the rules might be expected to occur in the heat of the moment. Whether the conduct is sufficiently serious to justify criminal liability is an objective issue which did not depend on the views of individual players. In deciding whether the conduct justified criminal liability the court would look at the circumstances of the case, including the type of sport, the level at which it was played, the nature of the conduct, the degree of force used, the extent of the risk of injury and the defendant's state of mind. Criminal liability was not always

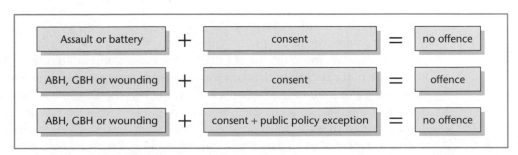

Figure 13.6 Consent and the non-fatal offences

necessary because most organised sports had their own disciplinary procedures and an award of damages could be available from the civil courts.

In **R** v **Moss** (2000) criminal liability was felt to be necessary. The defendant was playing rugby when he punched an opponent in the face, fracturing his eye socket. The Court of Appeal commented that sport was 'not a licence for thuggery and was a game covered by strict rules; the offence involved an assault off the ball and after play had moved on; serious injury had been inflicted'. The defendant was convicted of inflicting grievous bodily harm in breach of s. 20 of the Offences Against the Person Act 1861. In **Attorney-General's Reference (No. 6 of 1980)** two men had got into an argument and had proceeded to have a fist fight; it was held that, although they both fought voluntarily, they could not rely on the defence of consent. On the other hand, fights that take place within the Queensberry Rules do fall within a recognised exception.

Rough horseplay

The defence of consent has been allowed where serious injuries occur following what the courts describe as 'rough horseplay', though others might call it bullying. In **Jones** (1986) a gang of schoolboys threw their victims up to ten feet into the air, with the result that one victim suffered a ruptured spleen and broke his arm. The defence was allowed on the basis that there was no intention to cause injury, and on appeal convictions for grievous bodily harm were quashed.

Tattooing

R v **Wilson** (1996) was the first major case of the Court of Appeal to interpret the implications of **R** v **Brown** on the law of consent. Wilson had, at his wife's request, used a hot knife to brand his initials onto her buttocks. The scars were found during a medical examination and he was subsequently charged with the offence of assault occasioning actual bodily harm contrary to s. 47 of the Offences Against the Person Act 1861. At the trial it was argued in his defence that his wife had consented to his conduct. The judge felt bound by **R** v **Brown** to rule that the defence of consent was not available on the facts. Wilson was convicted but his appeal was allowed by the Court of Appeal which stated that this conduct fell within the recognised exception identified by **R** v **Brown** of tattooing. In addition, the court observed that it was not in the public interest to impose a criminal sanction on such consensual activity between husband and wife carried out in the privacy of their matrimonial home and without any aggressive intent.

Non-violent sexual relations

A victim can consent to the risk of serious harm resulting from sexual intercourse. They can therefore consent to the risk of catching a sexually transmitted disease, such as AIDS. In the case of **R** v **Dica** the defendant was accused of recklessly infecting two women with HIV contrary to s. 20 of the Offences Against the Person Act 1861. At his initial trial the defendant intended to argue that the women had known of his HIV positive status and had consented to sexual intercourse with him despite this. However, the trial judge ruled that as a matter of law a defence of consent could not succeed because under the case of **Brown** a victim could not consent to such serious harm unless their conduct fell within one of the recognised exceptions, and it did not do so here. Dica was convicted and sentenced to eight years' imprisonment. The Court of Appeal allowed his appeal, on the basis that the trial judge should not have withdrawn the issue of consent from the jury. Modern society was not prepared to criminalise adults who willingly accepted the risks taken by consenting to sexual intercourse. Criminalisation would undermine the understanding that sexual relationships were pre-eminently private and personal to the individuals involved in them. A retrial was ordered. A person could consent to the risk of being infected by a sexually transmitted disease, and this consent would provide a defence to a charge under s. 20 of the Offences Against the Person Act 1861 of recklessly inflicting grievous bodily harm on another.

The Court of Appeal in **Dica** drew a distinction between violent and non-violent sexual conduct. For violent conduct the harm is caused intentionally. For non-violent conduct any injury caused is only caused recklessly. The defence of consent would not be available for intentional violent conduct, but it would sometimes be available for reckless non-violent conduct. Thus the defence could, where appropriate, be available to a s. 20 charge under the Offences Against the Person Act 1861, but not to a s. 18 charge. **Brown** was concerned with violent sexual conduct for which the defence of consent was never available. **Dica** was concerned with non-violent sexual conduct for which the defence could sometimes be available:

> . . . violent conduct involving the deliberate and intentional infliction of bodily harm is and remains unlawful notwithstanding that its purpose is the sexual gratification of one or both participants. Notwithstanding their sexual overtones, these cases were concerned with violent crime, and the sexual overtones did not alter the fact that both parties were consenting to the deliberate infliction of serious harm or bodily injury on one participant by the other. To date, as a matter of public policy, it has not been thought appropriate for such violent conduct to be excused merely because there is a private consensual sexual element to it.

There are some risks linked to having sexual relations to which the victim can consent, but there are other risks to which the courts are not prepared to allow a defence of consent. In **Emmett** (1999) a man had been convicted of causing actual bodily harm to his fiancée. During sexual relations he had asphyxiated her with a plastic bag, causing internal bleeding in her eyes, and poured lighter fluid over her breasts, causing a serious burn. His appeal against his conviction was unsuccessful. The Court of Appeal considered that the 'actual or potential damage to which the appellant's partner was exposed in this case plainly went far beyond that which was established by the evidence in **Wilson**'.

There is no need to rely on the defence of consent where the defendant lacked the *mens rea* for an offence anyway. This point was made in a first instance decision of **R v Simon Slingsby** (1995). The defendant met a woman in a nightclub. They later had vaginal and anal intercourse to which she consented. She also consented to him penetrating her vagina and anus with his hand. Neither of them thought about the fact that he was wearing a signet ring but the ring caused her internal cuts. She did not realise the seriousness of her injuries, which went septic and caused her death. Slingsby was charged with unlawful and dangerous act manslaughter. The trial judge ruled that **Brown** could be distinguished, as in the case before him the defendant lacked the *mens rea* for any offence, thus there was no need to consider the defence of consent.

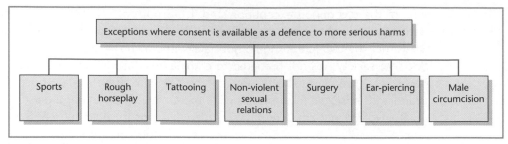

Figure 13.7 Consent

Criticism

Sexual relations

The role of the criminal law in policing sexual relations is very controversial. Peter Tatchell, a spokesperson for the gay rights group *Outrage*, has commented, following the House of Lords judgment in **R** v **Brown**, 'The state has no legitimate business invading the bedrooms of consenting adults and dictating how they should have sex.'

There has been concern that the criminal law is discriminating against homosexual behaviour to which the defence of consent was not allowed in **Brown**, as opposed to heterosexual relations for which the defence of consent was allowed in **Wilson**. In the latter case the Court of Appeal stated: 'Consensual activity between husband and wife, in the privacy of the matrimonial home, is not, in our judgment, a proper matter for criminal investigation, let alone criminal prosecution.'

Homosexuals do not have the option of getting married in England (though they can now form a civil partnership). In **Emmett** the Court of Appeal explicitly denied any discrimination stating that there was no logical basis for the law: 'to draw any distinction between sado-masochistic activity on a heterosexual basis and that which is conducted in a homosexual context'.

There is also a danger that, in prosecuting HIV transmission under the non-fatal offences legislation, the law may be discriminating against vulnerable members of our society. It is acceptable for the criminal law to require individuals to reveal their HIV status before having unprotected sexual intercourse so that their partner can genuinely consent or refuse to consent to this risk taking. But no such obligation should be imposed where the parties are going to use a condom.

The Court of Appeal appeared to state in **Dica** that the shorter the relationship between the defendant and the victim, the more likely the victim would be treated as impliedly accepting the risk of contracting a sexually transmitted disease. The Court stated:

> Given the long-term nature of the relationships, if the appellant concealed the truth about his condition from [the two women whom he infected], and therefore kept them in ignorance of it, there was no reason for them to think that they were running any risk of infection.

This could be interpreted as suggesting that a different view would be taken if the defendant and victim had a 'one-night stand'. Such an approach would suggest an inappropriate value judgement regarding an individual's sexual relations. The courts would be drawing a distinction between a couple living together and a one-night stand. In the later case of **Konzani**, the Court of Appeal did not place any emphasis on the duration of the relationship, and in fact one of the victims had only known the defendant for ten minutes before having sexual relations, but the defence of consent still needed to be considered.

The academic David Feldman (1993) has highlighted the inconsistency of allowing the defence for the bullying behaviour in **Jones**, to which it is hard to see any real consent, and not for the fully consensual behaviour in **Brown**. He points out that while bullying is reckless behaviour with substantial risks being foolishly taken, sado-masochistic activity is very ritualistic and disciplined, so that risks are carefully calculated and minimised. In addition, free expression of sexuality is considered desirable in a free society, whereas bullying is merely an expression of aggression. Under proposals by the Law Commission the defence would not be available for horseplay and it would continue to be unavailable for sado-masochistic activity.

Serious injury and consent

It has been questioned how a person can have a defence of consent to assault and battery but no defence to s. 47 of the Offences Against the Person Act 1861, when an essential element of the latter offence is proof of either of the former.

Consent and euthanasia

Euthanasia arises where a person consents to another taking their life, which is most likely to arise where an individual is terminally ill and in pain. There is an ongoing debate as to whether euthanasia should be legalised. At the moment euthanasia can constitute the offence of murder, unless it is committed by omission (see the case of Tony Bland at p. 14) or it is only the secondary result of the medical treatment administered (see p. 65).

Those in favour of the legalisation of euthanasia have argued it offers a person the opportunity to select the time and manner of their dying in order to secure a peaceful end to their life, unencumbered by intrusive medical technology. The practice of providing patients with potentially lethal drugs is becoming increasingly common. A survey of 300 doctors carried out for the *Sunday Times* ('Doctor will you help me die?' *Sunday Times*, 15 November 1998) suggests that 15 per cent of Britain's 36,000 GPs have assisted patients to die. The danger of this practice being abused has been highlighted by the conviction in 2000 of Harold Shipman, who killed a large number of his female patients by giving them an overdose of morphine.

In practice individuals are rarely convicted following an act of euthanasia. This is because either the jury refuse to convict or the prosecution choose not to proceed. Thus in March 1996 the prosecution against the care worker, Rachael Heath, for the attempted murder of a 71-year-old cancer victim was dropped. On 11 May 1999, David Moor, a Newcastle-upon-Tyne GP, was acquitted of the murder of George Liddell, an elderly and terminally ill patient. The prosecution had alleged that Dr Moor had injected Mr Liddell with a potentially lethal dose of diamorphine with the intention of causing death. The defence argued that the drug had been provided for purely therapeutic reasons – to relieve Mr Liddell's pain. In interviews he had apparently admitted that he administered diamorphine to hundreds of other terminally ill patients. The prosecution of David Moor was opposed by members of George Liddell's family. Mr Liddell's daughter said that Dr Moor was 'a hard-working and dedicated GP who doesn't deserve to be at the centre of a police investigation. The police should concentrate on catching criminals and not prosecuting this marvellous doctor.'

But doctors are still in a very vulnerable position before the law. It should be noted that the defence of diminished responsibility – which is sometimes used by spouses and others who kill loved ones in order to relieve suffering – will seldom be available to medical practitioners. In the case of **R** v **Cox** (1992) Dr Cox carried out the wishes of his dying patient and deliberately injected her with strong potassium chloride, a drug which causes death but has no therapeutic value. She died soon afterwards. Her family felt that, by giving her the injection, Dr Cox had released her from her pain and allowed her to die with dignity. The jury convicted, though their reluctance to do so could be seen from the fact that some of them wept openly when the verdict was returned.

Many people would like to see the law in this area reformed. Sixty per cent of doctors questioned in the *Sunday Times* survey agreed with the proposition that 'Doctors should have the power to assist death without fear of prosecution . . . by prescribing lethal drugs for patients to take themselves.' Hazel Biggs (1996) has suggested that the criminal law should look at the harm caused in each situation. In most instances of homicide, death is the harm caused by the conduct of the killer. With euthanasia, the indignity of a living death in a persistent vegetative state, or the protracted and painful dying process associated with terminal disease, can appear more harmful than death itself.

In the Netherlands, euthanasia has been legalised. The effect of this is that doctor-assisted suicide is available in the Netherlands, subject to guidelines made by the courts and the Dutch Medical Association. In Germany, euthanasia does not give rise to liability for murder but to a lesser offence with a reduced sentence. Such an approach has, however, been rejected by the Criminal Law Revision Committee in 1980 which decided to reject proposals for a new offence of mercy killing subject to a maximum sentence of two years' imprisonment. Another approach would be to have a defence of mercy killing available.

Lawful chastisement

Under common law, parents or any other person acting *in loco parentis* were allowed to use a moderate level of physical punishment on their children. The application of this defence has now been significantly reduced following the passing of s. 58 of the Children Act 2004. Under this section, the defence is no longer available to the more serious offences under s. 47, 20 and 18 of the Offences Against the Person Act 1861 and s. 1 of the Children and Young Persons Act 1933 (cruelty to persons under 16). The defence can still be relied upon where the defendant is charged with battery. The current law therefore still allows parents to smack their children provided they do not cause a bruise, as this would then amount to actual bodily harm.

For the defence to succeed where a person is charged with battery, the amount of force used must not be excessive. In **R** v **Hopley** (1860) it was stated that the force would be unlawful if it was:

'administered for the gratification of passion or rage or if it be immoderate or excessive in its nature or degree, or if it be protracted beyond the child's powers of endurance or with an instrument unfitted for the purpose and calculated to produce danger to life and limb'.

School teachers are banned from using corporal punishment in schools, but the Education Act 1996 allows school staff to use reasonable force to restrain pupils who are violent or disruptive. In **R (on the application of Williamson and others)** v **Secretary of State for Education and Employment**, the House of Lords rejected a claim by teachers and parents of children at four Christian schools in England that the ban on corporal punishment breached their right to religious freedom under Art. 9 of the European Convention on Human Rights. The appellants had claimed that an education based on the Bible required the use of corporal punishment. Lady Justice Hale commented: 'If a child has a right to be brought up without institutional violence, as he does, that right should be respected whether or not his parents and teachers believe otherwise.'

● Criticism

The existence of the defence of lawful chastisement has been very controversial and it is pleasing that its scope has been significantly reduced by the Children Act 2004. Before the Act was passed, the defence was available even where the physical abuse caused actual bodily harm, or even potentially serious bodily harm. This situation was severely criticised by the European Court of Human Rights. In **A** v **United Kingdom** (1998) the applicant was 9 years old and had been beaten regularly by his stepfather. The beatings had been carried out using a stick. The stepfather was charged with causing actual bodily harm and offered the defence of lawful chastisement. He was acquitted and the applicant took his case to the European Court of Human Rights arguing that the state had failed to protect the child from physical abuse. The European Court held that Art. 3 of the European Convention of Human Rights, prohibiting torture or inhuman and degrading treatment, had been violated. The Court felt that the defence of lawful chastisement as it then applied did not provide adequate protection to children, who were vulnerable members of society.

This is a delicate area of the law as views are strongly held by the public on the subject and very polarised. Some people still think physical force is a useful method of child discipline, though there is no evidence to suggest physical punishment improves a child's behaviour. Others would like the rights of children to be fully respected so that they were treated as equal citizens who could not be smacked, in the same way as the law considers it unacceptable for one adult to smack another adult.

The criminal law states the behaviour of which a society disapproves. Outlawing all violence against children would be a crucial step in public education. Twelve European countries have a complete ban on smacking children. A report by Christina Lyon (2000) called *Loving Smack or Lawful Assault* considered the impact of the ban on rates of domestic violence and juvenile violence in those countries. It found that the ban consistently led to a reduction in child abuse, domestic violence and violence outside the home. The ban in Sweden outlawing such violence has apparently been very successful in changing the attitudes and behaviour of parents.

Professional and voluntary bodies who work with children and other social service groups almost all wish to see the complete abolition of the defence of chastisement.

? Answering questions

1 **F and G agreed to beat up X who had recently displaced G in G's former girlfriend's affections. F and G waited for X as he came home from work. They jumped on X. X punched F rendering him unconscious. X fought with G who fell and hit his head on a wall. X walked away leaving F and G on the pavement.**

Advise the parties of their criminal liability. What difference, if any, would it make to your advice if (a) F, who had a thin skull, had died from X's blow; or, alternatively, (b) G had died of exposure? *(London External LLB)*

When F and G agreed to beat up X they entered into a criminal conspiracy to assault X, probably with actual or grievous bodily harm. When F and G jumped on X in furtherance of their agreement they committed offences under the Offences Against the Person Act 1861.

X punched F. This could have amounted to a non-fatal offence, the type of offence depending on the gravity of the harm actually caused. He will have a self-defence or a public defence (see p. 346) as long as he only used a reasonable amount of force.

If F had died because he had a thin skull, the rule in **Blaue** would apply so that X would have to take his victim as he found him. The thin skull would not break the chain of causation and X could be liable for murder or manslaughter depending on his *mens rea* and the success of any public or private defence.

If G had died of exposure, you would need to consider whether X had a duty to act and seek help for his victims. You could look at the case of **R v Miller** at p. 13. On the issue of causation you could consider the test of foreseeability and the case of **Pagett** (see p. 56).

2 **Maggie and Bert are both staying in a hospital. Maggie is expecting her first child and is of low intelligence. She is trying to read a book and Bert starts to taunt her about her inability to read and the fact that her unborn child is illegitimate. In a violent rage Maggie throws a plate at Bert but it strikes Rose, a doctor, who is killed.**

Bert is being treated for epilepsy. He walks into the hospital grounds and is approached by a policeman, PC Scott. He mistakes him for an alien from another planet and attacks him, and he dies two weeks later from his injuries.

Consider the criminal liability of
(a) Maggie
(b) Bert.

Problem questions like this commonly combine the general defences discussed in this chapter with specific defences such as provocation for murder. You need to keep the divisions used in the question, so divide your answer into two parts, (a) and (b). In part (a) consider whether Maggie could be liable for murder. Look first of all at whether she has the *actus reus*, and then the *mens rea* of the offence. On the facts, she would appear to have both. However, she would seek to rely on a defence. The most relevant defence would be provocation. Applying the subjective test first, she seems to have had a sudden and temporary loss of self-control. As regards the objective limb, a court may not take into account the fact that she is of low intellect, is pregnant with an illegitimate child and has difficulty reading – **Camplin, Attorney-General for Jersey** *v* **Holley**. Even if this defence should succeed it is only a partial defence and she would still be liable for voluntary manslaughter.

In part (b) you would need to consider Bert's liability for murder. Again, he would appear to have both the *actus reus* and *mens rea* of the offence and the crucial issue would be whether he has any defence. The partial defence of diminished responsibility and the complete defence of insanity would both be relevant here and you would need to look at these in detail. Mention should be made of the case of **Sullivan** on epileptics and insanity. You also ought to discuss the different effects of a successful defence of diminished responsibility and a successful defence of insanity.

3 **Critically evaluate the M'Naghten Rules. Are they an appropriate test for insanity in the modern world?** *(OCR)*

This is a fairly easy question to deal with if you are properly prepared. As is so often the case, the question is divided very clearly into parts and so your answer should also be divided in this way. In the first part, you need to state what the rules are, and critically evaluate them – this means highlighting the strengths and weaknesses of the law. You can answer the second part by discussing, among other things, the criticisms made of the rules by medical experts, and the movement in America for the abolition or restriction of a defence of insanity.

4 **Should the defence of insanity be abolished?**

This question requires similar material to the previous one, but here the emphasis of your argument will be whether the defence should be abolished, rather than whether it is out of date, though the two issues overlap. With a question such as this you will still want to show the examiner that you know what the current law of insanity is, but you should use this material as part of your argument that the defence still has/no longer has a useful function in today's society.

5 **K, who is attending a lecture by L, a well-known hypnotist, agrees to be hypnotised. L tells K that he intends to induce a state of aggression in him by means of a keyword 'bananas'. K agrees and is duly hypnotised. When L mentions the keyword 'bananas', K reacts by smashing the microphone on L's head, causing bruising. N, a member of the audience, attacks and kills P, who is sitting beside him. P had been calling N 'a stupid loony'. N is in fact severely retarded and lost his self-control when P taunted him. Doctors are prepared to give evidence that N is not insane although he has a mental age of seven.**

Advise K, who is charged with assault occasioning actual bodily harm to L and criminal damage to the microphone *(25 marks)*

and N, who is charged with murder. *(25 marks) (OCR)*

You need to divide your answer into two clear parts, the first considering K's liability and the second considering N's liability. Looking first at K, we are told that he has been charged with assault occasioning actual bodily harm and criminal damage. You need to discuss these offences in detail. As regards assault occasioning actual bodily harm, since its *mens rea* is subjective (either intention or subjective recklessness as to an assault or a battery) K could argue that he lacked the *mens rea* at the time. In relation to the offence of criminal damage the *mens rea* required used to include **Caldwell** recklessness, but, following the case of **R v G and another** (2003), subjective recklessness will need to be proven.

K's main defence would appear to be automatism, but this is narrowly interpreted and the courts are reluctant to allow it when the automatist state is self-induced.

Moving to the second part of your answer, you would need to consider first whether N had the *actus reus* and *mens rea* of murder. He would appear to do so. You could then consider whether he had the partial defences of either diminished responsibility or provocation. Because we are told that the doctors will give evidence that he is not insane, you should only look at the issue of insanity very briefly, though you should point out that the legal definition of insanity is not the same as the medical definition.

6 **Are the criminal defences defined too narrowly, so that people who have public sympathy are facing criminal sanction instead of benefiting from a defence?** *(LLB)*

A wide range of approaches could be taken to answering this question. The most obvious defence to discuss is the public/self-defence which has been controversial following the case of **Martin** and the question of how much force can be used to protect one's property. You could also consider the defence of necessity and whether this defence has been broadened following the case of **Re A (Children)**. As regards the defence of duress, there remains the question of whether this defence is available to a charge of murder, and the issue of self-induced duress. The defence of consent may be too narrow following the case of **Brown** in its approach to homosexual activity, when compared to the case of **Wilson**. The defence of insanity has historically been very narrowly defined, with many people suffering recognised mental ill-health being excluded from its remit.

7 **Penny, Alice and Colin were standing on a bridge with nothing to do during their Christmas holiday. Penny is 11 years old, Alice is 9 years old and Colin is 15 years old. There was a large concrete slab lying by the side of the road and Penny pulled it over to the edge of the bridge. She waited for a bus to approach and Colin shouted 'Go on, throw it.' Penny threw the concrete slab down onto the road. The concrete slab broke through the front window of the bus and killed the bus driver. Alice had a mobile telephone and she telephoned her mother, Jemma, to let her know what had happened and suggested that perhaps her mother should call an ambulance. The children then ran away. Jemma is suffering from clinical depression and schizophrenia and fails to call an ambulance. An ambulance was called about an hour later, by a passer-by, but the bus driver is dead on arrival at the hospital. He would probably have survived if medical assistance had reached him sooner.**

When questioned by the police about the incident, Penny is adamant that she was only playing and thought throwing the concrete 'would be a laugh'. She never intended anybody to be hurt.

Discuss the criminal liability of Penny, Alice, Colin and Jemma. *(LLB)*

The bus driver has been killed, and therefore this question raises the issue of liability for a homicide offence. Looking first at Penny's criminal liability for this incident, Penny does not appear to have intended to kill or to have intended to cause grievous bodily harm, and therefore she could not be liable for murder. You are therefore required to examine her liability for unlawful and dangerous act manslaughter and gross negligence manslaughter. It is unlikely that Jemma's omission to act would break the chain of causation.

As regards Alice's liability, she is only 9 years old and therefore has a complete defence of being a minor.

In relation to Colin, he was present at the time of the crime and shouted 'Go on, throw it.' He could therefore be liable as a secondary party. His level of liability would depend on his own *mens rea*.

Jemma's liability is dependent on an omission. Her liability would therefore depend on whether the criminal law would impose a duty on her to act in these circumstances. A prosecution could be brought on the basis of gross negligence manslaughter, as there is no act upon which to base liability for unlawful and dangerous act manslaughter. The question would therefore be whether it was reasonably foreseeable that the bus driver would be harmed by her failure to call the ambulance.

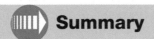 ## Summary

Infancy
Children under 10 years of age cannot be criminally liable.

Insanity
The rules on the defence of insanity were laid down in the **M'Naghten** case back in 1843. The starting point of the rules is that everyone is presumed sane. In order to rebut this presumption the accused must prove, on a balance of probabilities, that, when the offence was committed, they were suffering from a defect of reason, caused by a disease of the mind, so that either: (a) they did not know the nature and quality of their act; or (b) they did not know that what they were doing was wrong in law. The courts are now drawing a distinction between a disease of the mind caused by an internal factor and one caused by an external factor. In the former the relevant defence is insanity; in the latter it is automatism.

Automatism
This defence arises where the crime was committed by an involuntary act caused by an external factor (such as being banged on the head by a hammer or stung by a bee). The defence of automatism may not be available if the automatism was caused by the accused's own fault, such as by drinking too much.

Mistake
The issue of mistake is relevant in two contexts: it may mean that the accused could not have had *mens rea*, or it may be relevant in deciding whether a person has another defence such as self-defence. The mistake must be one of fact, not of law, so that a mistaken belief that your conduct is not illegal will not suffice as a defence.

Intoxication

Intoxication can be caused by alcohol or drugs. The defence of intoxication is allowed only in a limited number of circumstances, and only where it means that the defendant lacked the *mens rea* of the offence. If defendants lack *mens rea*, criminal liability can still be imposed if they were intoxicated at the relevant time and would have had *mens rea* if they had been sober. The starting point is that if the defendant did actually have the *mens rea* of the crime, then intoxication cannot be a defence. This was made very clear by the House of Lords in **R** v **Kingston** (1994).

Even where intoxication means that the accused lacks the *mens rea* of a crime, in some circumstances they can still be found liable, forming an exception to the rule that both *mens rea* and *actus reus* are required. In this respect, the courts distinguish between crimes of basic intent and crimes of specific intent; intoxication will usually be a defence to crimes of specific intent where the defendant lacked *mens rea*, but not usually to crimes of basic intent. The leading case in this area is **DPP** v **Majewski** (1977). If the defendant is treated as being involuntarily intoxicated, then intoxication may be a defence to any crime, whether one of basic or specific intent, provided the defendant lacks *mens rea*.

There is one circumstance where intoxication will not even be a defence to an offence of specific intent. This is where a person gets intoxicated in order to summon up the courage to commit a crime – often called getting 'Dutch courage'.

Self-defence and public defence

Parliament has attempted to clarify this area of law by passing s. 76 of the Criminal Justice and Immigration Act 2008.

Public defence

This is a statutory defence contained in s. 3 of the Criminal Law Act 1967. Under this section a person has a defence where they use reasonable force in the circumstances to prevent crime, or lawfully to arrest or assist the lawful arrest of offenders, suspected offenders or persons unlawfully at large.

Self-defence

This term covers the common law defences of self-defence and defence of another, again using such force as is reasonable in the circumstances.

Elements of the defence

Defendants can only rely on these defences if their action was necessary because of a threat of unjustified harm to themselves, to someone else or to property, or because of a need to prevent crime in one of the ways listed above. In deciding whether or not the behaviour was necessary, the courts will take into account three key issues: whether the person could have retreated from the situation; whether the threat was imminent; and whether the defendant made some mistake which caused them to think the action was justified. A defendant will only be justified in reacting to a threat which is imminent. If a defendant makes a mistake which leads them to believe there are circumstances which make defensive action necessary, the courts will assess the necessity of the defence on the basis of the facts as the defendant believed them to be, even if the mistake is not a reasonable one to make, as in **R** v **Williams (Gladstone)** (1987). However, the defendant must have used no more than reasonable force.

Duress

Duress is the defence that applies where a person commits a crime because they are acting under a threat of death or serious personal injury to themselves or another. The most important recent case on duress is the House of Lords judgment of **R** v **Hasan** (2005) which restricted its availability. There are now two forms of this defence: duress by threats and duress of circumstances.

Duress by threats

This traditional defence of duress covers situations where the defendant is being forced by someone else to break the law under a direct threat of death or serious personal injury to themselves or someone else.

Two-part test

In order to try to find the balance between the seriousness of the harm threatened to the accused and the seriousness of the consequent illegal behaviour, a two-part test was laid down in **Graham** (1982):

1 Was the defendant forced to act as he or she did because he or she feared that otherwise death or serious personal injury would result to the defendant, an immediate relative or someone for whom the defendant reasonably regarded him or herself as responsible?
2 Would a sober person of reasonable firmness, sharing the defendant's characteristics, have reacted to that situation by behaving as the defendant did?

The subjective part of the test

The defendant must have had no opportunity to avoid the threat, except by complying with it. There may not be any actual imminent threat. If there is no such threat, but the defendant makes a mistake and honestly and reasonably believes there is an imminent threat, the defence of duress can be available.

Voluntary exposure to duress

Following the House of Lords case of **R** v **Hasan** (2005) the defence of duress is not available when:

> as a result of the accused's voluntary association with others engaged in criminal activity, he foresaw or ought reasonably to have foreseen the risk of being subjected to any compulsion by threats of violence.

The objective part of the test

In applying the second, objective, limb of the **Graham** test, the reasonable person can be given some of the characteristics of the defendant but not all.

To which crimes does duress allow a defence?

The defence of duress is not available to murder, attempted murder or treason.

Duress of circumstances

The basic rules for this defence are the same as for duress by threats, except that it applies where there is no express threat of 'do this or else' but the circumstances threatened death or serious personal injury unless the crime was committed. The defence is relatively new, originating in **R** v **Willer** (1986).

Necessity

This defence essentially applies to situations in which defendants are faced with the choice of committing a crime, or allowing themselves or someone else to suffer or be deprived in some way. The courts, in the past, have been reluctant to recognise a general defence of necessity. In the high-profile case of **Re A (Children)** (2000), involving the medical separation of Siamese twins, the Court of Appeal paved the way for an established, general defence of necessity. It expressly stated that a defence of necessity existed at common law.

Consent

A victim's consent to the defendant's behaviour can exempt the defendant from liability.

An informed consent

For the defence to be allowed the defendant must know what they are consenting to – you cannot consent to something of which you are not aware: **R** v **Dica** (2004).

Capacity to consent

Certain people do not have the capacity to consent to the use of physical force over their body. They may lack this capacity due, for example, to their youth or mental ill-health.

The nature and degree of harm

Following the leading case of **Brown**, in deciding whether to allow the defence the courts will look at the nature and degree of harm consented to by the defendant. This is primarily a question of public policy, and the courts seek to strike a balance between the seriousness of the harm consented to, and the social usefulness, if any, of the conduct. The defence of consent is generally available to very minor harms of assault and battery. It is not available to more serious harms, unless the conduct involved falls within a recognised exception.

Euthanasia

Suicide is no longer a criminal offence in England. A person can choose to take their own life. But it is unlawful to do a positive act to assist a person to commit suicide (known as euthanasia or mercy killing).

Exceptions

A victim cannot consent to injury (other than assault and battery) unless the activity causing that injury falls into certain exceptions which are considered to have some social usefulness, in which case the defendant can consent to conduct which might otherwise constitute a serious offence. The exceptions include:

- sports
- rough horseplay
- tattooing
- non-violent sexual relations
- surgery
- ear-piercing, and
- male circumcision.

Lawful chastisement

Lawful chastisement consists of a parent, or person acting *in loco parentis*, using physical force to punish a child. Following the passing of the Children Act 2004, s. 58 this defence is available to a charge of assault or battery but it is not available for more serious offences against the person.

Reading list

Beyleveld, D. and Brownsword, R. (2007) *Consent in the law*, Oxford: Hart Publishing.

Biggs, H. (1996) 'Euthanasia and death with dignity: Still posed on the fulcrum of homicide' [1996] *Criminal Law Review* 878.

Butler Committee (1975) *The Report of the Committee on Mentally Abnormal Offenders* (Cm 6244), London: HMSO.

Child, J. (2009) 'Drink, drugs and law reform: a review of Law Commission Report No. 314' [2009] Crim LR 488.

Clarkson, C.M.V. (2004) 'Necessary action: A new defence' [2004] *Criminal Law Review* 80.

Dennis, I. (2000) 'What should be done about the law of self-defence?' [2000] *Criminal Law Review* 417.

Elliott, C. and De Than, C. (2007) 'The case for a rational reconstruction of consent in criminal law' 70 *Modern Law Review* 225.

Gardner, S. (2005) 'Direct action and the defence of necessity' [2005] *Criminal Law Review* 371.

Home Office (1975) *Report of the Committee on Mentally Abnormal Offenders* (Cmnd 6244), London: HMSO.

Law Commission (1977) *Defences of General Application* (Law Com No. 83), London: HMSO.

Law Commission (2009) *Intoxication and criminal liability* (Law Com. No. 314) London: Law Commission.

Leverick, F. (2002) 'Is English self-defence law incompatible with Article 2 of the ECHR?' [2002] *Criminal Law Review* 347.

Leverick, F. (2002) 'The use of force in public or private defence and Article 2: A reply to Professor Sir John Smith' [2002] *Criminal Law Review* 963.

Leverick, F. (2008) *Killing in Self-Defence*, Oxford: Oxford University Press.

Livings, B. (2007) 'A Different Ball Game – Why the Nature of Consent in Contact Sports Undermines a Unitary Approach' [2007] *Journal of Criminal Law* 71, 534.

Mackay, R. (1995) *Mental Condition Defences in the Criminal Law*, Oxford: Oxford University Press.

Mackay, R. (2007) 'Epilepsy and the defence of insanity: time for change?' [2007] *Criminal Law Review* 782.

Mackay, R. (2009) 'Righting the wrong? – some observations on the second limb of the M'Naghten Rules' [2009] *Criminal Law Review* 80.

Mackay, R., Mitchell, B. and Howe, L. (2006) 'Yet more facts about the insanity plea' [2006] *Criminal Law Review* 399.

Norrie, A., 'Criminal Law', in Grigg-Spall, I. and Ireland, P., *The Critical Lawyers' Handbook, Volume* 1, http://www.nclg.org.uk/book1/contents.htm.

Ost, S. (2005) 'Euthanasia and the defence of necessity: advocating a more appropriate legal response' [2005] *Criminal Law Review* 355.

Parish, S. (1997) 'Self defence: The wrong direction?' [1997] *Criminal Law Review* 201.

Patren, E. (1995) 'Reformulating the intoxication rules' [1995] *Criminal Law Review* 382.

Rogers, J. (2002) 'A criminal lawyer's response to chastisement in the European Court of Human Rights' [2002] *Criminal Law Review* 98.

Sangero, B. (2006) *Self-Defence in Criminal Law*, Oxford: Hart Publishing.

Simester, A. (2009) 'Intoxication is never a defence' [2009] *Criminal Law Review* 1.

Smith, J.C. (1993) '*R v Brown*: Case comment' [1993] *Criminal Law Review* 583.

Smith, J.C. (2002) 'The use of force in public or private defence and Article 2' [2002] *Criminal Law Review* 958.

Uniacke, S. (2001) 'Was Mary's death murder?' 9 *Medical Law Review* 237.

Weait, M. (2005) 'Criminal law and the sexual transmission of HIV: R v Dica' 68(1) *Modern Law Review* 120.

Reading on the internet

The leaflet, *Householders and the use of force against intruders*, is available on the website of the Crown Prosecution Service at:

http://www.cps.gov.uk/publications/prosecution/householders.html

The House of Lords judgment of **R** *v* **Hasan**, on duress, is available on Parliament's website at:

http://www.publications.parliament.uk/pa/ld200405/ldjudgmt/jd050317/hasan-1.htm

The case of **Pretty** *v* **UK** (2002), on euthanasia, is available on the website of the European Court of Human Rights at:

http://cmiskp.echr.coe.int/tkp197/view.asp?item=1&portal=hbkm&action=html&highlight=Pretty%20%7C%20v%20%7C%20UK&sessionid=10158303&skin=hudoc-en

---

Visit **www.mylawchamber.co.uk/elliottcriminal** to access multiple choice questions, flashcards and practice exam questions to test yourself on this chapter.

Use **Case Navigator** to read in full some of the key cases referenced in this chapter:

- AG for Jersey *v* Holley [2005] 2 A.C. 580
- DPP *v* Majewski [1977] A.C. 443
- Morgan [1976] AC 182
- R *v* Blaue – [1975] 3 All ER 446
- R *v* Brown [1993] 2 All ER 75
- R *v* G [2003] UKHL 50; [2004] 1 AC 1034
- R *v* Hennessy [1989] 2 All ER 9
- R *v* Pagett (1983) 76 Cr. App. R 279
- R *v* Quick [1973] 3 All ER 347

14 Codification of the criminal law

This chapter discusses efforts made, particularly by the Law Commission, to codify the criminal law.

Introduction

The criminal law is an area of law of particular significance to every member of society, as under this law an individual's freedom can be removed and they can be placed in prison. It is therefore of particular importance that members of the public either know what the law is in this field or are able to find out what the law is. At the moment, however, the criminal law is contained in a wide range of legislation and judicial decisions which can be difficult for lawyers to understand, let alone lay people. This has led some to favour the creation of a criminal code which would bring together in one accessible book the key legislative provisions of the major criminal offences. The criminal law in most other countries is codified.

The Law Commission was created in 1965. Under the Law Commission Act of that year its task is to codify the law, but to date the Commission has only had very limited success. In the field of criminal law, from 1968 to 1974, the Commission produced a series of working papers, but in 1980 it announced that its shortage of resources would not allow it to continue, and appealed for help with the task. The Society of Public Teachers of Law responded, and established a committee of senior academics, headed by Sir J.C. Smith. The team set out the aims of codification as being to improve the accessibility, comprehensibility, consistency and certainty of the criminal law. A first draft was produced in 1985. Following wide consultation a final Draft Code was published in 1989, but this has never been legislated as law.

The Draft Code incorporates not only the existing law, but also recommendations for reform made by law reform bodies. Thus it takes into account reform proposals made by the Law Commission, the Criminal Law Revision Committee and the Butler Committee on Mentally Abnormal Offenders (1975). Reform proposals were incorporated where the existing law was inconsistent or arbitrary or where a recent official report recommended reform. It established a dictionary of key fault terms (for example, intention and recklessness) which Parliament henceforth would be presumed to have intended unless it indicated to the contrary.

Much to the irritation of the academics involved in this project, the Draft Code has never been presented to Parliament. The Law Commission's response to this failure has been to produce a series of 'mini-codes' in relation to specific areas of criminal law in the hope that this will prove more attractive to Parliament. These mini-codes have covered such areas as the offences against the person, intoxication and involuntary manslaughter. If enacted they could together form a single criminal code.

Until recently there was no tangible sign of progress in implementation of any of the Law Commission's major reports dating back to 1993. Decisions of the courts continued to draw attention to defects in the substantive law in areas on which the Law Commission had already proposed legislation. A former chairperson of the Law Commission had written in the Criminal Law Review in 1995 that the reports of the Commission 'were being shelved because there was no general perception, particularly among non-lawyers, that there was anything much wrong with the criminal law that needed reform, let alone that large sums of money were being wasted, and countless unfairnesses perpetrated, because important parts of our basic criminal law were so difficult to access'. He concluded that no government would use precious parliamentary time to pass the technical law reform Bills because such legislation did not win votes or advance ministerial careers.

In 2001 the Government published an official paper, *Criminal Justice: the Way Ahead*. This paper was presented to Parliament by the Home Secretary in February of that year as the Government's vision of the future for criminal justice. It includes an express commitment to codification of the criminal law. This would be a 'consolidated, modernised core criminal code to improve public confidence and make for shorter, simpler trials'. It states that 'codification could begin with some valuable proposals already made by the Law Commission on offences against the person, involuntary manslaughter and corruption'. Following the Government's stated commitment to codify the criminal law, the Law Commission carried out a review of its Draft Code.

However, in its *Tenth Programme of Law Reform* (2008) the Law Commission has dropped its efforts to codify the law because codification has become 'evermore difficult' due to the complexity of the common law and the increased pace of legislation. Instead the Law Commission has decided to focus on specific projects to reform and simplify the criminal law, with the aim of returning to codification at a future date. Indeed, the Law Commission has had some success with the introduction of legislation which is a direct response to its recommendations to reform the criminal law, including provisions in the Fraud Act 2006, the Serious Crime Act 2007 and the Coroners and Justice Act 2009.

 Summary

At the moment the criminal law is inaccessible to the public because it is contained in a wide range of legislation and judicial decisions which can be difficult for lawyers to understand, let alone lay people. This has led some to favour the creation of a criminal code which would bring together in one accessible book the key legislative provisions of the major criminal offences. The criminal law in most other countries is codified. The Law Commission continues to undertake a considerable amount of work towards the development of an English Criminal Code, but for the time being there does not appear to be the political will to introduce such a Code.

 Reading list

Bingham, Lord Justice (1998) 'A criminal code: must we wait for ever?' [1998] *Criminal Law Review* 694.

Ferguson, P. (2004) 'Codifying criminal law (2): The Scots and English Draft Codes compared' [2004] *Criminal Law Review* 105.

Hare, I. (1993) '*R v Savage, DPP v Parmenter*, A compelling case for the code' [1993] 56 *Modern Law Review* 74.

Mackay, R.D. and Mitchell, B.J. (2006) 'Sleepwalking, automatism and insanity' [2006] *Criminal Law Review* 901.

Appendix: Answering examination questions

At the end of each chapter in this book, you will find detailed guidelines for answering exam questions on the topics covered. Many of the questions are taken from actual A level past papers, but they are equally relevant for candidates of all law examinations, as these questions are typical of the type of questions that examiners ask in the field.

In this section, we aim to give some general guidelines for answering questions on criminal law.

Citation of authorities

One of the most important requirements for answering questions on the law is that you must be able to back the points you make with authority, usually either a case or a statute. It is not good enough to state that the law is such and such, without stating the case or statute which lays down that law.

Some examiners are starting to suggest that the case name is not essential, as long as you can remember and understand the general principle that the case laid down. However, such examiners remain in the minority and the reality is that even they are likely to give higher marks where the candidate has cited authorities; quite simply, it helps give the impression that you know your material thoroughly, rather than half-remembering something you heard once in class.

This means you must be prepared to learn fairly long lists of cases by heart, which can be a daunting prospect. What you need to memorise is the name of the case, a brief description of the facts, and the legal principle which the case established. Sometimes it is useful to know the court, particularly if it is a House of Lords judgment. Learning the cases is often a slow and dull process, but is necessary in order to perform well in the examination.

Knowing the names of cases makes you look more knowledgeable, and also saves writing time in the exam, but if you do forget a name, referring briefly to the facts will identify it. It is not necessary to learn the dates of cases, though it is useful if you know whether it is a recent or an old case. Dates are usually required for statutes.

You need to know the facts of a case in order to judge whether it applies to the situation in a problem question. However, unless you are making a detailed comparison of the circumstances of a case and the facts of a problem question, in order to argue that the case should or could be distinguished or applied, you should generally make only brief reference to facts, if at all – long descriptions of facts waste time and earn few marks.

When reading the 'Answering questions' sections at the end of each chapter in this book, bear in mind that, for reasons of space, we have not highlighted every case which you should cite. The skeleton arguments outlined in those sections *must* be backed up with authority from cases and statute law contained in the relevant chapter.

There is no right answer

In law exams, there is not usually a right or a wrong answer. What matters is that you show you know what type of issues you are being asked about. Essay questions are likely to ask you to 'discuss', 'criticise' or 'evaluate', and you simply need to produce a good range of factual and critical material in order to do this. The answer you produce might look completely different from your friend's but both answers could be worth 'A' grades.

Breadth and depth of content

Where a question seems to raise a number of different issues – as most do – you will achieve better marks by addressing all or most of these issues than by writing at great length on just one or two. By all means spend more time on issues which you know well, but be sure at least to mention other issues which you can see are relevant, even if you can only produce a paragraph or so about them.

The structure of the question

If a question is specifically divided into parts, for example (a), (b) and (c), then stick to those divisions and do not merge your answer into one long piece of writing.

Law examinations tend to contain a mixture of essay questions and what are known as 'problem questions'. Tackling each of these questions involves slightly different skills, so we will consider each now in turn.

Essay questions

Answer the question asked

Over and over again, examiners complain that candidates do not answer the question they are asked – so if you can develop this skill, you will stand out from the crowd. You will get very few marks for simply writing all you know about a topic, with no attempt to address the issues raised in the question, but if you can adapt the material that you have learnt on the subject to take into account the particular emphasis given to it by the question, you will do well.

Even if you have memorised an essay which does raise the issues in the question (perhaps because those issues tend to be raised year after year), you must fit your material to the words of the question you are actually being asked. For example, suppose during your course you wrote an essay on the advantages and disadvantages of strict liability, and then in the exam you find yourself faced with the question 'Should strict liability offences be abolished?' The material in your coursework essay is ideally suited for the exam question, but if you begin the main part of your answer with the words 'The advantages of strict liability include . . .', or something similar, this is a dead giveaway to the examiner that you are merely writing down an essay you have memorised. It takes very little effort to change the words to 'Abolition of strict liability would ignore certain advantages that the current law has . . .', but it will create a much better impression, especially if you finish with a conclusion which, based on points you have made, states that abolition is a good or bad idea, the choice depending on the arguments you have made during your answer.

In your essay, you should keep referring to the words used in the question – if this seems to become repetitive, use synonyms for those words. This makes it clear to the examiner that you are keeping the question in mind as you work.

Plan your answer

Under pressure of time, it is tempting to start writing immediately, but five minutes spent planning each essay question is well worth spending – it may mean that you write less overall, but the quality of your answer will almost certainly be better. The plan need not be elaborate; just jot down everything you feel is relevant to the answer, including case names, and then organise the material into a logical order appropriate to the question asked. To put it in order, rather than wasting time copying it all out again, simply put a number next to each point according to which ones you intend to make first, second and so forth.

Provide analysis and fact

Very few essay questions require merely factual descriptions of what the law is; you will almost always be required to analyse the factual content in some way, usually highlighting any problems or gaps in the law, and suggesting possible reforms. If a question asks you to 'analyse whether the defence of insanity is satisfactory', you should not write everything you know about the defence of insanity and finish with one sentence saying the defence is or is not satisfactory. Instead you should select your relevant material and your whole answer should be targeted at answering whether the defence is satisfactory, by, for example, pointing out any gaps or problems in it, and highlighting changes which have improved it as a defence.

Where a question uses the word 'critically', as in 'critically describe' or 'critically evalu-ate', the examiners are merely drawing your attention to the fact that your approach should be analytical and not merely descriptive; you are not obliged to criticise negatively every provision you describe. Having said that, even if you do not agree with particular criticisms which you have read, you should still discuss them and say why you do not think they are valid; there is very little mileage in an essay that simply describes the law and says it is perfectly satisfactory.

Structure

However good your material, you will only gain really good marks if you structure it well. Making a plan for each answer will help in this, and you should also try to learn your material in a logical order – this will make it easier to remember as well. The exact construction of your essay will obviously depend on the question, but you should aim to have an introduction, then the main discussion, and a conclusion. Where a question is divided into two or more parts, you should reflect that structure in your answer.

A word about conclusions: it is not good enough just to repeat the question, turning it into a statement, for the conclusion. So, for example, if the question asks 'Is the law on rape satisfactory?', a conclusion which simply states that the law is or is not satisfactory will gain you very little credit. Your conclusion should summarise your argument, so, for example, in the rape question you could say something like: 'The reforms of the law on male rape and the definition of penetration have substantially improved the law on rape, bringing it up to date and addressing some of the gaps in the previous law. However, problems with consent, an overly narrow *actus reus* and the procedural rules mean that it is still far from satisfactory. Further reforms are clearly necessary, but even these will not be entirely successful in protecting women from rape unless social and judicial attitudes change as well' (assuming of course that you have made these points in your essay).

Problem questions

In problem questions, the exam paper will describe an imaginary situation, and then ask what the legal implications of the facts are – usually by asking you to advise one of the parties involved. For example, 'Jane hits Peter who falls back and knocks over Deirdre who hits her head on the pavement and dies. Advise Jane and Peter as to their criminal liability.'

Read the question thoroughly

The first priority is to read the question thoroughly, at least a couple of times. Never start writing until you have done this, as you may well get halfway through and discover that what is said at the end of the question makes half of what you have written irrelevant – or at worst, that the question raises issues you have no knowledge of at all.

Answer the question asked

This includes paying close attention to the words printed immediately after the situation is described. If a question asks you to advise one or other of the parties, make sure you advise the right one – the realisation as you discuss the exam with your friends afterwards that you have advised the wrong party and thus rendered most of your answer irrelevant is not an experience you will enjoy. Examiners do sometimes show mercy when they feel a genuine mistake of this kind has been made in the heat of the moment, but you cannot rely on that, and you will certainly not get a good mark for work done in this way. Similarly, if a criminal law question states that you should consider liability for murder, for example, then that is what you should discuss, even if the problem seems to you to raise issues of other offences – part of the skill is sorting out what is and is not relevant. However, where there is no such limitation, you should discuss all the possible options.

Spot the issues

In answering a problem question in an examination you will often be short of time. One of the skills of doing well is spotting which issues are particularly relevant to the facts of the problem and spending most time on those, while skimming over more quickly those matters which are not really an issue on the facts, but which you clearly need to mention.

Apply the law to the facts

What a problem question requires you to do is to spot the issues raised by the situation, and to consider the law as it applies to those facts. It is not enough simply to describe the law without applying it to the facts. Do not start your answer by copying out all the facts, or keep referring to them at great length. This is a complete waste of time, and will gain you no marks.

Unlike essay questions, problem questions are not usually seeking a critical analysis of the law. If you have time, it may be worth making the point that a particular area of the law you are discussing is problematic, and briefly stating why, but if you are addressing all the issues raised in the problem you are unlikely to have much time for this. What the examiner is looking for is essentially an understanding of the law and an ability to apply it to the particular facts given.

Use authority

As always, you must back up your points with authority from case or statute law.

Structure

The introduction and conclusion are much less important for problem questions than for essay questions. Your introduction can be limited to pointing out the issues raised by the question, or, where you are asked to 'advise' a person mentioned in the problem, what outcome that person will be looking for. You can also say in what order you intend to deal with the issues. It is not always necessary to write a conclusion, but you may want to summarise what you have said, highlighting whether, as a result, you think a person is liable or not for a criminal offence.

There is no set order in which the main part of the answer must be discussed. Sometimes it will be appropriate to deal with the problem chronologically, in which case it will usually be a matter of looking at the question line by line; while in other cases it may be appropriate to group particular issues together. A clear way to do this with criminal law questions, for example, is to take the possible offences in descending order of seriousness, or in descending order of relevance to the facts, so that you take the most likely offence first. If you are asked about the liability of more than one person, it is best to consider each one in turn, unless they have done exactly the same things and have the same characteristics.

If the question is broken down into clear parts – (a), (b), (c) and so on – the answer must be broken down into the same parts; whether this is the case varies with different examining boards.

Whichever order you choose, try to deal with one issue at a time – if you choose to consider each person or each offence in turn, for example, finish what you have to say on each before going on to the next. Jumping backwards and forwards gives the impression that you have not thought about your answer. If you work through your material in a structured way, you are also less likely to leave anything out. In criminal law questions, for example, it is a good idea when considering each possible offence to ask first whether the defendant has committed the *actus reus*, then whether he or she had the *mens rea*, and finally whether any defences are available – you should certainly never start considering possible defences before you have explained what the offence is.

No right answer

It is particularly important with problem questions to realise that there is often no single right answer. In the Jane/Peter/Deirdre problem, for example, you are not required to prove beyond doubt that Jane or Peter would or would not be guilty of murder; you are simply required to spot the issues that the courts will take into account in deciding this, and the rules they will use to make that decision, giving authority for all those points.

In most cases, you will need to specify the possible implications of different issues. In the Jane/Peter/Deirdre problem, for example, you might say that the court first needs to discover whether causation can be proved, explaining the rules on causation as they apply to these facts. You then have two possible situations: where causation is proved, and where it is not. Simply discuss them in turn: first state that if causation is proved, the court will need to consider whether Jane had the *mens rea* for murder, and then go on to explain what this entails; then state that if causation is not proved, Jane may be liable for a non-fatal offence, and explain what is required for this liability.

Select bibliography

Aldridge, P. (1997) 'The Sexual Offences (Conspiracy and Incitement) Act 1996' [1997] *Criminal Law Review* 30.

Ashworth, A. (1976) 'The doctrine of provocation' [1976] *Criminal Law Journal* 292.

Ashworth, A. (1995) Editorial comment [1995] *Criminal Law Review* 185.

Ashworth, A. (1995) *Principles of Criminal Law*, Oxford: Clarendon Press.

Ashworth, A. (2002) 'Robbery re-assessed' [2002] *Criminal Law Review* 851.

Becker, B.C. (1974) 'Criminal attempts and the law of crimes' 3 *Philosophy and Public Affairs* 262.

Bennett, T. and Holloway, K. (2004) 'Gang membership, drugs and crime in the United Kingdom', 44 *British Journal of Criminology* 305.

Beyleveld, D. and Brownsword, R. (2007) *Consent in the law*, Oxford: Hart Publishing.

Biggs, H. (1996) 'Euthanasia and death with dignity: still posed on the fulcrum of homicide' [1996] *Criminal Law Review* 878.

Bingham, Lord Justice (1998) 'A criminal code: must we wait for ever?' [1998] *Criminal Law Review* 694.

Bird, S. and Brown, A. (2001) 'Criminalisation of HIV transmission: implications for public health in Scotland' [2001] *British Medical Journal* 323, 1174.

Blogg, A. and Stanton-Ife, J. (2003) 'Protecting the vulnerable: legality, harm and theft', 23(3) *Legal Studies* 402.

Box, S. (1983) *Power, Crime and Mystification*, London: Tavistock.

Brady, J. (1980) 'Punishing attempts', 63 *The Monist* 246.

Brereton, D. (1997) 'How Different are Rape Trials? A Comparison of the Cross-Examination of Complainants in Rape and Assault Trials', 37 *British Journal of Criminology* 242.

Brownmiller, S. (1976) *Against Our Will: Men, Women and Rape*, London: Penguin.

Buchanan, A. and Virgo, G. (1999) 'Duress and mental abnormality' [1999] *Criminal Law Review* 517.

Budd, T. and Mattinson, J. (2000) *The Extent and Nature of Stalking: Findings from the 1998 British Crime Survey*, Home Office Research Study 210, London: HMSO.

Bullock, K. and Tilley, N. (2002) *Gangs, Shootings and Violent Incidents in Manchester: Developing a Crime Reduction Strategy*, Crime Reduction Research Series 13, London: Home Office.

Burns, S. (2009) 'How certain is death', 159 *New Law Journal* 459.

Butler Committee (1975) *The Report of the Committee on Mentally Abnormal Offenders* (Cm 6244) London: HMSO.

Carson, D. (1970) 'Some sociological aspects of strict liability' [1970] *Modern Law Review* 225.

Chambliss, W.J. (1984) *Criminal Law in Action*, New York/London: Wiley.

Clarkson, C. and Cunningham, S. (2008) *Criminal Liability for Non-Aggressive Death*, Aldershot: Ashgate.

Clarkson, C.M.V. (1998) 'Complicity, *Powell* and manslaughter' [1998] *Criminal Law Review* 556.

Clarkson, C.M.V. (2004) 'Necessary action: A new defence' [2004] *Criminal Law Review* 80.

Clarkson, C. and Keating, M. (2003) *Criminal Law: Text and Materials,* London: Sweet & Maxwell.

Cobley, C., Sanders, T. and Wheeler, P. (2003) 'Prosecuting cases of suspected "shaken baby syndrome" – a review of current issues' [2003] *Criminal Law Review* 93.

Corporate Manslaughter and Corporate Homicide Bill (2006) House of Commons Library Research Paper 06/46, London: House of Commons.

Criminal Law Revision Committee, Fourteenth Report (1980) *Offences Against the Person,* London: HMSO.

Criminal Statistics, England and Wales (2000), London: HMSO.

Crosby, C. (2008) 'Recklessness – the continuing search for a definition' (2008) *Journal of Criminal Law* 72, 313.

Crown Prosecution Service (2001) *Householders and the use of force against intruders,* London: CPS.

Cunningham, S. (2002) 'Dangerous driving a decade on' [2002] *Criminal Law Review* 945.

Davies, M. (1996) *Textbook on Medical Law,* London: Blackstone.

Davies, M. (2004) 'Lawmakers, Law Lords and legal fault: Two tales from the (Thames) river bank: Sexual Offences Act 2003; R v G and Another' [2004] *Journal of Criminal Law* 130.

Dennis, I. (2000) 'What should be done about the law of self-defence' [2000] *Criminal Law Review* 417.

Douglas, C. *et al.* (2001) 'The intention to hasten death: A survey of attitudes and practices of surgeons in Australia', 175 *Medical Journal of Australia* 511.

Downes, D. (1966) *The Delinquent Solution: A Study in Subcultural Theory,* New York: Free Press.

Dripps, D. (1992) 'For a Negative Normative Model of Consent, with a Comment on Preference – Skepticism, 2 *Legal Theory* 113.

Edwards, S. (2004) 'Abolishing provocation and reframing self defence – the Law Commission's options for reform' [2004] *Criminal Law Review* 181.

Eekelaar, J. and Bell, J. (eds) (1987) *Oxford Essays in Jurisprudence,* Oxford: Clarendon Press.

Elliott, C. (2004) 'What future for voluntary manslaughter?' [2004] *Journal of Criminal Law* 253.

Elliott, C. and De Than, C. (2006) 'Prosecuting the drug dealer when a drug user dies: R v Kennedy (No. 2)', 69 *Modern Law Review* 986.

Elliott, C. and De Than, C. (2007) 'The case for a rational reconstruction of consent in criminal law', 70 *Modern Law Review* 225.

Elliott, C. and De Than, C. (2007) 'The case for a rational reconstruction of consent in criminal law', 70 *Modern Law Review* 225.

Elliott, C. and Quinn, F. (2002) *English Legal System,* Harlow: Longman.

Elliott, R. (2002) *Criminal Law, Public Health and HIV Transmission: A Policy Options Paper,* UNAIDS.

Ellison, L. (1998) 'Cross-Examination in Rape Trials' [1998] *Criminal Law Review* 605.

Ewing, C.P. (1987) *Battered Women who Kill,* Lexington, MA: Lexington Books.

Feldman, D. (1993) *Civil Liberties and Human Rights in England and Wales,* Oxford: Oxford University Press.

Ferguson, P. (2004) 'Codifying criminal law (2): The Scots and English Draft Codes compared' [2004] *Criminal Law Review* 105.

Finch, E. (2002) 'Stalking the Perfect Stalking Law: An evaluation of the efficacy of the Protection from Harassment Act 1997' [2002] *Criminal Law Review* 703.

Finch, E. and Munro, V.E. (2004) 'The Sexual Offences Act 2003: Intoxicated consent and drug assisted rape revisited [2004] *Criminal Law Review* 789.

Finch, E. and Munro, V. (2005) 'Juror Stereotypes and Blame Attribution in Rape Cases Involving Intoxicants (2005) 45 *British Journal of Criminology* 25.

Fletcher, G. (1978) *Rethinking the Criminal Law,* London: Little Brown.

Gardner, S. (2001) 'Compassion without respect? Nine fallacies in *R v Smith*' [2001] *Criminal Law Review* 623.

Gardner, S. (2005) 'Direct action and the defence of necessity' [2005] *Criminal Law Review* 371.

Glazebrook, P. (1969) 'Should we have a law of attempted crime?' 85 *Law Quarterly Review* 28.

Gobert, J. (2008) 'The Corporate Manslaughter and Corporate Homicide Act 2007 – Thirteen years in the making but was it worth the wait?' (2008) 71 *Modern Law Review* 413.

Green, S.P. (2006), *Lying, cheating and stealing: a moral theory of white collar crime,* Oxford: Oxford University Press.

Griew, E.J. (1985) 'Dishonesty – the objections to *Feely* and *Ghosh*' [1985] *Criminal Law Review* 341.

Grigg-Spall, I. and Ireland, P. (eds) (1992) *The Critical Lawyers' Handbook,* London: Pluto Press.

Gross, H. (2007) 'Rape, moralism and human rights' [2007] *Criminal Law Review* 220.

Grubin, D. (1999) *Sex Offending Against Children: Understanding the Risk,* Home Office, Police Research Series, Paper 99.

Hall, J. (1963) 'Negligent behaviour should be excluded from penal liability', 63 *Columbia Law Review* 632.

Hall, R.E. (1985) *Ask Any Woman, a London Enquiry into Rape and Sexual Assault,* Bristol: Falling Wall Press.

Haralambous, N. (2004) 'Retreating from Caldwell: restoring subjectivism' [2004] *New Law Journal* 1712.

Hare, I. (1993) '*R v Savage, DPP v Parmenter.* A compelling case for the code', 56 *Modern Law Review* 74.

Harris, J. and Grace, G. (1999) *A Question of Evidence? Investigating and Prosecuting Rape in the 1990s,* Home Office Research Study 196, London: Home Office.

Hart, H. (1968) *Punishment and Responsibility,* New York: Oxford University Press.

Hearnden, I. and Magill, C. (2004) *Decision-making by House Burglars: Offenders' Perspectives,* London: Home Office.

Heaton, R. (2001) 'Anything goes' [2001] *Nottingham Law Journal* 50.

Heaton, R. (2001) 'Deceiving without thieving' [2001] *Criminal Law Review* 712.

Heaton, R. (2004) 'Principals? No principles!' [2004] *Criminal Law Review* 463.

Herring, J. (2005) 'Mistaken Sex' [2005] *Criminal Law Review* 519.

Herring, J. (2007) 'Human rights and rape: a reply to Hyman Gross' [2007] *Criminal Law Review* 228.

Herring, J. (2007) 'Familial Homicide, Failure to Protect and Domestic Violence: Who's the Victim' [2007] *Criminal Law Review* 923.

Herring, J. and Palser, E. (2007) 'The duty of care in gross negligence manslaughter' [2007] *Criminal Law Review* 24.

Hirst, M. (2008) 'Causing death by driving and other offences: a question of balance' [2008] *Criminal Law Review* 339.

Hirst, M. (2008) 'Murder under the Queen's Peace' [2008] *Criminal Law Review* 541.

HM Crown Prosecution Service Inspectorate (2002) *A Report on the Joint Inspection into the Investigation and Prosecution of Cases Involving Allegations of Rape,* London: HMCPSI.

Hogan, B. (1978) 'The mental element in crime; strict liability' [1978] *Criminal Law Review* 74.

Home Office (1975) *Report of the Committee on Mentally Abnormal Offenders* (Cmnd 6244), London: HMSO.

Home Office (1998) *Reforming the Offences Against the Person Act 1861*, London: HMSO.

Home Office (1998) *Speaking up for Justice, Report of the Interdepartmental Working Group on the Treatment of Vulnerable or Intimidated Witnesses in the Criminal Justice System*, London: Home Office.

Home Office (1998) *Violence: Reforming the Offences Against the Person Act 1861*, London: Home Office.

Home Office (2000) *British Crime Survey*, London: HMSO.

Home Office (2000) *Reforming the Law of Involuntary Manslaughter: The Government's Proposals*, London: HMSO.

Home Office (2000) *Setting the Boundaries: Reforming the Law on Sex Offences*, Home Office, London.

Home Office (2001) *Criminal Justice: The Way Ahead* (Cm 5074), London: HMSO.

Home Office (2002) *Protecting the Public: Strengthening Protection Against Sex Offenders and Reforming the Law on Sexual Offences* (Cm 5668), London: HMSO.

Home Office (2003) *British Crime Survey*, London: HMSO.

Home Office (2003) *Safety and Justice: The Government's Proposals on Domestic Violence*, Cm. 5847, London: Home Office.

Home Office (2005) *Review of the Road Traffic Offences Involving Bad Driving*, London: Home Office.

Home Office (2006) *Convicting Rapists and Protecting Victims – Justice for Victims of Rape*, London: Home Office.

Home Office (2006) *Crime in England and Wales 2005/06*, London: Home Office.

Horder, J. (1992) *Provocation and Responsibility*, Oxford: Clarendon Press.

Horder, J. (ed.) (2007) *Homicide Law in Comparative Perspective*, Oxford: Hart Publishing.

Jackson, B. (1982) 'Storkwain: a case study in strict liability and self-regulation' [1991] *Criminal Law Review* 892.

Jefferson, M. (2001) 'Corporate criminal liability: the problem of sanctions' [2001] *Journal of Criminal Law* 235.

Jones, T., MacLean, B. and Young, J. (1986) *Islington Crime Survey: Crime, Victimisation and Policing in Inner-City London*, Aldershot: Gower.

Kalvin, H. and Zeisel, H. (1996) *The American Jury*, New York: Legal Classics Library.

Keating, H. (1996) 'The Law Commission Report on Involuntary Manslaughter (1) The restoration of a serious crime' [1996] *Criminal Law Review* 535.

Kibble, N. (2005) 'Judicial discretion and the admissibility of prior sexual history evidence under section 41 of the Youth Justice and Criminal Evidence Act 1999: Sometimes sticking to your guns means shooting yourself in the foot: Part 2' [2005] *Criminal Law Review* 263.

Kibble, N. (2005) 'Judicial perspectives on the operation of s. 41 and the relevance and admissibility of prior sexual history evidence: four scenarios: Part 1' [2005] *Criminal Law Review* 190.

King, M. and Mezey, G. (1992) *Male Victims of Sexual Assault*, Oxford: Oxford University Press.

Kinsey, R. (1984) *First Report of the Merseyside Crime Survey*, Liverpool: Merseyside County Council.

Kinsey, R., Lea, J. and Young, J. (1986) *Losing the Fight Against Crime*, Oxford: Basil Blackwell.

Langan, P. and Farrington, D. (1998) *Crime and Justice in the United States and in England and Wales, 1981–96*, United States Department of Justice.

Law Commission (1977) *Defences of General Application* (Law Com No. 83), London: HMSO.

Law Commission (1993) *Assisting and Encouraging Crime* (Consultation Paper No. 131), London: Law Commission.

Law Commission (1996) *Legislating the Criminal Code: Involuntary Manslaughter* (Law Com No. 237), London: HMSO.

Law Commission (2002) *Fraud* (Law Com No. 276, Cm 5560) London: HMSO.

Law Commission (2003) *Children: Their Non-accidental Death or Serious Injury (Criminal Trials)* (Law Com No. 279), London: HMSO.

Law Commission (2003) *Partial Defences to Murder: A Consultation Paper*, No. 173, London: HMSO.

Law Commission (2004) *Partial Defences to Murder*, No. 290, London: HMSO.

Law Commission (2005) *A New Homicide Act for England and Wales?* (Consultation Paper No. 177) London: TSO.

Law Commission (2006) *Inchoate Liability for Assisting and Encouraging Crime* (Cm 6878), London: TSO.

Law Commission (2006) *Murder, manslaughter and infanticide* (Law Com No. 304), London: TSO.

Law Commission (2006) *Inchoate Liability for Assisting and Encouraging Crime*, Law Com. No. 300, London: Law Commission.

Law Commission (2007) *Participating in Crime*, Law Com. No. 305, London: Law Commission.

Law Commission (2007) *Conspiracy and Attempts*, Consultation Paper No. 183, London: Law Commission.

Law Commission (2009) *Intoxication and criminal liability*, Law Com. No. 314, London: Law Commission.

Lea, J. and Young, J. (1984) *What is to be Done About Law and Order?* London: Penguin Books.

Lees, S. (1996) *Carnal Knowledge Rape on Trial*, London: Hamish Hamilton.

Leverick, F. (2002) 'Is English self-defence law incompatible with Article 2 of the ECHR?' [2002] *Criminal Law Review* 347.

Leverick, F. (2002) 'The use of force in public or private defence and Article 2: A reply to Professor Sir John Smith' [2002] *Criminal Law Review* 963.

Leverick, F. (2008) *Killing in Self-Defence*, Oxford: Oxford University Press.

Levi, M. and Handley, J. (1998) *The Prevention of Plastic and Cheque Fraud Revisited*, Home Office Research Study No. 182, London: HMSO.

Livings, B. (2007) 'A Different Ball Game – Why the Nature of Consent in Contact Sports Undermines a Unitary Approach' [2007] *Journal of Criminal Law* 71, 534.

Lyon, M. (2000) *Loving Smack or Lawful Assault: A Contradiction in Human Rights and Law*, London: Institute for Public Policy Research.

Mackay, R. (1995) *Mental Condition Defences in the Criminal Law*, Oxford: Oxford University Press.

Mackay, R. (2007) 'Epilepsy and the defence of insanity: time for change?' [2007] *Criminal Law Review* 782.

Mackay, R. (2009) 'Righting the wrong? – some observations on the second limb of the M'Naghten Rules' [2009] *Criminal Law Review* 80.

Mackay, R.D. and Mitchell, B.J. (2003) 'Provoking diminished responsibility: Two pleas merging into one?' [2003] *Criminal Law Review* 745.

Mackay, R.D. and Mitchell, B.J. (2005) 'But is this provocation? Some thoughts on the Law Commission's Report on Partial defences to murder' [2005] *Criminal Law Review* 44.

Mackay, R., Mitchell, B. and Howe, L. (2006) 'Yet more facts about the insanity plea' [2006] *Criminal Law Review* 399.

Matza, D. (1964) *Delinquency and Drift*, London: Wiley.

Mirrlees-Black, C. (1999) *Domestic Violence: Findings from a New British Crime Survey Self-completion Questionnaire*, Home Office Research Study No. 191, 1999, London: Home Office.

Mitchell, B. (2000) 'Further evidence of the relationship between legal and public opinion on the law of homicide' [2001] *Criminal Law Review* 814.

Morrison, S. and O'Donnell, I. (1994) *Armed Robbery*, Occasional Paper 15, University of Oxford Centre for Criminological Research.

Nash, S. and Furse, M. (1995) 'Companies' human rights' [1995] *Business Law Review* 31.

Norrie, A., 'Criminal Law', in Grigg-Spall, I. and Ireland, P., The Critical Lawyers' Handbook Volume 1, http://www.ncig.org.uk/book1/contents/htm.

Norrie, A. (1999) 'After Woollin' [1999] *Criminal Law Review* 532.

Norrie, A. (2001) 'The structure of provocation' [2001] *Current Legal Problems* 307.

Ormerod, D. (2007) 'The Fraud Act 2006 – Criminalising Lying' [2007] *Criminal Law Review* 193.

Ormerod, D. and Taylor, R. (2007) 'The Corporate Manslaughter and Corporate Homicide Act 2007' [2007] *Criminal Law Review* 589.

Ost, S. (2005) 'Euthanasia and the defence of necessity: advocating a more appropriate legal response' [2005] *Criminal Law Review* 355.

Padfield, N. (1995) 'Clean water and muddy causation: Is causation a question of law or fact, or first a way of allocating blame?' [1995] *Criminal Law Review* 683.

Parish, S. (1997) 'Self defence: The wrong direction?' [1997] *Criminal Law Review* 201.

Parrot, A. and Bechhofer, L. (1991) *Acquaintance Rape*, New York: John Wiley & Sons.

Parsons, S. (1998) 'Criminal Liability for the Act of Another: Accessorial liability and the doctrine of joint enterprise' *Journal of Criminal Law* 352.

Patren, E. (1995) 'Reformulating the intoxication rules' [1995] *Criminal Law Review* 382.

Pedain, A. (2003) 'Intention and the terrorist example' [2003] *Criminal Law Review* 579.

Plumstead, I. (2002) Paper for the NSPCC Conference, 'Which of you did it?'

Power, H. (2006) 'Provocation and Culture' [2006] *Criminal Law Review* 871.

Queen's Bench Foundation (1976) *Rape: Prevention and Resistance*, San Francisco.

Rock, P. (1993) *The Social World of the English Crown Court*, Oxford: Clarendon Press.

Rodwell, D.A.H. (2005) 'Problems with the Sexual Offences Act 2003' [2005] *Criminal Law Review* 290.

Rogers, J. (2002) 'A criminal lawyer's response to chastisement in the European Court of Human Rights' [2002] *Criminal Law Review* 98.

Rogers, J. (2006) 'The Law Commission's Proposed Restructuring of Homicide' [2006] *Journal of Criminal Law* 223.

Rogers, J. (2008) 'The codification of attempts and the case for "preparation"' [2008] *Criminal Law Review* 937.

Rumney, P.N.S. and Morgan-Taylor, M.P. (1998) 'Sentencing in cases of male rape' *Journal of Criminal Law* 263.

Sangero, B. (2006) *Self-Defence in Criminal Law*, Oxford: Hart Publishing.

Simester, A. (ed.), (2005) *Appraising Strict Liability*, Oxford: OUP.

Simester, A. (2009) 'Intoxication is never a defence' [2009] *Criminal Law Review* 1.

Simester, A. and Sullivan, R. (2007) *Criminal Law: Theory and Doctrine*, Oxford: Hart Publishing.

Smart, C. (1989) *Feminism and the Power of Law*, London: Routledge.

Smith, J.C. (1989) 'Necessity and Excuse' published in *Justification and Excuse in the Criminal Law*, London: Stevens.

Smith, J.C. (1993) 'R v Brown: Case Comment' [1993] *Criminal Law Review* 583.

Smith, J.C. (1994) 'R v Adomako' [1994] *Criminal Law Review* 757.

Smith, J.C. (1997) 'Obtaining cheques by deception or theft' [1997] *Criminal Law Review* 396.

Smith, J.C. (1997) *Law of Theft*, London: Butterworths.

Smith, J.C. (1999) 'Commentary on *Klineberg and Marsden*' [1999] *Criminal Law Review* 417.

Smith, J.C. (2001) 'Withdrawal in complicity: a restatement of principles' [2001] *Criminal Law Review* 769.

Smith, J.C. (2002) 'The use of force in public or private defence and Article 2' [2002] *Criminal Law Review* 958.

Smith, J.C. and Hogan, B. (2005) *Criminal Law*, London: Butterworths.

Smith, K.J.M. (1994) 'The Law Commission consultation paper on complicity (1) A blue print for rationalism' [1994] *Criminal Law Review* 239.

Stanko, E. (2000) 'The Day to Count: A Snapshot of the Impact of Domestic Violence in the UK', *Criminal Justice* 1, p. 2.

Stark, E. and Flitcraft, A. (1995) 'Killing the beast within: Woman battering and female suicidality', 25(1) *International Journal of Health Services* 43.

Sullivan, B. (2001) 'Corporate killing – some government proposals' [2001] *Criminal Law Review* 31.

Sullivan, G.R. (2008) 'Participating in crime: Law Com No. 305 – joint criminal ventures' [2008] *Criminal Law Review* 19.

Tadros, V. (2006) 'Rape without consent', 26 *Oxford Journal of Legal Studies* 449.

Taylor, R. (2008) 'Procuring, causation, innocent agency and the Law Commission' [2008] *Criminal Law Review* 32.

Temkin, J. (1987) *Rape and the Legal Process*, London: Sweet & Maxwell.

Temkin, J. and Ashworth, A. (2004) 'The Sexual Offences Act 2003 (1) Rape, sexual assaults and the problems of consent' [2004] *Criminal Law Review* 328.

Temkin, J. and Krahe, B. (2008) *Sexual Assault and the Justice Gap: A Question of Attitude*, Oxford: Hart Publishing.

Transport Research Laboratory (2002) *Dangerous Driving and the Law*, Road Safety Research Report No. 26.

Uniacke, S. (2001) 'Was Mary's death murder?' 9 *Medical Law Review* 237.

Victim Support (1996) *Women, Rape and the Criminal Justice System*, London: Victim Support.

Walby, S. (2005) *The Cost of Domestic Violence*, London: Department of Trade and Industry.

Walker, L.E. (1999) *The Battered Woman Syndrome*, New York: Springer.

Walker, N. (1999) 'The end of an old song'? 149 *New Law Journal* 64.

Warshaw, B. (1984) *The Trial Masters: a Handbook of Strategies and Techniques that Win Cases*, Englewood Cliffs, NJ: Prentice-Hall.

Watson, M. (1998) 'Cannabis and the Defence of Necessity', 148 *New Law Journal* 1260.

Watson, M. (1999) 'A case of medical necessity', 149 *New Law Journal* 863.

Weait, M. (2005) 'Criminal law and the sexual transmission of HIV: R v Dica', 68(1) *Modern Law Review* 120.

Wells, C. (1996) 'The corporate manslaughter proposals: pragmatism, paradox and peninsularity' [1996] *Criminal Law Review* 545.

Wells, C. (1997) 'Stalking: The Criminal Law Response' [1997] *Criminal Law Review* 30.

Williams, G. (1961) *Criminal Law: The General Part*, London: Stevens.

Williams, G. (1983) 'The problems of reckless attempts' [1983] *Criminal Law Review* 365.

Williams, G. (1983) *Textbook of Criminal Law*, London: Stevens.

Williams, G. (1991) 'Criminal omissions – the conventional view', 107 *Law Quarterly Review* 86.

Williams, G. (1992) 'Rape is Rape', 142 *New Law Journal* 11.

Wilson, W. (2003) *Criminal Law: Doctrine and Theory*, London: Longman.

Wilson, W. (2008) 'A rational scheme of liability for participating in crime' [2008] *Criminal Law Review* 3.

Without Consent: Her Majesty's Crown Prosecution Service Inspectorate and Her Majesty's Inspectorate of Constabulary Thematic Report, London: Home Office.

Wootton, B. (1981) *Crime and the Criminal Law: Reflections of a Magistrate and Social Scientist*, London: Stevens.

Yearnshire, S. (1997) 'Analysis of Cohort', in Bewley, S., Friend, J. and Mezey, G. (eds) *Violence Against Women*, London: Royal College of Obstetricians and Gynaecologists.

Glossary

Acceleration principle. This is where the actions of the defendant speed up or accelerate the death of the victim, for example, a doctor giving a terminal cancer patient an extra dose of morphine. See **R** v **Adams** (1957) and the decision in **Re A (Conjoined twins)** (2000).

Accomplices.
- Where there are others involved in the commission of the offence.
- They are not the main party (the principal).

Action. This is usually voluntary and involves the defendant being aware of what he is doing in order for it to be deemed blameworthy.
    See **R** v **Church** (1966).

Actus reus. Actions or omissions required to form part of the offence. It can also be described as everything required to commit the offences other than the state of mind.
    It can include the circumstances of the offence, such as consent, and can also include the consequence of the offence, such as Death or Grievous Bodily Harm.
    See **R** v **Malcherek and Steel** (1981), **R** v **Cheshire** (1991).

Aggravated burglary.
- Where the defendant commits a burglary with a firearm or imitation firearm.
- Section 10 Theft Act 1968.

Aggregation principle. Where the actions and intentions of a group of people could be accumulated to lead to vicarious liability.

Appropriation. Where a person acts in a way towards property that is at odds with the interest of the owner, controller or possessor of the property.

Assault. This can occur when a victim thinks that he is likely to suffer imminent harm.

Attempt.
- Where the defendant carries out actions more than merely preparatory to an offence.
- Maximum sentence is the same as for the main offence.

Automatism. Where the defendant commits a crime because of an involuntary action.

Battery. This is where the victim suffers harm; there need be no fear or anticipation of harm.

Belonging to another. Where the property can be owned, controlled or possessed, this means that it can be stolen from a person who is looking after an item rather than the registered keeper as in a car.

Burden of proof.
- This is the obligation usually placed on the prosecution to demonstrate that the defendant is guilty beyond all reasonable doubt.
- It can be reversed in certain cases to place the burden on the defendant to show that he did not commit the offence on the balance of probability.

Burglary. Two types:
- Section 9(1)a

  Where the defendant will be found guilty because he has entered the property as a trespasser with the intention to steal, cause GBH or criminal damage.
- Section 9(1)b where the defendant entered the property as a trespasser, the defendant does steal or inflict GBH or attempts to complete either offence.

The difference is that in (a) all that is required is that the defendant intends the offences whereas in (b) the defendant has to do something!

Carries a 10-year sentence for ordinary properties and 14 for domestic burglary.

Automatic sentence on third offence.

Causation. The link between what the defendant does and the consequence to the victim of the defendant's actions. See **R** *v* **Jordan** (1956).

Causing/allowing the death of child or vulnerable adult.
- Section 5 Domestic Violence, Crime and Victims Act 2004.
- This was enacted in order to ensure that responsibility was taken for the deaths of individuals in care and controls of others where the death was not accidental but it was difficult to prove the guilt.
- See the decision in **Lane and Lane** (1986).

Causing death by dangerous driving.
- Section 1 Road Traffic Act 1988.
- *Actus reus*: objective test as to competence and awareness.
- No *mens rea* as to the likelihood of death.
- Proof that the defendant drove dangerously within the legislative definition.

Causing death by careless driving under the influence of drink or drugs.
- Section 3 Road Traffic Act 1988.
- *Actus reus*: driving without due care and attention.
- Mechanically propelled vehicle.
- Road or public place.
- Whilst under the influence (not inebriated) of intoxicants.
- Objective negligence test.

Consent.
- Can be a complete defence.
- Obtained through the victim understanding the event and what was being asked of him or her.
- **R** *v* **Konzani** (2005).
- Victim must have the capacity to consent.
- Can have consent to common law assault and battery, but not to s. 47 OAPA 1861.

Consent (in relation to rape).
- Defined in s. 74 of the Sexual Offences Act 2003, as where the victim agrees by choice and has freedom to make that choice.
- This is a test which is not subjective and does not depend on what the defendant thinks.
- Must be real and not submission, see **R** *v* **Olugboja** (1981).
- Force in obtaining consent negatives the consent, see **R** *v* **Larter and Castleton** (1998).
- **R** *v* **R** – consent in marriage is not automatic.

Consent obtained by fraud.
● Where the consent was obtained in this way there may be no consent.
● See **R** v **Tabassum (Naveed)** (2000) but also **R** v **Richardson** (1999).

Conspiracy. Where the defendant, with at least one other, agrees to commit an offence. Two types:
1 Statutory – s. 1 Criminal Law Act 1977.
2 Common Law – for example, to corrupt public morals or outrage public decency.

On the whole they are mutually exclusive.

Constructive manslaughter. See unlawful and dangerous act.

Corporate liability. Where a corporation, a body with a separate and legal identity, is held blameworthy for the actions of its employees or linked individuals or other subsidiary corporations, where the employees have carried out actions on behalf of the company.

Criminal damage.
● For full discussion see the decision in **R** v **G**.
● Causing damage to another's property.
● Can be damage or destruction of the property.
● Basic intention is all that is required.
● Cunningham recklessness.
● Limited defence of lawful excuse See **Jaggard** v **Dickinson** (1981).
● **R** v **Jones** (2004).

Criminal damage endangering life.
● Criminal Damage Act s. 1(2).
● Criminal damage AND . . .
● Intent or reckless as to endangering life.
● No need to show that it was endangered and that the defendant was reckless.

De minimis **principle.** Based on factual causation, where the courts look at the link between what the defendant did and whether or not this was a significant element in the death of the victim.

Death. There is no clear definition as to what death is, but see the decision in **R** v **Malcherek and Steel** (1981).

Defect of reason. Where the defendant cannot reason, see **R** v **Clarke** (1972).

Delegated management.
● This is where the management of a particular action or issue has been assigned with all apt powers to another to carry out that action.
● Usually where there is a statutory power to carry out the action in question there will be delegation and therefore vicarious responsibility for the actions carried out under that delegation.

Deviation from offence. Where the principal deviates from the plan, it is possible that if the consequences to the victim are not foreseeable, then the defendant may escape liability.

Diminished responsibility. Burden of proof is placed on the defendant to show that they satisfy the criteria set out in s. 2 of the Homicide Act 1957. It requires:
- Abnormality of the mind (psychiatric evidence may help).
- Which causes substantial mental impairment when the killing took place.
- Can be caused by internal or external factors.
- Including injury, illness, for example, depression. Does not include drink or drugs unless these affected the capacity of the individual, for example, alcoholism not intoxication.
- Leading to arrested: retarded development.
- See **R** v **Dietshcmann** (2003) and **R** v **Gittens** (1984).

Disease of the mind.
- Malfunctioning of the mind and can include arteriosclerosis (sleep walking).
- Not the brain in the physical sense.
- Usually linked to internal factors (INsanity = INternal try to remember it this way).

Dishonesty. The **Ghosh** test determines this:
- Was the defendant dishonest by the standards of ordinary people?
- Did the defendant know that he was dishonest by those standards?

Doctrine of identification.
- Where the statute allows the *actus reus* and the *mens rea* of the delegate to be assumed as that of the body corporate.
- The body must be able to delegate the duty given to it under statute.
- Limited liability as there is a clear criteria as to who can be a delegate.

Doli incapax.
- Where there was a presumption that a child between 10 and 14 did not have the *mens rea* for the offence.
- This could be rebutted (denied) using evidence.
- Abolished by s. 34 Crime and Disorder Act 1998.

There is a suggestion that this section only affected the common law position.

Duress.
- Two types.
- Duress by threat.
- Duress by circumstance.
- Closely linked with the defence of necessity.
- Not available to murder or attempted murder.

Duress by circumstance.
- As with duress by threat, but there is no expressed threat.
- Here the main issue is the seriousness of the circumstance threatened death or other serious consequence.
- See **R** v **Willer** (1986), **R** v **Conway** (1988) and **R** v **Martin** (1989).

Duress by threat.
- Objective and subjective (combination test as with self-defence, see also link with provocation), the **Graham** test.
- Was the defendant forced to act because of likelihood of harm to self or person (subjective)?
- Would a sober person of reasonable firmness, with the same characteristics as the defendant, have responded in the same way (objective)?

Entry. There must be entry to the property but this does not have to be substantial, effective or indeed complete, see the decisions in **R** v **Ryan** and **R** v **Brown**.

Euthanasia. The unlawful killing of an individual, see the decision in **Re Diane Pretty**.

External cause. On the issue of causation, where there is an external factor which is linked directly to the action, for example, a bang on the head, an attack by spiders!

Factual causation. This is where the defendant, as a matter of fact, causes the actual harm to the defendant. See **R** v **Smith** (1959).

Fraudulent property offences. Found in the Fraud Act 2006.

General defences. These are defences which can be applied to a broad range of offences.

Gross negligence manslaughter.
- Where the defendant has a duty of care to the victim.
- Fails to comply with the ordinary standard required to carry out that duty.
- The victim dies.
- The failure is so significant that the jury warrants it to be criminal.
- See the decision in **R** v **Adomako** (1994).

Imminent (in relation to self-defence).
- Must be about to happen.
- Can get retaliation in first in limited cases, for example, **McInnes** but see **Malnik** v **DPP**.

Inchoate offences. Where the offences are incomplete but there is still blameworthy conduct.

Incitement. A common law offence that was abolished by the Serious Crime Act 2007. It existed where the defendant tried to persuade or encourage a third party to commit a crime.

Indirect intention. The jury are entitled to find indirect intention when the:
1 Defendant foresaw death or serious injury as a virtual certainty of his actions.
2 And the defendant appreciated that this was the case.

See the decisions in **R** v **Nedrick** (1986), **R** v **Woolin** (1997) and **R** v **Matthews and Alleyne** (2003) for further discussion.

Infancy. This is where the defendant is under the age of 10.

Innocent agent. Where a person is not liable for an offence, despite apparently carrying out its *actus reus*, because he or she:
- Lacks *mens rea*.
- Has a relevant defence.

Instead, another person, the principal offender, is treated as being responsible for their innocent acts.

Insanity.
- Insane automatism.
- No psychiatric definition.
- No real medical definition therefore it can be and has been broadly interpreted.
- Available to summary and indictable offences where *mens rea* is required.
- Not available to strict liability matters.

- Requires evidence of a defect of reason caused by disease of the mind leading to the defendant not knowing what he was doing was wrong or not understanding the nature and quality of the actions.
- Burden of proof is on the defendant.

Intention to permanently deprive.
- Where the defendant intends to ensure that the property does not go back to the victim, if at all and certainly not in the same state as when it was stolen.
- The item can therefore be returned but it may have been stolen if it cannot be used again, for example, rail ticket.

Intoxicated mistake. No defence, see **O'Grady** (1987) and **R** v **Kingston** (1994).

Involuntary act. Where the defendant is not responsible for his actions as the mind is not in control. See **Attorney-General's Reference (No. 2 of 1992).**

Involuntary manslaughter.
- This is where the defendant satisfies the *actus reus* for murder, but does not satisfy the *mens rea*.
- Gross negligence manslaughter.
- Unlawful and dangerous act manslaughter.

Involuntary intoxication.
- Only available as a defence if the *mens rea* for the offence does not exist because of the involuntary intoxication.
- Soporific drugs, prescribed drugs and laced drinks will provide the necessary level of involuntariness.

Irrebuttable presumption in relation to rape. This is where there is a presumption that there was no consent and that the defendant had the necessary *mens rea*.

Where there was:
- Intentional deceit about the actions
- Intentional inducement of the victim to give consent

Joint Enterprise. Where the parties work together, with a communicated common intention, to commit an offence.

Legal causation. This is where the defendant is deemed in law to be responsible for the consequences to the victim. See the decision in **R** v **Cheshire** (1991). One key test is whether or not the actions of the defendant were the 'substantive and operative cause of the injury to the defendant'. It need not be sole responsibility.

Legal person. This can include an individual, company or body recognised in law, such as a charity.

Make off. No need for the defendant to run off.

Making off without payment.
- Where the defendant leaves premises without making payment when payment are due and are known to be due.
- Section 3 of the Theft Act 1978.
- Can be goods or services that are not paid for.

Maliciously (in relation to non-fatal offences). Where the defendant has the intention to:

- Cause/inflict some harm *or*
- Where the defendant is reckless as to causing some harm, albeit not serious harm.

Mens rea. This is the state of mind required to commit an offence.

There are several descriptions in respect of *mens rea* but it is often referred to as the 'guilty mind'. It should coincide with the event of the *actus reus*, see the decisions in **Fagan** *v* **Metropolitan Police Commission** (1969).

Mens rea **for involuntary manslaughter.** Each offence has different needs from this element:

- Gross negligence manslaughter: no *mens rea* is required as the offence is based on the premise of negligence and omission.
- Unlawful and dangerous act manslaughter: where the *mens rea* is the same as the *mens rea* required for the unlawful act which lead to the death – for example, the *mens rea* for the burglary or a robbery.

Mens rea **for murder.** The *mens rea* for murder is set out by the phrase 'malice aforethought'. This requires the defendant to have:

- Intended to kill the victim *or*
- Intended to cause GBH to the victim.

Mental disorder.

- Potential defence that will take over from insanity.
- Range of actions where there is no causal link between the mental illness and the actions.
- Butler Committee.
- Adopted partially in the Draft Criminal Code.

Mistake.

- Needs to be an honest mistake, see **DPP** *v* **Morgan** (1976).
- Not necessary for it to be reasonable but it might help with a jury.
- Not available to strict liability offences where *mens rea* is the issue.
- Separate statutory rules in relation to rape.

More than merely preparatory. Not defined in legislation, but in **R** *v* **Jones** (1990) it was suggested that there needs to be a course of action where the natural consequence is the commission of an offence.

Motive. Motive is not relevant to the *mens rea* of an offence, see the decision in **R** *v* **Steane** (1947).

Murder. This is a common law offence: Coke's definition (excluding the rule about the victim dying within a year and a day which has been abolished) indicates that the murder is:

- An unlawful killing.
- Of a person in being.
- Under the Queen's Peace.
- With malice aforethought, express or implied.

Necessity.

- Where the court has to decide between the defendant choosing to commit a crime or be subject to a crime.
- The lesser of two evils defence.
- Courts reluctant to allow this.

- But see **A (Children) (Conjoined twins)**, **R** *v* **Dudley and Stephens** (1884), **R** *v* **Shayler** (2001).

Requirements:
- Act needed to avoid irreparable and inevitable evil.
- Only what was necessary to avoid above was completed.
- Evil used was no more than that which was faced.
- **Shayler** addition:
  - Evil to be directed against those who threatened it.

Negligence. This is where the defendant has acted in a way that has fallen below the standard that is required. It mainly links to strict liability offences but also has been found to be relevant to gross negligence manslaughter as set out in **R** *v* **Adomako** (1994).

Non fatal offences against the person.
- This is where the victim suffers an injury, mental or physical, that can be attributed to the defendant.
- Main legislation is the Offences Against the Person Act 1861 and the Criminal Justice Act 1988.

Non-fraudulent property crime. Seen as blue collar crime. Includes:
- Theft.
- Robbery.
- Burglary.
- Blackmail.
- Taking without consent.
- Criminal damage.

Novus Actus Interveniens. This is a way to describe an intervening act which breaks the chain of causation. It must be a significant action which clearly separates the actions of the defendant from an unforeseeable event.

Objective. This is the opposite of subjective. Here the court is looking at what a reasonable person would have made of the defendant's conduct, see the decisions in **Metropolitan Police Commission** *v* **Caldwell** (1982).

Omission. This is important in criminal law as it bridges the gap between Tort (civil wrong) and Crime. Here the defendant must have owed a duty of care to the victim and has failed, for a reason perceived to be criminal, by the jury to have carried out the duty.

Traditionally, a failure to act does not give rise to criminal liability. However, some omissions do give rise to criminal liability, and they include the following:
- Where there is a contractual duty and failure to comply will lead to harm or death, see **R** *v* **Pittwood** (1902).
- Where there is a relationship between the parties which is recognized as leading to responsibility, for example, a parent, see **R** *v* **Gibbins and Proctor** (1918).
- Where there is failure to carry out duties that the defendant accepted as, for example, in **R** *v* **Stone and Dobinson** (1977).
- Where the defendant causes a situation to arise which is dangerous or harmful, see **R** *v* **Miller**.
- Where there is a statutory obligation to do something, and the defendant does not comply, for example, driving without an MOT.

Person in being. The victim needs to be alive at the time of the defendant's *actus reus* to give rise to liability for a homicide; see the decision **Attorney-General's Reference (No. 3 of 1994), Airedale National Health Service Trust** v **Bland** (1993) and **R** v **Church** (1966) for further discussion.

Private defences.
● Common law defences such as self defence, where actions relate to defending oneself or another.
● Overlap with public defence.

Property. For the purposes of theft:
● This can include a chose in action, for example, bank accounts, any property including land but in limited circumstances.
● Money.
● Parts of bodies unless they have been donated for medical purposes.

But cannot include:
● Anything wild, not tamed or kept in captivity.
● Anything that has been taken from woodland without being sold or passed on for profit.
● For further discussion see Section 4 of the Theft Act.
● Cannot include electricity or information, see the decision in **R** v **Lloyd** (1985).

Provocation. It is a statutory defence which is found in s. 3 Homicide Act 1957 and is **only applicable** to MURDER. This is where the defendant must show:
● A sudden and temporary loss of self-control.
● Provocation.
● A reasonable person with the same legally relevant characteristics as the defendant would have responded in the same way.
● See the decision in **R** v **James and Karimi** (2006) for further discussion.
● Can be carried out by words/acts or a combination of the two.
● It does not have to come from the victim, see the decision in **R** v **Pearson**.

Public defences. Where there is a statutory defence, for example, s. 3 Criminal Law Act 1967 – self-defence.

Queen's Peace. Within the jurisdiction of England and Wales.

Rape. Definition found in s. 1 of the Sexual Offences Act 2003. The definition makes it an offence when the defendant:
● Intentionally penetrates the vagina, anus or mouth of another with a penis.
● No consent to the penetration.
● The defendant does not reasonably believe that the victim consents.

Rebuttable presumption for rape.
● Where certain conditions/events exist there is a presumption that the defendant had the *mens rea* and that the victim was not consenting.

This is unusual and exists in the following situations:
● Where there is violence or threat of violence against the complainant or a third party.
● Complainant was unlawfully detained.
● The complainant was asleep when the offence took place.

- Due to physical disability the capacity to communicate consent was restricted or not available.
- Complainant incapacitated by an action of the defendant.

If these conditions exist then the defendant has to show that there was no *mens rea* and that there is evidence to suggest consent.

Recklessness. This is where the defendant appreciates that there is a risk of harm and yet still unreasonably continues with the course of conduct, see the decision in **R** v **G and another** (2003).

Regulatory offences. Where there is a clear statutory provision (usually) which seeks to control or regulate actions or behaviour.

Robbery.
- This is theft with force or threat of force (no force needs to be carried out).
- A maximum sentence of life imprisonment.

Secondary party.
- Aiding – Providing support or assistance, before the crime takes place.
- Abetting – Encouragement at the time of the offence.
- Counselling – Encouraging, advising, providing information in order for the offence to go ahead.
- Procuring – Taking steps to ensure that a crime is committed, to produce the end result (the crime) by defendant's endeavour.

Section 8 Criminal Justice Act 1967. This provision allows for the jury not to have to infer intention or foresight just because a consequence was probable. The jury can look at all factors in order to determine what they think the defendant thought/intended/foresaw at the time of the offence.

Section 18 Offences Against the Person Act 1861.
- This is often called wounding with intent.
- There are, however, other aspects to the offence such as assaulting a police officer with intent to resist arrest or with the intent to stop another from being arrested.
- *Mens rea* is usually an intention to cause grievous bodily harm.
- It is an indictable offence and carries a maximum sentence of life imprisonment.
- It is necessary to show that the victim suffered serious harm, for example, a broken leg or severe psychiatric trauma or wounding.

Section 39 Criminal Justice Act 1988.
- Common law assault.
- Common law battery.
- Can be charged under this as a summary offence.

Section 20 Offences Against the Person Act 1861. This is where the defendant unlawfully and maliciously inflicts grievous bodily harm or wounding on the victim. It carries a maximum sentence of five years and is triable either way. The *mens rea* that is required can be intention or subjective recklessness, there is no need to intend the particular harm that the victim suffers; all that is necessary is the foresight that some type of harm is likely to occur.

Section 47 Offences Against the Person Act 1861. This occurs where the defendant causes the victim to suffer actual bodily harm.

- *Actus reus* can include assault or battery.
- *Mens rea* is intention or recklessness as to the assault or battery.

Self defence.
- Only where the actions are necessary and reasonable in the circumstances.
- Two tests: objective as to the amount of force that is used.
- Subjective in determining whether force was necessary.
- See **R** *v* **Martin** (2003) and **R** *v* **Jones** (2004).

Sentencing (in relation to murder). Provisions for sentencing are found in the Criminal Justice Act 2003. Mandatory sentence is still set out.

Sexual Offences Act 2003. Legislation passed in order to codify and clarify the law on sexual offences.

Stalking. Campaign of harassment, frequently with sexual undertones.

Subjective. This is where the main concern is to look at what the defendant saw or perceived as a consequence of his actions.

Survivor of a suicide pact. Section 4 of the Homicide Act 1957 allows the court to determine that the person who is a survivor of the suicide pact be found guilty of the offence.

Taking without consent.
- S. 12 of the Theft Act.
- Taking a vehicle without the consent of the owner.
- Can relate to the passenger of the vehicle as well as the taker.
- There is an aggravated offence.

Theft.
- Defined in the s. 1 of the Theft Act.
- Dishonest appropriation of property belonging to another with the intention of permanently depriving the other of it.
- Carries seven years and is a triable either way offence.

Transferred malice. Malice is another way to describe intention or recklessness.
  In a situation where a defendant has intended that his actions cause a consequence which does not happen to the expected victim, but another does suffer then this will still cause liability to stay with the defendant, for example, if A intends to kill B, but misses and kills C he will still have the intention to kill immaterial of the victim.

Trespasser.
- Civil law definition: where on property without the other's permission.
- Can be limited to that which is expected of you when on the premises, for example, **DPP** *v* **Walkington: R** *v* **Jones and Smith**.
- Must be a trespasser at the time that the defendant entered the building or part of it.

Unlawful and dangerous act manslaughter.
- Where the defendant carries out an unlawful act.
- The act was dangerous (objective assessment) and the reasonable person should have the same knowledge as the defendant, see the decision in **R** *v* **Watson** (1989).
- The victim died because of the act, see **Kennedy (No. 1 and No. 2)**.
- Can be a strict liability offence, see the decision in **R** *v* **Andrews** (2003).

Vicarious. Where the actions of one person are carried out in substitute of another.

Vicarious liability.
- Where one person is held responsible for another's actions.
- In law the actions are those of a legal person.
- This can be expressly stated by statute, for example, the Licensing Act 1964.
- Or implied – this is known as the extensive construction principle (for strict liability matters only).

Voluntary intoxication.
- Only a defence to specific intent offences where the defendant has to form the necessary *mens rea* for the crime, see **DPP** v **Majewski** (1977).
- Never a defence to basic intent or reckless offences – it is therefore a reason to impose liability where a person might appear to have lacked *mens rea*, see **R** v **Kingston** (1994).

Voluntary manslaughter.
- Voluntary manslaughter is unusual in that the defendant can never be charged with it but can be found guilty of it!
- It requires all the elements of murder but there is a reason which will reduce the offences from murder to manslaughter.
- The reasons are found in the Homicide Act 1957 and are the partial defences of provocation, diminished responsibility and a suicide pact.

Withdrawal. Where secondary parties seek to deny liability because of their decision to withdraw. Must be carried out in the following ways:

Spontaneous crime:
- Not participating.
- No need for communication.

Planned crime:
- Must communicate.
- More likely to be accepted if withdrawal takes place a considerable time before the commission of the offence.

See the decision in **R** v **Mitchell and King** (1999) as well as **R** v **Becerra** (1975).

SWINDON COLLEGE

LEARNING RESOURCE CENTRE

Index

The essential reference for all students of law

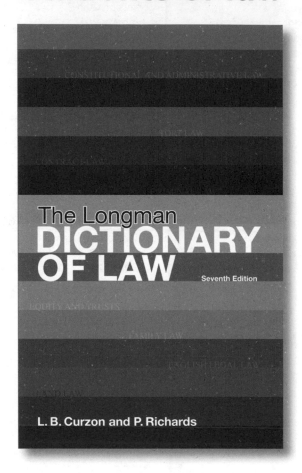

* Fully comprehensive entries on all aspects of English Law
* Clear definitions of specialised legal terminology
* Cross-referenced, giving full references for cases and statutes

The dictionary is fully supported by a companion website which links to additional legal information, and provides updates to definitions.

Available from all good bookshops or order online at:
www.pearsoned.co.uk/law